Corporate Governance Post–Sarbanes-Oxley

Regulations, Requirements, and Integrated Processes

ZABIHOLLAH REZAEE

BICENTENNIAL

1807

WILEY

2007

BICENTENNIAL

John Wiley & Sons, Inc.

Library of Congress Cataloging-in-Publication Data:

Zabihollah, Rezaee, 1953-
    Corporate governance post–Sarbanes-Oxley : regulations, requirements,
and integrated processes / Zabihollah Rezaee.
        p. cm.
    Includes index.
    ISBN: 978-0-471-72318-9 (cloth : alk. paper)
    1.   Corporate governance–United States.   2.   Corporations–Auditing–
Law and legislation–United States–Criminal provisions.   3.   United
States. Sarbanes-Oxley Act of 2002.   I. Title.
    HD2785.T83 2007
    658.4001–dc22   2006024004

This book is dedicated to my daughter Rose

About the Author

ZABIHOLLAH (ZABI) REZAEE is the Thompson-Hill Chair of Excellence and Professor of Accountancy at the University of Memphis. He received his Ph.D. from the University of Mississippi, his M.B.A. from Tarleton State University in Texas, and his B.S. degree from the Iranian Institute of Advanced Accounting in Iran. Dr. Rezaee holds several certifications, including Certified Public Accountant (CPA), Certified Management Accountant (CMA), Certified Internal Auditor (CIA), Certified Fraud Examiner (CFE), and Certified Government Financial Manager (CGFM), and is a member of numerous professional organizations. Dr. Rezaee is a former member of the Standing Advisory Group of the Public Company Accounting Oversight Board (PCAOB), created by the Sarbanes-Oxley Act (SOX) of 2002, and a member of the PCAOB Financial Reporting Fraud project synthesis group.

Dr. Rezaee has published over 160 articles in a variety of accounting and business journals, including the *Journal of Accounting and Economics*; *Contemporary Accounting Research*; *Journal of Business, Finance and Accounting*; *Journal of Accountancy*; *Journal of Accounting, Auditing and Finance*; *Management Accounting Quarterly*; *Internal Auditor*; *Advances in Accounting*; *Advances in Public Interest Accounting*; *Journal of Forensic Accounting*; *Auditing: A Journal of Practice and Theory*; *Research in Accounting Regulations*; *Internal Auditing*; *The CPA Journal*; *Journal of Accounting Education*; *Critical Perspectives on Accounting*; and *Accounting Horizons*. Dr. Rezaee has served on the editorial boards of several journals. He received the 1998 Distinguished Research Award at Middle Tennessee State University and the Lybrand Bronze Medal for outstanding article in 1999, awarded by the Institute of Management Accountants. He was selected by the Institute of Internal Auditors for the 2003 Outstanding Contributor Award for his article, "The Three Cs of Fraudulent Financial Reporting" published in *Internal Auditors*.

Active within the accounting profession and the academic and business communities, Dr. Rezaee has made over 150 presentations at conferences and workshops throughout the world. He teaches financial, management, and international accounting and auditing, and has been involved in financial and management consulting with national and international organizations, such as the United Nations. Dr. Rezaee is the author of a book entitled *Financial Institutions, Valuations, Mergers and Acquisitions* (John Wiley & Sons, 2001). In 2002, he published a book entitled *Financial Statement Fraud: Prevention and Detection* (John Wiley & Sons), which has also been translated into the Korean and Chinese languages, and in 2004 he coauthored the third edition of the U.S. Master Auditing Guide, *CCH*. Dr. Rezaee's recent book, entitled *Audit Committee Oversight Effectiveness Post Sarbanes-Oxley Act*, was published in the fall of 2006 by the Bureau of National Affairs, Inc.

Contents

Acknowledgments

Many people have generously contributed their time, knowledge, and talents during the development, writing, revisions, and production stages of this book. I am most grateful to all of them, and without their valuable assistance and contributions this book would not have come to fruition. There is one person, however, who deserves special thanks.

Lynn E. Turner. Lynn is a former chief accountant at the SEC whose contributions to matters affecting corporate governance have been even more significant in the post-SOX era than when he was with the SEC. Lynn's time, talents, and skills have been vital to the publication of this book. He is my mentor who has educated me about corporate governance by furnishing relevant and updated materials, invaluable comments, technical review, and advice in the development of different phases of the book. Lynn's unique view points relevant to corporate governance and his passion for investor protection through robust regulations are reflected throughout the book. I remember days that I received more than 15 emails from Lynn on book-related materials that several times overwhelmed my computer. I cannot thank him enough for his friendship, mentorship, and tireless support; without his advice and furnished materials the book would not have been made possible.

This book has also benefited, *inter alia*, from permission to quote from several references and publications of a variety of professional organizations and standard-setting bodies including the Securities and Exchange Commission (SEC), the Public Company Accounting Oversight Board (PCAOB), the Financial Accounting Standards Board (FASB), the American Institute of Certified Public Accountants (AICPA), the Institute of Internal Auditors (IIA), the Institute of Management Accountants (IMA), the Committee of Sponsoring Organizations of the Treadway Commission (COSO), the National Association of Corporate Directors (NACD), the Conference Board, the Big Four public accounting firms (Deloitte & Touche, Ernst & Young, KPMG, and PricewaterhouseCoopers), national stock exchanges (NYSE, Nasdaq, AMEX), institutional investors (CalPERS, TIAA-CREF, AFL-CIO SBA of Florida), the Business Roundtable (BRT), Financial Executives International (FEI), the Council of Institutional Investors (CII), the Charted Financial Analyst (CFA) Institute (formerly the Association for Investment Management and Research (AIMR)), the International Corporate Governance Network (ICGN), the Investor Responsibility Research Center (IRRC), Corporate Library, U.K. Financial Reporting Council, and Glass, Lewis & Co., LLC.

I would also like to thank the members of the editorial staff of John Wiley, including Tim Burgard, Natasha Andrews-Noel, Julie Burden, L. Haviland, and Helen Cho, for their editorial guidance, and my assistant, Barbara Haertl, and two graduate students, Joseph Nowell and Siddhi Shastri, for their hard work, dedication, and invaluable assistance. My sincere thanks are due to my family: wife Soheila, son Nick, and daughter Rose, for their love and support.

PREFACE

Historically, the dispersed capital ownership structure, robust and effective corporate governance reforms including regulations and market mechanisms, and the friendly corporate environment in the United States have made the U.S. capital markets home to public companies worldwide. Effective corporate governance reforms have also led to greater investor protection and confidence as well as high shareholder value and corporate market capitalizations Corporate and accounting scandals of the late 1990s and early 2000s caused losses of hundreds of billions of dollars in market capitalizations and investor confidence in the capital markets. Subsequent congressional responses (the Sarbanes-Oxley Act of 2002, a.k.a. SOX) and regulatory rules issued by the Securities and Exchange Commission (SEC), as well as increased accountability requirements in the listing standards of national stock exchanges and best practices, have turned the spotlight onto the issue of corporate governance. Corporate governance is regarded as the most influential theme of the 21st century, having transformed from a compliance requirement to a strategic business imperative. Corporate governance reforms including state and federal statutes, SOX, SEC rules, listing standards, and best practices are at the center stage of corporate accountability.

Corporate governance can be narrowly defined as a company's extent of compliance with these reforms or widely defined as a company's relations with a wide range of corporate governance participants including the board of directors, management, auditors, legal counsel, financial advisors, regulators, standard setters, shareholders, and other stakeholders. The latter definition is adopted in this book. Effective corporate governance cannot be achieved merely through compliance with laws and regulations. Rather, it is achieved by the commitment to do the right thing, observe moral and ethical principles and professional conduct, and accept accountability.

Corporate governance's role in restoring public trust in corporate America is critical and has become mandated by the capital markets. While the effects of regulations and the threat of severe penalties for corporate wrongdoers help reduce investor anxiety, still more is required. Corporations must earn back investor confidence and demonstrate a proactive stance on ensuring accurate and reliable financial reports to their shareholders. To win back public trust, a framework must be developed that encompasses all key participants and processes. This book provides this framework by examining the oversight, managerial, compliance, internal auditing, advisory, external auditing, and monitoring functions of corporate governance, and introduces a blueprint for various functions of corporate governance designed to create sustainable shareholder value while protecting the interests of other stakeholders. Effective corporate governance is required for the efficient functioning of the financial markets to attract and retain capital. The corporate governance concepts, principles, guidelines, structure, regulatory requirements, functions, and best practices presented in this book focus primarily on public companies although they may well apply to all entities whether for-profit, not-for-profit, or private companies planning to go public in the future.

This book presents essential and fundamental concepts of corporate governance focusing on an integrated approach that addresses fiduciary duty and professional responsibilities of all financial market participants. Corporate governance has moved from purely internal managerial issues and compliance requirements to a broad strategic business imperative, risk assessment, and reporting issues concerning the board of directors, board committees, executives, internal auditors, external auditors, legal counsel, financial analysts, investment bankers, governing bodies, investors, and other stakeholders. The suggested integrated approach to corporate governance will assist corporations in demonstrating that they must in fact hold themselves to high standards of professional accountability, integrity, ethical conduct, and honorable behavior that exceed all applicable regulations. This book is intended to promote the corporate governance reforms that should already be in place and provide an integrated approach towards effective corporate governance structure that will aid in regaining investor confidence in corporate America and maintaining the global competitiveness and leadership of U.S. capital markets.

The 14 chapters of this book are organized into three parts. The first part contains two chapters that present the rise of corporate governance. Chapter 1 discusses corporate governance and its important role in improving public trust and investor confidence in corporate America, its capital markets, and financial reporting. Chapter 2 examines fundamentals of corporate governance including structure, principles, functions, and mechanisms.

Part II includes Chapters 3 through 10, which constitute the heart of the book and provide a framework for integration of all of the important functions of corporate governance. Chapter 3 examines the oversight function assumed by the board of directors in holding management accountable for creating shareholder value and in overseeing strategic decisions, operational performance, financial reports, internal controls, and audit activities. Chapter 4 discusses board committees established to perform and coordinate oversight functions including the three mandatory audit, compensation, and nominating/governance committees. Chapter 5 discusses the managerial function in managing, directing, and controlling corporate affairs. Chapter 6 presents the compliance function to ensure compliance with all applicable regulations, standards, procedures, and best practices. Chapter 7 discusses the internal audit function typically assigned to internal auditors to provide assurance and consulting services through ongoing monitoring of corporate governance, operations, risk management, internal control, and financial reporting. Chapter 8 presents the advisory function in providing legal and financial advice to the board of directors and executives. Chapter 9 examines the external audit function assumed by external auditors in providing high-level assurance regarding true and fair presentation of financial statements. Chapter 10 presents the monitoring function assumed by shareholders, including individual and institutional investors, who elect the board of directors and can exert pressure on independent directors to replace nonperforming executives. This chapter also discusses the role of other stakeholders in corporate governance.

Part III consists of Chapters 11–14 and focuses on the contemporary issues in corporate governance including the disclosure of key financial and nonfinancial performance indicators, assurance provided by audit functions, executive compensation, and election of directors. Chapter 11 focuses on the corporate governance of not-for-profit organizations. Chapter 12 examines business ethics and its role in corporate governance. Chapter 13 examines globalization, technology, and corporate governance. This section concludes with Chapter 14 discussing future trends and emerging initiatives in corporate governance.

I hope you find that this book is a valuable resource in creating an integrated model of corporate governance that allows all participants to fulfill their responsibilities while adding value to their organizations. Anyone who is involved with corporate governance, the financial reporting process, investment and voting decisions, legal and financial advising, audit functions, and corporate governance education will be interested in this book. Specifically, corporations, their executives, the boards of directors, board committees, internal and external auditors, accountants, lawmakers, regulators, standard-setters, users of financial statements (investors, creditors, and pensioners), investor activists, business schools, and other professionals (attorneys, financial analysts, and bankers) will benefit from this book.

As this book was going to production, some efforts were being made to roll back some provisions of SOX and/or relax its implementation rules on the grounds that its requirements are overly costly and often onerous and detrimental to the global competitiveness of the U.S. capital markets. These efforts recommend rolling back corporate governance reforms, limiting class-action lawsuits against companies and their auditors, and reducing criminal prosecution of companies by the government. Indeed, the U.S. Senate, in April 2007, rejected SOX changes and instead encouraged regulators to resolve implementation challenges of SOX and to fine-tune its Section 404 on internal controls. This raises the question of whether the historical trend of financial scandals, usually caused by relaxed regulations and ineffective corporate governance measures including market mechanisms, is doomed to repeat itself. Any potential future financial scandals would be extremely significant and devastating to about 100 million American investors and the U.S. capital markets and economy. Corporate governance reforms, including regulations such as SOX, in protecting investors and improving the global competitiveness of the U.S. capital markets are successful in the long term when they are perceived and proven to be cost-effective, efficient, and scalable. There should be a proper balance between robust corporate governance reforms in protecting investors from corporate scandals and the cost of compliance with such reforms. Ineffective corporate governance reforms may cause loss of investor confidence and thus loss in the performance of the capital markets. Similarly, excessive compliance costs can force corporations to move to capital markets abroad.

Zabihollah (Zabi) Rezaee, Ph.D., CPA, CMA, CIA, CFE, CGFM
Memphis, TN
May 2007

Since corporations first gained widespread acceptance in the United States in the later 1800s, corporate governance has been an important evolving issue. And with each episode of major corporate scandals, how oversight of executives chosen to run corporations is conducted has faced increased scrutiny. From the McKesson Robbin case of the late 1930s to the Penn Central debacle preceding the 1972/73 bear market to the Enrons and WorldComs of the current century, corporate governance has changed dramatically. And the pace of change is increasing.

In today's global capital markets and economy, where shareholders are both diverse and widely dispersed, active and engaged corporate governance is important to increasing and protecting shareholder value. Yet at the same time, good corporate governance demands the directors walk a fine line that balances the role of active oversight with avoiding unnecessary meddling in day-to-day corporate affairs that rightly are the responsibility of management. In carrying out this balancing act, boards of directors are also required to fulfill a multitude of tasks that run from reviews of corporate business strategies, to consideration of acquisitions, to oversight of the quality of financial reporting, to assessment of compliance programs, hiring of executives and planning their succession, as well as establishing pay for top level executives in light of their performance or lack thereof.

It is with all in of this in mind that Professor Zabi Rezaee has created and presented a comprehensive model of an effective corporate governance structure for consideration by those affected by corporate governance. The model and Professor Rezaee bring together all the elements of corporate governance and its constituents including management and the board of directors, those responsible for compliance programs including the role of the internal audit function. It also discusses the role in corporate governance of key advisors such as the legal and accounting professions.

Professor Rezaee's model is built from the foundation up. He provides readers with an understanding of the fundamentals of corporate governance including the structure of governance. That structure is expanded on in a discussion of the roles played by the directors in fulfilling their fiduciary responsibilities to investors as opposed to the managerial function in corporations.

But one would be remiss to think corporate governance will remain unchanged with increasing business risks posed by the global economic and capital market environment we live in. To that end, *Corporate Governance Post–Sarbanes-Oxley* appropriately provides the reader with a useful discussion of emerging and contemporary issues confronting those involved with corporate governance including those in the monitoring function, as well as those in the growing field of not-for-profit organizations. And it adds an international flavor to its pages, which is unquestionably important and useful as today's largest investors as well as accomplished management teams and directors come from a multitude of countries. In fact, in taking up the issue of corporate governance in an international environment, Dr. Rezaee does us all a favor in reminding us that best practices in corporate governance are not constrained by any lines on a paper map, in a digital world of business and investors.

Lynn E. Turner, CPA
April 17, 2007
Managing Director of Research
Glass, Lewis & Co., LLC
Former Chief Accountant of the SEC

The Rise of Corporate Governance

One

The Rise of Corporate
Governance

CHAPTER 1

Financial Markets, Investor Confidence, and Corporate Governance

INTRODUCTION

The U.S. financial markets are characterized by a widespread ownership structure where about 100 million Americans, directly or indirectly, through retirement plans, mutual funds, or active trading, participate in the capital markets. This type of ownership structure can be influenced by a typical agency problem of separation of the decision control assigned to management and the ownership control retained by a wide range of shareholders.[1] The integrity and efficiency of financial markets depend on the quality and reliability of financial information disseminated to the markets by public companies as well as investor confidence in such information. Congressman William Lacy Clay (D-MO) states:

> *Over a hundred million Americans have investments in our markets. The confidence of these investors is paramount to the continued viability of the markets. This confidence is buoyed by the accuracy, reliability, and transparency of our financial reporting.[2]*

The primary role of all corporate governance participants as defined in this book centers around the fundamental theme of protecting investors, creating long-term shareholder value, restoring investor confidence, and supporting strong and efficient capital markets. Corporate governance measures (e.g., independent directors, competent and ethical executives, effective internal controls, credible external audits) can play an important role in minimizing the agency problem and ensuring that management's interests are aligned with those of shareholders. The pervasiveness of financial scandals and the related loss of billions of dollars of shareholder value have received extensive media coverage and attention from regulators and standard setters. This chapter discusses the importance of financial markets and the free market system, investor confidence, public trust, and effective corporate governance.

3

SIGNIFICANCE OF FINANCIAL MARKETS

About half of all households in the United States are now participating in the securities markets through private investing in public company shares, mutual funds, and public and private pension funds. Regarding the U.S. capital markets, the U.S. Treasury secretary, Henry M. Paulson, states that as the lifeblood of the nation's economy, the capital markets function as a conduit connecting

> *those who need capital with those who invest or lend capital. They play a vital role in helping entrepreneurs implement new ideas and businesses expand operations, create jobs. They give our citizens the confidence to invest, earn higher return on their savings, and reduce the costs of borrowing for student loans, mortgages, and consumer credit. Our capital markets are the deepest, most efficient, and most transparent in the world ... competitive capital markets will pave the way for continued economic growth that benefits all Americans.*[3]

The U.S. financial markets are an important sector of the nation's economy. Consider these facts:

1. The U.S. financial services industry's gross domestic product (GDP) in 2006 exceeded $1 trillion, accounting for 8.1 percent of the U.S. GDP.
2. The securities industry accounted for more than $175 billion, about 17 percent of the total for financial markets.
3. The financial services sector employed about 6 million workers in the United States in 2005, accounting for 5 percent of the total private sector employment.[4]

As employers continue to shift the responsibility for funding retirement to individual workers, the national trend of increasing inflows into mutual funds is only expected to grow and employees will need to become more knowledgeable about investing.

The financial markets play an important role in society by:

- Efficiently allocating a scarce resource of capital.
- Enabling public companies to raise capital for establishing or expanding their businesses.
- Providing a financial marketplace for individual investors to invest money in an attempt to fund their retirement goals or try to save enough for their children's education.[5]

The free enterprise system in the United States is developed and promoted to create jobs and wealth, enable growth, foster innovation, reward initiatives and risks, and effectively use resources. It has been transformed from

> *a system in which our businesses were generally owned and controlled by small groups of people—and often managed by those same people—to*

> *a system in which our businesses are owned by public investors, each of whom share a stake in the prosperity of new business opportunities and innovations. The U.S. has achieved this widespread participation by maintaining high quality disclosure standards and enforcement policies that protect the interests of public investors.*[6]

The liquidity, integrity, safety, efficiency, transparency, and dynamics of capital markets are vital to the nation's economic welfare, since the markets act as signaling mechanisms for capital allocation. The capital markets have been vibrant because investors have confidence in them and are able to obtain, analyze, and price securities based on the information provided about public companies and the economy. Information is the lifeblood of the capital markets. Without information, stocks would be mispriced, capital markets would be inefficient, scarce resources (capital) would be inefficiently used and allocated, and economic growth would not be possible.

Capital markets provide public companies the opportunities to raise capital to establish or expand their businesses as well as finance their investments and other public projects while enabling investors to put their capital to work.[7] Their efficiency, liquidity, and integrity depend on their "ability to obtain, digest, and price securities derived from information about companies and the economy."[8] Lynn Turner, a former chief accountant at the Securities and Exchange Commission (SEC), in testifying before the Senate Banking Committee, states, "[T]he ability of the U.S. capital markets to attract capital depends on investors having confidence in the integrity and transparency of the markets. Confidence is earned over time through honest and fair markets that provide investors with the material information they need to make informed decisions."[9] However, as three former chief accountants of the SEC have said: "In our capital markets a single catastrophic reporting failure is a disaster in which losses to investors and the public can be, and often are, overwhelming, wiping out decades of hard work, planning, and saving."[10]

PUBLIC TRUST AND INVESTOR CONFIDENCE

Public trust and investor confidence in the nation's economy and its capital markets are the key drivers of economic growth, prosperity, and financial stability. Investors are confident when stock prices are high, the news about future stock performance is optimistic, and financial information is perceived to be reliable. The wave of financial scandals in the late 1990s and the early 2000s coupled with the economic downturn had a substantial negative impact on investor confidence. Corporate and accounting scandals are still a major concern among investors. In May 2006, more than 71 percent of investors felt that accounting issues negatively affected the capital markets (down from 91 percent in 2002).[11] Corporate governance reforms, including the Sarbanes-Oxley Act of 2002 (SOX), SEC-related rules, listing standards of national stock exchanges, and best practices, have been established to rebuild public trust and investor confidence in corporate America. Investors would like to see changes in the corporate governance structure that not only require compliance with these reforms but also address managerial incentives and pressures, vigilance and independence of boards of directors, quality and independence of auditors, objectivity of financial analysts, and shareholder democracy in director elections. Public trust and investor confidence in public financial information is a complex issue that "cannot be legislated . . . the investment community is requiring individual companies, one by one, to earn back market trust."[12]

High-quality financial information contributes to investor willingness to invest in the capital markets, facilitates investment activities of public companies at a justifiable cost of capital, enables efficient capital markets and proper allocation of capital, contributes to business growth and expansion, and eventually supports economic growth and stability for the nation. Four factors can contribute to efficient, fair, and full disclosures and to the flow of high-quality information to the capital markets.

1. Public companies have strong incentives to disseminate high-quality financial information about their financial position and results of operations to enable them to raise capital at the lowest possible cost.
2. Federal securities laws, including the Securities Act of 1933 and the Securities Exchange Act of 1934, require fair and full disclosures of financial information, and they enforce an efficient flow of information to the capital markets by penalizing companies for furnishing misleading information.
3. Legislators have intervened through SOX to ensure public trust and investor confidence in financial information and the capital markets.
4. The capital markets have utilized mechanisms and technological advances to enable market participants to efficiently receive and use information in their investment activities and trading decisions.

The efficient functioning of the capital markets is based on the premise that all market participants comply with a set of laws, rules, regulations, standards, and best practices known as corporate governance. Investors must have confidence that corporate governance measures are effectively enforced and that public financial information disclosed by corporations is reliable. One factor that has contributed to the gradual decline of public confidence in corporate America is the public's heightened awareness of the importance of corporate accountability and responsibility as it relates to financial reporting. This can be explained in several ways. First, many institutional investors have relied less on companies to provide them with transparent, reliable, and useful information in making sound investment and voting decisions and are now relying more on themselves to make their own decisions. Corporations should focus on this trend and become trustworthy and valuable by providing high-quality financial information.

Second, investors are more inclined to look to individuals, such as directors and officers, and trust them rather than "faceless" corporations. A survey reveals that "Americans are consistently more favorable towards people than towards the institutions they represent."[13] For example, Americans place more confidence in members of the military (soldiers) than the military, a police officer than the police, the president than the presidency, and executives in major corporations than major corporations themselves. This fact suggests that a company's directors and officers, rather than the company itself, are more instrumental in influencing investor confidence and public trust. This trust can be badly damaged when executives of high-profile companies (e.g., Enron, WorldCom, Global Crossing, and Tyco among others) are convicted of crimes that harm investors.

Third, "Americans express the most confidence in people and institutions which are sworn to protect the public."[14] This finding suggests that professionals—public accountants, doctors, attorneys, financial stock brokers, and executives—are expected to be more trustworthy than laypeople. Unfortunately, the recent wave of corporate and accounting scandals, indictments, and convictions of executives has adversely affected corporate culture and the attitude of future corporate leaders. A survey shows that: (1) only 2 percent of surveyed investors reported that they believe highly in the trustworthiness of the chief executive of large companies; (2) only 9 percent said they had full trust in financial services in 2005 compared with 14 percent in 2004; and (3) over 90 percent believed that big companies have too much influence on the government.[15] Despite the low confidence that investors, both sophisticated and average, had in the ethics and corporate governance of U.S. companies, this confidence is even lower for non-U.S. companies.[16]

In its recommendations to improve corporate governance and public trust in corporate America, the Committee for Economic Development (CED) states:

> *We are unwavering advocates for the free market system, but we are just as firm in our belief that businesses and their leaders must earn the public's trust. Perceptions that firms flout rules, behave unethically, and use deceptive business processes weaken confidence in, and support for, the free enterprise system. ...We acknowledge at the outset that no laws or policies will ever be sufficient to end all corporate misbehavior (or, for that matter, misbehavior in any segment of public life). We are confident, however, that truly independent and inquisitive boards of directors will provide the best safeguard against corporate wrongdoing.*[17]

The heads of the six largest global audit networks—PricewaterhouseCoopers, KPMG, Ernst & Young, Deloitte & Touche, Grant Thornton, and BDO—believe that six important attributes make the capital market stable, efficient, and prosperous:

1. Investor need for information is well defined and met.
2. The roles of the various stakeholders in the capital markets (preparers, investors, regulators, standard setters) are aligned and supported by effective forums for continuous dialogue.
3. The auditing profession is vibrant and sustainable in adding value to the efficiency and growth of the capital markets.
4. A new business reporting model reflecting both financial and nonfinancial performance measures is developed to provide relevant and reliable information in a timely manner.

. 5. Large, collusive frauds, particularly financial statement frauds, are increasingly rare.

6. Financial information is reported and audited pursuant to globally consistent standards.[18]

The two key contributing factors to the efficient functioning of the financial markets are entrepreneurs and reliable financial information, both of which are provided by public companies. The next section presents the important role that corporations play in the financial markets.

CORPORATIONS' ROLE IN SOCIETY

Corporations with entrepreneurial spirit are the main engines that drive the nation's economy and its capital markets to long-term sustainable prosperity. Corporations have contributed to the creation of millions of jobs, which have helped to maintain unemployment at below 5 percent for many years in the United States. Corporations and their financial information contribute to the safety, integrity, and efficiency of capital markets. The financial markets provide a means of ensuring retirement funds for senior citizens, college tuition funds for the younger generation, and income for the workforce. Thus, the safety, integrity, and efficiency of the capital markets can benefit everyone. As depicted in Exhibit 1.1, corporations in the United States are viewed as creators of sustainable economic value. Public companies have a set of contractual relationships with a broad range of participants, including shareholders, creditors, vendors, customers, employees, governmental agencies, auditors, and global communities and societies.[19] Corporations are viewed as a nexus of contracts with their stakeholders.[20] Contracting participants pursue their own goals and continue their relationships with the company only so long as there is a mutual interest and the company creates value for them. Society in general and the government in particular create an environment in which corporations are able to fulfill their social responsibility and tax obligations.

Public companies are vital to the nation's economic growth and prosperity. Sustainable performance of public companies depends on the willingness of investors to invest in them. Such willingness has been undermined by a loss of confidence in corporations and their directors and officers to look after the interests of investors. Public companies rely on public sources of funding through issuing stocks as opposed to private funding through banks or selected groups of investors. For this open financial system to function effectively there should be an appropriate system of checks and balances, namely an effective corporate governance structure. The separation of ownership and control in the open financial system can result in the agency problem between management and shareholders, where management's interests may not be aligned with those of shareholders, or where management withholds important information from shareholders (information asymmetry). Under the open system, shareholders invest in a corporation and elect the board of directors, which then hires management to run the corporation.

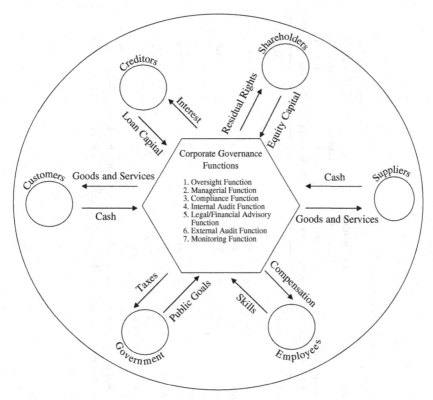

EXHIBIT 1.1   Corporations' Role in Society
Source: Extracted from Z. Rezaee, *Financial Statement Fraud: Prevention and Detection* (Hoboken, NJ: John Wiley & Sons, 2002)

Exhibit 1.2 shows the distribution of 9,428 public companies by market capitalization as of June 2005. The exhibit indicates that about 77.1 percent of total public companies and about 5.5 percent of the total U.S. equity market capitalization are made up of public companies with less than $700 million market capitalization whereas 22.9 percent of the total U.S. public companies and about 94.5 percent of the total U.S. equity market capitalization have greater than $700 million market capitalization. The majority of new jobs in the public sector are created by smaller companies, which constitute about 80 percent of all public companies. As smaller companies grow, the integrity and quality of their financial reporting become more important to investors who provide capital for them.

Corporations are separate legal entities. Shareholders are not involved in day-to-day corporate decision making and thus cannot know enough about the company's condition to evaluate management's performance. The agency theory implies that the board of directors is elected to manage the potential conflict

EXHIBIT 1.2 Distribution of Companies, by Market Capitalization (March/June 2005)

Market Capitalization	Number of Companies	Average Market Capitalization (in millions)	Median Market Capitalization (in millions)	Percent of Companies (%)	Cumulative Percent of Number of Companies (%)	Percent of Market Capitalization (%)	Cumulative Percent of Market Capitalization (%)
$ 0 to $ 25m	2,641	$8.2	$6.3	28.0	28.0	0.1	0.1
$ 25m to $ 50m	965	36.1	35.0	10.2	38.2	0.2	0.3
$ 50m to $ 75m	565	62.0	62.0	6.0	44.2	0.2	0.5
$ 75m to $100m	418	86.9	86.5	4.4	48.7	0.2	0.8
$100m to $200m	1,020	143.3	140.9	10.8	59.5	0.9	1.6
$200m to $500m	1,270	325.0	314.6	13.5	73.0	2.4	4.1
$500m to $700m	393	597.8	601.8	4.2	77.1	1.4	5.5
$700 to $ 1b	408	839.1	831.8	4.3	81.5	2.0	7.5
$1b to $ 5b	1,195	2,173.6	1,839.3	12.7	94.1	15.4	22.9
$5b to $ 10b	234	7,099.6	6,851.2	2.5	96.6	9.8	32.7
$10b or more	319	35,637.8	18,803.5	3.4	100.0	67.3	100.0

Source: Adapted from Securities and Exchange Commission, Final Report of the Advisory Committee on Smaller Public Companies to the U.S. Securities and Exchange Commission, April 23, 2006. Available at: www.sec.gov/info.smallbus/acspc/acspc-finalreport.pdf.

of interests between management and shareholders. It further assumes that this internal mechanism is designed to align the interests of management with those of the shareholders without the need for external mechanisms (e.g., regulations and rules). The first wave of financial scandals at the turn of the twenty-first century and the second rash of option backdating scandals in 2006 prove that internal mechanisms alone may not be adequate. There should be a set of laws, rules, regulations, standards, and best practices that lead management to act ethically and responsively, in the best interest of shareholders, and to provide market participants with accurate, complete, timely, and useful information. It is unrealistic to expect all corporate directors and officers to provide accurate and complete financial information all the time. Indeed, the reported financial scandals and highly publicized financial restatements prove that directors and officers can be motivated to provide misleading and fraudulent financial reports when the opportunities exist. Thus, corporate governance measures are designed to create a culture of ethical conduct and compliance and to ensure that investors receive accurate, complete, and timely information to make investment and voting decisions.

Investors are responsible for providing needed capital to facilitate the effective operation of the company and have a right to elect their representatives, the company's board of directors. The board of directors is authorized to make decisions on behalf of its constituents (investors) and is directly responsible for selecting and continuously monitoring management's decisions and actions without micromanaging. Management is authorized to run the company and is responsible and accountable for decisions made and actions taken with the primary purpose of creating and enhancing sustainable shareholder value. Corporate governance provides the opportunity for shareholders to monitor the company's board of directors and enables the board to oversee management and facilitate management's decision-making process, which creates shareholder value. Corporate governance should create an appropriate balance of power-sharing that:

- Provides shareholder democracy in freely electing directors (e.g., the majority voting system).
- Enables the board of directors to make strategic decisions and oversee and consult with management without micromanaging.
- Empowers management to run the company.

The separation of ownership and control in the modern corporate structure, the diffuse nature of ownership, and the focus on protecting the interests of a wide range of stakeholders (investors, creditors, employees, management, customers, suppliers, government, and others) necessitate the need for an effective corporate governance structure that addresses, manages, and minimizes potential conflicts of interest among corporate governance participants. These conflicts of interest are commonly referred to as an agency problem resulting from differences in incentives and goals of corporate governance participants and information asymmetry among those participants. The primary goal of corporate governance is not simply to reduce agency costs, but to create an equitable balance of power and access to relevant information among all corporate governance participants, particularly shareholders, directors, and management. Recent financial scandals have raised serious concerns about how this balance is being managed and who is watching over the companies to ensure that shareholders' interests are being protected.

SOURCES OF INFORMATION TO THE CAPITAL MARKETS

Technological advances, including the Internet, enable investors to have real-time online access to a large volume of information about public companies—their governance, operations, and investment choices—and capital markets. The Internet facilitates the flow of fair and transparent information to all investors, individuals, and institutions, small or large. Investors have online access to companies' financial disclosures filings and auditor and analyst reports, and they rely on information public companies disseminate to the capital markets in making investment and voting decisions. Information from public companies flows into the marketplace from three fundamental sources: regulated disclosures, voluntary disclosures, and research analyst reports.[21]

Regulated Disclosures

The United States Congress established the capital markets as a disclosure-based system rather than a merit-based system. That is, the SEC regulates the capital markets by establishing rules and regulations that require public companies to disclose material information that may impact investors' investment decisions. The SEC does not regulate by determining the merits of whether it is appropriate for a company to be public and sell its stock to the public. Accordingly, in the late 1990s, the SEC permitted dot-com companies to make initial public offerings (IPOs) despite questionable business plans, recurring losses, and little or no revenue streams, provided they made the required disclosures.

Regulated disclosures include filings with the SEC of annual audited financial statements on Form 10-K, quarterly reviewed financial reports on Form 10-Q, extraordinary transactions on a current basis on Form 8-K (e.g., auditor changes, resignation or death of a director or an officer, bankruptcy), and internal control reports for large public companies (Sections 302 and 404). These filings are discussed in detail in Chapter 6. Financial statements and internal control reports should be prepared from the perspective of shareholders who have residual claims on a company's assets. These regulated financial disclosures are a vital source of information to investors. These disclosures create a way for public companies to communicate with their shareholders about financial and corporate governance issues that affect their financial condition and results of operations. SEC-mandated filings have been criticized for encouraging public companies to focus on the short-term performance of meeting earnings forecasts and creating a check-box compliance mentality in order to ensure minimum compliance with SEC rules rather than focusing on improving earnings quality and quantity.[22]

Donald T. Nicolaisen, the former chief accountant of the SEC, stated regarding the importance of high-quality financial information that "financial reporting can be a matter of life and death ... If this [the wave of accounting scandals and corporate fraud] happened in the medical profession, we wouldn't stand for it. It's time for the accounting profession and the business community to catch up."[23] Financial disclosures under SEC regulations are a step forward in providing investors with reliable financial information. William McDonough, the former chairman of the Public Company Accounting Oversight Board (PCAOB), stated, "[C]onfidence in the accuracy of accounting statements is the bedrock of investors being willing to invest, in lenders to lend and for employees knowing that their firms' obligations to them can be trusted."[24] The SEC, through its EDGAR online filing and disclosure system, has the potential to facilitate electronic access and the ability to compare financial reports of public companies. The SEC is also promoting the use of tagged financial reporting data by utilizing the eXtensible Business Reporting Language (XBRL) to enable investors and other market participants to access and analyze financial data from different software platforms. The move toward the use of the XBRL format should provide investors with online real-time access to a large volume of standardized tagged financial information. On September 25, 2006, the SEC announced that it awarded three separate contracts totaling $54 million to transform its filing disclosure system from a form-based electronic filing cabinet to a dynamic real-time system with interactive capabilities.[25] The three contracts are intended to: (1) modernize and maintain the EDGAR database to use interactive data using the XBRL language; (2) complete XBRL code writing for U.S. GAAP (generally accepted accounting principles) financial statements by preparing XBRL taxonomies that can be used by all companies in all industries; and (3) develop interactive data tools for investors on the SEC's Web site to enable investors to view and analyze companies' financial data that are filed in XBRL.

The value of investors' investment and quality of their voting decisions depend on the accuracy of information they used in the decision-making process. It is expected that in the post-SOX era, investors will have more access to better-quality financial information for four reasons:

1. New corporate governance reforms (SOX, SEC rules, listing standards), which promote more shareholder democracy (e.g., majority voting, declassified boards)
2. More vigilant oversight responsibility by boards of directors, particularly the audit committee
3. Executive certifications of internal controls and financial statements
4. Improved audit objectivity and independence (the PCAOB, SEC rules)

The SEC's self-filing financial disclosures have worked well in requiring public companies to file their quarterly reviews and annual audited financial statements and in punishing companies for filing misleading financial reports or violating securities laws. The SEC, by moving toward convergence and principles-based global accounting standards, can facilitate the flow of capital across national borders and enable investors to gain access to more easily available, less complex, and more comparable global financial information. The SEC's success in achieving its mission of protecting investors from receiving misleading financial and regulated disclosures and maintaining efficient, transparent, and competitive capital markets can only be measured in terms of investor confidence in the markets. Establishing appropriate securities laws and maintaining effective enforcement of the laws is essential in sustaining investor confidence. Securities laws that are not cost-effective, efficient, and scalable and are not effectively enforced can erode investor confidence.

Voluntary Disclosures

Public companies often voluntarily release earnings guidance regarding projected performance and other financial and nonfinancial information in addition to their mandated disclosures. Public companies have traditionally provided investors and analysts with earnings guidance. This practice was initiated during the 1970s, when many companies began privately communicating their earnings forecasts to large investors; it become a common practice during the stock market boom of the 1990s, particularly when Congress protected companies from liability for their earnings forecasts.[26] Earnings announcements, even though not required, provide valuable information to market participants and motivate companies to meet their earnings expectations. Voluntarily released earnings guidance is expected to result in higher valuations, lower volatility, and improved liquidity.[27] However, a study reveals that while corporate earnings guidance may increase trading volumes in the short term, it does not increase valuations and has no lasting effect on stock price volatility or liquidity.[28] The 2006 survey of 213 finance executives who prepare financial reports including earnings guidance indicates that: (1) the majority (53 percent) issuing earning guidance, about 37 percent, do not issue such guidance and more than 10 percent while still issuing earnings guidance are considering issuing it less frequently; and (2) the majority (59 percent) do not think that eliminating quarterly reports (10-Qs) and keeping just annual reports (10-Ks) would serve shareholder interests of focusing companies on long-term performance.[29]

Several prominent public companies (e.g., Coca-Cola, Intel, Ford, General Motors, Google, and Citigroup) have discontinued the practice of issuing earnings guidance and instead issue more detailed performance measures.[30] These companies have decided to focus on sustainable goals and long-term performance instead of short-term earnings achievements. They are attempting to avoid both the costs associated with releasing earnings guidance and the possible negative impacts on stock price if earnings guidance targets are not met. However, the majority of surveyed companies (83 percent) that are already issuing earnings guidance plan to continue to do so. About 75 percent of the surveyed companies believe that earnings guidance helps to satisfy requests from investors and analysts, and over half report that the guidance facilitates management's focus on financial goals.[31]

Surveyed executives do not agree on the costs and benefits of releasing earnings guidance. The perceived benefits of issuing earnings guidance include:

- Satisfying requests from investors and analysts.
- Maintaining a channel of communication with investors.
- Intensifying management's focus on achieving financial targets.
- Moderating the volatility of the company's share price.[32]

Ironically, potential benefits did not include achieving higher valuations, building a wider shareholder base, or increasing liquidity.[33] The executives surveyed mentioned costs associated with issuing earnings releases, including the cost of management time, the shortcomings of focus on short-term earnings, and the cost of employee time.[34] The survey also reveals that sell-side analysts demand earnings guidance more insistently than mutual/pension funds and hedge funds and that discontinuing earnings guidance releases may decrease the company's visibility and cause analysts to reduce coverage.[35]

Merrill Lynch believes it would be in investors' best interests if companies dropped quarterly earnings guidance. It claims that market participants need to see earnings guidance for what it is—a rough assessment of one indicator of a company's well-being. Earnings guidance dictates an outcome and discourages debate.[36] It is not accurate and is constructed in such a way that companies have "either [met] or 'beat[en]' their guidance in 56 of the last 59 quarters."[37]

Large public companies, their analysts, and fund managers are in favor of discontinuation of quarterly earnings guidance. This discontinuation is expected to change the relationship between company's executives and financial analysts, as well as the way fund managers are evaluated and rewarded. Quarterly earnings guidance has been provided because it: (1) assists management to focus on short-term results; (2) makes forecasting by analysts easier; and (3) enables hedge funds to profit from discrepancies between actual earnings and forecasted earnings. However, earnings guidance, by focusing on the company's short-term performance at the expense of its long-term health, is detrimental to sustainable shareholder value creation and enhancement.

The CFA Institute Center for Financial Market Integrity and the Business Roundtable Institute for Corporate Ethics issued a report that calls on corporate leaders (CEOs, CFOs), asset managers, investors, and others to: (1) break the short-term obsession that is detrimental to corporate governance effectiveness and sustainable shareholder interest; (2) reform practices involving earnings guidance, compensation, and communications to investors; and (3) adopt practices to promote sustainable and enduring shareholder value creation and enhancement.[38] The report outlines a broad set of recommendations, suggesting that companies, their leaders, institutional investors, analysts, and asset managers deemphasize short-term performance. The nine specific recommendations are to:

1. Reform earnings guidance practice by reconsidering the benefits and consequences of providing earnings guidance and making adjustments to earnings guidance that best reflect shareholders' sustainable interests.
2. Develop long-term incentives across the board by linking compensation for corporate executives and asset managers to the achievement of long-term strategic and value-creation goals.
3. Demonstrate corporate leadership by focusing on sustainable shareholder value creation and enhancement.
4. Improve communications and transparency by providing more meaningful and frequent information regarding the company's strategy and long-term value

drivers that could effectively lessen the financial community's dependence on earnings guidance.
5. Promote broad education for all market participants about the benefits of long-term thinking and the costs of short-term thinking.
6. End the practice of providing quarterly earnings guidance.
7. Align corporate executive compensation with long-term shareholder interests.
8. Improve disclosure of asset managers' incentive metrics, fee structures, and personal ownership of funds they manage.
9. Endorse the use of corporate long-term investment statements to shareholders that adequately reflect the company's operating model.[39]

The report states: "The obsession with short-term results leads to the unintended consequences of destroying long-term value, decreasing market efficiency, reducing investment returns and impeding efforts to strengthen corporate governance."[40] William Donaldson, former SEC chairman, while supporting recent efforts to convince public companies to stop issuing quarterly earnings, warned that any movement in this direction should be balanced by increasing disclosure about the company's key performance indicators, including long-term strategic goals.[41] Christopher Cox, the chairman of the SEC, says that "recent calls for public companies to stop issuing quarterly earnings guidance are healthy recommendations."[42] However, any efforts in reforming earnings estimates should not make public companies less transparent or their disclosures less frequent to investors. Relevant, timely, and forward-looking information is vital to the financial market and is instrumental in reducing financial risk and uncertainty over corporate prospects.

Technological advances enable corporations to utilize a variety of means to communicate with their shareholders and other users of their financial and nonfinancial information. An increasing number of high-profile companies publish corporate blogs and online diaries to disseminate relevant information. SEC disclosure rules including Regulation Fair Disclosure (Reg. FD) allow public companies to provide information by any broad and nonexclusionary methods including blogs, Web sites, webcasts, news releases, and regulatory filings that reach a broad audience. Indeed, in the first official communication posted to a blog by Christopher Cox, the chairman of the SEC encourages companies to disclose significant financial information through blogs as a way to expand investors' access to relevant information.[43] As of November 2006, more than 30 Fortune 500 companies, including Amazon.com, Cisco Systems, Oracle, Boeing, and General Motors, were utilizing blogs to disseminate relevant, broad, nonexclusionary, timely, and robust information to the investing public.[44]

Research Analyst Reports

Financial analysts who follow and project companies' future earnings and evaluate their short-term quarterly performance are an important source of information and are essential to transparent and efficient capital markets. Analysts forecast for both long-term and short-term earnings quality and quantity. The mere focus on short-term analyst forecasts and quarterly earnings guidance when such earnings numbers can be easily managed through either acceleration of revenue recognition or deferral of investments (e.g., technology, research, and development) can create an illusion of value relevance of earnings releases. Management has traditionally manipulated earnings disclosures by establishing or promoting a low threshold for earnings forecasts and then attempting to beat the forecasts through actual lower-than-optimum performance or earnings management. This process can lead to the misallocation of investor capital when reported earnings are higher than management-forecasted earnings.

Academic research documents that sell-side analysts' earnings estimates and forecast revisions provide an important source of information to the marketplace, with a stronger market reaction to upward rather than downward forecast revisions.[45] During the economic and market boom of the 1990s, the objective and skeptical mental attitude of analysts became almost irrelevant. The perception was that the analysts' research was not influenced by investment banking concerns. However, reported financial scandals of the early 2000s raised three concerns regarding analysts' conflicts of interest:

1. While the Nasdaq Composite Index was dropping by more than 60 percent, less than 1 percent of analysts' recommendations in 2000 were to sell.
2. About 99 percent of all recommendations by sell-side analysts were to hold, buy, or strong buy.
3. Public companies often withheld business from firms whose analysts issued unfavorable reports.[46]

SOX and SEC-related rules on Regulation Analyst Certification (Reg. AC) address the objectivity of analysts' forecasts and forecast revisions; the topic is discussed in detail in Chapter 8. Reg. AC requires that research reports distributed by brokers and dealers certify that the views expressed in the reports accurately reflect authors' personal views of the securities or issuers and state whether the authors' compensation was, is, or will be directly or indirectly related to the expressed recommendations or views.[47] The National Association of Securities Dealers (NASD) in 2006 issued its guide to understanding securities analyst recommendations, which suggests that analysts' ratings do not have clear and standardized meanings (e.g., "underperform" means different things to different analysts) and a potential conflict of interest may influence an analyst's recommendations.[48] Thus, investors should be aware of both the nature (potential conflicts) and content (meanings) of analyst recommendations.

The current system of financial disclosures—which consists of mandated disclosures of quarterly, annual, and other filings with the SEC; voluntary disclosures of earnings guidance above and beyond the required disclosures by the SEC; and analyst reports—has served the capital markets, investors, public companies, and regulators well. Nonetheless, this model captures only financial information regarding financial conditions and results of operations. A corporate reporting model that captures both financial and nonfinancial key performance indicators is needed. Nonfinancial information disseminated to the capital markets by public companies includes:

- Market information, such as market growth, market share, and regulatory environment.
- Corporate governance information, such as board of directors' composition, structure, and committees.

- Strategic information, such as goals and objectives.
- Information about management, such as track record, compensation plans, and incentive plans.
- Value-creating information, such as customers, employees, suppliers, innovative brands, and supply chain.
- Corporate responsibility information, such as environmental, ethical, and social information.
- Forecasts, projections, and other technical and quantitative market information.

Investors demand forward-looking financial and nonfinancial information, and companies have strived to provide such information. PricewaterhouseCoopers has recently published a practical guide based on best practices of providing a view of the future that investors need.[49] PwC's guide is based on the seven pillars of effective communication by public companies to their stakeholders, including shareholders:

1. Resources available to the company and how they are managed.
2. Key risk and uncertainties that may affect the company's sustainable performance in creating long-term value for its shareholders.
3. The significant relationships with principal stakeholders (e.g., shareholders, customers, suppliers, employees, governments, and society) that are likely to affect the company's sustainable performance.
4. Quantified data pertaining to trends and factors that are likely to influence the company's future prospects.
5. Any uncertainties underpinning forward-looking information.
6. Targets relating to key performance indicators (both financial and nonfinancial) used to manage the company's business.
7. How the report reflects the company's long-term objectives and the strategies to achieve those objectives.[50]

The ever-growing complexity of business transactions (e.g., derivatives fair-value measurements), recent regulatory reforms, and litigious environment have contributed to the complexity of accounting standards. Overly complex accounting standards may not provide the necessary guidance for the preparers and auditors to produce high-quality financial information and can create a significant cost burden with little value to investors. Regulators (SEC), standard setters, and the business community should work together to address the complexity. While regulators should review the accuracy and completeness of financial reports as well as proper disclosures of business transactions, they should avoid second guessing management's judgments. When issuing accounting and auditing standards to assist in the preparation of high-quality financial information, standard setters should make their standards cost-effective, efficient, and scalable. Corporations should regard the preparation and dissemination of high-quality financial reports as their ultimate goal and fiduciary duty to the investing public. Any improvements in this system—such as more timely and ready access to relevant information by using the XBRL format, greater focus on a principles-based approach to financial reporting, or less complexity in and convergence toward globally accepted accounting standards—enable public companies to provide better-quality financial information to investors.

The capital markets in the United States, the strongest in the world, cannot survive without public trust and investor confidence in the reliability of the financial information disseminated to them. The reported financial scandals and financial restatements have underscored how vital these qualities are. The reliability, relevance, usefulness, and transparency of information disseminated to the marketplace depend on personal integrity, competence, and professional accountability of those involved in the financial reporting process. These participants are management, boards of directors (including the audit committee), independent auditors, and financial and legal advisors. Management is primarily responsible for the reliability and completeness of financial and nonfinancial reports; the other participants are corporate gatekeepers, as discussed in the next section. These gatekeepers play an important role in influencing the quality of information corporations disseminate to the marketplace.

CORPORATE GATEKEEPERS

True corporate governance reforms and best practices require the establishment of four key gatekeepers that ensure proper checks and balances and accountability for financial reporting. These gatekeepers are:

1. An independent and competent board to oversee management's strategy and financial reporting performance.
2. An independent and competent external auditor to provide a high level of assurance as to the reliability, quality, and transparency of the financial reports of public companies.
3. Competent legal counsel to provide ethical legal advice and to ensure that there is more than mere technical compliance with applicable laws, regulations, rules, and standards.
4. Competent and ethical financial advisors and investment bankers to advise companies in conducting their business affairs.

These gatekeepers play a key role in the effective and efficient functioning of the capital markets. Investors look to and often rely on the gatekeepers to protect their interests; regulators hold them accountable for guarding against corporate malfeasance and misleading financial information. It should be noted that legal counsel and financial advisors are generally viewed as advocates for those they represent as opposed to being investors' representatives. The other two gatekeepers—the board of directors and the independent auditor—are legally and conceptually regarded as representing investors with the purpose of protecting investor interests.

A look at the recent high-profile financial scandals shows that the failures of these gatekeepers were significant contributory factors. The question often heard during the reported financial scandals at the turn of the twenty-first century, "where were gatekeepers," is being asked again as more than 200 companies are being investigated by federal authorities for their practice of backdating employee stock option grants. Backdating practices enable the company's executives and key personnel to profit by retroactively locking in a low purchase price for stock.

To fulfill their responsibilities effectively, gatekeepers should:

- Be objective and fully independent from the company.
- Exercise professional skepticism when dealing with the company's management or relying on management representations.
- Effectively discharge their professional responsibility to the company and its investors.
- Withdraw from any engagement when the integrity of their work is compromised due to conflicts of interest or if they become aware that misleading representations have explicitly or implicitly been made to investors due to factors beyond their control.

The value-adding activities, roles, and responsibilities of gatekeepers and other corporate governance participants are examined in more detail in Chapters 3 through 10. No corporate governance would be necessary if management acted in the best interests of shareholders and if corporate gatekeepers (board of directors, lawyers, and accountants) effectively discharged their fiduciary duties and professional responsibilities. Corporate governance is needed to avoid concentration of power in the hands of management and to create an effective system of checks and balances to balance power-sharing authority among shareholders, boards of directors, and management. Due to corporate governance reforms, all gatekeepers have increased responsibility and accountability to work toward the achievement of sustainable shareholder value creation and enhancement. The effectiveness of these reforms depends on the quality of the value-adding professional judgment of all gatekeepers.

Corporate governance is conceived broadly in this book in terms of institutional arrangements and mechanisms that affect and are affected by the role of corporate governance participants, particularly all corporate gatekeepers. Public companies have recently undergone a series of reforms intended to improve the effectiveness and objectivity of corporate gatekeepers. Corporate governance has been a central issue within those companies, and it is becoming a process through which shareholders induce management to act in the best interests of the company and its shareholders. A study of more than 300 global institutional investors reveals that corporate governance concerns are still very much on the rise even in the post-SOX era.[51] The study also indicates that "corporate governance means different things to different people," which is the topic that will be discussed in the remainder of this chapter.[52]

CORPORATE GOVERNANCE

Philosophy

The corporate governance philosophy adopted herein does not advocate a "one-size-fits-all" approach to governance and management of the company. Instead, it focuses on a conceptual and integrated approach to creating an appropriate balance between the two complementary, and yet often conflicting, forces of the decision control vested in the company's board of directors and management and its ownership control exercised by shareholders. Shareholders elect directors to govern the company; then directors hire top management and other key professionals, such as financial advisors, legal counsel, and auditors, among others, to operate the company for the benefits of the shareholders. Thus, shareholders place trust in management to act in their best interests, and they rely on corporate governance mechanisms to reinforce this trust, although it may be adversely affected by conflicts of interest and information asymmetries between management and shareholders. The principal-agent relationship can be aligned and strengthened through a proper system of checks and balances and accountability provided by corporate governance.

The effectiveness of corporate governance depends in part on compliance with appropriate state and federal statutes as well as listing standards and best practices suggested by investor activists and professional organizations. Failure to comply with such standards could result in fines, delisting penalties, and bad press, causing a substantial devaluation of the share price and ultimately bankruptcy. While compliance is required, it does not guarantee effective corporate governance. Effective corporate governance can be achieved only when all participants:

- Add value to the company's sustainable long-term performance.
- Effectively carry out their fiduciary duty and professional responsibilities.
- Are held accountable and personally responsible for their performance.
- Develop a practice of compliance combined with a commitment to the highest ethical standards with a goal of avoiding potential conflicts of interest and acting in the best interests of the company and its shareholders.

The 2006 Global Study by the Institutional Shareholder Services (ISS) finds that corporate governance has transformed from a compliance obligation to a business imperative, and it is now regarded as being a part of the ownership responsibility.[53] This business imperative philosophy is advocated and discussed throughout this book. As one would expect, well-governed companies outperform weak-governed companies over the long term. A study by Governance Metrics International reveals that companies with less effective corporate governance, measured in terms of less board oversight, were more likely to restate their earnings and financial statements and were less compliant with corporate governance reforms than well-governed companies.[54] Academic research suggests that good (poor) corporate governance is associated with higher (lower) profits, less (more) risk, less (more) stock price volatility, higher (lower) values, and larger (smaller) cash payouts; and that firms with stronger corporate governance experienced higher stock returns (an average abnormal return of 8.5 percent per year) than those with weaker corporate governance during the 1990s.[55]

Definition

The business literature has defined corporate governance in different ways and from different perspectives. Some authors define corporate governance from a regulatory perspective as "the system of laws, rules, and factors that control operations at a company."[56] Others define it from the point of view of corporate governance participants and the related constraints of dealing "with the ways in which suppliers of finance to corporations assure themselves of getting a return on their investment."[57] Yet others view corporate governance as more than merely the relationship between the company and its capital providers, by focusing on the broader aspects of stakeholders. In the areas of law and economics, corporate governance investigates how to secure and motivate efficient management of corporations by the use of incentive mechanisms, such as contracts, organizational design, and legislation.[58] Corporate governance can also be defined in the context of the agency theory, as a process designed to align interests of management (agent) with those of shareholders (principals), and to hold management accountable to the company's equity owners.

In essence, corporate governance is a legal concept used to describe corporate oversight accountability and the balance of power that exists among shareholders, management, and directors. The legal definition of corporate governance focuses on the enforcement of shareholders' rights, stating that "the field of corporate governance is concerned with the rules and principles that regulate the power relationship among owners [shareholders], directors, and managers."[59] Thus, corporate governance defines shareholders' rights and their enforcement and the fiduciary duties of the company's directors and officers to its shareholders. State laws have traditionally provided the definition and enforcement of shareholders' rights. Nonetheless, federal laws and regulations (SOX, SEC rules), through proxy rules and public filings, have significantly influenced the enforcement of shareholders' rights.[60] Institutional investors have used the federal proxy rules in an effort to shape and improve corporate governance practices at individual companies. Thus, from a legal point of view, corporate governance is influenced by state and federal laws as well as regulations and the listing standards of national stock exchanges.

In practice, effective corporate governance can be described as a vigorous set of checks and balances that establish responsibilities, require accountability, and enforce consequences. In this context, the term "corporate governance" refers to the company's decision-making and control processes as determined by its board of directors. Thus, it can be more narrowly defined as the extent of a company's compliance with applicable laws, rules, regulations, standards, and best practices, or it can be more widely defined as a company's relationship with a wide range of corporate governance participants, including the board of directors, management, auditors, legal counsel, financial advisors, regulators, standard setters, shareholders, and other stakeholders. Corporate governance is a process effected by legal, regulatory, contractual, and market-based mechanisms and best practices to create substantial shareholder value while protecting the interests of other shareholders. This definition is adopted in this book and implies that there is a dispersed ownership structure and thus the role of corporate governance is to limit opportunistic behavior of management. In a capital structure where there is concentrated ownership and a small group of shareholders can exercise ownership control, corporate governance should ensure alignment of interests of controlling shareholders with those of minority or individual shareholders.

Corporate Governance Drivers

The corporate governance structure in the United States is a hybrid system of laws, regulations, and best practices. The primary drivers of corporate governance are state corporate laws, federal and state securities law, judicial process, stock exchange listing standards, best practices, and market correction mechanisms. These drivers are synthesized next and discussed more thoroughly in Chapter 6.

State Corporate Laws Corporations are incorporated in a particular state. Each state establishes its own corporate laws, and its court system interprets that law. State corporate laws establish a minimum standard of conduct for corporations and their directors, officers, and shareholders; they also specify the fiduciary duties, authorities, and responsibilities of each. State corporate laws influence corporate governance by creating a balanced power-sharing situation among company shareholders, directors, and management. Corporate law specifically affects corporate governance issues relating to company formation, rights of shareholders, fiduciary duties of directors and officers, financial reporting and disclosures, proxy rights at annual shareholder meetings, voting procedures, rights of foreign creditors and shareholders, and rights of minority shareholders. For example, according to Delaware general corporate law requirements:

- The board of directors must have at least one member.
- The board has the authority to run the business and affairs of the corporation.
- The board has the authority to designate new members if a current member is disqualified or resigns.
- Any committee can create a subcommittee, given that there is at least one committee member on the subcommittee.
- Directors are protected while performing their duties as long as they accept documents from officers, employees, and others in good faith and exercise due care.
- The company can loan money or provide other assistance to any director or employee.
- Nonindependent directors and directors with interests in other corporations are allowed as long as the relationship is disclosed and is not detrimental to the company.[61]

Federal Securities Laws During the early 1900s and prior to the establishment of the SEC in 1934, financial markets in the United States were primarily unregulated. Prior to the market crash of 1929, there was not much interest in federal regulation of the securities markets.[62] Investors did not have much of an appetite for the regulations requiring financial disclosure or the federal oversight of the securities market. The Securities Act of 1933 was passed by Congress with the primary purpose of requiring that investors receive adequate financial and other information regarding securities offered for public sale, prohibiting misinterpretations, deceit, and other fraud in the sale of securities. The Securities Exchange Act of 1934 provided protection for investors who trade securities by creating the SEC to oversee the securities industry. SOX was passed by Congress in July 2002 to further hold public companies accountable for their financial reports.

Federal securities laws are passed by Congress and are intended to protect investors and improve investor confidence. Lawmakers can influence corporate governance in two ways: (1) through their legislation, such as the passage of securities laws; and (2) through their efforts, often motivated by lobbyists, to influence the SEC's rule-making process. Legislation has been very effective and beneficial in protecting investors from corporate malfeasance and in creating an environment in which corporations conduct their legitimate business of creating shareholder value. Efforts by lawmakers to influence the SEC have been controversial and contra-effective, as stated by former SEC chairman Arthur Levitt:

> *Every day, the SEC would receive letters from lawmakers opposing some proposed regulatory change—[auditing reforms, expensing of stock options]—letters that eerily mimicked the rhetoric of one industry trade group or another ... Many of the reforms that were thwarted in this way could have saved investors some of the pain from the scandals of the past five years.*[63]

The two fundamental federal securities laws pertaining to public companies are the Securities Act of 1933 and Securities Exchange Act of 1934. These Acts are primarily disclosure-based statutes that require public companies to file periodic reports with the SEC and to disclose certain information to shareholders. Since its inception in 1934, the SEC has influenced corporate governance beyond its mandatory disclosure requirements through establishing rules to regulate the disclosures and processes for proxy statements. The federal securities laws, while providing a regulatory environment within which public companies operate, do not generally "address rules of corporate conduct affecting the market place, except as to matters such as disclosure and fraud."[64]

Judicial Process   Court cases brought under both state and federal laws have had some positive impacts on public companies' governance. For example, as part of the settlement negotiated by public pension funds (the California Public Employees' Retirement System, the New York State Common Retirement Fund, and the New York City Pension Funds) in *In re Cendant*, in addition to a $3.2 billion cash settlement, Cendant agreed to several corporate governance reforms to prevent further occurrence of financial fraud.[65] The measures adopted at Cendant required:

- The majority of directors to be independent directors.
- The establishment of audit, compensation, and nominating committees composed solely of independent directors.
- The elimination of the staggered board.
- Shareholder approval regarding the repricing of underwater options.[66]

Another example of the influence of courts on the development of corporate governance is the recent decision by the Second Circuit Court of Appeals, on

September 5, 2006.[67] The court decision overturned the SEC's staff interpretations that allow public companies to exclude shareholder proposals on nomination of directors from proxies. Indeed, the court ruled that under the existing SEC rules, shareholders may access the proxy for purposes of submitting proposals regarding the nomination of their choice of a candidate for director. The SEC, in October 2003, released a proposed rule that would require public companies to include in their proxy material shareholder nominees for election as director in order to enhance shareholders' ability to participate in the proxy process for the nomination and election of directors.[68] As of April 2007, no further actions had been taken by the SEC to finalize its proposal. It is expected that the court's decision will encourage the SEC to improve disclosure regarding nominees of long-term shareholders.

Listing Standards   Listing standards adopted by national stock exchanges establish corporate governance standards for companies in order to promote high standards of corporate democracy, corporate responsibility, and accountability to shareholders, and to monitor the operation of the securities markets. Corporate governance listing standards address a variety of issues, from uniform voting rights to the mandatory audit committee formation and shareholder approvals of broad-based option plans. These listing standards are regarded as "rules" under the 1934 Exchange Act, and as such they must be approved by the SEC before they become effective.

Listing standards of national stock exchanges (NYSE, Nasdaq, and AMEX) go beyond provisions of SOX in establishing corporate governance rules for listed companies.[69] The seven key provisions of these listing standards follow.

1. Listed companies must have a majority of independent directors (e.g., two-thirds independent directors). However, investor advocates argue that the definition of "independent directors" adopted by national stock exchanges should be further strengthened.
2. An independent director is one who has no material relationships (e.g., financial, affiliation) with the company.
3. Independent directors must meet regularly (e.g., at least four times a year) without the presence of management.
4. Listed companies must have at least three mandatory board committees, including audit, compensation, and nominating/governance.
5. The three mandatory board committees must:
   a. Be composed solely of independent directors.
   b. Have a written charter addressing their purpose, goals, roles, authority, responsibilities, and resources.
   c. Conduct the entire board and the committees' annual performance evaluation.
6. Listed companies must adopt and disclose their corporate governance guidelines.
7. Listed companies must adopt and disclose a code of ethics and business conduct for their directors, officers, and employees, and must promptly disclose any noncompliance with the code by their directors or officers.

Enforcement of listing standards has been criticized primarily because there has rarely been a delisting resulting from noncompliance with standards. These and other aspects of self-regulatory organizations are further discussed in Chapter 6.

Best Practices Corporate governance best practices suggested by professional organizations (Conference Board, the National Association of Corporate Directors, Business Roundtable) and investor organizations (Council of Institutional Investors, International Corporate Governance Network) are nonbinding guidelines intended to improve corporate governance policies and practices of public companies above and beyond the state and federal statutes and listing standards. Corporate governance best practices should not substitute for state or federal statutes or listing standards; rather they should be viewed as supplemental to those statutes and standards. However, the use of best practices should be encouraged, and corporate governance rating agencies do systematically grade public companies for their compliance with best practices. Furthermore, these best practices have assisted public companies in enhancing their long-term financial performance.

Market Correction Mechanisms It has been suggested that corporate governance does not need reform, since markets are efficient and ultimately they will adopt the best corporate governance practices. Essentially, there is no need for reforms beyond state statutes because market competition provides incentives for public companies to adopt the most efficient and effective corporate governance structure. Companies that do not adopt effective corporate governance are presumably less efficient in the long term and ultimately are replaced. This proposition may not be true for three reasons.

1. The numerous financial scandals in the late 1990s and the early 2000s prove that market-based mechanisms alone are not sufficient to solve corporate governance problems.
2. By the time the markets are able to make such a correction for ineffective corporate governance, investor confidence has been lost along with perhaps trillions of dollars of market capitalization, often caused by bankruptcy. This is exactly what occurred when capital markets hit rock bottom in the early 2000s.
3. A large percentage of pension fund assets are usually passively managed through indexed funds and therefore cannot sell poorly governed or poorly performing companies.

The primary causes of reported scandals were market correction mechanisms, lax regulations and oversight, and poorly developed disclosure standards that failed to protect investors. Market correction mechanisms are often initiated and enforced after the occurrence of substantial management abuse and after shareholders either lose millions of dollars as a result of accounting and other frauds or sell some of their actively managed shares. Selling shares has associated transaction costs and does not directly remove the assets from management's control, since sales simply pass shares to other investors who ultimately suffer the same management malfeasance. Accordingly, market correction mechanisms may affect corporate governance only after significant wealth is transferred or destroyed as a result of management misconduct and corporate malfeasance. In addition, there are often considerable transaction costs for other stakeholders, including employees, in the form of layoffs, lost wages, and the permanent loss of retirement funds by individuals and large pension funds, and society in the form of lost taxes and large-scale bankruptcies.

Market mechanisms failed to prevent the corporate debacles of Enron, World-Com, and Global Crossing, which were devastating to shareholders, employees, pensioners, and society. A report by Glass Lewis & Co. shows that investors have suffered significant losses caused by fraudulent financial statements in the past decade.[70] As indicated in Exhibit 1.3, the lost market capitalization of 30 high-profile financial scandals caused by fraud during the period 1977 to 2004 is more than $900 billion and resulted in a negative impact on stock returns for 77 percent of the fraud-prone companies.[71] Thus, corporate governance reforms should create an environment that promotes strong marketplace integrity and efficiency and restores and promotes investor confidence and public trust.

CORPORATE GOVERNANCE REFORMS

The erosion in investor confidence in the early 2000s has been caused by many factors, among them the collapse of the dot-com market, an economic downturn, reported financial scandals, and numerous earnings restatements of high-profile companies. Several new corporate governance reforms in the United States have been established: SOX, SEC-related implementation rules, revised listing standards of national stock exchanges, guiding principles of professional organizations, and best practices. These reforms are intended to restore investor confidence by improving the vigilance and effectiveness of corporate governance and the reliability, integrity, transparency, and quality of financial reports.

Regulatory Bodies

Corporate governance reforms are fully discussed in Chapter 6. Exhibits1.4 to 1.6 provide a list of regulatory agencies, standard setters, and organizations that either develop or promote these reforms. Investors often consider investment in companies a high risk when the information about the company is not favorable (e.g., financial restatement, internal control deficiencies). Thus, companies could benefit from corporate governance reforms that improve investor confidence in their financial reporting and help them achieve a wider and more diverse investor base. Corporate governance reforms should provide a "right balance" between effectiveness in protecting investors and efficiency in providing such protection.

The pre-SOX financial environment can be characterized as the era of ample incentives and opportunities for engaging in conflicts of interest that caused financial manipulations and fraud. A list of problems follows.

- There was a lack of vigilant boards of directors to oversee managerial functions, particularly financial reporting.
- Excessive management compensation, linked to reported earnings, provided incentives for management to manipulate earnings.

EXHIBIT 1.3 Fraud-Prone Companies and Their Market Capitalization Loss

Company Name	Ticker	Stock Price Peak Date	Price of Stock at Peak	Stock Price Bottom Date	Price of Stock at Bottom	Lost Market Cap ($ in million)	Cumulative Return (%)
WordCom	WCOM	6/30/99	$61.93	7/21/02	$0.00	($119,874)	−100
Bristol-Myers Squibb	BMY	12/29/00	$73.94	7/24/02	$20.55	($104,615)	−72
Tyco	TYC	1/30/01	$62.80	7/25/02	$8.25	($ 93,312)	−85
Nortel	NT	7/26/00	$83.88	10/10/02	$0.44	($ 67,157)	−99
Enron	ENE	8/23/00	$90.00	12/2/01	$0.00	($ 66,501)	−100
AIG	AIG	6/7/04	$74.80	4/29/05	$50.85	($ 62,653)	−32
Qwest	Q	7/5/00	$58.00	8/13/02	$1.11	($ 48,942)	−96
Xerox	XRX	5/3/99	$63.69	12/7/00	$4.44	($ 39,068)	−93
El Paso	EP	2/21/01	$74.50	2/13/03	$3.45	($ 35,172)	−94
Cendant	CD	3/24/98	$41.00	10/8/98	$7.50	($ 27,717)	−81
Fannie Mae	FNM	2/19/04	$79.88	4/4/05	$51.46	($ 27,675)	−36
Waste Management	WMI	5/4/99	$59.00	3/28/00	$13.06	($ 27,661)	−77
Global Crossing	GX	5/19/99	$58.25	1/28/02	$0.00	($ 25,356)	−100
MicroStrategy	MSTR	3/14/00	$2,920.00	7/26/02	$4.50	($ 22,803)	−100
Elan	ELN	6/20/01	$62.87	10/9/02	$1.17	($ 20,187)	−98
Dynegy	DYN	5/1/01	$57.95	7/25/02	$0.51	($ 18,700)	−99

28

Company	Symbol	Purchase Date	Price	Date	Value	(Loss)	%
Purchase Pro	PROEQ. PK	12/28/99	$395.94	9/13/02	$0.00	($12,353)	– 100
Rite Aid	RAD	1/8/99	$50.94	10/31/02	$1.79	($12,258)	– 93
Homestore	HOMS	1/25/00	$122.25	2/11/02	$0.69	($8,500)	– 99
Peregrine Systems	PRGN	3/27/00	$79.50	9/22/02	$0.00	($8,350)	– 100
Network Associates	MFE	12/24/98	$66.00	12/28/00	$4.13	($8,301)	– 94
Adelphia	ADELQ	1/4/01	$50.31	6/25/02	$0.00	($7,699)	– 100
Health South	HLSH	8/29/01	$18.26	3/31/03	$0.07	($7,117)	– 100
Oxford Health Plans	OHP	8/4/97	$85.81	8/13/98	$6.63	($6,185)	– 92
Lernout & Hauspie	LHSP	3/14/00	$65.00	11/29/00	$0.00	($6,098)	– 100
Critical Path	CPTH	8/31/00	$309.00	11/9/04	$0.00	($4,907)	– 100
McKensson HBOC	MCK	10/6/98	$94.69	5/26/00	$16.06	($4,848)	– 52
Sunbeam	SOC	3/4/98	$52.00	10/25/01	$0.05	($4,442)	– 100
Symbol Technologies	SBL	3/5/01	$34.47	10/10/02	$4.99	($4,001)	– 78
Krispy Kreme	KKD	8/18/03	$49.37	2/24/05	$5.36	($2,578)	– 89
Total						($905,030)	– 77

Source: Adapted from Glass Lewis & Co. 2005. Restatements: Traversing Shaky Ground. An Analysis for Investors. (June 2). Available at: www.glasslewis.com.

EXHIBIT 1.4 Regulatory Organizations Influencing Corporate Governance

Name	Description	Web Site
American Stock Exchange (AMEX)	The AMEX has been a pioneer in market innovation for more than a century and remains committed to developing successful new investment products and innovative services for companies and investors. As the nation's most diversified financial marketplace, AMEX conducts trading through an advanced centralized specialist system and is committed to providing a superior marketplace for the investing public and its members.	www.amex.com
Committee of the Sponsoring Organizations of the Treadway Commission (COSO)	COSO was originally formed in 1985 to sponsor the National Commission on Fraudulent Financial Reporting, an independent private sector initiative that studied causal factors that can lead to fraudulent financial reporting and developed recommendations for public companies and their independent auditors, for the SEC and other regulators, and for educational institutions.	www.coso.org
Financial Accounting Standards Board (FASB)	The mission of the FASB is to establish and improve standards of financial accounting and reporting for the guidance and education of the public, including issuers, auditors, and users of financial information.	www.fasb.org
International Accounting Standards Board (IASB)	The IASB is an independent, privately funded accounting standard setter based in London. Board members come from nine countries and have a variety of functional backgrounds. The IASB is committed to developing, in the public interest, a single set of high-quality, understandable, and enforceable global accounting standards that require transparent and comparable information in general-purpose financial statements. In addition, the IASB cooperates with national accounting standard setters to achieve convergence in accounting standards around the world.	www.iasb.org
Municipal Securities Rulemaking Board (MSRB)	The MSRB was established in 1975 by Congress to develop rules regulating securities firms and banks involved in underwriting, trading, and selling municipal securities: bonds and notes issued by states, cities, and counties or their agencies to help finance public projects. The MSRB which is composed of members from the municipal securities dealer community and the public, sets standards for all municipal securities dealers. Like the NYSE and NASDS the MSRB is a self-regulatory organization that is subject to oversight from the SEC.	www.msrb.org

New York Stock Exchange (NYSE)	The NYSE is the world's leading and most technologically advanced equities market. A broad spectrum of market participants, including listed companies, individual investors, institutional investors, and member firms, create the NYSE market. Buyers and sellers meet directly in a fair, open, and orderly market to access the best possible price through the interplay of supply and demand.	www.nyse.com
Nasdaq	Nasdaq is the largest electronic screen-based equity securities market in the United States, both in terms of number of listed companies and in traded share volume. With approximately 3,200 listed companies, it is home to category-defining companies that are leaders across all areas of business, including technology, retail, communications, financial services, transportation, media, and biotechnology industries.	www.nasdaq.com
National Association of Securities Dealers (NASD)	As the world's leading private sector provider of financial regulatory services, NASD has helped bring integrity to the markets—and confidence to investors—for more than 60 years. It has served as the primary private sector regulator of America's securities industry, overseeing the activities of more than 5,100 brokerage firms, approximately 109,300 branch offices and more than 657,690 registered securities representatives. In addition, NASD provides outsourced regulatory products and services to a number of stock markets and exchanges.	www.nasd.com
National Futures Association (NFA)	The NFA is the industrywide, self-regulatory organization for the U.S. futures industry. It strives every day to develop rules, programs, and services that safeguard market integrity, protect investors, and help members meet their regulatory responsibilities.	www.nfa.futures.org
Public Company Accounting Oversight Board (PCAOB)	The PCAOB is a private-sector, nonprofit corporation, created by the Sarbanes-Oxley Act of 2002, to oversee the auditors of public companies in order to protect the interests of investors and further the public interest in the preparation of informative, fair, and independent audit reports.	www.pcaob.com
Securities and Exchange Commission (SEC)	The mission of the U.S. SEC is to protect investors; maintain fair, orderly, and efficient markets; and facilitate capital formation.	www.sec.gov

Source: Extracted from Web sites presented in the exhibit.

EXHIBIT 1.5 Investor-Driven Organizations

Name	Description	Web Site
Bernstein Litowitz Berger & Grossmann LLP (BLB&G)	BLB&G is the trusted securities fraud-monitoring and litigation counsel for many of America's public pension plans as well as other institutional investors. Institutional clients rely on BLB&G to evaluate and litigate their securities claims vigorously and to keep them fully informed.	www.blbglaw.com/html/portfolio_monitoring.html
Business for Social Responsibility (BSR)	BSR is a global organization that helps member companies achieve success in ways that respect ethical values, people, communities, and the environment.	www.bsr.org/index.cfm
California Public Employees' Retirement System (CalPERS)	CalPERS' mission is to advance the financial and health security for all who participate in the system. It aims to fulfill this mission by creating and maintaining an environment that produces responsiveness to all those whom it serves.	www.calpers.ca.gov/
Conference Board (CB)	The CB creates and disseminates knowledge about management and the marketplace to help businesses strengthen their performance and better serve society. Working as a global, independent membership organization in the public interest, the CB conducts research, convenes conferences, makes forecasts, assesses trends, publishes information and analysis, and brings executives together to learn from one another.	www.conference-board.org/
Corporate Library (CL)	The CL is a unique and superior information resource. Its analysts are expert practitioners in the fields of corporate governance, executive compensation, ratings analysis, takeover defenses, social networking, and corporate leadership profiling.	www.thecorporatelibrary.com
CorpWatch	CorpWatch counters corporate-led globalization through education, network building, and activism. It works to foster democratic control over corporations by building grassroots globalization—a diverse movement for human rights and dignity, labor rights, and environmental justice.	www.corpwatch.org
Council of Institutional Investors (CII)	The CII is an organization of large public, labor, and corporate pension funds that seeks to address investment issues that affect the size or security of plan assets. Its objectives are to encourage member funds, as major shareholders, to take an active role in protecting plan assets and to help members increase return on their investments as part of their fiduciary obligations.	www.cii.org/about/

Glass Lewis & Co. (GLC)	GLC is an independent research firm focused on identifying business, legal, governances, and financial statement risks at public companies in time for investors to act.	www.glasslewis.com/
Institutional Shareholder Services (ISS)	ISS is the world's leading provider of proxy voting and corporate governance services with over 20 years of experience. ISS serves more than 1,600 institutional and corporate clients worldwide with its core business: analyzing proxies and issuing informed research and objective vote recommendations for more than 33,000 companies across 115 markets worldwide.	www.issproxy.com
Interfaith Center on Corporate Responsibility (ICCR)	For over thirty years the ICCR has been a leader of the corporate social responsibility movement. ICCR's membership is an association of 275 faith-based institutional investors, including national denominations, religious communities, pension funds, endowments, hospital corporations, economic development funds, and publishing companies. ICCR and its members press companies to be socially and environmentally responsible. Each year ICCR-member religious institutional investors sponsor over 100 shareholder resolutions on major social and environmental issues.	www.iccr.org
Investor Responsibility Research Center (IRRC)	IRRC is the leading source of high-quality, impartial information on corporate governance and social responsibility. Founded in 1972, IRRC provides proxy research and analysis, benchmarking products, as well as proxy voting services to more than 500 institutional investors, corporations, law firms, foundations, academics, and other organizations.	www.irrc.org
Social Accountability International (SAI)	SAI is a nongovernmental, international, multi-stakeholder organization dedicated to improving workplaces and communities by developing and implementing socially responsible standards. SAI convenes key stakeholders to develop consensus-based voluntary standards, conducts cost-benefit research, accredits auditors, provides training and technical assistance, and assists corporations in improving social compliance in their supply chain.	www.sa-intl.org
State Board of Administration (SBA)	The SBA is committed to providing superior investment and trust services through prudent financial management and administration of assets while adhering to high ethical, fiduciary, and professional standards.	www.sbafla.com/

Source: Extracted from Web sites presented in the exhibit.

33

EXHIBIT 1.6 Nonregulatory Organizations

Name	Description	Web Site
American Association of Accountants (AAA)	The AAA promotes worldwide excellence in accounting education, research, and practice.	www.aaahq.org
American Institute of Certified Public Acountants (AICPA)	The AICPA is the national, professional organization for all certified public accountants. Its mission is to provide members with the resources, information, and leadership to enable them to provide valuable services in the highest professional manner to benefit the public as well as employers and clients.	www.aicpa.org
American Society for Women Accountants (ASWA)	The mission of ASWA is to enable women in all accounting and related fields to achieve their full personal, professional, and economic potential and to contribute to the future development of their profession.	www.aswa.org
Association of Government Accountants (AGA)	AGA serves government accountability professionals by providing quality education, fostering professional development and certification, and supporting standards and research to advance government accountability.	www.agacgfm.org
Institute of Management Accountants (IMA)	The IMA is the world's leading organization dedicated to empowering management accounting and finance professionals to drive business performance.	www.imanet.org
Institute of Internal Auditors (IIA)	The IIA aims to be the global voice of the internal audit profession: advocating its value, promoting best practices, and providing exceptional service to its members.	www.theiia.org
National Association of Corporate Directors (NACD)	NACD is a national nonprofit membership organization dedicated exclusively to serving the corporate governance needs of corporate boards and individual board members.	www.nacdonline.org

Source: Extracted from Web sites presented in the exhibit.

- Independent auditors' objectivity was adversely affected by high nonaudit fees (e.g., consulting, internal control outsourcing).
- The system of internal controls and disclosures was inadequate and ineffective.
- There was a lack of proper accounting standards to deal with and recognize complex and significant off–balance sheet financial transactions.
- The gap between reported earnings and pro forma earnings, commonly referred to as operating earnings, was widening.
- The involvement in the financial reporting process of financial analysts and advisors was conflicted.
- Institutional investors were inattentive in scrutinizing and monitoring their investment in companies and their financial reports.
- There was lax enforcement and ineffective investigation and disciplining of substandard audits.

Regarding the landscape leading to the passage of SOX, Senator Paul S. Sarbanes (D-MD) stated:

The roots of the problem lay not with the legendary "few bad apples" but rather with system and structural defects that required a statutory remedy. There was a remarkable consensus among our witnesses on the nature of the problems, notably lack of auditor independence, ineffective regulatory oversight of accountants, lax standards of corporate governance and securities analysts' conflicts of interest.[72]

Sarbanes-Oxley Act of 2002

Traditionally, state rather than federal legislation has significantly shaped corporate governance by specifying requirements for incorporation and defining the fiduciary duty of directors and officers. However, in light of the growing participation of millions of Americans in the capital markets, and the widespread impact of financial scandals in those markets, Congress and the American public recognized the need for a more proactive federal role. In response, the Sarbanes-Oxley Act of 2002 was signed into law on July 30, 2002, to reinforce corporate accountability and rebuild investor confidence in public financial reports. The reported financial scandals at the turn of the century and congressional responses (i.e., SOX) are not unprecedented. Similar events led to the enactment of the Securities Act of 1933, the Securities Exchange Act of 1934, and the creation of the SEC.

SOX was designed primarily to do six things:

1. Establish an independent regulatory structure for the accounting profession.
2. Set high standards and new guiding principles for corporate governance.
3. Improve the quality and transparency of financial reporting.
4. Improve the objectivity and credibility of the audit function and empower the audit committee.

5. Create more severe civil and criminal penalties for violations of the federal securities laws.
6. Increase the independence of securities analysts.[73]

Exhibit 1.7 provides a summary of the provisions of SOX pertaining to corporate governance, financial reporting, and audit activities of public companies.

In describing the long-term benefits of compliance with the provisions of SOX, then chairman of the SEC William A. Donaldson stated:

> The Sarbanes-Oxley reforms should yield extraordinary long-term benefits in the form of improved financial reporting, better management control, and more ethical behavior by companies and gatekeepers. This, in turn, should lead to sounder corporate governance, better and more reliable reporting, improved corporate performance, enhanced investor confidence, and ultimately, a lower cost of capital.[74]

In assessing the positive impact of SOX on corporate governance, Ira M. Millstein, the well-known leader in corporate governance, states:

> SOX did directly what it was supposed to do: take the best practices in director independence and audit procedures and make them mandatory.... All that Sarbanes did was to take "should" and "could" and turned it into "must." And it worked.[75]

Christopher Cox, the chairman of the SEC, in support of SOX, states:

> We have come a long way since 2002 [passage of SOX]. Investor confidence has recovered. There is greater corporate accountability. Financial reporting is more reliable and transparent. Auditor oversight is significantly improved.... The Act is not perfect in every respect. But the vast majority of its provisions are net contributors to the nation's economic health.... While competitors in other countries are using Sarbanes-Oxley as a reason for foreign companies to list in their jurisdictions, many of those same countries are adopting provisions of the Act as part of their own regulatory regimes.... We will do our best to honor your legacy by ensuring that Sarbanes-Oxley works for every stakeholder—for investors, for issuers, for our economy, and for our country.[76]

Indeed, many aspects of the best practices of corporate governance (e.g., board independency, and audit committee formation) promoted by professional organizations, such as the Business Roundtable, were incorporated into the provisions of SOX. A Government Accountability Office (GAO) report concludes that regulators, investors, public companies, and auditors are in general agreement that SOX has had a positive impact on investor confidence and investor protection although its compliance cost may be disproportionately higher for smaller companies.[77] The 2006 CFO survey of 213 finance executives reveals that: (1) the

EXHIBIT 1.7 Summary of Provisions of SOX

Corporate Governance	Financial Reporting	Audit Functions	Others
1. Enhanced audit committee responsibility for hiring, firing, compensating, and overseeing auditors and preapproval of non-audit services	1. CEO/CFO certification of financial reports	1. Establishment and operation of the Public Company Accounting Oversight Board (PCAOB), an independent non-governmental agency that regulates and oversees the audit of public companies	1. Professional responsibilities for attorneys appearing and practicing before the SEC
2. Disclosure, in periodic reports, of whether the audit committee has at least one member who is a "financial expert" and if not, why	2. Internal control report by management	2. Registration with the PCAOB of public accounting firms that audit public companies	2. Disclosures of corporate code of ethics
3. CEO and CFO certification of the accuracy and completeness of quarterly and annual reports	3. Attestation and report by auditors on management's assessment of internal controls	3. PCAOB authority to issue auditing standards, inspect registered accounting firms' operations, and investigate potential violations of securities laws	3. Collection and administration of funds for victim investors
4. Management assessment and reporting of the effectiveness of disclosure controls and procedures	4. Disclosures of off–balance sheet arrangements	4. Requirement that auditors be appointed, compensated, and overseen by the audit committee	4. Analyst conflicts of interest (Regulation AC)
5. Ban on personal loans by companies to their directors or executives other than certain regular consumer loans	5. Disclosures of contractual obligations	5. Many nonaudit services are prohibited from being performed contemporaneously with an audit	5. Whistleblower protection
	6. Disclosures of reconciliation of non-GAAP financial measures pertaining to pro forma financial information	6. Rotation of the lead (or coordinating) audit partner and the lead review partner every five years	6. Debts non-dischargeable in bankruptcy
	7. Disclosures of material correcting adjustments by auditors		7. Temporary freeze authority for SEC
	8. Disclosures of transactions involving management and principal stockholders		8. SEC censures or bars any person who is not qualified, lacks the requisite character or integrity, or engages in unethical conduct, from appearing before the SEC.
			9. Lengthened statute of limitations for securities fraud
			10. Criminalization of corporate misconduct

(continued overleaf)

EXHIBIT 1.7 (*Continued*)

Corporate Governance	Financial Reporting	Audit Functions	Others
6. Establishment of procedures by each audit committee for receiving, retaining, and handling complaints received by the company concerning accounting, internal controls, or auditing matters	9. Accelerated filing of changes in beneficial ownership by insiders	7. Auditors report to the audit committee	11. Criminal penalties for defrauding shareholders of public companies
7. Review of each quarterly and annual report (Forms 10-Q and 10-K) by officers	10. Real-time disclosures of information concerning material changes in financial condition or operations (Form 8-K disclosures)	8. One year cooling-off period before audit staff can take a principal officer position.	12. Retaliation against informants
8. Forfeiture by CEO or CFO of certain bonuses and profits when the company restates its financial statements due to its material non-compliance with any financial reporting requirements	11. Periodic review of published financial statements by the SEC at least once every three years	9. Auditor attestation to and reporting on management assessment of internal controls	13. Increased criminal penalties under securities laws and mail and wire fraud
9. Improper influence on conduct of audits	12. SEC-enhanced authority to determine what constitutes U.S. GAAP	10. Limitations on partner compensation	14. Future studies on consolidation of public accounts by firm, audit firm rotation, accounting standards, credit rating agencies, and investment banks
10. Insider trades during pension fund blackout periods		11. Disclosure of fees paid to the auditor	
11. Officer and director penalties for violations of securities laws or misconduct		12. Requirements for pre-approval of audit and permitted nonaudit services by the audit committee	
		13. Retention of audit work papers and documents for five years	
		14. Increased penalties for destruction of corporate audit records	

Source: Extracted from the Sarbanes-Oxley Act of 2002. (July 30). Available at: www.sec.gov/about/laws/sox2002.pdf

majority (almost 70 percent) believe that they have seen at least some improvement in their business processes resulting from compliance with provisions of SOX; (2) the vast majority, while having realized some benefits of SOX, failed to consider those benefits in the form of a lower cost of capital; and (3) more than 82 percent said they disclose more information on their financial statements (e.g., footnotes, proxies, income statement, balance sheet) in the post-SOX period.[78]

In summary, SOX is considered as a process whose impact on improving the effectiveness of corporate governance will continue for years to come. In its infancy, SOX was viewed as a compliance document that often caused complications and substantial compliance costs for many companies regardless of size. As SOX is approaching its stage of maturity, it will encourage: (1) public companies to move away from their practice of checklist compliance mentality and move toward incorporating its provisions into their sustainable business strategies and governance practices; (2) regulators (SEC) and standard setters (Financial Accounting Standards Board [FASB], PCAOB, national stock exchanges) to establish more effective, efficient, and scalable implementation rules, accounting and auditing standards, and corporate governance standards to ease complexities and compliance costs of adopting its provisions; and (3) global adoption of many of its key provisions that are considered worldwide as cost-justified.

Several attempts have been taken to roll back some provisions of SOX despite the continuing corporate scandals. The Committee on Capital Markets Regulation was formed in September 2006 to study the impacts of recent regulatory reforms, including SOX, on U.S. global competitiveness, the extent to which U.S. capital markets are losing ground to foreign markets, the causes of such decline, and its effects on the financial industry and the economy.[79] The committee, while not calling for any statutory changes to SOX, recommends that the SEC relax implementation rules pertaining to Section 404 of SOX on internal controls, strengthen shareholder rights, curtail the role of state authorities, and limit auditor liability.[80] The committee's recommendations are driven by the main objective of strengthening global competitiveness of U.S. capital markets rather than protecting investors, whose role is vital to the vibrancy of the capital markets. The committee suggests that the SEC conduct a thorough cost-benefit analysis of SOX implementation rules (Section 404) that may impose a high cost on businesses, particularly smaller companies. Arthur Levitt, the former SEC chairman, believes that such analysis could impair the SEC's ability in issuing effective rules as "cost-benefit analysis is Washington speak for 'slow down the regulator'."[81] The former SEC commissioner Harvey Goldschmid said that if regulators (SEC, Treasury Department) pursue the committee's recommendations, "the recent drive for accountability and deterrence would be replaced by a world where almost anything goes."[82]

It has been argued that SOX is not the problem; SOX authorizes the SEC to issue rules to implement its provisions. Some of these rules—for example, rules concerning internal controls of Section 404—cost at least 100 times more than what was originally estimated by the SEC (e.g., SEC's estimated cost of $91,000 per company to the first-year actual costs of on average $9.8 million). Thus, while rolling back provisions of SOX is not desirable, making SEC-related implementation rules more effective and scalable is a step in the right direction in ensuring sustainable efficacy of SOX. Indeed, the SEC, on December 13, 2006, approved its proposed interpretive guidance that would assist public companies of all sizes and complexity to plan and perform their annual management assessment of internal control over financial reporting under Section 404 of SOX.[83] This proposed interpretive guidance is intended to help public companies make their compliance more cost-effective and efficient by focusing on risk and materiality and applying a risk-based and top-down approach to internal control reporting by both management and auditors. It is expected that the SEC and the PCAOB will continue to examine ways to improve cost-effectiveness, efficiency, and scalability of Section 404 compliance. Improvements are needed in the areas of: (1) focusing on key controls, particularly company-level controls; (2) using a top-down, risk-based approach in testing only significant accounts and risks; and (3) testing important business functions including information technology systems, accounting systems, and application of complex accounting standards (e.g., derivatives, taxes), whistleblowing function, and business reviews by directors and officers.

Regulatory reforms in the United States are aimed at improving the integrity, safety, and efficiency of the capital markets while maintaining their global competitiveness. To inspire investor confidence, regulations should be perceived as being fair and in balance.[84] Fairness of regulations, while creating a level playing field for market participants and ensuring investors receive reliable information, does not guarantee success. Regulations should strike the right balance of: (1) not being so extensive so as to discourage innovation, impose unnecessary costs on affected companies and their investors, or stifle competitiveness and job creation; and (2) not being so lax so as to engage in a regulatory race to the bottom of eliminating necessary safeguards for investors. In the words of Henry Paulson, the U.S. Treasury secretary, "the right regulatory balance should marry high standards of integrity and accountability with a strong foundation for innovation, growth, and competitiveness."[85] As this book was going to press, the U.S. Senate voted not to change SOX provisions by making Section 404 compliance optional for smaller companies, instead asking regulations to fine-tune Section 404. This symbolic support of SOX by the Senate was reviewed by many as a continuous effort by policymakers to protect investors from corporate malfeasance.

CORPORATE CULTURE AND GOVERNANCE

Corporate culture is a continuous process in which corporate leadership, including the board of directors and the top management team, sets a "right tone at the top." It is often an informal process that establishes powerful norms and standards that influence employee behavior. Laws, regulations, rules, and standards are effective measures in changing the structure, process, and composition of corporate governance, whereas the corporate culture is developed over time and derived from shared values. The engaged board of directors can significantly influence the corporate culture by:

- Setting an appropriate tone at the top by promoting personal integrity and professional accountability.

- Rewarding high-quality and ethical performance.
- Disciplining poor performance and unethical behavior.
- Promoting reliable, relevant, and transparent financial reports.
- Maintaining the company's high reputation and stature in the industry and in the business community.

One of the most important objectives of SOX is to improve the corporate culture of public companies by requiring these companies to set the appropriate tone at the top and promote ethical behavior. In discussing the importance of setting a right tone, Stephen M. Cutler, the SEC's director of the Division of Enforcement, states:

> *"Tone at the top" seems to have become a panacea for what is ill in corporate America, and an explanation for much of what has gone wrong. [In the two years post-SOX], the SEC has brought more than 1,300 civil cases and has obtained orders for disgorgement and penalties in excess of $5 billion.*[86]

Cutler suggests several ways managers can set an appropriate tone:

- Comply with the letter and the spirit of laws, rules, and regulations.
- Make character a part of the company's hiring policies and criteria.
- Make integrity, ethics, and compliance integral components of the evaluation, promotion, and compensation processes.
- Allow no tolerance for compliance risk.
- Resolve ethical violations quickly and firmly.
- Create a culture of compliance by holding managers accountable for setting the right example.
- Cultivate the culture of compliance through continuous monitoring, follow-up, and reassessment.
- Avoid a checklist mentality.[87]

In the words of SEC's director of the Office of Compliance Inspections and Examinations, Lori A. Richards:

> *It's not enough to have policies. It's not enough to have procedures. It's not enough to have good intentions. All of these can help. But to be successful, compliance must be an embedded part of your firm's culture.*[88]

Compliance just for the sake of compliance and the development of a "compliance check-box" mentality is not enough. Corporations should create an ethical environment that encourages all corporate governance participants to do the right thing and to understand that this is vital to the company's sustainable financial performance. Indeed, a culture of compliance and ethics should be integrated into the company's corporate governance structure. Although steady progress has been made to improve the culture of ethics and corporate governance measures for many corporate boards in the post-SOX era, significant changes have occurred more slowly than expected.[89] To integrate the culture of ethics and compliance into corporate governance effectively, corporations should set an appropriate tone at the top that promotes:

- The development of roles and responsibilities for all corporate governance functions (oversight, managerial, auditing, compliance, assurance, monitory).
- Directors, officers, and employees doing the "right thing" and understanding that this is vital to the company's sustainable performance.
- Directors, executives, and employees accepting responsibility and accountability for their actions and the actions of those under their supervision.
- Personnel freely raising concerns and issues without fear of retaliation.
- Proper consideration of ethical issues throughout the company when difficult and complex decisions are made.
- Understanding of the incentives, opportunities, and rationalization factors affecting individuals' decisions when the pressure exists that may drive unethical behavior.
- Proper oversight and management of all compliance activities, including ongoing monitoring of compliance programs, policies, and procedures in order to ensure their effectiveness and adoption of any changes in applicable laws and regulations.
- Directors and top officers exemplifying an ethical tone.
- Reporting of unethical and noncompliance instances through the proper channels, up to top-level management and, if necessary, to the board of directors or its designated committee (e.g., audit committee).
- Promoting the ethical culture and best practices by demonstrating ethical business decision making and cultivating ethical role models.

Warren Buffet, a veteran of corporate governance, rightfully stated that the five most dangerous words in the business culture are "Everybody else is doing it" as a rationale for business decision making.[90] This phrase has often been used to justify the morality and legitimacy of business actions. One obvious misuse of this phrase is the rationale by many companies for providing backdated or manipulated option grants to their directors and officers.

SUMMARY

Corporate governance involves a set of relationships and power-sharing among a company's board, management, and shareholders. These relationships determine the way the board oversees management's running of the company and how directors are accountable to shareholders. Good corporate governance should provide proper incentives for the board and management to pursue the objectives that are in the best interests of the company and its shareholders. It also lays the foundation for the integrity and efficiency of the financial markets. Conversely, poor corporate governance reduces a company's potential and can even pave the way for financial difficulties and fraud. Simply stated, good corporate governance improves investor confidence and strengthens market integrity and efficiency, thereby promoting economic growth and financial stability. The ultimate effect of good corporate governance and moving beyond having merely an effective compliance culture is based on ethical behavior and decisions made by the company's board of directors and management and the impact of those decisions in protecting investors.

Effective corporate governance should create an appropriate balance between the shareholders, board of directors, and management while complying with market-based mechanisms, state and federal statutes, and best practices. The question that remains on the minds of many corporate governance activists is whether the historical trend of financial scandals, caused by relaxed regulations and ineffective corporate governance measures, is doomed to repeat itself. Examples of these financial scandals include corporate and accounting scandals of the early 1930s, which promoted congressional responses that included the passage of the Securities Act of 1933, the Securities Exchange Act of 1934, and the creation of the SEC; the savings and loan debacles of the 1980s, which resulted in the Federal Deposit Insurance Corporation Improvements Act of 1991; and the wave of financial scandals of high-profile companies in the late 1990s and the early 2000s, which prompted the passage of SOX. The author believes that the impacts of any potential future financial scandals would be extremely significant, since the majority of U.S. households now invest in the financial markets.

Today's investors demand more accountability, and public companies have responded by making improvements to their corporate governance practices and accountability above and beyond the regulatory compliance mandated in the post-SOX era. The emerging reforms have significantly improved the corporate governance policies and practices of many companies and thus investor confidence in corporate America. The long-term success of these reforms will best be achieved when they are perceived and proven to be effective, efficient, and scalable.

NOTES

1. According to the *Financial Dictionary*, agency theory is a theory concerning the relationship between a principal (shareholder) and an agent of the principal (company's managers). Essentially it involves the costs of resolving conflicts between the principals and agents and aligning interests of the two groups. Agency problem is a conflict of interest arising among creditors, shareholders, and management because of differing goals. These definitions can be found at: financial-dictionary.thefreedictionary.com/Agency+Theory.
2. Clay, W. L. 2006. Statement of the Honorable William Lacy Clay before the Subcommittee on Capital Markets, Insurance, and Government Sponsored Enterprises. "Fostering Accuracy and Transparency in Financial Reporting." (March 28). Available at: financialservices.house.gov/media/pdf/032906cl.pdf.
3. Paulson, H. M. 2006. Remarks by Treasury secretary on the competitiveness of U.S. capital markets. Economics Club of New York, New York. (November 20). Available at: http://www.treas.gov/press/releases/hp174.htm.

4. The Committee on Capital Markets Regulation. 2006. Interim report of the Committee on Capital Markets Regulation. (November 30). Available at: www.capmktsreg.org/research.html.

5. Lackritz, M. E. 2006. Testimony of President, Securities Industry Association, before the Subcommittee on Capital Markets of Committee on Financial Services of U.S. House of Representatives (March 29). Available at: financialservices.house.gov/media/pdf/060204ml.pdf.

6. Niemeier, C. D. 2006. *American competitiveness in international capital markets.* Background Paper for the Atlantic's Ideas Tour Commemorating the Magazine's 150th Anniversary. Washington, DC: U.S. Public Company Accounting Oversight Board (PCAOB).

7. Lackritz, 2006. Testimony of President.

8. Ibid.

9. Turner, L. E. 2006. Hearing on: Stock Options Backdating before U.S. Senate Committee on Banking, Housing, and Urban Affairs (September 6).

10. Schuetze, E., M. Sutton, and L. Turner. 2003. Letter sent to the PCAOB by the three former chief accountants of the SEC (January 4).

11. U.S. Government Accountability Office (GAO). 2006. Consideration of key principles needed in addressing implementation for smaller public companies. Available at: www.gao.gov/news/items/do6361.pdf.

12. Woodward, R., J. Dittmar, and C. Munoz. 2003. The currency of good governance. *Platts Energy Business and Technology* 5(4): 30.

13. Wirthlin. 2002. Current trends in public opinion from Wirthlin worldwide. *The Wirthlin Report* 12(2) (July–August).

14. Ibid.

15. Deutsch, C. 2005. New surveys show that big business has a P.R. problem. *New York Times* (December 9). Available at: www.nytimes.com.

16. Ibid.

17. Committee for Economic Development (CED). 2006. Private Enterprise, Public Trust: The State of Corporate America after Sarbanes-Oxley (March 21). Available at: www.ced.org/docs/summary/summary_2006corpgov.pdf.

18. International Audit Networks. 2006. Global capital markets and the global economy: A vision from the CEOs of the International Audit Networks (November).

19. Rezaee, Z. 2002. *Financial Statement Fraud: Prevention and Detection.* John Wiley & Sons, Hoboken, NJ.

20. Jenson, M., and W. Meckling. 1976. Theory of the firm: Managerial behavior, agency costs and ownership structure. *Journal of Financial Economics* 3(4): 305–360. Available through the Science Direct database at www.sciencedirect.com.

21. Lackritz, M. E. 2006. Testimony of the President.

22. Ibid.

23. PricewaterhouseCoopers (PwC) (2005) Director's College. 2005. Boardroom Exchange. Presented by the University of Delaware and PricewaterhouseCoopers (October 27). Available at: www.pwc.com/extweb/pwcpublications.nsf/docid/BBE7CBD55C8AM33D85257060006DD24F.

24. Solomon, D., and C. Bryan-Low. 2003. 'Tough' cop for accounting beat. *The Wall Street Journal* (April 16): C1.
25. U.S. Securities and Exchange Commission (SEC). 2006. SEC to rebuild public disclosure system to make it interactive (September 25). Available at www.see.gov/news/press/2006/2006-158.htm.
26. McKinsey Quarterly. 2006. Weighing the pros and cons of earnings guidance: A McKinsey Survey. (April 2). Available at www.mckinseyquarterly.com/article_page.aspx?ar=1752&62=5.
27. Ibid.
28. Hsieh, P., T. Koller, and S. R. Rajan. 2006. The misguided practice of earnings guidance. (March). *McKinsey Quarterly*. Aummary avialable at: www.mckinseyquarterly.com/article_abstract_visitor.aspx?ar=1759&L2=5& L3=5.
29. Fink, R., and D. Durfee. 2006 Could it be that finance executives really don't mind regulation? *CFO Magazine* (September 1).
30. Roberts, D. 2006. Guidance falling out of favor on Wall Street. *Financial Times* (March 12).
31. McKinsey Quarterly, 2006.
32. Ibid.
33. Ibid.
34. Ibid.
35. Ibid.
36. Browning, C. 2006. Statement of the head of global securities research and economics for Merrill Lynch Submitted to the Subcommitte on Capital Markets, Insurance, and Government Sponsored Enterprises Committee on Financial Services. U.S. House of Representatives (March 29). Available at: financialservices.house.gov/media/pdf/032906cb.pdf.
37. Ibid.
38. CFA Institute Center and Business Roundtable Institute for Corporate Ethics. 2006. Breaking the short-term cycle (July 24). Available at http://www.cfapubs.org/toc/ccb/2006/1.
39. Ibid.
40. Ibid.
41. Whitehouse, K. 2006. Former SEC head supports efforts stop quarterly guidance. *The Wall Street Journal* (July 25). Available at online.wsj.com/article/BT_Co_20060725_712995.html.
42. Hughes, S. 2006. SEC Chairman: Recommendations to end earnings view's healthy. *The Wall street Journal* (July 25). Available at online.wsj.com/article/BT_Co_20060725_713932.html.
43. Gordon, M. 2006. SEC Chief Suggests Blogs for Disclosures. PhysOrg (November 7). Available at: physorg.com/news82126753.html.
44. Ibid.
45. Lang, M., and R. Lundholm. 1996. Corporate disclosure policy and analyst behavior. *Accounting Review* 71 (October): 467–491.
46. Arkin, S. S. 2002. Analysts' conflicts of interest: What's the crime? *New York Law Journal*. (February): 3.

47. Securities and Exchange Commission. 2003. Regulation analyst certification. (February 20). Available at: www.sec.gov/rules/final/33-8193.htm.

48. National Association of Securities Dealers. 2006. NASD guide to understanding securities analyst recommendations. Available at: www.nasd.com/web/idcplg ?IdcService=SS_GET_PAGE&nodeId=580.

49. PricewaterhouseCoopers (PwC). 2006. Guide to forward-looking information: Don't fear the future—Communicating with confidence (January). Available at: www.pwc.com/Extweb/pwcpublications.nsf/docid/E97847126DD93E1380257 0FA004100D7.

50. Ibid.

51. Murray, A. 2006. Business: Corporate governance concerns are spreading and companies should take heed. *Wall Street Journal* (April 12): A2.

52. Ibid.

53. Institutional Shareholder Services. 2006. Global Investor Study: From compliance obligation to business imperative. Available at: www.issproxy.com/ globalinvestorstudy/theme1.jsp.

54. Governance Metrics International. 2005. GMI ratings reports. Available at: www.gmiratings.com/.

55. Brown, L. D., and M. L. Caylor. 2004. Corporate governance and firm performance. Working Paper, Georgia State University. Gompers, P. A., J. L. Ishii, and A. Metrick. 2003. Corporate governance and equity prices. *Quarterly Journal of Economics* 118(1): 107–155.

56. Gillan, S. L., and L. T. Starks. 1998. A survey of shareholder activism: Motivation and empirical evidence. *Contemporary Finance Digest*. 2 (3 Autumn): 10–34.

57. Shleifer, A., and R. Vishny. 1997. A survey of corporate governance. *Journal of Finance* 52 (2 June): 737–775.

58. What is corporate governance? 2005. Available at: www.encycogov.com/What-IsCorpGov.asp.

59. Goodman, A., and B. Schwartz. 2004. *Corporate governance: Law and practice.* Albany, NY: Matthew Bender & Co.

60. Ibid.

61. Delaware General Corporate Law Requirements. Available at: www.delcode. state.de.us/title8/c001/sc04/index.htm=TopofPage.

62. U.S. Securities and Exchange Commission (SEC). 2006. Introduction—The SEC: Who we are, what we do. Available at: http://sec.gov.

63. Levitt, A. 2006. Cutting the corruption. *Washington Post* (January 23).

64. American Bar Association. 2002. Special study on market structure listing standards and corporate governance. A Special Study Group of the Committee on Federal Regulation of Securities. American Bar Association, Section of Business Law. (August). 57 *Business Law*. 1487.

65. Leibell, J. N., and R. D. Poliakoff. 2000. In re Cendant: The dawning of a new age. *Advocate. BLB&G Institutional Investors* 2 (First Quarter). Available at: www.blbglaw.com.

66. Ibid.

67. United States Court of Appeals, for the Second Circuit. 2006. American Federation of State, County and Municipal Employees, Employees Pension Plan vs. American International Group, Inc. (September 5). Docket No. 05-2825-cv.
68. U.S. Securities and Exchange Commission (SEC). 2003. Proposed Rule: Security Holder Director Nominations (October 14). Available at: www.sec.gov/rules/proposed/34-48626.htm.
69. New York Stock Exchange. 2004. Listing standards. Available at: www.nyse.com/pdfs/finalcorpgovrules.pdf. Nasdaq Stock Market. 2004. Listing standards and fees.
70. Glass Lewis & Co. 2005. Restatements: Traversing shaky ground: An analysis for investors. (June 2). Available at: www.glasslewis.com.
71. Ibid.
72. Sarbanes, P. 2006. Senator Paul S. Sarbanes' Remarks on the Sarbanes-Oxley Act before consumer Federation of America Lifetime Consumer Hero Award (March 23). Available at: www.glasslewis.com/downloads/415-47.pdf.
73. Sarbanes-Oxley Act. 2002. (July 30). Available at: www.sec.gov/about/laws/soa2002.pdf.
74. Donaldson, W. H. 2005. Speech by SEC chairman: Remarks before the Financial Services Roundtable. U.S. Securities and Exchange Commission. (April 1). Available at: www.sec.gov/news/speech/spch040105whd.htm.
75. Spencer Stuart Board Index. 2005. What's really changed in the three years since the Sarbanes-Oxley Act (SOX). (December 5). Available at: www.spencerstuart.com.
76. Cox, C. 2006. Chairman Christopher Cox of U.S. Securities and Exchange Commission Testimony Concerning the Impact of the Sarbanes-Oxley Act. Before the U.S. House Committee on Financial Services (September 19). Available at www.sec.gov/news/testimony/2006/ts091906cc.htm.
77. United States Government Accountability Office. 2006. Sarbanes-Oxley Act challenges for small companies. (April) GAO-06-361. Available at: www.gao.gov/cgi_bin/getrpt?GAO-06-361.
78. Fink, R. and D. Durfee. 2006. Could it be that finance executives really don't mind regulation? *CFO Magazine* (September 1).
79. Committee on Capital Markets Regulation. 2006. Interim report of the Committee on Capital Markets Regulation (November 30). Available at: www.capmktsreg.org/research.html.
80. Ibid.
81. Westbrook, J. 2006. Senate's Dodd Cautions against Sarbanes-Oxley Changes (November 30). Bloomberg News.
82. Ibid.
83. U.S. Securities and Exchange Commission. 2006. SEC Votes to Propose Interpretive Guidance for Management to Improve Sarbanes-Oxley 404 Implementation (December 13). Available at: www.sec/gov/news/press/2006/2006-206.htm.
84. Paulson, H. M. 2006. Remarks by Treasury secretary.
85. Ibid.

86. Cutler, S. M. 2004. Speech by SEC Director of Division of Enforcement. Second Annual General Counsel Roundtable: Tone at the top: Getting it right. (December 3). Available at: www.sec.gov/news/speech/spch1203004smc.htm.
87. Ibid.
88. Richards, L. A. 2003. Speech by SEC Staff: The culture of compliance. Spring Compliance Conference: National Regulatory Services. (April 23). Available at: www.sec.gov/news/speech/spch042303lar.htm.
89. Corporate Board Member/PricewaterhouseCoopers. What directors think 2005. Corporate Board Member/PwC survey. Available at: www.boardmember.com.
90. *Financial Times*. 2006. "Full text of Warren Buffet's memorandum" (October 9). Available at: www.ft.com.

CHAPTER 2

Fundamentals of Corporate Governance

INTRODUCTION

Public companies are a major engine of economic growth and prosperity in a free enterprise system in advanced capitalist economies, such as the United States. Shareholders who invest capital are usually remote, by distance or knowledge, from those managing the corporation. The wave of financial scandals of the late 1990s and early 2000s was devastating. It resulted in billions of dollars in financial losses and the erosion of investor confidence and public trust in financial reports disseminated by public companies. Financial scandals of high-profile companies such as Enron, WorldCom, Global Crossing, and Qwest (better known as the Big Four scandals) alone cost investors and pensioners more than $460 billion.[1] They also raised a fundamental question: Where were the directors, officers, auditors, outside legal counsel, financial analysts, investment banks, and even standard-setting bodies and regulators? More specifically, questions were raised concerning the lack of ethical, vigilant, and effective corporate governance, which played a major role in these scandals. The Conference Board states:

> *The Enron bankruptcy, accompanied by the WorldCom debacle and other corporate scandals, has caused a sea change in the attention given corporate governance and in how directors are viewed by the public, shareholders, employees, and the courts.*[2]

This chapter presents a model of an effective corporate governance structure and explains how it should work to improve corporate accountability to shareholders and improve the quality of publicly disclosed financial reporting.

CORPORATE GOVERNANCE STRUCTURE

Corporate governance has traditionally been seen as the mechanism for aligning the interests of management with those of shareholders. More specifically, the role

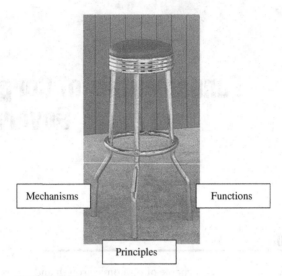

Mechanisms   Functions   Principles

EXHIBIT 2.1   Corporate Governance Structure

of corporate governance has been to reduce agency costs and to create long-term shareholder value by focusing on the decision-monitoring responsibilities of the board of directors and the decision-management functions of senior executives. In this book, an integrated approach to corporate governance is adopted by focusing on the value-increasing role of corporate governance participants, including the board of directors, management, auditors, financial advisors, legal counsel, standard-setting bodies and regulators, and investors. The corporate governance structure presented in this chapter is based on three interrelated components of corporate governance: principles, functions, and mechanisms, as depicted in Exhibit 2.1. A well-defined and effective functioning of these three components contributes to the effectiveness of corporate governance in creating sustainable shareholder value and protecting the interests of other stakeholders as well.

Corporate Governance Principles

There is no single globally accepted corporate governance code, yet there is a growing set of principles that can be applied across a broad range of board structures, business practices, and legal, political, and economic environments. In 2004, the Organization for Economic Co-operation and Development (OECD) released its revised Principles of Corporate Governance. The OECD principles are intended to assist both OECD and non-OECD governments in their efforts to evaluate and improve the legal, institutional, and regulatory framework for corporate governance in their countries and to provide guidance and suggestions for stock exchanges, investors, corporations, and other parties that have a role in the process of developing good corporate governance.[3] Exhibit 2.2 outlines the

EXHIBIT 2.2 OECD Principles of Corporate Governance (2004)

Principle	Subprinciple
The corporate governance framework should:	
I. Promote transparent and efficient markets, be consistent with the rule of law, and clearly articulate the division of responsibilities among different supervisory, regulatory, and enforcement authorities.	■ The corporate governance framework should be developed with a view to its impact on overall economic performance, market integrity, and the incentives it creates for market participants and the promotion of transparent and efficient markets.
	■ The legal and regulatory requirements that affect corporate governance practices in a jurisdiction should be consistent with the rule of law, transparent, and enforceable.
	■ The division of responsibilities among different authorities in a jurisdiction should be clearly articulated and ensure that the public interest is served.
	■ Supervisory, regulatory, and enforcement authorities should have the authority, integrity, and resources to fulfill their duties in a professional and objective manner. Moreover, their rulings should be timely, transparent, and fully explained.
II. Protect and facilitate the exercise of shareholders' rights.	■ Basic shareholder rights should include the right to secure methods of ownership registration, convey or transfer shares, obtain relevant and material information on the corporation on a timely and regular basis, participate and vote in general shareholder meetings, elect and remove members of the board, and share in the profits of the corporation.
	■ Shareholders should have the right to participate in, and to be sufficiently informed on, decisions concerning fundamental corporate changes such as amendments to the statutes or articles of incorporation or similar governing documents of the company, the authorization of additional shares, and extraordinary transactions, including the transfer of all or substantially all assets that in effect result in the sale of the company.

(continued overleaf)

EXHIBIT 2.2 (*Continued*)

Principle	Subprinciple
	■ Shareholders should have the opportunity to participate effectively and vote in general shareholder meetings and should be informed of the rules, including voting procedures, that govern general shareholder meetings.
	■ Capital structures and arrangements that enable certain shareholders to obtain a degree of control disproportionate to their equity ownership should be disclosed.
	■ Markets for corporate control should be allowed to function in an efficient and transparent manner.
	■ The exercise of ownership rights by all shareholders, including institutional investors, should be facilitated.
	■ Shareholders, including institutional shareholders, should be allowed to consult with each other on issues concerning their basic shareholder rights as defined in the principles, subject to exceptions to prevent abuse.
III. Ensure the equitable treatment of all shareholders, including minority and foreign shareholders. All shareholders should have the opportunity to obtain effective redress for violation of their rights.	■ All shareholders of the same series of a class should be treated equally.
	■ Insider trading and abusive self-dealing should be prohibited.
	■ Members of the board and key executives should be required to disclose to the board whether they, directly, indirectly, or on behalf of third parties, have a material interest in any transaction or matter directly affecting the corporation.

IV. Recognize the rights of stakeholders established by law or through mutual agreements and encourage active cooperation between corporations and stakeholders in creating wealth, jobs, and the sustainability of financially sound enterprises.

- The rights of stakeholders that are established by law or through mutual agreements are to be respected.
- Where stakeholder interests are protected by law, stakeholders should have the opportunity to obtain effective redress for violation of their rights.
- Performance-enhancing mechanisms for employee participation should be permitted to develop.
- Where stakeholders participate in the corporate governance process, they should have access to relevant, sufficient, and reliable information on a timely and regular basis.
- Stakeholders, including individual employees and their representative bodies, should be able to freely communicate their concerns about illegal or unethical practices to the board, and their rights should not be compromised for doing this.
- The corporate governance framework should be complemented by an effective, efficient insolvency framework and by effective enforcement of creditor rights.

V. Ensure that timely and accurate disclosure is made on all material matters regarding the corporation, including the financial situation, performance, ownership, and governance of the company.

- Disclosure should include, but not be limited to, material information on the financial and operating results of the company; company objectives; major share ownership and voting rights; remuneration policy for members of the board and key executives, and information about board members, including their qualifications, the selection process, other company directorships and whether they are regarded as independent by the board; related party transactions; foreseeable risk factors; issues regarding employees and other stakeholders; governance structures and policies, in particular, the content of any corporate governance code or policy and the process by which it is implemented.

(continued overleaf)

EXHIBIT 2.2 (*Continued*)

Principle	Subprinciple
	■ Information should be prepared and disclosed in accordance with high-quality standards of accounting and financial and nonfinancial disclosure.
	■ An annual audit should be conducted by an independent, competent, and qualified auditor in order to provide external and objective assurance to the board and shareholders that the financial statements fairly represent the financial position and performance of the company in all material respects.
	■ External auditors should be accountable to the shareholders and owe a duty to the company to exercise due professional care in the conduct of the audit.
	■ Channels for disseminating information should provide for equal, timely, and cost-efficient access to relevant information by users.
	■ The corporate governance framework should be complemented by an effective approach that addresses and promotes the provision of analysis or advice by analysts, brokers, rating agencies, and others that is relevant to decisions by investors and free from material conflicts of interest that might compromise the integrity of their analysis or advice.

VI. Ensure the strategic guidance of the company, the effective monitoring of management by the board, and the board's accountability to the company and the shareholders.

- Board members should act on a fully informed basis, in good faith, with due diligence and care, and in the best interests of the company and the shareholders.
- Where board decisions may affect different shareholder groups differently, the board should treat all shareholders fairly.
- The board should apply high ethical standards. It should take into account the interests of stakeholders.
- The board should fulfill certain key functions, including: reviewing and guiding corporate strategy, major plans of action, risk policy, annual budgets and business plans; setting performance objectives; monitoring implementation and corporate performance; overseeing major capital expenditures, acquisitions, and divestitures; monitoring the effectiveness of the company's governance practices and making changes as needed; selecting, compensating, monitoring, and, when necessary, replacing key executives and overseeing succession planning; and ensuring a formal and transparent board nomination and election process.
- The board should be able to exercise objective independent judgment on corporate affairs.
- In order to fulfill their responsibilities, board members should have access to accurate, relevant, and timely information.

Source: Adapted from OECD, Principles of Corporate Governance (2004). Available at: www.oecd.org/dataoecd/32/18/31557724.pdf.

current principles and subprinciples that have been established by the OECD as guidance for corporate governance. The set of core principles of the OECD are applicable to a wide range of jurisdictions. The International Corporate Governance Network (ICGN) has adopted these principles as the minimum acceptable standards for companies and investors worldwide.[4] The ICGN highly recommends that companies use the OECD corporate governance principles including honesty, resilience, responsiveness, and transparency as best practices to improve their own governance.

Honesty   Honesty means telling the truth at all times, regardless of the consequences. Honesty is important in establishing a trusting relationship among all corporate governance participants (directors, management, auditors, financial advisors, legal counsel, employees, customers, and government). It also means that corporate communications with both internal and external audiences, including public financial reports, should be accurate, fair, transparent, and trustworthy. A reputation for honesty can be earned over time through truthful and transparent corporate communication, and it can be easily destroyed through a pattern of lies, deception, malfeasance, concealment, and fraud. Thus, public companies should continuously and consciously strive to develop and maintain an ethical culture based on honesty and integrity that starts at the top of the organization, where actions speak louder than words.

Resilience   A resilient corporate governance structure is sustainable and enduring in the sense that it will easily recuperate from setbacks and abuse. One possible impediment to corporate governance structure is abuse to its flexibility, openness, and responsiveness. Corporate governance mechanisms, both internal and external, are designed to prevent, detect, and correct such abuses. Internal mechanisms include a vigilant board of directors, effective internal controls, and a robust system of checks and balances with related policies and procedures. External mechanisms are applicable laws, regulations, rules and standards, the capital markets, the market for corporate control, the labor market, and stakeholder monitoring.

Responsiveness   The company's timely and appropriate responses to the concerns, requests, or desires of investors, customers, employees, auditors, suppliers, corporate governance and social responsibility activists, and other stakeholders demonstrate that it respects the concerns of others. Effective corporate governance is responsive to reasonable requests that have a proper business purpose, from all corporate governance participants, emerging issues, and changes in regulatory, social, and environmental issues. The emerging corporate governance structure emphasizes value creation for all participants and maximizes the returns to both human and physical capital.

Transparency   Plain English, nonboilerplate disclosures to both internal and external audiences can create trust. In essence, transparency means that the company is being forthright with its intended audience and not attempting to hide relevant but potentially negative information by disclosing it in vague sentences buried in the middle of a voluminous document. It also means that disclosures are fair, accurate, reliable, and understandable by individual stakeholders. Transparent communication should be easy to understand for all concerned parties in terms of its goals and message. An important principle of effective corporate governance is its transparency and well-balanced, fair disclosure, not only of financial information, but also of information related to operations, structures, and executive compensation linked to long-term financial performance. One important element of the financial reporting process is the disclosure of important events, transactions, and conflicts of interest to shareholders that could possibly affect the judgment and decisions of the board of directors or management. An obvious example is identification and disclosure of related parties and related party transactions where self-dealing by management or directors may be involved, such as with chief financial officer Andy Fastow's off–balance sheet partnerships with Enron (i.e., JEDI, CHEWCO, etc.).

In October 2004, the European Community (EC) released a proposal intended to improve corporate governance transparency in these ways:

- The company's board of directors would be directly responsible for financial statements.
- Proper disclosure of all material off–balance sheet arrangements would be required in the notes to the financial statements.
- Proper disclosure of transactions with related parties would be required.
- A corporate governance statement as an integral part of annual reports would be required to reflect information about the company's risk management system, internal controls, shareholders' rights and meetings, and the board of directors and its committees.[5]

A joint report by the CFA Institute and the Business Roundtable Institute for Corporate Ethics suggests five recommendations for improving corporate communications and transparency:

1. Encourage companies to provide more meaningful and frequent communications about their long-term vision, strategic goals, and performance metrics including key financial indicators, and more transparent financial reports.
2. Encourage greater use of plain-language communications as opposed to the current communications dominated by legal and accounting language.
3. Endorse the use of corporate sustainable investment statements to shareholders above and beyond the requirements of the current practice reporting and operating model.
4. Improve corporate disclosure and communication processes to adequately inform investors and analysts rather than create complexity and confusion regarding the company's sustainable performance.
5. Encourage institutional investors to provide sustainable investment statements to their beneficiaries similar to those that companies are required to make to their shareholders.[6]

Effective corporate governance should be developed based on nine key principles:

1. *Value-adding philosophy.* Corporate governance should provide the foundations for all seven corporate governance functions (oversight, managerial, compliance, internal audit, advisory, external audit, monitoring) to add value to the company's sustainable and enduring performance.
2. *Independence.* This concept determines the extent to which the corporate governance process and its related mechanisms minimize or avoid conflicts of interests and self-dealing actions of its directors, officers, auditors, legal counsel, financial analysts, investment bankers, and other key personnel. Corporate governance reforms (Sarbanes-Oxley [SOX], SEC rules, best practices, and listing standards) regard independence as the backbone of corporate governance. Other corporate governance principles, functions, and mechanisms evolve around and are affected by the concept of independence in both appearance and in fact.
3. *Ethical conduct.* Corporate governance should promote ethical conduct for all corporate governance participants throughout the company. Doing so entails an appropriate tone at the top and a firm commitment from corporate governance participants to adhere to ethical behavior and conduct. A corporate culture of compliance and ethics should be integrated into the company's corporate governance structure to encourage all personnel to do the "right thing" and to understand that this is vital to the achievement of sustainable performance.
4. *Accountability.* Accountability forms the cornerstone of corporate governance by continuously monitoring best practices and by effectively discharging responsibilities. The main drivers of accountability are the acceptance of responsibility, ethical decision making, transparency, and candor, which result in the establishment of trust and a mutually beneficial working relationship between the company and its shareholders. Corporate governance should foster accountability and responsible decision making throughout the company. All corporate governance participants should be held accountable for their decisions, actions, and performance.
5. *Shareholder democracy.* Corporate governance should promote shareholder democracy in director elections by recognizing and respecting the rights of shareholders. It can be achieved through the requirements of declassified boards, nomination of directors by shareholders, and the majority-vote election procedures for directors. In addition, the rights and interests of all stakeholders should be acknowledged and respected. These requirements, among others, are discussed further in Chapters 3 and 10.
6. *Integrity of financial reporting.* Corporate governance should safeguard the integrity of financial reporting by enhancing the quality, reliability, and transparency of financial reports. Under the Exchange Act rules, public companies must disclose required information by filing annual and quarterly reports and other current reports when certain events occur. The required disclosure should be adequate to inform the marketplace about the company's performance and to protect investors.
7. *Transparency.* The company's actions, governance, and the financial and nonfinancial aspects of its business should be easily available and understandable by

all parties concerned. SEC chairman Christopher Cox, regarding the usefulness and transparency of both financial and nonfinancial information provided to investors, states:

> *A proxy statement today may well contain all the required information, and yet still not tell anybody much of anything....Investors and their directors have a right to the information. Complete. Clear. Comprehensible....If someone orders a steak, you don't give them a cow and a meat cleaver. Investors should get all the information they need—and they should get it in a form they can use.*[7]

8. *Competence and integrity.* The effectiveness of corporate governance depends on the integrity and competence of those who carry out key functional responsibilities (the seven corporate governance functions discussed in this book).
9. *Effective system of checks and balances.* The existence of an effective system of checks and balances ensures proper alignment of the interests of management with those of the shareholders as well as division of responsibilities among shareholders, the board of directors, and management.

Corporate Governance Functions

Corporate governance functions constitute an important element of the corporate governance structure. Exhibit 2.3 shows the seven essential corporate governance functions of oversight, managerial, compliance, internal audit, advisory, external audit, and monitoring. A well-balanced implementation of these seven interrelated functions produces responsible corporate governance, reliable financial reports, and credible audit services. This integrated approach underscores and reaffirms the primary goal of corporations to create sustainable shareholder value while securing the interests of other stakeholders. Given that the primary purpose of any business, particularly public companies, is to create substantial and enduring value, then the goal of corporate governance is to ensure that all participants are working to achieve this goal.

The interactive functions shown in Exhibit 2.3 are discussed separately in the next eight chapters. These interrelated and interwoven functions should be integrated into the overall corporate strategy and accountability. Three of these functions, however, are crucial to the achievement of sustainable corporate performance: the oversight function assumed by the board of directors, the managerial function delegated to management, and the monitoring function exercised by shareholders. A well-balanced operation of the corporate governance functions discussed in the next subsections can contribute to the effectiveness of corporate governance.

Oversight Function The board of directors has a fiduciary duty to oversee management to ensure it is acting in the best interests of the company and its shareholders. The board's effectiveness depends in large part on a director's independence, qualifications, skill sets, and resources. Public companies' day-to-day operations are managed by executive management under the oversight of the board of directors. The oversight function is thoroughly examined in Chapters 3 and 4.

EXHIBIT 2.3   Corporate Governance Function

Managerial Function   Management holds the responsibility to run the company and manage its resources and operations to create sustainable shareholder value. The effectiveness of this function depends on the alignment of management's interests with those of shareholders (the owners). Management of the company by senior executives may give rise to potential conflicts of interest (i.e., self-dealing) and other motivational problems (agency problems) that may be detrimental to corporate governance balance of power. The managerial function is further discussed in Chapter 5.

Compliance Function   The compliance function is based on a set of laws, regulations, rules, standards, and best practices developed by state and federal legislators, regulators, standard-setting bodies, and professional organizations to create a compliance framework of minimum standards to be followed by public companies. The corporate compliance environment is framed by federal statutes passed by Congress (e.g., Securities and Exchange Acts of 1933 and 1934, SOX), state statutes (e.g., state corporate laws defining the fiduciary duties of directors and officers), regulators (e.g., SEC, PCAOB, and FASB), national stock exchanges (e.g., listing standards), courts (e.g., interpreting laws and enforcing director and officer breaches of those legal duties for the benefit of shareholders), and best practices advocated by investor activists and professional organizations (e.g., Conference Board, Council of Institutional Investors, International Corporate Governance Network). The compliance function is thoroughly addressed in Chapter 6.

Internal Audit Function   Internal auditors provide both assurance and consulting services to the company in the areas of operational efficiency, risk management, internal controls, financial reporting, and governance processes. The effectiveness of the internal audit function depends on the independence, objectivity, competence, experience, and integrity of the company's internal auditors. The internal audit function is examined in Chapter 7.

Legal and Financial Advisory Function   Legal counsel provides legal advice and assists the company and its directors, officers, and employees in complying with applicable laws, regulations, and other matters, including strategic planning. Lawyers are generally viewed as advocates for those they represent. However, the effectiveness of corporate legal counsel depends on their professional objectivity, competence, and integrity. Financial advisors provide financial planning and advice to the company. The effectiveness of financial advisors depends on their professional objectivity, independence, training and experience. The advisory function is examined in detail in Chapter 8.

External Audit Function   The external audit function is required for public companies and is conducted by a public accounting firm. External auditors are supposed to be independent and are hired by the company to opine whether financial statements truly and fairly represent, in all material respects, the company's financial position and results of operations in conformity with generally accepted accounting principles. External auditors lend credibility to the company's financial reports and thus add value to its corporate governance. The effectiveness of this function depends on the independence, objectivity, competence, and integrity of external auditors in providing a high-quality integrated audit of both the company's internal controls and its financial statements. The external audit function is thoroughly examined in Chapter 9.

Monitoring Function   The monitoring function is exercised by shareholders, particularly institutional shareholders, who are empowered to elect directors. Shareholders can influence corporate governance through their proposals and nominations to the board of directors, when permitted. Other stakeholders can also affect corporate policies and practices. The effectiveness of this function depends on the participation and attentiveness of shareholders (owners). The monitoring function is discussed in detail in Chapter 10.

Corporate Governance Mechanisms

The separation of control and ownership in corporations has caused agency problems, and a series of corporate governance mechanisms have been implemented to mitigate them. Agency problems may develop for four reasons.

1. Managers may have the incentives for higher earnings, and when provided with opportunities, they may attempt to serve their own personal interests at the expense of the company's long-term well-being.

2. There may be an information asymmetry between management and the company's shareholders as management may be motivated to disclose good news and withhold bad news that might adversely reflect on its performance.
3. Management may be motivated, particularly when its compensation is linked to the company's reported earnings, to focus on short-term performance and to manipulate financial information to generate positive stock price changes or prevent an adverse effect on stock prices, which is frequently tied to management bonus payments.
4. Management may provide the company's board of directors with inaccurate and incomplete information in an attempt either to have better control over the board or to keep directors in the dark.

The agency theory implies that the board of directors is elected to manage the potential conflict of interests between management and shareholders. It further assumes that this internal mechanism alone works effectively without the need for external mechanisms (e.g., regulations and rules). Recent financial scandals indicate that a combination of both internal and external corporate governance mechanisms is needed to protect investors and other stakeholders from management misconduct and fraud. The corporate governance structure consists of a set of both internal and external mechanisms designed to manage, monitor, control, reward, and discipline arrangements and relationships among all corporate governance participants in order to create sustainable and enduring value for shareholders and to protect the interests of other stakeholders. Examples of internal governance mechanisms are the board of directors (particularly independent directors, the audit committee composed solely of independent directors at public companies), internal controls, and internal audit functions. Examples of external mechanisms are the capital market, the market for corporate control, the labor market, state and federal statutes, court decisions, shareholder proposals, and best practices of investor activists.

The capital markets, by representing an important source of funds to public companies, can act as an external corporate governance mechanism in monitoring and disciplining management. For the company to raise capital with minimum cost, capital markets must view management as a "good risk."[8] If senior executives are not viewed as "good risks," capital markets would discipline them by limiting their opportunities to raise capital or make capital more expensive. For example, if investors are not satisfied with the company's performance, they may be able to sell their shares. However, most institutional investors cannot do the "Wall Street walk" (i.e., sell their shares) because they are in passive index funds, such as the Russell 3000, and generally cannot selectively sell their stock in a particular company that is part of the index. However, if, for example, a large hedge fund sells its shares in a particular company, other investors may follow suit and the company's stock price may drop, which could force management to change course. Inefficient and poorly performing corporations are often a target for a hostile takeover.

Financial scandals of high-profile companies indicate that market-correction mechanisms alone cannot solve principal agent problems, asymmetric information, or conflicts of interest that exist among corporate governance participants. Market failures and the resulting financial scandals provide justifiable grounds for policy intervention to prevent management from adopting a suboptimal level of corporate governance. Regulations, the judicial process (courts), and local, state, and federal governments have significantly influenced the corporate governance structure.[9]

In summary, an effective corporate governance structure depends on a sharing of power between the board of directors, management, and shareholders. In addition, it includes appropriate interactions between internal mechanisms (e.g., board of directors, internal controls), external mechanisms (e.g., capital markets, market for corporate control, labor markets), and compliance requirements, including state and federal statutes, related regulations, best practices, and proposals put forward by shareholders at the annual shareholder meeting.

The corporate governance structure should be based on these premises, which are to be discussed throughout the book:

- The primary purpose of corporate governance is to create and enhance sustainable shareholder value while also protecting the interests of other stakeholders.
- The board of directors, as a representative of the owners (shareholders), has direct authority and responsibility to govern the business affairs of the company and is ultimately accountable to shareholders for the company's strategic performance, achievement of goals, financial performance, and prevention of negative surprises.
- The board of directors delegates the authority of managing the company to the top management team (senior executives, CEO, CFO, general counsel) and holds senior executives accountable for their decisions, actions, and performance.
- The independent chairperson of the board of directors (as is the entire board) is directly responsible for setting the board agenda, coordinating the board's activities, and overseeing the performance of the CEO.
- The position of chairman of the board and the CEO should be separate.
- The three mandatory board committees of audit, compensation, and nominating should be composed solely of independent directors.
- The CEO is directly responsible for managing the day-to-day operations of the company and is ultimately accountable to the board for the assigned managerial functions and decisions.
- The role of corporate governance participants (e.g., oversight, managerial, compliance, legal, internal audit, advisory, external audit, and monitoring) should be viewed as "value-added."
- Corporate governance should promote and facilitate shareholder democracy through simple majority voting and shareholders' access to proxy materials.
- Proper communications and public disclosures through proxy statements and periodic financial reports assist shareholders in making informed investment and proxy voting decisions.
- Well-governed companies outperform poorly governed companies in the long term. Thus, effective governance is a competitive advantage in the marketplace, and more capital will flow to companies with good governance.
- Directors' and officers' accountability should be achieved through a proper performance evaluation system that rewards good and ethical performance

while correcting or in some egregious cases punishing poor performance and misconduct.
- Directors and senior executives own a significant amount of the company stock.
- The independent auditor is annually ratified by shareholders.
- A shareholder advisory vote should be required for the approval of performance-based compensation plans for directors and officers.

CORPORATE GOVERNANCE REPORTING

Corporate governance reporting entails assessing the quality of the organization's corporate governance and presenting findings to interested stakeholders, including the board of directors, executives, auditors, regulatory agencies, and shareholders. Standards should be developed to assess, attest to, and report on the effectiveness of this process. Public companies do not usually report their corporate governance activities. However, in the post-SOX era, many companies have begun to disclose their corporate governance policies along with other information on their Web sites. Such reporting goes beyond the mandatory periodic financial reports or filings with regulatory bodies (the SEC). Corporate governance reports disclose: the company's vision, strategies, and missions in creating sustainable stakeholder value; the composition, independence, and functions of its board of directors; and additional information pertaining to financial, economic, social, and environmental indicators.

The Council of Institutional Investors (CII) believes that public companies should have written, disclosed corporate governance policies and procedures as well as a code of ethics that applies to their directors, officers, and employees.[10] The disclosed structure, policies, and procedures should provide adequate protection to investors and hold corporations accountable to their stakeholders. The guiding principles and best practices adopted by a number of national stock exchanges require expanded corporate governance practice disclosures, leading many public companies to reexamine their practices and provide disclosures of such practices. The Deloitte & Touche 2003 survey, however, reveals that while only about 23 percent of surveyed companies disclose their corporate governance practices on their Web sites, an additional 14 percent are planning to expand their practice disclosures above and beyond what is required by the SEC.[11]

The Commission of the European Communities requires that listed companies include in their annual report a comprehensive statement reflecting the major elements of their corporate governance structure and practices, including:

- The operation of the shareholder meetings.
- A description of shareholder rights and how they can be exercised.
- The composition of the board of directors and its committees (e.g., audit, compensation, nomination/corporate governance).
- The shareholders with major holdings, their voting and control rights, and related major agreements.
- Any direct or indirect relationships between major shareholders and the company.

- Any material transactions with related parties.
- The existence and nature of a risk management system.
- A reference to the company's code on corporate governance.[12]

In August 2006, the SEC issued its final rules to expand its requirements of corporate governance disclosures.[13] These consolidated disclosure requirements include board meetings and committees; particular disclosures regarding audit, nominating, and compensation committees; and a narrative description of the company's procedures for determining director and executive compensation, related person transactions, director independence, and other corporate governance matters. Previous rules required disclosures of nominating and audit committees; this rule requires the same disclosure of the compensation committee, including:

- The scope of authority of the compensation committee.
- The extent to which the compensation committee may delegate any authority to other persons, specifying what authority may be so delegated and to whom.
- If their authority is set out in a charter or other document, and where to access it.
- Any executive officers who have a say in the compensation committee's agenda.
- The role of any consultants and who hired them.
- The independence of each member.[14]

In addition to the aforementioned items, the corporate governance report should include:

- The company's objectives and management visions to achieve these objectives.
- Summary of financial position and results of operations.
- Compensation policy for directors and officers including shareholder advisory vote on executive pay.
- Board committees' policies, procedures, and disclosures.
- Significant issues relevant to employees and other stakeholders.
- Corporate governance structure including aspects, principles, and functions.
- Material information on sustainability performance of multiple bottom lines in areas of economic, ethical, social, and environmental activities.
- Company's initiatives on risk management including foreseeable risk factors and responses.
- The company's voting system (majority versus plurality).
- Duality of CEO positions or separation of the positions of the independent chair of the board and the CEO.
- The percentage of independent directors.
- The number of meetings of the board of directors and its committees.
- The annual evaluation of the board of directors, its committees, and the committee members.
- The company's compliance with corporate governance reforms including SOX, SEC-related rules, exchange listing standards, and best practices.
- The company's code of conduct and ethics for directors, officers, and all other key personnel.

- The company's whistleblower policies and procedures.
- All relevant information about the effectiveness of the company's corporate governance.
- Summary information on financial and nonfinancial key performance indicators (KPIs).
- Assessment of the company's responsiveness to the needs of all of its stakeholders.
- Other information deemed necessary and relevant to the company's shareholders and other stakeholders pertaining to corporate governance.

CORPORATE GOVERNANCE RATINGS

The well-publicized rash of high-profile financial scandals caused some institutional investors to be more active in monitoring companies in which they invested, including paying more attention to corporate governance and considering its effectiveness in their investment decisions.[15] The well-deserved, long-awaited investor focus on corporate governance generated a demand for the development of ratings metrics or systems that gather, analyze, rank, and compare corporate accountability practices of public companies.[16] National and international organizations, including Glass Lewis & Co. (Glass Lewis), Institutional Shareholder Services (ISS), Governance-Metrics International (GMI), The Corporate Library, Standard & Poor's (S&P), and Moody's Investment Service, have developed and published variations of corporate governance ratings that are often used by institutional shareholders in assessing their stock returns and by bondholders in determining the costs of lending.

Exhibit 2.4 presents a list of these organizations with their related corporate governance rating services as presented in the 2005 State Board of Administration of Florida Pension Fund Annual Corporate Governance report.[17] The report shows that many of these ratings are correlated; the Glass Lewis pay-for-performance analysis and the Board Analysts' CEO compensation rating found low correlation.[18] Corporate governance ratings are evolving and, as such, some inconsistencies in ratings among these providers may exist. For this reason, caution should be exercised in using ratings from several providers.[19]

The Credit Agency Reform Act (CARA) was signed into law on September 29, 2006, amending the Securities Exchange Act of 1934. The CARA is intended to improve the quality of credit ratings and to protect investors by enhancing accountability, competition, and transparency in the credit rating industry.[20] The CARA establishes a registration process which grants the SEC's authority to register nationally recognized statistical rating organizations (NRSROs).[21] Five of the provisions of the CARA are:

1. The SEC has exclusive authority for NRSRO registration and qualification.
2. NRSROs must meet criteria set forth in the CARA to be registered as a credit rating agency.
3. The SEC will oversee the registered NRSROs through examinations and enforcement actions.
4. The SEC is directed to issue rules concerning conflicts of interest and the misuse of nonpublic information by NRSROs.

EXHIBIT 2.4 Corporate Governance Rating Organizations

Organization	Description	Web Site
Glass Lewis & Co. (GLC)	■ Provides global proxy research and advice for approximately 8,000 public companies and several stock indexes including the Russell 3000, S&P 500, S&S Mid Cap 400, Wilshire 5000, S&P Small Cap 600, among others. ■ Focuses on the economic consequences of corporate governance issues (e.g., board independence, executive compensation, majority voting, and their potential effect on shareholder value. ■ Establishes a proprietary method for rating public companies' executive compensation practices by using a pay-for-performance model focusing on several performance measures of one-year total shareholder return, two-year change in book value, two-year stock price performance, one-year ROE, two-year EPS growth, and one-year ROA. The compensation of the top five officers in a company is compared to the median paid by competition in its own industry, sector, and similar-size firms. A letter grade from A to F is then assigned to the company's overall compensation practice. ■ Provides corporate governance services to institutional investors, mutual funds, and pension funds, without seeking consulting services.	www.glasslewis.com

(*continued overleaf*)

EXHIBIT 2.4 (*Continued*)

Organization	Description	Web Site
Institutional Shareholder Services (ISS)	■ Provides several services including corporate governance quotient (CGQ) ratings, proxy recommendations, research services, and voting analytics as well as consulting services. ■ Provides company ratings based on corporate governance practices that assist institutional investors in assessing the effectiveness of public companies' governance and quality of corporate boards. ■ Gathers corporate governance data about 5,000 public companies and classifies them into 63 ratings criteria based on their corporate governance practices and structures. ■ Calculates the raw score for each company and then compares companies on a relative basis to an index and industry group to determine the separate index and industry CGQ scores.	www.issproxy.com
Council of Institutional Investors (CII)	The CII annually publishes a focus list of underperforming companies. The companies included in the focus list should have the largest underperformance relative to their industry group's five-year median return, and they must lag both their market index and industry group returns for one-, three-, and five-year periods ending June 30.	www.cii.org

The Corporate Library	www.thecorporatelibrary.com

- Provides data on more than 2,000 U.S. and 500 large international companies.
- Provides comparative corporate governance data for large companies and their directors, a corporate governance best practices score, and a unique board effectiveness rating system.
- Performs no consulting services. It is fully independent and it does not offer any investment or proxy recommendations.
- Identifies potential areas of the board's ineffective oversight rated from A to F where firms with F ratings have exhibited major governance-related problems.
- Determines how well a company meets generally accepted governance practices suggested by professional organizations.
- Provides the CEO compensation ratings by identifying red flags such as base pay over $1 million, CEO bonus more than double the annual salary, excessive amounts of options granted to the CEO, high tax payments (gross-ups), a declining number of shares owned by the CEO, and lack of adequate disclosure on CEO compensation.

(continued overleaf)

EXHIBIT 2.4 (*Continued*)

Organization	Description	Web Site
Governance Metrics International (GMI)	■ GMI provides corporate governance ratings and research on more than 3,200 global companies. Its rating criteria are based on securities regulations, stock exchange listing standards, and various corporate governance principles and best practices. ■ GMI establishes global ratings and has market ratings by using hundreds of data points to determine an overall GMI score and separate scores for each of GMI's six research categories of board accountability, financial disclosure and internal controls, shareholder rights, remuneration, market for control, and corporate behavior. GMI ratings are ranked from 1 to 10, where 10 score indicates the highest ratings.	www.gmiratings.com
Equilar	Equilar provides detailed compensation data based on more than 75 unique data elements gathered from proxy and annual reports for all top executives of 4,000 companies, including Russell 3000. Executive compensation elements included in the database are cash compensation, long-term awards, option grants using the Black-Scholes and Binomial Lattice models, employment agreements, and company financial performance.	www.equilar.com

FTSE/ISS Corporate Governance Indexes (CGI)	Financial Times Stock Exchange (FTSE), an independent company owned by Financial Times and London Stock Exchange, in collaboration with ISS has developed global corporate governance index since April 2004. The CGI covers about 2,200 large and mid-cap stocks in the 24 developed countries of the FTSE Global Equity Index Series. The CGI rating system covers about 60 corporate governance criteria regarding five general areas: (1) board of directors (composition, nominating committee, voting policies, succession planning, and size); (2) audit (audit committee, audit fees, and auditor rotation); (3) shareholder rights and protections (capital structure and antitakeover provisions); (4) compensation (director compensation, cost of equity awards, pension provisions); and (5) ownership (percentage of total equity owned by directors and director/executive ownership guidelines).	www.ftse.com
Standard and Poor's/Glass, Lewis & Co. Board Accountability Index (BAI)	The Board Accountability Index (BAI) is structured based on correlation between stock performance and the extent to which boards are accountable to their shareholders. The BAI is regarded as an enhanced corporate governance index because it tracks its benchmark index closely through quantitative algorithms and because of its robustness in controlling for risk. The BAI covers only the S&P 500 companies and makes constant updates on its weightings and closing prices. The BAI evaluate S&P 500 companies (underweights and overweights) based on five corporate governance criteria: (1) staggered boards; (2) ability of shareholders to amend corporate bylaws; (3) poison pills; (4) golden parachutes; and (5) supermajority merger requirements. The BAI overweights companies with less than three of these criteria classified as good governance companies and underweights them with three or more entrenching provisions reflecting bad governance companies.	www.glasslewis.com/ solutions/bai.php

Source: Extracted from Web sites presented in the exhibit.

5. Registered NRSROs are subject to disclosure requirements to improve transparency and disclosure of conflicts of interest, procedures, and methodologies used in determining credit ratings.[22]

The CARA defines an NRSRO as a credit rating agency that: (1) has been in business as a credit rating agency for at least three consecutive years prior to the date of its application for registration under Section 15 E; and (2) issued credit ratings certified by qualified institutional buyers with respect to financial institutions, brokers, dealers, insurance companies and corporate issuers, issuers of asset-backed securities, issuers of government securities, and a combination of these obligors.[23] Examples of NRSROs are Standard and Poor's (S&P) and Moody's Investor Service, Inc. (Moody's), which rate more than 99 percent of the debt obligations and preferred stock issues by public companies in the United States. The CARA is viewed as a reasonable approach in regulating credit agencies, providing transparency and objective standards for NRSROs, and promoting competition in the credit rating industry by opening the field to further entrants.

CONVERGENCE IN CORPORATE GOVERNANCE

Financial scandals of the early 2000s were not unique to the United States. The revelation of global financial scandals (Parmalat, Royal Ahold, etc.) encouraged regulators worldwide to recognize the need to address the global corporate governance deficiencies and work together to improve the quality, reliability, and transparency of global financial reports to enhance the integrity and efficiency of the global markets. Several initiatives have been taken to improve corporate governance worldwide, while many specifically address a country's improvements in its corporate governance. No globally accepted set of corporate governance principles or global regulatory framework governs corporations, global financial institutions, or capital markets worldwide. As of 2006, regulators in the United States, the SEC, the International Organization of Securities Commission (IOSCO), and the World Federation of Exchanges (WFE) have yet to agree on a global regulatory framework or a global corporate governance structure. The OECD's international standards of corporate governance have not achieved enough global acceptance to be included in the global regulatory framework even though the ICGN highly recommends them as corporate governance best practices.

The Commission of European Communities suggests that the European Union (EU) should actively coordinate the corporate governance efforts and reforms of its member states, requiring each member state to take four steps:

1. Identify its corporate laws, securities laws, listing rules, codes of conduct, and best practices.
2. Make progress toward designating a code of corporate governance, intended for use at the national level, with which listed companies should either comply or disclose noncompliance.

3. Coordinate its code of corporate governance with other member states.
4. Participate in the coordination process established by the EU.[24]

Several issues need to be addressed to promote convergence in global corporate governance.[25] The first and most important issue is whether corporate governance principles and provisions should be mandatory as a set of rules that all companies must comply with as opposed to recommendations and disclosure practices that require companies to disclose whether and how they have complied with the recommendations. This issue should be addressed in determining which approach will prevail in global corporate governance. In the United States, the emerging reforms are either regulated by Congress and regulators (SOX and SEC-related rules) or mandated by the national stock exchanges (the listing standards of the NYSE, Nasdaq, and AMEX). Corporate governance reforms in other countries (the Cadbury Report and the Combined Code in the United Kingdom) are mostly in the context of recommendations for best practices, which encourage compliance rather than being imposed on corporations.

The second issue is the rules-based versus principles-based approach to corporate governance convergence. The structure in the United States is viewed as a rules-based approach, whereas other countries are promoting a principles-based approach. These principles-based approaches are very broad and comprehensive without specifying specific rules in terms of the number of independent nonexecutive directors and their term limits, but they are steps in the right direction in improving corporate governance and accountability and reinforcing investors' rights. It appears that convergence would be more feasible when countries agree on the principles-based approach rather than having to reconcile voluminous and often irreconcilable rules.

The third issue is the consensus on the primary purposes of global corporate governance. The primary goal and focus in the United States is on the creation and enhancement of shareholder value; in some other countries, the protection of the interests of all stakeholders is considered the main goal of corporate governance. Convergence would be possible if all nations agree that the primary purpose is the enhancement of shareholder value while protecting the interests of other stakeholders.

Convergence is likely not feasible for all provisions of corporate governance. Some provisions that have already been converged or are good candidates for convergence are:

- Director independence where the majority of directors should be independent.
- The audit committee financial expertise requirement.
- The oversight responsibility of the audit committee to appoint, compensate, dismiss, and oversee the work of independent auditors.
- Board committees and their oversight responsibilities (audit, compensation, and nomination/governance).

Major differences that make convergence more difficult are: (1) the fact that in many countries, such as the United Kingdom, the position of the CEO and the chair of the board must be separate, but there is no such requirement in the United States; and (2) the independence requirement for the majority or all members of various board committees.

The European Commission encourages the coordination and convergence of national codes of corporate governance through high-level meetings of the European Corporate Governance Forum. These meetings typically are chaired by the Commission and include representatives from all member states, European regulators, investors, issuers, and academics.[26] The United States is already participating in efforts toward convergence of global accounting and auditing standards. More specifically, seven issues should be resolved to facilitate global convergence in corporate governance:

1. Corporate governance focus
   - Creation of shareholder value. The primary goal of corporate governance in the United States is to create and enhance sustainable shareholder value by focusing on improving the key financial performance indicators (earnings, stock prices, market capitalization).
   - Protection of stakeholder interests. The main goal of corporate governance in Europe is to protect the interests of all stakeholders including shareholders, creditors, suppliers, employees, customers, governments, and society.
2. Board system
   - Unitary board system, where the board of directors and management are the same (e.g., Singapore board system).
   - Two-tier board system, where there are two boards of supervisory and management, and the supervisory board oversees the management board. The European two-tiered model of corporate governance consists of an executive board and a supervisory board. The executive board comprises senior executives and inside directors, and is primarily responsible for managing the company. The supervisory board is typically composed of outside directors who represent shareholders, employees, and lenders (banks); this board appoints and oversees the activities of the executive board.
   - Oversight board system where the board of directors appoints management and oversees its activities (in the United States).
3. Compliance with the code
   - Voluntary compliance, where the listed companies are required to comply with the code or explain noncompliance. The listed companies should tailor their corporate governance practices to the circumstances and choose the most suitable practices while attempting to conform corporate governance to the code. The listed companies should view the code as benchmarks and suggestions for good governance practices and justify noncompliance; unjustifiable deviations from the code should be penalized by the capital markets (Singapore code).
   - Compulsory compliance, where the listed companies are required to comply with the code and noncompliance is penalized and punished. The U.S. compulsory compliance approach permits no flexibility, which presents a one-size-fits-all approach to corporate governance.

4. Corporate governance approach
   - ○ Rules-based approach to corporate governance, where corporate governance reforms and listing standards are very rigid, are applicable to all listed companies, detail requirements for compliance, and prescribe a specific set of rules to be observed by all companies.
   - ○ Principles-based approach to corporate governance, where principles establish benchmarks and norms for good governance practices, but companies are given the flexibility to establish their own corporate governance rules tailored to their circumstances. This approach may create more room for manipulation and even noncompliance with minimum standards.
   - ○ The U.K. approach to corporate governance reforms is more principles-based, which requires companies to "comply or explain why not." This flexible approach to corporate governance, coupled with the fact that U.K. shareholders are in a much stronger position than their U.S. shareholders to nominate directors and forward their resolutions, has recently made the U.K. capital market more attractive to global IPOs.
   - ○ Different types of corporate governance structure are exposed to different financial misconduct and scandals. For example, the dispersed ownership system of governance in the United States is prone to earnings management schemes (e.g. Enron, WorldCom), whereas concentrated ownership systems are more vulnerable to the appropriation of private benefits of control (e.g. Parmalat).[27]

5. Director independence
   - ○ At least one-third of the board should comprise independent directors (Singapore code).
   - ○ The majority of the board must consist of independent directors (U.S. stock exchange listing standards).
   - ○ At least half of the board, excluding the chair, must be independent directors. For smaller companies, at least two independent directors should be on the board (U.K. code).

6. Plurality vs. majority voting process
   - ○ U.S. corporate governance reforms allow plurality voting whereas reforms in European countries require majority voting for a director's election.
   - ○ The election of a director is a vital role of shareholders in corporate governance, as directors serve as their agents. Under plurality voting, only one "For" vote will ensure the candidate's seat on the board regardless of the number of "Withheld" or "Against" votes for the candidate.
   - ○ Plurality voting may work fairly when there are more candidates than available board seats, and it can be alternatively ineffective when the candidate is ensured approval with as little as one vote. Majority voting empowers shareholders by requiring that the candidate be elected through the approval of a majority of shareholders.

7. CEO duality
   - ○ The European corporate governance initiators require the separation of the positions of chair of the board and the CEO. U.S. reforms do not require this separation.

The most important step in the convergence process is the statutory power to implement and enforce the globally accepted corporate governance principles, rules, or best practices. Different nations have different enforcement processes and criminal sanctions for the violation of corporate governance principles. To address this important global issue, in 2005 the United Nations (UN) Secretary-General invited a group of representatives from 20 investment organizations in 12 countries to establish a set of global best practice principles for responsible investment (PRIs).[28] The process of developing principles for responsible investment was coordinated and overseen by the UN Financial Initiative and the UN Global Compact. The PRIs are voluntary and aspirational rather than prescriptive. They provide a framework for incorporating environmental, social, and governance (ESG) issues into investment decision-making and ownership practices.[29] Compliance with the PRIs is expected to lead not only to a more sustainable financial return, but also to a close alignment of the interests of investors with those of global society at large. The PRIs consist of six principles:

1. Integration of ESG issues into investment analysis and the decision-making process.
2. Incorporation of ESG issues into investment ownership policies and practices.
3. Promotion of appropriate disclosure on ESG issues by the entities in which institutional investors invest.
4. Promotion of acceptance and implementation of the principles within the investment industry.
5. Collaboration among institutional investors to enhance the effectiveness of implementing the principles.
6. Reporting on initiatives, activities, and progress toward implementing these principles.[30]

Exhibit 2.5 presents these six PRIs along with the possible actions that should be taken to achieve these principles and the related interpretation. It is expected that these PRIs will receive global acceptance as a framework for integrating ESG into the corporate governance structure.

SUMMARY

Developments of the late 1990s and the early 2000s have reinvigorated the focus on effective corporate governance to protect shareholders and other stakeholders from managerial misconduct and corporate malfeasance. These reforms require professional accountability, personal responsibility, and integrity for all corporate governance participants. These developments aim at improving public trust and investor confidence in corporate America, its corporate governance, its capital markets, and financial reporting. This chapter presents the corporate governance structure consisting of principles, mechanisms, and seven interrelated functions to achieve a primary goal of creating sustainable shareholder value. These functions are further discussed in Chapters 3 to 10.

EXHIBIT 2.5 Principles of Responsible Investment

Principles	Possible Actions	Interpretations
Integration of environmental, social, and governance (ESG) issues into investment analysis and decision-making process	1. Address ESG issues in investment policy statements. 2. Support development of ESG-related tools, metrics, and analyses. 3. Assess the capabilities of internal investment managers to incorporate ESG issues. 4. Assess the capabilities of external investment managers to incorporate ESG issues. 5. Ask investment service providers (e.g., financial analysts, consultants, brokers, research firms, or rating companies) to integrate ESG factors into evolving research and analysis. 6. Encourage academic and other research on this theme. 7. Advocate ESG training for investment professionals.	Despite much important work in this area for several years by asset owners and investment managers, large institutional investors lack a framework for the systematic integration of ESG issues into investment decision-making and ownership practices. The PRIs provides this framework. The aim is to help integrate consideration of ESG issues by institutional investors into investment decision-making and ownership practices, and thereby improve long-term returns to beneficiaries.
Incorporation of ESG issues into investment ownership policies and practices	1. Develop and disclose an active ownership policy consistent with the principles. 2. Exercise voting rights or monitor compliance with voting policy (if outsourced). 3. Develop an engagement capability (either directly or through outsourcing).	The principles are based on the premise that ESG issues can affect investment performance and that the appropriate consideration of these issues is part of delivering superior risk-adjusted returns and is therefore firmly within the bounds

(continued overleaf)

EXHIBIT 2.5 (*Continued*)

Principles	Possible Actions	Interpretations
	4. Participate in the development of policy, regulation, and standard setting (e.g., promoting and protecting shareholder rights). 5. File shareholder resolutions consistent with long-term ESG considerations. 6. Engage with companies on ESG issues. 7. Participate in collaborative engagement initiatives. 8. Ask investment managers to undertake and report on ESG-related engagement.	of investors' fiduciary duties. The principles clearly state they are to be applied only in ways that are consistent with those duties. The principles are designed to be compatible with the investment styles of large, diversified institutional investors that operate within a traditional fiduciary framework. The principles apply across the whole investment business and are not designed to be relevant only to SRI products. However, the principles do point to a number of approaches—such as active ownership and the integration of ESG issues into investment analysis—that SRI and many corporate governance fund managers also practice.
Promotion of appropriate disclosure on ESG issues by the entities in which institutional investors invest	1. Ask for standardized reporting on ESG issues (using tools such as the Global Reporting Initiative). 2. Ask for ESG issues to be integrated within annual financial reports. 3. Ask for information from companies regarding adoption of/adherence to relevant norms, standards, codes of conduct, or international initiatives (e.g., the UN Global Compact). 4. Support shareholder initiatives and resolutions promoting ESG disclosure.	The principles suggest a policy of engagement with companies rather than screening or avoiding stocks based on ESG criteria (although this may be an appropriate approach for some investors). No legal or regulatory sanctions are associated with the principles. They are designed to be voluntary and aspirational. There may be reputational risks associated with signing up and then failing to take any action.

| Promotion of acceptance and implementation of the principles within the investment industry | 1. Include principles-related requirements in requests for proposals (RFPs).
 2. Align investment mandates, monitoring procedures, performance indicators, and incentive structures accordingly (e.g., ensure investment management processes reflect long-term time horizons when appropriate).
 3. Communicate ESG expectations to investment service providers.
 4. Revisit relationships with service providers that fail to meet ESG expectations.
 5. Support the development of tools for benchmarking ESG integration.
 6. Support regulatory or policy developments that enable implementation of the principles. | For institutional investors to make these principles work, they will need to encourage a change in the way that their agents incorporate ESG issues into their processes.

 The objective is for the principles to be integrated within the mainstream investment and ownership practices across the investment functions of an entire organization. They are not just applicable within specific asset classes or product lines. (This applies for all categories of signatory.) The principles have been designed as a commitment from the top-level leadership of the whole investment business.

 Investors will choose to implement the principles in different ways, and those choices will affect resource requirements. At a minimum, institutions should allocate sufficient staff time to properly understand the types of activities that are suggested in the principles, investigate how other investors have used them, and begin the im21lementation process.

 While these principles are designed to enhance the delivery of long-term returns to beneficiaries, their implementation will also focus greater attention on ESG issues throughout the investment and corporate sectors. New research and better metrics will be developed to support investors as |

(*continued overleaf*)

EXHIBIT 2.5 (*Continued*)

Principles	Possible Actions	Interpretations
		they become increasingly active owners. Encouraged to adopt a more systematic approach to managing ESG issues, corporate management will take more interest in these extrafinancial drivers of risk and reward, which will come to define corporate profitability in the medium and longer term. In this way, the principles for responsible investment will contribute to improved corporate performance on environmental, social and governance issues.
Collaboration among institutional investors to enhance the effectiveness of implementing the principles	1. Support/participate in networks and information platforms to share tools, pool resources, and make use of investor reporting as a source of learning. 2. Collectively address relevant emerging issues. 3. Develop or support appropriate collaborative initiatives.	Implementing the principles will lead to a more complete understanding of a range of material issues, and this should ultimately result in increased returns and lower risk. Signatories will be part of a network that creates opportunities to pool resources, lowering the costs of research and active ownership practices. The principles also allow investors to work together to address a range of systemic problems that, if remedied, may then lead to more stable,

	accountable, and profitable market conditions overall. The PRIs provide investors with a high-level framework for integrating ESG issues into investment decisions. And as signatories develop policies and procedures for integration, the PRIs secretariat will be available to help investors implement them.
Reporting on initiatives, activities, and progress toward implementing these principles	1. Disclose how ESG issues are integrated within investment practices. 2. Disclose active ownership activities (voting, engagement, and/or policy dialogue). 3. Disclose what is required from service providers in relation to the principles. 4. Communicate with beneficiaries about ESG issues and the principles. 5. Report on progress and/or achievements relating to the principles using a "Comply or Explain" approach. 6. Seek to determine the impact of the principles. 7. Make use of reporting to raise awareness among a broader group of stakeholders.

Source: The United Nations Environment Programme Finance Initiative (UNEPFI) and the UN Global Compact 2006. Principles for Responsible Investment (April 27). Available at: http://www.unpri.org.

NOTES

1. Rezaee, Z. 2004. Corporate governance role in financial reporting. *Research in Accounting Regulation* 17: 107–149.
2. Brancato, C. K., and C. A. Plath. 2002. Corporate governance best practices: A blueprint for the post-Enron era. Conference Board. Available at: www.conferenceboard.org.
3. Organization for Economic Cooperation and Development. 2004. Principles of corporate governance. Available at: www.oecd.org/dataoecd/32/18/31557724.pdf.
4. International Corporate Governance Network. 2005. Statement on global corporate governance principles (July 8). Available at: www.icgn.org/organisation/documents/cgp/revised_principles_jul2005.php.
5. European Commission. 2004. Audit of company accounts: Commission proposes directive to combat fraud and malpractice. Available at: http://europa.eu.int/rapid/pressReleasesAction.do?reference=IP/04/340&format=HTML&aged=0&language=EN&guiLanguage=en.
6. CFA Institute Center and Business Roundtable Institute for Corporate Ethics. 2006. Breaking the short-term cycle. (July 24). Available at: http://www.cfapubs.org/toc/ccb/2006/1.
7. Cox, C. 2005. SEC's chairman speech: Remarks before the Economic Club (December 12). Available at: www.sec.gov/news/speech/spch121205cc.htm.
8. Schleifer, A., and R. W. Vishny. 1997. A survey of corporate governance. *Journal of Finance* 52: 737–783.
9. Ibid.
10. Council of Institutional Investors. 2004. Corporate governance policies (October 13). Available at: www.cii.org.
11. Deloitte & Touche. 2003. Audit committee financial expert designation and disclosure practice survey. Available at: www.deloitte.com/dtt/article/0,1002,sid%253D2006%2526cid%253D13514,00.html.
12. Commission of the European Communities. 2003. Modernizing company law and enhancing corporate governance in the European Union: A plan to move forward. *COM* 284 final (May 21).
13. Securities and Exchange Commission. 2006. Executive compensation and related party disclosure. (January 17). FILE NO. S7-03-06. Available at: www.sec.gov/rules/proposed/33-8655.pdf.
14. Ibid.
15. Goodman, A., and Schwartz, B. 2004. *Corporate governance: Law and practice*. New York: Matthew Bender & Co.
16. Ibid.
17. State Board of Administration of Florida. 2005. SBA 2005 corporate governance report. Available at: www.sbafla.com/pdf/investment/CorpGovReport.pdf.
18. Ibid.
19. Millstein, I. M. 2005. "Beware the 'box tickers.'" Spencer Stuart US Board Index 2005. Available at: http://content.spencerstuart.com/sswebsite/pdf/lib/SSBI-2005.pdf.

20. House Committee on Financial Services. 2006. Credit Agency Reforms Act (September 29). Available at: www.financialservices.house.gov/news.asp.
21. Ibid.
22. Ibid.
23. Ibid.
24. European Commission. 2003. Audit of company accounts: Commission sets out ten priorities to improve quality and protect investors. Available at: http://europa.eu.int/rapid/pressReleasesAction.do?reference=IP/03/715& format=HTML&aged=0&language=EN&guiLanguage=en.
25. Ibid.
26. Ibid.
27. Coffee, J. C. 2005. A theory of corporate scandals: Why the U.S. and Europe differ. Columbia Law School. Working Paper Series (March). Available at: www.law.columbia.edu/center_program/law_economics.
28. United Nations Environment Programme Finance Initiative and the UN Global Compact. 2006. Principles for responsible investment. (April 27). Available at: www.unepfi.org/principles or www.unglobalcompact.org/principles.
29. Ibid.
30. Ibid.

Functions of Corporate Governance

CHAPTER 3

Oversight Function

INTRODUCTION

T he oversight function of corporate governance is vested in the company's board of directors, which is elected by its shareholders to oversee the managerial function. The Conference Board states: "The ultimate responsibility for good corporate governance rests with the board of directors."[1] A vigilant board of directors that proactively participates in strategic decisions; asks management tough questions; oversees management's plans, decisions, and actions; and monitors management's ethical conduct, financial reporting, and legal compliance, can be very effective in achieving good governance and protecting stakeholders' interests. Their primary oversight function is the appointment of the chief executive officer (CEO) and concurrence with the CEO's selection of other senior executives (top management team) to run the company. Corporations are legally required to have a board of directors, and many not-for-profit organizations (e.g., churches, universities) also have a similar governing board.

Boards of directors have experienced unprecedented challenges and opportunities in the post-Sarbanes-Oxley (SOX) era, and some boards still struggle to find the right balance between engaging in the strategic decisions of advising management without micromanaging and monitoring its managerial decisions and actions. The success of the board in fulfilling its oversight responsibility depends on the ethics, independence, composition, structure, resources, diligence, experience, and skill sets of the entire board, as well as members' working relationships with other participants in the corporate governance structure (e.g., management, external auditors, and investors), as depicted in Exhibit 2.3 in the last chapter. The Committee for Economic Development (CED) states: "[W]e are confident that truly independent and inquisitive boards of directors will provide the best safeguard against corporate wrongdoing."[2] This chapter presents the corporate governance oversight function of boards of directors to fulfill their fiduciary duty, maintain their independence, ensure compliance with corporate governance reforms, and achieve effective boardroom processes and committee activities.

ROLE OF THE BOARD OF DIRECTORS

The board of directors should establish sustainable strategic goals to create long-term shareholder value and direct management to implement these strategic goals. Directors can also rely on management to initiate these strategic goals. However, they should be approved and monitored by the company's board of directors. Thus, the primary responsibilities of the board of directors are to: (1) hire a competent and ethical CEO; (2) ensure other top executives (CFO, controller, treasurer, and operational managers) are being hired; and (3) monitor management's sustainable strategic, financial and operational goals in achieving long-term shareholder value. In performing their oversight function, boards of directors should be careful not to micromanage by involving themselves in managerial and operational decisions. They should oversee managerial strategies but should not be responsible for the actual implementation of strategies. However, even though directors should not micromanage, in today's ever-changing and complex business environment, the traditional model of the board of directors of just overseeing the financial reporting of public companies is no longer adequate. Directors should be more involved in the corporate governance function and building and maintaining an ethical company culture to ensure their company is prepared to be successful and able to build long-term shareholder value.

To fulfill their oversight function effectively, directors should develop the right balance between their advisory role of engaging in the company's strategic decisions while allowing management sufficient latitude to run the company's operations and still fulfill their fiduciary role by scrutinizing management's performance and the quality, reliability, and transparency of both financial and nonfinancial information provided by management. Charles O. Holiday, the chairman and chief executive officer (CEO) of DuPont, describes the role of directors as "noses in, fingers out," meaning that directors should strike an appropriate balance between overseeing managerial decisions and actions, by having the vision and courage to challenge management, while effectively advising management on strategic plans without micromanaging.[3]

The board of directors usually is comprised of both insiders (senior executives) and outsiders (independent directors). Nevertheless, the entire board is considered representative of shareholders, responsible for protecting shareholders' rights and interests, and should be engaged in an oversight function rather than a managerial function. The board is ultimately responsible for the company's business affairs and governance as stated in its governing documents, including the articles of incorporation, the bylaws, and shareholder agreements. State laws generally require the formation of a board of directors for corporations to represent shareholders and make decisions on their behalf. The Delaware General Corporate Law Code states:

The business and affairs of every corporation organized under this chapter shall be managed by or under the direction of a board of directors, except as may be otherwise provided in this chapter or its certification of incorporation.[4]

The board of directors is the cornerstone of the company's corporate governance structure and has the primary role of safeguarding the interests of shareholders and other stakeholders. State statutes and corporate governance reforms assign the oversight function of corporate governance to the board of directors. Almost all states have a similar statute authorizing and empowering the board to direct, oversee, and control a company's business affairs and to govern its activities. Shareholders have the statutory right to nominate and elect the board, and in many states to approve major decisions and/or transactions, such as the sale of major assets, mergers and acquisitions, or dissolution of the company. It is expected that the move toward the majority voting system and the decision by the Second Circuit Court of Appeals on September 5, 2006, enables shareholders to engage more effectively in the nomination and election of directors.[5]

In the past, boardrooms of many companies were viewed as "gentleman's clubs" composed of white males and characterized by a tendency and desire to please the CEO and rubber-stamp matters at the CEO's discretion, rather than being a forum for robust inquiry and discussion that adds value to effective corporate governance processes. The board, in overseeing management, should be able to establish and influence the company's vision, mission, strategies, and goals as well as management's plans, decisions, and implementation plan to achieve these goals. The Conference Board describes the board's role as being:

> ... *to focus on* guidance *and* strategic oversight, *while it is* management's duty to run *the company's business, with the goal of increasing shareholder value for the long term* ... *The ultimate responsibility for directing the company, however, lies with the board, since most state corporate statutes generally provide that the business of the company shall be managed under the direction of the board.*[6]

The 2004 National Association of Corporate Directors (NACD) report summarizes 11 roles of boards:

1. Approving the company's philosophy, vision, and mission.
2. Appointing, monitoring, evaluating, compensating, and, when warranted, replacing the company's CEO and other senior executives, and ensuring the management succession.
3. Reviewing and approving management's strategic plans, decisions, and actions.
4. Reviewing and approving the company's financial objectives, plans, decisions, and actions, including significant capital allocations and expenditures.
5. Reviewing and approving material nonrecurring, extraordinary business transactions (e.g., mergers and acquisitions, special purpose entities).
6. Monitoring corporate sustainable and enduring performance.
7. Ensuring the company's compliance with all applicable laws, regulations, rules, and standards, including ethical auditing and accounting standards.
8. Evaluating the board's oversight effectiveness, the performance of each of the board committees, and individual directors.

9. Forming board committees (e.g., audit, compensation, governance, nominating) to promote effective accountability for each committee and its members.
10. Communicating with shareholders by attending the annual meetings and responding to shareholders' questions and concerns.
11. Performing such other functions as required by law or assigned to the board in the company's governance documents.[7]

In a 2005 survey of 1,468 respondents of both publicly and privately held companies, "directors expressed an eagerness to spend more time on topics such as their companies' talent, skills, and current performance," and 64 percent claim that there has been an overall increase in their board's involvement.[8] Most respondents feel that the directors had improved their understanding of the company specifically in the areas of strategy, financial position, and risk. However, a very small number feel that their directors have a complete understanding of the risk (18 percent); and while the numbers are higher for strategy and finance (34 percent and 48 percent, respectively), still below half of the directors have a complete understanding of these areas. A McKinsey survey indicates that boards of directors in the post-SOX era are becoming more knowledgeable and engaged in their companies' core performance and value-creating activities, including strategy and finance.[9] Nevertheless, two corporate governance activities that demand more board knowledge and involvement are risk management and executive compensation.[10] The Treasury Secretary, Henry M. Paulson, believes that in the post-SOX era:

> *Corporations are better governed today. Directors are more independent, more aware of real and perceived conflicts, more diligent about their fiduciary responsibilities, and they spend much more time engaged in compliance processes. One important indicator of the effectiveness of corporate governance changes will be the ability of companies to attract experienced, competent board members who can add real value—and who are able to spend more time at board meetings overseeing the business and developing strategies, and less time on regulatory compliance.*[11]

The Working Group on Corporate Governance, about two decades ago, suggested five corporate governance guidelines for board of directors of public companies, and they are still relevant to the effective oversight function of the board of directors:

1. The board of directors should evaluate the performance of the chief executive officer regularly against established goals and strategies.
2. This evaluation should be performed by "outside" directors.
3. All outside directors should meet alone, at least once a year, coordinated by a leader.
4. Directors should establish appropriate qualifications for board members and communicate those qualifications clearly to shareholders.
5. Outside directors should screen and recommend candidates based on qualifications established by the board.[12]

FIDUCIARY DUTIES OF THE BOARD OF DIRECTORS

Fiduciary duty is the legal concept that is constantly refined by courts to address potential conflicts between the principals (owners) and their agents (directors/ management). The most comprehensive definition of fiduciary duty is "[a] duty to act for someone else's benefit, while subordinating one's personal interests to those of the other person."[13] Directors should realize that their primary duty is to be the corporate gatekeeper by protecting investors and working toward the achievement of shareholder value creation and enhancement while protecting the interests of other stakeholders. The fiduciary duties of boards of directors are specified in the laws of the state of incorporation, generally also contained in the company's charter and bylaws, and interpreted by courts when there is litigation alleging breach of fiduciary duty. The two primary fiduciary duties of directors are the duty of loyalty and the duty of care.[14] The company's directors and officers are bound to exercise their corporate powers as trustees for the benefit of the company and its shareholders.

Duty of Loyalty

The duty of loyalty requires directors to act in good faith and refrain from activities that put their own interests ahead of the interests of the company. This duty requires directors to:

- Act in the best interest of the company and its shareholders.
- Not compete with the company on whose board they serve.
- Subordinate their personal interests to the interests of the company.
- Refrain from benefiting at the company's expense in any transactions involving their companies.

Duty of Care

The duty of care requires directors to exercise due diligence and prudence in carrying out their oversight function, meaning they must run the company honestly and in good faith by exercising the level of care that a reasonably prudent person would use under the same circumstances. Failure to be well informed, exercise vigilant oversight, assure a reliable information and reporting process, or monitor compliance may constitute a breach of the fiduciary duty of care expected of directors. For example, directors on WorldCom's board failed to perform adequate due diligence on the largest bond offering in the history of the United States. Enron directors twice waived the company's code of ethics in order to allow one of its senior executives (Fastow) to enter into related-party off–balance sheet transactions that disguised the failing financial health of Enron.

Other Fiduciary Duties

Recent literature and law cases suggest several other related fiduciary duties for directors, including the duty of obedience, the duty of good faith, and the duty of fair disclosure, among others.

Duty of Obedience   This duty requires directors to act within the scope of the powers of the organization, as specified in its charter and by law or the mission statement. The duty of obedience is unique to not-for-profit organizations (NPOs) to ensure that directors effectively oversee NPOs and protect public interest.[15] This provides a standard of legal accountability for NPOs similar to that of enhancing long-term shareholder value for corporations.[16]

Duty of Good Faith   The two primary fiduciary duties of loyalty and care require directors to act in good faith. An evolving body of legal literature and Delaware case law assert there is a separate fiduciary duty of good faith that goes above and beyond the two primary fiduciary duties of care and loyalty. There is no one-size-fits-all definition of the duty of good faith. However, it is well recognized that any irresponsible, irrational, reckless, and disingenuous behavior or conduct by directors can breach this duty. The fiduciary duty of good faith can be violated by actions indicating a conscious or intentional disregard for risk to the company.

Duty of Fair Disclosure   This duty requires directors to provide timely, reliable, relevant, and transparent financial and nonfinancial information to shareholders and other stakeholders. The Securities and Exchange Commission (SEC), in August 2000, passed Regulation Fair Disclosure (Reg. FD) which requires that public companies not disclose material information to select investors or securities professionals.[17] The intent of Reg. FD is to eliminate superior trading opportunities for beneficiaries of the company's selective disclosures while promoting disclosure of reliable, relevant, and transparent financial information to all market participants including shareholders and leveling the playing field for individual investors.

Fiduciary Duties and the Business Judgment Rule

Directors, in effectively fulfilling these fiduciary duties, operate under the legal doctrine of the "business judgment rule." The business judgment rule provides directors with broad discretion to make good faith business decisions. Under this rule and in the absence of evidence of gross negligence, business misconduct, or fraud, directors are typically provided with broad discretion to make decisions and carry out their fiduciary duties of care, obedience, good faith, and loyalty without facing challenges of legal liability.

Generally speaking, directors (officers) have a duty to the company to perform their oversight (managerial) functions in good faith, in a manner that reasonably represents the best interests of the company, and with the care, skill, and diligence that a prudent person would use under similar circumstances. In fulfilling their oversight functions, directors are entitled to rely on information, reports, financial statements, advice, and opinions provided to them by the company's management, independent auditors, legal counsel, and other advisors (e.g., independent compensation consultants). The duty of good faith has not been fulfilled when a director relies on information while knowing or suspecting that the information is not reliable. The business judgment rule implies that directors, when making business decisions, are reasonably informed and rational in such a manner that a prudent person would concur with the decision. The general perception is that directors (officers), in performing their oversight (managerial) functions, will not usually be held liable for losses caused by their decisions, and courts usually do not interfere with their activities and business decisions.

Directors may be held liable under the federal securities laws for engaging in the production and distribution of materially false, fraudulent, or misleading information to investors, which then influence the company's stock prices.[18] SOX prohibits directors from fraudulently misleading investors or from trading during pension blackout periods.[19] The Enron fraud raised serious questions about the breach of the fiduciary duties of its board of directors in representing and protecting shareholder interests. Traditionally, directors of failed companies did not incur personal liability and were able to find directorships in other boardrooms easily. However, this tradition is starting to change in the post-Enron era. Lawsuits filed on behalf of aggrieved investors resulted in 8 outside directors of Enron agreeing to pay $13 million in personal funds; 12 directors of WorldCom agreed to pay $18 million out of their own pockets to settle shareholder litigation without admitting or denying any liability. These directors also suffered damages to their reputations and future careers, and they were barred from serving on any boards. At one point, prior to Enron's collapse, "11 of its outside directors held board seats at a total of 21 other companies. Today [2006], two of the former Enron directors hold a total of four directorships."[20] Thus, ineffective oversight of the board of directors can cause not only company bankruptcy and result in permanent shareholder losses but can also damage board members' reputations and careers, and may even create personal liability.

Since 2000, the SEC has gone to court seeking to bar 696 directors and officers from serving on other corporate boards. Although it has sought to bar Enron's executives, so far the directors have escaped notice.[21] The Committee on Capital Market Regulation suggests that the SEC provide protections from lawsuits for directors who rely in good faith on corporate officials and auditors in fulfilling their fiduciary duties.[22] It is eventually up to the shareholders, particularly institutional investors, to assess the oversight effectiveness, personal integrity, and professional accountability of the board of directors. Investors use their voting power to elect only those directors who are fit to serve on the board and should withhold their votes from those who are not qualified to serve. Directors may be regarded as unfit to serve on boards when the companies they serve are in violation of the securities laws, display unethical conduct, undergo a major bankruptcy, have financial restatements, have ineffective corporate governance, or fail to protect investors' long-term interests.

Directors' Duties in the United Kingdom

The U.K. Companies Act of 2006 provides more prescriptive duties of directors, which require them to act in good faith in the best interests of the company in such a way that promotes the success of the company for the benefit of its shareholders. Specifically the seven general duties of directors are:

1. *Duty to act within powers.* Directors must act in accordance with the company's constitution and exercise their powers for the purposes for which they are conferred.

2. *Duty to promote the success of the company.* Directors must act in good faith to promote the success of the company for all of its shareholders. In effectively fulfilling this duty, a director must have regard to: (1) the likely consequences of any decision in the long term; (2) the interest of the company's employees; (3) the need to foster the company's business relation with its stakeholders including suppliers and customers; (4) the effects of the company's operations on the community and the environment; and (5) the company's reputation of high standards of business conduct and fairness.

3. *Duty to exercise independent judgment.* Directors must exercise independent judgment in fulfilling their duties.

4. *Duty to exercise reasonable care, skill, and diligence.* Directors must exercise the care, skill, and diligence expected of reasonable and diligent person.

5. *Duty to avoid conflicts of interest.* Directors should avoid situations and opportunities that may conflict with the interests of their company.

6. *Duty not to accept benefits from third parties.* Directors must not accept benefits from any persons other than their company when acting on the company's behalf.

7. *Duty to declare interest in proposed transaction or agreement.* Directors must disclose the nature and extent of their interest in their company to the other directors.[23]

BOARD ATTRIBUTES

The board of directors is the most essential component of corporate governance in providing advisory and oversight functions. Thus, the quality of these functions is a very important determinant of corporate governance effectiveness. Several attributes of the board, including its authority, leadership, independence, compensation/equity holdings, resources, separation of the role of the chair of the board from the CEO, and other attributes (e.g., leadership skills, business knowledge, financial expertise, character, and ethics), are considered to affect the quality of the oversight function performed by the company's board.

Authority

The decision-making authority of the board of directors is granted when shareholders elect directors to govern the company's business affairs on their behalf. The board is authorized to hire, evaluate, compensate, and fire the CEO and approve the top management team which manages the company's day-to-day operations. Myron T. Steele, Chief Justice of the Delaware Supreme Court, stated:

> [T]he most pressing business issues facing the courts of Delaware involve determining the proper balance between the authority and the accountability of directors. ...Delaware will not test the judgment of members of the board of directors so long as no credible issue is raised about the objectivity

of the directors' decision-making or their candor in starting the basis for their decision-making.[24]

SOX substantially expands the authority of directors, particularly audit committee members, since they are now directly responsible for hiring, firing, compensating, and overseeing the work of the company's independent auditor. SOX changed the balance of power between management and the audit committee, empowering the audit committee by enhancing its independence and increasing its responsibilities. Audit committees are also responsible for hiring and firing the chief audit executive (CAE) and overseeing the budget and the audit plans of the company's internal audit function.

Leadership

Public companies are required to have a board of directors led by a chairperson. The norm in the past has been for companies to combine the positions of the chairperson and the CEO (CEO duality), but this is starting to change due to shareholder concerns that CEO duality results in ineffective corporate governance, fraud, and other malfeasance. This dual position concentrates too much power in the hands of one person by allowing the company's CEO to undertake the two most important functions of corporate governance—the managerial and oversight functions—which empowers the CEO to oversee the direction of the company while managing its operations. The chair of the board and the CEO both should be leaders with vision, strategy, business acumen, motivation, and problem-solving ability. Ideally, two qualified individuals should assume these two separate positions. It is better to have an independent chair of the board to ensure the maximum protection for investors, although it is not necessary in every case. A survey shows that almost half of the responding 1,103 directors believe that the board leadership should emanate from the CEO; 38 percent felt that leadership should come from a nonexecutive chair other than the CEO.[25]

There are two separate concepts of leadership. The first is board leadership, which should be assumed by a nonexecutive director (e.g., lead or presiding director) to ensure effective fulfillment of the board responsibility as the guardian of shareholder interests. The second is corporate leadership, which belongs to the CEO, who should be in the driver's seat to lead the company to achieve its mission of sustainable performance. Many investor activists and organizations (the Conference Board, National Association of Corporate Directors) have called for more independent board leadership through either the separation of the position of the CEO and the chairperson, or through the establishment of a lead or presiding director position, but only if there is no history of problems at the company. This issue is becoming increasingly important as institutional investors, including pension funds, now assess board independence and board leadership in their investment decision-making process.

Authoritative guidance (SOX, listing standards) in the United States does not directly address the responsibilities of the board chair but gives full flexibility to the board of directors to decide on the chair's responsibilities. The 2003 U.K. Combined Code suggests eight responsibilities for the chair of the board:

1. Manage the board and set its forward-looking agenda, focusing on strategic issues and decisions rather than formulating approvals of management proposals.
2. Ensure the board and its directors receive accurate, timely, and transparent information regarding the company's performance.
3. Facilitate the board's effective communication with shareholders and support directors' understanding of the views of the major investors.
4. Operate the board effectively by allowing sufficient time for thorough discussion of complex or contentious issues.
5. Facilitate the development of properly constructed induction programs for new directors.
6. Consider the development needs of the company's board in order to improve its overall effectiveness.
7. Promote active engagement by all directors of the board.
8. Ensure the annual evaluation of the board, its committees, and individual directors.[26]

The board of directors is required to meet regularly to discuss the company's business affairs and financial reports with and without the presence of management (CEO). The effectiveness of board meetings depends largely on the chair's ability to lead and set an agenda and direct discussions. The chair's leadership style and ability determine whether the meetings will be short or lengthy, formal or informal, friendly or adversarial, relaxed or tense, efficient or inefficient, productive or nonproductive, responsive or nonresponsive, relevant or irrelevant, decisive or indecisive, and predetermined or deliberative. In some situations, the chairperson and/or the CEO can dominate the meeting agenda and make decisions prior to the meeting, impose their views and decisions on other directors, and then request approval for decisions that have already been made. In these situations, directors have two choices: They can: (1) oppose the predetermined decision on its merits and view it as disruptive and uncollegial, or (2) rubber-stamp it and become irrelevant and subservient.

More than half (51 percent) of directors participating in the 2006 survey of Corporate Board Member/PwC reported they prefer a board led by the chair/CEO to ensure effective board leadership while still being able to control the board's agenda.[27] When the chair of the board and CEO are competent, honest, and ethical, and exercise due diligence in protecting stakeholder interests, their domination and aggressiveness in pushing their agenda through the meeting, and the tendency for directors to be subservient, can improve the effectiveness of meetings and may be beneficial in the long term to the well-being of the company in creating stakeholder value. However, when the board chair and/or CEO are dishonest, incompetent, or self-serving, the subservient attitude of directors can be detrimental to the long-term well-being of the company and its purpose of creating sustainable stakeholder value. In any case, the subservient board cannot be successful in the long term when there is an inability or lack of willingness to stand up to an imperial CEO who is not performing. Thus, the deliberative board, in which directors individually add value and contribute to the board deliberations and collectively work toward stakeholder value creation, assumes responsibilities and holds itself accountable for its decisions, making it more effective and successful in the long term. The effectiveness of board meetings is also influenced by being informed and engaged rather than just taking a historical perspective of past events or focusing too much attention on process and administrative procedures rather than tackling difficult substantive issues.

The board agenda is usually prepared by the independent chair of the board, in close coordination and collaboration with the CEO (when the CEO is not also the board chair) to ensure its relevance and appropriateness, and with the support of senior executives. In the case of CEO duality, the independent lead or presiding director should work with the CEO to prepare the board agenda to ensure its relevance and appropriateness. The minutes of the board meeting should include attendees, a description of issues discussed, the deliberation process and time devoted to discussing these issues, including voting, decisions, and actions taken by the board.

Separation of Chair and CEO Roles

The separation of the offices of the chairperson of the board and the CEO has remained a challenge for many public companies even in the post-SOX era. The positive but slow trend toward the separation of the roles continues in Standard & Poor's (S&P) 500 boards. During 2005, about 71 percent (338 boards) of these boards had a combined chair/CEO, which is down from 74 percent and 77 percent in 2004 and 2000, respectively. Only 43 (9 percent) out of the 140 companies that have separated the roles had a truly independent chair. In the other 94 companies (3 did not list a chairperson) where the chair was not independent, the chair was a former company CEO, received significant other compensation from the company, or was a relative of the CEO.[28] This situation is in stark contrast to the United Kingdom, where the majority of public companies (90 percent) have separate chairs and CEO roles.[29]

Investors generally favor separation of the positions of the CEO and the chairperson as a means of strengthening the board's independence and reducing the potential conflicts of interest, particularly when the company is perceived to be managed poorly. An example of a successful shareholder attempt to decouple CEO duality is at the 2004 Disney annual meeting where shareholders, owning 43 percent of Disney's stock, cast record-setting "withhold" vote on the reelection of Michael Eisner to the board as chair. This action subsequently caused the board to separate the two jobs of CEO and chair by removing the chair title from Mr. Eisner's employment contract, although he did remain Disney's CEO for some time thereafter. The Conference Board, while acknowledging that no single board structure has been demonstrated superior in providing oversight leading to sustainable and enduring shareholder value creation and enhancement as well as stakeholder protection, recommends three alternatives for board structures:

1. The separation of the offices of the chairperson of the board and CEO.
2. Two separate individuals perform the roles of chairperson of the board and CEO. If the chairperson is not "independent," according to the definition provided in listing standards (e.g., the New York Stock Exchange), a lead independent director should be appointed.
3. A presiding director position should be established where boards choose not to separate the positions of the chairperson and CEO, or where they are in transition to such a separation.[30]

Decoupling the roles of the chairperson and the CEO is receiving more acceptance. More than 29 percent of S&P 500 companies, in 2005, have separated the roles of the chairman and the CEO compared to only 21 percent nine years ago.[31] The 2006 Corporate Governance report of the State Board of Administration (SBA) of Florida reports that for companies in the Russell 3000 index: (1) over 48 percent combined the chairman and CEO roles; (2) about 20 percent separated the chairman and CEO roles with an independent chair; (3) more than 14 percent separated the roles with an insider chair; (4) about 10 percent separated the chairman and CEO roles with an affiliated chair; and (5) the remaining 7 percent did not disclose any separation.[32]

The benefits of the separation of the CEO and chair positions are:

- Corporate governance standards in other countries (e.g., the United Kingdom) and best practices in the United States (e.g., the Conference Board) recommend splitting these two important roles, and such separations align U.S. corporate governance with that of other countries.
- Improvement in the CEO's accountability.
- The reduction in the CEO's potential conflicts of interest that have caused some of the recent financial scandals.
- Having two individuals (CEO and chair) in the corporate leadership role should improve corporate governance and operations.
- The board responsibility is to oversee management for shareholders' benefit, and this oversight responsibility would be more effective when the chair of the board assumes no executive role.

The potential costs of the separation are: (1) the likelihood of a reduction in the CEO's authority when the CEO's power is shared with a nonexecutive director who is less informed and possibly less experienced in a leadership role; and (2) the introduction of a more complex and new relationship into the company's commitment to a unitary board, which may negatively affect the status and oversight responsibility of outside directors.[33]

Lead/Presiding Directors

In the post–corporate governance reforms era, the demand for an independent lead director has increased substantially, particularly in the presence of CEO duality. The demand has arisen from the growing concern that CEO duality places too much power in the hands of one person, which may impede board independence. Thus, the position of an independent lead or presiding director is widely supported as an acceptable alternative to an independent chair if the company has no history of governance or other significant problems. An independent lead director's responsibilities are to:

- Manage and facilitate the board's governance process.
- Provide a measure of the board's independence from the CEO.
- Develop the board's agenda for meetings.
- Act as a liaison among the board, the CEO, and shareholders.
- Preside over executive sessions.
- Oversee governance-related activities and processes.
- Oversee significant issues and risks between board meetings and inform the entire board about these issues and risks.
- Set the agenda and identify items for executive session consideration.
- Lead the discussion in executive sessions.
- Engage with the CEO on identifying items and the agenda for executive sessions.
- Serve as a liaison between the board and the CEO by providing feedback to the CEO on executive sessions.
- Present the CEO's views, concerns, and issues to the independent directors.
- Collaborate with the CEO in taking proactive actions to deal with special situations and to set processes to engage independent directors.
- Take lead and proactive actions on important issues pertaining to CEO performance assessment and goal setting, CEO succession planning, and board and individual director assessment.[34]

The post-SOX era has witnessed an upward trend in the adoption of the lead and presiding director roles to strengthen board independence, particularly when the positions board chair and CEO are not separated. The 2005 survey of the Spencer Stuart Board Index (SSBI) reveals that about 94 percent of all S&P 500 boards in 2005 had an independent lead or presiding director.[35] However, several issues relevant to lead/presiding directors deserve further consideration, according to George M. C. Fisher, the presiding director of General Motors (GM) Corporation.[36] The first issue is using the title of "lead" or "presiding" director. GM, like many other public companies, has opted for "presiding director" because, according to Fisher, "calling someone a lead director potentially singles that person out as a super-director, and implies that other directors must communicate through that person to the CEO."[37] The term "presiding director" may signify a less permanent leadership role and more of a rotation position for the lead director.

The 2005 SSBI survey also shows that two-thirds of S&P 500 boards prefer the title "presiding director" over "lead director."[38] The 2005 survey of S&P 500 boards reveals that rotation is more common among presiding directors than among lead directors; only 4 percent of 144 boards with a lead director rotate the role regularly whereas over 32 percent of the 303 boards that have a presiding director rotate that role.[39] Of the 163 boards (more than 20 percent) that opted to rotate the role of lead/presiding directors, the majority (60 percent) rotate the role among committee chairs at each board meeting; the remainder rotate the role among all independent directors each meeting, quarterly, or annually.[40] Additional compensation (e.g., annual cash retainers in the range of $85,000 to $300,000) was paid to 46 percent of the lead directors compared to only 3 percent of presiding directors in 2005 by S&P 500 companies.[41]

Regardless of the title, the second issue is what the role of such directors should be. According to Fisher, the role is twofold:

> ... to help the company succeed and to help the CEO to be a winner ... in good times, the responsibilities tend to be limited to presiding over meetings, and liaising with management.... In challenging times, however, the role becomes very time consuming and very demanding.[42]

The primary role of the lead/presiding director is to preserve board independence where the positions of the chair and the CEO are combined, particularly when the CEO is relatively inexperienced or unduly aggressive and possessive or during a management transition. When the roles are combined, the board should appoint an independent lead/presiding director who:

- Is responsible for the board's operations (e.g., meetings, agendas, communications).
- Provides leadership during a chair/CEO transition or when the company is in a crisis.
- Chairs meetings of nonexecutive and independent directors.
- Serves as the liaison between the chair and the independent directors.
- Presides over board meetings in the absence of the chair.
- Leads the board of directors and CEO performance evaluation process to prevent the chair/CEO from being placed in the conflicted position of evaluating his or her own performance.

An independent lead director can be an acceptable alternative only if a company does not have a history of problems (i.e., financial restatements, litigation, etc.); even in such cases, this position is acceptable only if the lead director has real duties similar to an independent chair and rotation of this position does not occur more frequently than on an annual basis.

Resources

The board of directors should have adequate resources to fulfill its oversight functions effectively, including financial, legal, information, and administrative resources. It must have adequate financial resources to compensate the company's directors and officers and to hire external auditors, legal counsel, and other advisors to assist the entire board and its committees (audit, compensation, and nominating/governance) in effectively discharging their oversight function. The information resources are provided to the board from a variety of corporate governance participants, including management, internal auditors, external auditors, legal counsel, financial advisors, and investors. To ensure the objectivity and independence of the advice, independent consultants should be hired by and report to the company's board and not receive their assignments from management. The board should have adequate staff support, internal or external advisors, and legal counsel to assist it in preparing for meetings, setting the agenda, identifying the relevant and important corporate governance issues that will be addressed in meetings, providing analysis and assessment of these issues, and making possible recommendations.

The primary source of information to the board of directors comes from management. Such information may not always be relevant, complete, uncensored, or provided on a timely basis. In some cases when the CEO sets the agenda, important issues may get buried in voluminous documents or at the end of a long agenda without receiving the required attention from the board. To carry out their duties effectively, directors delegate decision-making authority to management and rely on information furnished to them. Directors are not expected to know everything or even be experts in every aspect of the company's business and affairs. They are expected to fulfill their fiduciary duties by being informed and diligent in identifying and considering facts based on the information they receive from management and others, and make judgments about facts and events. Under the business judgment rule, directors are expected to exercise due care and to make informed decisions. Courts generally do not second-guess informed decision making even if the business decision later turns out to be wrong.

Board Independence

The independence of the company's board of directors is a critical aspect of corporate governance and has a significant impact on the board's effectiveness. The national stock exchanges (NYSE, Nasdaq, and AMEX) require a majority of directors of a listed company to be independent. Exhibit 3.1 summarizes director independence rules, standards, and best practices of a variety of sources. However, the listing standards' definition of *independent* is weaker than the definition adopted by the Council of Institutional Investors (CII), as explained next.

Several definitions of "independent director" are provided in the literature and by authoritative sources. The most comprehensive definition has been adopted by the CII:

> *An independent director is someone whose only nontrivial professional, financial, or non-financial connection to the corporation, its chairman, CEO, or any other executive officer is his or her directorship.*[43]

This definition, which is promoted in this book and, in practice, has been adopted by the majority of institutional investors, simply states that to be independent, a director should not have any connections (financial, social, institutional) with the company other than his or her directorship that may compromise his or her objectivity and loyalty to the company's shareholders. A ruling by the Delaware Court of Chancery provides insights into connections and affiliations that might compromise a director's independence.[44] The court finds social and institutional

EXHIBIT 3.1 Comparison of the Definition of "Director Independence"

Securities and Exchange Commission	New York Stock Exchange	Nasdaq	Council of Institutional Investors
Nonemployee	Nonemployee and no family members are an executive officer	Nonemployee of the company, its parent, or subsidiaries	Neither is, nor in the past 5 years has been, or whose relative is, or in the past 5 years has been, employed by the corporation or employed by or a director of an affiliate
Other than as a director, does not directly or indirectly receive any compensation	Neither they nor their family receive over $100,000 in any given year in direct compensation	Neither they nor their family members receive over $60,000 per year from the company, its parent, and/or subsidiaries	Neither they nor their family has been paid or received more than $50,000 in the past 5 years under a personal contract with the corporation, an executive officer or any affiliate of the corporation
	Neither they nor their immediate family are employed by a current or previous auditor (last three years) of the company (internal or external)	Neither they nor their immediate family are employed by a current or previous auditor (last three years) of the company (external)	Has not had a relative who is, or in the past 5 years has been, an employee, a director, or a 5 percent or greater owner of a third-party entity that is a significant competitor of the corporation
	Neither they nor their immediate family are executive officers of a company that has on its compensation committee an executive of this company	Neither they nor their immediate family are executive officers of a company that has on its compensation committee an executive of this company	Have not in the past 5 years been employed by or had a 5 percent or greater ownership interest in a third party that provides payments to or receives payments from the corporation that account for 1 percent of the third party's or 1 percent of the corporation's consolidated gross revenues in any single fiscal year, or if the third party is a debtor or creditor of the corporation,

Has no required disclosure of a business relationship	Neither they nor their immediate family employed by a company that has transactions with this company exceeding the greater of $1 million or 2 percent of gross revenues	Neither they nor their family members may have a controlling interest in any company that has transactions with this company exceeding the greater of $200,000 or 5 percent of gross revenue	the amount owed exceeds 1 percent of the corporation's or the third party's assets	Neither is, nor in the past 5 years has been, or whose relative is, or in the past 5 years has been, an employee, director, or owner of a firm that is one of the corporation's or its affiliate's paid advisors or consultants or that receives revenue of at least $50,000 for being a paid advisor or consultant to an executive officer of the corporation
Has no interest or service to the company		No family member may be an executive officer of the company, its parent or subsidiary		Not an employee or director of a foundation, university, or other nonprofit organization that receives significant grants or endowments from the corporation or one of its affiliates or has been a direct beneficiary of any donations to such an organization
Is not an "interested person" according to the 1940 Investment Company Act		Is not an "interested person" according to the 1940 Investment Company Act		Is not a party to a voting trust, agreement, or proxy giving his/her decision-making power as a director to management except to the extent that there is a fully disclosed and narrow voting arrangement, such as those that are customary between venture capitalists and management regarding the venture capitalists' board seats

Sources: Securities and Exchange Commission.

New York Stock Exchanges, *NYSE Listed Company Manual*, Section 303A, "Corporate Governance Rules," November 3, 2004. Available at: www.nyse.com/pdfs/section303A_final_rules.pdf.

National Association of Securities Dealers, "Director Independence: Proposal to Provide Additional Transparency to Certain Preferential, Ordinary-Course Payments Made by Financial Institutions," 4200(a)(15)(B), June 22, 2004. Available at: www.nasdaq.com/about/RuleFilingsListings/FilingsListing2004.stm.

Council of Institutional Investors, "Council Policies: Independent Director Definition," 2006. Available at: www.cii.org/policies/ind_dir_defn.htm.

connections may preclude director independence, as in the Oracle case, where a special litigation committee was made up of two directors who were professors at Stanford University.[45] Thus, factors such as social and institutional connections above and beyond financial motives might compromise director independence.

On January 17, 2006, the SEC released its proposed rule, and subsequently on July 26, 2006 voted to require:

- Disclosure of whether each company's director or director nominee is independent.
- A description of any undisclosed relationships that were considered when determining whether each director or director nominee is independent.
- Disclosure of any audit, compensation, and nominating committee members who are not independent.
- A narrative explanation of the independence status of directors.
- Disclosure regarding the compensation committee's process and procedures for the consideration of the company's directors and executive compensation.[46]

SEC rules require that companies identify and disclose the independent directors and director nominees as determined by the definition of independence in their applicable listing standards (e.g. NYSE, Nasdaq). Public companies should also disclose any member of their audit, compensation, or nominating committee who is not independent. If the company is not "listed," it must disclose the information based on the definition of independent used by either a national stock exchange or a national securities association. The company has to make sure the definition is used consistently and uniformly for each director, and must disclose the definition used at least every three years. Public companies are required to disclose "a description of any transactions, relationships or arrangements" for directors that are designated as "independent" that the board took into consideration before making the decision on independence.[47]

Anecdotal evidence and surveys show a significant pattern toward director independence pursuant to the passage of SOX. The 2005 SSBI survey reveals that:

- The number of new independent directors recruited by S&P 500 companies in 2005 dropped by about 25 percent to 333 compared with 443 in 2004 primarily because most companies had already met the SOX, SEC rules, and listing standards requirements for greater board independence and financial expertise.
- About 40 percent of the boards in 2005 had one nonindependent director, namely the CEO, compared with 12 percent in 2000.
- More than 45 percent of independent directors come from strong financial and operational backgrounds as active or retired CEOs or chief operating officers (COOs).[48]

Evidence of improvement in director independence which was made possible by recent corporate governance reforms, particularly SOX, is the decision made by the five independent directors at the Atmel Corporation, a Silicon Valley semiconductor company, to fire the CEO and chairman of the board along with three other executives.[49] This suggests significant changes in the balance of power-sharing between management and the board of directors in the post-SOX era as the CEO of Atmel called a special shareholders' meeting to fire the five independent directors who subsequently fired him.[50] One example of violation of director independence was at Hewlett-Packard Co., when the board chairwoman, Patricia C. Dunn, ordered investigators to spy on the outside directors who possibly leaked the confidential information to reporters.[51] Investigators used deception to obtain confidential telephone records of directors and reporters.[52] To prevent further occurrence of eavesdropping or spying in the form of pretexting on directors who dissent or even vote the wrong way, directors should obtain a promise from their boards that they will not seek access to directors' confidential telephone or other records without their written permission. The board of directors should set an appropriate tone at the top in promoting ethical and legal behavior throughout the company. Any attempt to spy on directors is not only unethical and potentially illegal but also violates director independence.

To discharge their oversight responsibilities effectively, "directors must be made not only *independent of insiders* but also *dependent on shareholders*. ...[W]hat is necessary is better disclosure but also a fundamental reform in allocation of power between boards and shareholder" (emphasis added).[53] While addressing directors' independence from the company and its management, the current corporate governance reforms have not tackled director dependence on shareholders; thus directors do not recognize that their actual boss is the owners of the company. A lack of director accountability and allegiance toward management is evidenced by:

- The inability of shareholders to remove directors under the plurality-voting standards.
- Shareholders' inability to place candidates on the corporate ballot.
- Staggered boards.
- Shareholders' inability to initiate and adopt changes in corporate governance measures set in the company's charter.[54]

Director Compensation/Equity Holdings

Director compensation has recently received significant attention as public companies have significantly increased the number of independent directors on their boards. A study shows that director pay at more than 2,000 public companies increased over 16.5 percent in 2005 whereas total annual board pay jumped 20 percent and in some companies reached $801,000 in 2005.[55] The 2005 SSBI survey indicates that:

- The trend toward paying directors per meeting has decreased in the past decade as more companies are paying higher retainers in lieu of meeting fees.
- 62 percent of S&P 500 companies paid meeting fees in 2005, down from 74 percent in 2000.

- The median payment was $1,500 per meeting in 2005, up from $1,000 in 2000. The minimum payment was $750 and the maximum was $7,500.
- Companies usually pay lower fees for telephonic meetings.
- The average retainer paid to audit committee members in 2005 was 42 percent higher than the retainer paid to members of other committees.
- 83 percent of S&P 500 boards pay retainers to committee chairs. This figure is higher than the average retainer paid to other committee members.
- The majority of boards (61 percent) pay committee meeting fees of about $1,500. They usually pay higher meeting fees to their audit committee, with an average of $2,150 per meeting.
- The meeting fee premium for audit committee members is on average $1,000; the premium for the audit committee chair is about $1,500.[56]

The survey of SSBI shows that:

- Director compensation is determined most often by either the compensation committee or by the nominating/governance committee of the board.
- The majority (93 percent) indicated that their compensation committee consults with an outside advisor in handling director compensation.
- More than 66 percent of surveyed boards are expecting to make changes in director compensation in order to compensate for the increased time commitment, the increased director liability, and the desire to change the mix between cash and equity.
- 37 percent of surveyed boards are planning to increase director compensation by up to 10 percent; 33 percent and 19 percent anticipate a 10 to 20 percent and a 20 to 30 percent increase, respectively.[57]

There is no magic way of determining how and how much to pay directors. However, the general perception and best practices suggest that any increases in stock ownership, reductions in cash payments, and changes in compensation should be aligned with shareholders' long-term interests determined by the board, approved by shareholders, and fully disclosed in public reporting. Traditionally, director compensation has consisted of a retainer for board membership and fees for being a committee chair and attendance of board and committee meetings. The ever-increasing amounts of time, commitment, and liability required of directors to fulfill their fiduciary duties in recent years have had positive effects on their compensation. Exhibit 3.2 summarizes director compensation guidelines provided by several institutional investors. These guidelines suggest that:

- Director compensation consists of a combination of both cash and stock.
- All directors should own stock in the company.
- Director pay should be comparable to peer market groups.
- All unusual compensation should be reviewed and approved by the independent directors and disclosed in the proxy statement.
- Pensions and postretirement benefits should not be granted to outside directors.
- Shareholders should approve director compensation.

EXHIBIT 3.2 Institutional Investors' Guidelines on Director Pay

Council of Institutional Investors	California Public Employees Retirement System (CalPERS)	TIAA-CREF	Domini Social Investments
1. All directors should own stock in the company.	1. Director compensation consists of a combination of cash and stock.	1. All unusual compensation should be reviewed by independent directors and disclosed in the proxy statement.	1. Directors should own stock in the company, but directorships should not be limited due to financial reasons.
2. Directors should be compensated only in cash and stock, with the majority being in stock.	2. Director compensation should be examined on a case-by-case basis to ensure accountability to the shareholders.	2. The board should establish a fixed retirement policy for directors	2. Outside directors should not receive pension plans.
3. Pay should be indexed to peer/market groups.	3. Stock options for independent directors will be approved if reasonable, and are more favorable if they replace cash compensation.	3. Directors must own a material amount of company stock, equal to one year's compensation as a board member.	3. Outside directors should not receive over $100,000 per year in compensation.
4. Boards should consider options with forward contracts to align management and shareholder interests.	4. Refrain from providing pensions to nonemployees without shareholder approval.	4. Payment of directors should be at least partly in stock.	
	5. Shareholders should analyze and approve directors' compensation.		
	6. Retirement plans should be only for employee directors.		
	7. At least half of director's annual income should be from stock.		

Sources: Council of Institutional Investors, "Council Policies: Director Compensation," September 30, 2005. Available at: www.cii.org/policies/dir_compensation.htm.

CalPERS, "U.S. Corporate Governance Principles," April 6, 2005, p. 6. Available at: www.calpers-governance.org/principles/domestic/us/page06.asp.

Teachers Insurance and Annuity Association, College Retirement Equities Fund, "TIAA-CREF Policy Statement on Corporate Governance," 2005. Available at: www.tiaa-cref.org/pubs/pdf/governance_policy.pdf.

Domini Social Investments, "Proxy Voting Guidelines and Procedures," 2005. Available at: www.domini.com/common/pdf/ProxyVotingGuidelines.pdf.

Directors should be given the opportunity or even be required to purchase a reasonable share of the company's common stock. The compensation committee should determine the amount and percentage of director stock ownership that will motivate directors to position their long-term interests with those of shareholders. Many companies have adopted target ownership plans; one mandates that a defined percentage of the company's common stock be owned by its directors in order to focus their efforts and performance toward shareholder value creation and enhancement. Common sense suggests that directors' equity ownership should motivate better performance. Stock ownership is normally regarded as a long-term incentive plan for the company's directors. The perception is that when a meaningful portion of directors' current and future net worth is linked to the company's success as measured in terms of capital gains (e.g., stock price appreciation, dividends), they consider themselves shareholders and thus work toward creating and enhancing long-term shareholder value. Nonetheless, too low a portion of stock ownership may not create adequate incentives for performance enhancement, and too high a portion may create entrenchments.

Other Attributes of the Board of Directors

Various attributes of the boards of directors can influence their oversight effectiveness. Directors' business knowledge, gender, ethnicity, diversity, age, and independence are important attributes of the board.

Business Knowledge and Legal and Financial Expertise   The business knowledge and legal and financial expertise of directors can significantly improve their effectiveness in dealing with complex business, governance, regulatory, legal, accounting, and auditing issues. Corporate governance reforms post-SOX require that all members of audit committees have financial literacy and expertise, and at least one member must be designated as the audit committee financial expert as defined by SEC rules.[58] Theoretically, additional experience obtained by directors resulting from a longer tenure should enhance their knowledge about the firm's practices, operations, and culture and thus improve the effectiveness of their oversight functions. Nevertheless, the likelihood of directors being entrenched with top management may increase as their tenure increases. Furthermore, newly hired directors can bring new perspectives, diversity in terms of experience as well as gender and ethnic backgrounds, and ideas to the board, and are more likely to be independent from management.

The number of financial experts on public company boards is expected to increase significantly because, in the post-SOX era, companies must disclose whether they have financial expert(s) on their audit committees.[59] The 2004 SSBI survey indicates that:

- 91 percent of S&P public company boards identified at least one financial expert, a significant increase from only 21 percent in 2003.
- In all S&P 500 companies, there were 832 identified financial experts in 2004 compared with 146 in 2003.

- More than 33 percent of the financial experts on audit committees are directors who are new to the committee.
- Among the 154 financial experts new to audit committees, more than 47 percent are new to the board. This indicates that boards are adding directors who meet the financial expert requirements.[60]

Diversity of the Board of Directors The diversity of the company's board of directors in terms of the age, percentage of women serving on the board, and the number of minorities (African Americans, Hispanics, and Asians) is addressed sufficiently in the literature. Diversity of the board has received considerable interest and attention in the business community, and attempts are being made to add more female directors to company boards. The number of female directors on Fortune 500 company boards has increased in the past decade from 9.6 percent of board seats in 1995 to 14.7 percent in 2005.[61] With the current rate of progress of board gender diversity being, on average, one-half of one percentage point per year for the past decade, however, at that rate it could take nearly 70 years for women to reach parity with men on corporate boards.[62]

The 2005 annual survey of the British Equal Opportunities Commission reveals that while the number of women in senior management positions is continuing to rise, without further legislation parity with males will be decades away.[63] In the United Kingdom, only 10.5 percent of directors (nonexecutive and executive) of Britain's largest listed companies were women in 2005 compared with 8.6 percent in 2003.[64] More diversity in gender on boards is desirable. A study of large U.S. companies finds that boards with women directors:

- Are better than all-male boards at influencing management.
- Are better at recruiting and retaining women employees.
- Have a competitive advantage in the war for talent.[65]

The 2005 survey of SSBI shows that: (1) the majority (73 percent) of the surveyed boards have at least one minority director; among this majority, 75 percent have at least one African American director, and 34 percent and 11 percent have at least one Hispanic director or one Asian director, respectively; (2) about 35 percent of the respondents have a non-U.S. citizen on the board; among them, about 55 percent are from Europe and the rest are from Mexico and Canada.[66] Overall, director diversity has increased slightly in the post-SOX period, but the proportion of seats held by women continues to remain low in comparison with their representation in the nation's management positions and entire workforce.

Age of the CEO and Directors The age of the CEO and directors has been discussed and debated in corporate governance literature, professional standards, guiding principles, and corporate governance reforms. The general consensus among companies is that there should be mandatory retirement ages for both CEOs and directors as well as term limits for their positions.[67] The perception is that as directors and CEOs get older, they become more complacent and are less willing and likely to initiate changes when needed. Furthermore, older CEOs may lose touch with the current business environment, technical advances, global competition, emerging corporate governance reforms, and current stakeholders. Younger directors and CEOs, however, may not have the adequate experience and reputation, and may have a tendency to be less risk averse, which could have a negative impact on monitoring and controls. Therefore, diversity of the company's board of directors in terms of age can create a well-balanced functioning of the board, although a keen focus should be on the qualifications, knowledge, experience, and effectiveness of directors as opposed to their age.

The 2005 survey of SSBI shows that (1) the average age of independent directors on S&P 500 boards increased to 60.8 years in 2005 compared to 60.00 in the pre-SOX period; (2) the average age of the newly recruited independent directors was 56.4 years; and (3) about 70 percent of these boards had an average age of 60 or older compared with 61 percent in 2000, which may reflect a greater appointment of retired executives as board members.[68] The mandatory retirement age for directors of public companies in the post-SOX era is becoming more prevalent and rising. The 2005 survey of S&P 500 boards conducted by the SSBI reveals that in 2005, 78 percent of S&P 500 boards established a mandatory retirement age, up from 58 percent in 2000.[69] The survey also shows that the target retirement age is rising in the post-SOX era: In 2005, 45 percent of S&P 500 boards set the retirement age at 73 or older compared with 9 percent and 3 percent in 2004 and 2000, respectively.[70] Among the 185 proxy statements of S&P 500 companies that reported departing directors in 2005, (1) 58 disclosed no reason for the departure of one or more directors; (2) 90 percent cited retirement as the reason for such departures; and (3) the remainder disclosed a variety of reasons, such as death or other personal and business commitments and conflicts of interest.[71]

Founding Family CEO   The CEO as part of the founding family can have an impact on the corporate governance structure and the ability of shareholders to participate effectively in monitoring and controlling the company's affairs. Traditionally, founders have employed professional management rather than their heir as the new CEO upon the departure of the company's founder. The motivation to appoint family members to the company's board is to keep control within the family, which is detrimental to the independence of the board and may lead to entrenchment, less monitored and effective corporate governance structure, and worse financial performance over the long-term.

CEOs as Board Members   One question that is often asked is whether a company benefits: (1) when its CEO holds a directorship in other companies; and (2) when CEOs of other companies sit on its board of directors.[72] The 2005 SSBI survey of reveals that:

- More than half of the surveyed boards said they limit the number of other boards on which their CEO may serve as an independent director.
- The limitation of CEO membership on other boards ranges from one other board to as many as six with an average of two to three other boards.

- The board typically reviews and approves the CEO's membership on other boards.[73]

The best corporate governance practices dictate that CEOs' fiduciary duties and primary responsibilities are to their company and its shareholders. As such, they should focus on their own stewardship functions and consult with their board before serving as nonexecutive directors on boards of other companies. Nonetheless, the corporate governance literature points out seven reasons for CEOs' desire to sit on other boards:

1. Board service provides education and experience for CEOs, particularly those who are not chairs of boards, in learning how boards operate.
2. Directorships and board service provide an opportunity to learn strategic and policy-making at another level.
3. Directorships and outside board services enable CEOs to learn about different corporate governance practices, their implications, and their effectiveness.
4. Outside board service enables CEOs to make contacts that may help their companies.
5. Directorships should not impair CEOs' accountability to their companies and shareholders.
6. Directorships and board services allow CEOs to meet fellow business leaders in a more collegial and neutral environment.
7. CEO directorships can cause reciprocal interlocking boards when the CEO of Company A serves as a director of Company B and the CEO of Company B sits on the board of Company A.[74]

Board interlocks, either directional or nondirectional, occur when a person associated with one company serves on the board of another company. Directional interlocks can be formed when a corporate executive (sending partner) sits on the board of another company (receiving partner). Nondirectional interlocks occur when a nonexecutive director of Company A sits on the board of Company B. Multiple director interlocks continue to dominate the U.S. corporate board network. Twenty-seven boards in 2005 were involved in three or more multiple interlocks with other boards, sharing at least two directors with another board.[75] After the Grasso Gate scandal at the New York Stock Exchange was investigated, it was determined that interlocking board relationships were a contributing factor. A study conducted by the Corporate Library, a corporate governance resource, shows that more than 40 percent of the 120 companies under investigation for backdating their stock option grants shared directors with other implicated companies.[76] Thus, one common corporate governance attribute of backdated companies is the director interlocking relationships and the fact that they share a network of directors.

Board Declassification Many boards are currently divided into classes or staggered groups with only a portion of members up for reelection each year. Recent trends have seen a strong push toward the declassifying of boards. Declassification calls for the removal of a staggered system and election of the entire board on an annual basis. Investor activists have promoted board declassification for several years as a way to hold directors more accountable. Board declassification has continued to gain momentum, and maintaining a classified board in the future will be difficult for a public company to justify to its shareholders. Thus, public companies should assess the benefits and detriments of the board declassification format in light of their own corporate governance structure and consider moving toward declassifying their board in the near future.

Number of Directors   State law normally specifies a minimum number of directors. For example, Section 141(b) of the Delaware General Corporation Law states:

> *The board of directors of a corporation shall consist of* 1 *or more members. The number of directors shall be fixed by, or in the manner provided in the bylaws, unless the certificate of incorporation fixes the number of directors, in which case a change in the number of directors shall be made only by amendment of the certificate.*[77]

The U.K. Companies Act of 2006 requires public companies to have at least two directors; private companies must have at least one director, who must be a natural person.[78] The range of directorship is typically specified in the company's bylaws, which often are amended by the board without shareholder approval. The size of the board can also affect its efficiency and effectiveness. Anecdotal evidence and the results of academic research regarding the size and the effectiveness of boards are inconclusive, and the direction is not clear. On one hand, a small board size is considered to be efficient because the process of deliberation becomes time consuming and unwieldy with large boards.[79] On the other hand, a large board can be more effective in monitoring managerial actions primarily because by increasing the number of directors involved with monitoring, management may decrease the opportunity for wrongdoing, and collusion becomes more difficult. A board size of 9 to 15 directors is normally considered to be an adequate range to satisfy the number of board standing committees (audit, compensation, and nomination/governance), the size of the company, and the extent of its operations, although a board size of less than 9 directors may work well for small companies. The 2005 SSBI survey indicates that:

- The average board size for S&P 500 companies remains at 10.7 directors for the post-SOX era.
- The board range is narrowing; two-thirds of boards now have between 9 and 12 directors compared with 59 percent in the pre-SOX period.
- 82 percent of boards have 12 or fewer directors, up from 70 percent in 2000.
- Financial services tend to have the largest boards, with as many as 29 directors; technology companies have the smallest boards, with about 5 directors.[80]

The total number of directors for 5,825 U.S. public companies as of the end of 2006 was 49,783 directors, which represents an average of 8.6 directors per board. Boards of larger companies averaged about 12 directors compared with 7 for smaller companies.[81] U.S. boards had an average 1.59 inside directors and 6.96 outside directors per company with almost even 50 percent inside/outside chairs.[82] Academic research suggests that:

- Poor performance is positively related to smaller boards and fewer outside members.
- Outside directors are often added after a period of poor performance.
- It normally takes longer for members to be added than for directors to leave.
- Powerful CEOs are often able to exert significant influence over board appointments to ensure that the new director will support, or at least not challenge, executive decisions.[83]

Who Can Be a Director?   The question of "who can be a director" is not properly addressed in the business and corporate governance literature. The current British company law permits any legal person (e.g., other companies) to be company directors as if they are individuals. This flexibility has been criticized for its inability to identify and hold individual directors accountable for their actions. The new U.K. Corporations Act of 2006 requires at least one of the company's directors to be a natural person of at least 16 years old.[84] The term "director" has a broad meaning under English law; it includes any person, firm, company, or other entity that: (1) exercises management control over a U.K. company; or (2) participates in the management of a U.K. company in the manner usually expected of a director.[85] The concept of "shadow directors" continues to be recognized in the Companies Act of 2006; a shadow director is defined as a person in accordance with whose directions or instructions the directors of a company are accustomed to acting. For example, an officer of a parent company could qualify as a shadow director of a U.K. subsidiary company where the subsidiary is accustomed to acting in accordance with the instructions of that officer. The average age of a chairperson, nonexecutive directors, CEOs, and executive directors is 62, 59, 54, and 51 years, respectively. In the United Kingdom, women make up about 1 percent of listed chairs, 11 percent of nonexecutive directors, and 2.5 percent of executive directors.[86]

Number of Directorships   Directors of public companies in the pre-SOX era were criticized for serving on many boards and not devoting adequate time to fulfill their directorship responsibilities. In the post-SOX era, it is expected that public companies will be less likely to retain directors who serve simultaneously on too many boards. The Council of Institutional Investors issued its 2006 policies regarding the number of directors:

> *Companies should establish and publish guidelines specifying on how many other boards their directors may serve. Absent unusual, specified circumstances, directors with full-time jobs should not serve on more than two other boards. Currently serving CEOs should only serve as a director of one other company, and then only if the CEO's own company is in the top half of its peer group. No person should serve on more than five for-profit company boards.[87]*

In the boardroom, "multitasking" refers to a situation where a person sits on the board of several companies. About 0.7 percent (350) of the nation's 50,000 company directors sit on four boards; the majority sit on one or two boards.[88] However, James Johnson, a former chairman of Fannie Mae, serves on the boards of six companies, including Gannett, Goldman Sachs, KB Home, Target, Temple-Inland, and UnitedHealth Group. In all these boards he holds key committee posts as a chairman of the compensation committee.[89] A 2004 survey indicates that:

- 76 percent of the 100 largest U.S. public companies addressed the issue of service by their directors on other boards by including a requirement for notifying the board before joining another board and limiting the number of boards.
- About 29 percent require a maximum limit, ranging from three to seven boards, on which a director may serve.
- At 42 percent of the Fortune 100 companies, at least one director serves on five or more public company boards.[90]

Number of Meetings   The frequency of meetings of the board of directors can provide an estimate of the amount of time devoted to the board's oversight function. However, such an estimate does not capture the quality of the work performed during meetings or the amount of monitoring conducted outside of meetings. It is expected that boards of public companies are required to devote more time to carrying out their oversight responsibilities effectively in the post-SOX era. There is no magic number of times that boards should meet to fulfill their fiduciary duties, but they should meet at least five times a year to review quarterly financial reports and attend the annual shareholders' meeting. A 2004 survey shows that the number of the 100 largest U.S. public companies boards meeting 10 or more times increased from 20 percent in 2002 to 29 percent in 2003.[91] The audit committee of these companies met almost twice as many times as other board committees, including the nominating and compensation committees.[92] The 2005 SSBI survey indicates that:

- The median number of board meetings for S&P 500 boards remained steady at seven in the post-SOX period.
- About 47 percent of these boards met six to eight times a year with the maximum of 24 and the minimum of three meetings.
- Over 10 percent of the boards met at least once a month.[93]

Executive sessions of the outside directors have received a widening acceptance as a means of promoting an independent culture in the boardroom. Listing standards of national stock exchanges (e.g., NYSE, Nasdaq) also require nonexecutive directors hold regular executive sessions. The primary purpose of executive sessions is to encourage nonexecutive directors to have open and frank discussion regarding issues concerning management, performance, evaluation, compensation, competence, and credibility. The head or presiding director should provide leadership and the agenda for executive sessions, allow candid and informal discussion, take minutes of the sessions and whenever appropriate report back to the company's CEO and other key executives. A 2006 PwC survey of 1300 directors reveals that: (1) about 69 percent of respondents reported that their executive sessions were very useful to the board and their CEO clearly understood their value; (2) while finding their executive sessions useful to the board, more than 22 percent were unsure whether their CEO appreciates them; (3) 7 percent believed their executive sessions were not valuable to the board; and (4) about 1 percent felt that executive sessions were not only valuable but also strained the CEO/board relationship.[94]

The corporate governance issues brought before the board for deliberation whether by management or others(e.g., auditors) should be submitted to the board prior to the meetings. The advance submission of meeting materials allows directors to have sufficient time to study, analyze, understand, and be prepared to ask relevant questions, discuss the issues, and deliberate on them. Taking proper minutes of the board meetings is crucial in presenting different views on the deliberated issues, the consensus of the board on the decisions made, dissents, and actions taken. The corporate secretary may take the minutes of the meetings and, with the advice of the company's legal counsel, prepare the board minutes and include them in the company's records. If the company's bylaws require the approval of minutes before they are official, the minutes should be approved at the next board meeting.

Director Attendance   Public companies in the post-SOX era are stricter and more transparent about director attendance at board meetings in general and at the annual meeting in particular by having formal policies requiring director attendance and disclosing proper information about it. The SSBI 2005 survey of S&P 500 boards reveals that:

- 54 percent of the boards reported that all of their directors attended the previous year's annual meeting of the company.
- Of the remaining 46 percent that had less than full attendance of directors, about half had only one director miss the annual meeting.
- About 60 percent of S&P 500 boards in 2005 had a formal policy requiring attendance at their annual meetings.
- More than 92 percent of S&P 500 companies reported board attendance in 2005 compared with 75 percent in 2004.[95]

A 2006 survey of directors reveals that support for virtual meetings through safe and secure Internet environment is growing; about 43 percent of surveyed directors said they would feel comfortable with a virtual meeting compared with 36 percent in 2002.[96]

BOARD SELECTION

The board should be composed of directors with attributes relevant to the company's mission. For example, the board of a healthcare company may include individuals from the medical community (hospitals), the insurance industry, and the local business community who can bring diversity and expertise to the board. Shareholders elect directors and empower and entrust them to hire competent and ethical executives to manage the business and make decisions on their behalf. Thus, the reputation, expertise, competence, and integrity of directors are important in gaining and maintaining the trust and confidence of shareholders. The 2005 survey of SSBI indicates that: (1) the majority of the surveyed boards (87 percent) plan to add one or two directors; (2) more than half of their new directors will be replacing retiring directors; (3) 20 percent intend to increase financial expertise on the board; (4) 16 percent plan to bring more independent directors; and (5) about 12 percent aim to increase gender and race diversity.[97]

The election process of directors can also affect the board's effectiveness in the sense that the process enables shareholders to replace unsatisfactory directors. The majority of public companies currently use the plurality voting system, which is permitted by state laws. Under the plurality voting system, shareholders receive ballots enabling them to vote "for" a director or cast a symbolic "withhold" vote without being given the legal right to vote "against" a director. As a result, shareholder election of directors is not a democratic process. Management usually nominates a director. If the election is uncontested, nominated directors can be elected with just a single vote cast in their favor.

A staggered board structure in which only a portion of the board is elected each year may contribute to the continuity of the board's monitoring function but does not maximize board accountability. Investors typically do not like staggered boards, and many shareholder proposals ask boards to declassify. The staggered structure makes the annual reelection of the entire board more difficult because under a typical staggered structure, only one-third of the board is elected each year for a three-year term. Glass Lewis & Co. tracked director elections and prepared a 2005 director elections scorecard consisting of results for 17,168 individual director elections. The scorecard indicates that:

- 19 directors (about 0.1 percent) received a withhold vote of more than 50 percent.
- 54 directors received a withhold vote of between 10 and 50 percent.
- On average, directors received about a 4.5 percent withhold vote with a median of 2.2 percent.[98]

In the post-SOX era, and in response to concerns raised by investor activists, particularly institutional ones, many public companies are modifying their director election process. One example is Pfizer, which in June 2005 revised its corporate governance principles by requiring that any director who receives a majority of withheld votes submit an official resignation to the board. Then the board must review the resignation and decide how to rectify the situation.[99] Several other boards followed Pfizer's lead and revised their board election process, including Office Depot, Circuit City, ADP, and Disney, and it is expected that more will follow suit. However, investors would prefer that companies adopt a majority voting director election standard in the company's bylaws as opposed to adopting a policy that can be modified only with shareholder approval.

The practice of director election is changing in two important ways. First, the majority voting in various forms is gaining momentum; second, shareholder proposals demand companies adopt workable majority voting policies through changing their bylaws. The initiative for majority voting started in 2005, when 55 shareholder proposals called for majority voting election, and investor activists sent a letter to the 1,500 largest public companies requesting the voluntary adoption of majority voting standards.[100] The trend toward the adoption of such policies is expected to continue. Two forms of majority voting policies have received support: the majority-of-votes-cast standard and the majority-of-outstanding-votes standard. The full implementation of majority voting and a middle-ground approach of requiring directors who receive more "withhold" than "for" votes to tender their resignation to the board of directors is expected to improve board elections. Under the plurality voting system, directors encounter few, if any, challenges and little chance of losing an election. Academic research suggests that directors do not usually suffer reputational damages from low votes as their lower votes have no effect on the appointment of directors or any change in firm governance or performance.[101] Nonetheless, directors who attended less than 75 percent of board meetings or received a negative ISS recommendation obtained 15 percent and 18 percent fewer votes, respectively.[102]

Under the current SEC rules, shareholders can either vote for the nominated directors or withhold their support, which in either case results in the director nominee being elected. A decision by the United States Court of Appeals for the Second Circuit, in September 2006, facilitates more shareholder power in director election by allowing the shareholders to submit proposals for inclusion on ballots and to seek access to the company's proxies concerning director nomination and elections. In the absence of clear guidance on technical issues by state corporate laws in replacing the plurality vote standard with a majority vote standard, companies should consider voluntarily adopting the corporate governance director election standard in their bylaws of a majority-of-votes-cast "for" standard. For example, in January 2006, Intel's board amended the company's bylaws to replace its plurality vote standard with a majority vote standard for the election of directors.[103] This move by Intel is viewed positively by its shareholders in holding its directors more accountable and in bringing democracy to its boardroom.

Best Practices

The company's board of directors, in collaboration with its top management team, particularly the CEO, should decide on and tailor the board model to fit its corporate governance structure, based on what model best fits the board's oversight function. David A. Nadler, the chairman of Mercer Delta, a New York–based management consulting firm, describes five types of board models.

1. *The passive board.* The passive board is the traditional model, characterized by minimal engagement by directors, and only at the CEO's discretion. Board members have the role of ratifying management's decisions with a limited accountability.
2. *The certifying board.* The certifying board model certifies to shareholders that the CEO meets the expectations of the board in properly managing the company,

oversees an orderly succession process, and focuses on protecting investors and promoting independent directors.

3. *The engaged board.* This model emphasizes the importance of collaboration between the company's board and its CEO in providing insight, advice, and support on major decisions; oversees managerial functions and company performance; and continuously redefines its roles, responsibilities, and boundaries.

4. *The intervening board.* This type of board model works best in crisis situations where the board holds frequent and intensive meetings to make important decisions about the company's governance and operations.

5. *The operating board.* This model is most appropriate in the early stage of start-up companies where executives have specialized expertise but insufficient board management experience. In this model, the board makes all key decisions, and management implements the strategic decisions and plans made by the board.[104]

These five different boards provide best practices ranging from the least involved to the most involved boards. Companies should choose which board practice best fits their corporate governance oversight function. Real-world boards may be a hybrid of these practices and vary across time, key issues, and decisions. Indeed, "a passive or certifying board in crisis, for instance, may morph temporarily into an intervening board to remove the CEO and then into an operating board until a new leader is in place."[105] The engaged board model can work best in many situations.

A corporate governance publication of the London Stock Exchange and RSM Robson Rhodes identifies seven practices of boards, ranging from the practices of an effective board to those of a board that is not achieving their full potential.[106] Exhibit 3.3 presents types of boards, their focus, and their attributes. Companies should evaluate their own board, identify its focus and attributes, determine its best practices, assess its strengths and weaknesses, and determine how it can best move toward the most effective model for their company.

BOARD OF DIRECTORS' EDUCATION AND EVALUATION

Corporate governance guiding principles and best practices issued by a number of organizations and national stock exchanges recommend continuous education and evaluation of the board of directors. Listing standards (NYSE, Nasdaq) require listed companies to disclose their corporate governance guidelines, including their requirements for director orientation and continuing education.[107] In addition, directors who serve on audit committees should maintain their education in financial literacy as required by SOX Section 407 and SEC rules.[108] Director continuing education is often regarded as an indication of effective corporate governance. Professional organizations are incorporating this into their rating of companies' governance, and companies should allocate an annual budget amount for it. For example, the ISS, the Corporate Library, Standard & Poor's, and Moody's Investor Service have all graded boards in the area of corporate governance, including director continuing education.

EXHIBIT 3.3 Types of Boards, Their Focus and Attributes

Type	Focus	Attributes
The Effective Board	▪ Strategic discussions ▪ Oversight functions	▪ Clear strategy aligned to capabilities.
The Dreamers	▪ Strong focus on future ▪ Long-term strategies ▪ Consider social and environmental implications	▪ Insufficient focus on current concerns ▪ Fail to identify and/or manage key risks ▪ Unrealistically optimistic
The Adrenaline Groupies	▪ Clear decisions taken ▪ Decisions implemented	▪ Lurch from crisis to crisis ▪ Focus on short-term only ▪ Lack of strategic direction ▪ Internal focus ▪ Tendency to micro-manage
The Semidetached	▪ Strong focus on external environment ▪ Intellectually challenging	▪ Out of touch with the company ▪ Little attempt to implement decisions ▪ Poor monitoring of decision making ▪ If out of touch with external environment, board becomes totally detached

(continued overleaf)

EXHIBIT 3.3 (*Continued*)

Type	Focus	Attributes
The Number Crunchers	■ Short-term needs of investors considered ■ Prudent decision making	■ Focus on financial impact ■ Lack of blue-sky thinking ■ Lack of diversity of board members ■ Impact of social and environmental issues largely ignored ■ Risk averse
Talking Shop	■ All opinions given equal weight ■ All options considered	■ No effective decision-making/implementation process ■ Lack of direction from the chairman ■ Lack of focus on critical issues ■ No evaluation of previous decisions
The Rubber Stamp	■ Makes clear decisions ■ Listens to in-house expertise ■ Ensures decisions are implemented	■ Does not consider alternatives ■ Dominated by executives ■ Relies on fed information ■ Focuses on supporting evidence ■ Does not listen to criticism ■ Role of nonexecutive directors limited

Source: Extracted from Figures 1 to 4, "Board Games of the London Stock Exchange, Practical Guide to Corporate Governance" (2004). Available at: www.rsmi.co.uk.

Board education is essential in providing professional development for directors and ensuring that they keep abreast with emerging issues, rules, standards, and best practices affecting their performance. The majority of responding directors (83 percent) felt that directors should attend director training and education seminars while 29 percent prefer outside the boardroom seminars where they can meet other directors; 11 percent are in favor of bringing board education into the boardroom to deal with sensitive issues, and 52 percent prefer a combination of outside and internal training.[109]

The performance evaluation of the company's board of directors should be completed formally and regularly (at least annually) through self-evaluation, independent committee evaluation (audit, compensation, nominating), or outside consulting evaluations. Each of these approaches has advantages and disadvantages. For example, self-evaluation of the board can be more in depth; outside consultant evaluations can be perceived to be more independent. Assessment of individual directors' performance is very sensitive and often subjective, primarily because no generally accepted criteria are established for the board evaluation. If there is a possibility that these evaluations may show the board to be ineffective in monitoring management, directors are typically leery of making any of this information public to shareholders, due to litigation concerns. However, some type of summary aggregate evaluation information for shareholders would be very helpful. Thus, companies may want to start with evaluating the performance of the entire board, then its committees, and finally individual members of the committees.

The company's board evaluation and training is an important component of its accountability. The 2005 survey of 1,103 directors reveals that about 30 percent reported that their company had no formal training program for them, whereas 55 percent reported they were encouraged or required to participate in outside director training.[110] The 2005 survey of SSBI shows that almost all (99 percent) of the surveyed boards used a formal process to evaluate the performance of their board in 2005 compared with 90 percent in 2004; and only about 33 percent of surveyed boards formally assessed the performance of individual directors.[111] These results suggest that while the board performance evaluation is becoming a norm for best practices, individual directors' assessment and accountability is not widely practiced.[112]

Some of the generally accepted and commonly viewed benchmarks for the entire board evaluation are:

- Fulfillment of oversight functions.
- Transparency and accountability of oversight functions.
- Overseeing conflicts of interest.
- Establishment of goals and strategies.
- Assessment of management's performance.

A 2006 survey of 1300 directors indicates that: (1) about 86 percent report that performance is formally evaluated on a regular basis; (2) more than 59 percent use their general counsel to execute their performance evaluation whereas 15 percent employ an outside attorney and another 1.4 percent utilize either an internal officer or outside advisors; (3) all surveyed boards have usually implemented the NYSE requirements for their board evaluations; and (4) about 60 percent took proper actions based on the board evaluation indicating that they take the process seriously.[113] The committees of the board of directors should be evaluated according to their assigned oversight functions and the fulfillment of their responsibilities. The individual members of each board committee should be evaluated based on their governing ability, integrity, financial literacy, strategic perspective, decision making and judgment, teamwork, communication, leadership, and business acumen. Exhibit 3.4 provides benchmarks and criteria for evaluating the board, its committees, and directors.

DETERMINANTS OF AN EFFECTIVE BOARD

To fulfill their oversight function effectively, boards should be competent, ethical, committed, responsible, and accountable. The business and academic literature suggests these 27 determinants of an effective board of directors:[114]

1. *Competency of the board.* The effectiveness of the board in shaping a company's strategic direction and providing advice to management and performing its oversight functions largely depends on the competency of its members (directors), including their experience, knowledge, information, and decision-making ability. Directors should have sufficient understanding and knowledge of the company's business; competitive environment; and social, legal, and technological advances affecting the company's business and operation. They should also have knowledge of the internal financial and human resources available to the company in implementing its strategy and achieving its goals. Thus, the nomination and election process of directors is critical in checking nominees' education and experience background and electing competent directors. The board should have an appropriate mix of backgrounds, skills, and knowledge bases in order to effectively carry out its oversight responsibilities, including the timely response to corporate problems and open, honest, and constructive challenges to management.

2. *Ethical conduct of directors.* The company's directors should set an appropriate tone at the top of practicing and promoting ethical behavior, legal compliance, and professional conduct. Ethically and legally obedient directors create a business environment that encourages and rewards ethical conduct and compliance with applicable laws and regulations and disciplines unethical behavior and illegal actions. To monitor the ethical and legal performance of the company effectively, the board should have access to the information and have knowledge of the company's structure and business process. There should be a communication process and mechanism for the board to gain knowledge of potential unethical and illegal issues and actions throughout the company. SOX provides several mechanisms that boards can use to prevent and detect unethical and illegal conduct.[115]

EXHIBIT 3.4 Board Performance

Benchmarks	Criteria
Board Independence	▪ No more than two inside directors. ▪ No insiders on audit, nominating, and compensation committees. ▪ No outside members who directly or indirectly draw consulting, legal, or other fees from the company. ▪ No interlocking directorships (CEOs who sit on each other's boards). ▪ It is desirable for outside directors to meet regularly without the CEO.
Board Quality	▪ Fully employed directors sit on no more than four corporate boards and retired directors, on no more than seven. ▪ More kudos are given if the board has at least one outside director experienced in the company's core business. ▪ It is a plus if at least one director is a CEO of a company of similar size. ▪ A higher rating is given if all directors attended 75% or more of meetings or if a board has no more than 15 directors.
Board Activism	▪ Boards should meet regularly without management present and should evaluate their own performance every year. ▪ Audit committees should meet at least four times a year. ▪ Boards should be frugal on executive pay. ▪ Boards should be decisive when planning a CEO succession. ▪ Boards should be diligent in oversight responsibilities. ▪ Boards should be quick to act when trouble strikes.
Board Accountability	▪ All board directors must own a minimum of U.S. $150,000 of stock, ensuring an alignment of their interests with those of investors. ▪ More kudos, are given if the company does not offer pension benefits to its directors—a benefit that many believe makes directors less likely to challenge the CEO. ▪ Board stands for election every year. ▪ Boards that fail to evaluate their performance rate lower.

Source: Adapted from Ernst & Young, Corporate Governance Workshop: Board Performance, 2002. Available at: www.ey.com.

   a. Section 405 of SOX directed the SEC to issue rules requiring public companies to disclose whether it has a code of ethics for its principal financial officers, controller, or principal accounting officers.

   b. According to Section 307 of SOX and SEC-related implementation rules, if the company's outside attorney becomes aware of a material violation of the securities laws and similar illegal acts, he or she is required to report the violation to the company's chief legal officer and ultimately to the board of directors or its representative, the audit committee.

   c. National stock exchanges require their listing companies to have a code of ethical conduct.

   d. Section 806 of SOX provides a civil action for employees who have been subject to retaliation by their employers for disclosing the company's illegal activities. SOX and the SEC-related implementations rules require the company's audit committee to establish a whistleblower program.

3. *Directors' independence.* One way to improve directors' objectivity is to require the majority of directors (at least two-thirds) to be nonexecutive and independent with no financial or familial relationships with the company's senior management. Independent directors have less incentive to engage in actual or potential conflicts of interest with management. The emerging corporate governance reforms (SOX, SEC rules, and listing standards) require that the majority be independent and that all directors who serve on the audit, compensation, and nominating committees be independent and nonexecutive directors to ensure better accountability and reduce the likelihood of potential conflicts of interest between executive and nonexecutive directors. The author suggests that all directors who serve on the board except the CEO be independent.

4. *Directors' accountability.* Individual directors should be accountable to shareholders by requiring a record of their votes on material corporate resolutions in the proxy statements. Records of individual directors' votes and public disclosures of them would likely improve the vigilant attitude and behavior of directors, particularly when investor activism and professional organizations keep track of their pattern of voting and develop director voting scorecards.

5. *CEO duality.* In most industrial countries other than the United States, corporate governance requires the separation of the positions of chair and CEO. This separation can provide a better balance in the boardroom and greater board independence.

6. *Reinvigorate shareholders.* Shareholders play a crucial role in monitoring the function of corporate governance. Shareholder engagement in the monitoring function through the nomination and election process can substantially improve the effectiveness of corporate governance.

7. *Independent investigation of wrongdoing.* The Conference Board suggests that the independent investigation of the alleged wrongdoing is vital to the company's well-being.[116] Companies should hire outside counsel to conduct investigations involving their executives. To ensure a fair and effective investigation, this special counsel should not be the company's regular outside counsel or a firm that receives a significant amount of revenue from the company. Internal investigation

can serve as damage control to minimize the negative impacts of alleged wrong-doing, particularly when the company is under investigation by regulators.

8. *Focus on long-term success.* The Conference Board recommends that corporate boards, executives, and shareholders focus on the company's long-term success and sustainable and enduring performance rather than on short-term market expectations.[117] Companies should pay more attention to their long-term investors and should be receptive to shareholder nominations of candidates for the board, and they should consider implementing shareholder proposals receiving a substantial number of "for" votes. Companies should also respond to a wide variety of stakeholders, including creditors, employees, customers, suppliers, competitors, and communities.

9. *Directors' responsibility.* Directors' responsibility and fiduciary duties should be clearly defined and should include approving the company's strategic decisions and overseeing the managerial function. A good balance of powers should exist between the company's board and its CEO. The outside directors should be empowered to carry out their oversight responsibility effectively.

10. *Transparent nomination and election process.* The nomination and election process should be fair and transparent, and shareholders should exercise their voting rights to nominate, support, endorse, and elect candidates for directors. The nominating committee should nominate the most qualified individuals to the board. Availability of directors' annual performance evaluation could be a great help to shareholders in assessing the qualifications, credentials, and suitability of candidates put forth by the board for election or reelection.

11. *Provide boards with funding, advisors, and administrative staff.* SOX requires that the audit committee of the company's board of directors be provided with funding to pay for independent auditors and other advisors deemed necessary. It is expected that for routine business affairs, management educates and informs the board in carrying out its oversight function, although the board has its own independent obligation to be informed of key company issues. However, like audit committees, the other board committees should be provided funding and have access to advisors when deemed necessary. Thus, board oversight effectiveness can be significantly improved by providing budgets and independent advisors to the entire board to deal with complex issues, management, and shareholder proposals that warrant additional research or an independent opinion.

12. *Annual formal evaluation of the board.* The company's board should tailor its annual evaluation process for the entire board, each of its committees, and individual directors. A combination of internal reviews, peer reviews, and external reviews (e.g., consulting firms) can be used to assess board oversight effectiveness in ensuring shareholder value creation and enhancement as well as stakeholders' value protection. To ensure the effective oversight function, there should be a three-tier evaluation process for the board that includes assessment of the performance of the entire board, each committee of the board, and each individual director. The non-CEO chair, the lead independent director, or the presiding director in collaboration with the chair should initiate and oversee the fairness, transparency, and effectiveness of the board evaluation process.

13. *Meeting attendance and participation.* Regular meeting attendance and participation in discussions and decisions not only shows the directors' commitment but also improves their oversight effectiveness in evaluating management proposals and improves their responsiveness to shareholder proposals. Good attendance and compelling participation of directors is important to both the company's success and their prestige and reputation.

14. *Stock ownership.* It can be argued theoretically that when directors own a significant portion (more than 10 percent) of the company's outstanding shares, they will be more vigilant in their oversight responsibilities. Academic research, however, does not suggest that directors' stock ownership is a good measure for differentiating good boards from bad boards.[118] Nonetheless, directors' stock ownership can align their interests with those of shareholders.

15. *Directors' skills.* Directors' knowledge, experience, skills, and utilization of these qualifications in carrying out their oversight responsibilities can significantly affect their oversight effectiveness. Possession of these qualifications is necessary, but their utilization can differentiate good boards from bad boards. For example, Enron's board comprised mostly prominent individuals with impressive financial competencies, experience, and achievements (e.g., former Stanford dean, CEO of an international bank, a hedge fund manager), yet they claimed that they were confused by Enron's hedging, off–balance sheet, and special purpose entities financial transactions, and they subsequently settled lawsuits brought against them by Enron's shareholders for their ignorance and lack of participation and vigilant oversight function. They also waived the company's ethics policy on three separate occasions.

16. *Director's age.* The general perception among companies is that the board becomes less effective in its oversight function as the average age of its members increases over a certain number of years (e.g., 70 years).[119]

17. *Holdover CEO.* Having the past CEO serving on the current company's board is rarely beneficial, yet it may improve the board oversight effectiveness in the short run. Past CEOs tend to continue to act in their former role, attempting to run and mange the company, rather than carry out their new oversight responsibilities. Nevertheless, during a short transition period, the retired CEO can bring experience to the board, assist in guiding the new directors, and bring more cohesiveness to the board.

18. *Succession planning.* Succession planning is an important responsibility for the corporate board. It entails the continuous evaluation of the CEO's performance and the process for the replacement of the CEO on demand (e.g., ineffective performance, sudden death, incapacity, or quitting). Almost half of the 1,103 responding directors (47 percent) reported that they were not satisfied with their succession planning efforts; 66 percent did not address this important issue; and 26 percent chose not to consider the issues because their CEO was uncomfortable with the topic.[120]

19. *Board size and committees.* Given that many public companies have at least three board committees (audit, compensation, nominating/corporate governance) and each committee should have at least 3 independent directors, and no committee member should serve as the chair of another committee, public companies need

to have between 6 and 9 independent directors serving on their board commit-tees. Assuming that two-thirds of the directors are independent and nonexecu-tive directors, the normal size of the company's board is then in the range of 9 to 15 directors.

20. *Executive sessions.* Independent directors should have executive sessions with internal auditors and external auditors to discuss financial reporting and audit activities without CEO interference. The general counsel should also have the right to speak to independent directors in the executive session.

21. *Boardroom climate.* Developing a culture of trust and candor in the company's boardroom enables executives to share important information with directors in advance and to discuss strategic issues and decisions. Directors should trust and respect each other and be able to work effectively as a team in overseeing the managerial function. A necessary change in the boardroom culture requires a better understanding of the important role that directors play in ensuring the effectiveness of corporate governance. Boards must create the right tone at the top in their cultural, structural, and procedural reforms; practice constructive skepticism; accept individual directors' accountability; and, under rare circumstances, impose personal director liability for breach of their fiduciary duty where fraud is pervasive.

22. *Allow dissent.* Constructive discussions in the boardroom should view dissent as an opportunity to openly debate the company's strategic issues and decisions and should not view being skeptical as a sign of disloyalty. Healthy and open debate should be the norm in the boardroom.

23. *Individual director accountability.* The board can promote accountability by giving individual directors particular oversight responsibility, such as: overseeing internal control, whistleblower programs, tax transactions, financial reporting, codes of business ethics and risk assessment; requiring directors to report to the entire board on their assigned oversight responsibility; rotating directors on their assigned responsibilities; providing them with a sufficient budget to hire professional advisors as deemed necessary; and holding them accountable for their decisions and actions.

24. *Director liability.* Directors should be held accountable for knowingly breaching material fiduciary duties of obedience, loyalty, and due care and/or engaging in: corporate misconduct; malfeasance; fraudulent activities; violations of applica-ble laws, rules, or regulations; or intentionally misleading investors. Director liability is discussed further in the next section of this chapter.

25. *Executive compensation.* Executive compensation remains a challenging issue for many corporate boards. More than 70 percent of 1,103 responding directors felt that they were having trouble controlling the level of executive compensa-tion; 14 percent wanted to spend more time on these issues whereas 84 percent believed they were doing a good job of managing executive compensation.[121] The majority of surveyed directors (75 percent) believed their boards were having a difficult time managing CEO compensation.[122] Another issue relevant to executive compensation is that the compensation consultant should work directly for the compensation committee and should be prohibited from work-ing for management simultaneously. Situations where consultants can be the

company's board consultant on one project and then a management consultant on another project should be avoided.

26. *Multiple bottom lines.* Many U.S. company boards are being criticized for focusing solely on financial matters and information and ignoring other aspects of the business. The 2005 survey of 1,103 directors reveals that the majority (89 percent) reported they receive financial and business data; only 47 percent of directors receive information on employee values and satisfaction, and 42 percent receive information about customer satisfaction. The board of directors should consider the company's performance in all areas, including economic, ethics, governance, social, and environmental.

27. *Risk management.* Risk management is an important aspect of business strategies, and corporate boards should be involved in risk management. A survey shows that more than half of the 1,103 directors who responded reported that they do not have any action plan if their company faces a major crisis; 8 percent were not sure if they had such a plan.[123]

BOARD ACCOUNTABILITY

The existing corporate governance reforms in the United States do not typically empower investors to hold directors accountable (e.g., lack of majority voting and shareholder access to proxy materials). Federal authorities (SEC, DoJ) have not been aggressive enough to bring charges against the outside directors of fraud-prone companies such as Enron, WorldCom, Adelphia, Qwest, and Global Crossing, among others. Lack of proper regulations and ineffective enforcement procedures not only contribute to a system of unaccountability for outside directors but also make the right "tone at the top" meaningless as many outside directors have received backdated or otherwise manipulated stock option grants. More than 1,400 outside directors at 460 public companies might have received options with grant dates manipulated.[124] It is surprising that these gatekeepers who are expected to protect shareholders from excessive and manipulated executive pay participated in the same scheme to defraud investors.

Accountability of the company's board of directors can be classified into three areas:

1. Accountability to shareholders for protecting their long-term interests.
2. Accountability for the effectiveness of the board's operation.
3. Accountability for implementation of the company's strategic plan to ensure sustainable and enduring performance and success.

Accountability to Shareholders

The company's board of directors is accountable to shareholders for protecting their long-term interests by aligning management's interests with those of shareholders. To discharge its accountability to shareholders effectively, the board should:

- Consider adopting shareholder proposals that received a majority of votes cast for and/or against.
- Take actions on recommendations approved by the majority of shareholders.
- Interact with the large shareholders, respond to communications from shareholders, and consider their views, inputs, and insights on important governance and oversight functions.
- Attend the annual shareholders' meeting and be willing to respond to shareholder questions.

Accountability for Board Operation

The company's board of directors should be accountable for its own operation to:

- Ensure directors are working toward the achievement of the company's mission and strategic objectives of attaining sustainable and enduring performance.
- Perform regular evaluation of the board and its individual directors, including an assessment of the board's technical skills, financial expertise, experiences, and other qualifications to fulfill its fiduciary responsibilities effectively.
- Require continuing professional development and education for directors.
- Set high standards for attendance at board and committee meetings.

Accountability for Strategic Decisions and Performance

The company's board of directors should oversee the appropriateness and soundness of all managerial strategic plans, decisions, actions, and performance to ensure sustainable and enduring performance in the multiple bottom-line activities of economic, governance, ethical, social, and environmental measures. The board should obtain necessary information about the company's operations and its financial reporting process and maintain familiarity with the company's business affairs and reporting requirements.

DIRECTOR LIABILITY

Directors are usually subject to liability exposure under state and federal law. State law imposes on directors the fiduciary duties of obedience, loyalty, good faith, and due care. Breaches of these mandatory duties can result in litigations against directors where the court determines the nature and extent of directors' liability. Federal securities laws (e.g., Sections 20(a) and 10(b) of the Exchange Act of 1934) impose duties and obligations on directors for upholding these laws. Under such laws, directors are potentially liable where the company discloses misleading public reports. Directors can be held liable under pension law if their company's retirement plan suffers significantly as a result of overinvestment in the company's own shares.

Sections 305 and 1105 of SOX give the SEC authority to bar directors from serving on the board of public companies if they are deemed "unfit."

It is very rare that outside directors serving on board committees come under scrutiny and investigation by federal authorities for their decisions on the board. However, the three outside directors of Mercury Interactive Corp. who served on both its compensation and audit committees and signed off on the alleged illegal and intentional backdated options are under investigation by the SEC.[125] The SEC, in June 2006, advised these directors that it was considering filing a civil complaint against them regarding their involvement and approval of manipulated stock options grants.[126] It would be the first time that all the members of the compensation and audit committees could face civil charges, if the SEC decides to take further action against these directors for conduct that did not even happen in high-profile scandals of Enron and WorldCom.[127]

Until recently, it was extremely rare for directors to be compelled to pay a portion of settlements from their own pockets. In the WorldCom settlement case, 12 of the company's outside directors agreed to pay $24.75 million from their personal funds; in the Enron case, 10 of the outside directors agreed to pay $13 million in personal contributions. Agreements reached for personal contributions in these two cases may have profound and unprecedented implications for and effects on the determination of future directors' personal liability. Many have argued that the existing securities litigation trend will have a chilling effect on recruiting outside directors and maintaining existing directors who face the exposure of losing personal assets.[128] The general consensus is that in these two cases, the board of directors in general and outside directors in particular failed to effectively discharge their oversight responsibilities and acquiesced entirely to the company's CEO and thus did not prevent corporate wrongdoings. The signal sent by the Enron and WorldCom settlements is that, as the guardians for protecting investors' interests, directors will be held accountable and personally liable when they allow fraud and violations of securities laws to be committed by their company's management.

A survey of a small sample (75) of directors indicates that:

- The majority (65 percent) of responding directors were surprised by the settlement requiring outside directors of Enron and WorldCom to pay damages out of their own pockets.
- 75 percent felt that the right decision was made to hold outside directors personally liable for corporate fraud.
- 95 percent thought that the WorldCom and Enron cases were extreme exceptions.
- 61 percent reported that personal financial penalties by directors will affect their willingness to serve on other boards.
- 79 percent said their personal assets are more at risk because of the Enron and WorldCom settlements.[129]

These results and other anecdotal evidence suggest that directors who fulfill their fiduciary duties, exercise due diligence, perform their oversight function, exercise good faith, and use independent judgment should not be adversely affected by these settlements. However, the Enron and WorldCom settlements should encourage directors to be more skeptical and conscientious about their job by effectively discharging their oversight function, consulting with legal and financial advisors, understanding and reviewing management's strategic and operating decisions and actions, paying attention to unusual and nonrecurring business transactions (mergers, acquisitions, related parties), complying with applicable rules and regulations, maintaining their independence, reviewing and approving executive compensation, communicating with key shareholders, and avoiding self-serving and self-dealing.

The Enron and WorldCom cases were rare situations of outside directors suffering liability. In both companies:

- Outside directors' oversight responsibility was not adequately fulfilled.
- Even though they were not directly engaged in fraudulent activities, they sold their shares of the company during a time when share prices were high due to the fraud.
- The potential liability cost exceeded available D&O insurance.
- Outside directors were collectively wealthy.
- Plaintiffs were either motivated to force directors to disgorge profit gained from fraudulent financial activities they failed to prevent and detect, or they wanted to send the clear message to outside directors that they could be held personally liable for failing to effectively discharge their oversight responsibilities.[130]

Lessons learned from the Enron and WorldCom director settlement cases for outside directors are that:

- In rare circumstances, they are not immune to personal liability and resulting out-of-pocket costs.
- They should thoroughly investigate the company's culture and management's integrity before accepting a directorship or continuing to serve on an existing board.
- They should be vigilant and effectively discharge their fiduciary duties and oversight function.
- In order to ensure that they have the proper amount of time, effort, and commitment necessary to do the job right, they should not serve on too many boards.
- They should ensure that the company carries adequate D&O insurance.[131]

Lessons learned by plaintiffs, particularly institutional investors, are:

- Outside directors play a vital role in ensuring the effectiveness of corporate governance.
- Do not create undue fear for qualified individuals to serve as outside directors.
- Go after the personal assets of outside directors only in the rare case of pervasive fraud or deliberate self-dealing in carrying out their oversight responsibilities.[132]

Corporations often protect their directors from liability for decisions made on behalf of the company with either an indemnification provision in the corporate charter or with directors' and officers (D&O) insurance. The prescriptive approach used in the Companies Act of 2006 in specifying directors' duties along with the higher standard of skill, care, and due diligence expected of directors could expose directors of U.K. companies to a greater risk of liability.[133] To mitigate such a risk, the Companies Act allows U.K. companies to agree to indemnify directors against claims and liabilities resulting from negligence, default and breach of duty including associated legal costs brought by third parties, or unsuccessful claims brought by the company. Nonetheless, directors are not usually released from such claims and cannot be protected against criminal liabilities and liabilities owed to the company. Companies are allowed to buy directors' and officers' liability insurance for the benefit of directors.[134] It has been argued that recent corporate governance requirements along with the fear of lawsuits and potential legal liabilities have discouraged many potential candidates from accepting outside director job offers. The availability of directors' liability insurance can influence individuals' decisions to accept or reject a directorship. The 2005 survey of SSBI shows that more than half of the surveyed boards in 2005 (51 percent of 149) have changed their D&O insurance coverage in the post-SOX period; about 45 percent have increased the amount of coverage, 17 percent have added Side A (executives' personal assets protection), and another 17 have added a severability provision.[135]

Under the business judgment rule, directors who make decisions in good faith, based on rational reasoning and an informed manner, can be protected from liability on the grounds that they have effectively fulfilled their fiduciary duty of care. In a recent court case decided by the Delaware Chancery Court trial of the Walt Disney Company, the plaintiffs claimed that the directors breached their duties of due care and good faith in failing to sufficiently oversee generous compensation and severance packages for former Disney president Michael Ovitz. The court's decision was that directors did not breach their fiduciary duties to shareholders in deciding to hire Ovitz and then fire him 14 months later at a cost to shareholders of $140 million. The relevant question is to what extent outside directors can breach their fiduciary duties and how irresponsible they can be before facing legal liability. One may be surprised by the answer interpreted by the Delaware Court and a special committee of Krispy Kreme Doughnuts. While harshly criticizing outside directors for nonperformance of their duties, they found that they had acted legally and were not facing any legal responsibility.[136] In the Disney case, the Delaware judge had harsh criticism for Disney directors, but concluded that they had acted legally. In contrast, in the Krispy Kreme Doughnuts case, the special committee strongly criticized the directors' performance but suggested that the company should oppose suits against those directors.[137]

The general consensus in courts and society's perception is that directors are not held liable for ordinary negligence arising from honest mistakes, omission, or taking prudent risks for potentially rewarding business strategies as long as they act on a reasonably informed basis, in good faith, and free of self-serving and conflicts of interest. Therefore, it is a widely accepted proposition under the business judgment rule that directors cannot and are not expected to guarantee corporate success and compliance. Instead, they should be expected to exercise due diligence, avoid conflicts of interest, and act in good faith to build profitable, sustainable performance and should adhere to the letter and spirit of applicable laws, regulations, rules, and corporate governance best practices.

In the absence of director liability reform and clear standards of fiduciary duties of due care and loyalty, directors of public companies should:

- *Exercise due diligence before accepting a board seat.* Candidates for directorship should consider:
  - ○ Corporate culture and the "tone at the top" that govern the CEO and the rest of the company.
  - ○ Time required to carry out fiduciary duties effectively (at least 150 to 200 hours per year).
  - ○ Interest in and knowledge of the company's industry and financial reporting process.
- *Take corporate governance seriously.* Obtain sufficient knowledge of the company's governance structure, board of directors, and board committees, and assess the company's corporate governance measures by comparing them with listing standards and best practices.
- *Pay close attention to transactions with management.* Obtain and review the company's related party transactions and ensure they are properly approved by the board of directors and are fully disclosed. Aggressive related party transactions (e.g., Enron's special purpose entities) can cause problems for directors.
- *Pay close attention to executive compensation.* Review the company's executive compensation schemes to ensure they are properly approved by the board and are fully disclosed. Any excessive executive compensation package can be problematic for the board. Obtain shareholder advisory vote on executive compensation.
- *Focus on compliance.* Review the company's compliance with applicable laws, rules, regulations, and ethical standards, and ensure the company's board of directors oversees the corporation's compliance effectively.
- *Keep the audit committee on the hot seat.* Corporate governance reforms have expanded the roles and responsibilities of the audit committee and the qualifications for their members (e.g., independence, financial expertise). Committee members should ensure that they can meet all enhanced audit committee oversight duties and attributes before considering joining the committee.
- *Pay attention to news about the company.* Review significant press stories and other publications (favorable and unfavorable) about the company.
- *Listen to the company's major shareholders.* Directors, as shareholders' representatives, should communicate with shareholders, pay attention to concerns and issues raised by institutional investors, and consider implementing shareholder proposals that received high "for" votes.
- *Think about independent leadership for the board.* In situations of CEO duality, the independent leadership (e.g., leading or presiding director) of the board should be setting board agendas, evaluating directors and officers, and objectively running the board.

- *Review D&O policies and indemnification provisions.* Obtain sufficient understanding of the company's D&O policies and indemnification provisions to ensure adequate protection is provided. Regarding their liability coverage and claims, the company's directors and others should consider whether:
  - The coverage is adequate for the liability assumed by the D&O.
  - There is a D&O policy that conforms to the company's bylaws.
  - There is a provision in the D&O policy in the case of bankruptcy.
  - Defense costs can be advanced under the D&O policy.
- *Pay attention to emerging developments in corporate governance.* Obtain sufficient knowledge and update their understanding of emerging corporate governance measures including SOX, SEC-related rules, listing standards of national stock exchanges, and best practices.[138]

SUMMARY

Corporate governance reforms have fostered and will continue to enhance directors' oversight effectiveness and accountability. Nevertheless, there is much room for improvement. Many boards need to utilize best practices to empower themselves and become more independent from management, which includes seeking out information about a company from other sources rather than relying exclusively on management. Boards should engage more in strategic decisions including CEO succession, risk management, and consulting executives without micromanaging. The two most prevailing and challenging issues relevant to many boards in the United States continue to be board independence and executive compensation, specifically where pay is effectively linked to financial performance in the post-SOX era. Only the board can address and deal with these two issues effectively.[139] The future trend in the boardroom is toward more outside directors, more diverse representation in terms of expertise and race, an average board size of 10 to 15 directors, and more transparent director election and evaluation.

The six lessons that directors can learn from this chapter are:

1. Understand your fiduciary duties and responsibilities as representatives of shareholders and guardians of their interests in creating sustainable value.
2. Observe all applicable corporate governance reforms (state and federal statutes) and utilize best practices to discharge your oversight responsibilities effectively.
3. Identify your largest shareholders (e.g., institutional investors, pension funds), listen to them, and address their concerns.
4. Maintain appropriate board independence (at least two-thirds), especially when the CEO fills two roles by also serving as chair of the board.
5. Appoint a competent and ethical top management team to run the company, do not micromanage, and have a plan for CEO and director succession.
6. Promote high-quality, reliable, and transparent financial and nonfinancial information in order to earn and maintain public trust and investor confidence.

NOTES

1. Conference Board. 2003. Commission on Public Trust and Private Enterprise. (January). Available at: www.conference-board.org/pdf_free/SR-03-04.pdf.
2. Committee for Economic Development. 2006. Private enterprise, public trust: The state of corporate America after Sarbanes-Oxley. Available at: www.ced. org/newsroom/press/press_2006corgov.pdf.
3. Director's College. 2005. Boardroom Exchange. Presented by the University of Delaware and PricewaterhouseCoopers. (October 27). Available at: www.pwc.com.
4. The State of Delaware. 2005. General Corporation Law. Title 8, Ch. 1, §141 (b). Available at: delcode.delaware.gov/title8/c001/sc04/index.shtml.
5. United States Court of Appeals. For the Second Circuit. 2006. American Federation of State, County and Municipal Employees, Employees Pension Plan vs. American International Group, Inc. (September 5). Docket No. 05-2825-cv.
6. Conference Board. 2003. Corporate governance best practices: A blueprint for the post-Enron era. Available at: www.conference-board.org.
7. National Association of Corporate Directors. 2004. NACD Blue Ribbon Commission report on director professionalism. Available at: www.nacdonline.org.
8. *McKinsey Quarterly*. 2006. What directors know about their companies: A McKinsey survey. (March). Available at: www.mckinseyquarterly.com/article_page.aspx?ar=1769&L2=39.
9. Ibid.
10. Ibid.
11. Paulson, H. M. 2006. Remarks by Treasury Secretary on the competitiveness of U.S. capital markets. Economics Club of New York, New York, (November 20) hp-174. Available at: www.treas.gov/press/releases/hp174.htm.
12. The Working Group on Corporate Governance. 1991. A New Compact for Owners and Directors. *Harvard Business Review* (July-August):141–143.
13. *Black's Law Dictionary*. 1990. 625 (6th edition).
14. Traverse, S. E. 2002. Fiduciary duties of corporate directors and officers. Sacks Tierney, P.A. Attorneys (October). Available at: www.sackstierney.com/articles/fiduciary.htm.
15. Sasso, P. 2003. Searching for trust in not-for-profit boardroom: Looking beyond the duty of obedience to ensure accountability. *UCLA Law Review* 50. Available at: www.uclalaw-review.org/articles/?view=50/6+detail=1.
16. Ibid.
17. Securities and Exchange Commission (SEC). 2000. Selective disclosures and insider trading. Release Nos. 33-7881, 34-43154. Available at: www.sec.gov/rules/final/33-7881.htm.
18. Securities Act of 1933. Available at: www.sec.gov/about/laws/sa33.pdf. Securities Exchange Act of 1934. Available at: www.sec.gov/about/laws/sea34.pdf.
19. Sarbanes-Oxley Act of 2002. Available at: www.sec.gov.about/laws/soa2002.pdf.

20. Morgenson, G. 2006. Sticky scandals, Teflon directors. *New York Times.* (January 29). Available at: select.nytimes.com/2006/01/29/business/business special3/29gret.html.
21. Ibid.
22. The Committee on Capital Markets Regulation. 2006. Interim report of the Committee on Capital Market Regulation. (November 30). Available at: www.capmktsreg.org/research.html.
23. Office of Public Sector Information. The Companies Act 2006. Available at: http://search.opsi.gov.uk/search?q=companies+act+2006+pdf&output=xml_no_dtd&client=opsisearch&proxystylesheet=opsisearch&site=default_collection.
24. Director's College. 2005. Boardroom Exchange. Presented by the University of Delaware and PricewaterhouseCoopers. (October 27). Available at: www.pwc.com.
25. Corporate Board Member/PricewaterhouseCoopers. 2005. What directors think 2005. Corporate Board Member/PwC survey. Available at: www.boardmember.com.
26. UK Combined Code. 2003. Available at: www.frc.org.uk/corporate/combined-code.cfm.
27. Corporate Board Member/PricewaterhouseCoopers 2006 Survey. 2006. What directors think (December). Available at: www.boardmember.com or www.pwc.com/vs.
28. Spencer Stuart. 2006. Spencer Stuart Board Index 2005. *CFO Direct* (January 12). Available at: www.cfodirect.pwc.com/CFODirectWeb/Controller.jpf?NavCode=USAS-6BG34 T.
29. UK Combined Code. 2003.
30. Conference Board. 2003. Commission on Public Trust and Private Enterprise: Corporate governance principles, recommendations, and specific best practice suggestions (January 9). Available at: www.conference-board.org/knowledge/governanceCommission.cfm.
31. Deutsch, C. 2006. Fewer chiefs also serving as chairmen. *New York Times.* Available at: www.nytimes.com/2006/03/17/business/17ceo.html.
32. State Board of Administration (SBA) of Florida. 2006. Corporate Governance Annual Report 2006. Available at: www.sbafla.com.
33. Deutsch, C. 2006. Fewer chiefs also serving as chairmen. *New York Times.* Available at: www.nytimes.com/2006/03/17/business/17ceo.html.
34. Gross, P. M. 2005. Presentation at Stanford Graduate School of Business: Executive education, corporate governance program. (June 3). Available at: www.ced.org.
35. Spencer Stuart. 2006. Spencer Stuart Board Index 2005. *CFO Direct.*
36. Fisher, G. M. C. 2005. Commentary: 2005 Survey of Spencer Stuart Board Index (December 5). Available at: www.spencerstuart.com.
37. Ibid.
38. Spencer Stuart. 2006. Spencer Stuart Board Index 2005.

39. Ibid.
40. Ibid.
41. Ibid.
42. Fisher, G. M. C. 2005. Spencer Stuart Board Index (December 5). Available at: www.spencerstuart.com.
43. Council of Institutional Investors. 2004. Corporate governance policies. (October). Available at: www.cii.org/policies/ind_dir_defn.htm.
44. In re: Oracle Derivative Litigation, C. A. No. 1871, Strine, V. C. (Del. Ch. June 17, 2003). Available at: http://courts.delaware.gov/OPINIONS/(dbwbju55gm max1akkocwit45)/download.ASPx?ID=54350.
45. Ibid.
46. Securities and Exchange Commission. 2006. Executive compensation and related party disclosure. (January 17). FILE NO. S7-03-06. Available at: www.sec.gov/rules/proposed/33-8655.pdf.
47. Ibid.
48. Spencer Stuart. 2006. Spencer Stuart Board Index 2005.
49. Norris, F. 2006. Atmel's mess: You're fired. No, you are. *New York Times* (August 11). Available at: www.nytimes.com.
50. Ibid.
51. Norris, F. 2006. Don't like a director? Spy on him. *New York Times* (September 8). Available at: www.nytimes.com.
52. Ibid.
53. Bebchuk, L. 2006. The SEC: Beyond disclosure. Forbes.com. (January 19). Available at: www.forbes.com/columnists/2006/01/18/sec-executive-comp-comment-cx_lb_0119bebchuk.html.
54. Bebchuk, L. 2005. The myth of the shareholder franchise. Available at: http://papers.ssrn.com/sol3/papers.cfm?abstract_id=829804.
55. Morgensen, G. 2006. Behind every underachiever, an overpaid boar? *New York Times* (January 22). Available at: www.nytimes.com/2006/01/22/business/yourmoney/22suits.html.
56. Spencer Stuart. 2006. Spencer Stuart Board Index 2005.
57. Ibid.
58. Securities and Exchange Commission. 2003. *Audit Committee Financial Expert* (January). Final Rule No. 34-47262: IC-25914. Available at: www.sec.vog/rules/final/34-47262.htm.
59. Ibid.
60. Daum, J. H., and T. J. Neff. 2005. Key trends drive board composition. Spencer Stuart Board Index (SSBI): *Directors and Board* 29 (2 Winter): 58–62.
61. *Catalyst*. 2006. 2005 Catalyst census of women board directors of the Fortune 500 shows 10-year trend of slow progress and persistent challenges. (March 29). Available at: www.catalystwomen.org/pressroom/press_releases/3_29_06%20-%20WBD%20release.pdf.
62. Ibid.

63. *Financial Times*. 2006. The wisdom of diversity: Companies should be more imaginative in recruiting directors. (January 6). Available at: www.financialtimes.com.
64. Ibid.
65. Ibid.
66. Spencer Stuart. 2006. Spencer Stuart Board Index 2005.
67. Allen, T. 2005. Governance Weekly: More companies adopt board age limits. Institutional Shareholder Services (ISS). Available at: www.issproxy.com/governance/publications/2005archived/134.jsp.
68. Spencer Stuart. 2006. Spencer Stuart Board Index 2005.
69. Ibid.
70. Ibid.
71. Ibid.
72. National Association of Corporate Directors. 2004. NACD Blue Ribbon Commission report on director professionalism. Booth, J., and D. Deli. Factors affecting the number of outside directorships held by CEOs. *Journal of Financial Economics* 40: 81–104.
73. Spencer Stuart. 2006. Spencer Stuart Board Index 2005.
74. Ibid.
75. Corporate Library. 2006. Board analyst alert. Available at: www.thecorporatelibrary.com.
76. Corporate Library. 2006. The spread of options backdating: A closer look at the boards and directors involved (October 2). Available at: www.thecorporatelibrary.com.
77. State of Delaware. 2005. General Corporation Law. Title 8, Ch. 1, §141 (b). Available at: delcode.delaware.gov/title8/c001/sc04/index.shtml.
78. Office of Public Sector Information. The Companies Act 2006. Available at: http://search.opsi.gov.uk/search?q=companies+act+2006+pdf&output=xml_no_dtd&client=opsisearch&proxystylesheet=opsisearch&site=default_collection.
79. Jensen, M. C. 1993. The modern industrial revolution: Exit, and the failure of internal control systems. *Journal of Finance* 3: 831–880.
80. Spencer Stuart. 2006. Spencer Stuart Board Index 2005.
81. Corporate Board Member/PricewaterhouseCoopers 2006 Survey. 2006. What directors think (December).
82. Ibid.
83. Pearce, J. A., and S. A. Zahra. 1992. Board composition from a strategic contingency perspective. *Journal of Management Studies* 29: 411–438. Hermalin, B., and M. Weisbach. 1988. The determinants of board composition. *RAND Journal of Economics* 19(4): 589–606.
84. Office of Public Sector Information. The Companies Act 2006.
85. Ibid.
86. London Stock Exchange. 2004. A practical guide to corporate governance. Available at: www.rsmi.co.uk.

87. Council of Institutional Investors. 2006. Council policies: Board of directors. Available at: www.cii.org/policies/boardofdirectors.htm.
88. McTague, J. 2006. Meet Mr. Generosity. *Barron's* (August 11). Available at: http://users2.barrons.com/lmda/do/checkLogin?mg=evo-barrons&url=http%3A%2F%2Fonline.barrons.com%2Farticle%2FSB115594752153140046.html%3Fmod%3Dseekingalpha.
89. Ibid.
90. Sherman & Sterling LLP. 2004. Trends in the corporate governance practices of the 100 largest US public companies. Available at: www.sherman.com/.
91. Ibid.
92. Ibid.
93. Spencer Stuart. 2006. Spencer Stuart Board Index 2005.
94. Corporate Board Member/PricewaterhouseCoopers. 2006 Survey. What directors think.
95. Spencer Stuart. 2006. Spencer Stuart Board Index 2005.
96. Corporate Board Member/PricewaterhouseCoopers 2006 Survey. What directors think.
97. Spencer Stuart. 2006. Spencer Stuart Board Index 2005.
98. Glass Lewis & Co. 2005. Available at: www.glasslewis.com.
99. Foran, M. M. 2005. Commentary: The 2005 Survey of the Spencer Stuart Board Index (December 5). Available at: www.spencerstuart.com.
100. Katz and McIntosh. 2006. Corporate update. Available at: www.law.com/jsp/nylj/corporateUpdateArchive.jsp.
101. Cai, J., J. L. Garner, and R. A. Walking. 2006. Electing directors. Working paper. LeBow College of Business, Drexel University.
102. Ibid.
103. Intel News Release: Intel board adopts majority vote standard for election of directors. 2006. Available at: www.intel.com/pressroom/archive/releases/20060119corp.htm.
104. Nadler, D. A. 2004. Building better boards. *Harvard Business Review*. (May): 102–111.
105. Ibid.
106. London Stock Exchange. 2004. A practical guide to corporate governance.
107. Nasdaq. 2004. Listing standards. Available at: www.nasdaq.com/about/nasdaq_listing_req_fees.pdf. New York Stock Exchange. 2004. Final NYSE corporate governance rules. Available at: www.nyse.com/pdfs/finalcorpgovrules.pdf.
108. Sarbanes-Oxley Act of 2002, Section 407. Available at: www.sec.gov/about/laws/soa2002.pdf. Securities and Exchange Commission. 2003. (January 23).
109. Corporate Board Member/PricewaterhouseCoopers 2006 Survey. What directors think.
110. Corporate Board Member/PricewaterhouseCoopers. 2005. What directors think 2005. Corporate Board Member/PwC survey. Available at: www.boardmember.com.

111. Spencer Stuart. 2006. Spencer Stuart Board Index 2005. *CFO Direct.*
112. Ibid.
113. Corporate Board Member/PricewaterhouseCoopers 2006 Survey. What directors think.
114. Montgomery, C. A., and R. Kaufman. 2003. The board's missing link. *Harvard Business Review* (March): 86–93 and Sonnenfeld, J. A. 2000. What makes great boards great. *Harvard Business Review* (September): 106–113.
115. Sarbanes-Oxley Act. 2002. (July 30). Available at: www.sec.gov/about/laws/soa2002.pdf.
116. Brancato, C. K., and C. A. Plath. 2003. Corporate governance best practices: A Blueprint for the Post-Enron Era. *Conference Board* (May). Available at: www.conference-board.org.
117. Ibid.
118. Yermack, D. 1995. Do corporations award CEO stock options effectively? *Journal of Financial Economics* 39: 237–269.
119. Duryee, T., and K. Peterson. 2004. Younger voices are getting a platform. (October 3). *Seattle Times.* Available at: http://texis.seattletimes.nwsource.com/nw100/static/boards/youngboards.html.
120. Corporate Board Member/PricewaterhouseCoopers. 2005. What directors think.
121. Ibid.
122. Ibid.
123. Ibid.
124. Steffy, L. 2006. Sarbanes-Oxley stifling? Say it with a straight face. *Houston Chronicle* (December 21). Available at www.chron.com.
125. Dash. E. 2006. Who signed off on those options? *New York Times* (August 27). Available at: www.nytimes.com.
126. Ibid.
127. Ibid.
128. Lebowitz, A. P. 2005. The WorldCom directors settlement: The lead plaintiff's perspective. *NAPPA Report* 9 (3 August).
129. Engen, J. R., and C. Deitch. 2005. "Chilling" (What directors think of the Enron/WorldCom settlements). *Corporate Board Member Europe* (Winter). Available at: www.boardmembereurope.com/issues/archive.pl?article_id= 10087.
130. Ibid.
131. Ibid.
132. Ibid.
133. Gibson, Dunn, & Crutcher. 2006. New Companies Act of 2006 ("Companies Act"): Impacts Upon Directors of U.K. Companies (December 7). Available at: www.gibsondunn.com.
134. Ibid.
135. Spencer Stuart. 2006. Spencer Stuart Board Index 2005. *CFO Direct.*
136. Norris, F. 2005. Inept boards need have no fear. *New York Times.* (August 12). Available at: http://events.nytimes.com/2005/08/12/business/12norris.html? 8dpc.

137. Ibid.
138. Dunn, G. 2005. The director settlement at Enron and World Com: Lessons for directors (January 18). Available at: www.gibsondunn.com/practices/publications/detail/id/7661?PublicationID=7701.
139. Clapman, P. 2005. Commentary: The 2005 Survey of Spencer Stuart Board Index (SSBI). (December 5). Available at: www.spencerstuart.com.

CHAPTER 4

Board Committees

INTRODUCTION

The oversight function of corporate governance is typically delegated by the board of directors to various board committees. However, the entire board remains responsible for the oversight of these delegated functions. Each stock exchange has listing standards that require publicly traded companies listed on the exchange (e.g., New York Stock Exchange [NYSE]) to form at least three board committees, including the audit committee, the compensation committee, and the nominating/governance committee, which must consist solely of independent directors, as defined by the exchange. Public companies may also form other special committees (e.g., executive, finance, budget, risk management, litigation, and mergers and acquisition) to address special board projects or conduct independent investigations of alleged misconduct as needed. This chapter discusses the three mandatory committees plus various other committees the board may create.

TYPES OF BOARD COMMITTEES

Boards of directors generally perform their oversight function through committees in order to make efficient use of time and to take advantage of the expertise of individual directors. Committee formations and assignments depend on the size of the company, its board, and assumed responsibilities. Committees of the board of directors are a subset of the board; as such, they address relevant issues and make recommendations for final approval by the entire board of directors. Board committees normally function independently from each other and should have sufficient authority, resources, and delegated responsibilities to effectively assist the entire board in fulfilling its oversight function. These committees are usually formed as a means of improving board effectiveness and efficiency in areas where more focused, specialized, and technically oriented groups are deemed necessary and beneficial for the company. Board committees can bring more focus to the board's oversight function; however, ultimately the entire board remains responsible for fulfilling this function, which includes holding management accountable for the performance of the company.

The 2005 survey of the Spencer Stuart Board Index (SSBI) reveals that:

- The median number of board standing committees for Standard & Poor's (S&P) 500 boards remains at four with 29 percent having four committees; 28 percent have five committees.
- The number of S&P 500 boards with six or more committees is down to 15 percent in the post-SOX period from 45 percent in 2000.
- In nearly 100 percent of S&P 500 boards, the three mandatory committees (audit, compensation, nominating/governance) are composed entirely of independent directors.
- Besides the three mandatory board committees, the executive and finance committees are most common.
- A small but growing number of S&P 500 boards have added committees focused on science and technology (5 percent); environment, health, and safety (5 percent); and legal/compliance issues (4 percent).[1]

Audit Committee

An audit committee comprising at least three independent directors is required under the listing standards to implement and support the oversight function of the board, specifically in areas related to internal controls, risk management, financial reporting, and audit activities.

Compensation Committee

A compensation committee comprising at least three independent directors is required to implement and support the oversight function of the board, particularly in areas relevant to the design, review, and implementation of directors' and executives' evaluation and compensation plans.

Nominating/Governance Committee

A nominating committee comprising at least three independent directors is required under the listing standards to implement and support the oversight function of the board pertaining to identifying and recommending candidates for nomination to the board and to oversee the director election process. This committee is also involved with: (1) internal corporate governance matters at the company, such as drafting an ethics code of conduct and a corporate governance policy; and (2) communications with or from shareholders, including responding to individual proposals voted on by shareholders at the annual meeting.

Special Committees

The board of directors may form special committees to assist the board in carrying out its strategic and oversight functions, including financing, budgeting, investment, risk management, special litigation or investigative issues, and mergers and acquisitions.

Special committees should consist only of independent, nonexecutive directors. The finance committee can be formed to:

- Approve the company's major transactions with defined characteristics (e.g., mergers and acquisitions, research and development) or a specified threshold (e.g., above $100,000).
- Provide guidance on the company's financial decisions and policies.
- Advise management on enterprise risk management activities.

The board's risk management committee is usually established to provide oversight of the company's risk management matters regarding credit, market, operations, legal compliance, liquidity, and reputation. A special litigation or investigation committee comprising solely independent directors may be formed to hire outside legal counsel to conduct an independent investigation in the event of allegations of misconduct involving directors, officers, or employees or to oversee complex litigation matters that have the potential to expose the company to large losses.

The remainder of this chapter discusses in detail the three mandatory independent board committees.

AUDIT COMMITTEE

The analysis of the reported financial scandals of the late 1990s and the early 2000s points to a consistent pattern of lapses in the audit committee oversight function. This raises the question: Where was the audit committee? Audit committees should function to protect investors' interests by taking the lead on oversight responsibilities in the areas of internal controls, financial reporting, audit activities, and compliance with applicable laws, and regulations. Over the years, the audit committee has evolved from a voluntary committee to a required committee.[2]

Corporate governance reforms have provided new challenges and opportunities for audit committees. To address these challenges and opportunities effectively, audit committees are seeking an appropriate balance between advising management and overseeing its performance in the areas of financial reporting; risk management; internal controls; audit functions; legal compliance; and the establishment of a whistleblowing program and an business code of ethics. Securities and Exchange Commission (SEC) rules prohibit the listing of any security of an issuer (public company) that is not in compliance with the audit committee requirements established by the Sarbanes-Oxley Act (SOX). These requirements pertain to:

- The independence of audit committee members.
- The audit committee's responsibility to appoint and oversee the company's independent accountant.
- Procedures for handling complaints regarding the company's accounting practices.
- The authority of the audit committee to engage advisors.
- Funding for the independent auditor and any outside advisors engaged by the audit committee.

Audit Committee Relationships with Other Corporate Governance Participants

Relationship with the Board of Directors   The audit committee is one of the major standing committees on a company's board of directors and as such works with the other board committees (compensation, nomination/governance) to fulfill the board's fiduciary duties to shareholders and other stakeholders. Members of the audit committee often interact with members of other board committees in oversight functions pertaining to financial reporting, compensation, and the nomination process. In addition, minutes of meetings of all committees are presented and approved by the entire board.

Working Relationships with Management   The audit committee should interact with management by asking relevant and thought-provoking questions pertaining to the company's strategy, financial performance, corporate governance structure, internal controls, financial reporting, audit activities, legal matters, risk assessment, codes of ethics, and whistleblower programs. Senior executives (chief executive officer [CEO], chief financial officer [CFO], and general counsel) should inform the audit committee of significant events and transactions that substantially affect the company's risk management. Prior to SOX, audit committees were criticized for not sufficiently overseeing the legal and risk management function, including the impact of weak internal controls on the quality of publicly disclosed financial reports.

Working Relationships with External Auditors   As a result of SOX, the audit committee is now responsible for the hiring, firing, and compensation of the independent auditors as well as overseeing their work. External auditors are held ultimately accountable to the entire board. However, the audit committee as a representative of the board facilitates the efficient and effective functioning of the board in overseeing auditors. The open and candid communications between the audit committee and external auditors should preserve the independence of the auditors from undue management influence and empower the audit committee to discharge its oversight responsibilities effectively on behalf of the entire board of directors. Audit committees must approve all audit and any permissible nonaudit consulting services, if any, provided by the external auditors to the company or its senior executives or directors, and they should also review the auditors' audit scope, plan, and findings. The audit committee should also not agree to permit the external auditors to artificially limit their liability for a failed audit in advance of conducting the audit through the use of limitation of liability provisions in the engagement letter or other side agreements with the company.

As part of the audit of internal controls, the external auditors evaluate the effectiveness of the audit committee. Ineffective committees may be considered material weaknesses in internal control.[3] Thus, a dual evaluation of the committee's performance by the external auditors creates a check-and-balance process that should be guarded from potential conflicts of interest. The audit committee should have access to and, when warranted, review all engagement letters signed between the independent auditors and their clients for providing all preapproved audit and any nonaudit consulting services. In addition, the committee should receive from the independent auditors a detailed summary of each engagement describing the service involved, related fees, and rationale that show the provided services are compatible with the auditor independence rules. In the post-SOX era, independent, external auditors work with management at the direction of the audit committee which is a significant improvement.

Working Relationships with Internal Auditors The audit committee is responsible for the hiring, firing, overseeing, and compensation of the head of the internal audit department (chief audit executive [CAE]). Internal auditors should report their audit findings directly to the audit committee and ultimately be accountable to that committee rather than management. This working relationship requires open, readily accessible, and candid communication between the internal auditor and the audit committee without undue influence from management. The committee should have a clear understanding of internal auditing policies, processes, practices, and findings.

Audit Committee Principles

The ten audit committee principles that follow provide comprehensive guidance for audit committees to fulfill their oversight function effectively. These principles are extracted from SOX, SEC-related rules, the Blue Ribbon Committee (BRC) recommendations, and KPMG Audit Committee Institute's publication.

1. *Audit committee formation.* Public companies should establish audit committees tailored to their corporate governance structure and unique corporate culture and characteristics—one size does not fit all.
2. *Independence.* Audit committees should be composed solely of independent directors.
3. *Members' qualifications.* At a minimum, all members of the audit committee should be financially literate with one member designated as the committee financial expert; members should also be knowledgeable, experienced, informed, vigilant, and diligent, possessing these qualities:
   a. General understanding of the company's major economic, business, operating, legal, and financial risk.
   b. A broad knowledge of the interrelationship of the company's operations and financial reporting.
   c. A clear understanding of the difference between the company's decision-making function delegated to management and its oversight function assumed by the audit committee.
   d. Ability to formulate and ask probing questions about the company's operations, business, internal control, financial reporting process and audit activities.
   e. Courage to challenge management when necessary.
4. *Authority.* The board of directors should delegate to the audit committee authority to carry out its assigned oversight responsibilities, including the

authority to: hire, compensate, and fire both the independent auditor and the internal auditor; engage independent counsel and other advisors; and conduct any investigations deemed necessary to fulfill its oversight responsibilities.

5. *Funding.* The audit committee should be provided with sufficient funding for payment and compensation to the independent auditor, the internal auditor (CAE), legal counsel, and other advisors.

6. *Oversight function.* At a minimum, the audit committee should be responsible for overseeing internal control, financial reporting, risk assessments, internal auditing, codes of ethics, whistleblower programs, and external auditing.

7. *Accountability.* The audit committee should be ultimately accountable to the board of directors as representative of all stakeholders, particularly shareholders. To fulfill this accountability, the committee should report quarterly to the board, and annually to shareholders, about its activities, achievements, and performance. The committee should also be evaluated annually for the achievement of its objectives.

8. *Charter.* The audit committee should have a written charter tailored to the company that clearly describes its authority, resources, funding, duties, oversight responsibilities, structure, process, independence, membership qualifications and requirements, and relationship with management, the internal auditor, and the independent auditor.

9. *Agenda.* A comprehensive, written, and well-developed agenda will help the audit committee focus on its mission and fulfillment of its oversight responsibilities. The agenda should be prepared in advance with inputs from the management, internal auditor, independent auditor, legal counsel, and other personnel involved. It also should be effectively carried out and properly documented.

10. *Orientation, training, and continued education.* There should be an orientation program for newly appointed audit committee members, and all members should participate in annual training and continuing education programs to keep abreast of emerging initiatives and developments affecting their job performance.[4]

Audit Committee Composition

The composition of the audit committee can have a significant impact on its effectiveness. The sections that follow cover audit committee composition in terms of size, independence, qualifications, attributes, and resources.

Committee Size   The audit committee should consist of at least three independent directors. The size of the audit committee usually ranges from three to six members, whereas SEC rules and listing standards for public companies require at least three independent members. The average number of audit committee members has remained constant in the post-SOX period at about four per company board. The 2004 SSBI survey shows that:

■ The average number of directors on the audit committee of S&P 500 companies was 4.17 in 2004 compared with 4.23 and 4.35 in 2003 and 2002, respectively.

- About 26 percent of audit committee members are active chairs, presidents, or CEOs.
- 21 percent of the audit committee members are retired chairs, presidents, and CEOs.
- The number of audit committee members with accounting backgrounds including CFOs rose to 9 percent in 2004 from 5 percent in 2003.
- About 12 percent of audit committee members are active and retired human resources, strategy, and operations professionals.[5]

Independence The audit committee should be composed of independent, nonexecutive, outside directors. SEC rules and listing standards require audit committee members to be independent by not:

- Receiving any compensation other than what they are paid as a board member.
- Providing any advisory or consulting services to the company they serve or its affiliates or other business ties.
- Having been employed by the company or its affiliates within the past five years.
- Having been a member of the immediate family of the company's executives or its affiliates within the past five years.[6]

Member Qualifications At least one of the members of the audit committee should be designated as a financial expert. However, the other members of the audit committee should be financially literate. The SEC defines the term "audit committee financial expert" and how that term applies to the committee, especially in relationship to required disclosures.[7] The final rules define an audit committee financial expert as a person who has all of these attributes:

- An understanding of generally accepted accounting principles (GAAP) and financial statements.
- The ability to assess the general application of such principles in connection with the accounting for estimates, accruals, and reserves.
- Experience in preparing, auditing, analyzing, or evaluating financial statements that present a breadth and level of complexity that are generally comparable to the breadth and complexity of issues that can reasonably be expected to be raised by the registrant's financial statements, or experience actively supervising one or more persons engaged in such activities.
- An understanding of internal controls and procedures for financial reporting.
- An understanding of audit committee functions.

Under the SEC rules, a person must have acquired such attributes in any one or more of these ways:

- Education and experience as a principal financial officer, principal accounting officer, controller, public accountant, or auditor or experience in one or more positions that involve the performance of similar functions.

- Experience actively supervising a principal financial officer, principal accounting officer, controller, public accountant, auditor, or person performing similar functions.
- Experience overseeing or assessing the performance of companies or public accountants with respect to the preparation, auditing, or evaluation of financial statements.
- Other relevant experience.

A company that discloses that it does not have an audit committee financial expert must explain the reason why. If a company discloses that it has an audit committee financial expert, it also must disclose the expert's name. The SEC rules permit, but do not require, a company to disclose that it has more than one audit committee financial expert on its audit committee. The SEC rules also require a company to disclose whether the person(s) identified as the audit committee financial expert is independent of management.

The trend toward the increasing number of audit committee designated financial experts has continued in the post-SOX era. A 2006 survey of 700 audit committees members at 178 public companies reveals that: (1) the majority of surveyed audit committees have at least one designated member as audit committee financial expert; (2) about 23 percent of designated financial experts have an accounting background; (3) the number of audit committee members who are accountants doubled from 5 percent in 2002 to 11 percent in 2005; (4) the number of audit committees with at least one accountant increased from 20 percent in 2002 to 38 percent in 2005.[8] This survey suggests that accountants are steadily infiltrating audit committees.

Member Attributes   All members of the audit committee should have these attributes:

- Ability to understand financial reports.
- Commitment and availability in terms of time and effort required to serve.
- Status as an independent party.
- Integrity and objectivity.
- Due diligence.
- Ability to maintain confidentiality.
- Ability to accept assigned oversight responsibilities.
- Ability to assume accountability.
- Ability to use informed judgments.
- Ability to demonstrate leadership ability.
- A sufficient understanding of the legal and regulatory framework of public companies.

Authority/Resources   SOX, in recognizing the increased responsibilities assigned to audit committees, authorized them to engage independent counsel and other outside advisors as they determined necessary and required the company to provide appropriate funding for such advisors. Given that at least one member of the audit committee is designated as a financial expert and the audit committee receives accounting advice from both internal and external auditors, should the committee be authorized to have an accounting advisor? In normal circumstances, the committee should obtain financial and accounting assistance from the company's management and internal and external auditors. In a limited situation, when significant matters arise that indicate the use of overly aggressive accounting treatments and the possibility of fraudulent financial activities involving management and possibly the external auditors, or in understanding complex accounting rules, policies, and practices (derivatives, leases, pensions, postretirement), the audit committee should be in a position to retain its own independent accounting advisor or forensic investigator.

Audit Committee Responsibility

The audit committee carries out responsibilities delegated to it by the entire board of directors. Thus, the primary responsibility of the committee is to represent shareholders (owners) and other stakeholders and protect their interests. Responsibilities usually delegated to the audit committee pertain to corporate governance, internal controls, financial reporting, and audit activities. It is important to note that: (1) audit committee responsibilities pertain to oversight functions rather than managerial functions; and (2) any of the listed responsibilities can be assumed by the company's board of directors or assigned to other committee(s) of the board.

Audit committee responsibilities may include but are not necessarily limited to:

- Overseeing the effectiveness of corporate governance.
- Appointing, compensating, and retaining independent auditors and overseeing their activities, including audit and permissible nonaudit services.
- Reviewing financial reports, including the annual audited financial statement and quarterly reviewed financial statements by independent auditors.
- Overseeing the effectiveness of the design and operations of internal control over financial reporting.
- Reviewing management and auditor reports on internal control over financial reporting.
- Approving audit and permissible nonaudit services.
- Overseeing the internal audit function, including hiring, compensating, and firing the CAE (the head of internal audit department).
- Overseeing the establishment and operation of whistleblower programs and procedures.
- Overseeing the establishment and implementation of the company's code of ethical conduct.
- Reviewing earnings releases and information provided to analysts and credit rating agencies.
- Overseeing management risk assessment relevant to financial reporting and antifraud programs.

- Communicating with the company's legal counsel matters related to possible violation of laws and regulations, and informing independent auditors regarding these matters.
- Reporting audit committees' roles, responsibilities, functions, and performance quarterly to the company's board of directors and annually to the shareholders.
- Other responsibilities assigned to the audit committee by the company's board of directors.[9]

These oversight responsibilities can be grouped into eight categories.

1. *Corporate governance.* The audit committee, as one of the crucial and influential participants of the company's corporate governance, should participate with other board committees (compensation, nominating) in overseeing the effectiveness of corporate governance without assuming a managerial responsibility.
2. *Internal controls.* The audit committee should oversee the effectiveness of both design and operation of the company's internal control structure. The audit committee's oversight of Sections 302 and 404 on internal control over financial reporting is becoming more important as management certifies internal controls and reports on their effectiveness over financial reporting. The audit committee should:
   a. Know the senior executive who is directly responsible and ultimately accountable for Sections 302 and 404 compliance.
   b. Understand the process of establishing and maintaining adequate and effective internal control.
   c. Understand procedures for assessing the effectiveness of both the design and operation of internal control over financial reporting.
   d. Understand the proper documentation of compliance with Section 404.
   e. Review management's report on the effectiveness of internal control over financial reporting.
   f. Review auditor reports expressing an opinion on management's assessment of the effectiveness of internal control over financial reporting.
   g. Evaluate the identified significant deficiencies and material weaknesses in internal control.
   h. Be satisfied with management and auditor efforts and reports on internal control over financial reporting.
   i. Ensure that management has properly addressed the identified material weaknesses and taken remediation actions to correct them.
3. *Financial reporting.* The audit committee should oversee the financial reporting process by reviewing annual and quarterly financial statements including: management discussion and analysis (MD&A), accounting principles, practices, estimates, and reserves, and independent auditors' suggestions, comments, adjusting, and classification entries. The audit committee is responsible for overseeing the integrity, reliability, quality, and transparency of the company's financial disclosures.

4. *Audit activities.* The audit committee is responsible for overseeing both internal and external audit activities. It has the direct responsibility for hiring, compensating, and firing the company's independent auditor and CAE. Sections 201 and 202 of SOX require the company's audit committee to preapprove all audit and permissible nonaudit services. The preapproval of permissible nonaudit services may be delegated to a member of the audit committee, who must present preapproved nonaudit services to the full committee in its regular meeting. Thus, the audit committee must establish preapproval policies and procedures to:
   a. Increase the audit committee knowledge and understanding of all permissible nonaudit services.
   b. Evaluate the qualifications of providers of preapproved nonaudit services.
   c. Select the best provider considering reinforcement of auditor independence from management.

   Both the independent auditor and the CAE should be held ultimately accountable to the audit committee, which should receive and review reports of the independent auditors on financial statements and internal control over financial reporting. The audit committee should also receive and review significant internal audit reports.

5. *Code of ethics conduct.* The audit committee is responsible for overseeing the establishment and enforcement of the company's code of ethical conduct to ensure that an appropriate "tone at the top" policy is designed and implemented to promote ethical conduct throughout the company. Corporate governance reforms (SOX, SEC rules, listing standards, best practices) discussed in Chapter 1 requires that public companies adopt and disclose codes of ethical conduct for their directors, officers, and employees. The audit committee should oversee the company's compliance with the requirements for establishing and disclosing this code.

6. *Whistleblower program.* The audit committee is responsible for overseeing the establishment and enforcement of whistleblower programs in compliance with the requirements of SOX and SEC-related rules. SOX created the opportunity for confidential and anonymous submissions of complaints by requiring that the company's audit committee establish procedures for receiving, recording, retaining, and treating such complaints. Section 301 of SOX requires audit committees of public companies to establish effective programs and procedures for handling the concerns and complaints of whistleblowers.[10] Pursuant to the passage of SOX, concerned employees are enabled to report financial and accounting irregularities as well as fraud without undue fear of suffering demotion, suspension, harassment, threats, loss of job, or any other form of retribution. To implement provisions of SOX pertaining to whistleblowers effectively, public companies should establish whistleblower programs and procedures that enable employees to report suspected incidents of misconduct anonymously. These programs and procedures encompass establishing an effective hotline with a toll-free number and the capability to accept collect calls, a fax number, a regular mail address or post office box, and a confidential Web site.

7. *Enterprise risk management.* The audit committee is responsible for overseeing the company's enterprise risk management and making sure it is suitable in identifying business events and transactions, their related risks and opportunities, management risk tolerance and actions taken to monitor and minimize risks threatening the integrity and reliability of financial reports. Boards of directors and audit committees have been criticized for not paying proper attention to the company's risk management and risk appetites and their potential impacts on the integrity, reliability, and quality of financial reports even in the post-SOX era.

8. *Financial statement fraud.* A vigilant oversight function of the board of directors, particularly the audit committee, can play an important role in the prevention, detection, and deterrence of financial statement fraud. KPMG suggests that the audit committee oversight function can assist in the prevention and detection of financial statement fraud in nine ways:

   a. Assessing management's process designed for the identification and mitigation of fraud risk as well as prevention and detection of fraud.

   b. Promoting the tone at the top and reinforcing a zero-tolerance policy for fraud.

   c. Evaluating employment opportunities and procedures to recruit competent and ethical employees including background checks on key personnel.

   d. Overseeing management's internal control over financial reporting, including contemplating the incentives and opportunities for management override of and inappropriate influence over internal control.

   e. Analyzing the reasonableness of financial results in comparison with prior or forecasted results, including a review of material resources.

   f. Assessing management's policies, accounting practices, and documentation for material estimates used in financial statements.

   g. Assessing management's policies, accounting practices, and documentation regarding processing of journal entries and reporting cycle closing process.

   h. Establishing a whistleblower program and process for receipt, retention, and investigation of confidential information and concerns about fraud and unethical behavior.

   i. Overseeing management's processes and procedures for the design, implementation, and documentation of antifraud programs and measures.[11]

The audit committee's role in financial reporting, internal controls, and auditing activities is more commonly accepted, but its role in risk management activities, whistleblower programs, financial statement fraud, and business ethics is not yet fully utilized.

Audit Committee Effectiveness

PricewaterhouseCoopers (PwC) suggests six ways in which audit committee effectiveness can be significantly improved.

1. *Making the work plan risk-oriented.* Audit committee effectiveness will be improved if it focuses on the top risk areas, including the key financial risks, and areas with less robust control functions.

2. *Understanding the business.* Audit committee members should be sufficiently knowledgeable about the company's operations, particularly in diversified or geographically diffuse areas.
3. *Providing an objective view in reporting judgments.* Executives (CEOs, CFOs) make inherently subjective assessments and judgments in producing external financial reports in order to make the company look good financially. It is the audit committee's job to challenge the quality of financial reports where necessary by overseeing the financial reporting process.
4. *Gauging the "health" of the corporate culture.* Audit committees should be involved in companies' codes of conduct and ethical guidance by setting an appropriate tone at the top of promoting ethical conduct and compliance with applicable rules, regulations, and standards.
5. *Keeping up to date.* The ever-increasing laws, regulations, rules, standards, and other requirements for public companies necessitate that audit committee members keep abreast of these measures and their relevance to their companies.
6. *Assessing performance.* Audit committees' performance should be assessed periodically. The method(s) of assessments can be formal or less formal self-assessment, peer review, or via an outside facilitator. The purpose of the performance assessment is to identify and address deficiencies and improve audit committee effectiveness.[12]

Audit Committee Meetings/Agendas

Audit committee meetings should provide a forum for candid, open, and constructive dialogue among committee members, management, internal auditors, and external auditors. The committee's chair should set the tone for the nature, content, substance, flow, agenda, discussion, frequency, and the length of these meetings. The quality and quantity of audit committee meetings can have a significant impact on its effectiveness in fulfilling the board's oversight responsibilities. Those individuals who typically should participate in meetings are all of the members of the audit committee, senior executives (CEO, CFO, controller, and general counsel), internal auditors (CAE), external auditors, and others who can contribute to or be responsible for issues discussed in the meetings.

The audit committee should also have private or executive meetings with both internal and external auditors as needed when there are major issues that would be better addressed without management present. A combination of formal audit committee meetings with senior executives present and executive meetings with just internal and/or external auditors should improve the effectiveness of audit committee oversight functions. The perception of internal auditors as the "eyes and ears" of the audit committee suggests that the head of the internal audit department should attend all formal committee meetings. The emergence of the integrated audit of financial statements and internal control over financial reporting underscores the importance of the attendance of the audit firm's lead partner at all important formal audit committee meetings, particularly those pertaining to the oversight function of financial risk, internal control over financial reporting, and audit activities directly affecting the integrity, reliability, quality, and transparency of financial statements audited by the independent, external auditors.

The frequency of audit committee meetings and how members should participate depend on the extent of the audit committee's involvement in the company's oversight functions, the responsibilities assigned to it, and the activities it undertakes. The committee should meet at least four times a year to review the company's quarterly financial reports and as needed to address other important issues and engage in other oversight functions (internal control, audit activities, whistleblower programs, and risk assessment). A 2006 survey of 700 audit committee members of 178 public companies shows that the average number of audit committee meetings almost doubled in the post-SOX period from 5 in 2002 to 10 in 2005.[13]

The audit committee should have a well-defined, well-structured, and well-conducted written agenda for all of its meetings. The agenda should cover:

- The minutes of the previous meeting.
- A review of current financial statements and the related audit report, treatment of complex and unusual transactions, accounting principles, policies and practices, and the valuation of assets, determination of liabilities, and estimates of reserves.
- A review of the current management and independent auditor reports on internal control over financial reporting, including the identified significant deficiencies and material weaknesses in the design and operation of internal controls and management responses to reported material weaknesses by the independent auditor.
- A review of the established whistleblower programs, such as the consideration of reported complaints or concerns pertaining to internal control, corporate governance, audit activities, and financial reporting, and the appropriate responses to those complaints.
- A review of the company's enterprise risk management to ensure objectives are defined, risks are identified and assessed, and proper policies and procedures are designed to minimize the risks.
- A review of both internal and external auditors, audit plans, scope, and findings.

Audit Committee Reporting

There are typically three formal audit committee reports: regular status reports, the annual report to the board, and the annual report to shareholders.

The audit committee's regular reports or minutes of its meetings to the company's board of directors should describe the committee's agenda, activities, deliberations, and recommendations. In addition to this regular report, the audit committee should prepare and submit a formal annual report to the board, summarizing its authorities, duties, oversight responsibilities, resources, funding, diligence process, performance, activities, recommendations, and deliberations for the past year and its agenda for the coming year. Also, the audit committee should prepare and submit a formal annual report to the company's shareholders, recommending that financial statements prepared in accordance with generally accepted accounting principles (GAAP) be included in the annual report on Form 10-K or Form 10-KSB. The committee should adopt a charter and show that it has satisfied its oversight responsibilities in compliance with the established charter as specified in the proxy statement. The audit committee's reporting responsibilities are primarily to the board of directors and shareholders, even though it should communicate with a variety of corporate governance participants, including management, internal auditors, legal counsel, financial advisors, and external auditors.

The audit committee should indicate in its report to shareholders whether the committee has:

- Reviewed and discussed the audited financial statements with management.
- Discussed with the independent auditor those matters required to be communicated with the audit committee in accordance with applicable standards (e.g., Public Company Accounting Oversight Board [PCAOB] auditing standards, independence rules).
- Received from the independent auditor the independent disclosures and discussed with him or her matters relevant to auditor independence.
- Recommended to the company's board of directors, based on discussions with management and the independent auditor, that audited financial statements be included in the annual report on Form 10-K or Form 10-KSB to be filed with the SEC.[14]

The format and content of the report depend on the size of the audit committee, its assumed oversight responsibilities, the number of meetings during the year, and the number of designated audit committee financial experts (a minimum of one). The audit committee should tailor its report according to the oversight responsibilities assumed and its performance during the year. A typical audit committee report to shareholders consists of five paragraphs.

Paragraph 1. Describes the formation and composition of the audit committee.

Paragraph 2. Describes the responsibilities of the company's management, the independent auditor, and the audit committee pertaining to internal control over financial reporting and the preparation of financial statements.

Paragraph 3. States that the audit committee has met with both the company's management and the independent auditor to discuss the preparation of financial statements in conformity with GAAP and the performance of a financial audit in accordance with PCAOB auditing standards. This paragraph also explains the committee's communication about accounting, auditing, and internal control issues with both management and the independent auditor.

Paragraph 4. Addresses auditor independence, and states that the company's independent auditor has provided to the audit committee the written disclosures required by the Independent Standard Board Standard No. 1 and has discussed auditor independence with the external auditor. This paragraph also describes provisions of nonaudit services that are compatible with maintaining auditor independence.

Paragraph 5. States that, based on the audit committee's discussion with the company's management and the independent auditor, the committee recommended that the board of directors include audited financial statements in its filings with the SEC on Form 10-K.

The audit committee report to the shareholders should be tailored to the company's corporate governance structure and meet the SEC's regulatory requirements and listing standards of the national stock exchanges. A review of several recent audit committee reports including the 2006 audit committee report of The Home Depot, suggests that these reports should contain eight key themes.

1. *Composition of the audit committee.* This section includes the number and names of all audit committee members, the name of the designated audit committee financial expert (at least one member), and a statement that all members are independent and meet the independence requirements of the SEC and listing standards.
2. *Audit committee charter.* The audit committee should act under a written charter that sets forth its duties, oversight responsibilities, composition, meetings, authority, and resources. The audit committee charter should be attached to the company's proxy statement once every three years and/or made available on the company's Web site and available in print, free of charge, upon request.
3. *Audit committee meeting.* This section states the number of times the audit committee met during the year, including meetings with principal financial officers (CEO, CFO), internal auditors, external auditors, general counsel, and others.
4. *Review of financial reports.* This section includes a statement that the audit committee reviews the company's quarterly and annual reports, including MD&A of financial condition and results of operations. This review section should indicate that the committee discusses the annual reports with the company's management, and reviews audit reports on financial statements and internal control over financial reporting as well as quarterly financial reports reviewed by the auditor, and related matters, such as the quality (not just the acceptability) of the company's accounting principles, critical accounting policies, alternative methods of accounting under GAAP, and other financial disclosures.
5. *Audit committee's role in internal control reporting.* The audit committee should review management's report on internal control required under Section 404 of SOX, including plans for documenting, testing, and assessing internal controls, results of the assessment, deficiencies discovered, and remediation taken. The committee should also review the audit report on internal control over financial reporting, including the scope of the audit, the opinion issued, control deficiencies, and material weaknesses identified by the auditors.
6. *Policy-making responsibility of the audit committee.* In compliance with relevant SEC rules and listing standards, the audit committee often engages in establishing certain policies, including procedures for the receipt, retention, and

anonymous consideration of complaints regarding financial and control matters and recruiting of personnel who were formerly employed by the company's public accounting firms. The committee should also oversee the appropriateness of management policies pertaining to the financial reporting process, including risk management and the use of derivative instruments.

7. *Matters discussed with the independent auditors.* To oversee the company's audit activities effectively, the audit committee may address these issues with the independent auditors:

 a. Whether any significant judgments made by management in the preparation of the financial statements would have been made differently had the auditors themselves been responsible for the preparation.

 b. Whether the company's financial statements fairly present to investors its financial position and performance for the reporting period in accordance with GAAP and SEC disclosure requirements.

 c. Whether the company has implemented and maintained adequate and effective internal controls.

 d. Whether the auditors received any communication or discovered any information indicating any improprieties regarding the company's accounting and reporting procedures and financial reports.

 e. That the auditor will be retained and may raise any concerns about the company's financial reporting directly with the audit committee.

8. *Audit committee activities during the reporting period.* Committee activities should include:

 a. Review and discussion of the audited financial statements with management and the independent auditor.

 b. Review of the auditor independence.

 c. Any recommendation regarding the audited financial statements.

 d. Review of the fees paid to the independent auditors.

 e. Consideration of the company's policy regarding the retention of the auditor.

Even in the post-SOX era audit committees are not being effectively utilized, according to the report by PricewaterhouseCoopers (PwC) that calls for an audit committee discussion and analysis (ACD&A) in annual reports.[15] The ACD&A should address accounting policy and practice issues that were discussed with the company's management and its auditors (both internal and external), financial risks and related internal controls being considered, and how the audit committee satisfies itself that financial reports are accurate, complete, and transparent. Audit committee reports to shareholders should further discuss:

- Management and the independent auditor reports on internal control over financial reporting.
- The audit committee's oversight responsibility over internal controls.
- The company's preapproval policies and procedures for both audit and nonaudit services.
- Audit committee whistleblower programs.

- Audit committee involvement in hiring, retaining, and overseeing the work of independent auditors, and the overall assessment of the audit quality and the effectiveness of independent audit of financial statements.

Legal Liability of Audit Committees

Some question whether the enhanced oversight responsibility of the audit committee—particularly its direct responsibility for appointment, retention, compensation, and oversight of the work of independent auditors—creates any new legal exposures for the committee as a subset of the entire board of directors. The answer is probably not, since the audit committee has been empowered by SOX and now has better-defined authority and responsibilities to assist it in being more effective. Nonetheless any remote potential for increased legal exposure should:

- Not have an adversarial impact on audit committee members' decision-making attitude and process in the sense that members should continue to base their decisions and actions on sound and justifiable professional standards, ethical behavior, and professional judgments.
- Encourage the audit committee to prepare proper documentation of its agenda for meetings, discussions, deliberation processes, minutes of meetings, and decisions made and actions taken by the committee to fulfill its oversight responsibility.
- Promote the preparation and retention of detailed meeting minutes and sufficient deliberation and discussion of issues related to the board's oversight decisions and function.

Audit Committee Fees

The increased audit committee efforts and commitments in terms of the frequency and length of meetings along with the remote potential for increased board of director and audit committee liability have had some positive impact on committee member fees. The 2004 SSBI survey shows that:

- The average retainer amount paid to audit committee members by S&P 500 companies in 2004 increased more than 32 percent compared with 2003.
- The average retainer fee paid to audit committee members was about 6 percent higher than the amount paid to members of other committees in 2004.
- The average retainer of audit committee chairpersons was about 85 percent higher than the average retainer paid to chairpersons of other committees.
- The highest audit committee chairperson retainer paid in 2004 was $96,000 by Monster Worldwide.[16]

Audit Committee Performance Evaluation

Although SOX and SEC rules do not directly address audit committee performance evaluation, listing standards require that the audit committees of listed companies perform an annual performance assessment, including a self-assessment by the full board. Listing standards, however, do not provide any guidance pertaining to the format, content, or the method of such assessment. Thus, the board of directors and the audit committee can tailor this evaluation to the company's corporate governance structure. The board of directors should decide who will perform the audit committee performance assessment, the format of the evaluation process, and the documentation process. The self-evaluation of audit committee members should be discussed with each member of the committee and reviewed by the entire board of directors. Recommendations are made for further consideration by the board. Criteria typically used in the audit committee self-evaluation are:

- Knowledge, skill sets, experience, and expertise.
- Leadership ability and judgment.
- Commitment to achieve audit committee's mission, duties, and oversight responsibilities.
- Meeting attendance.

COMPENSATION COMMITTEE

The compensation committee usually is formed to determine the compensation and benefits of directors and executives. To be effective and objective, the compensation committee should be composed solely of independent outside directors with sufficient human resources experience in compensation and related issues. This committee should hire outside compensation advisors who report directly to and are compensated by the committee to ensure objectivity and independence from management. The recent debate over the reasonableness of executive compensations, recognition of stock-based compensations as a compensation expense, and the pervasiveness of the illegal backdating of executive stock option grants have continued to generate a considerable amount of interest in the formation and function of the compensation committee. Shareholders believe the link between executive pay and company financial performance needs to be strengthened. In addition, the growing gap between executive pay and average worker pay (430 to 1) must be addressed. The compensation committee is responsible for disclosing the company's pay philosophy and performance metrics and establishing compensation plans that retain qualified directors, executives, and employees while motivating optimal performance that creates long-term shareholder value.

Compensation Committee Principles

The Council of Institutional Investors (CII) suggests these principles and practices for ensuring the effectiveness of the compensation committee:

- *Structure.* The compensation committee should be composed solely of independent directors who rotate periodically, are knowledgeable or take responsibility to become knowledgeable regarding compensation and related issues, and can exercise due diligence and professional judgment in effectively carrying out their assigned responsibilities.

- *Responsibilities.* Compensation committee responsibilities include:
  - ○ Developing, approving, monitoring, and disclosing the company's executive pay philosophy, which considers the full range of pay components, desired mix of cash and equity awards, and relation of executive pay to compensation of other employees.
  - ○ Vigilantly overseeing all aspects of executive compensation for top executives, including the company's CEO, CFO, and other highly paid executives of subsidiaries, special purpose entities, and other affiliates to ensure fair, nondiscriminatory, rewarding, and forward-looking pay.
  - ○ Implementing pay-for-performance executive compensation driven predominately by performance and rewarding superior performance.
  - ○ Reviewing annually the performance of individuals in the oversight group (directors) and approving their bonuses, severance, equity-based award, death/disability, retirement, termination with and without cause, changes of control, and voluntary termination.
  - ○ Assuming accountability for the committee's operations, including attending all annual and special shareholder meetings, being available to respond directly to questions regarding executive compensation, reporting on its activities to the independent directors of the company's board, and preparing and being responsible for the compensation committee report included in the annual proxy materials.
  - ○ Assuming the responsibilities for hiring, retaining, and firing outside independent experts including legal counsel, financial advisors, and human resources consultants when negotiating contracts with executives.
- *Proxy statement disclosure.* The compensation committee is directly responsible for ensuring that all aspects of the company's executive compensation are fully and fairly disclosed in plain English in the annual proxy statement to enable shareholders to clearly understand how and how much directors and executives are paid, including salary and short- and long-term incentive compensation. The compensation committee should properly disclose the executive compensation philosophy that drives its policies. If the committee uses a criterion in determining and justifying executive compensation, such as the benchmarking of companies in peer groups, it should be properly disclosed.[17]

Compensation Committee Responsibilities

Responsibilities of the compensation committee can be generalized into three areas: evaluation and compensation of directors; evaluation and compensation of executives; and disclosure of the work of the compensation committee.

Evaluation and Compensation of Directors Assessment of individual directors' performance is sometimes viewed as a sensitive topic because a "bad" evaluation could be embarrassing for the entire board and/or an individual director if such information become publicly available or was obtained by shareholders for use in a legal proceeding against the company. However, stock exchange listing standards and best practices established by various organizations (e.g., the Council of Institutional Investors, the Conference Board, and National Association of Corporate Directors [NACD]) either require or strongly recommend a formal, annual evaluation process for the board of directors, each major committee of the board, and each member of the board committees. A proper evaluation process selected by the compensation committee in assessing the performance of directors can vary from company to company, depending on the board's independence from the CEO, corporate governance structure, board composition, and executive power within the company. Use of an independent facilitator can greatly increase the effectiveness of the board self-evaluation process. The purposes of board and director performance evaluations are to: identify areas of concern, poor performance or absence of needed skill sets or expertise; make constructive suggestions for improvements in the directors' oversight function or board composition; and use the evaluations as part of the process for determining overall director compensation.

There are no mandated guidelines for the evaluation of director and board performance. Thus, the compensation committee has the flexibility to tailor the evaluations to the company's corporate governance structure and attributes. The committee should consider six issues pertaining to the annual evaluation of the company's board of directors:

1. Should the evaluation be a self-assessment, or should outside consultants be hired?
2. Should the evaluation be performed for each director in addition to the entire board and its committees?
3. Who should oversee the evaluation?
4. What benchmark should be used to determine effective and successful evaluation?
5. How should the board document the evaluation?
6. Should the entire evaluation or a synopsis be disclosed to shareholders?

The compensation committee often uses these benchmarks or criteria in the evaluation process:

- Knowledge, experience, gender and ethnic diversity, and expertise of directors.
- Teamwork and leadership ability.
- Maturity, objectivity, judgment, and independence.
- Value-added contribution to the company's welfare.
- Understanding of the company's business and industry, including legal and financial literacy.
- Firm commitment and dedication to working toward the achievement of the company's goals.
- Safeguarding of the company's assets, ensuring integrity of its financial reports, and protecting the interest of shareholders.
- Creating long-term shareholder value.

- Protecting the interests of other stakeholders.
- Setting an appropriate tone at the top in promoting ethical conduct.

Compensation for directors and officers has received significant scrutiny from investors and regulators; however, compensation for nonemployee, outside directors has not been sufficiently addressed in the literature. To increase responsiveness and accountability of directors to shareholders (owners) and to improve the effectiveness of board committees, companies are changing their compensation policies and practices by paying per-meeting fees to members of board committees (audit, compensation, governance, nominating) and increasing the use of restricted and deferred stock that require ownership holding periods that exceed the director's term on the board to ensure greater alignment of interests with shareholders (owners).

Evaluation and Compensation of Senior Executives   Evaluation of senior executive performance is one of the most important functions of the compensation committee to ensure executives are working toward the achievement of the company's goal of creating sustainable shareholder value and protecting the interests of shareholders and stakeholders. The committee should link executive compensation to the company's performance and provide transparency and plain-English disclosures on a multiyear basis as to the nature and extent of executive compensation and objective performance measures, including the value of the use of corporate jets, automobiles, and housing and supplemental executive pension plans that oftentimes are unfunded liabilities. Executive evaluations have five objectives:

1. Identify areas of concern and poor executive performance.
2. Direct managerial activities and strategic objectives toward achieving the company's goals of creating and enhancing sustainable shareholder value.
3. Align executive interests with those of long-term shareholders.
4. Ensure executive compliance with applicable laws, rules, regulations, and standards as well as ethical conduct.
5. Use the evaluation as a basis for determining executive pay that closely links pay with financial performance.

Executives should be evaluated based on:

- Motivation and desire to do the right thing.
- Professional accountability and responsibility for financial performance and meeting strategic objectives.
- Competence.
- Ethical leadership.
- Ability to represent shareholders' interests.
- Compliance with applicable laws and regulations.
- Personal integrity.
- Community outreach.
- National recognition.
- Other achievements.

To link CEO compensation to performance, the compensation committee should:

- Prepare and use "tally sheets" calculating each component of compensation and tallying it all up.
- Implement internal pay equity policies and procedures, and ask internal audit and/or human resources departments to conduct internal pay equity audits.
- Use stock options as ownership incentives, not as components of current compensation.
- Consider all components of CEO compensation, including retirement benefits to executives beyond the amounts that would be payable under the company's retirement plan to all other employees, including perks that the CEO may be receiving (e.g., personal use of company aircraft), excessive severance (e.g., pay for failure that includes granting unearned years of service credit to artificially boost pension payouts at companies heading for bankruptcy), and other termination payouts (e.g., pension payouts and life insurance payment provisions that include payments for the lifetime of the executive's spouse).[18]

Proper design and implementation of fair and equitable executive compensation plans consisting of base salaries, annual bonuses, and long-term incentive packages can significantly influence the effectiveness of the managerial function and employee morale. The compensation committee should determine whether executives are eligible for annual bonuses or benefits under long-term incentive plans. Annual executive bonuses should be based on relevant and objective performance criteria in order to improve the company's financial performance and to enhance long-term shareholder value. Annual executive bonuses are commonly paid in cash; they can also be paid as company shares to be held for a substantial period of time to reduce short-term incentives and enhance longer-term incentive structures. These bonuses should have upper limits, be approved by shareholders, and be fully disclosed in the company's proxy statements. Long-term incentive plans can be in terms of shares granted, nonvested deferred remuneration, and nonexercisable options to be held for several years (at least a three-year vesting period, but preferably five or more years). The shares or options should be held for a significant period after vesting or exercise. These long-term incentive plans should be approved by shareholders, fully disclosed, and nonpensionable. As a general rule, only the basic salary of executives should be pensionable. In addition, executives should not be permitted to artificially boost their own pension plans while at the same time cutting the pension benefits of the average worker.

In light of these trends, commonsense executive compensation programs should include:

- *Salary.* The CEO's salary should be based on the mean of salaries paid at peer group companies, not exceeding $1 million annually, with close linkage to the financial performance of the company. No senior executive should be paid more than the CEO, and the gap between CEO and average worker pay should be a factor that is taken into consideration.

- *Annual bonus.* The annual bonus paid to senior executives should be linked to performance based on both quantitative (financial) and qualitative (nonfinancial) measures as a percentage of salary capped at 100 percent.
- *Long-term equity compensation.* Long-term equity compensation to senior executives should:
  - ○ Be in the form of restricted shares, not stock options.
  - ○ Be based on justifiable, objective performance criteria that cannot be changed midstream and on challenging performance benchmarks.
  - ○ Contain a vesting requirement of at least three years and preferably five or more years.
  - ○ Require executives to hold all shares awarded under the program for the duration of their employment.
  - ○ Ensure that the value of a restricted share grant does not exceed $1 million on the date of the grant.
- *Severance.* The maximum severance payment to a senior executive should not exceed one year's salary and bonus.
- *Disclosure.* Key components of the executive compensation plan should be specified in plain English for multiyear periods in the compensation committee's report to shareholders.[19]

Statistics show that: the top five executives at U.S. public companies received compensation that, on average, amounted to 10.3 percent of their company's net income compared with 4.8 percent in 1993; the average CEO received a 91 percent raise in 2004 while the other employees' raises amounted to less than 4 percent on average; in 2004, CEOs earned an average about 431 times higher than the pay of the average worker compared to 42 times in 1980.[20] Representative Barney Frank (D-MA), on November 10, 2005, introduced legislation entitled "The Protection against Executive Compensation Abuse Act" aimed at bringing executive pay in line with the company's performance. The legislation, if passed, would require public companies to do five things:

1. Provide details about components of executive annual pay including cash, incentives, stock options, and perks.
2. Submit the entire executive pay package for shareholder approval, which gives shareholders veto power over executive pay packages.
3. Disclose the full market value of company-paid perks, including an executive's personal use of a company jet.
4. Report the specific criteria by which executives earn incentive pay.
5. Disclose to shareholders the amount that executives would earn on a proposed takeover or acquisition that requires shareholder consent. [21]

Academic studies present two distinct views on executive compensation. The dominant view is that the design and implementation of an optimal compensation package may provide management with efficient incentives to create and enhance long-term shareholder value.[22] The second view is that executives have considerable influence over the design and the amount of their own pay, which enables them to extract rents. This view suggests there is no relationship between executive compensation and performance primarily because managerial power determines executive compensation. Another study finds that CEO compensation is higher when: the board is large, making it more difficult for directors to organize in opposition to the CEO; many outside directors have been selected by the CEO, who feel obligated to him or her; and outside directors serve on three or more boards, creating more demands on their time.[23]

Three recent developments have started to address the excessive compensation based on financial performance or lack thereof that is being paid to corporate executives. The first is SEC rules that require public companies to provide more disclosures regarding executive pay. On July 26, 2006, the SEC approved comprehensive changes in the disclosure requirements for: (1) the compensation of directors and officers; (2) related-person transactions; (3) director independence; (4) ownership of securities by officers and directors; and (5) other corporate governance matters.[24] To comply with these requirements, companies should provide greater disclosure in their proxy statements, annual reports, and registration statements regarding total compensation of their directors, principal executive officer, principal financial officer, and three highest-paid officers. Other requirements pertain to disclosure of the grant-date fair value of the stocks options, changes in pension values and nonqualified deferred compensation earnings, and the company's compensation discussion and analysis (CD&A) section. The primary purpose of the CD&A section is to accurately and completely disclose the board's process of determining executive compensation and to make executive compensation transparent to shareholders.

The second development is the wave of executive stock option (ESO) grant backdating practices scandals. More than 250 public companies were being investigated by federal authorities (SEC, IRS, Department of Justice) as of April 2007.[25] The backdating of ESOs is a process by which grant dates and exercise prices of stock options are managed retroactively to precede a run-up in underlying shares in order to maximize the options' value. It is considered an illegal way of boosting options' value. Another scheme often used in maximizing options' value is known as spring-loading by setting options dates and prices ahead of news. Both practices of backdating and spring-loading stock options are an attempt to manipulate options' values; in the best scenario, these practices can be regarded as improper accounting and, in the worst scenario, as fraud or inside trading. Backdating ESOs grants may have the effect of benefiting executives by securing low stock price by essentially using "stockholder money to buy high and sell *even lower* than their filings previously disclosed."[26] The backdating ESOs probe is still in its early stage; more companies are being scrutinized and questioned about their backdating policies and practices. Prior to the passage of SOX, options grants did not need to be disclosed for weeks or even months, which could allow executives to retroactively choose favorable grant dates. In the post-SOX period, companies are required to disclose their executive options within two business days of being granted. The board of directors, particularly the compensation committee, should be more actively involved in: (1) authorizing and approving ESOs; (2) setting the grant dates; (3) getting the approval of shareholders on award option grants; (4) assuring proper filing with the SEC on Form 4 on the date an option grant is made; and (5) providing full transparency of option grants by disclosing plausible reasons for grants on a certain date (e.g., shareholders' annual meetings) or on a periodic basis (e.g., monthly, quarterly, annually).

Third, a study by Mercer Human Resource Consulting indicates that more companies are imposing performance targets on options and the restricted stock they grant to their CEOs.[27] This study suggests that neither additional disclosure nor linking executive pay to performance would cure the problem; additional disclosure may provide more ammunition for executives and their consultants to find ways to justify additional increases, and performance metrics may encourage executives to manage earnings and focus on short-term performance at the expense of sustainable performance.

The Florida State Board of Administration (SBA) pension fund encourages companies' compensation committees to establish stock ownership guidelines for their officers and directors.[28] The guidelines suggest that:

- Senior executives obtain and maintain an ownership interest expressed as a multiple of their salary from the president and chief executive officer (15 times salary) to other senior executives (5 times salary).
- The desired level of stock ownership should be met or exceeded within three years of becoming a director or officer.
- Shares owned include phantom shares into which compensation is deferred.
- Personal shares obtained, restricted shares, and other shares acquired through stock-based performance arrangements are included in determining compliance with stock ownership targets.
- For participants (directors, officers) who have not met their stock ownership target, any performance-based shares that would otherwise be received are deferred into phantom stock units (career shares) and will be held in these career shares until their employment ends.
- Executives who have not met the stock ownership target within three years will be required to defer 50 percent of their annual incentive compensation into phantom stock units and retain all shares realized through stock option exercises until they meet the target stock ownership.[29]

The Committee for Economic Development (CED) believes that executive compensation is excessive and that the solution to this problem should address both the process and the disclosure of executive compensation.[30] The CED makes these recommendations regarding executive compensation:

- The company's compensation committee should establish measurable, specific, and attainable performance objectives and assess management's performance in achieving these objectives.
- The company's compensation committee, composed of independent directors with direct authority to control all forms of executive compensation, should run the compensation process.

- Compensation consultants should be entirely independent of management and work for the compensation committee.
- Senior executives should have a significant equity interest in their companies to effectively align their interests with those of shareholders.
- Choices of forms of executive compensation should promote the company's sustainable value creation rather than exploit favorable tax and accounting treatment.
- Severance compensation should also be overseen by the company's compensation committee and disclosed fully to shareholders.
- Companies should have the right to recapture executive bonuses influenced by misleading financial statements that are subsequently restated.[31]

Compensation Committee and Consultants

The role that the compensation committee plays in corporate governance is becoming more crucial as the issues concerning executive compensation are becoming more complicated, and as the committee receives more advice from outside consultants. The relationship between the committee and its outside consultants is important, particularly when consultants provide advice to both the committee and management. The SEC rules require public companies to describe their compensation committee processes and procedures including: (1) the scope of authority of the compensation committee; (2) the nature and extent of authority being delegated by the compensation committee to other persons; and (3) any role that compensation consultants play in determining or recommending the amount or form of executive and director compensation. This information regarding compensation consultants should disclose: (1) the name of each consultant; (2) whether the consultants were engaged and retained directly by the compensation committee; (3) the nature, extent, and scope of consultants' assignment; and (4) the extent and nature of guidelines and instructions given to the consultants regarding their responsibilities and performance.

The best practices suggest that the compensation committee: (1) must ensure that consultants are independent of management and provide objective and relevant advice to the committee; (2) must retain and control all aspects and terms of the committee-consultant relationship, including consultant appointment, retention, dismissal, the scope of the work, and oversight and monitoring of work; and (3) may allow, in a rare case, a consultant to perform limited services for management as long as such services are properly disclosed in their reports to the committee.[32]

An influential group of institutional investors representing $849.5 billion in assets sent a letter to the compensation committees of at least 25 high-profile S&P 500 companies requesting information concerning disclosure practices of their committee's use of compensation consultants. The letter addresses the issue of the independence of consultants particularly where they also provide consulting services to the management.[33] Independent consultants play an important role in providing fair, unbiased, and independent advice to the company's compensation committee in light of recent requirements by the SEC mandating compensation committees to sign off on the CD&A included in the proxy statement. The institutional investors requested a response from the chairs of the compensation committees of S&P 500 companies, including AT&T, Bank of America, Cisco, Citigroup, ExxonMobil, General Electric, and Microsoft, to these two questions:

1. Does the consultant employed by the company's compensation committee provide other consulting services to its management? If any, describe the nature of the work and whether it is properly disclosed in the CD&A.
2. Does the company's board of directors have a policy prohibiting the compensation committee's consultant from providing other services to its management, and if not, would the board adopt such a policy and disclose it in its CD&A?[34]

Compensation Committee Report

The compensation committee should prepare pay philosophy procedures and reward the outstanding performance of executives. The U.K. Department of Trade and Industry suggests seven key disclosures in the compensation report:

1. Names of the compensation committee members and those who provide advice to it.
2. Statement of compensation policy for the following and subsequent years.
3. Statement of objective performance measures, including share options and long-term incentive plans for individual executives.
4. The trend of total shareholder return relative to broad equity market index for the past five financial years.
5. Details of executives' service contracts, including potential early termination payments.
6. Individual executives' compensation, trading in share options, pension, and holdings in long-term incentive plans.
7. Trends of total compensation and its components over time as well as the linkage between pay and financial performance over the long term.[35]

The American Federation of State, County and Municipal Employees (AFSCME) plan has submitted proposals at 26 companies for the 2006 proxy season that include advisory shareholder votes on executive compensation reports and programs to align executive compensation with shareholders' interests.[36] By urging corporate boards to establish an annual shareholder advisory vote to either approve or reject their company's compensation committee report, the AFSCME is attempting to bring U.S. compensation committee reports in line with the requirements in the United Kingdom and Australia.

In July 2006 the SEC adopted amendments that would refine currently tabular compensation disclosure and combine it with the improved narrative disclosure to enhance transparency of disclosure of compensation of the company's directors and senior executives. Public companies are required to provide compensation disclosure in the form of a CD&A that: (1) specifies the objectives and implementation of executive compensation programs; (2) addresses the most important factors underlying the compensation policies and decisions; (3) will be filed and be a part of disclosure subject to certification by the company's CEO and CFO; (4) will require a statement of whether the compensation committee has reviewed and discussed the CD&A with management and recommended that it be included in the company's annual report on Form 10-K and proxy statement; (5) separates the "performance graph" from the executive compensation disclosure and moves it to the disclosure role covering the market price of common equity and related matters; (6) organizes executive compensation disclosures into three broad categories of: (a) compensation over the last three years; (b) holdings of outstanding equity-related interests received as compensation that are the source of future gains; and (c) retirement plans, deferred compensation and OPEB; and (7) provides in tabular and narrative disclosure columns for salary, bonus, stock, stock options, grant date fair value of option, and a more complete picture of compensation.[37]

The SEC rules on executive compensation require proper disclosures of public companies' executive compensation without imposing or even assessing the nature and extent of the compensation. These rules are intended to assist investors to obtain complete accurate and transparent information on executive compensation in order to make sound investment and voting decisions. SEC rules improve executive compensation disclosure by requiring public companies to: (1) prepare and include the new CD&A in their proxy statements and annual reports on Form 10-K filed with the SEC; (2) refine their disclosure controls and procedures concerning executive compensation by gathering and analyzing the new expanded compensation information; and (3) hold their compensation committee directly responsible for establishing executive compensation plans, getting the approval of the entire board regarding those plans, and disclosing the committee's authority, responsibility, roles, functions, and resources in its new compensation committee report (CCR). The CCR, which is effectively modeled on the required audit committee report (ACR), must be furnished, not filed, and should contain these two statements: (1) whether the company's compensation committee has reviewed and discussed the CD&A with management; and (2) whether the compensation committee, based on its review and discussions, recommends to the board of directors that the CD&A be included in the company's annual report on Form 10-K and proxy statement.

The author suggests that the company's compensation committee properly disclose in the compensation report included in the annual report 10 major aspects of the committee:

1. The composition of the compensation committee, including the number of members, their names, their qualifications, and their independence.
2. Objectives and implementation programs of director and executive compensations, including "say on pay" policy of shareholder advisory votes.
3. The compensation committee policies and procedures.
4. The details of compensation of individual directors and officers, including salaries, bonuses, shares, and options.
5. Approval by the shareholders of stock-based compensation plans and costs of such plans.

6. Accounting policies and practices for the recognition or disclosure of the expenses related to stock-based compensation.
7. Means of contacting the company's board of directors, particularly compensation committee members.
8. Relevant information about the independent compensation consultants.
9. The company's policies in recapturing executive bonuses influenced by misleading financial statements that are subsequently restated.
10. Procedures for approval of key employees' and executives' stock options plans by either shareholders or its representative board of directors, the administration of those plans and the determination of their grant dates by the compensation committee.

Determinants of Effective Compensation Committees

The author suggests 12 determinants of an effective compensation committee:

1. All public companies must have a compensation committee on their board of directors, which is directly responsible for determining the appropriate level and structure of executive compensation plans for the company's principal executive and principal financial officers, including the CEO, CFO, chief operating officer (COO), general counsel, and other highly paid executives, both corporate and subsidiary. The committee may also consider compensation for the company's directors.
2. The compensation committee must be composed solely of independent directors who are not affiliated with and do not receive any other compensation or items of value from the company aside from board meeting or committee-related fees.
3. The compensation committee should have a charter stating its roles, responsibilities, and functions. The charter should be approved by the entire board of directors and fully disclosed to shareholders.
4. The compensation committee should have authority and budgetary resources to hire experts, advisors, and consultants as it deems necessary to design and implement executive compensation arrangements. Management should not control the company's budgetary resources, and the same consultant should not be hired by management.
5. The compensation committee should develop pay-for-performance goals for the company's executives, establish executive compensation plans to achieve the stated goals, evaluate executive performance, and revise compensation plans as necessary to provide incentives for high executive performance.
6. The compensation committee should ensure executive compensation disclosures are sufficient and compliant with SEC disclosure requirements. Backdating of executive stock options in the post-SOX era has created new challenges for compensation committees as more than 250 companies have been implicated for their option backdating. The CFA, Center for Financial Market Integrity, requested that the SEC bring enforcement actions against these companies and adopt additional disclosures and rules to prevent such practices, including requiring companies to disclose:

    a. Dates for all prior-year compensation committee meetings in the proposed compensation discussion and analysis.

    b. Dates on which compensation committees approve share-based awards through 8-K filings.

    c. Effective grant dates for all share-based awards if different from the approval dates.

    d. Any information about whether executives were permitted to select or recommend grant dates for their options.[38]

7. The compensation committee should ensure that executives repay to the company any portion of their compensation affected by restatements of the company's financial results.

8. The compensation committee should establish policies addressing the appropriate mix of salary bonuses and long-term incentive compensation, including severance and retirement arrangements, which are fully disclosed to and approved by the shareholders.

9. The compensation committee should establish pay-for-performance metrics based on appropriate performance measures such as economic value added (EVA), shareholder value added (SVA), return on equity (ROE), return on assets (ROA), residual income (RI), earnings, and cash flow growth (ECG). These performance measures should exclude any gains resulting from market-wide and/or industry-wide movements.

10. The compensation committee should strongly encourage executive stock ownership and promote equity-based compensation (stock options, restricted stock). The committee should annually review the company's target stock ownership levels for each officer level, typically as a multiple of salary (e.g., 5 to 15 times salary), and adjust these levels as deemed appropriate to align interests of executives with those of shareholders.

11. The committee should have a charter stating its policies, procedures, composition, authority, resources, and responsibilities as well as the requirement for producing an annual report on executive compensation for inclusion in the company's proxy statement.

12. The committee should provide a compensation disclosure and analysis and require that it be included in the company's annual report on Form 10-K and proxy statements.

NOMINATING/GOVERNANCE COMMITTEE

The nominating/governance committee is usually responsible for identifying, evaluating, and nominating a new director to the board, and it also facilitates the election of the new directors by shareholders. The committee may use staffing support provided by the CEO in identifying and recruiting new members of the company's board of directors. An effective nominating committee can substantially reduce the traditional role played by the CEO in selecting new directors who may not be independent from management.

Responsibilities of the Nominating/Governance Committees

In theory, shareholders elect directors who appoint senior executives to run the company. In reality, management chooses the company's directors. Several suggestions are made to bring more democracy into the boardroom to hold the nominating committee directly responsible for the nomination of directors and empower shareholders to elect directors. One suggestion is to permit large shareholders with 3 to 5 percent of the company's stock (e.g., pension funds) to directly nominate candidates to compete with management's nominees. This approach, while enabling larger shareholders (pension funds) to elect directors opposed or not supported by management, may not bring cohesiveness and effectiveness to the boardroom and may not serve the best interests of all shareholders where there is a conflict between large shareholders (5 percent ownership) and other shareholders. A more practical and less controversial approach is to: (1) establish an objective evaluation system to effectively assess the performance of existing directors; and (2) assign to the independent nominating committee the responsibility of director evaluation and nomination. This approach is more in line with recent corporate governance reforms and is strongly endorsed by the CED.[39]

The nominating committee is responsible for:

- Reviewing the performance of the current directors.
- Assessing the need for new directors.
- Identifying and evaluating the skills, background, diversity (gender, ethnic background, and experience), and knowledge of candidates for the board.
- Having an objective nominating process for qualified candidates to the board.
- Assisting in the election of qualified new directors.
- Establishing corporate governance policies (e.g., majority-vote policies).
- Communicating with shareholders regarding board candidates and other shareholder concerns and issues.
- Determining whether the entire board of directors meets the independence requirements set by listing standards in terms of the majority of directors (at least two-thirds) being independent.

The board's nominating committee should lead the process for directors' assessment and election. Issues that the nominating/governance committee should consider in this evaluation process include but are not limited to:

- The gender and ethnic diversity of the board in creating a right balance to enable directors to address the current and future business challenges and reflect the company's customer base as a competitive advantage.
- The experience necessary to effectively operate board committees. The nominating committees should have at least one director with a human resources background.
- Future expertise needs of the company's board. For example, if the company expects future mergers and acquisitions, having a director with knowledge

and background in valuation models will be very helpful. A company's future challenges in enterprise risk management and social and environmental responsibility also require consideration of directors knowledgeable in those areas.

- Requirement of two terms of several (e.g., three to five) years' directorship for nonexecutive directors to ensure the maintenance of their independence.
- A proper combination of director qualifications and behavioral characteristics.[40]

There should be an appropriate mix of personality types and experiences to generate proactive discussions of corporate issues and alternative courses of actions. Behavioral characteristics and experiences of a qualified director include:

- Asking difficult, probing questions.
- Having well-developed interpersonal and communication skills.
- Having industry experience and awareness.
- Providing valuable input.
- Being available when needed.
- Being alert, inquisitive, and informed.
- Having business knowledge and needed skill sets.
- Contributing to committee work.
- Attending and actively participating in meetings.
- Speaking out appropriately at board meetings.
- Preparing for meetings.
- Making long-range strategic planning contributions.
- Contributing overall.
- Ensuring responsibility and accountability.
- Being familiar with, or willing to learn about, emerging corporate governance issues and applicable laws, rules, regulations, standards, and best practices.
- Communicating effectively with and being available to shareholders and other stakeholders, including executives and other employees, creditors, suppliers and customers.
- Supporting the company's economic, performance, ethical, environmental, social, and governance objectives.[41]

Selection and Nomination of New Directors

The nominating committee is responsible for selecting and nominating a new director. The company's CEO often informally participates on the nominating committee and thus may identify and suggest a new director for membership. The committee, with staff support from the company's CEO and/or consulting with independent advisors, should annually determine the gender and ethnic diversity, independence, expertise, knowledge, and other attributes needed on the board. The comparison of the desired and existing board profiles determines the needed profile in addition to gender and ethnic diversity for a competitive advantage. For example, if the nominating committee decides to increase the percentage of independent directors, or if there is a need for a particular functional expertise or to increase gender or ethnic diversity on the board, then the selected candidate should meet the needed profile.

A pool of candidates who meet the board's desired profile should be selected. Their backgrounds, knowledge, expertise, diversity, ethical values, and character should be reviewed by the nominating committee and references checked thoroughly before potential nominees are selected. The selected candidates should then be approved by the entire board before being finalized as director candidates for election by shareholders at the company's annual meeting. The candidates should also be interviewed by the nominating committee to ensure that they are not only a good fit, but also have the time and interest to be effective members of the company's board of directors and that they are not members of too many boards. During their interview with the committee, candidates can meet with existing directors, and learn about the company's facilities, top management team, and opportunity to serve on the board. The company benefits from this interview; management can assess potential candidates, and other directors can get to know candidates and perhaps try to convince them to accept the directorship.

As indicated in the 2005 survey of Spencer Stuart Board Index, the recruiting task of the nominating committee of the board is becoming more challenging and complex in the post-SOX era for four reasons:

1. The move toward supermajority independent directors (all independent directors except for the CEO) is gaining more acceptance from public companies, demanded by investor activists, and supported by regulators and standard setters.
2. The pool of traditional candidates for directorship is shrinking as the active senior executives (CEOs, corporate operating officers, CFOs) now serve on no more than one outside corporate board.
3. There is a growing demand for specific director expertise to assist with the ever-increasing complex business issues (cutting edge manufacturing, corporate governance, environmental expertise).
4. There is greater scrutiny and heightened sensitivity about the director selection process in order to avoid real or potential conflicts and improve the transparency of the nomination and election process.[42]

Election of Directors

The candidates for directorship are normally disclosed in proxy materials prepared by the company for the annual meeting of shareholders where shareholders will vote to elect director candidates to the board of directors. The shareholders elect directors, particularly independent directors, to represent their interests. The company's bylaws normally authorize the board to fill interim vacancies on the board for the remainder of the unexpired terms or until the next annual meeting of shareholders. Directors' terms usually begin and expire on the date of the annual meeting of shareholders and are specified for an annual term, which shareholders view as desirable because it enhances director accountability unless the company has not yet declassified its board to eliminate longer, staggered board terms. Once a director is elected at the annual meeting, the director completes his or her elected term, unless otherwise removed or forced to resign for a proper cause, which is a rare event. Recent corporate governance reforms suggest that, in order to better represent shareholder interests, directors should be elected or reelected annually under a majority-vote rule with no staggered terms for directors and the elimination of the classified board structure.

Under the current plurality default standard for director elections under Delaware law and other state corporate laws, individual directors are elected even if they only cast one vote for themselves, as the plurality standard does not permit shareholders to vote against a director candidate. Shareholders are only permitted under current law to cast a symbolic withhold vote if they oppose the election of an individual director on the basis of lack of independence, lack of qualifications, or some other proper business reason. Because of this significant limitation, the plurality default standard has been criticized by shareholders as not being very democratic; it also unfairly gives incumbent directors a significant reelection advantage when change may be warranted. The move toward companies voluntarily adopting majority voting for the election of directors has received a tremendous amount of attention and support from institutional investors because it will:

- Put real voting power in the hands of shareholders (owners).
- Democratize the public company director election process.
- Make the corporate board more accountable to and more representative of shareholders.
- Be consistent with the emerging global standard of majority voting for director elections already in place in developed countries such as the United Kingdom, Germany, Canada, Australia, and France.

There has been continuing momentum by shareholders to encourage companies to voluntarily adopt a majority-vote standard for the election of public company directors. For example, the California Public Employees' Retirement System (CalPERS) board recently adopted a three-pronged plan to advocate for adoption of a majority-vote standard for the election of public company directors. According to CalPERs board president Rob Feckner, "Majority vote will give shareowners the power to hold directors accountable for their actions and their performance, and elect the best person for the job."[43] CalPERs' majority-vote plan suggests:

- Implementing majority-vote policies and procedures at public companies through the company's bylaw and charter amendments.
- Making changes to state laws to implement majority vote where feasible.
- Implementing the majority-vote policies at the SEC and national stock exchanges.
- Amending CalPERs Corporate Governance Core Principles and Guidelines to promote majority votes for corporate directors.[44]

In the 2005 shareholders' meetings, about 82 public companies received majority-voting shareholder proposals; from them, 9 companies approved majority votes on their proposals.[45] During the 2005 proxy season (January 1 through June

30, 2005), a total of 64 majority-vote proposals were voted on with an average support of about 44 percent,[46] which is significant shareholder support for a new shareholder proposal.

Two types of amendments to the plurality voting system have been proposed and voted on during the 2005 proxy season. The first type is to amend a company's bylaws to implement a majority-vote default standard, which can be amended subsequently only by shareholder approval, which shareholders prefer. The second way is by amending a company's corporate governance principles, which is less desirable to shareholders because the principles can be unilaterally amended by the board of directors at any time without shareholder approval, and it does not require directors to resign if they receive a majority of "withhold" votes if the board decides to override the will of its shareholders. Under the second approach, often referred to as the Pfizer-type majority-vote standard, directors who receive a majority of "withhold" votes submit their resignation to the company's board of directors, the board considers the resignation, and then it makes a final determination regarding whether to accept the resignation or not. The Pfizer approach has been criticized by shareholders for failing to give investors the right to vote "no" and because it still gives the board final decision-making authority on director selections and not shareholders (owners).

The Canadian Coalition for Good Governance (CCGG), which represents 46 institutional investors managing more that $1 trillion in assets, has convinced more than 20 major Canadian companies to adopt a policy requiring directors to tender their resignations if they fail to obtain majority support from shareholders in board elections.[47] The CCGG urges companies to require their directors to resign voluntarily if they do not receive at least 50 percent support from shareholders in board elections but allows the board to decide whether to accept the resignations.[48] The CCGG has decided to ask companies to change their voting systems and policies to send a strong message that shareholders are concerned about the current system of board elections and their views should count, and because it is easier to convince companies to voluntarily change their policies than to lobby the federal government to change regulations regarding board elections.[49] The CCGG has been very successful in contacting the 150 largest Canadian companies, and 17 of Canada's top 50 companies have agreed to adopt the new majority-voting policy. Perhaps investor activists and corporate governance organizations in the United States should follow suit to promote changes in companies' current voting policies for director elections.

Reelection of Incumbent Directors

In the past, boards of directors traditionally had staggered terms of three years with no term limits. Although the directors' positions on the board are not tenured, the bylaws do not usually mention term limits. Thus, incumbent directors have traditionally been reelected unless they retire or are removed for cause, which is a very rare occurrence. At such time when annual performance evaluations of individual directors and entire boards of directors become a more meaningful and widespread exercise fully disclosed to shareholders, it may then be appropriate to use those evaluations as a factor for determining whether it is appropriate for an incumbent director to run for reelection as an effective representative of shareholders' interests. Several suggestions have been made to ensure the proper and objective nomination of the incumbent director for elections, including:

- Establish a mandatory retirement age for all new, incumbent, inside, and outside directors. Currently there are no laws, listing standards, or other external requirements mandating the standard retirement age for directors. Thus, public companies, in following corporate governance best practices (e.g., CII policy statements), should individually decide what mandatory retirement age works best for their directors (perhaps in the range of 70 to 75 years).
- Use the annual board evaluation as a vehicle for assessing the qualifications, knowledge, credentials, and changes in the status of the existing directors and their eligibility to be nominated for reelection.
- Use term limits for reelections of incumbent directors.
- Require annual certification from directors to disclose any changes in their primary employment circumstances, potential conflicts of interest, and engagement in any illegal act or unethical behavior that could be embarrassing to the company.
- Provide incentives and opportunities for directors to resign from the board prior to renomination and reelection in circumstances when they are ineffective, have engaged in unethical conduct or illegal acts, or are associated with any conflicts of interest.
- Encourage shareholders, particularly institutional investors, to include their board nominees on the company's official ballot.
- Strongly encourage annual continuing director education to ensure that director knowledge of corporate governance and financial literacy remains current.

Succession Planning Process

The company's nominating committee should establish an effective and routine succession planning process designed to ensure proper planning for orderly succession to the company's board and other senior executive positions. The key features of such a process include:

- Continuous improvement.
- Proper oversight and approval by the board.
- CEO input, involvement, and collaboration, as appropriate, without dominating or unduly influencing the committee.
- Efficient execution of an established succession plan in the event of a company crisis.
- Alignment with the company's strategic and business plan.
- Ability to identify or recruit the proper ethical leadership at the right time.
- The continuous development of employee talent pools at lower levels of the organization.

- Having an effective program in place to identify and professionally develop internal candidates as part of a formal performance evaluation and career development process.
- Avoidance of a "horse race" mentality that may lead to loss of key employees when a new CEO is selected.[50]

In the post-SOX era, the nominating committee has faced the challenges of establishing a more effective, objective, and transparent process of recruiting and nominating candidates who are more carefully and thoroughly evaluating the time, commitment, risks, and rewards associated with directorships. The stock exchange listing requirement that a majority of directors be independent and not have financial or personal ties to management, particularly the CEO, makes the nomination process more objective and effective, but also more time-consuming. Thus, the committee should give proper consideration to the skills, expertise, leadership, and gender and ethnic diversity needed on the board in light of the company's corporate culture, character, strategic goals, and customer base. The committee should continue to focus on establishing an effective and targeted recruitment process.

Nominating Committee Disclosures

In October 2003 the SEC proposed rule amendments that would, under certain circumstances, allow shareholders representing at least 15 percent voting shares to include their own board nominees along with management's choices on the company's official ballot. The proposal was adopted by the SEC in November 2003.[51] The amendments expand the current proxy statement disclosure regarding a company's nominating or similar committee to include:

- Whether the company has a nominating or similar committee, and if not, the rationale behind the decision and who among the directors performs that duty.
- A copy of the nominating committee's charter or listing on its Web site if it is available; if the charter is not available, why not; and if it does not exist, a statement to that fact.
- A statement as to the independence of the directors on the nominating committee.
- Whether the nominating committee has a policy with regard to the consideration of any director candidates recommended by security holders, and if so, the particulars of the policy.
- The minimum qualifications and skills necessary to be considered for nomination.
- How the nominating committee goes about nominating directors.
- Who recommended the nominee.
- If a third party was involved, any fees paid.
- How to conduct the board of directors and its committees, including the nominating committee.[52]

More than three years after the first SEC-proposed rules for shareholder access to company proxy material were released, the SEC, under pressure, is reconsidering its original proposal to find a meaningful way to ensure board accountability to shareholders. The shareholder access rules should create an appropriate balance of power between shareholders and management by empowering shareholders with a meaningful role in the election process without having to encounter an expensive proxy contest. The decision by the Court of Appeals for the Second Circuit, in September 2006, prompted the SEC to reconsider its rules concerning shareholder access and encouraged shareholders to propose bylaw amendments enabling them to nominate directors to be included on the company's proxy. The Committee on Capital Markets Regulation recommended that the SEC resolve whether shareholders should get access to their company's proxies for director elections.[53] The SEC has yet to deliberate on this important issue affecting shareholder democracy.

The author suggests that public companies prepare a written charter for their nominating committee and make it available on the company's Web site and/or include a copy in the proxy statement. If the company does not have a charter for its nominating committee, it should state so in its proxy statement, and also explain why it does not have such a charter. If the company is listed on an exchange, it should disclose whether all members of its nominating committee are independent, as defined in the listing standards. If the company is not listed, it should disclose whether each member of its nominating committee is independent, as determined by its board and consistent with the requirements of the listing standards. The nominating committee should establish policies and procedures for considering director candidates recommended by shareholders. If the committee does not have such policies and procedures, it should so state in the proxy statement, and explain the board's justification and reasons for not having such policies and procedures.

OTHER BOARD STANDING COMMITTEES

The board of directors may form special committees to assist it with special matters, transactions, or events. The due process for the board special committee is important; courts carefully scrutinize a special committee process to ensure that the committee has a clear mandate, performs its responsibilities with due diligence, and is truly disinterested. On December 21, 2005, the Delaware Chancery Court issued its decision in *In re: Telecommunications, Inc.* (TCI), which found that the entire special committee was flawed and that certain disclosures regarding the special committee's work were misleading.[54]

The Delaware Chancery Court's TCI opinion provides guidance regarding the establishment and process of the board special committee:

- If a board delegates matters to a special committee, the committee members must be selected carefully to ensure there is no conflict of interest.
- Boards should consider carefully whether the compensation paid to special committee members may taint the special committee process or otherwise give the appearance of impropriety or undue influence.

- The mandate of the special committee must be clear, in writing, and in the form of a resolution by the entire board, and the committee must act on behalf of the constituency it represents.
- A special committee acting in an "interested" merger transaction, or a transaction involving a controlling shareholder, in the absence of extraordinary circumstances, should retain its own financial and legal advisors, separate from the advisors retained by the company or its controlling shareholder.
- A special committee must perform its role on an informed basis through meeting enough times to address the assigned matters and hiring outside counsel and financial advisors to thoroughly analyze, assess, and understand the issues under consideration.
- Where fairness of the price being paid to a class of shares is at issue, the courts will review a board's analysis, including its reliance on a fair opinion, to ensure that the considerations being paid to shareholders (e.g., preference or premium) are fair.[55]

Public companies may form other standing or special committees to deal with issues requiring particular expertise. For example, a company may establish a finance committee to oversee its financing activities, capital structure, or strategic and planning activities. Special committees can also be established to deal with emerging issues, such as environmental issues, mergers, acquisitions, and investigation of alleged wrongdoing by directors and officers. The most commonly utilized special committees are governance/strategic, litigation, and special investigation committees composed solely of independent directors.

Governance/Strategic Committee

The governance/strategic committee should be in charge of establishing the agenda for the company's board of directors to determine what issues the board should discuss with management and to what extent. Traditionally, management has controlled and dictated the board's agenda. At many companies, the agenda is dictated by the CEO; board members have inadequate information, short meetings, and less constructive, meaningful discussion. The governance/strategic committee should collaborate with the company's CEO in designing a mutually agreed-upon agenda for board meetings. The governance committee should be formed to facilitate and coordinate the activities of the entire board and all other committees.

The governance/strategic committee should:

- Control the agenda and the meeting.
- Review the past agendas and minutes of meetings to ensure adequate time and discussion were devoted to each issue.
- Revise the agenda as necessary and set priorities for meetings.

The governance/strategic committee, in collaboration with top-level management, should each year identify several top priorities for the board, including strategic direction, financing activities, investment opportunities, succession planning, and sustainable growth. These priorities should be then placed at the top of the board's agendas for meetings. Management should submit proposals and recommendations for each of the priorities, provide sufficient information and briefing materials in advance for each of the major issues, allow appropriate debates and discussions, and seek board approval on these issues.

Outside Independent Directors' Committee

When the company's CEO also serves as the chair of the board of directors, an outside, independent directors' committee should be formed to maintain the board's independence from management and the CEO. The outside, independent directors' committee should be composed solely of nonexecutive directors and should engage in an oversight function; inside directors—including the CEO—assume the responsibility of managing the day-to-day operations of the company. The independent presiding or lead director of the board should be elected by the entire board.

Executive Committee

The executive committee usually meets between board meetings to review and approve managerial decisions, plans, and actions on behalf of the entire board. It has been suggested that the executive committee be utilized, when it is difficult to gather the entire board, to deal with an emerging or time-sensitive issue, and an executive committee consisting of available independent directors can make decisions on behalf of the company's entire board. The committee can be composed of the chairs of other committees to coordinate their activities and set an agenda for the entire board. The executive committee can act as a senior board to address all issues before they are presented to the entire board. In this situation, the executive committee serves best when there is a large board of directors.[56]

Disclosure Committee

The SEC recommends that public companies establish a disclosure committee to assist the company's executives (e.g., CEO, CFO) in complying with Section 302 of SOX internal control and financial statement certifications.[57] A disclosure committee should consist of personnel who are knowledgeable of the company's periodic filing requirements, business and legal disclosure practices, and disclosure controls and procedures. Individuals qualified to serve on the committee are the general counsel and the chief accounting officer, CAE, controller, risk management officer, outside legal counsel, and investor relations. The responsibilities of the disclosure committee include, but are not limited to:

- Overseeing the appropriateness of all disclosures that are made publicly available and the process of disseminating public information.
- Assisting executives in the preparation of and compliance with SOX executive certification requirements.
- Assisting management in the assessment of the effectiveness of the design and operation of internal control over financial reporting.

- Ensuring compliance with laws, regulations, rules, and standards related to the company's periodic filings.
- Assisting management with the assessment of control deficiencies and their classifications to significant deficiencies that should be communicated to the audit committee or material weaknesses that should be disclosed in the SEC filings.

Information Technology Committee

Post September 11, 2001, corporate boards began to pay more attention to information technology (IT) security and business continuity. Implementation of Section 404 on internal control over financial reporting underscores the importance of IT in financial reporting. Some companies have started to develop a separate IT board committee to address and oversee IT issues. A survey of 2,143 public companies in 2006 shows that only 86 of these companies had a technology committee overseeing IT projects and functions as well as evaluating future technologies and strategic opportunities.[58]

SUMMARY

Effective compliance with new corporate governance reforms, complexity of business, globalization, and technological advances have encouraged the board to establish standing committees to best utilize the expertise, knowledge, and efforts of its directors. Several standing committees of the board have emerged. The three mandatory committees for listed companies are audit, nominating/governance, and compensation committees. Other board committees, such as budget, finance, executive, special litigation, disclosure, or investment committees, may also be established by some public companies. Recent developments in corporate governance reforms have boosted the relevance, importance, and public profiles of all three mandatory committees for public companies. Thus, as corporate governance remains an integral element of ethical public company leadership, the need for a better understanding of these committees and their activities is becoming increasingly important. Board committees are normally formed to assist the company's board of directors in effectively fulfilling its fiduciary duty of protecting investor interests with the keen understanding that the entire board is responsible for the company's oversight function, as described in Chapter 3.

NOTES

1. Spencer Stuart. 2006. Spencer Stuart Board Index 2005. *CFO Direct* (January 12). Available at: www.cfodirect.pwc.com/CFODirectWeb/Controller.jpf?Nav Code=USAS-6BG34T.
2. Much of the discussions in this section come from: Rezaee, Z. (2006). *Audit committee oversight effectiveness post-Sarbanes-Oxley Act: Resources, attributes, functions, and accountability*. Bureau of National Affairs. Chapter 1.

3. Public Company Accounting Oversight Board. 2004. Auditing Standard No. 2: *An Audit of internal control over financial reporting performed in conjunction with an audit of financial statements* (Paragraph 17). Available at: www.pcaob.org/standards.
4. Sarbanes-Oxley Act of 2002. Available at: www.sec.gov.about/laws/soa2002.pdf. Securities and Exchange Commission. 2003. SEC Release Nos. 33-8220; 34-47654: *Standards relating to listed company audit committees*. Washington, DC: U.S. Government Printing Office. Blue Ribbon Committee on Improving the Effectiveness of Corporate Audit Committees. 1999. Report and recommendations of Blue Ribbon Committee on improving the effectiveness of corporate audit committees. NYSE and Nasdaq. KPMG. 2003. Audit Committee Roundtable: Building a framework for executive audit committee oversight. Audit Committee Institute. (Spring): 4. Available at: www.kpmg.com/aci.
5. Daum, J. H., and T. J. Neff. 2005. Key trends drive board composition. Spencer Stuart Board Index: *Directors and Board* 29 (2): 58–62.
6. Securities and Exchange Commission. 2003. Release No. 33-8183: Strengthening the commission's requirements regarding auditor independence. Available at: www.sec.gov/final/33-8183.htm.
7. Securities and Exchange Commission. 2003. SEC Release Nos. 33-8177; 34-47235: Disclosure required by Sections 406 and 407 of the Sarbanes-Oxley Act of 2002. Washington, DC: U.S. Government Printing Office.
8. Taub, S. 2006. Missing: Audit committee accountants. Available at: www.cfodirect.com/CFODirectweb/cfocontent.
9. Rezaee, Z. 2006. *Audit committee oversight effectiveness post-Sarbanes-Oxley Act.* Bureau of National Affairs.
10. Sarbanes-Oxley Act of 2002. Section 301. Available at: www.sarbanes-oxley.com/section.php?level=1&pub_id=Sarbanes-Oxley.
11. KPMG. 2004. Forensic fraud survey. Available at: www.kpmg.com/aci/docs/Fraud%20Survey_040855_R5.pdf.
12. PricewaterhouseCoopers. 2006. *World Watch: Governance and Corporate Reporting* (Issue 1). Available at: www.cfodirect.pwc.com/CFODirectweb/cfocontent/content6.
13. Taub, S. 2006. Missing: Audit Committee Accountants. Available at: www.cfodirect.com/CFODirectweb/cfocontent.
14. Rezaee, Z. 2006. *Audit committee oversight effectiveness post-Sarbanes-Oxley Act. Tax Management Inc.* Bureau of National Affairs.
15. PricewaterhouseCoopers (PwC). 2006. Audit committees: Are we using them effectively? Available at: www.uk.pwc.com.
16. Daum and Neff. Key trends drive board composition.
17. Council of Institutional Investors. 2005. Role of compensation committee (August). Available at: www.cii.org/policies/compensation/role_comp_committee.htm.
18. Corporate Counsel. 2005. The new standards for compensation committees. (September–October). *Executive Press.* Available at: www.compensationstandards.com.
19. Ibid.

20. Kristof, K. M. 2005. Bill targets executive compensation. *Los Angeles Times.* (November 14). Available at: www.latimes.com.
21. Ibid.
22. Bebchuk, L. A., and J. M. Fried. 2003. Executive compensation as an agency problem. *Journal of Economic Perspectives* 17 (3): 71–92.
23. Core, J., R. Holthausen, and D. Larcker. 1999. Corporate governance, chief executive officer compensation and firm performance. *Journal of Financial Economics* 51: 371–406. Available at: accounting.wharton.upenn.edu/spring2006/acct920/class%2013%20core-holthausen-larcker%201999.pdf.
24. Securities and Exchange Commission (SEC). 2006. SEC votes to adopt changes to disclosure requirements concerning executive compensation and related matters (July 26). Available at: www.sec.gov/news/press/2006/2006-123.htm.
25. Glass Lewis & Co. 2007. Stock-Option Backdating Scandals. Yellow Card Trend Alert (March 16). Available at: www.glasslewis.com.
26. Morgenson, G. 2006. Options fiesta, and investors paid the bill. *New York Times* (July 30). Available at: www.nytimes.com.
27. Akst, D. 2006. Why rules can't stop executive greed. *New York Times* (March 5). Available at: www.nytimes.com/2006/03/05/business/yourmoney/05cont.html.
28. State Board of Administration of Florida. 2005. SBA 2005 corporate governance report. Available at: www.sbafla.com/pdf/investment/CorpGovReport.pdf.
29. Ibid.
30. Committee for Economic Development. 2006. Private enterprise, public trust: The state of corporate America after Sarbanes-Oxley. Available at: www.ced.org.
31. Ibid.
32. The Conference Board. 2006. The evolving relationship between compensation committees and consultants (September). Available at: www.conference-board.org.
33. A letter sent by institutional investors to the chair of compensation committees of the 25 top S&P 500 companies concerning their compensation committee policies.
34. Ibid.
35. London Stock Exchange. 2004. Practical guide to corporate governance. Available at: http://investaquest.londonstockexchange.com/en-gb/products/companyservices/Practical+Guides.htm.
36. AFSCME, 2006. AFSCME Plan 2006 shareholder proposals: Board accountability needed to rein in excessive executive pay. Available at: www.afsme.org/press/2005/207.htm.
37. Securities and Exchange Commission. 2006. SEC votes to adopt changes to disclosure requirements.
38. CFA Institute. 2006. Re: Executive compensation and related party disclosures (Ref. S7-03-06). Available at: www.cfainstitute.org.
39. Committee for Economic Development (CED). 2006. Private enterprise, public trust: The State of corporate America after Sarbanes-Oxley. (March). Available at: www.ced.org/docs/report/report_2006corpgov.pdf.

40. London Stock Exchange. 2004. Practical guide to corporate governance (July). Available at: www.londonstockexchange.com/en-gb/products/companyservices/Practical+Guides.htm?wbc_purpose=Basic.
41. Many of these characteristics are extracted from Conference Board. 2003. Corporate governance best practices: A blueprint for the post-Enron era.
42. Spencer Stuart. 2006. Spencer Stuart Board Index 2005.
43. CalPERs. 2005. Majority vote election plan. Available at: www.calpers.ca.gov/index.jsp?bc=/about/press/pr-2005/march/majority-vote.xml.
44. Ibid.
45. Ibid.
46. Mishra, S. 2005. Shareholders give board support to board election reform in 2005. Investor Responsibility Research Center. *IRRC Corporate Governance Bulletin.* (September 1). Available at: http://oa.irrc.com/members/newsletters/data/2/JulySep_05-Reform.html?PRINT=YES.
47. McFarland, J. 2006. Director elections closer. Globeandmail.com (March 9). Available at: http://theglobandmail.com/servlet/story/RTGAM.20060309.wxrvotes09/EmailBNstory/Business/home.
48. Ibid.
49. Ibid.
50. UK Combined Code on Corporate Governance. 2003. The Combined Code on Corporate Governance (July). Available at: www.fsa.gov.uk/pubs/ukla/lr_comcode2003.pdf. Conference Board. 2003. Corporate governance best practices: A blueprint for the post-Enron era.
51. Securities and Exchange Committee. 2003. Disclosure regarding nominating committee functions and communications between security holders and boards of directors. (November). Available at: www.sec.gov/rules/final/33-8340.htm.
52. Ibid.
53. The Committee on Capital Markets Regulation. 2006. Interim report of the Committee on Capital Market Regulation. (November 30). Available at: www.capmktsreg.org/research.html.
54. Wilkie Farr & Gallagher, LLP. 2006. Delaware chancery court highlights pitfalls of a flawed special committee process in interested merger transactions. Shareholders, Litig. Civ. A. No. 16740 (Del. Ch. Dec. 21, 2005) (January 9). Available at: www.willkie.com.
55. Ibid.
56. Colley, J., J. Doyle, W. Stettinius, and G. Logan. 2003. *Corporate governance: The McGraw-Hill executive MBA series.* New York: McGraw-Hill.
57. Securities and Exchange Commission. 2002. Certification of disclosure in companies' quarterly and annual reports. (August 29). Available at: www.sec.gov/rules/final/33-8124.htm.
58. The Corporate Library conducted its analysis for Tapestry Networks on June 9, 2006, on a database of 2,143 public companies that it follows.

CHAPTER 5

The Managerial Function

INTRODUCTION

The managerial function of corporate governance consists of achieving operational efficiency, enhancing the quality, reliability, and transparency of financial reports, and ensuring compliance with applicable laws, regulations, rules, and standards. Shareholders may lack reasons to trust management because of information asymmetries, potential conflicts of interests, self-interest, and opportunistic behavior. Corporate governance mechanisms should be established and maintained to properly align management's interest with those of shareholders by reducing the extent of opportunistic behavior and information asymmetries. Management may have motives that differ from shareholders and be influenced by factors such as financial rewards (outsized executive compensation, including bonuses linked to short-term reported earnings) and relationships with other corporate governance participants (directors). When the opportunity is provided, management acts in an optimistic and self-interested manner as opposed to acting in the best interest of the company and its shareholders. Appropriate corporate governance mechanisms should be in place to identify, manage, or eliminate these potential conflicts of interest. This chapter addresses the managerial function and its vital role in improving corporate governance effectiveness and the reliability of financial reports.

MANAGEMENT RESPONSIBILITIES

Management, under the oversight direction of the board of directors, is fully responsible for all managerial functions, including the development and execution of corporate strategies, safeguarding resources, financial performance assessment, fair presentation of financial reports in all material respects, and increasing long-term shareholder value. The management team, led by the chief executive officer (CEO) and supported by the chief financial officer (CFO) and other senior executives (general counsel, controllers, treasurers, operating managers), assumes the functions of managing the business, running the day-to-day operations of the company and ensuring effective and responsible corporate governance. The management responsibilities described in this chapter are organized into three areas: operations, corporate reporting, and compliance, with a keen focus on financial reporting.

Operations

Operations involves the execution of a company's strategic plan, and may involve decisions by management to improve the efficiency, effectiveness, and cost structure of an organization's operations, including design, production, sale, and marketing of company products and services. The operations process should be a value-creation function that generates profit and enhances shareholder wealth in a responsible and ethical manner. Management, as a key participant in corporate governance, is responsible for managing the day-to-day operations of the company which may involve analyzing market trends, competition, domestic and global markets, and economic indicators. Operations may entail:

- Designing products and services, marketing and delivering them, and invoicing products and servicing customers.
- Investing in both human and capital resources.
- Financing investments and expenditures through internal growth, issuing stock, or incurring debt.

Corporate Reporting

Corporate reporting is much broader than financial reporting as it encompasses both financial and nonfinancial reports. Exhibit 5.1 presents the relationship between financial statements, financial reporting, and corporate reporting.

- Financial statements reporting focuses on providing historical financial information regarding the financial condition and results of operations in four basic financial statements: balance sheet, income statement, cash flow statement, and the statement of owner's equity.
- Financial reporting provides financial statement information and other financial information, including analysis of financial aspects and internal control over financial reporting. It is broader than financial statements reporting.
- Corporate reporting provides financial, contextual, and nonfinancial information on key performance indicators (KPIs) that enables investors to better understand the company's financial and nonfinancial measures (market share, new product development, customer retention, social responsibility, environmental performance).

Both financial statements reporting and financial reporting capture only financial information about the company's financial position and results of operations. Corporate reporting, on the other hand, captures not only financial information but also nonfinancial information relevant to KPIs used in making operational, financing, and investment decisions. There is a strong need for the development of a globally accepted corporate reporting model to record and disclose

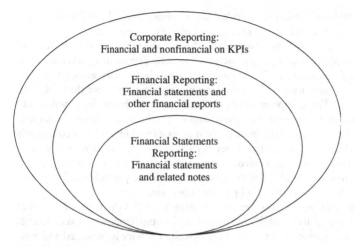

EXHIBIT 5.1 Corporate Reporting

a company's multiple bottom lines (MBL) performance regarding economic, governance, ethical, social, and environmental activities.

The American Institute of Certified Public Accountants (AICPA) Special Committee on Enhanced Business Reporting (EBR) established the Enhanced Business Reporting Consortium, which is in the process of developing a voluntary framework for the disclosure of key financial and nonfinancial performance indicators driven by business strategy, plans, opportunities, and risks. The EBR will establish voluntary guidelines for reporting performance indicators into four categories:

1. *Business landscape.* The company's perspectives on the business and economic environment are identified, as well as all relevant external forces that could influence the company's business strategy for achieving sustainable performance and enduring success. For the business landscape, a company needs to:
   a. Identify the boundaries of the market(s) in which the business operates in terms of industry sectors, markets served, market size and growth potential, geographic locations, market stability, range of products, and services and competitors.
   b. Discuss the effects of market conditions on past performance and management's expectations for the future.
   c. Discuss the company's capacity to withstand changes in forces beyond its control.

   It then needs to focus on competition, specifically the key factors necessary to be successful, the opportunities and threats, and suggestions regarding new products or improved quality that will make the company more competitive in the market; and customers, specifically the effects of changing customer needs and expectations and the effect of environmental, demographic, social, or cultural trends on the company's customer base. Other aspects of the business landscape

include technological change, shareholder relations, capital availability, legal environment, political environment, and regulatory environment.

2. *Strategy.* Based on the defined business landscape, strategies are established and executed to enable the company to achieve success. The strategy section builds on the business landscape and communicates not only the business strategy, but also how the organization and the underlying structures support the execution of the strategy. The company needs to examine how the business will make money and create value—what differentiates its product from those of competitors. It also must describe how management assesses and updates the company's business model. Next the company needs to examine the organization, specifically its structure, values and culture, corporate governance, risk management, handling of environmental and social issues, the business portfolio and its future direction, resource allocation, and product life cycle.

3. *Competencies and resources.* Here the company identifies the value drivers that facilitate managing its available resources and competencies in executing its strategies. The company must assess how customer service is managed and how customers' changing needs are identified and handled. Other areas that should be explored include: people, innovation, supply chain, intellectual property, information and technology, financial assets, and physical assets.

4. *Performance.* Assessment of performance of the company and its management team is accomplished by linking its achievement of sustainable shareholder value creation and other stakeholder value protection to its business landscape, strategy, competencies, and resources. Performance assessment provides insight into whether the company and its management team have produced results in line with stakeholder expectations. Ultimately, the key performance indicators or narrative about qualitative factors enable stakeholders to better assess sustainable business practices and the quality and variability of a company's cash flows and profitability. Four factors of performance are examined: profitability, liquidity, operating, and segment.[1]

Initiatives to Improve Corporate Reporting

Several initiatives have been taken to improve the quality of corporate reports and make them relevant, useful, reliable, and transparent for decision making. Among these initiatives are:

Forward-Looking Information   Investors like to have forward-looking financial and nonfinancial information and companies have strived to provide such information. PricewaterhouseCoopers (PwC) has recently published a practical guide that is based on seven pillars of effective communication by public companies to their stakeholders, including shareholders:

1. Resources available to the company and how they are managed
2. Key risk and uncertainties that may affect the company's sustainable performance in creating long-term value for its shareholders

3. The significant relationships with principal shareholders (e.g., shareholders, customers, suppliers, employees, governments, and society) that are likely to affect the company's sustainable performance
4. Quantified data pertaining to trends and factors that are likely to influence the company's future prospects
5. Any uncertainties underpinning forward-looking information
6. Targets relating to key performance indicators (both financial and nonfinancial) used to manage the company's business
7. How the report reflects the company's long-term objectives and the strategies to achieve those objectives.

Management Commentary   Financial reporting includes both qualitative and quantitative financial information in addition to financial statements in order to provide a full understanding of business performance. The International Accounting Standards Board (IASB) has issued a discussion paper on management commentary (MC) which supports the financial reporting concept.[2] MC is expected to explain the main trends, key performance indicators, and factors that are likely to influence the company's long-term performance and current performance position. MC accompanies financial statements and provides additional financial information about the nature of business, objectives, strategies, main resources, related risks and relationships, performance measures, results, and prospects.

Comprehensive Business Reporting Model   The Chartered Financial Analysts Institute (CFA) has published a paper that sheds light on the future corporate reporting. It consists of 12 principles:

1. The company must be viewed from the perspective of its shareholders.
2. Fair-value information is the only information relevant for financial decision-making.
3. Accounting standards should provide guidance for the measurement, recognition, and disclosure of relevant information for decision making.
4. All events and economic transactions should be accurately and completely recognized as they occur in the financial statements.
5. Investors' wealth assessment must determine the materiality threshold of what is significant to the informed investor.
6. Financial reporting must be neutral—in particular, accounting standards should not be influenced by the outcome of the reporting.
7. All changes in net assets must be reported in a single statement of changes in net assets.
8. The statement of changes in net assets should include timely recognition of all changes in fair values of assets and liabilities.
9. The cash flow statement should be prepared using the direct method.
10. Changes affecting each of the financial statements must be reported and explained on a disaggregated basis.

11. Individual line items should be reported based on the nature of the items rather than their function.
12. Disclosures must provide all the additional information shareholders need to understand the item being reported on financial statements.[3]

Financial reporting transparency, quality, reliability, and integrity can be improved and its complexity can be reduced by:

- Cooperative efforts by the Financial Accounting Standards Board (FASB) and the International Accounting Standards Board (IASB) to move toward the convergence of accounting standards in promulgating a single, globally accepted set of reporting standards.
- Discontinuation of the current practices of quarterly earnings forecasts driven by the earnings guessing game, and based on a short-term goal of meeting earnings targets. Instead, there should be a move toward providing transparent and timely information on the fundamental long-term drivers and economic factors that will affect the company and its prospects.
- The use of fair value for financial reporting measurements.
- The move toward the eXtensible Business Reporting Language (XBRL) format by establishing a taxonomy that enables consistent and reliable reporting across all companies and industries.

Compliance

Compliance with both the spirit and the requirements of applicable rules, regulations, and laws, including legal, regulatory, and tax and accounting rules, is one of the primary responsibilities of management. The focus of the investing community and the financial markets will continue to be on a public company's financial performance; however, recently companies' social responsibility performance has also started to receive attention. In some cases, particularly in Europe where it may be required by law, management has been asked to start providing sustainability reporting focusing on the company's compliance with social, ethical, and environmental regulations. There has been growing international interest in corporate social responsibilities, including environmental, social, and, governance (ESG) issues.[4] The ESG issues can affect the financial performance of investments, and thus such information should be considered as a factor in the investment decision-making process.

CORPORATE EXECUTIVES/OFFICERS

Corporations usually have a management team consisting of a CEO, general counsel, CFO, controller, treasurer, and other key members, including chief compliance/governance officer, chief risk officer, chief operations officer, chief development officer, and chief ethics officer.

Chief Executive Officer

The top executive is typically the chief executive officer (CEO). The managerial function is usually carried out by a management team that also consists of other senior executives.[5] All employees look to the CEO for direction and guidance, and to establish the tone-at-the-top conduct, as actions speak louder than words. The CEO should promote ethical, professional conduct throughout the entire company and be held accountable for the long-term success of the company. The CEO is in a significant leadership role and typically is well compensated for these responsibilities. The CEO should also have a strong ethical value system and character, in addition to the appropriate skill sets, in order to lead the company and build long-term shareholder value.

Corporate governance reforms presented in Chapters 1 and 2 address many challenges facing CEOs, including holding them more accountable to shareholders and avoiding real, or even the appearance of, conflicts of interests that may impair their objectivity, fairness, and transparency. This section presents key CEO challenges, including: fiduciary duties; pay and skill; self-serving and self-dealing CEOs; succession planning; duality; financial knowledge and understanding; and diversity.

Fiduciary Duties   Executives are considered agents of the company and its owners (shareholders). This agency relationship creates a fiduciary duty. A number of key executives may have employment agreements with their employers. As an officer of the company, they have a fiduciary duty to act in the best interests of the company and its shareholders. Breach of these legal duties may result in litigation by shareholders (owners) to recover losses caused by well-compensated executives, who should be acting in the best long-term interests of shareholders rather than, for example, engaging in self-dealing that may violate their fiduciary duty to the company, including tort actions against the agent for losses caused by the breach.[6] One of these fiduciary duties is the duty of loyalty, which requires executives to act solely for the benefit of the company and its shareholders. This duty of loyalty obligates executives not to:

- Act adversely to the principal (shareholders) without consent, or on behalf of a person whose interests are adverse to the principal without consent.
- Compete with the principal.
- Use or wrongly communicate confidential information.[7]

On May 25, 2006, former Enron senior executives Ken Lay and Jeffrey Skilling were found guilty of lying about their company's finances in the second largest bankruptcy in the history of the United States. The verdict was announced four years after the Enron bankruptcy and about four months on trial. Skilling was found guilty of 19 counts of fraud, conspiracy, making false statements, and inside trading and was convicted on nine criminal counts that could result in a maximum sentence of 185 years. Lay, who subsequently passed away, was found guilty on four bank fraud charges for illegally using the company's money to buy stock. The only good thing that came out of the Enron bankruptcy and subsequent conviction of its executives is the recognition that public companies' directors and officers have fiduciary duties of loyalty and care to investors. They must be conscientious of their duty because they will eventually be held accountable for their actions.

Pay and Skill   There has been much discussion on the relationship between CEO performance and compensation and concerns about excessive CEO pay. In 1992 CEOs were paid 82 times the average of blue-collar workers; in 2004 they were paid more than 400 times this average.[8] This excessive pay coupled with the perceived decline in their performance as measured by total shareholder return has raised severe concerns about equity and the fairness of executive compensation, particularly as worker pay remains flat. The excessive executive compensation is evidenced by the fact that Lee R. Raymond, the retired CEO of Exxon, was compensated more than $686 million from 1993 to 2005, which amounts to $144,573 per service day.[9] On January 18, 2006, the judge overseeing the United Airline Corporation's reorganization approved an executive compensation package of at least $115 million; the airline company is emerging from Chapter 11 bankruptcy and other employees (pilots, flight attendants, mechanists, ticket agents) took pay cuts.[10]

Outsized executive pay is, unfortunately, a common occurrence in the United States. In the United Kingdom, there is a smaller albeit growing gap between the highest-paid and lowest-paid workers as they follow the U.S. example of overpaid CEOs: Executives at the largest 100 companies earned 54 times as much as the typical worker in 2004 compared with only 10 times as much in 1979.[11] An academic study reveals that the sales of the top 100 quoted companies on the U.K. stock exchange increased by an annual 2.7 percent from 1983 to 2002, pretax profiting rose by the same amount, and company market valuation increased by 18.2 percent, while executive pay rose by 26.2 percent.[12] These facts suggest that the role of CEOs has been regarded as "value skimming" rather than "value increasing" for shareholders, as CEOs "mak[e] a big show of doing all the things beloved of the management gurus but in reality quietly enriching themselves for mediocre performance."[13]

Self-Serving and Self-Dealing CEOs   Several CEOs of high-profile companies have been indicted, and in some cases convicted, for self-serving, self-dealing, and engaging in fraud, conspiracy, and filing false financial reports. On July 14, 2005, Qwest's former finance chief, Robin Szeliga, who was charged during an inquiry into the company's accounting policies, pleaded guilty to insider trading. Former WorldCom CEO Bernard Ebbers got 25 years in prison for his involvement in overseeing the largest corporate fraud in U.S. history. This sentence was handed down three years after WorldCom went bankrupt in an $11 billion accounting fraud. John Rigas, the founder of Adelphia, received 15 years of prison time for his role in the fraud. Timothy Rigas, Adelphia's CFO, was sentenced to 20 years in prison. Calisto Tanzi, the founder and CEO of Parmalat, the Italian dairy and juice giant that collapsed in an $18 billion fraud, will stand trial for alleged market securities violations. Tyco's Dennis Kozlowski and Mark Swartz got 8 and 25 years jail time, respectively, for their corporate misconduct. Kirk Shelton of Cendant received 10 years for involvement with accounting scandals. Ken Lay and Jeffrey Skilling, executives of bankrupt Enron, were found guilty of fraud and conspiracy and are also facing years in prison; however, Ken Lay died in 2006. These cases of executive indictments and convictions have greatly damaged the integrity and reputation of CEOs generally, while creating a high demand for competent, ethical, and accountable CEOs. However, the responsible and ethical actions of many executives have made U.S. companies the most productive and competitive in the global market and have made the U.S. financial markets the most vibrant and efficient in the world.

Succession Planning There was unprecedented CEO turnover in 2005: 1,228 CEOs left their posts in 2005, more than double the 663 who left in 2004.[14] The upward trend in CEO turnover has resulted from either the voluntary planned retirement or unexpected departure due to illness, accident, or failure to fulfill the assumed responsibility (e.g. wrongdoings, not meeting the forecasted earnings). Without proper succession planning, this turnover can be detrimental to sustainable performance and effectiveness of governance. This growing trend has brought the vital issue of CEO succession to the attention of the boards. David A. Nadler suggests that:

> *CEOs and boards ought to start the succession planning process at least four to five years before the CEO plans to retire ... Boards want to be involved in setting the criteria for assessing CEO candidates. After all, they're the ones who have to live with the consequences of the decision, not the incumbent CEO.*[15]

A 2006 survey of 1,330 directors conducted by Corporate Board Member and PwC indicates that: (1) 20 percent of the surveyed directors reported their company did not have a succession plan; (2) about 23 percent believed that their CEO was uncomfortable with the topic of succession; and (3) more than 43 percent said they were dissatisfied with their company's succession plan.[16] Business surrounded with significant uncertainties, a CEO's tenure is not guaranteed. Thus, the company's board of directors, and particularly the CEO, should, in advance, search for and develop internal talented and qualified executives to succeed the CEO, provide opportunities for candidates to gain experience in all aspects of the business, and motivate them to develop the required skills to become a successful CEO.[17] Effective CEO succession planning contributes to sustainable company performance, the effectiveness of its corporate governance, better performance of the current CEO, smoother and seamless transition, and the success of the new CEO.

The entire board of directors, particularly the nominating/governance and compensation committees, should be involved in the CEO succession planning. The 2005 Spencer Stuart Board Index (SSBI) survey indicates that: 38 percent of Standard & Poor's (S&P) 500 boards assigned the responsibility for CEO succession planning to their compensation committee whereas 35 percent and 26 percent said that their nominating/governance and the entire board or the independent directors deal with this issue, respectively; about 48 percent of surveyed boards indicated that they use a formal process (e.g., benchmarking internal candidates against external ones) to evaluate internal candidates for CEO; and more than 66 percent said that their compensation committee deals with CEO evaluation.[18]

CEO Duality   CEO duality—where the CEO also holds the position of the chair of the company's board of directors—has a few advantages and a number of disadvantages, as discussed in Chapter 3. CEO duality remains a challenge for many U.S. public companies attempting to establish the right balance of power among executives, directors, and shareholders. It is expected that the trend toward the separation of the positions of the chair of the board and the CEO will continue to increase, eventually bringing U.S. practice in line with that of European countries (e.g., the United Kingdom).

Financial Knowledge and Understanding   CEOs in the post-SOX era are expected to have sufficient knowledge and understanding of their company's financial risks, internal controls, and financial reporting in addition to other managerial skills. According to a survey conducted by *CFO Magazine*, 31 percent of 341 CFO participants believed that prior to the passage of SOX, their CEOs might have been ignorant of financial statement fraud in their companies; 44 percent said that would have been impossible.[19] In the post-SOX period, the majority of CFOs (95 percent) believe that their CEOs are either moderately or significantly involved in important corporate finance decisions. The survey reports that CEOs in the post-SOX era understand financial issues very well or extremely well.[20] Today's CEOs cannot plead ignorance of their company's financials because of the new penalties for false filings and executive certification requirements on both internal controls and financial statements.

Diversity   CEO positions in large public companies traditionally have been dominated by males. There is a need for more diversity in the CEO position. The year 2005 was not a good one for female CEOs of Fortune 500 companies. For two consecutive years (2004, 2005), stocks of companies led by female CEOs on average underperformed the benchmark S&P 500's index, and the number of female CEOs of Fortune 500 companies fell to seven in 2005 compared to nine in 2004.[21] More work needs to be done in addressing why there are so few female CEOs, particularly when women represent more than 47 percent of today's workforce.[22]

Chief Financial Officer

Traditionally, the role of CFOs has been primarily accounting and finance driven, covering controllership, financial reporting, decisions support, and regulatory compliance. However, this is changing and expanding into both business and strategic corporate decision making. The role of the CFO has evolved into a major corporate governance participant engaging in internal control, financial reporting, strategy execution, value creation and enhancement for shareholders, and value protection for all other stakeholders. CEOs and directors rely on CFOs to help them in developing and executing corporate strategies. CFO Research Services issued a report entitled "The Activist CFO—Alignment with Strategy, Not Just with the Business," in April 2005, which details the trend toward activist CFOs who participate with both business and strategy authorities.[23] According to the report:

The activist CFO may sound a lot like a CEO, an overall leader of the enterprise and a super-line manager . . . . focus first on the strategy, not just on business support . . . . recent executive appointments suggest that the activist CFO is ideally suited to an expanded role.[24]

CFOs now function beyond the traditional role as control agents, scorekeepers, or decision supporters. They participate in strategic decisions and help attain goals by becoming active and working closely with the board of directors. The CFO Research Services report also identifies four CFO profiles:

1. Growth navigators who work closely with CEOs with a keen focus on growth rather than cost control.
2. Executive maestros who primarily focus on operational excellence.
3. Turnaround surgeons who rise to the challenge of making difficult decisions to restore ailing companies to financial health.
4. Business model transformers who identify opportunities for strategic innovation and take full advantage of these opportunities.[25]

A survey of directors indicates that the CFO's key role in corporate governance is to ensure that the letter of the law is met (often relying on the general counsel) to promote effective corporate governance above and beyond the letter of the law to include the spirit of the law, to ensure effective and candid communication between the CFO and the board, and to behave ethically.[26] The top five professional qualities of CFOs in terms of importance are:

1. Strategic sense.
2. Financial knowledge and expertise, particularly SEC disclosure rules and accounting and auditing standards.
3. Budgeting and planning ability.
4. Management skill.
5. Capital market knowledge.[27]

Indeed, CFOs are aware of their strategic role in corporate governance and the increasing opportunities of becoming tomorrow's CEO.[28] Despite the current trend toward the involvement of CFOs in strategic decision making and corporate governance, their primary responsibility is to ensure the effectiveness of internal control over financial reporting as well as the reliability, integrity, quality, and transparency of both internal and external financial reports.

CFO Transition to CEO Historically, less than 15 percent of CFOs get promoted to CEO. However, in the post-SOX era, boards "are less interested in the swashbuckling executive of the 1990s and more apt to choose a trusted manager who shows the right blend of operational and financial expertise. With more CFOs gaining hands-on experience managing business, they have become contenders."[29] The dot.com bubble of the 1990s favored CEOs with a background in engineering, marketing, and sales.

The dot.com debacles and financial scandals of the late 1990s and early 2000s have made finance an essential part of the CEO's job.

There are several advantages to having former CFOs as CEOs:

- CFOs tend to focus more on shareholder value creation and enhancement by considering all aspects of the business; CEOs with more marketing or operations backgrounds tend to focus on growth and cost efficiency.
- CFOs pay close attention to metrics and focus on economic value-added activities and ways to improve performance and generate a return that exceeds the company's cost of capital.
- CFOs may be regarded as investor-friendly because of their financial and market-analysis experience and their attention to investors' return on investment and stock price indicators (e.g., price/earnings multiple).
- CFOs are better equipped to identify business risk, assess the challenges and opportunities presented by the business risk, determine the company's risk appetite and tolerance, and manage the risk according to the company's tolerance.[30]

Corporate Development Officer

Recent corporate governance reforms as well as the increased investor scrutiny and the emerging requirements for commitment to excellence in corporate governance necessitate the establishment of a new position of the corporate development officer (CDO), particularly for companies actively engaged in mergers and acquisitions. According to the Ernst & Young study *Striving for Transaction Excellence: The Emerging Role of the Corporate Development Officer*, there is a need for another "C" in the C-suites of Corporate America, the CDO, to assist the CFO in remaining focused on financial reporting and compliance with applicable laws and regulations.[31] The study indicates that about 37 percent of existing CDOs report directly to the CEO or the company's boards; 86 percent of CDOs are a primary source of generating transaction opportunities such as mergers and acquisitions, sales of subsidiaries, carve-outs and spin-offs; and the proliferation of the CDO role is likely to continue.[32]

An Ernst & Young study also presented ten attributes of corporate development functions in averting risk, meeting the emerging challenging transaction market, and improving their outcomes:

1. *Alignment of strategic planning and corporate development activities.* CDOs assist the individual business units to formulate transaction strategies that meet their business unit objectives and annually assess corporate strategies.
2. *Robust pipeline management.* CDOs facilitate a formal pipeline management process to incorporate inputs from key business unit leaders to establish metrics and measures to determine cost, time resources, bottlenecks, and other components of pipeline management and eventually to consummate the transaction deals.

3. *Realistic synergy analysis in modeling transactions.* Providing that synergy planning drives transaction pricing, CDOs establish models focusing on discounted cash flow analysis, liquidation analysis, analytical analysis for comparable transactions and companies, adjusted book value, pricing analysis, consummating the deal, and due diligence analysis to attain the underlying strategic objectives and preserve identified value.

4. *Full-scope due diligence.* CDOs focus on "full-scope due diligence" as encompassing both financial and nonfinancial determinants of corporate development strategies, including management competence and continuity, market trends, production capability, supplier contracts, potential litigation, value drivers, and strategic imperatives in making informed decisions.

5. *Continuous measurement and feedback.* CDOs assist in identifying and quantifying business opportunities where value will be created, enhanced, and maintained through synergy planning and developing monitoring systems to identify opportunities for continuous improvement, ongoing measurement and meaningful processes.

6. *Well-developed integration road map.* CDOs design a comprehensive road map to mitigate integration risk, increase value, and manage time constraints, and should prioritize those activities that will achieve key objectives.

7. *High-performing virtual teams.* CDOs establish and maintain high-performing virtual teams representing members from all business units to formalize and document processes, create sophisticated tools, and align individual metrics with transaction measures and goals.

8. *Interaction with the board of directors and executive committee.* CDOs interact with executive management and directors and make periodic presentations to the board in order to review the pipeline motion and its alignment to corporate strategy and to seek preliminary approval for potential transaction opportunities.

9. *Documentation for accountability.* CDOs prepare documentation of formal procedures for decision making, controls, communication protocols, and retention policies to measure and reward functional and individual performance in all phases of the transaction life cycle and to promote a culture of accountability.

10. *Robust financial models.* CDOs establish expandable and flexible financial models through all stages of the transaction life cycle, including postdeal integration, quantitative analysis of key value drivers, and the benchmark for look-back processes to ensure anticipated synergies have been realized.[33]

Chief Risk Officer

Enterprise risk management (ERM) was originally used by organizations to identify and manage financial and litigation risks that impede production or negatively affect revenues.[34] In the post-SOX period, ERM takes a broader strategic approach to promote corporate governance effectiveness of not only controlling risks but also revealing growth opportunities. A chief risk officer can be appointed to oversee ERM overall strategies and proper implementation of their various policies related to financial risk, operational risk, internal audit, and compliance. The majority of financial service institutions (over 80 percent) are creating the position of chief risk officer (CRO) to manage their risks resulting from regulations, outsourcing, off-shoring, mergers, and lending activities.[35] The number of financial institutions with CROs has increased about 30 percent since 2002. A tougher regulatory environment and increased scrutiny by customers and investors have encouraged financial institutions to pay more attention to risk management. Public companies may consider combining the position of the CRO with the chief governance officer (CGO), discussed in the next section, to ensure that corporate governance policies and practices are in line with the emerging corporate governance reforms. The combined positions of the CRO and CGO can set a right tone at the top promoting compliance with all applicable laws, regulations, rules, listing standards, and best practices of corporate governance, and can ensure that noncompliance risks are managed.

Chief Governance Officer

The emerging corporate governance reforms have underscored the importance of corporate governance measures and compliance with these measures. To comply with corporate governance measures effectively, it may be feasible and desirable to have one individual take on the role of a chief governance officer. The essential responsibilities of the CGO may include:

- At a minimum, ensuring knowledge of corporate governance regulations and best practices, particularly as governance moves from compliance to a business imperative.
- Improving corporate governance practices and communication with investors.
- Aligning corporate governance practices with global best practices.
- Fostering positive relationships between the company's board of directors and its management and investors, particularly institutional investors.
- Assisting in achieving the corporate governance objective of creating and enhancing long-term shareholder value while protecting the interests of other stakeholders (e.g., creditors, employees, customers, suppliers, government).
- Establishing effective corporate governance practices for the board of directors, its committees (audit, compensation, nominating), and staff.
- Conducting training and ethics for the company's personnel on its corporate governance structure and measures.

Chief Ethics and Compliance Officer

The compliance culture can be promoted through the establishment of a centralized chief ethics and compliance officer (CECO) who is primarily responsible for ensuring compliance with all applicable laws, regulations, rules, standards, codes of ethics, policies, and procedures, and who oversees all compliance functions. The CECO should report directly to the board and should maintain a close working relationship with the company's directors to aid in setting compliance strategies; establishing compliance programs, policies, and procedures based on the determined compliance strategies; properly communicating compliance policies and procedures to business units' compliance officers; and continuously monitoring and enforcing the effective functioning of compliance policies and procedures. The compliance culture can also be promoted locally through each business unit, to ensure that management complies with all applicable laws, regulations, rules, standards, codes of ethics, policies, and procedures. Regardless of how the culture is organized, it should be integrated throughout the organization.

The 2006 survey conducted by the Ethics and Compliance Officer Association (ECOA) and Salary.com indicates that: (1) organizations recognize the importance of their ethics and compliance office; (2) the compensation of ethics and compliance officers, on average, increased by 12 percent in 2006; (3) top global ethics and compliance executives earned a median annual salary of $206,800, median total cash compensation of $285,000, and median long-term incentives of $132,100; (4) top domestic ethics and compliance executives earned a median annual salary of $180,000 with a median total cash compensation of $202,300 and median long-term incentives of $81,600; and (5) ethics and compliance officers add value to their organizations as reflected in their increased compensation.[36]

EXECUTIVE COMPENSATION

The year 2006 is regarded as the year of executive compensation scrutiny and reforms. Many consider executive pay as the single most important issue facing corporate governance after accurate financial reporting and board independence. Pay-for-performance decisions are an integral component of the monitoring function of corporate governance and an important way for shareholders to assess the performance of executives. The establishment of attainable, reasonable, and objective goals and proper structure of the company's pay-for-performance programs that reward executives for sustainable, enduring, and outstanding performance can contribute to the effectiveness of corporate governance. The general philosophy is that executives should receive proper incentives and be paid for their good performance to create sufficient motives for outstanding performance, and they should not be paid excessively for poor performance or underperformance.[37] A joint report of the CFA Institute and the Business Roundtable Institute for Corporate Ethics: (1) suggests that corporate executives' compensation be aligned with sustainable enduring shareholder value creation and enhancement supported by the company's long-term goals and strategies; and (2) encourages institutional investors and asset managers to establish processes to ensure that the companies in which they invest use effective, sustainable pay-for-performance criteria in determining executive compensation.[38]

A survey of 55 institutional investors representing $800 billion in assets, conducted by consulting firm Watson Wyatt Worldwide in 2005, indicates that: the vast majority of respondents (90 percent) reported that corporate executives are dramatically overpaid; about 85 percent believed that current pay models are not linked to performance and have hurt corporate America's image; and more than 87 percent believed that directors' and officers' pay is heavily influenced by management.[39]

These results suggest that the survey respondents are not satisfied with current executive pay, compensation standards, severance-pay packages, and compensation disclosure practices, but they do regard pay-for-performance models (e.g., stock awards) as favorable. A vast number of shareholder groups and the employee pension plan for the American Federation of State, County and Municipal Employees (AFSCME) and institutional investor TIAA-CREF focus more on executive compensation by withholding votes based on "poor" compensation practices.

Glass Lewis & Co., in September 2006, released its review of 2005 executive compensation practices.[40] The report is based on the analysis of 2,375 companies that were in either Standard & Poor's 500 index or the Russell 3000 index. Glass Lewis & Co. established its proprietary pay-for-performance model by analyzing six indicators of shareholder wealth and business performance. These indicators are two-year stock-price change, two-year change in book value per share, two-year growth in earnings per share, one-year return on assets, one-year return on equity, and one-year total return. The model then evaluates compensation of the top five executives by benchmarking that against compensation of the top five executives at peer companies. The model calculates a weighted-average executive compensation percentile and compares them with performance percentile in calculating the "pay-for-performance gap." The gap scores are placed on a forced curve and then each company is assigned a letter grade A through F with 20 percent of companies receiving an A and 10 percent receiving an F.

The 2006 executive compensation report indicates that: (1) at the 25 companies with overpaid compensation, CEO compensation pay averaged $16.7 million in 2005 while the stocks at these companies fell an average of 14 percent and their net income dropped 25 percent on average; (2) at the top 25 underpaid companies, CEO compensation pay averaged $4.4 million while these companies' stock increased by 38.5 percent and their net income rose by 43.8 percent on average; (3) in the top 25 overpaid companies, CEO compensation is about 6.4 percent of their reported net income, whereas in the top 25 underpaid companies, their executive pay is about 0.2 percent of the reported net income; (4) a large number of companies continue to pay outsized compensation to their executives, whereas the worst pay-for-performances scores for 2005 include Interpublic Group of Cos., Morgan Stanley, Ariba Inc., and Vitesse Semiconductor Corp; (5) companies with the best pay-for-performance scores for 2005 consist of Goggle Inc., Caterpillar Inc., Nordstrom Inc., and Titanium Metals Corp; (6) 98 executives in 2005 received more than $20 million in annual compensation; and (7) some companies with poor pay-for-performance practices have experienced severe problems in other areas of their corporate governance or financial reporting.[41]

Anecdotal evidence is mixed regarding the relation between CEO pay and the nation's economic performance. A survey of directors documented that 65 percent believed the executive pay has contributed to positive U.S. economic performance in the sense that good executives help to create jobs and sell products that contribute to the prosperity of the nation.[42] A survey of institutional investors, on the other hand, found that only 22 percent reported that the executive pay system has helped the nation's economic growth; 90 percent felt top executives are significantly overpaid.[43] The contrasting views of investors and directors on reasonableness and relevance of executive pay suggest: (1) despite recent corporate governance reforms, management decides who gets on the board, and thus directors have incentives to support pay arrangements that favor senior executives; (2) directors are more aligned with CEOs than with shareholders; and (3) outsized executive pay will continue to grow until shareholders are empowered to easily replace directors.

Components of Executive Compensation

Corporate executives are generally paid on three levels: for their position, performance and purpose.[44] First, executives, regardless of their performance (e.g. good or bad), are paid annual salaries for their position according to their employment contract. Second, executives are awarded with a bonus or profit sharing, for recognition of their performance above and beyond their salary base, which is typically tied to the company's performance in terms of profits or achievement of goals. Finally, executives are rewarded for achieving the primary purpose of creating sustainable shareholder value through their stock options, which are normally tied to stock price performance as designated to align executives' interest with those of shareholders. Any other means of compensating executives, including backdating of option grants, not only weakens the bond between executives and shareholders but also guarantees executives a low entry point that is not available to the average shareholder.[45]

Executive compensation includes: salary; annual incentive compensation (bonus); long-term incentive compensation; stock option awards and stock award units; employment contracts, severance, and change-of-control payments; retirement arrangements; and stock ownership.[46]

Salary   Salary is the major component of executive compensation. It should be set at a level that reflects responsibilities, tenure, and past performance yielding highest value for the company. Salary paid to executives should be comparable with their peer group, and the compensation committee should publicly disclose its justification and rationale for paying the company's executives and high-paid personnel above the median of the peer group.

Annual Incentive Compensation   The annual, short-term, cash-incentive compensation plans should be designed both to reward superior performance that meets or exceeds predetermined and disclosed performance targets and to align executive interests with the company's objectives and strategic goals. The compensation committee should structure the methodology for bonus plans containing specific qualitative and quantitative performance-based operation and strategic measures; get board approval on incentive formula plans; and fully disclose the description of the qualitative and quantitative measures, benchmarks used, targets set, performance cycle determined, and details on the determination of final payouts. Shareholders should approve the establishment of and any significant amendments to the company's annual incentive compensation plans for directors and officers. Section 304 of SOX requires that executives repay incentive compensation to the company when they engage in corporate scandals, malfeasance, or fraudulent financial activities that cause restatements of financial statements or significant harm to the company.

Long-Term Compensation   Long-term compensation plans are designed to achieve several long-term objectives, including retaining productive and highly qualified executives, aligning executives' financial interests with those of shareholders, and promoting and rewarding superior long-term performance. The compensation committee should evaluate the costs and benefits of long-term incentive compensation plans thoroughly to ensure that they are designed effectively and efficiently and that they are achieving their intended long-term strategic goals. The committee should fully disclose the philosophy and strategy for the plans, including the criteria and grant timing for the company's directors and officers in the annual proxy statement. Shareholders should approve the establishment of any material amendments to the company's long-term incentive plans, including equity-based plans. The compensation committee should incorporate disgorgement provisions for repaying provided compensation into the long-term incentive plans in the event of material corporate malfeasance or fraudulent financial activities involving directors and officers.

Stock Option Awards   Stock option awards are considered long-term incentive plans granted to executives to attract and retain talented executives and reward superior performance. Stock options grant holders the right, but not the obligation, to buy stock in the future. Thus stock options have costs to the company that should be recognized as an expense on the income statements according to the provisions of the Statement of Financial Accounting Standards (SFAS) 123(R). SFAS 123(R) requires stock options to be recognized as expenses and subtracted from earnings in the same way as other salary and benefits costs. The effect of recognizing stock option expenses on reported earnings of public companies will be significant. For example, earnings for companies in the S&P 500 index would have decreased 6 percent and 8 percent in 2004 and 2003, respectively, had all stock options been expensed.[47] Accounting for stock options will be discussed further later in this chapter.

Investors may have the perception that options are awarded at fixed dates and the exercise price of options equals the market value of the underlying stock on the same date. This perception may not hold true in the case of backdated options granted at below-market prices. Backdating or pre-emptive timing of options can cause a substantial increase in the value of backdated options. Option backdating practices enable companies to issue so-called "in-the-money" discounted options without shareholder approval and proper disclosure, which have already resulted in internal investigations, probes by federal authorities, late filings, financial restatements, internal deficiencies, shareholder lawsuits, and executive departures. These detrimental effects of option backdating, along with the opportunity for executives to benefit at the expense of investors, can have negative effects on shareholder wealth.

Stock Ownership   Executive stock ownership is a useful incentive plan and an important component of executive pay. The agency theory suggests that the level of executive stock ownership in the company may provide incentives for management to align its interests with those of shareholders as it approaches high levels but may have negative impacts on other corporate governance mechanisms as management becomes entrenched. Academic research suggests that earnings quality may be lower at entrenchment levels of between 30 and 50 percent of executive stock ownership.[48] The board of directors and particularly the compensation committee can alleviate these concerns by restricting executive stock sales, requiring executive long vesting holding periods for shares obtained through exercise of stock options, or mandating strong executive stock ownership requirements. SEC rules require that public companies disclose the stock holdings and exercises of previously awarded equity compensation, including stock appreciation rights (SARs). The SEC's amendments require disclosure of the number of shares purchased by the company's management as well as the inclusion of directors' qualifying shares in the total amount of securities owned.[49]

The recent trend in the executive compensation structure is toward greater use of restricted shares and less focus on stock options. A report indicates that about 66 percent of the top 250 U.S. public companies used restricted shares in their executive compensation structure in 2005 compared with 49 percent in 2003.[50] This trend is expected to continue as companies are required to expense their stock option grants on a fair-value basis in compliance with SFAS No. 123(R).

Employment Contracts, Severance, and Change-of-Control Payments   These payment arrangements should be made on a limited basis. For example, employment contracts should be provided only to a newly hired or recently promoted executive and should not be longer than three years. Severance payments should be made only in noncontrol change situations in the event of wrongful termination, death, or disability, not for poor performance, failure to renew the contract, or resignation under pressure. The company's compensation committee must fully disclose the descriptions, terms, and conditions of employment contracts and other arrangements covering directors and officers along with the committee's rationale and the total dollar value of such payments. The committee should disclose new executive employment contracts or amendments to existing contracts in the company's 8-K and subsequent 10-Qs filed with the SEC. All employment contracts and other arrangements made for severance, change-of-control, or other special payments to executives in excess of 2.99 times the average annual salary plus an annual bonus for the previous three years of employment should be ratified by shareholders.

Retirement Arrangements   Retirement arrangements consist of deferred compensation plans, supplemental executive retirement plans (SERPS), retirement packages, and other retirement arrangements specially designed for high-paid executives. The compensation committee should review these executive special retirement arrangements to ensure that they are in the best interests of shareholders and are reasonable and consistent with programs and benefits offered to the company's general workforce. The committee should not structure or authorize executive special retirement arrangements that contain provisions such as above-market wages, excess service credits for time not actually worked, deferred compensation plans, and other postretirement benefits that are not offered under plans covering other employees.

Pension and other postemployment benefits (OPEB) for executives of high-profile companies (General Motors, General Electric, AT&T, and Exxon Mobil) have substantially increased while the companies are announcing that their pension and

OPEB obligations are putting them at a competitive disadvantage and they are planning to end pensions for their workers.[51] For example, at Bellsouth Corp., while the liabilities for pensions for ordinary workers have decreased by 3 percent since 2002, the obligation for pensions for its executives has increased by 89 percent over the same period.[52] Furthermore, at many companies, executive pensions make up a significant portion of pension obligations (e.g., 58 percent at Aflac, Inc., 19 percent at Federated Department Stores, 12 percent at Exxon Mobil, 12 percent at Pfizer, and 9 percent at MetLife).[53]

Executive perquisites normally include both financial and nonfinancial benefits in addition to salary and incentive bonuses paid to top executives, and in some cases they can be significant. Executive perquisites include such benefits as car usage or allowance, member dues, housekeeping, personal travel expenses, and other support services.[54] Despite the SEC requirement for full disclosure of these perquisites (Regulation S-K), many companies fail to report them. For example, Colgate failed to disclose more than $150 million in executive perquisites, and the SEC fined Tyson Foods because of its failure to disclose over $3 million in perquisites given to its former chairman.[55] These perquisites not only provide no incentive for high executive performance that would create shareholder value, but also are regarded as poor governance and ineffective board oversight function. Another important issue facing executive compensation is the proper disclosure and transparency of so-called tax gross-ups, where companies pay extra sums to cover executives' personal tax bills. Many companies (e.g., The Home Depot) are currently paying taxes due on core elements of executive pay, including stock grants, severance packages, and signing bonuses, or reimbursing taxes on corporate perquisites.[56] Patrick McGurn, an executive vice president of Institutional Shareholder Services, Inc., states that "This smacks of Leona Helmsley–like treatment, that only little people pay taxes.... [companies] are removing taxes from the list of inevitable life experiences, leaving only death."[57]

Executive Compensation Disclosure

Warren Buffett, a prominent corporate governance activist, states that "executive compensation is the acid test of corporate governance."[58] However, until very recently, investors were not provided with sufficient disclosures to assess how public companies "score on this critical test." The issue of the extent, nature, and disclosure of executive compensation has been of great concern and has received extensive scrutiny, and it is ultimately viewed as the directors' responsibility. Because boards of directors have not adequately addressed the issue of excessive CEO compensation in the post-SOX era, they have encouraged regulatory initiatives. In November 2005 a bill was introduced in the House of Representatives by Congressman Barney Frank (D-MA) that would require expanded disclosure and shareholder approval of executive compensation.[59] The SEC, in January 2006, issued proposed rules that would require companies to disclose more relevant information and explain objectives and policies regarding executive compensation. [60]

In August 2006 the SEC issued rules that require more relevant and transparent disclosure of executive pay, including total compensation figure incentive stock-and-options-based rewards, pension and other OPEB plans, and perquisites for the company's CEO, CFO, and the three other highest-paid executive officers as well as all directors.[61] These rules also require a new compensation discussion and analysis (CD&A) to replace the current compensation committee report and performance graph. The CD&A would have to be filed with regulators (SEC) and thus would require a sign-off certification from the CEO and CFO. Public companies must comply with these disclosure requirements in Forms 8-K for triggering events occurring on or after November 7, 2006, and in Forms 10-K and 10-KSB for fiscal years ending on or after October 15, 2006. These requirements address only the proper disclosure of executive compensation. It is ultimately the board's responsibility to understand the concerns of investors and the public about outsized executive compensation, address these concerns, develop reasonable executive compensation plans linked to performance and aligned with interests of investors, and get shareholder approval on these plans. The SEC rules require four types of executive compensation disclosures: (1) a compensation discussion and analysis; (2) a summary compensation table disclosing compensation relevant to the last three fiscal years; (3) tabular disclosures covering holdings of equity-based awards as of the end of the last fiscal year, including stock and nonstock incentives plan awards; and (4) tabular and narrative disclosure of retirement and other postemployment compensation.[62]

The SEC rules on executive compensation are intended to ensure shareholders and other users of financial statements receive complete, accurate, and transparent disclosures regarding public companies' executive compensation and related issues. These disclosure requirements pertain to executive and director compensation, related-person transactions, security ownership of officers and directors, and director independence and other corporate governance matters. These rules do not suggest or regulate how much executives should be paid. Instead, they require proper disclosures of such executive pay. Public companies are required to file the company's CD&A with the SEC. The CD&A is principles-based, and should be tailored to the company's specifications and should cover compensation for the past fiscal years, including the objectives of compensation programs, elements of compensation, and implementation of executive compensation policies and practices. SEC rules require public companies to disclose policies and procedures governing their related person transactions. To comply with these rules effectively, public companies should: (1) integrate the policy with other company policies pertaining to the company's code of conduct and conflict of interest resolution; (2) determine which board committee (preferably the nominating and governance committee) is responsible for administering these policies and procedures; and (3) review and approve all compensation for executive officers.[63] Exhibit 5.2 compares current SEC rules on executive compensation with prior rules.

Best practices of executive compensation disclosures are emerging as high-profile companies, including GE and Pfizer, disclose information above and beyond SEC requirements regarding their compensation consultant services. These companies in their 2006 proxy material disclosed: (1) names of compensation consultants; (2) what they are engaged for; (3) other work done for the company and service fees; (4) the responsibility of the company's compensation committee to engage

EXHIBIT 5.2 Comparison of Prior Rules with New Rules on Executive Compensation

	Prior Rules	New Rules
Scope	Chief Executive Officer (CEO) and the four other most highly compensated exective officers	Principal Executive Officer (PEO), Principal Financial Officer (PFO), and three other most highly compensated executive officers
Disclosures/Tables	Disclosure of Board Compensation Committee Report on Executive Compensation	Older Compensation Committee Report eliminated; replaced by (1) new Compensation Committee Report, and (2) narrative Compensation Discussion and Analysis section
	Audit Committee Report required by item 306 of Regulation S-K	No changes to format; moved to disclosure under item 407(d) of Regulation S-K
	Performance of Graph required by item 402 of Regulation S-K	No changes to format; moved to disclosure under item 201 of Regulation S-K
Summary Compensation Table	■ Salary and bonus	■ Salary and bonus
	■ Other annual compensation	■ Dollar-value of stock awards
	■ Dollar-value of restricted stock awards	■ Fair value of option/SAR awards
	■ Securities underlying options/SARs	■ Non-equality incentive plan payouts
	■ Long-term incentive plan payouts	■ Change in pension value and nonqualified deferred compensation earnings
	■ All other compensation	■ All other compensation (refined)
		■ Total compensation
Supplemental Tables	■ Long-Term Incentive Plan Awards	■ Grants of Plan-Based Awards
	■ Option and SAR Grants	■ Outstanding Equity Awards at Fiscal Year-End

Category		
	- Ten-Year Report on Repricing of Options/SARs - Aggregated Option/SAR Exercises and FYE Option/SAR Value - Pension Plan	- Option Exercises and Stock Vested - Pension Benefits - Nonqualified Deferred Compensation - Director Compensation
Severance Benefits/Change-in-Control	Narrative disclosure of employment contracts and termination of employment and change-in-control arrangements	Narrative disclosure regarding potential payments upon termination and change-in-control provisions
Other Director Compensation	Narrative format	- New Director Compensation Table - Narrative disclosures required
Related-Person Transactions	- Disclosure threshold of $60,000 - Not required to disclose policies/procedures for approval	- Disclosure threshold of $120,000 - Disclosure policies/procedures for approving related party transactions
Director Independence/Corporate Governance	Various disclosures required by items 306, 401, 402 and 404 of Regulation S-K	New and reorganized disclosure regarding corporate governance matters (i.e., independence of directors, compensation committee processes and procedures)

Source: CFOdirect Network www.CFOdirect.com.

211

the compensation consultants; and (5) consultants' involvement with compensation committee meetings. The author suggests that these best practices could be improved if companies provided the total fees paid to their compensation consultants along with a breakdown of the fees for compensation consulting and other services. This would bring transparency to the same level as is currently required for independent auditors (e.g., total auditor fees, audit-related, tax, and nonaudit services).

Moody's Corporate Governance Assessment (CGA) focuses on a long-term creditor's (bondholder) views of leverages as opposed to riskier short-term strategies measured in terms of short-term changes in stock prices. Moody's takes into consideration the company's executive compensation strategies, policies, practices, and structures, including incentives that increase credit risk, and regards excessive, undisciplined executive pay patterns as an indication of weak corporate governance. Moody's pays attention to 11 aspects of executive compensation policies and practices in its corporate governance assessment report:

1. A long-term orientation in executive pay structure, policies, and practices.
2. A clear link between the company's strategy and its executive pay structure.
3. Moderation in potential pay package. Any excessive, outsized nonperformance executive rewards may be viewed as signs of ineffective corporate governance that adversely affect the company's credit ratings. Excessive pay to senior management is more troublesome than such pay to the company's founders/entrepreneurs.
4. Restraint in the use of stock options. Moody's typically views the use of restricted shares more favorably than overemphasis on stock options, which may cause executives to focus too much on short-term stock performance.
5. Balance in performance metrics. While the optional mix of performance metrics depends on the company's specifications and its industry, executive compensation plans that make greater use of credit-friendly metrics such as cash flow and return on assets and place less focus on earnings per share (EPS) and total shareholder return (TSR) are considered more favorably.
6. Discipline in pay practice over time. The presence or absence of well-disciplined executive pay linked to the company's performance and its pattern over time affect the company's credit rating. The effectiveness of the company's compensation committee in linking executive pay to performance is very important.
7. Clarity of pay structure. Proper disclosure and transparency of the company's executive compensation policies and practices are viewed favorably for credit rating purposes.
8. Relative balance in top executives' pay. A significant discrepancy between CEO pay and the compensation of other senior executives may be viewed as a personal risk for the CEO, too much power embodied in the CEO position, and a potential succession challenge.
9. Quality in pay structure disclosure and decision making and the effectiveness of the company's compensation committee.
10. The overall structure of the company's executive compensation package, including the requirements for stock ownership, long vesting in equity award, stock sale restriction policies, holding periods for shares obtained through equity

awards, and requirements for stock ownership while the executive remains employed at the company.

11. The aggressive executive sale of shares regarding a potential focus on short-term gains as well as hedging against holdings in the company stock.[64]

The author suggests seven best practices of executive compensation in order to align management interests with long-term interests of shareholders:

1. No tenure for senior executives—senior executives, including the CEO and the CFO, should not have multiyear contracts.
2. Senior executives' performance should be reviewed annually and continuation of their employment and reappointment should be approved either annually or every few years.
3. Senior executive compensation should be linked to performance.
4. Senior executive compensation packages, including, salary, short-term bonuses, long-term incentives (stock options, restricted stocks), pension and postemployment benefits, and perquisites, should be fully disclosed to shareholders.
5. The influence of outside consultants on compensation committee decisions should be limited, and the entire board of directors should consider the committee's recommendation in approving senior executive compensation.
6. Chief executives' pay should be reasonable relative to that of their peers and should be limited to the predetermined and preferably relatively small multiple (5 to 10 times) of the compensation of the company's top 20 most senior managers.
7. Stock options should be awarded at fixed grant date schedules (e.g quarterly or annual meetings), be approved by the board, and receive shareholder advisory votes.

FINANCIAL REPORTING REQUIREMENTS

Public companies with more than $10 million of assets whose shares are held by more than 500 investors are required to file annual audited financial reports (Forms 10-K or 10-KSB) and quarterly reviewed financial reports (Forms 10-Q or 10-QSB) with the SEC. The SEC's role in corporate financial reporting, according to the 1977 Report of the SEC Advisory Committee on Corporate Disclosure, is to ensure public availability of all corporate-oriented information (including financial reports) to the investing public.[65] In addition to filings with the SEC, public companies also disseminate both annual reports and quarterly reports to shareholders. The basic information in filings with the SEC and financial reports to shareholders is the same even though the format and the depth of the financial information provided may be different. Financial reports submitted to shareholders usually contain, in addition to financial information, nonfinancial information about the company's markets, products, and people; SEC filings normally contain more detailed financial information.

A company's annual meeting provides its shareholders with an opportunity to communicate with management and the board of directors by asking questions about the company's performance and also gives management the opportunity to present its views. The annual report of public companies normally contains this financial information:

- Audited financial statements including notes to the financial statements.
- Management's discussion and analysis (MD&A) of financial condition and results of operations.
- Management certifications of financial statements.
- Management assessments of the effectiveness of internal control over financial reporting.
- Audit committee report.
- Independent auditor's report on financial statements.
- Independent auditor's report on management assessment of the effectiveness of internal control over financial reporting.[66]
- Five-year summary of selected financial data.
- Summary of selected quarterly financial data for the past two years.
- Quarterly market data for the past two years, including high and low stock prices for common stock, dividends paid, and price/earnings ratio.

Two provisions of SOX pertain to executive certifications of financial reports. Section 302 of the act requires the principal executive and financial officers of the company (CEO, CFO) to certify each periodic (quarterly and annual) report filed with the SEC.[67] This is also referred to as the civil certification, because the certifying officers may face civil liability for false certifications. Under Section 906 of SOX, each periodic report containing financial statements filed by a reporting company must be accompanied by a certification of the CEO and CFO of the company.[68] Section 302 executive certification is signed by both the company's CEO and CFO and contains statements that both officers certify that:

- Financial reports (quarterly and annual) are reviewed by them.
- Financial reports are materially accurate and complete.
- Based on their knowledge, financial statements, including footnotes and other financial information, such as selected financial data, MD&A analysis of financial condition, and results of operations contained in the report, fairly present in all material respects the company's financial condition, results of operations, and cash flows. The fair presentation of financial reports, including financial statements and other financial information, is broader than fair presentation of financial statements under generally accepted accounting principles (GAAP).
- They: (a) are responsible for establishing and maintaining the company's "disclosure controls and procedures" and "internal control over financial reporting"; (b) have assessed the effectiveness of the company's disclosure controls and procedures within 90 days prior to the filing of the report; and (c) have presented in the report their conclusions about the effectiveness of disclosure controls and procedures.
- They have disclosed to the company's independent auditors and the audit committee of the board of directors: (a) all significant deficiencies and material

weakness in the design and operation of the internal control over financial reporting; and (b) any fraud that involves management or other employees with a significant role in internal control over financial reporting.

FINANCIAL REPORTING CHALLENGES

Financial reporting challenges are numerous. This section focuses on some of the most prevailing challenges.

Complexity in the Financial Reporting Process

The financial reporting process is becoming more complex and complicated as public companies are required to comply with numerous regulations and standards. Complexity has been regarded as a contributing factor to the occurrences of financial restatements and scandals by encouraging form over substance in the financial reporting process. Sources of complexity in financial reporting are:

- Lack of neutral and fair reporting on diverse and complicated business events and transactions.
- The continuing focus on achieving short-term earnings.
- The diverse and often conflicting interests of market participants.
- An evolutionary standard-setting process with no compromise and consistent application.
- A rules-based approach in the standard-setting process.
- The use of accounting-motivated structuring to generate form-over-substance results.
- Resistance to change and use of technology in the financial reporting process.[69]

Complexity of accounting standards not only makes the preparation of transparent financial statements more difficult but also impedes the ability of users to understand financial information. A contributing factor to the complexity and extent of accounting rules is the reluctance on the part of management and accountants to use their judgment, instead asking for clarification and more rules from standard setters. Management should use professional judgment driven by the most transparent accounting treatment for a particular business transaction rather than the most advantageous treatment. Scott Taub, deputy chief accountant with the SEC, said, "We've gone from 'where does it say this is wrong?' to 'where does it say this is ok?' in the application of accounting standards."[70] Accounting standard setters (e.g. FASB) and regulators (e.g. SEC) are moving toward principles-based and transparent accounting standards by addressing accounting for leases, derecognition, pensions, and financial investments.

Accounting and auditing standard setters (SEC, FASB, and PCAOB) have attempted to address the complexity by working toward simplification and codification. Nonetheless, some of the accounting standards and rules on measuring and recognizing financial transactions are unduly complex (e.g., derivatives), so that they do not allow preparation of high-quality financial statements. Several suggestions have been made to resolve this complexity, including the establishment of a sound conceptual framework, formal rule making by regulators, addressing the litigious environment, and active participation by preparers and auditors.[71] On March 28, 2006, a bill (H.R. 5024) was introduced entitled "Promoting Transparency in Financial Reporting Act of 2006." The act would intend to reduce the complexity in financial reporting and improve transparency of financial reports.

The FASB has taken five initiatives to reduce complexity and improve reliability, relevance, and transparency of financial reporting:

1. The revision of several Statements of Financial Accounting Standards (SFAS) that are regarded as being overly complex, being rules based, and not reflecting the underlying economic activity (e.g., accounting for pensions and postemployment benefits, derivatives, revenue recognition).
2. The development of a comprehensive and integrated codification of all existing accounting literature to enable an easily retrievable single electronic-based source for all GAAP.
3. The use of more principles-based standard-setting approaches, including a major project to strengthen the conceptual framework and the convergence of accounting standards.
4. Working with the XBRL Consortium to develop and further the use of XBRL and other emerging technologies in financial reporting.
5. Working with the SEC, PCAOB, and other interested parties to reduce complexity in the financial reporting process.[72]

Disaster Recovery Plans

Natural disasters, such as severe floods, hurricanes, and earthquakes, can be devastating to individuals and businesses. The disasters of the past several years (September 11, 2001 terrorist attacks, Hurricane Katrina in 2005) made companies develop sound disaster recovery plans to ensure the safety and security of their employees, minimize the impact on operations, and protect important electronics and other information from destruction. Management should identify potential risks, assess their possible impacts, and design controls to manage their exposure. The board of directors should oversee the company's risk management assessment and ensure appropriate processes are designed to deal with high-risk areas. The impacts of actual and potential unexpected disasters on financial reporting should be assessed.

Financial scandals of the early 2000s and recent world events including the September 11 terrorist attacks and natural disasters have generated more interest in the issue of overall enterprise risk management (ERM), including increased interest in the traditional risks (e.g., strategic, financial, operational, information security, and reputational). The Committee of Sponsoring Organizations of the Treadway Commission (COSO) defines "enterprise risk management" as:

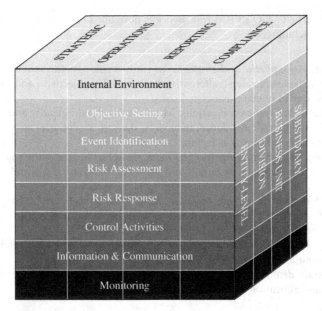

EXHIBIT 5.3 Relationship of Objective and Components of Enterprise Risk Management

Source: Adapted from COSO Enterprise Risk Management Framework. Available at: www.cpa2biz.com/CS2000/Products/CPA2BIZ/Publications/COSO+Enterprise+Risk+Management+-+Integrated+Framework.htm.

A process, effected by an entity's board of directors, management and other personnel, applied in strategy setting and across the enterprise, designed to identify potential events that may affect the entity, and manage risks to be within its risk appetite, to provide reasonable assurance regarding the achievement of entity objectives.[73]

The relationship between ERM's objectives and its related components is depicted in Exhibit 5.3 in a three-dimensional matrix. The vertical column represents the four objectives of strategy, operations, reporting, and compliance. The horizontal rows depict the eight components of internal environment, objective setting, event identification, risk assessment, risk response, control activities, information and communication, and monitoring. The third dimension of the cube shows the ERM ability to focus on the entire entity, its business subsidiaries, business units, divisions, and entity levels.

The ERM framework enables management to achieve the entity's goal of creating stakeholder value by effectively managing uncertainty and related risk and opportunity. The COSO's ERM framework is developed based on six premises and capabilities, including:

1. *Aligning risk appetite and strategy.* An entity's risk appetite should be considered in assessing strategic alternatives, establishing objectives, and developing mechanisms to manage associated risks.
2. *Enhancing risk response decisions.* Management should identify and select risk responses (e.g., risk avoidance, reduction, sharing, acceptance) associated with the uncertainty its entity is facing.
3. *Reducing operational surprises and losses.* In achieving the entity's goals, management should minimize pitfalls and surprises that cause losses and additional costs.
4. *Identifying and managing multiple and cross-enterprise risks.* Management should effectively identify and manage interrelated and integrated risks threatening the entity's operations and performance.
5. *Seizing opportunities.* Management should identify and proactively realize opportunities provided by uncertainties.
6. *Improving deployment of capital.* Management should assess overall capital needs and allocation of capital to manage risk.[74]

Disclosing Off–Balance Sheet Items

The 2006 CFO survey of 213 finance executives shows that: (1) about 43 percent of responding CFOs reported that between 1 and 25 percent of their debt or other liabilities is not reflected on their balance sheet in 2006 compared with 20 percent in 2002; and (2) the vast majority support the FASB's proposals to put leases and pensions on the balance sheet even though about 40 percent believe such changes could hurt their companies' stock prices.[75] The SEC has already adopted amendments to its rules that require public companies to provide an explanation of their off–balance sheet arrangement in their MD&A section. The SEC staff, in June 2003, released a report and recommendations pursuant to Section 401(c) of SOX on arrangements with off–balance sheet implications, special purpose entities, and transparency of filings by public companies. The SEC report identifies several initiatives intended to improve transparency of financial reporting and also makes several recommendations for standard setters (PCAOB, FASB) in setting future auditing and accounting standards on off–balance sheet transactions.

The three off–balance sheet transactions of pensions and other postemployment benefits, leases, and stock options are estimated at a total of $1.5 trillion in off–balance sheet assets and $2.3 trillion in off–balance sheet liabilities for the S&P 500 companies alone.[76] Their aggregate off–balance sheet assets are estimated at 6 percent of the total assets; their off–balance sheet liabilities are forecasted as 11 percent of the total liabilities.[77] The significance of these transactions, their relevance to investors in making investment decisions, and their usefulness to the capital markets in allocating scarce resources have encouraged regulators and standard setters to add overhauling accounting for these transactions to their agenda.

Leases   After 30 years of FASB's standards on leases specifying four criteria for differentiating operating leases (off–balance sheets) from capital leases (on–balance sheets), in July 2006 the FASB decided to add a major project on lease accounting to its standards-setting agenda that would overhaul the accounting practices for leases by bringing off–balance sheet operating leases on balance sheet. The FASB is expected to jointly work with the IASB on the project in an attempt toward international convergence in financial reporting. The final standard on leases is expected to be issued in 2009. Leasing is a big business, and the FASB initiative should have a positive impact on investor confidence that improvements to lease accounting eventually will be made. Many critics believe that this is long overdue as the current practice fails to reflect the underlying economics of many lease transactions and treats leases as another way to finance the acquisition of an asset.[78]

Leasing is a growing industry. The global equipment leasing market is a $600 billion to $700 billion business, with the United States accounting for about one-third of the global market.[79] The current accounting for leases depends on how the lease is structured, not its underlying economics. There are two fundamental ways to account for a lease from the lessee's perspective: either as an operating lease or a capital lease. An operating lease is reflected on the income statement as a rent expense, and the statement of cash flow is reflected as operations cash overflows. A capital lease, however, affects all three financial statements the same way as transactions for borrowing and buying except that buying or borrowing transactions affect cash flow from investing whereas capital lease transactions affect cash flow from operations. Accounting for leases should reflect the economic reality of lease transactions. While the choice of accounting method for lease transactions does not change, the economic reality of these transactions can affect the behavior of companies that generate accounting numbers and investors who use these numbers to make investments and voting decisions.

Fair-Value Measurements   On September 15, 2005, the FASB issued Statement of Financial Accounting Standards (SFAS) No. 157 entitled "Fair Value Measurements".[80] SFAS No. 157 provides enhanced guidance for using fair value to measure assets and liabilities and expanded transparent information concerning the definition of fair values, the extent to which companies measure fair value for their assets and liabilities, the information used to measure fair value and the impact of fair-value measurements on their earnings. The definition of fair value, in SFAS No. 157, focuses on the price that "would be received to sell the asset or paid to transfer the liability at the measurement data (at exit price), not the price that would be paid to acquire the asset or received to assume the liability at the measurement date (an entry price)."[81] The key provisions of SFAS No. 157 are: (1) enhanced guidance for using fair value to measure assets and liabilities; (2) proposed transparent disclosures concerning fair-value measurements; (3) disclosure of the effect of fair-value measurements on earnings; (4) clarification of the definition of fair value based on an exit price instead of an entry price on the measurement data; (5) requirement that fair value is a market-based measurement, not an entity-specific measurement; (6) market participant assumptions used in determining fair value should include the risk inherent in a particular valuation technique, the effect of a restriction on the sale or use of an asset; (7) clarification that a fair-value measurement for a liability reflects its nonperformance risk, such as credit risk; and (8) disclosures concerning the use of fair value to measure assets and liabilities in interim and annual periods subsequent to initial recognition.[82]

Convergence of Financial Reporting

Financial accounting standards have evolved in different countries based on their political, cultural, social, and regulatory environment. Nonetheless, the primary purpose should be to provide relevant, useful, transparent, reliable, and timely information to users of financial statements. Public financial information should assist investors in making sound investment and voting decisions. The convergence in accounting standards is feasible when this primary goal is shared by the global investors. Thus, the FASB, the IASB, the SEC, and the Council of European Securities Regulators (CESR) have worked toward accounting convergence.[83] Convergence in accounting facilitates comparability across borders that may result in a move toward the efficient flow of capital on a global basis.

Convergence of different sets of accounting standards means that some or all of these standards will be modified or changed. Changes or modifications of standards require changes in accounting policies and practices and the assessment of the risks involved with the interpretation and application of these changes. The IASB and FASB both agreed to eliminate some of the major differences in their accounting standards to promote a set of globally comparable financial statements.[84] It is expected that by 2009 foreign companies using the International Financial Reporting Standards (IFRS) issued by the IASB will not have to reconcile their financial statements to GAAP. The IASB and FASB released a joint Memorandum of Understanding (MOU) that lists 11 specific areas where the convergence progress is expected to be achieved by 2008.[85] The MOU indicates that in order to effectively and timely achieve the road map, which has already been agreed on by the SEC and the European Union Internal Market Commission, all parties involved should coordinate their efforts and actions. The MOU also establishes guidelines for both IASB and FASB to work toward convergence.

MD&A Guidance

The SEC has provided more guidance to improve the transparency and informativeness of public companies' MD&As. The management commentary section of financial reporting, better known as MD&A in the United States, is regarded as an important source of information to investors in making investment and voting decisions.[86] MD&As present management's views of the company, its plans for the year ahead, and its assessment of risks and risk management, and set the tone of the company. MD&As should go beyond superficial analyses and reviews of information presented in the accompanying financial statements to provide relevant and forward-looking information on operational strategies, liquidity and capital resources, research and development, enterprise risk management, and related party transactions. Listed companies in the United States are required to publish an

MD&A; companies listed on stock exchanges throughout the world have no such requirements.[87] In the United States the value relevance of MD&As is diminishing as management is becoming aware and concerned about its legal liability toward any misleading statements associated with financial forecasts.[88]

In April 2006 the IASB issued its discussion paper on management commentary (MC) that provides both financial and nonfinancial information in annual reports.[89] The focus of MC is on corporate reporting, including key financial and nonfinancial performance indicators, to assist all participants in the global capital markets to make sound economic and investment decisions. The development of MC necessitates the participation of all global securities regulators (SEC, IOSCO), standards setters (FASB, IASB), analysts, investors and management. Standards on MC would encourage consistency in corporate reporting, improve transparency of business performance, strengthen corporate governance, encourage good practice disclosure, and enhance the quality of annual corporate reporting.

eXtensible Business Reporting Language

In the United States, both regulators (SEC) and standard setters (FASB, AICPA, PCAOB) have taken initiatives to address online real-time financial reporting using the eXtensible Business Reporting Language (XBRL) format and electronic or continuous auditing. Recently the SEC has promoted XBRL voluntary reporting and provided a faster review for companies using XBRL. It is expected that XBRL taxonomies for different industries will be further developed and the use of the XBRL format will gain more momentum in 2007 and onward.

XBRL makes it easier to generate, compile, validate, and analyze business and financial information. These features of XBRL improve the quality, completeness, comparability, and timeliness of business and financial information in making decisions. XBRL has developed an international public consortium of about 2500 organizations from 27 countries worldwide. XBRL uses an electronic tag, similar to bar codes on merchandise, to explicitly define information in a standard way so that it can be easily read by a variety of software applications. Since the fall of 2005, more than 8200 financial institutions in the United States have submitted their quarterly call reports, also known as risk-oriented filings, to federal banking regulators in XBRL format. These institutions have substantially reduced their filing compliance costs and provided higher quality data, better analytical procedures (ratios), and more relevant benchmarking data. In addition, about 25 public companies (e.g. Ford, General Electric, Microsoft, PepsiCo, Bristol-Myers Squib, and United Technologies) have filed their annual (10-K) and quarterly (10-Q) reports in XBRL as part of a voluntary SEC pilot program.[90] Other countries (e.g. Australia, Canada, China, the European Union, India, and Japan) are following suit.

The SEC's efforts to encourage public companies to use XBRL-tagged documents for their filings with the commission in the first year (2004 filing) attracted only 9 company participants; in the second year, 17 companies participated in this XBRL pilot program, including MCO, Bristol Meyers, Squibb, Dow Chemical Co., and Xerox Corp. To improve the quality of its technical materials and its standard-setting process, XBRL International is establishing the XBRL Standards Board (XSB).[91] The XSB's primary responsibilities will be to:

- Increase the quality, consistency, and stability of technical materials of XBRL International.
- Enhance the level of openness and formality of the standard-setting process of the XBRL.
- Improve the effectiveness of the standard-setting process, which should accelerate adoption of XBRL standards.

The use of XBRL in financial reporting is further discussed in Chapter 11.

Accounting Pensions and Other Postretirement Employee Benefits

Providing postemployment benefits to employees and their accounting have been a challenge for public companies and are now becoming a struggle to survive. Some companies have eliminated, frozen, or amended their plans (e.g., Sprint, Nextel, Verizon, and IBM); other financially distressed companies (e.g., United Airlines, Pittsburgh Brewing) have shifted their pension obligations to the Pension Benefit Guarantee Corporation (PBGC) to subsidize pension funding. The FASB has initiated its two-phase project of improving accounting practices by requiring recognition of unfunded pension and OPEB obligations. Many of the OPEB and pension plans were developed several decades ago with observable costs and obligations for companies. Today, fulfilling OPEB and pension obligations diverts companies' operating capital intended for growth, expansion, and operating purposes. To compete effectively in the global market and particularly with companies in countries where the labor is cheap and pension and OPEB plans are practically nonexistent, U.S. companies may have to reduce employees' retirement benefits and freeze or terminate their defined benefit plans.

The two sources of funding retirement are lifetime corporate pensions and private 401(k) employee contribution plans. Both sources are in crisis as baby boomers live longer and their income shrinks.[92] About half of the nation's workforce is not covered by any private sector retirement plan, 30 percent invest in employee contribution plans of 401(k)s, 10 percent have lifetime corporate pensions, and the remaining 10 percent have a combination of 401(k) and pension plans.[93] In order to be able to maintain their standard of living after retirement, Americans with 401(k) and pension plans need to save 15 to 18 percent of their annual salary for 30 years by accumulating at least 6 to 10 times of their annual pay before retirement.[94] In the past several decades there has also been a significant shift in the cost and responsibility for retirement saving from corporations to employees. For example, in 1978, employees put in about 11 percent of total retirement contribution; the remaining 89 percent was invested by corporations. In 2000, the employee share had increased to 51 percent; the company share had fallen to 49 percent.

Several factors have contributed to this significant shift in retirement contributions, including bankruptcy of high-profile companies (Enron, WorldCom), which legally terminated lifetime pension programs; well-publicized financial restatements of prominent companies (Xerox, AOL, Tyco), which caused the underfunding of pensions and OPEB; and company decisions to reduce or terminate their pension plans and transfer their unfunded retirement plans to the PBGC, which already has a deficit of more than $23 billion. This perceived retirement crisis will worsen due to the fact that the majority of pension and OPEB plans are unfunded and soon will be required to be presented on company balance sheets, which will substantially reduce shareholders' equity in public companies.

One of the shortcomings of the current accounting standards on pension is that they allow companies to estimate their pension funds' investment returns at the beginning of the year and then, regardless of the year's actual returns, at the end of the year, factor the pension assumption into reporting earnings. The incorporation of these assumptions into earnings can significantly inflate earnings. For example, Lucent reports $1.2 billion in earnings from operations in 2004 when, in fact, about $1.1 billion of the reported earnings resulted from pension calculations.[95] Academic research finds that companies tend to ratchet up their assumptions of pension fund returns to exaggerate their earnings just before certain corporate events, such as acquisitions, exercise of stock options by executives, or secondary stock offerings where a higher stock price is desirable.[96]

On March 31, 2006, the FASB issued its phase-one proposal to improve accounting for pensions and OPEB.[97] The issuance of SFAS No. 158, on September 29, 2006, entitled "Employers' Accounting for Decision Benefit Pension and Other Post Retirement Plans," completed the first phase of the FASB's comprehensive project on pensions.[98] SFAS No. 158 requires companies to recognize a net liability or asset to report the funded status of their defined benefit pension and other postretirement benefit plans on their balance sheet. Companies are required to disclose the expected effect of SFAS No. 158 in their Form 10-Qs that are filed after September 30, 2006. Also, calendar year-end public companies are required to adopt the recognition and disclosure provisions of SFAS No. 158 as of December 31, 2006. SFAS No. 158 could have significant effects as many companies are required to recognize on their balance sheets the funded status of OPEB and pension plans. SFAS No. 158 also requires fiscal-year-end measurements of plan assets and benefit obligations.

The FASB will address recognition of pension and OPEB costs on the income statements in its second phase. However, any changes in fair value of the plan assets and obligations should be shown in other comprehensive income, and the measurement date for the pension plan should be the same as the company's fiscal year. It is estimated that the disclosure of the funded status of both the OPEB and pension plans on the balance sheet would reduce shareholder equity for the S&P 500 companies by 7 percent, or about $255 billion in 2006.[99] This possible reduction in owners' equity would ultimately spark changes in companies' pension and OPEB plan policies and practices. Companies may attempt to change their sponsor-defined benefit pension plans by shifting asset allocations, freezing the plans, terminating pension and OPEB plans, or closing plans to new employees.[100]

In the second phase, which is considered the overhaul of pensions and OPEB accounting standards, and a significant move toward converging U.S. and other international accounting standards, the FASB would address four areas:

1. Recognition and reporting in earnings and other comprehensive income the cost of providing pension and OPEB benefits to employees.
2. Measurement of pension and OPEB obligations under plans with lump-sum settlement options.
3. Guidance regarding measurement assumptions.
4. Whether OPEB trusts should be consolidated by plan sponsors.

The first phase is regarded as a temporary fix of pensions and OPEB disclosure problems as companies would be required to book only the net difference between the fair value of their pension plan assets and estimated amount of their pension and OPEB plans' future obligations to employees. The author suggests that the FASB expedite its second-phase project by addressing the perceived "glaring measurement problems"; providing guidelines for the measurement and recognition of future retirement benefit obligations to employees; and addressing assumptions that companies are making in estimating future interest rates and salary inflation. The primary concern regarding pension accounting is the determination of a company's pension capability by projecting future salary increases and other costs through the projected benefit obligation (PBO) method. The PBO is determined by calculating the present value of the future benefit payments, including expected salary. It is not clear why future pay increases should be regarded as a current liability on the balance sheet. Perhaps the accumulated benefit obligations (ABO) method, which does not require an estimate of future obligations, is a better method to use in calculating pension liabilities.

Principles-Based versus Rules-Based Accounting Standards

The rules-based approach was criticized for providing opportunities for management to find loopholes in the rules in order to manipulate financial information. Thus, the FASB has released proposals on the use of the principles-based approach to standard setting in order to improve the quality and transparency of financial information.[101] Principles-based accounting standards are expected to be more understandable, allow the use of more professional judgment by auditors on the quality of financial information, make it more difficult to structure transactions, and facilitate convergence in financial reporting. The principles-based approach requires accountants, management, and auditors to consider the substance of business transactions and the principles governing them rather than the specific forms and rules that may apply to them. The principles-based approach promotes the use of participants' professional judgment in the financial reporting supply chain, including management, accountants, auditors, legal counsel, and analysts, rather than attempts by these participants to interpret accounting rules and sometimes bend these rules.

SOX requires the SEC to conduct a study on the adoption of a principles-based accounting system in U.S. financial reporting. On July 25, 2003, the SEC issued a study that suggests that U.S. generally accepted accounting principles are excessively rules-based; as such, they could produce financial information that is inconsistent with the underlying economic substance of events and transactions.[102] Nevertheless, the study concludes that the exclusive use of a principles-based set of standards could result in: inconsistent accounting treatment of similar transactions, a lack of comparability of financial results of different companies, and inadequate guidance or structure for exercising professional judgment by accountants, and could create implementation difficulties.

The SEC's study recommends a hybrid of focusing on an "objectives-based" approach in establishing accounting standards. The recommended objectives-based approach:

- Enables accounting standards to be based on an improved and consistently applied conceptual framework.
- Clearly states the accounting objective of the standards.
- Provides sufficient structure and details to make the standard operational and applied on a consistent basis.
- Minimizes the use of exceptions from the standards.
- Avoids the use of percentage tests to prevent manipulations of standards by achieving technical compliance while evading the intent of the standards.
- Holds management responsible for capturing within the company's financial reports the economic substance of business events and transactions.
- Establishes objectives and an accounting model for business transactions while providing sufficiently detailed guidance for management and auditors to comply with standards.

On March 29, 2006, Bill Gradison, the acting chairman of the PCAOB, in testimony before the U.S. House of Representatives Committee on Financial Services, stated:

> The terms "principles-based" and "rules-based" typically are used to refer to the two ends of a spectrum of specificity. On one end of that spectrum are principles-based standards that contain comparatively fewer details and prescriptions and, on the other end are rules-based standards that are highly prescriptive in their requirements, and leave fewer decisions to professional judgment. . . . I firmly believe that a system of rules without principles is unworkable. . . .[103]

Principles-based standards, while allowing more flexibility and professional judgment in applying accounting standards, may encourage variability in financial disclosures that reduces comparability of financial statements. Rules-based accounting standards, however, may encourage companies to use them in engineering transactions to achieve particular results. Rules-based auditing standards can encourage auditors to focus primarily on technical compliance rather than professional judgment. There should be a right balance between rules-based and principles-based accounting and auditing standards to foster quality, reliability, usefulness, and transparency of financial disclosures while reducing their complexity.

Financial Restatements

The wave of recent financial restatements by high-profile companies has raised serious concerns about the reliability of financial reports and the effectiveness of corporate governance and internal control and the credibility of audit services. These restatements usually erase billions of dollars of previously reported earnings. Research by the SEC's office of the Chief Accountant documents that the majority of restatements (55 percent) were due to misapplication of basic accounting rules (e.g., leases) and lack of proper accounting records whereas about one-third of restatements were due to errors in judgment related to more complex accounting issues (e.g., derivatives); only 5 percent were due to deliberate misstatements and fraud.[104] These restatements are caused by many factors, including:

- Tremendous pressures on management to meet or exceed analysts' earnings forecasts to avoid adverse affects on stock prices.
- The need to preserve executive compensation incentives.
- Outdated accounting and rule-based standards.
- Complex corporate financing arrangements, including off–balance sheet assets and liabilities.
- Audit failures resulting from compromised auditor independence.[105]

About 10 percent of listed U.S. public companies restated their financial statements in 2006. Financial restatements hit a new record in 2006 as 1,356 public companies filed 1,538 restatements, which was up 13 percent compared to 2005.[106] In the post-SOX period: (1) about 2,931 U.S. companies filed at least one restatement and 683 restated two or more times; (2) restatements by accelerated companies required to comply with SOX declined by 14 percent, whereas non-Section 404 compliance companies rose 40 percent; (3) about one-third of large companies (accelerated) and two-thirds of smaller companies that restated claimed they have effective internal control over financial reporting; (4) restatements by large companies with $75 million or more in revenue are down 20 percent, whereas for smaller companies, they are up 49 percent; (5) restatements by companies audited by Big Four accounting firms are down 32 percent, whereas for non–Big Four audit clients, they are up 76 percent; (6) restatements for companies listed on the national stock exchanges are down 20 percent, whereas for companies listed on the over-the-counter stock markets, they are up 76 percent.[107]

The increasing number of financial restatements can be interpreted in four ways.

1. The implementation of corporate governance reforms, including SOX, SEC rules, PCAOB standards, and listing standards, created an unprecedented environment of extensive scrutiny, which brought financial errors, irregularities, and fraud to light.

2. These corporate governance reforms were a continuous process, and their full impact in preventing financial problems and improving the financial reporting process has not yet materialized, as about 15 percent of these restatements were made by repeat filers.

3. For many public companies, 2004 was the first year of the mandatory internal control reporting under Section 404 of SOX. The fact that more than 580 companies reported material weaknesses in their internal controls suggests the ineffectiveness of their financial reporting process.

4. The implementation of SFAS No. 154 requires companies to restate their prior-period statements for changes in accounting principles as if the company had always used the new principle. These types of discretionary restatements driven by changes in accounting principles are expected to increase in the future. However, they should be differentiated from restatements driven by errors and fraud management. Reports should properly disclose the reasons for various types of restatements. Auditors should assess management's disclosures on restatements and place more attention on restatements resulting from correction of errors and fraud.

INTERNAL CONTROL REPORTING AND EXECUTIVE CERTIFICATION

SOX and SEC-related implementation rules require public companies to design and maintain adequate and effective internal controls and disclosures for assessment and reporting of their "disclosure controls and procedures" and "internal control over financial reporting." Disclosure controls and procedures defined in Rules 13a-15 and 15d-15 of the Securities Exchange Act of 1933 are designed by public companies to ensure that information required to be disclosed is accurate and complete and is gathered, recorded, processed, summarized, and reported with the required time period.[108] Internal control over financial reporting is defined as a process designed to ensure that transactions are recorded properly in accordance with management's authorization and that financial statements are prepared in accordance with GAAP.[109] Thus, the definition of internal control over financial reporting is broader than that of disclosure controls and procedures in the sense that disclosure controls and procedures may include or exclude some components of internal control over financial reporting (disposition and safeguarding assets).

The COSO report broadly defined internal control as "a process effected by an entity's board of directors, management, and other personnel—designed to provide reasonable assurance regarding the achievement of objectives in the following categories: effectiveness and efficiency of operations; reliability of financial reporting; and compliance with applicable laws and regulations."[110] This definition is very comprehensive and addresses four aspects of internal control:

1. The process.
2. Individuals who affect internal control.

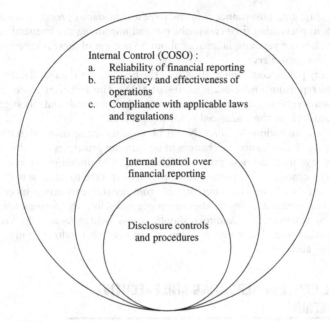

EXHIBIT 5.4   Internal Control

3. Limitations of internal control.
4. Objectives of internal control.

As shown in Exhibit 5.4, the COSO definition of internal control is broader in the sense that it encompasses both "internal control over financial reporting" and "disclosure controls and procedures" defined by the Sarbanes-Oxley Act and related SEC rules.

Management's Responsibility under Section 302 of SOX

Section 302 of SOX requires the management (CEO, CFO) of public companies to assess and report on the effectiveness of disclosure controls and procedures of both quarterly and annual reports. The principal executive (CEO) and financial (CFO) officers must certify that they:

- Have reviewed the report (annually and quarterly filed with the SEC), believe that the report neither contains untrue statements nor omits material facts, and believe that it fairly presents the financial statements and other financial information.
- Are responsible for designing, establishing, and maintaining disclosure controls and procedures, and have assessed and presented in the report their conclusions about the company's effectiveness of disclosure controls and procedures.

- Have disclosed to the audit committee and external auditors all significant deficiencies and material weaknesses in internal controls that could adversely affect the company's ability to record, process, summarize, and report financial information and any fraud, whether material or not, that involves management or other employees who have a significant role in the company's internal controls and financial reporting.
- Have indicated whether there have been significant changes in internal control over financial reporting subsequent to the date of their evaluation, including remediations of their previously identified significant deficiencies and material weaknesses.

Management Responsibilities for Section 404 Compliance of SOX

Section 404 of SOX requires management (CEO, CFO) to document and assess the design and operation of the company's internal control over financial reporting and report on its assessment of its effectiveness. This mandatory internal control report must be integrated into the company's annual reports and include six assertions:

1. Management's responsibility for establishing and maintaining adequate and effective internal control over financial reporting.
2. The framework used by management in its assessment of the effectiveness of design and operation of internal control over financial reporting.
3. Management's assessment of the effectiveness of the design and operation of the company's internal control over financial reporting.
4. Disclosure of any identified material weaknesses in the company's internal control over financial reporting.
5. Disclosure that the company's independent auditor has issued an attestation report on management's assessment of the effectiveness of internal control over financial reporting.
6. The attestation report of the company's independent auditor.

Sections 302 and 404 of SOX required the company's executives (CEO, CFOs) to "sign off" on and thus certify their company's financial statements and internal control over financial reporting. Lord and Benoit conducted a study on the relationship between Sections 302 and 404 that indicates that only 47 of the 586 companies that reported ineffective internal controls under Section 404 in 2005 disclosed ineffective controls in their prior-year Section 302.[111] The study also shows that only 75 of the 586 companies disclosed ineffective controls in the previous quarter (just 45 days before Section 404 compliance). The study concludes that "one would have expected far greater number of Section 302 significant deficiency disclosures than have been observed to date" primarily because the threshold for "significant deficiencies" is lower than for "material weaknesses" under Section 404. The study, however, finds a 92 percent correlation between Sections 302 and 404 in reporting ineffective disclosure controls in the first quarter when both sections' compliance were performed. The study concludes that:

> *It was only after a company was faced with having to report ineffectiveness under Section 404, part of which is the independent auditor assessment, that companies self reported deficiencies under Section 302. Under the legislation, one would expect that most companies would first report deficiencies under Section 302, and then potentially never report under Section 404 because of remediation activities.*[112]

Auditor Report on Internal Control over Financial Reporting

Section 404 of SOX requires the independent auditor to attest to and report on management's assessment of the effectiveness of the company's internal control over financial reporting. The independent auditor report must state the auditor's opinion as to whether management's assessment of the effectiveness of internal control over financial reporting is fairly stated in all material respects, or it must state that an overall opinion cannot be expressed and provide an explanation why.

The auditor attestation report on internal control over financial reporting must be filed with the company's annual report filings. This attestation should be conducted by applying the appropriate audit procedures to assess the effectiveness of both the design and operation of internal control over financial reporting in accordance with PCAOB Auditing Standard No. 2 and the proposed Auditing Standard No. 5, which are discussed in Chapter 9. The effective evaluation and reporting of the company's internal control over financial reporting by both management and the independent auditor requires them to coordinate processes and procedures for documenting and testing internal control over financial reporting. This cooperation in documenting internal controls should not violate external auditor independence rules as long as management is actively involved in the process and assumes full responsibility for the effectiveness assessment.

Public companies and independent auditors are taking several steps to fulfill their internal control reporting requirements, including:

- Cooperative efforts between management and independent auditors in documenting internal control over financial reporting while preserving auditor independence.
- Adoption of a suitable evaluation framework for internal control over financial reporting (e.g., COSO framework).
- Implementation of an effective oversight function of internal control over financial reporting by the audit committee.
- Establishment of adequate disclosures for reporting on internal control over financial reporting.

Feasibility of Section 404

The average total implementation costs of first-year (2004) compliance with Section 404 for large public companies with market capitalization of greater than $700 million was estimated at $7.3 million, or 0.09 percent of their reported revenues.[113] The average costs for smaller public companies with market capitalization between $75 and $700 million was estimated as $1.5 million, or 0.46 percent of their revenues. Audit fees associated with Section 404 compliance for larger companies were about one-quarter of the total compliance costs; for smaller companies, audit fees represented over one-third of those costs.[114] The total compliance costs consist of audit fees and costs associated with management's assessment of internal controls, including travel, recruiting, hiring staff, training fees paid to service providers other than external auditors, and software purchases. In the first year, Section 404 compliance costs were driven mostly by substantial documentation of previously undocumented internal controls, assessment of control deficiencies and related remediation actions, and understanding of the requirements and guidelines, training staff, and assessing the effectiveness of internal control over financial reporting.[115]

Compliance with Section 404 leads to five benefits:

1. Improvements in internal control over financial reporting resulting from identifying and remediating internal control deficiencies and weaknesses.
2. Improvements in reliability of financial statements by restating previously erroneous financial statements.
3. Expanding the scope of internal control beyond the finance and accounting functions to the operating, management, business unit, and executive levels.
4. Enabling the board of directors, particularly the audit committee, to effectively oversee internal control over financial reporting.
5. Promoting transparency regarding the design and operation of internal control and reliability of financial statements resulting in more efficient use of capital and improvements in investor confidence.[116]

The Big Four accounting firms sponsored a survey conducted by CRA International Inc. on the second-year implementation costs of Section 404.[117] The survey found that:

- The total Section 404 costs decreased substantially in the second year: by 43.9 percent and 30.7 percent for large (market capitalization of more than $700 million) and small (market capitalization of less than $700 million) companies, respectively.
- Section 404–related audit fees in year two declined by 22.3 percent and 20.6 percent for large and small companies, respectively, even though the total audit fees in proxy materials were flat or declined slightly.
- Section 404 audit fees accounted for 33 percent and 39 percent of the total Section 404 costs in the second year for large and small companies, respectively. These results indicate that non–Section 404 audit fees increased substantially in the second year of Section 404 compliance. This increase is attributed to:

○ Additional audit procedures required by new auditing standards other than Section 404.
○ Higher salary costs paid to audit personnel.
○ Higher practice protection costs.
○ Additional costs pertaining to compliance and independence monitoring systems.

The substantial decline in Section 404 audit-related fees is caused by:

■ Increased efficiencies resulting from the learning curve effect in implementing and testing of controls from year one to year two.
■ Substantial reduction in the required documentation in the second year compared with the first year.
■ A reduction in the use of outside parties in the company's readiness activities in year two.
■ A decline in the number of key controls tested in the second year of Section 404 compliance.
■ A greater reliance on the work of others (e.g., internal auditors) in year two.

Disclosure of Material Weaknesses in Internal Controls

The majority (85 percent) of the 3,400 accelerated filers that filed their mandatory internal control reporting as of November 15, 2005, reveal no material weaknesses in their internal control over financial reporting.[118] The other 15 percent that reported material weaknesses, and thus received adverse opinions, identified problems in areas of material year-end adjustment, personnel, segregation of duties, information technology processing and access, and accounting issues pertaining to income taxes, revenue recognition, leases or commitments, consolidations, inventory and cost of sales, fixed or intangible assets, and related depreciation and impairments. Exhibit 5.5 shows that the number of companies that disclosed material weaknesses in their internal control over financial reporting appears to be decreasing in 2006, particularly larger companies and small-cap companies that were required to comply with Section 404 on mandatory internal control reporting.

Lessons Learned

The implementation of provisions of SOX, particularly Section 404 on internal controls, is expected to help improve the reliability of financial statements, detection and prevention of fraud, investor confidence in financial reports, and, thus, the efficiency of the capital markets. The second year of compliance, 2005, was a learning curve experience with some progress toward a more sustainable process as public companies and their auditors learned from their first-year assessment, documentation, and audit, and adapted to the more detailed guidance provided by the SEC and the PCAOB in May 2005. As a result, the second-year compliance costs of Section 404 declined by about 40 percent, on average, for public companies as they began integrating Section 302 into the Section 404 process. Independent auditors

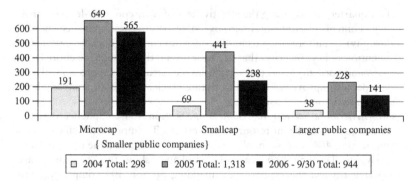

EXHIBIT 5.5 Number of Companies that Disclosed Material Weaknesses, by Company Size
Note: Size categories are based on the recommendations of the SEC Advisory Committee on Smaller Public Companies. Microcap includes companies with $128M or less in market capitalization; Smallcap includes companies with more than $128M to $787M in market capitalization; Larger public companies include those with more than $787 in market capitalization.
Source: Glass Lewis & Co. 2006.

also gained more experience in integrating audits of both internal control over financial reporting and financial statements, thus improving their audit efficiency and effectiveness.

The year 2006 is the third year of compliance with Section 404. It is expected that Section 404 compliance will evolve from "a project-based effort to a more sustainable process strategy."[119] To make this transition effectively, public companies should integrate Section 404 compliance into their business strategy by embracing five lessons learned from compliance in years one and two:

Lesson 1: *Identify control deficiencies.* The reports of the first year of Section 404 compliance revealed about 15 percent of accelerated filers received an adverse opinion indicating they had material weaknesses in their internal control over financial reporting. Significant deficiencies and material weaknesses should be identified, the level of risk associated with these deficiencies realized, and the control needed to mitigate their risk understood.

Lesson 2: *Remediate control deficiencies.* The first two years of compliance with Section 404 have proven that remediation often takes longer than anticipated and investors appear to be more concerned about uncorrected and pervasive material weaknesses than remediated and isolated control deficiencies. Public companies should not take a "quick-fix" approach but rather should focus on assessing the causes and effects of control deficiencies and develop well-documented remediation initiatives to correct the deficiencies.

Lesson 3: *Focus early on company level controls and information technology general controls.* Public companies should focus earlier in the year (e.g., first quarter) on assessing the effectiveness of their company-level controls (e.g., control environment, board oversight effectiveness, management philosophy) and information technology general controls (documentation and retention policy, security) that are operational throughout the entire company and normally affect transaction-level controls. This approach will help companies improve resource and testing efficiency of both company-level and transaction-level controls.

Lesson 4: *Attribute Section 404 ownership.* Section 404 compliance is costly and requires significant resources and efforts. To improve the efficiency of the Section 404 process, public companies should determine its ownership early on. The first two years of compliance show that companies are moving toward the process of embedding Section 404 compliance into each business line's operations in order to generate synergistic benefits. The assignment of responsibility for compliance should be driven by the company's culture, organizational structure, functional responsibilities, and operating needs (e.g., creating a separate compliance officer position), and should be decided early in the process.

Lesson 5: *Adopt across-the-board training.* The Section 404 sustainable compliance process can be achieved where compliance is embedded into each business line's operation and where those who are affected by the process, particularly those at a managerial level, fully understand the compliance requirements and their impact on their day-to-day operations and activities. This understanding can be achieved through continuous training provided by self-assessment programs or process improvement initiatives.[120]

The 2006 FEI survey asked participants for suggestions on ways that Section 404 compliance can be improved. These nine suggestions are listed in order of their importance:

1. Reduce the degree of documentation.
2. Allow greater reliance on internal audit resources and data.
3. Use roll-forward procedures.
4. Clarify the definition of "key controls."
5. Allow cumulative reliance on year-one testing and documentation.
6. Make exceptions for new systems installed in the second half of the fiscal year.
7. Clarify of the definition of "significant deficiency."
8. Clarify of the definition of "material weakness."
9. Allow remediation of controls in the fourth quarter.[121]

Small Businesses and Section 404

Smaller companies should benefit from management and auditor reporting on internal control over financial reporting (ICFR) in compliance with requirements of Section 404 of SOX for four reasons: (1) their ICFR is typically weaker than that of larger companies; (2) they have almost twice the risk of restating their financial statements; (3) they are more likely to have material weaknesses in their ICFR;

and (4) they are more likely to be the subject of fraud. The compliance costs of Section 404 of SOX for smaller companies are estimated to be disproportionately high (about 2.5 percent of their annual revenues); for larger companies, such costs are estimated to be about 1/10 to 2/10 of 1 percent. Ten initiatives have been taken to address these concerns for smaller companies:

1. The SEC has extended the implication of the Section 404 deadline for smaller companies with less than $75 million in market capitalization on three occasions, with the latest extension to 2008. On August 9, 2006, the SEC proposed further Section 404 relief for nonaccelerated filers and newly public companies in order to assist them to comply effectively and efficiently with Section 404's reporting requirements.[122] The proposal postpones management's annual report regarding the assessment of the effectiveness of the company's ICFR from the fiscal year ending on or after July 15, 2007 to the fiscal year ending on or after December 15, 2007. The proposal would require smaller companies to provide in their annual report an auditor's report on management's assessment of ICFR for the fiscal year ending on or after December 15, 2008. This gives external auditors one year to provide their mandate internal control report after the filing of management's report on ICFR.

2. The SEC and the PCAOB issued guidance (May 16, 2005) to make the Section 404 compliance process more effective, efficient, and economical.

3. COSO has established guidance for smaller companies in implementing Section 404 in a more efficient and effective manner. The Committee of Sponsoring Organizations of the Treadway Commission in June 2006 issued a report entitled "Internal Control over Financial Reporting—Guidance for Smaller Public Companies."[123] This report neither replaces nor modifies the previously issued framework on Internal Control Integrated Framework, but rather provides guidance on how to apply the framework to smaller public companies. The report guides management with establishing and monitoring effective ICFR as well as the assessment of the internal control effectiveness.

4. The SEC has established an advisory committee that made its recommendations regarding the implication of Section 404 for smaller companies. The SEC and the PCAOB sponsored a roundtable on May 10, 2006, to assess the feasibility of Section 404 and PCAOB Auditing Standard No. 2 for smaller companies. On May 17, 2006, the SEC announced it would take a series of actions to improve the implementation of SOX Section 404 internal control requirements.[124] Actions the SEC intends to take are to: (1) issue guidance for public companies and work with the PCAOB in revising its Auditing Standard No. 2 on ICFR; (2) postpone the compliance date for Section 404 requirements for smaller companies beyond July 2007; and (3) oversee PCAOB efforts to improve Section 404 implementation requirements.[125]

5. The Government Accountability Office recommends that the SEC:
   a. Evaluate the sufficiency of internal control guidance for smaller public companies.
   b. Coordinate with the PCAOB to ensure the consistent application of Auditing Standard No. 2 on the audit of ICFR.

c. Analyze the unique characteristics of smaller public companies and their investors to ensure the protection of investor interests and that any relief provided is targeted and limited.[126]

6. On July 18, 2006, the SEC released a proposed rule: the concept release concerning management's reports on ICFR.[127] The concept release is intended to provide a better understanding of the need and concerns of public companies regarding management's assessment of ICFR. The SEC anticipates that management would benefit from additional guidance on the form, extent, and nature of documentation to support its assessment.

7. A bill (H.R. 5405) has been introduced by Congressman Tom Feeney (R-FL) that modifies Section 404 of SOX by making compliance voluntary for public companies in five categories: (1) total market capitalization of less than $700 million for the relevant reporting period; (2) total product revenue of less than $125 million for the reporting period; (3) issuers with fewer than 1,500 record beneficial holders; (4) issuers subject to the requirements of Section 13(a) or 15(d) of the Securities Exchange Act of 1934 for a period of fewer than 12 calendar months; or (5) issuers who have not yet filed and were not required to file an annual report pursuant to Section 13(a) or 15(d) on the Securities Exchange Act of 1934. While this bill represents many of the recommendations of the SEC Advisory Committee on Smaller Public Companies, it does not require exemptions from compliance with Section 404. Instead, it suggests voluntary compliance.[128]

8. The advisory committee recommended exemption for public companies from compliance with Section 404 requirements unless and until a proper internal control framework for smaller companies is developed. The GAO report states that significant problems and challenges facing public companies, regardless of their size, relate to the implementation of Section 404 itself rather than the internal control itself.[129]

9. On December 13, 2006, the SEC proposed cost-effective and efficient interpretive guidance to assist public companies in complying with Section 404 regarding their management's annual assessment of internal control over financial reporting.[130] This guidance is intended to: (1) satisfy the SEC's mandatory internal control reporting requirements; (2) elaborate on factors for management to consider in identifying material risk that threatens the reliability of financial reporting and the controls that address those risks; (3) align the evaluation of the operating effectiveness of internal controls with the company's overall risk assessment; (4) address internal control deficiency evaluation, documentation, and disclosure; (5) provide principles-based and scalable guidance to enable the application of a top-down, risk-based approach appropriately tailored to all public companies of different size and complexity; and (6) require the auditor to provide an opinion only on the effectiveness of internal control over financial reporting, not management's assessment.[131]

10. On April 25, 2007, the U.S. Senate voted unanimously to require regulators to find-tune Section 404 to make its compliance more flexible and scalable for smaller companies.

Companies of all sizes should remain vigilant regarding the achievement of effective internal controls by identifying and correcting material internal control weaknesses. A higher level of investor confidence in public financial reports can be achieved when companies correct previously reported material weaknesses, and thus, the cost of capital goes down. Although the cost of compliance with Section 404 may be disproportionately high for smaller companies, noncompliance can diminish the quality of their financial reports and increase their exposure to fraud. Strong and effective corporate governance, including internal controls at smaller companies, is vital to their sustainable performance of creating shareholder value, particularly when the likelihood of financial fraud and irregularities is higher at smaller companies. The board of directors of smaller companies should set a right tone at the top by promoting compliance with corporate governance reforms, including Section 404 and other best practices.

SUMMARY

The managerial function is an important component of an effective corporate governance structure. The management team, led by the CEO and supported by the CFO, controllers, treasurers, operating managers, and general counsel, under the oversight direction of the board of directors, is primarily responsible for operation efficiency, internal control effectiveness, soundness of the accounting information system, reliability of financial reports, and compliance with all applicable laws, rules, regulations, and standards. Sustainable performance of creating and enhancing shareholder value can be achieved when the company's senior executives, particularly the CEO and the CFO, establish appropriate objectives with the vision set by its board of directors and communicate them in a transparent and engaging way to shareholders.

NOTES

1. Anderson, A., P. Herring, and A. Pawlicki. 2005. EBR: The next step. American Institute of Certified Public Accountants. Available at: www.aicpa.org/pubs/jofa/jun2005/anderson.htm.
2. International Accounting Standards Board (IASB). 2006 Discussion paper on Management Commentary CBI Response (April). Available at: http://www.iasb.org/uploaded_files/documents/16_230_mc-cl87.doc.
3. McEnally, R. 2006. Hearing before the U. S. House of Representatives Committee on Financial Services: Subcommittee on Capital Markets, Insurance, and Government Sponsored Enterprises. "Fostering Accuracy and Transparency in Financial Reporting" (March 29). Available at: http://www.cfainstitute.org/pressroom/pdf/WrittenStatementFinancialReporting.pdf.
4. United Nations Environment Programme Finance Initiative and the UN Global Compact. 2006. Principles for responsible investing. (April 27). Available at: www.unepfi.org/principles or www.unglobalcompact.org/principles.

5. American Law Institute. 1994. *Principles of corporate governance: Analysis and recommendations.* St. Paul, MN: ALI Publishers.

6. Johnson, L., and M. Sides. 2004. The Sarbanes-Oxley Act and fiduciary duties. *William Mitchell Law Review* 30 (4). Available at: http://ssrn.com/abstract= 528523.

7. Ibid.

8. Accounting Web. 2005. Study on CEO skill and excessive pay: A breakdown in corporate governance? (March 4). Available at: www.accountingweb.com/ cgi_bin/item/cgi?id=100612%d=65.

9. Movawad, J. 2006. For leading Exxon to its riches, $144,573 a day. *New York Times.* (April 15). Available at: www.nytimes.com.

10. *New York Times.* 2006. A little too close for comfort at UAL? (January 22). Available at: www.nytimes.com/2006/01/22/business/yourmoney/22suits. html.

11. Elliott, L. 2006. Nice work if you can get it: Chief executives quietly enrich themselves for mediocrity. *Guardian.* (January 23). Available at: www. guardian.co.uk.

12. Ibid.

13. Ibid.

14. Spencer Stuart. 2006. Spencer Stuart Board Index 2005. CFO Direct (January 12). Available at: http://www.cfodirect.pwc.com/CFODirectWeb/ Controller.jpf?NavCode=USAS-6BG34T.

15. Nadler, D. A. 2005. Commentary: The 2005 survey of Spencer Stuart Board Index (SSBI). (December 5). Available at: www.spencerstuart.com.

16. Corporate Board Member/PricewaterhouseCoopers 2006 Survey. 2006. What Directors Think (December). Available at: www.boardmember.com or www. pwc.com/vs.

17. Freeman, K. W. 2004. The CEO's real legacy. *Harvard Business Review* 82(2) (November). Available at: http://harvardbusinessonline.hbsp.harvard.edu/b02/ en/common/item_detail.jhtml?id=R0411B.

18. Spencer Stuart. 2006. Spencer Stuart Board Index 2005. CFO Direct (January 12). Available at: http://www.cfodirect.pwc.com/CFODirectWeb/ Controller.jpf?NavCode=USAS-6BG34T.

19. Frieswick, K. 2005. What does your CEO really know? *CFO Magazine.* (May 1). Available at: www.cfo.com/article.cfm/3907237.

20. Ibid.

21. Jones, D. 2005. Not so good year for female CEOs. *USA Today* (December 22). Available at: www.usatoday.com/money/companies/management/2005-12-22- women-ceos-usat_x.htm.

22. Williams, S. 2005. Background report A: Board diversity. Investor Responsibility Research Center. (February 9). Available at: http://oa.irrc.com/members/ pins/index.cgi?fun=show&File=:/data/2005/buckrept/123.html.

23. CFO Research Services. 2005. *The activist CFO—Alignment with strategy, not just with the business.* (April). CFO Publishing Corp. 253 Summer Street, Boston, MA 02210.

24. Ibid.

25. Ibid.
26. Harris, R. 2005. Spurred by regulatory change, directors and CFOs forge a new relationship. (January 1). Available at: www.cfo.com/article.cfm/3515695.
27. Ibid.
28. Brewis, J. 1999. How a CFO can graduate to CEO. (June). *Corporate Finance* 175 (13).
29. Durfee, D. 2005. The top spot. *CFO Magazine*. (October 6). Available at: www.cfodirect.com/cfopublic.nsf.
30. Ibid.
31. Ernst & Young. 2004. Striving for transaction excellence: The emerging role of the corporate development officer. (October). Available at: www.ey.com/global/content.nsf/us/media-release-10-04DC.
32. Ibid.
33. Ernst & Young. 2004. Ten attributes of world class corporate development functions. (October). Available at www.ey.com/global/content.nsf/us/TAS-Ten_Attributes_of_coporate_development_functions.
34. CFOdirect Network. 2006. Enterprise Risk Management: Making it over the Hurdle. Pricewaterhouse Coopers (PwC). (December 12). Available at: http://cfodirect.pwc.com/CFODirectWeb/Controller.jpf?ContentCode=MSRA-6W FQL8&ContentType=Content.
35. Deloitte & Touche. 2005. Global risk management survey. Available at: www.deloitte.com/dtt/research/0,1015,sid%253D2211%2526cid%253D713 16,00.html. (See attachment Global Risk Management Survey 2004.) Also available at: www.deloitte.com/dtt/cda/doc/content/us_Deloitte_2004_Global %20Risk_Management_Survey_fsi_0105.pdf.
36. Accounting Web. 2006. Ethics and compliance officers still valued in American corporations (September 20). Available at: www.accountingweb.com.
37. Van Clieaf, M., and J. L. Kelly. 2005. Myths of executive compensation: Returning to basic principles of pay for performance. *Corporate Governance Advisor* 13 (5) (September/October): 9–21. Retrieved September 8, 2005 from EbscoHost research database.
38. CFA Institute Center and Business Roundtable Institute for Corporate Ethics. 2006. Breaking the Short-Term Cycle. (July 24). Available at http://www.cfapubs.org/toc/ccb/2006/1.
39. Watson Wyatt. 2005. Finding the Right Balance: 2005/2006 Survey of institutional investors' views on executive compensation. Available at: www.watsonwyatt.com.
40. Glass Lewis & Co. 2006. Pay dirt: A review of 2005 executive-compensation practices (September 17). Available at: www.glasslewis.com.
41. Ibid.
42. Ibid.
43. Ibid.
44. Maskell, T. 2006. Backdating stock options deserves our derision. *Wall Street Journal* (July 21): page A15. Available at: http://online.wsj.com/article/SB115344720643113263.html.
45. Ibid.

46. Much of the discussion in this section comes from the Council of Institutional Investors' Corporate Governance Policies. 2004. Available at: www.cii.org. Also: IBM. 2005. Executive compensation. Available at: www.ibm.com/investor/corpgovernance/cgec.phtml#report. Poerio, M., and E. Keller. 2005. Executive compensation 2005: Many forces, one direction. Available at: www.xpay.net/XComp2005newBearings.htm. CalPERS. 2005. Executive compensation. CalPERS policy guidelines. Available at: www.calpers-governance.org/alert/exec-comp/proxy_policy.asp.

47. Beck, R. 2005. Companies review stock option accounting. *AP Business Writer.* (November 22). Available at: www.ap.org.

48. Pergola, T. M. 2005. Management entrenchment: Can it negate the effectiveness of recently legislated governance reforms? *Journal of American Academy of Business* 6(2): 177–185.

49. U.S. Securities and Exchange Commission (SEC). 2006. SEC votes to adopt changes to disclosure requirements concerning executive compensation and related matters (July 26). Available at: http://www.sec.gov/news/press/2006/2006-123.htm.

50. Moody's Investors Service. 2006. U.S. Executive Pay Structure and Metrics (June). Available at: http://www.moodys.com.

51. Schultz, E. and T. Francis. 2006. As workers' pensions wither, those for executives flourish. *Wall Street Journal* (June23). Available at: http://online.wsj/article/SB1151030625781888438.html.

52. Ibid.

53. Ibid.

54. State Board of Administration of Florida. 2005. SBA 2005 corporate governance report. Available at: www.sbafla.com/pdf/investment/CorpGovReport.pdf.

55. Ibid.

56. Maremont, M. 2005. Latest twist in corporate pay: Tax-free income for executives. *Wall Street Journal,\.* (December 22). Available at: www.careerjournal.com/salaryhiring/hotissues/20051223-maremont.html?mod=RSS_Career_Journal&cjrss=frontpage.

57. Ibid.

58. Bebchuk, L. 2006. How much does the boss make? *Wall Street Journal.* January 18). Available at: www.online.wsj.com.

59. Deutsch, C. H. 2005. Executive pay: My big fat C.E.O. paycheck. *New York Times* (April 3). Available at: www.nytimes.com.

60. Securities and Exchange Commission. 2006. Executive compensation and related party disclosure. (January 27). File No.: S7-03-06. Available at: www.sec.gov/rules/proposed/33-8655.pdf.

61. U.S. Securities and Exchange Commission (SEC). 2006. Executive Compensation and Related Person Disclosures Release No. 33-8732A (August 29). Available at: www.sec.gov/rules/final/2006/33-8732A.pdf.

62. Ibid.

63. Gibson, Dunn, & Crutcher. 2006. Policies and procedures for approving related party transactions (December 12). Available at: www.gibsondunn.com.

64. Moody's Investors Service. 2006. U.S. Executive Pay Structure and Metrics (June). Available at: http://www.moodys.com.
65. Securities and Exchange Commission. 1977. The report of the SEC Advisory Committee on corporate disclosure. Available at: www.sec.gov.
66. The independent auditor may issue an integrated report that combines items 6 and 7 in one comprehensive report on both financial statements and internal control.
67. Sarbanes-Oxley Act. 2002. Section 302: Corporate responsibility for financial reports. Available at: www.sec.gov/about/laws/soa2002.pdf.
68. Ibid.
69. Herz, R. H. 2006. Testimony of chairman of the Financial Accounting Standards Board before the Capital Markets, Insurance, and Government-Sponsored Enterprises Subcommittee of the Committee on Financial Services (March 29). Available at: www.fasb.org/testimony/03-29-06_full_text.pdf.
70. Taub, S. 2006. Financial Reporting: SEC Deputy Chief Accountant says Collective Demand Creates Complexity. Corporate Accountability Report (Vol. 4, No. 43): Page 1117 (November 3).
71. Cunningham, C. S. 2006. Testimony of the president and chief executive officer of Financial Executives International before the Subcommittee on Capital Markets, Insurance, and Government Sponsored Enterprises of the Committee on Financial Services of the United States House of Representatives (March 29). Available at: http://financialservices.house.gov/media/pdf/032906cc.pdf.
72. Herz. 2003. Testimony of chairman of the Financial Accounting Standards Board (June 3). Available at: http://www.fasb.org/testimony/06-03-03_attachments.pdf.
73. COSO Enterprise Risk Management Framework. Available at: www.cpa2biz.com/CS2000/Products/CPA2BIZ/Publications/COSO+Enterprise+Risk+Management+-+Integrated+Framework.htm.
74. Ibid.
75. Fink, R. and D. Durfee. 2006. Could it be that finance executives really don't mind regulation? *CFO Magazine* (September 1).
76. Zion, D., B. Carcache, and A. Varshney. 2006. Bring it on: Off balance sheet operating leases. (April 18). Credit Suisse. Available at: www.credit-suisse.com.
77. Ibid.
78. Ibid.
79. Ibid.
80. Financial Accounting Standards Board. 2006. Statement of Financial Accounting Standards No. 157, Fair Value Measurement (September 15). Norwalk, CT.
81. Ibid.
82. Ibid.
83. Financial Accounting Standards Board. 2006. FASB and IASB reaffirm commitment to enhance consistency, comparability, and efficiency in global capital markets. (February 27). Press release. Available at: www.fasb.org.
84. Rega, J., and V. Anand. 2006. U.S. International Accounting Boards vow to close gaps by 2008. (February 27). Available at: www.bloomberg.net.

85. Bullen, H. G., and K. Crook. 2005. Revisiting the concepts. Financial Accounting Standards Board. International Accounting Standards Board (May). Available at: www.fasb.org.
86. Fitch Ratings. 2006. Special report: Accounting and financial reporting risk: 2006 global outlook—Severity now? (January 24). Available at: www.fitchratings.com.
87. Ibid.
88. Ibid.
89. International Accounting Standards Board. 2005. Discussion paper: Management commentary: A paper prepared for the IASB by staff of its partner standard-setters and others (October). Available at: www.iasb.org/uploaded_files/documents/8_891_DPManComm.pdf.
90. U.S. Securities and Exchange Commission (SEC). 2006. Data submitted in the XBRL Voluntary Program on EDGAR. Available at: www.sec.gov/Archives/edgar/XBRL.html.
91. eXtensible Business Reporting Language. 2006. XBRL International forms standards board to strengthen its technical output (April 4). Available at: www.xbrl.org/Announcements/XSB-PR-final-4April2006.htm.
92. Press release. 2006. Baby boomers face retirement crisis as lifetime pensions wither and 401(k)s falter (May 8). Available at: www.pbs.org/frontline/retirement.
93. Ibid.
94. Ibid.
95. Walsh, M. W. 2005. A pension rule, sometimes murky, is under pressure. *New York Times.* (November 8). Available at: select.nytimes.com/gst/abstract.html?res=F30F14FF3E5A0 C7B8CDDA80994DD404482.
96. Bergstresser, D., M. A. Desai, and J. Rauh. 2004. Managerial opportunism and earnings manipulation: Evidence from defined benefit pension plans. Working paper, Harvard Business School (January). Available at: cowles.econ.yale.edu/behfin/2004-04-10/bergstresser-etal.pdf.
97. Financial Accounting Standards Board. 2006. Exposure draft to improve accounting for postretirement benefit plans, including pensions. (March 31). Available at: www.fasb.org.
98. Financial Accounting Standards Board (FASB). 2006. Statement of Financial Accounting Standards (FASB) No. 158: Employers' Accounting for Decision Benefit Pension and Other Post Retirement Plans (September 29). Available at: www.fasb.org/st/index.shtm.
99. Zion, D., B. Carcache, and A. Varshney. 2006. The quick fix: FASB issues pension and OPEB proposal: Phase I. Credit Suisse. (April 3). Available at: www.creditsuisse.com/researchdisclosures.
100. Ibid.
101. Financial Accounting Standards Board. 2002. Proposal for a principles-based approach to U.S. standard setting. Available at: www.fasb.org.
102. United States Securities and Exchange Commission. 2003. Study pursuant to Section 108(d) of the Sarbanes-Oxley Act of 2002 on the adoption by the United States Financial Reporting System of a principles-based accounting

system: Office of the Chief Accountant and Office of Economic Analysis. Available at: www.sec.gov/news/studies/principlesbasedstand.htm.

103. Gradison, B. 2006. Testimony of the acting chairman of Public Company Accounting Oversight Board before the U.S. House of Representatives Committee on Financial Services Subcommittee on Capital Markets, Insurance, and Government Sponsored Enterprises (March 29). Available at: http://financialservices.house.gov/media/pdf/032906bg.pdf.

104. Reilly. D. 2006. Restatement blame: Basic mistakes. *Wall Street Journal* (November 20). Available at: online.wsj.com/article/SB116398348172927897. html.

105. United States Government Accountability Office. 2002. Financial restatements. GAO-03-138. Available at: www.gao.gov/new.items/d03138.pdf.

106. Glass Lewis & Co. 2007. The Errors of Their Ways: Restatements Trend Alert, Yellow Card Trend Alert (February 27). Available at: glasslewis.com.

107. Ibid.

108. Securities Exchange Act. 1934. Sections 13a-15, 15D-15. Available at: www.sec.gov/divisions/corpfin/34act/sect13.htm and www.sec.gov/divisions/corpfin/34act/sect15 d.htm.

109. SEC Final Rule. 2003. Management's reports on internal control over financial reporting and certification of disclosure in Exchange Act periodic reports, Releases Nos. 33-8238, 34-47986. (June). Available at: http://www.sec.gov/rules/final/33-8238.htm.

110. Committee of Sponsoring Organizations of the Treadway Commission. 2004. Internal control issues in derivatives usage. The executive summary is available at: www.coso.org/publications/executive_summary_derivatives_usage.htm.

111. Lord and Benoit. 2006. The Lord and Benoit report: Bridging the Sarbanes-Oxley disclosure control gap. (March 31). Available at: www.section404.org.

112. Ibid.

113. CRA International. 2006. Sarbanes-Oxley Section 404 costs and implementation issue: Spring 2006 survey update. (April 17). Available at: www.crai.com.

114. Ibid.

115. PricewaterhouseCoopers. 2006. Current developments for audit committees 2006. (February). Available at: www.pwc.com/uscorporategovernance.

116. Ibid.

117. CRA International. 2005. Sarbanes-Oxley Section 404 costs and implementation issue (December 8). Available at: http://www.crai.com/pubs/pub_4896.pdf.

118. Audit Analytics as of November 2005. Available at: www.auditanalytics.com.

119. PricewaterhouseCoopers. 2006. Banking/capital market issue—Spring 2006. Sarbanes-Oxley Section 404: From project to process. PwC Banking & Capital Markets Group. (April 19). Available at: http://www.pwc.com/extweb/pwcpublications.nsf/docid/9e02dcfbfbfbda24852570890003247b/$File/spring2006_issues.pdf.

120. Ibid.

121. Financial Executives International. 2006. FEI Survey on Sarbanes-Oxley Section 404 Implementation (April 6). Available at: http://www2.fei.org/news/404_survey_4_6_06.cfm.

122. U.S. Securities and Exchange Commission (SEC). 2006. Internal Control over Financial Reporting in Exchange Act Periodic Reports of Non-Accelerated Filers and Newly Public Companies (August 9) Proposed Rules. Reference No. 34-54295. Available at: http://www.sec.gov/rules/proposed.html.

123. Committee of Sponsoring Organizations of the Treadway Commission (COSO). 2006. Internal control over Financial Reporting-Guidance for smaller public companies. Available at: http://www.aicpa.org/copyright.htm.

124. Securities and Exchange Commission (SEC). 2006. SEC Announces Next Steps for Sarbanes-Oxley Implementation (May 17). Available at: http://www.sec.gov/news/press/2006/2006-75.htm.

125. Ibid.

126. United States Government Accountability Office (GAO). 2006. Sarbanes-Oxley Act Challenges for Smaller Companies (April). GAO-06-361.

127. U.S. Securities and Exchange Commission (SEC). 2006. Concept Release Concerning Management's Reports on Internal Control over Financial Reporting (July 18). Available at: http://www.sec.gov.

128. U.S. House of Representatives. 2006. H.R. 5045 COMPETE Act (May 17). Available at: http://www.govtrack.us/congress/bill.xpd?bill=h109-5405.

129. United States Government Accountability Office (GAO). 2006. Sarbanes-Oxley Act Challenges for Smaller Companies (April). GAO-06-361.

130. U.S. Securities and Exchange Commission (SEC). 2006. SEC note to propose interpretive guidance for management to improve Sarbanes-Oxley 404 implementation (December 13). Available at: www.sec.gov/news/press/2006/2006-206.htm.

131. Ibid.

CHAPTER 6

Compliance Function

INTRODUCTION

Reported corporate and accounting scandals of the late 1990s and the early 2000s suggest that market-based correction mechanisms have failed to prevent those scandals and properly penalize corporate wrongdoers. Therefore, regulations, rules, standards, and best practices established by governing bodies, standard setters, and professional organizations are important external mechanisms in creating an environment that promotes, monitors, and enforces responsible corporate governance, reliable financial reporting, and credible audit functions. Corporate governance is evolving from a compliance function to a business imperative, as explained in Chapter 1. The compliance function eventually determines what information public companies must disclose to their shareholders for making sound investment and voting decisions and to other stakeholders for protecting their interests.

REGULATIONS AND COMPLIANCE WITH THEM

Primary sources of the compliance function of corporate governance are lawmakers, regulators, courts, standard setters, and enforcement agents. The fair and effective enforcement of compliance with applicable laws, regulations, rules, and standards governing public companies is the fabric of our financial markets. The enforcement should be aggressive and uncompromising enough to promote compliance yet not so rigid that it adversely affects the foundation of our free enterprise system. The Securities and Exchange Commission (SEC), in its new enforcement guidelines, is attempting to create a fair balance between effective compliance and severity of penalties.

Regulations that create an environment of better governance and are cost efficient in the long term can result in more sustainable performance. Regulations that require more effective governance (e.g., majority board independence, executive certifications of financial statements, and related internal controls) enable companies to make changes that create sustainable shareholder value. Laws affecting corporate governance can be established at both the state and/or federal level.

State Regulation

Corporations are created under state corporation statutes, which define the fiduciary duty of their boards of directors, describe rights of shareholders, and set other provisions, including sales of major assets and mergers and acquisitions. State courts and judges often interpret state corporate laws. State legislatures began regulating the securities markets in the early 1900s, before there were any regulations of securities markets.

The first comprehensive state securities law was enacted by Kansas in 1911. Known as the blue-sky law, some form was subsequently enacted in 23 states.[1] The blue-sky legislation was intended to mandate registration of securities and require companies to provide fair trading of securities and prevent fraud in the sale of securities. State corporate laws define directors' obligations, as almost all corporations (except for some banks and federally regulated entities) are incorporated by states. Corporate laws vary by state. The state of Delaware, where more than 50 percent of U.S. public companies are incorporated, has dominated with the issuance of corporate laws, regulations, and standards.

The Committee on Capital Markets Regulation recommends limiting how and when state law can pursue enforcement actions against auditing firms and financial institutions by suggesting that the Department of Justice (DoJ) have the ability to sign off on state indictments only in cases when the SEC chose not to take action, and the SEC have a final say on any settlement cases of national importance.[2] The committee proposes that state attorneys general coordinate prosecutions of companies with federal agencies (the SEC, DoJ). The DoJ should pursue corporate criminal indictments only as a last resort, with the rare possibility that companies waive their attorney-client privilege. The committee basically suggests that lawmakers and regulators should not be tough on the gatekeepers (management, directors, legal counsel, and auditors) who violate securities laws by relaxing some of the measures designed to protect investors from corporate malfeasance and wrongdoers and by promoting less-aggressive civil and criminal investigations. Investor protection measures provided through state law are vital to the effectiveness of corporate governance.

Federal Securities Regulation

Prior to the stock market crash in 1929, financial markets were primarily unregulated, and there was no support for federal regulations of the securities market as investors were not concerned about the threats of investing in an unregulated market.[3] The 1929 stock market crash and resulting Great Depression generated needed support and interest in federal securities legislation. Congress responded by passing the Securities Act of 1933. The primary purpose of the Act was to protect the initial purchaser of securities by requiring companies that offer securities for public sale to provide registration statements presenting adequate financial and other significant information about the securities.[4] Congress also enacted the Securities Exchange Act of 1934 to provide protection to all investors who trade securities (both buyers and purchasers) and created the Securities and Exchange Commission to register, regulate, and oversee the securities industry.[5]

In the United States, federal regulations of corporations started with the passage of the 1933 Securities Act and the Exchange Act of 1934. These acts apply to SEC registrants (public companies) and their financial reporting in providing accurate financial information to the capital markets for fair pricing purposes. This market pricing mechanism of corporate governance was intended to:

- Provide protection for investors against the threats of false information to the market influencing stock prices.
- Supplement inadequate investor rights under state law.
- Create a uniform and generally accepted framework for financial reporting and auditing.

Federal securities laws play an important role in corporate governance through disclosure requirements and the creation and approval of accounting and auditing standards, the latter through the formation of the Public Company Accounting Oversight Board (PCAOB) by SOX.

SARBANES-OXLEY ACT

The economic downturn of the early 2000s, coupled with several years of steady decline in the capital markets and numerous high-profile financial scandals, paved the road for regulatory actions. After several unsuccessful attempts by Congress to protect investors from receiving inaccurate financial information pursuant to the enactments of the securities laws, the wave of financial scandals and corporate malfeasance of the early 2000s, which caused the erosion of investor confidence, provided needed support for Congress to pass the Sarbanes-Oxley Act (SOX). The Act was intended to rebuild investor confidence and protect investors by improving the reliability, completeness, accuracy, and transparency of corporate disclosures, including financial reports.[6] President George W. Bush, in signing SOX into law, praised it as "the most far-reaching reforms of American Business Practices since the time of Franklin Delano Roosevelt."[7] SOX creates new and unprecedented requirements for public companies, measures that affect all corporate governance functions discussed in this book. The proper implementation of its far-reaching provisions is intended to address and affect the conduct of boards of directors, audit committees, executive, internal and external auditors, financial analysts, legal counsel, investment banks and other groups, and individuals associated with financial reports.

SOX is regarded as a continuous improvement process; many of its provisions (e.g., creation of the PCAOB, Section 404 of internal controls, mandatory improved audit committee, and executive certifications) will take time to cure the many corporate governance problems that contributed to the reported financial scandals. Thus, it is still too early to assess the net benefit (induced benefits – imposed costs), efficacy, and success of SOX in improving corporate governance effectiveness. The fundamental provisions of SOX can be divided into five categories:

1. Corporate governance.
2. Financial reporting.

3. Audit functions.
4. Federal securities law enforcement.
5. Others (e.g., legal counsel, financial analysts).

These provisions and related SOX Sections are summarized in Exhibit 6.1 and further discussed in the Sections that follow. In describing the long-term benefits of compliance with the provisions of SOX, former chairman of the SEC, William A. Donaldson, stated:

> [T]he Sarbanes Oxley reforms should yield extraordinary long-term benefits in the form of improved financial reporting, better management control, and more ethical behavior by companies and gatekeepers. This, in turn, should lead to sounder corporate governance, better and more reliable reporting, improved corporate performance, enhanced investor confidence, and ultimately, a lower cost of capital (... .) Section 404 may have the greatest long-term potential to improve financial reporting. At the same time, it may also be the most urgent financial reporting challenge facing corporate America and the audit profession in 2005.[8]

Corporate Governance Provisions

SOX directs the SEC to issue rules to implement its provisions and requirements for national stock exchanges to establish listing standards pertaining to listed companies' directors, officers, and financial and internal control reporting. SOX provisions, SEC-related rules, and listing standards influence corporate governance structure at least in three ways.

1. Auditors, analysts, and legal counsel, who were not traditionally considered components of corporate governance, are now brought into the realm of internal governance as the gatekeepers.
2. The legal status and fiduciary duties of the company's directors and officers, particularly the audit committee and chief executive officer, have been enhanced significantly.
3. Certain aspects of state corporate law were preempted and federalized. For example, Section 402 of SOX prohibits loans to directors and officers, although the state law permits such loans. Under Section 304, officers must reimburse certain compensation received if the company had to restate its financial statements as a result of fraud. Section 301 of SOX grants more direct statutory responsibilities (e.g., direct responsibility for hiring, compensating, firing independent auditors) to the audit committee than the state law.[9]

Financial Reporting Provisions

The primary focus of SOX is to improve the quality, reliability, and transparency of public financial reports. High-quality financial information can contribute

EXHIBIT 6.1 Sarbanes-Oxley Act of 2002 Provisions

I. Corporate Governance Provisions	
Section	**Provisions**
202	**Audit Committee preapproval of audit services**

All auditing services (which may entail providing comfort letters in connection with securities underwritings) and nonaudit services provided to an issuer by the auditor of the issuer shall be preapproved by the audit committee of the issuer.

205	**Amendments to the Securities Exchange Act 1934**

Defined Audit Committee and Registered Public Accounting Firm

301	**Public Company Audit Committees**

Each member of the audit committee shall be an independent member of the board of directors. The audit committee shall be directly responsible for the appointment, compensation, and oversight of the work of any registered public accounting firm associated by the issuer. The audit committee shall establish procedures for the receipt, retention, and treatment of complaints received by the issuer regarding accounting, internal accounting controls, or auditing matters and the confidential, anonymous submission by employees of the issuer or concerns regarding questionable accounting or auditing matters.

303	**Improper Influence on Conduct of Audits**

It shall be unlawful for any officer or director of an issuer to take any action to fraudulently influence, coerce, manipulate, or mislead auditors in the performance of financial audit of the financial statements.

304	**Forfeiture of Certain Bonuses and Profits**

CEOs and CFOs who revise company's financial statements for the material noncompliance with any financial reporting requirements must pay back any bonuses or stock options awarded because of the misstatements.

305	**Amendments to the Securities Exchange Act 1934**

Adapted the phrase "substantial unfitness" to read "unfitness."

306	**Insider Trades During Pension Fund Blackout Periods**

It shall be unlawful for any directors or executive officers directly or indirectly to purchase, sell, or otherwise acquire or transfer any equity security of the issuer during any blackout periods. Any profits resulting from sales in violation of this Section shall inure to and be recoverable by the issuer.

402	**Extended Conflict of Interest Provisions:**

It is unlawful for the issuer to extend credit or personal loans to any directors or executive officers.

(continued overleaf)

EXHIBIT 6.1 (*Continued*)

I. Corporate Governance Provisions

Section	Provisions
403	**Disclosures of Transactions Involving Management and Principal Stockholders**

Every person who is directly or indirectly the beneficial owner of more than 10 percent of any class of any equity security (other than an exempted security) which is registered pursuant to section 12, or who is a director or an officer of the issuer of such security, shall file the statements required by this subSection with the Commission.

406 **Code of Ethics for Senior Financial Officers**

The SEC shall issue rules to require each issuer to disclose whether it has adopted a code of ethics for its senior financial officers and the nature and content of such code.

407 **Disclosure of Audit Committee Financial Expert**

The SEC shall issue rules to require each issuer to disclose whether at least one member of its audit committee is a "financial" expert as defined by the commission.

705 **Study on Investment Banks**

Directs the comptroller general to conduct a study and report the findings to Congress regarding the role of investment bankers and financial advisors assisted public companies in manipulating their earnings and obfuscating their true financial condition.

806 **Whistleblower Protection**

Provides whistleblower protections for employees of any issuer who willingly provide evidence of fraud or violations of securities by that issuer.

1105 **Authority of the SEC**

The commission may prohibit a person from serving as a director or officer of a publicly traded company if the person has committed securities fraud.

1106 **Criminal Penalties for Violations of the 1934 Act**

Increases criminal penalties for violations of the 1934 act from $1 million to $5 million for individuals; from 10 years to 20 years imprisonment for each violation; and from $2.5 million to $25 million for each entity.

II. Financial Reporting Provisions

Section	Provisions
108	**Accounting Standards**

1. The SEC may recognized as "generally accepted" any accounting principles that are established by a standard setting body that meets the act's criteria.

2. The SEC shall conduct a study on the adoption of a principles-based accounting system.

EXHIBIT 6.1 *(Continued)*

302	**Corporate Responsibility for Financial Reports**

The signing officers (e.g., CEO, CFO) shall certify in each annual or quarterly report filed with the SEC that (a) the report does not contain any untrue statement of a material fact or omitted material facts that cause the report to be misleading; (b) financial statements and disclosures fairly present, in all material respects, the financial condition and results of operations of the issuer. The signing officers are responsible for establishing and maintaining adequate and effective controls to ensure reliability of financial statements and disclosures. The signing officers are responsible for proper design, periodic assessment of the effectiveness, and disclosure of material deficiencies in internal controls to external auditors and the audit committee.

401   **Disclosures in Periodic Reports**

Each financial report that is required to be prepared in accordance with GAAP shall reflect all material correcting adjustments that have been identified by the auditors. Each financial report (annual and quarterly) shall disclose all material off–balance sheet transactions and other relationships with unconsolidated entities that may have a material current or future effect on the financial conditions of the issuer.

404   **Management Assessments of Internal Controls**

1. Each annual report filed with the SEC shall contain an internal control report, which shall: (a) state the responsibility of management for establishing and maintaining an adequate internal control structure and procedures for financial reporting; (b) contain an assessment of the effectiveness of the internal control structure and procedures as of the end of the issuer's fiscal year.

2. Auditors shall attest to, and report on, the assessment of the adequacy and effectiveness of the issuer internal control structure and procedures as part of audit of financial reports in accordance with standards for attestation engagements.

405   **Exemptions**

Nothing in Section 401, 402, or 404, the amendments made by those sections, or the rules of the commission under those sections shall apply to any investment company registered under Section 8 of the Investment Company Act of 1940.

408   *Requires the SEC to review disclosures made to the SEC on a regular and systemic basis for the protection of investors including the review of the issuer's financial statements.*

409   **Real-Time Issuer Disclosures**

Each issuer shall disclose information on material changes in the financial condition or operations of the issuer on a rapid and current basis.

(continued overleaf)

EXHIBIT 6.1 *(Continued)*

1001   Corporate Tax Returns
        *The federal income tax return of public corporations should be signed by
        the CEO of the issuer.*

III. Audit Function Provisions
Section   Provisions
101   Establishment of Public Company Accounting Oversight Board (PCAOB)
          *The PCAOB is an independent, nongovernmental accounting oversight
          board to oversee the audit of publicly traded companies.*
102   Registration with the PCAOB
          *Register public accounting firms (foreign and domestic) that prepare
          audit reports for issuers.*
103   Functions of the PCAOB
          *The board shall establish, or adopt, by rule: auditing, quality control,
          ethics, independence, and other standards relating to the preparation
          of audit reports for issuers; conduct inspections of registered public
          accounting firms; conduct investigations and disciplinary proceedings
          and impose appropriate sections; enforce compliance with the act; and
          establish budget and manage the operations of the board and its staff.*
104   PCAOB Inspections of Registered Public Accounting Firms
          *The board shall conduct a continuing program of inspections to assess
          the degree of compliance of each registered public accounting firm and
          associated persons of that firm with this act, the rules of the board, the
          rules of the commission, or professional standards, in connection with
          its performance of audits, issuance of audit reports, and related
          matters involving issuers.*
105   PCAOB Investigations and Disciplinary Proceedings
          *The board shall establish, by rule, subject to the requirements of this
          section, fair procedures for the investigation and disciplining of
          registered public accounting firms and associated persons of such firms.*
106   Regulations of Foreign Public Accounting Firms
          *Any foreign public accounting firm that prepares or furnishes an audit
          report with respect to any issuer shall be subject to this act and the
          rules of the board and the commission issued under this act, in the
          same manner and to the same extent as a public accounting firm that is
          organized and operates under the laws of the United States.*
107   Commission Oversight of the Board
          *The SEC shall have oversight and enforcement authority over the
          PCAOB.*
109   Funding of the PCAOB
          *The board shall establish, with the approval of the commission, a
          reasonable annual accounting support fee (or a formula for the
          computation thereof), as may be necessary or appropriate to establish
          and maintain the board.*

EXHIBIT 6.1 (*Continued*)

201   Auditor Independence: Services Outside the Scope of Practice of Auditors
Registered public accounting firms are prohibited from providing any
nonaudit services to an issuer contemporaneously with the audit
including but not limited to: (a) bookkeeping or other services related to
the accounting record or financial statement of the audit client; (b)
financial information systems design and implementation; (c) appraisal
or valuation services; (d) actuarial services; (e) internal audit
outsourcing services; (f) management functions or human resources; (g)
broker or dealer, investment advisor, or investment banking; (h) legal
services and expert services unrelated to the audit; and (i) any other
services that the PCAOB determines, by regulation, is impermissible.

203   Audit Partner Rotation
The lead audit or coordinating partner and reviewing partner of the
registered accounting firm must rotate off of the audit every five years.

204   Auditor Reports to Audit Committees
The registered accounting firm must report to the audit committee: all
critical accounting policies and practices to be used; all alternative
treatments of financial information within generally accepted
accounting principles, ramifications of the use of such alternative
disclosures and treatments, and the preferred treatment; other material
written communication between the auditor and management.

206   Conflicts of Interest
The registered accounting firm is prohibited to perform audit for an issuer
who is CEO, CFO, controller, chief accounting officer, or person in an
equivalent employed by the accounting firm during the one-year period
preceding the audit.

207   Study of Mandatory Rotation of Registered Public Accounting Firms
The Comptroller General of the United States will conduct a study on the
potential effects of requiring the mandatory rotation of public
accounting firms.

208   Regulations and Independence Guidelines
The commission was given 180 days to implement final regulations
regarding the act. It shall be unlawful for any registered public
accounting firm (or an associated person thereof, as applicable) to
prepare or issue any audit report with respect to any issuer, if the firm
or associated person engages in any activity with respect to that issuer
prohibited by any of Subsections (g) through (l) of Section 10A of the
Securities Exchange Act of 1934, as added by this title, or any rule or
regulation of the commission or of the board issued thereunder.

209   Considerations by Appropriate State Regulatory Authorities
In supervising nonregistered public accounting firms and their associated
persons, appropriate state regulatory authorities should make an
independent determination of the proper standards applicable,

(*continued overleaf*)

EXHIBIT 6.1   (*Continued*)

particularly taking into consideration the size and nature of the business of the accounting firms they supervise and the size and nature of the business of the clients of those firms. The standards applied by the board under this act should not be presumed to be applicable for purposes of this Section for small and medium-size nonregistered public accounting firms.

701   **GAO Study and Report Regarding Consolidation of Public Accounting Firms**

The GAO shall conduct a study regarding consolidation of public accounting firms since 1989 and determine the consequences of the consolidation, including the present and future impact and solutions to any problems that may result from the consolidation.

IV. Securities Law Violations

Section   **Provisions**

601   **SEC Resource and Authority**

SEC appropriations for 2003 are increased to $776 million from which $98 million shall be used to hire an additional 200 employees to provide enhanced oversight of audit services.

602   **Practice before the Commission**

1. The SEC may censure any person, or temporarily bar or deny any person the right to appear or practice before the SEC if the person does not possess the requisite qualifications to represent others, has willfully violated federal securities laws, or lacks character or integrity.

2. The SEC shall conduct a study of securities of professionals (e.g., accountants, investment bankers, brokers, dealers, attorneys, investment advisors) who have been found to have aided and abetted a violation of federal securities laws.

3. The SEC shall establish rules setting minimum standards for professional conduct for attorneys practicing before the commission.

603   **Federal Court Authority to Impose Penny Stock Bars**

Amendment to the Securities Exchange Act of 1934 that allows the court to prohibit any person participating in, or, at the time of the alleged misconduct who was participating in, an offering of penny stock, from participating in an offering of penny stock, conditionally or unconditionally, and permanently or for such period of time as the court shall determine.

703   **Study and Report on Violators and Violations**

Directs the SEC to conduct a study and report its findings to Congress regarding the proliferation of violations of securities laws and associated penalties.

EXHIBIT 6.1 (*Continued*)

704	**Study of Enforcement Actions**
	Directs the SEC to analyze all enforcement actions over prior five-year period involving violations of reporting requirements and restatements of financial statements to identify areas of reporting that are most susceptible to fraud.
802	**Criminal Penalties for Altering Documents**
	Criminal penalties for document destruction, alternation, or concealment with the intent to impede federal investigations or in a federal bankruptcy case include fines and maximum imprisonment of 20 years.
803	**No Discharge of Debts in a Bankruptcy Proceeding**
	Liability for securities law or fraud violations may not be discharged under the U.S. Bankruptcy Code.
804	**Statute of Limitations for Securities Fraud**
	Statute of limitations to recover for a private action for securities fraud lengthened to the earlier of two years after the date of discovery or five years after the fraudulent activities.
807	**Criminal Penalties for Defrauding Shareholders of Publicly Traded Companies**
	Amended Chapter 63 of Title 18, United States Code, by adding Section 1348, Securities Fraud.
902	**Attempts and Conspiracies to Commit Criminal Fraud Offenses**
	Amended Chapter 63 of Title 18, United States Code, by adding Section 1349, Attempt and Conspiracy.
903, 904, 906	**White-Collar Crime Penalty Enhancements**
	1. Maximum penalty for mail and wire fraud is 10 years.
	2. The SEC may prohibit anyone convicted of securities fraud from being a director or officer of any public company.
	3. Financial reports filed with the SEC (annual, quarterly) must be certified by the CEO and CFO of the issuer. The certification must state that the financial statements and disclosures fully comply with provisions of securities acts and they fairly present, in all material respects, financial results and conditions of the issuer. Maximum penalties for willful and knowing violations of these provisions of the act are a fine of not more than $500,000 and/or imprisonment of up to five years.
1102	**Tampering with a Record or Otherwise Impeding an Official Proceeding**
	Whoever corruptly—(1) alters, destroys, mutilates, or conceals a record, document, or other object, or attempts to do so, with the intent to impair the object's integrity or availability for use in an official proceeding; or (2) otherwise obstructs, influences, or impedes any official proceeding, or attempts to do so; shall be fined under this title or imprisoned not more than 10 years, or both.

(*continued overleaf*)

EXHIBIT 6.1 (*Continued*)

1103	**Temporary Freeze Authority for the Securities and Exchange Commission**
	Whenever during the course of a lawful investigation involving possible violations of the Federal securities laws by an issuer of publicly traded securities or any of its directors, officers, partners, controlling persons, agents, or employees, it shall appear to the Commission that it is likely that the issuer will make extraordinary payments (whether compensation or otherwise) to any of the foregoing persons; the Commission may petition a Federal district court for a temporary order requiring the issuer to escrow, subject to court supervision, those payments in an interest-bearing account for 45 days.
1107	**Retaliation against Informants**
	"Whoever knowingly, with the intent to retaliate, takes any action harmful to any person, including interference with the lawful employment or livelihood of any person, for providing to a law enforcement officer any truthful information relating to the commission or possible commission of any Federal offense, shall be fined under this title or imprisoned not more than 10 years, or both."

V. Other provising not relations to other items not specifically
related to the above categories:

Section	Provisions
307	**Rules of Professional Responsibility for Attorneys**
	Require attorneys who appear or practice before the SEC to report violations of securities laws to the CEO or chief legal counsel and, if no action is taken, to the audit committee.
308	**Fair Funds for Investors**
	Allows the SEC to impose civil penalties on disgorged executives for the compensation of victims.
501	**Treatment of Securities Analysts**
	Registered securities associations and national securities exchanges shall adopt rules designed to address conflicts of interest for research analysts who recommend equities in research reports.
604	**Qualifications of Associated Persons of Brokers and Dealers**
	Amends the Securities Exchange Act of 1934 and refines the qualifications of associated oersons of Brokers and dealers.
702	**Credit Rating Study and Report**
	Directs the SEC to conduct a study and report its findings to Congress regarding the role, importance, and impact of rating agencies in the marketplace.
805, 905, 1104	**Review of Sentencing Guidelines**
	Authorizes the U.S. Sentencing Commission to review the sentencing guidelines for fraud, obstruction of justice, and other white-collar crimes and propose changes to existing guidelines.

significantly to the integrity and efficiency of the capital markets. Financial reporting provisions of SOX and SEC-related rules include:

- Certification of financial statements and internal controls by chief executive officers (CEOs) and chief financial officers (CFOs).
- Disclosure of off–balance sheet transactions.
- Disclosure pertaining to the use of non-GAAP (generally accepted accounting principles) financial measures.
- Disclosure of material current events affecting companies.
- Mandatory internal control reporting by management.
- A study of principles-based accounting standards.
- Convergence of accounting standards.
- Recognition of adequate funding for the Financial Accounting Standards Board (FASB) as an accounting standard-setting body.
- The oversight function of the FASB by the SEC.

Audit Function Provisions

A fundamental objective of SOX was to enhance the reliability and integrity of audit functions and the audit process as well as the credibility of audit reports provided in financial statements and to improve investor confidence in the auditing profession. Provisions of SOX and SEC-related rules addressing audit functions include:

- Creation of the Public Company Accounting Oversight Board to oversee the accounting profession.
- Adoption of new rules related to auditor independence.
- Issuance of new rules related to improper influence on auditors.
- Issuance of new rules pertaining to retention of records and audit evidence relevant to review and audit of financial statements.
- The oversight function of the PCAOB by the SEC.
- Attestation of and report on internal control over financial reporting.

On December 1, 2005, James S. Turley, the chairman and CEO of Ernst & Young, said in support of SOX and its positive impact on the accounting profession:

> *Certainly, the accounting profession, our firm included, has taken some ... shots from regulators and others over the last several years, and I'm here to tell you that we deserved some of those shots. I do feel somewhat fortunate, though, that my profession has faced some very tough times, and not only survived, but emerged better for the experience. The times have taught us the dangers of being arrogant ... of not listening. We have been reminded of the importance of engaging with others, not just with companies and boards, but with policymakers, opinion leaders, academicians, and the investor community. While what we have been through has been difficult, it has been to a positive end because it has encouraged us to do some soul-searching—as individuals and as a profession—to rediscover our roots.*

We have had time to ask ourselves, as accounting professionals, why we
do what we do...why it matters. What is our purpose and how does that
guide our decisions? *These are important questions in defining the culture
of any organization.*[10]

Enforcement of the Federal Securities Laws

SOX empowered the SEC to better enforce the federal securities laws in order to
improve public trust and investor confidence in the capital markets. SOX enabled
the SEC to use various means to bring enforcement actions against corporate wrongdoers, sanction them, obtain penalties and disgorgement, and compensate harmed
investors, and strengthened SEC efforts to conduct more thorough investigations of
corporate and auditing wrongdoers.

According to William Donaldson: "Two of the most powerful tools that the
Act gave the Commission to help meet this challenge [enforcement actions] are the
'Fair Funds' provision under Section 308(a) of the Act and the authority to seek
a temporary freeze of extraordinary payments by an issuer under Section 1103 of
the Act."[11] The Fair Funds Provision of SOX empowers the SEC to obtain civil
penalties resulting from enforcement cases and add them to disgorgement funds to
compensate injured investors who suffer losses due to securities law violations. Prior
to the passage of SOX, any collected civil penalties were given to the U.S. Treasury.
SOX authorizes the SEC, in certain circumstances, to use collected penalties for the
benefit of harmed investors. Section 1103 of SOX authorizes the SEC to obtain a
temporary order to escrow extraordinary payments by the company to its directors,
officers, partners, agents, controlling persons, or employees and to prevent the
payment of extraordinary rewards to executives and others while the company is
under investigation by the commission.

Provisions Addressing Conduct of Other Individuals

Several provisions of SOX address the conduct of all corporate governance participants in the financial reporting supply chain, including the board of directors,
the audit committee, management, internal auditors, external auditors, investment
banks, legal counsel, and financial analysts. Some provisions of SOX and SEC-related
rules address the conduct of gatekeepers other than directors, management, and
auditors, including the rules:

- Governing research analysts' potential conflicts of interest.
- Regarding standards of conduct for attorneys practicing before the SEC.
- Pertaining to rating agencies.

Whistleblower Provisions

Section 301 of SOX, SEC final rules, and listing standards all require that the audit
committee of public companies adopt procedures for: the receipt, retention, and
treatment of complaints received by the company related to accounting, internal

controls, and/or auditing matters; and the confidential, anonymous submission by employees of concerns regarding questionable accounting and/or auditing matters.[12]

Public companies can use a variety of ways to comply with whistleblower requirements, including the use of a telephone hotline, e-mail box, third-party services, and the company's Web site. Regardless of what means are used to facilitate whistleblower programs, the audit committee should ensure that employees, customers, suppliers, investors, and others are aware of such programs and their confidential disclosure options.

It is not clear whether the whistleblower provision of SOX stops at the U.S. border or if it can also be applied to foreign workers employed by U.S. multinational corporations. The U.S. Court of Appeals for the First Circuit decided that SOX provisions do not extend to foreign workers employed by the overseas subsidiaries of U.S. companies. Judge Levin Campbell wrote on behalf of the panel: "We believe if Congress had intended that the whistle-blower provision would apply abroad to foreign entities, it would have said so."[13] This ruling can be interpreted to mean that many employees of large U.S. multinational corporations (e.g., IBM, Coca-Cola, Wal-Mart, GE, GM, and Ford) will not be covered by the SOX whistleblower provisions.

SOX and Environmental Reporting

Although SOX does not directly address environmental reporting of public companies, any underreported environmental liabilities, particularly Superfund liabilities, may represent significant risk for executives (CEOs, CFOs) who certify the accuracy and completeness of financial statements under Section 302, executive certificate requirements of SOX. The Environmental Protection Agency (EPA) reports that companies and other entities spent $10 billion in 2005 in complying with environmental laws, 627 entities disclosed violations, and more than 600,000 businesses and individuals received EPA assistance in understanding and complying with environmental laws.[14] The only accounting guidance available on environmental accounting and reporting is Statement of Position (SOP) 96-1, entitled *Environmental Remediation Liabilities*, which focuses primarily on Superfund sites and related federal liability, whereas most environmental cleanup enforcement occurs on the state level.[15] Statement of Financial Accounting Standards (SFAS) No. 5 indirectly addresses environmental liabilities by requiring the accrual of liabilities if the liability was incurred prior to the balance sheet date or its amount can be reasonably estimated.

Evaluation of Sarbanes-Oxley Act

It is estimated that U.S. public companies spent about $6 billion in complying with the provisions of SOX in 2006. Anecdotal evidence shows that the cost of compliance with Section 404 of SOX on internal controls is, on average, about 0.10 percent of the total revenue of public companies.[16] Furthermore, William H. Donaldson has stated: "I believe it important to note that a substantial portion of the [compliance] cost may reflect initial start-up expenses as many companies, for the first time, conducted a systematic review and documentation of their internal controls."[17]

The cost of compliance with various provisions of SOX, particularly Section 404, has been extensively investigated. Estimations vary widely, from $5 million to $15 million per public company per year.

There are five common themes of various compliance cost estimates:

1. Much of the cost can be attributed to the deferred maintenance that had occurred in the years leading up to the passage of SOX (e.g., lack of adequate investment in the financial departments, as shown by reported material weaknesses in 2005).
2. The compliance cost is significantly higher than what was originally estimated and expected by regulators. (The SEC initially estimated compliance costs of less than $2 million.)
3. A great portion of the first-year compliance cost is considered as one-time charges that are expected to reduce substantially in year-two compliance and onward.
4. The audit fee has substantially increased under the integrated audit of both financial statements and internal controls for large accelerated public companies.
5. Regulators (SEC) and standard setters (PCAOB) were seemingly insensitive to the cost of rigid and cautious implementation and interpretation of provisions of SOX.

The cost of compliance with provisions of SOX dropped 23 percent in the second consecutive year from $4.51 million per company in 2004 to an average of $2.9 million in 2006.[18] The significant portion of SOX compliance costs in the first year (2004) is regarded as a one-time start-up cost that will diminish over time with costs averaging $7.3 million in 2005.[19] A report by the Government Accountability Office (GAO) found that smaller public companies are disproportionately burdened by SOX's compliance costs, particularly Section 404 on internal controls.[20] The report reveals that public companies with a market capitalization of below $75 million paid a median $1.14 in audit fees for every $100 of their revenue, whereas larger companies paid 13 cents.[21] The SEC has decided to postpone the requirement for compliance with Section 404 for smaller companies with a market capitalization of below $75 million until 2008; its Advisory Committee on Small Companies recommended that public companies with less than $128 million be exempted from Section 404 compliance.

Benefits of compliance with Section 404 are: (1) significant improvement in the quality of the financial reporting process in the sense that the first year of compliance (2004) revealed 1 in 6 large companies had material weaknesses in their internal control over financial reporting (ICFR) compared with only 1 in 15 companies in the second year of compliance (2005); (2) significant positive impacts on stock prices of companies that made improvements in their ICFR; (3) a deterrent to inappropriate financial reporting behavior by encouraging and enforcing compliance with adequate and effective ICFR on the part of employees; and (4) a mechanism through the independent audit of ICFR to oversee the quality of financial reporting more effectively.

The two key SOX Section 404 compliance issues, as identified by an Institute of Management Accountants (IMA)-sponsored survey, are: (1) a lack of practical management implementation guidance; and (2) the incomplete nature of the 1992 COSO framework in assessing the effectiveness of ICFR.[22] The survey further indicates that: (1) the majority of respondents (about 66 percent) reported lack of proper guidance and implementation of the COSO framework as the two key SOX compliance cost drivers; (2) more than half of the respondents reported that they did not use the COSO 1992 framework to assess the effectiveness of their ICFR assessment; (3) more than 45 percent of smaller companies and 35 percent of larger companies used the bottom-up approach rather than the risk-based approach for the assessment of the effectiveness of their ICFR; (4) about 38 percent of respondents did not believe that the COSO framework was guiding their internal control assessment whereas 68 percent relied on PCAOB Auditing Standard (AS) No. 2 for guidance; and (5) the majority (57 percent) of respondents did not believe the COSO framework alone was adequate guidance for assessing the effectiveness of internal controls.[23]

In the short term, SOX has had a positive impact on affected companies' internal controls and compliance practices and has restored investor confidence in the capital markets.[24] However, the long-term impact of SOX on corporate governance (the board of directors and audit committee oversight function), the financial reporting process (management reporting conservatism), and audit functions (audit quality, credibility, independence) likely will take at least 5 to 10 years to fully assess, although continued investor support for SOX has been overwhelmingly positive.

SOX Efficacy

Regulations including SOX and SEC-related rules should be effective, efficient, and scalable in order to generate sustainable effects and benefits. More than two years after the passage of SOX, William Donaldson, by then the former SEC chairman, expressed his views of the efforts of reform as an uphill fight. Specifically, Donaldson stated: "Too many are still intent on maintaining corporate prerogatives and preserving a narrow focus on short-term financial performance, often to the detriment of other goals of integrity and long-term performance defined by multiple measures."[25] Time will tell whether these vital corporate governance reforms will diminish in relevance. Nonetheless, what is obvious is that as more U.S. households invest in the capital markets, the next wave of scandals and their devastating effects could cripple the economy. It is the author's hope that public companies rise above the "check-box compliance" mentality and employ corporate governance best practices, in order to ensure sustainable and enduring performance and to create and enhance shareholder value.

The 2005 survey of the Spencer Stuart Board Index, an annual survey of corporate governance practices of Standard & Poor's (S&P) 500 companies, revealed that recent improvements in corporate governance practices go above and beyond regulatory compliance and move toward independence and proactive corporate accountability in the post-SOX era.[26] Examples of these improvements are:

■ Expanding the role of the lead and presiding director, which has made independent directors more accountable for and vested in the corporate governance process.

- Facilitating more direct interactions between institutional investors and the board to discuss concerns and improvements to corporate governance practices.
- Taking initiatives to improve corporate governance practices and making proactive changes rather than waiting for mandatory changes through legislation.[27]

Critics argue that SOX was passed hastily by Congress without proper public debate on its provisions and their substantial compliance costs. These critics ignore the fact that the initial roots of SOX can be traced back to 1972 and 1973, with the bear market and financial scandals of Penn Central, Equity Funding, and National Student Marketing as well as the corporate corrupt payments and bribes. During the 1970s Congress held many hearings regarding the accounting profession and corporate governance, and it prepared a staff report and subsequently introduced a bill (H.R. 13175) entitled "Public Accounting Regulatory Act" on June 16, 1978.[28] This bill was not passed, and it was further debated during the 1995 tort reform legislation of the Private Securities Litigation Reform Act (PSLRA). The 1978 bill suggested the establishment of a National Organization of Securities and Exchange Commission Accountancy to register public accounting firms that practice before the SEC and the authorization of disciplinary action against such accounting firms.[29] Many provisions of this bill were incorporated into SOX. Thus, the financial scandals of 2002 and many prior public hearings contributed to the passage of SOX, and many of its provisions had been unsuccessfully legislated on at least two occasions by Congress. It also should be noted that SOX was passed by Congress (334 ayes, 90 nays, 10 present/not voting) almost unanimously.

Some critics of SOX are attempting to ease some of its provisions. Congressmen Tom Feeney (R-FL), Mark Kirk (R-IL), and Gregory Meeks (D-NY) have told a House Government Reform Subcommittee that SOX has substantially increased company compliance costs and created some unintended problems, particularly for smaller companies, in complying with Section 404 on internal controls.[30] Congressional efforts have been made to either revise provisions of SOX or relax SEC rules designed to implement these provisions. For example, Representative Feeney believes that "external audits are totally redundant" in the post-SOX era because corporate officials now certify the accuracy and completeness of financial statements.[31] The threat of an audit would be enough to keep executives honest; a few companies can be chosen each year to be audited and the remainder can avoid the needless audit fees.[32] Scaling back some of the provisions of SOX (e.g., PCAOB) can lead to another wave of financial scandals similar to Enron and WorldCom. Congress held several hearings to: (1) examine the impact of SOX and SEC-related implementation rules on the U.S. capital markets in terms of liquidity, overall health, and competitiveness; (2) assess the net benefits of Section 404 of SOX; (3) compare safeguards provided by Section 404 with those of Section 302; (4) investigate the effect of SOX on resource allocation; and (5) address actions taken by the SEC to improve the efficiency and effectiveness of SOX.

SOX has been blamed for the recent decline of foreign initial public offerings (IPOs) in U.S. capital markets and for the seeming lack of U.S. competitiveness in global markets. Opponents of SOX (e.g., Feeney) attempt to blame high compliance costs of SOX as a key factor as why 24 of the top 25 IPOs of stock in 2005 were issued by exchanges abroad.[33] SOX alone, however, should not be blamed for IPO slowdown in the United States. The high fees charged by Wall Street investment banks in the United States, about 6.5 percent to 7 percent, compared with those of Europe, about 3 percent to 4 percent, and an even lower rate in Asia, are perhaps the key reason that the majority of IPOs were issued on exchanges outside of the United States.[34] Several additional factors have contributed to the recent decline in foreign IPOs and the perceived negative trend in U.S. competitiveness in the global markets: (1) more investor-friendly regulations and public policies in other countries (e.g., the United Kingdom); (2) the development of more active capital markets worldwide, particularly in London and Hong Kong; (3) a legal system in the United States that exposes market participants to undue litigation risk under the ineffective tort system; (4) a complex and confusing regulatory structure and enforcement procedures that are based on a rules-based system of focusing on compliance with specific rules, rather than compliance within the spirit of regulatory principles; and (5) unjustifiable compliance costs of new corporate governance and accounting rules.[35]

Corporate governance reforms were needed to identify and manage conflicts of interest among market participants and bring more accountability and transparency into public financial reports. However, to be effective, these reforms must be efficient, cost justifiable, and scalable. A recent *Wall Street Journal* reports that the premium investors pay for shares of foreign companies listed in the U.S. capital market have been significantly reduced since the passage of SOX in 2002.[36] Although investors are still paying premium, it has decreased to 31 percentage points in the post-SOX period from 51 percentage points in the pre-SOX period. Eliot Spitzer, New York's governor-elect, said, "We're failing in competitiveness because of failed business models and the lack of smart investment in technology. . . . The lesson of competitiveness is critical but let's not forget the lessons of integrity."[37]

The lowest cost of equity capital worldwide is made possible under the regulatory investor protections in the United States, including SOX, for three reasons:

1. Individual investors in the United States have provided companies with low-cost and long-term funding at a level unparalleled in any other country.
2. The high level of investor protection provided through regulations in the United States has promoted the cross-listing premium offered in the U.S. capital markets.
3. The benefits of the lost cost of equity capital in the United States exceed compliance costs associated with investor protection laws.[38]

The history of regulation in the United States appears to follow the pattern of lax regulation (early twentieth century) followed by corporate and accounting scandals (the stock market crash of 1929), responded to with more regulation (Securities Acts of 1933, 1934), relaxed or compromised regulation (the end of the twentieth century), yet another wave of financial scandals (the late 1990s and early 2000s), and then the resultant additional regulation (SOX, SEC rules, listing standards of the early 2000s). The intent of regulation has been to restore public trust and investor confidence in corporate America, its financial reports, and capital markets pursuant to the occurrences of massive financial scandals. It is expected that this endless cycle of financial scandals and government regulation will continue, as regulation is often compromised, leading to another wave of scandals. Nonetheless, the overwhelming support of SOX by the U.S. Senate in April 2007 is a good sign of continuous efforts by lawmakers to protect investors from such scandals.

OTHER RELEVANT FEDERAL LAWS

Another example of lawmakers' influences on corporate governance is the passage of the American Jobs Creation Act (AJCA) on October 11, 2004, by Congress. The AJCA is a response, in part, to a trade dispute with the European Union regarding the extraterritorial income provisions in the U.S. tax code that the World Trade Organization regarded as illegal. The AJCA includes several provisions that significantly affect business practices, tax planning schemes, and accounting for income taxes. Two important provisions of the AJCA are:

1. *Deduction for qualified domestic production activities.* The AJCA provides a deduction from taxable income equal to a stipulated percentage of qualified income from domestic production activities for companies that pay U.S. income taxes on their manufacturing activities. The eligible tax deduction cannot exceed 50 percent of the annual wages paid and should be phased in at rates of about 3 percent of qualified production income in 2005–2006, 6 percent in 2007–2009, and 9 percent in 2010 and thereafter.
2. *Repatriation of foreign earnings.* The AJCA creates temporary incentives for U.S. multinationals to repatriate accumulated income earned in other countries by allowing an 85 percent dividends-received deduction for certain dividends from controlled foreign subsidiaries.[39]

The Employee Retirement Income Security Act (ERISA) of 1974 is the major federal law that governs private sector retirement and health plans. The ERISA established requirements for participation, funding, vesting, fiduciary duties, financial disclosure, and reporting of private sector defined benefit pension plans. It also created the Pension Benefit Guarantee Corporation (PBGC) as a federal corporation that guarantees payment of basic pension benefits for millions of American workers, albeit typically at a much lower rate than originally promised by the employer. The PBGC's primary mission is to maintain voluntary private pension plans for the benefit of participants and to provide for payment of pension benefits to participants and their beneficiaries under covered plans when bankruptcy occurs.

SECURITIES AND EXCHANGE COMMISSION

The SEC is the federal agency in charge of administering and enforcing the federal laws governing securities markets in the United States. Its aim is to strengthen the integrity and soundness of securities markets. The goals of the SEC are to:

- Enforce compliance with federal securities laws by detecting problems in the securities markets, preventing and deterring violations of federal securities laws, alerting investors to possible wrongdoing, sanctioning wrongdoers, and returning funds to harmed investors.

- Promote healthy capital markets through an effective and flexible regulatory environment that facilitates innovation, competition, and capital formation, and improves investor confidence in the capital markets.
- Foster informed investment decision making by ensuring that investors receive complete, accurate, and transparent financial information and implementing a variety of investor education initiatives.
- Maximize the use of SEC resources through improvements in its organizational and internal controls effectiveness and sound investments in human capital and new technologies.[40]

Achievement of these goals contributes to improvements in the governance and integrity of public companies and the efficiency of the securities markets, economic growth, and prosperity for the nation. The SEC's leadership consists of a bipartisan five-member commission, including the chair and four commissioners. The SEC has 20 offices, including the office of the chair, who serves as the CEO, and 19 functional offices. Christopher Cox, the SEC chairman, describes the SEC's mission in this way:

> To protect investors; to maintain fair, orderly, and efficient markets; and to facilitate capital formation. ... Since we at the SEC most certainly are in the investor protection business, we've got to be vigilant in seeing to it that our actions do in fact contribute to America's productivity.[41]

Cox states that the SEC plays an important role in:

- Enforcement of the law by prosecuting fraud and unfair dealing to prevent corruption and bribery.
- Creation of a regulatory environment that promotes entrepreneurship and risk taking.
- Establishment of regulations for the capital markets to ensure their integrity and efficiency.[42]

SEC and Corporate Governance

The SEC has been empowered by Congress to influence corporate governance in several ways. As a governmental agency created for the protection of investors, the SEC, under Section 19(b) of the 1934 Exchange Act, is authorized to oversee listing standards of self-regulatory organizations (SROs) and approve any rule change proposed by SROs. Section 19(c) grants the SEC certain authority unilaterally to "abrogate, add to, and delete from" the rules of SROs.[43] Thus the SEC has the authority to impose new SRO rules, including corporate governance standards, or to amend or delete existing SRO rules whenever it deems necessary in order to ensure fair administration of the SRO, compliance with requirements of the Exchange Act relevant to SROs, or furtherance of the purpose of the Act. The opinion of the D.C. Circuit Court of Appeals in the Business Roundtable case practically limited the SEC's authority under Section 19(c) to impose corporate governance listing standards even though the interpretation of the opinion is controversial.[44]

The general consensus regarding the SEC authority to impose corporate governance listing standards on SROs can be summarized in this way:

1. Corporate governance listing standards are "rules" for purposes of the Exchange Act. As such, they must be adopted pursuant to Section 19 of the 1934 Exchange Act.
2. The Exchange Act does not empower the SEC to establish a comprehensive federal corporate law through SROs listing standards.
3. SEC authority over corporate governance listing standards under Section 19(c) of the Exchange Act is uncertain and limited to matters that are in furtherance of the purposes of the Act rather than unilaterally changing SRO rules or disapproving SRO rules relating to corporate governance.
4. Application of the consistency standard requires that a proposed rule change be consistent with the nondiscrimination requirement in Sections 6(b)(5) and 15A(b)(6).

Section 11A of the 1934 Exchange Act grants the SEC the authority to facilitate the establishment of a rational market system for securities, which indirectly affects SROs' corporate governance listing standards. Overall, the SEC has the authority to require the compliance (or noncompliance) of listed public companies with corporate governance listing standards and best practices disclosure in periodic reports, proxy materials, and other public filings. SROs will continue to receive attention as exchanges go from not-for-profit to for-profit, particularly as it relates to largely unregulated trading derivatives.

The SEC is also empowered by the 1934 Exchange Act to require public companies to disclose information that is relevant to shareholder voting and investment decisions, including governance practices (e.g., audit committee charters, composition, activities). SOX also directs the SEC to issue more than 50 rules in implementing its various provisions relevant to all corporate governance participants, including directors, management, internal auditors, external auditors, legal counsel, investment banks, financial analysts, and mutual funds. Finally, the SEC is authorized to oversee accounting standards issued by the FASB and audit standards adopted by the PCAOB for public companies. These accounting standards (e.g., accounting for stock-based compensation) and auditing standards (e.g., audit of internal controls over financial reporting) directly or indirectly affect corporate governance practices of public companies.

SEC Influence on Corporate Governance beyond U.S. Borders

The SEC actions against several high-profile European companies accused of financial fraud (e.g., Italian dairy giant Parmalat; Vivendi Universal based in Paris; Spiegel Inc. with controlling owners in Hamburg, Germany) indicate that the SEC is focusing on influencing corporate governance beyond U.S. borders, primarily due to the globalization of financial markets and reported violations of securities laws by many foreign issuers.[45] In a civil suit filed against Parmalat, the SEC accused the company of selling $1.5 billion in bonds and notes to U.S. institutional investors and, subsequently, misleading them by overstating its assets. As part of the settlement, in 2004, Parmalat agreed to have its board of directors elected by shareholders and have the majority of its directors be independent of the company's management.[46] On August 9, 2006, the SEC released its final rule stating the foreign practice issues (FPI) that are accelerated filers (but not large accelerated filers) are required to: (1) comply with the Section 404 requirement to include management's report on ICFR in their Form 20-F or 40-F annual report filed with the SEC for their fiscal year ending on or after July 15, 2006; and (2) provide an auditor's attestation report on ICFR in their annual reports until the fiscal year ending on or after July 15, 2007. [47]

SEC Financial Penalties/Enforcement

On January 4, 2006, the SEC issued a statement of guidance regarding financial penalties that followed the filing of two settled actions against two corporate issuers (McAffee and Matter of Applix). The SEC's decision to impose a penalty on the corporations is based on two principal considerations of:

1. The presence or absence of a direct benefit to the company as a result of the violation in the sense that the company itself has received a direct and material benefit from the offense (e.g., increased revenue, reduced expenses).
2. The degree to which the penalty will recompense or further harm the injured shareholders in order to protect innocent investors from further damages.

In addition to these two principal considerations, other factors in the SEC's decision are:

- The need to deter the particular type of offense to the extent that imposed penalties serve as an effective deterrent mechanism.
- The extent of injury to innocent parties in terms of the egregiousness of the harm done, the number of investors injured, and the degree of societal harm if the violation goes unpunished.
- Whether complicity in the violation is widespread throughout the company in terms of its isolation or pervasiveness.
- The level of intent on the part of the perpetrators to intentionally and knowingly mislead investors or not deliberately engage in the violation.
- The degree of difficulty in detecting the particular type of offense.
- The presence or lack of remedial actions taken by the company to correct and prevent further occurrences of the violation.
- The extent to which the company has cooperated with the SEC and/or other law enforcement.[48]

The SEC's corporate penalty guidelines are based on two sources of statutory authority: the Securities Enforcement Remedies and Penny Stock Reform Act of 1990, which granted the SEC the ability to seek civil penalties in its enforcement cases against public companies; and Section 308 of SOX on the fair funds provision, which allowed the SEC to use penalties paid and disgorgement obtained in enforcement activities to compensate victims of securities law violations.[49] In the post-SOX period, there has been a decreasing trend of SEC enforcement cases, as evidenced by the number of enforcement actions totaling 574 in 2006, compared with 630 in 2005, 639 in 2004, and 679 cases in 2003.[50] This declining trend coincides with the flat budget for the SEC in the post-SOX period and even reduction in its enforcement-division staff despite continuously increasing securities crimes and the wave of option grant backdating probes.

The SEC has the responsibility of maintaining the integrity, safety, and competitiveness of the capital markets as they have attracted trillions of dollars of investments from domestic and foreign sources. Recent corporate and accounting scandals that have eroded investor confidence have also caused the SEC to be aggressive in its enforcement actions against corporate malfeasance. The author suggests that the SEC should improve the effectiveness and fairness of its enforcement program in pursuing civil and criminal actions against corporate wrongdoers and in preventing, detecting, and correcting securities law violations that cause corporate malfeasance and scandals. The SEC, in continuing its strong and vigorous enforcement actions, should be mindful of the devastating consequences of the financial scandals of Enron, WorldCom, Global Crossing, Qwest, Adelphia, Tyco, Parmalat, Ahold, Fannie Mae, and AIG, among others, caused by securities law violations and, at the same time, be aware of unintended consequences of excessive enforcement that may have burned good and responsible companies that contribute to the efficiency, health, and competitiveness of the capital markets.

PUBLIC COMPANY ACCOUNTING OVERSIGHT BOARD

SOX created the PCAOB to regulate the auditing industry by overseeing auditors; setting auditing, quality control, and ethics standards; and registering public accounting firms. The PCAOB is established as an independent, not-for-profit organization under the oversight responsibility of the SEC and is treated as a self-regulatory organization, similar to the National Association of Securities Dealers (NASD). The SEC selected the five board members of the PCAOB with input from the Federal Reserve chairman and the treasury secretary. Only two of the five board members of the PCAOB can be certified public accountants (nonpracticing CPAs).

Section 107 of SOX authorizes the SEC to have oversight and enforcement authority over the PCAOB by stating that: (1) PCAOB adopted rules and standards should be approved by the SEC before they become effective; (2) the PCAOB's disciplinary actions must be communicated through the SEC upon final judgment; and (3) the SEC has censure authority of rescinding PCAOB authority, limiting its activities, functions, and operations.[51] Congress authorized the PCAOB to fund its expenses by imposing a fee on all public companies, determined in proportion to their market capitalizations, and from registration fees received from public accounting firms. Some criticized the rapid growth of the PCAOB's budget and employment levels and even suggested that the PCAOB's basic role of registering and inspecting public accounting firms and standard-setting activities should be transferred to the SEC.[52]

The PCAOB's primary functions are to:

- Register public accounting firms that audit public companies.
- Inspect the registered public accounting firms on a regular basis.
- Establish auditing, attestation, ethics, quality control, and independence standards.
- Conduct investigations and disciplinary proceedings.[53]

The PCAOB has also appointed a standing advisory group (SAG) of 30 members with expertise in accounting, auditing, corporate governance, investments, and corporate finance to assist the PCAOB in carrying out its standard-setting responsibilities.[54] These functions of the PCAOB are intended to protect investors from audit failures or receiving misleading audited financial statements. The PCAOB's activities pertain only to public accounting firms that audit public companies. These activities are discussed further in Chapter 9.

FEDERAL SENTENCING GUIDELINES FOR ORGANIZATIONS

In 1984 Congress created the U.S. Sentencing Commission (USSC) with the authority to issue guidelines for punishing organizations, including companies that have committed federal crimes.[55] The USSC's guidelines have been used by companies as a benchmark for reducing the risk of significant penalties if a violation of a law occurs. Pursuant to the passage of SOX, the Sentencing Commission revised its guidelines by focusing on an effective program to ensure companies' compliance with all applicable laws and regulations.[56] The revised guidelines, as summarized in Exhibit 6.2, are expected to have a significant impact on the effectiveness of corporate governance by requiring:

- Companies to establish and maintain an effective compliance program.
- Boards of directors to accept accountability to ensure compliance throughout the company.
- Companies to assign high-level individuals (e.g., executives) to oversee their compliance program.

COMMITTEE OF EUROPEAN SECURITIES REGULATORS

The European Commission (EC) established the Committee of European Securities Regulators (CESR) to ensure efficient and effective functioning of the European capital market. CESR's membership consists of the national securities regulators in the 25 member states and the securities authorities of Norway and Iceland. As an

EXHIBIT 6.2   Federal Sentencing Guidelines

For an Effective Compliance and Ethics Program, Organizations Should:	Minimum Requirements an Organization Should Have for the Program Are:
Exercise due diligence to prevent and detect criminal conduct.	The organization should establish standards and procedures to prevent and detect criminal conduct.
Promote an organizational culture that encourages ethical conduct and compliance with the law.	The governing authority should be knowledgeable about the content and operation of the program.
Design, implement, and enforce the program in a reasonable manner.	The governing authority should exercise reasonable oversight of the implementation and effectiveness of the program.
The failure to prevent/detect an instant offences does not necessarily mean the program is not effective.	Individuals with operational responsibility should periodically report to management and when appropriate to the governing authority on the effectiveness of the program.
	The organization should to the best of its ability not hire anyone to a position of authority who is known to have committed illegal or unethical acts.
	The organization should inform employees of the program and conduct periodic training sessions on the responsibility and role with the regard to the program.
	The organization should take reasonable steps to ensure the program is followed and to periodically evaluate its effectiveness.
	The organization should have and publicize a system for employees to report potential or actual criminal conduct without fear of reprisal.
	The organization should have appropriate incentives for compliance and disciplinary action for noncompliance.
	Once criminal conduct is detected the organization should take reasonable steps to prevent similar conduct, including modifying the program.
	The organization should periodically assess the risk of criminal conduct and take steps to reduce that risk.

Source: Adapted from U.S. Sentencing Commission, "2005 Federal Sentencing Guidelines," effective November 1, 2005. Available at: ussc.gov/2005guid/8b2_1.htm.

enforcement arm of the EC, CESR has observer status on several other regulatory bodies, including the European Securities Committee (ESC), the Accounting Regulatory Committee (ARC), and the European Financial Reporting Advisory Group (EFRAG). The three primary responsibilities of CESR are to:

1. Issue standards and guidance to national securities regulators for the implementation by member states.
2. Promulgate standards for the enforcement of financial reporting while allowing member states to take enforcement actions.
3. Issue implementation guidance on some of the key capital market directives (e.g., prospectus, transparency).

In May 2004 the SEC and CESR released a joint statement that specifies the terms of reference for future cooperation and coordination between the two bodies.[57] The three primary objectives of such cooperation, which are expected to improve global corporate governance, are to:

1. Identify and address emerging risks in the EU and U.S. markets at an early stage.
2. Discuss potential regulatory projects in order to facilitate converged ways of addressing common issues.
3. Set priorities for discussion and collaboration between the two bodies, including market structure issues, the role and responsibility of credit rating agencies and analysts, and mutual fund regulation.

On December 7, 2006, the new U.K. Companies Act of 2006 was published, which contains over 1,200 Sections and 15 appendices.[58] It represents the most significant reform of U.K. company law that affects both publicly and privately owned companies, and is intended to save U.K. companies an estimated £250 million per year through deregulation. The Act will be implemented in stages between January 2007 and October 2008, with the full implementation timetable expected to be published in February 2007. It is expected that some provisions of the Act regarding shareholder rights, directors' duties and liabilities, and audit report format will be considered by regulators in other countries, including the United States.

ROLE OF THE STATE AND FEDERAL ATTORNEY GENERAL

Federal regulators have been slow in responding to the recent wave of financial scandals, bringing enforcement actions against corporate wrongdoers, and preventing widespread effects of these scandals. Regulators are often slow to respond because of the bureaucratic processes involved. In early 2004 the SEC issued independence rules for mutual funds, which were subsequently appealed by the industry, and Congress requested that the SEC revisit them. The rules require that mutual funds have a board of directors composed of at least 75 percent independent directors with a chair who is an independent director. These rules are explained further in Chapter 10.[59]

The state attorney general can play an important role in enforcing compliance with applicable laws, rules, regulations, and corporate governance standards to protect investors. For example, the timely activities of the New York Attorney General Eliot Spitzer have had a significant impact on the mutual fund industry and its operations. Typically, following Spitzer's announcement of possible investigations, the concerned companies agree to pay fines for bad practices and correct their operations (e.g., 2002 Merrill Lynch analysts' practices). In July 2002 Spitzer, the comptroller of the state of New York, the treasurer of the state of California, and the treasurer of the state of North Carolina implemented new investment protection principles (IPPs) in their dealings with investment banks and broker/dealers.[60] The principles require broker/dealers who trade securities on the fund's behalf to:

- Sever the link between compensation for analysts and investment banking.
- Prohibit investment banking contribution (input) to analyst compensation.
- Establish a review committee to approve analysts' research recommendations.
- Disclose the coverage termination and the rationale for such termination upon discontinuation of research coverage of a company.
- Require disclosure in research reports whether the firm has received, or is entitled to receive, any compensation from a covered company over the past 12 months.
- Establish a monitory process to ensure compliance with the IPPs.[61]

Investment protection principles also require investment managers to:

- Disclose client relationships that could pose a conflict of interest in the evaluation of investment securities and the safeguards adopted to prevent or mitigate such conflicts.
- Disclose the manner in which investment managers and analysts are compensated.
- Disclose the amount of commission paid to broker/dealers.
- Disclose whether the broker/dealers have adopted the principles.
- Review the quality and integrity of financial data of companies under consideration for investment.
- Review the corporate governance practices of companies under consideration for investment.[62]

In February 2006 Spitzer settled one of the largest regulatory settlements with American International Group Inc. (AIG) for $1.64 billion to resolve allegations that the company's aggressive and deceptive accounting practices misled regulators and investors.[63] As part of the settlement, AIG, the largest global insurer, agreed to adopt improvements in its corporate governance and business practices, including retaining, for a period of three years, an independent consultant who will conduct a review of its accounting and internal controls to ensure the use of proper accounting procedures.[64] The SEC also worked with the state attorney general to settle allegations of accounting fraud brought against AIG. This settlement is much larger than the fines the SEC imposed on WorldCom ($750 million), Adelphia Communications Corp. ($715 million), and Time Warner ($300 million).

An example of the role of the federal attorney general in corporate governance is the recent settlement with KPMG regarding its tax shelter services. On August 30, 2005, more than three years after the passage of SOX, which was intended to regulate the auditing profession and improve the quality of audits, nine of the partners of KPMG were charged in the first indictments in the government's investigation of its tax shelters.[65] The U.S. Attorney's Office announced a $456 million settlement with KPMG, which was charged with a single count of conspiracy to defraud the government. KPMG admitted the criminal wrongdoing, and the firm will not be further prosecuted on this issue as long as it complies with the settlement requirements.[66] In addition to the non–tax-deductible and noninsurable $456 million penalties, KPMG's tax practices are substantially restricted; its compensation and benefits and personal financial planning units were closed, which were participating in the design and sale of aggressive tax shelter schemes.[67]

Despite these settlement requirements and the admission of criminal wrongdoing by KPMG, U.S. regulators, including both the Justice Department and the PCAOB, are seemingly confident about KPMG's ability to perform high-quality audits of public companies. U.S. Attorney General Alberto Gonzales states that the Department of Justice assessed "collateral consequences" in deciding not to indict KPMG and instead decided to settle for a deferred prosecution agreement with the firm. Gonzales specifically stated that "[the settlement] reflects the reality that the conviction of an organization can affect innocent workers and others associated with the organization and can even have an impact on the national economy."[68]

CORPORATE GOVERNANCE AND COURTS

Courts play a role in corporate governance by interpreting implications and applicability of corporate governance measures, rules, and regulations in disputed circumstances. The judicial process and court decisions in several landmark cases have affected the structure of corporate governance in the United States. Many of the cases have led to increased accountability and liability for a company's board of directors. For example, in *Escott v. Barrchris Construction Corp.*, directors were held liable for misleading financial statements in the registration statements; in *Gould v. American Hawaiian Steamship Co.*, directors were held liable for information in the proxy statement.[69] The U.S. District Court in *SEC v. Mattel* ruled that Mattel must restructure its board to include a majority of outside auditors and establish an audit committee.[70]

Courts play a vital role when there is a failure in the governance of public companies. In August 2005 the Delaware Chancery Court issued its opinion in the Disney litigation, in which its corporate governance was regarded by many as ineffective and a clearly flawed process.[71] The court concluded that while the Disney directors were ordinarily negligent, their negligence did not rise to the level of gross negligence to impose any liability them.[72] This recent court opinion suggests:

- Directors benefit under the business judgment rules intended to protect them from liability resulting from ordinary negligence, which is a sufficient basis for imposing liability on other professionals, including accountants.
- Investors should not look to courts under the business judgment rule for protection from corporate governance failures.
- Investors should consider other mechanisms (e.g., markets) for protecting their interests.[73]

The court's decision to hold directors liable only for gross negligence will probably work under the system that provides other legal arrangements and market mechanisms to protect investors from corporate governance failures.[74] For example, plurality voting in the United States makes it difficult for shareholders to replace undesirable incumbent directors. Other corporate laws, including many state laws, SEC rules, and charter provisions, do not empower shareholders to amend corporate bylaws to address corporate governance failures. Managements' ability to block takeover bids weakens or engineers mergers and acquisitions to serve their interests and weakens the monitoring and discipline that could be provided by the market for control. Thus, shareholders are left with the limited alternative of selling their shares, which are often indexed or adversely affected by corporate governance failures.[75] In this way, courts affect the corporate governance structure by interpreting corporate governance reforms (e.g., SEC rules, SOX) and their applicability and relevance in disputed circumstances.

CORPORATE GOVERNANCE AND SELF-REGULATORY ORGANIZATIONS

A self-regulatory organization (SRO) is a nongovernmental entity that represents registrants and is organized for the purpose of regulating their operations, standards of practice, and business conduct. The main objective of an SRO is to promote the protection of investors and the public interest based on a foundation of firm ethics and equality.[76] Exhibit 6.3 details SROs listed with the SEC.[77] Self-regulatory organizations, by establishing listing standards for their companies, including stock exchanges, can also influence corporate governance.

U.S. securities markets have changed significantly during the past several decades in response to globalization, technological advances, and greater investor demand for more transparent markets. The three primary national stock exchanges—the New York Stock Exchange (NYSE), the Nasdaq, and the American Stock Exchange—are competing for market share and have dominated the market for equity securities of U.S. issuers. The emergence of alternative trading systems (ATSs) has recently attracted increasing liquidity from the primary markets (the national stock exchanges). ATSs are electronic trading networks (ETNs), which operate as private

EXHIBIT 6.3 Listed Self-Regulatory Organizations

- American Stock Exchange (AMEX)
- Boston Stock Exchange(BSE)
- CBOE Futures Exchange, LLC (CFE)
- Chicago Board Options Exchange (CBOE)
- Chicago Mercantile Exchange (CME)
- Chicago Stock Exchange (CHX)
- Depository Trust Company (DTC)
- Emerging Markets Clearing Corporation (EMCC)
- Fixed Income Clearing Corporation (FICC)
- International Securities Exchange (ISE)
- Municipal Securities Rulemaking Board (MSRB)
- National Association of Securities Dealers (NASD)
- National Futures Association (NFA)
- National Market System Plans (NMS)
- National Securities Clearing Corporation (NSCC)
- National Stock Exchange (NSX)
- New York Stock Exchange (NYSE)
- NQLX (NQLX)
- OneChicago LLC (OC)
- Options Clearing Corporation (OCC)
- Pacific Exchange, Inc. (PCX)
- Philadelphia Stock Exchange (PHLX)
- Stock Clearing Corporation of Philadelphia (SCCP)

Source: Securities and Exchange Commission, "Self-Regulatory Organization Rule-making and National Market System Plans" (2005). Available at: http://sec.gov/rules/sro.shtml.

businesses rather than as SROs. ATSs provide a forum for automated and cheaper trading securities, including equities, corporate debt and options, and municipal and government securities. ATSs do not list public companies and thus do not maintain corporate governance standards. As trades are being increasingly executed off the primary markets and through ATSs, SROs may have fewer incentives and less ability to establish and maintain corporate governance listing standards.[78]

The NYSE began trading publicly on March 8, 2006, and by March 16, it was at its peak price of $90.25 per share. As of April 17 more than 1,328 shareholders owned about 155.6 million outstanding shares in the NYSE Group. On May 4 the NYSE Group, the parent of the NYSE, sold 25 million shares at $61.50 per share for a total of $1.54 billion.[79] The NYSE has presented a proposal to Euronext that would offer $10.2 billion in cash and shares for Euronext, and each NYSE share would be exchanged one for one with the new company's (NYSE Euronext) stock.[80] The proposal would create a transatlantic stock market worth $21 billion.[81] Mergers of stock exchanges, including the recent merger of the NYSE and Euronext and possible merger of Nasdaq and the London Stock Exchange, create challenges and opportunities for the U.S. capital markets, policymakers, and regulators that should be properly addressed. For example, non-U.S. exchanges may convince companies to leave the U.S. capital market to avoid compliance costs of SOX. Companies may choose non-U.S. capital markets for their capital fundraising or IPOs. In the absence of an agreement among the global regulatory bodies (SEC, EC), non-U.S. exchanges may be able to convince companies worldwide to list on their markets to avoid the compliance costs of SOX.

Two Sections of Rule 19 of the Exchange Act of 1934 provide the SEC with the authority to oversee self-regulatory organizations. Rule 19(6) requires SROs to file with the SEC any proposed changes in their rules; the SEC must approve the changes if they are consistent with the requirements of the Exchange Act. Rule 19(c) allows the SEC to amend the rules of SROs as it deems necessary or appropriate to ensure fair administration of SROs. Recently new rules have been proposed relating to the governance, administration, transparency, and ownership of SROs registered with the SEC.[82] Specifically, one item proposed would require that the board of directors of registered organizations be composed of a majority of independent members. Other items seek to amend existing reporting requirements of the Securities Exchange Act of 1934 with the requirement that an SRO file and disclose, on a frequent basis, information relating to its governance, regulatory programs, finances, ownership structure, and other items deemed essential. In order to improve SEC oversight and surveillance of SRO entities, the SEC has also proposed that quarterly and annual reports be filed that outline and detail the particular areas of regulatory programs.[83]

Pursuant to the passage of SOX, SROs proposed and adopted new corporate governance measures specified in their listing standards. The listing standards of the SROs govern the structure, composition, independence of listed companies' boards of directors, formation and functions of board committees (audit, compensation, nomination/governance committees), and communication with their shareholders.[84] These standards consist of: qualification requirements related to listed companies' annual revenues, assets, cash flow, public float, and/or market capitalization; and corporate governance measures relevant to listed companies' internal structure and conduct that are designed to promote high standards of corporate democracy and responsibility as well as integrity and accountability to shareholders.

These listing standards are intended to:

- Promote liquidity and transferability.
- Lend stability to the capital markets by permitting access only to listed companies with good corporate governance practices.
- Improve investor confidence in the capital markets by promoting listed companies with good governance and monitoring their corporate governance practices.[85]

Traditionally, listing arrangements between national stock exchanges and their listing companies have been the subject of private contracts. However, in the post-SOX era, with the well-deserved attention given to corporate governance in restoring public trust in corporate America, many corporate governance listing standards have been the subject of public discussion and regulatory scrutiny. In addition, the SEC has adopted a practice of encouraging exchanges to "voluntarily" adopt given corporate governance listing standards. In the process, it has urged the exchanges, listed companies, and shareholders to reach a consensus on those standards. This mode of activity has been called "regulation by raised eyebrow."[86] Examples of controversial corporate governance listing standards are the one-share, one-vote listing standard and the formation of an independent audit committee.

Listing standards are reasonably uniform among the national exchanges. It is desirable that these standards be consolidated with a keen focus on convergence to more principles-based listing standards. The SEC has attempted to create convergence in these standards. They are, to a large extent, still a matter of private contract between national stock exchanges and their listing companies. Nonetheless, noncompliance with these standards may result in delisting, which can be very costly and detrimental to the delisted company's survival. Recent financial scandals of high-profile companies (e.g., Enron, WorldCom, and Revco) have resulted in delisting from national stock exchanges.

SROs, through their listing standards, can shape companies' governance and influence boards' deliberations and operations. Both the NYSE and Nasdaq require notification when a company's executive officer becomes aware of any material noncompliance with listing standards. Furthermore, the NYSE requires annual affirmations and certifications of compliance with corporate governance listing standards from its listed companies. The requirements of listing standards appear to go beyond the SEC's implementation rules or provisions of SOX regarding director independence and oversight functions. They require that the majority of directors be independent, hold executive sessions, and form independent audit, compensation, and nomination committees.

BEST PRACTICES

The effectiveness of corporate governance depends on compliance with state and federal statues and listing standards as well as best practices suggested by investor activists and professional organizations. Public companies are required to comply with corporate governance requirements of state and federal statutes as well as listing standards of national stock exchanges. Nevertheless, mere compliance through rules, regulations, laws, and standards will not guarantee effective corporate governance. Companies should integrate best practices into their corporate governance structure. Best practices can be used as benchmarks to determine the best way to improve a business process and corporate governance by following the measures that leading organizations use to achieve excellent performance. Best practices should be viewed as sources of high achievements and creative insights for improvements while not being substituted for solutions to business problems. In addition, companies may be penalized by investors if they fail to consider best practices. The next sections discuss the best practices of the Conference Board, American Law Institute, American Bar Association, Institutional Investors, National Association of Corporate Directors, and Business Roundtable.

Conference Board

In the wake of financial scandals from 2000 to 2002, the Conference Board established a Commission on Public Trust and Private Enterprise, which has issued a three-part report relevant to executive compensation, corporate governance, audit, and accounting.[87] Some examples of recommendations pertaining to executive compensation are:

- Performance-based compensation should be linked to specific goals.
- The compensation committee should be responsible for all aspects of executive pay.
- Fixed-price stock options should be expensed.

Corporate governance recommendations state that:

- The board of directors should develop a structure that establishes an appropriate balance of power-sharing between the CEO and the independent directors.
- The board should be composed of a substantial majority of independent directors.
- It should establish a nominating/governance committee.
- It should establish a three-tier director evaluation mechanism to assess the performance of the entire board of directors, each committee of the board, and each member of the board committee.
- Shareholders, particularly long-term shareholders, should be more active in the governance of their companies.

Auditing and accounting recommendations address audit committees' oversight responsibilities relevant to financial reporting and auditing, including:

- The audit committee should be vigorous in complying with provisions of SOX.
- All companies should have an internal audit function.
- Public accounting firms should limit their nonaudit services to their audit clients.
- The auditing profession should establish a model to improve audit quality.

American Law Institute

In 1994 the American Law Institute (ALI) published its *Principles of Corporate Governance: Analysis and Recommendations*.[88] ALI's principles address the duties and responsibilities of directors and officers to both their company and its shareholders, including the objective and conduct of the company and its structure, directors' and officers' duty of care, the business judgment rule, and the duty of fair dealing. ALI's *Principles of Corporate Governance* is organized in seven parts with each part consisting of one or more recommended rules or principles plus comments on the rule or principle and on the related notes. The seven parts are:

Part 1 presents precise definitions for the essential terms used in the analysis and recommendations.

Part 2 defines the fundamental objective of the business corporation as enhancing corporate profit and shareholder gain.

Part 3 discusses the legal functions and powers of the company's directors and officers and the composition of the board of directors and its committees.

Part 4 elaborates on the duty of care of the company's directors and officers.

Part 5 presents the duty imposed on directors, officers, and controlling shareholders to deal fairly with the company.

Part 6 covers the role of directors and shareholders regarding transactions in control and tender offers.

Part 7 deals with corporate remedies.[89]

American Bar Association

The American Bar Association (ABA) issued its first "Model Business Corporation Act" in 1950 and has issued several editions of the *Corporate Director's Guidebook*, which provides guidance to corporate directors and officers in fulfilling their fiduciary duty and responsibilities.[90] *Corporate Director's Guidebook* is a valuable resource for directors to better understand their duties and obligations and how to fulfill their responsibilities effectively. It provides guidelines for board structure, its committees, leadership, meetings, size, and quality of information. The fourth edition of the *Guidebook* addresses recent developments affecting corporate governance in the post-SOX era. The ABA formed a task force on corporate responsibility to examine many corporate governance concerns (e.g., director independence, executives' responsibilities) that came to light with the bankruptcy of Enron and WorldCom, among others, and to make suggestions for improvement.[91] The recommendations of the ABA task force relating to board structure, composition, leadership, committees, and the professional conduct of lawyers were adopted as ABA policy in August 2003.[92]

Institutional Investors

The diversity in the shareholder base of public companies, the inability of average investors to exercise control over management decisions and actions, the reported managerial aggressive and unethical conduct, and the ever-increasing agency problems have encouraged the promotion of shareholder activism. Shareholder activism can assist in reducing agency costs by promoting effective corporate governance principles and monitoring compliance with corporate governance best practices. For example, the California Public Employee's Retirement System (CalPERS) has been an active institutional investor in promoting vigilant corporate governance. As a shareholder activist, CalPERS has published its Focus List since 1992. The Focus List is a list of public companies with poor corporate governance practices and poor financial performance. CalPERS selects these companies and asks them to implement voluntary corporate governance reforms (e.g., if a company has a staggered board, it asks the company to voluntarily eliminate the staggered board and hold annual director elections). Institutional investors have long been advocates for effective corporate governance at the companies in which they invest. Several institutional investors, including CalPERS, the Teachers Insurance and Annuity Association—College Retirement Equities Fund (TIAA-CREF), the Council of Institutional Investors (CII), the AFL-CIO, and the State Board of Administration (SBA) of Florida have adopted corporate governance guidelines, which they use for making voting decisions.

Conceptually, institutional investors represent small shareholders as pensioners or beneficiaries. To ensure that institutional investors effectively protect interests of their beneficiaries or trustees, they should disclose their corporate governance and voting policies as well as potential conflicts of interest and how they manage them. Institutional investors often rely on the proxy voting advisory services of others, including Glass Lewis & Co (GLC) and Institutional Shareholder Services, Inc. (ISS), for research on voting decisions.[93] GLC is a leading independent research and proxy advisory firm. It serves institutions that collectively manage more than $8 trillion, assisting them to make more informed investment and proxy voting decisions by assessing business, legal, governance, and financial statement risks at more than 10,000 companies worldwide.[94] Institutional investors have influenced corporate governance measures by demanding that corporate defendants improve corporate governance as part of their settlement agreements. Lawsuit settlement cases that had institutional investors as plaintiffs (e.g., Cendant Corp., Lucent Technologies, WorldCom, Oxford Health Plans, HealthSouth Corp., Siebel Systems, Broadcom Corp., and Daimler Chrysler AG) have been very successful. In these cases, institutional investors have played an important role as lead plaintiffs to:

- Significantly improve settlement recoveries (e.g., $3.528 billion at Cendant, $2.6 billion at WorldCom).
- Negotiate attorney's fee agreements from high percentage (e.g., 30 percent) to as low as single-digit fee percentages.
- Above all, demand improvements in corporate governance measures (e.g., appointment of lead independent directors, redesign of executive compensation plans).
- Prevent further occurrences of corporate malfeasance and misconduct through deterrence effects of shareholder litigation.[95]

Council of Institutional Investors

The Council of Institutional Investors (CII) was founded in 1985 in response to takeover activities that threatened the financial interests of pension fund beneficiaries. Its purpose was to encourage member funds to take an active role in protecting plan assets and to increase return on investment for its members.[96] The CII started with 20 members; by 2005 it had over 140 pension fund members, with total assets of more than $3 trillion and over 130 educational sustainers. The CII has played an important role in the development of emerging corporate governance reforms as a significant voice for institutional shareholder interests. The CII encourages every company to have written, transparent, and disclosed governance policies and procedures; an ethics code that is applicable to directors, officers, and employees; and provisions for strict enforcement of governance policies, procedures, and code of ethics.

National Association of Corporate Directors

Since 1996 the National Association of Corporate Directors (NACD) has established several blue-ribbon commissions on issues related to corporate governance, including the commissions on:

- Executive compensation and the role of the compensation committee.
- Audit committees.
- Board evaluation.
- CEO succession.
- Risk oversight.
- The role of the board in corporate strategy.

Business Roundtable

The Business Roundtable is an association of CEOs of leading U.S. companies and has addressed issues relevant to corporate governance. The Business Roundtable has several reports, including:

- The role and composition of the board of directors of large public corporations.
- Statements on corporate governance.
- Principles of corporate governance.
- Executive compensation.
- The nominating process and corporate governance committees.

These publications have addressed many corporate governance matters and established several best practices.[97]

State Board of Administration (SBA) of Florida

The State Board of Administration (SBA) of Florida, as a member of the Conference Board Governance Center and the International Corporate Governance Network (ICGN), issues annual corporate governance reports that provide best practice guidance for improving corporate governance. For example, the 2006 corporate governance report of the SBA of Florida identifies the following characteristics of effective corporate governance: (1) at least three-quarters of the directors are independent; (2) all mandatory board committees (audit, compensation, and nominating) consist solely of independent directors; (3) the chairman of the board is independent of management; (4) all directors are elected by a simple majority of voted shares on an annual basis or by plurality voting in the event of a contested election; (5) senior management is reviewed annually; (6) there are transparent vote tabulation policies, and individual shareholder votes are confidential from management; (7) there are no antitakeover schemes (e.g., supermajority voting thresholds, poison pills) without shareholder approval; (8) a company's bylaws or charter can only be amended by a simple majority of voted shares; (9) one share receives one vote; (10) there is no bundling of proxy issues; (11) all compensation plans are performance-based subject to shareholder approval; (12) all performance objectives and award thresholds used in equity-based compensation plans are transparent; (13) repriced or discounted stock options are prohibited; (14) all assumptions used in valuing the awards of options or other compensation plans must be fully disclosed; (15) directors and senior executives own significant amounts of company stock; and (16) the independent auditor is annually ratified by shareholders.[98]

SUMMARY

This chapter examines the compliance function of the corporate governance structure, which requires public companies to comply with federal and state statutes, SEC rules, and listing standards of national stock exchanges. Best practices of professional organizations and investor activists have also provided benchmarks for improving corporate governance. These corporate governance reforms have shaped and will continue to influence the corporate governance structure and practices.

NOTES

1. Nicklaus, D. 2006. Shareholders reap rewards of compliant companies. *St. Louis Post-Dispatch*. (March 3).
2. Committee on Capital Markets Regulation. 2006. Interim report of the Committee on Capital Markets Regulation. (November 30). Available at: www.capmktsreg.org/research.html.
3. Wisconsin Department of Financial Institutions. A brief history of securities regulations. Available at: www.wdfi.org/securities/regexemp/history.htm.
4. Securities and Exchange Commission. 2006. Introduction—The SEC: Who we are, what we do. Available at: www.sec.gov.
5. Ibid.
6. Sarbanes-Oxley Act of 2002. Available at: www.sec.gov/about/laws/soa2002.pdf.
7. Allen, M. 2002. Bush signs corporate reforms into law: President says era of "false profits" is over. *Washington Post*. (July 31).
8. Donaldson, W. H. 2005. Speech by SEC chairman: Remarks before the Financial Services Roundtable. U.S. Securities and Exchange Commission. (April 1). Available at: www.sec.gov/news/speech/spch040105whd.htm.
9. Mitchell, L. E. 2003. The Sarbanes-Oxley Act and the reinvention of corporate governance. *Villanova Law Review* 48 (4): 1189–1216.
10. Turley, J. S. 2005. Our role in the capital markets…and our purpose as professionals. Chairman and CEO of Ernst & Young speech before the United States Chamber of Commerce. Washington, DC. (December 1). Available at: www.ey.com/global/download.nsf/US/Turley_Speech_to_US_COC_12-01-05/$file/JST_COC_Speech_120105.pdf.

11. Donaldson, W. H. 2005. Testimony of the SEC chairman concerning the impact of the Sarbanes-Oxley Act before the House Committee on Financial Services (April 21). Available at: www.sec.gov/news/testimony/ts042105whd.htm.
12. Sarbanes Oxley Act. 2002. Section 301: Public Company Audit Committees. Available at: www.sarbanes-oxley.com/displaySection.php?level=2&pub_id=Sarbanes-Oxley&chap_id=PCAOB3&message_id=5. Securities and Exchange Commission. 2003. Standards relating to listed company audit committees: Release No. 33-8220. Available at: sec.gov/rules/final/33-8220.htm. New York Stock Exchange. 2004. Section 303A. Corporate governance listing standards. Available at: www.nyse.com/pdfs/Section303A_final_rules.pdf.
13. MacLean, P. A. 2006. Court Says Sarbanes-Oxley does not extend overseas. *Securities Class Action-Weekly News* (January 18). Available at: www.law.stanford.edu.
14. Securities Class Action. 2006. SOX and environmental reporting. *Weekly News*. (January 10). Available at: www.law.stanford.edu.
15. Ibid.
16. Charles River Associates. 2005. Sarbanes-Oxley Section 404 costs and remediation of deficiencies: Estimates from a sample of Fortune 1000 companies. (April). CRA No. D06155-00. Washington, DC. Submitted to April 2005 SEC Roundtable. Turner, L. 2005. Costs and benefits of the Sarbanes-Oxley Act. Submitted by Glass, Lewis & Co., LLC., to the April 2005 SEC Roundtable. Available at: www.glasslewis.com.
17. Donaldson, W. H. 2005. Testimony of the SEC chairman.
18. Financial Executives International (FEI). 2007. FES Survey (May) available at: www.fel.org/404survey.
19. Burns, J. 2005. Internal control compliance costs seen down 40%. Dow Jones News Services. (December 8). Available at: www.djnewswires.com.
20. Government Accountability Office (GAO). 2006. Consideration of Key Principles Needed in Addressing Implementation for Smaller Public Companies. Available at: www.gao.gov/new.items/do6361.pdf.
21. Ibid.
22. Institute of Management Accountants (IMA). 2006. COSO 1992 Control Framework and Management Reporting on Internal Control: Survey and Analysis Implementation Practices (October 18). Available at: www.imanet.org/research_SOX_Study.asp.
23. Ibid.
24. Whitman, R., L. Dittmar, and C. Munoz. 2003. The currency of good governance. *Platts Energy Business and Technology* 5 (4): 30.
25. Donaldson, W. H. 2004. Speech by SEC chairman: Remarks from the Conference Board's 2004 Annual Dinner (October 14). Available at: www.sec.gov/news/speech/spch101404whd.htm.
26. Spencer Stuart. 2006. Spencer Stuart Board Index 2005. *CFO Direct* (January 12). Available at: http://www.cfodirect.pwc.com/CFODirectWeb/Controller.jpf?NavCode=USAS-6BG34T.
27. Ibid.

28. House of Representatives. 1978. Public Accounting Regulatory Act. HR 13175. 95th Congress in Session (June 16). Available at: www.house.gov.
29. Ibid.
30. Schmidt, R. 2006. Accounting measure gets scrutiny at U.S. congressional hearing. Bloomberg. (April 5). Available at: www.bloomberg.net.
31. Morris, F. 2006. Trusting bosses not to cheat. *New York Times* (June 23). Available at: www.nytimes.com.
32. Ibid.
33. Murray, A. 2006. Fees may be costing Wall Street its edge. *Wall Street Journal* (August 2). Available at: www.online.wsj.com.
34. Ibid.
35. Paulson, H. M. 2006. Remarks by Treasury Secretary on the competitiveness of U.S. capital markets Economics Club of New York, New York. (November 20) hp-174. Available at: www.treas.gov/press/releases/hp174.htm.
36. Ip, G. 2006. Is a U.S. listing worth the effort? *Wall Street Journal* (November 28). Available at: online.wsj.com/article/SB116467408678033939.html.
37. Masters, B. 2006. Spitzer slams threat to corporate reforms. *Financial Times* (November 26). Available at: www.ft.com.
38. Niemeier, C. D. 2006. *American competitiveness in international capital markets*: Background Paper for the Atlantic's Ideas Tour Commemorating the Magazine's 150th Anniversary. Washington, DC. U.S. Public Company Accounting Oversight Board.
39. PricewaterhouseCoopers. 2004. Major accounting and reporting implications of the American Jobs Creation Act of 2004. *Dataline*. (October 21). Available at: www.cfodirect.com/CFOPrivate.nsf/vContentPrint/6306A13C2.htm.
40. U.S. Securities and Exchange Commission. 2005. 2005 performance and accountability report. Available at: www.sec.gov/about/secpar2005/shtml.
41. Ibid.
42. Ibid.
43. Rule 19(b)-3, Exchange Act Release No. 11, 203, 40 *Fed. Reg.* 7394, 7394 (January 23, 1975), and also Exchange Act § 19(c). 15 U.S.C. § 78s(c).
44. American Bar Association. 2002. Special study on market structure listing standards and corporate governance. A special study group of the Committee on Federal Regulation of Securities. American Bar Association, Section of Business Law. (August). 57 *Business Law* 1487.
45. Reisinger, S. 2004. SEC takes aim beyond U.S. borders: As the market becomes more global so does the enforcement. *National Law Journal* 26 (22): 8.
46. Parmalat in SEC accord on corporate reforms. 2004 verdicts and settlements. *National Law Journal* 26 (461): 13.
47. U.S. Securities and Exchange Commission (SEC) 2006. Internal control over financial reporting in Exchange Act Periodic Reports of foreign private issues that are accelerated filers: Final Rules. Reference No. 33-8730. Available at: www.sec.gov/rules/final.html.
48. Securities and Exchange Commission. 2006. Statement of the Securities and Exchange Commission lowering financial penalties. (January 4). Available at: www.sec.gov/news/press.shtm.

49. Baid, A. B., and D. B. H. Martin. 2006. Corporate penalty guidelines. Covington & Burling. (January 7). Available at: www.cov.com.
50. Burns. J. 2006. Enforcement Cases by SEC Fall Again; Focus on Late Filers. *Wall Street Journal* (November 3). Available at: www.online.wsj.com/article/SB116252597213012314.html.
51. Securities and Exchange Commission. 2002. Sarbanes-Oxley Act of 2002. Available at: www.sec.gov/about/lawsss/soa2002.pdf.
52. Wallison, P. J. 2005. Rein in the Public Company Accounting Oversight Board. *Financial Services Outlook.* (February 1).
53. Public Company Accounting Oversight Board. 2005. Available at: www.pcaobus.org.
54. Ibid.
55. Comprehensive Crime Control Act of 1984. Chapter 11 of Public Law No. 98-473. (October 12). Available at: www.ussc.gov/training/corpover.pdf.
56. U.S. Sentencing Commission. 2004. Amended organizational sentencing guidelines. (April 30). Available at: www.ussc.gov.
57. Committee of European Securities Regulators. 2004. Available at: www.cesr-eu.org/.
58. Office of Public Sector Information. The Companies Act 2006. Available at: http://search.opsi.gov.uk/search?q=companies+act+2006+pdf&output=xml_no_dtd&client=opsisearchproxystylesheet=opsisearch&site=default_collection.
59. Securities and Exchange Commission. 2004. Investment company governance, Investment Company Act Release No. 26520 (July 27). Available at: www.sec.gov/rules/finan/archive2004.shtml.
60. Anson, M., T. White, and H. Ho. 2003. The shareholder wealth effects of CalPERS' focus list. *Journal of Applied Corporate Finance.* (Winter): 8–17.
61. California State Treasurer's Office. 2004. Investment protection principles. (May 27). Available at: www.treasurer.ca.gov/news/releases/2004/052704_voting.pdf.
62. Pennsylvania State Employees' Retirement System. 2002. State employees' retirement board adopts investment protection principles. (October 31). Available at: www.sers.state.pa.us/sers/cwp/view.asp?A=303&Q=253956.
63. Powell, E. A. 2006. Government Announces $1.6B settlement with AIG. AP Associated Press. (February 9). Available at: www.ap.org.
64. Ibid.
65. Weil, J. 2005. Nine are charged in KPMG case on tax shelters. *Wall Street Journal.* (August 30).
66. Ibid.
67. Ibid.
68. Ibid.
69. See *Escott v. BarChris Constr. Corp.*, 283 F. Supp. 643, 696-98 (S.D.N.Y. 1968). See *Gould v. American-Hawaiian S.S. Co.*, 535 F.2 d 761 (3d Cir. 1976).
70. See *SEC v. Mattel, Inc.*, No. 74 Civ. 1185 (D.D.C. October 1, 1974).
71. *In re* Walt Disney Co. Derivative Litigation, August 9, 2005.

72. Bebchuk, L. 2005. The Disney verdict shuts out investors. *Financial Times*. (August 13). Available at: http://news.ft.com/cms/s/5e4 d3484-0a97-11 daaa9b-00000e2511c8.html.
73. Ibid.
74. Ibid.
75. Ibid.
76. Ontario Securities Commission. 2005. Self regulatory organizations. Available at: www.osc.gov.on.ca/MarketRegulation/SRO/sro_index.jsp. Investopedia.com. 2005. Self regulatory organization. Available at: http://investopedia.com/terms/s/sro.asp.
77. Securities and Exchange Commission. 2005. Self-regulatory organization (SRO) rulemaking and national market system (NMS) plans. Available at: http://sec.gov/rules/sro.shtml.
78. American Bar Association. 2002. Special study on market structure listing standards and corporate governance.
79. Reuters. 2006. Exchange shareholders sell $1.54 billion in stock. *New York Times*. (May 5). Available at: www.nytimes.com.
80. BBC News. 2006. Euronext attracted to NYSE bid. (May 22). Available at: http://news.bbc.co.uk/2/hi/business/5003558.stm.
81. Ibid.
82. Securities and Exchange Commission (SEC). 2005. Fair administration and governance of self-regulatory organizations; Disclosure and regulatory reporting by self-regulatory organizations; Recordkeeping requirements for self-regulatory organizations; Ownership and voting limitations for members of self-regulatory organizations; Ownership reporting requirements for members of self-regulatory organizations; Listing and trading of affiliated securities by a self-regulatory organization. Available at: http://sec.gov/rules/proposed/34-50699.htm.
83. Ibid.
84. New York Stock Exchanges. 2004. NYSE listed company manual Section 303A, Corporate governance rules. (November 3). Available at: www.nyse.com/pdfs/Section303A_final_rules.pdf. National Association of Security Dealers. 2004. Corporate Governance Standards Rule 4200(15).
85. American Bar Association. 2002. Special study on market structure listing standards and corporate governance.Available at: www.abanet.org/buslaw/corporateresponsibility/governance_relatedmat.html.
86. Ibid.
87. Conference Board. 2003. The Conference Board Commission on Public Trust and Private Enterprise: Findings and recommendations. Available at: www.conference-board.org/pdf_free/758.pdf.
88. American Law Institute. 1994. *Principles of corporate governance: Analysis and recommendations*. 2 vols. Available at: www.ali.org.
89. Ibid.
90. American Bar Association. 2004. *Corporate director's guidebook*, 4th ed. National Book Network.

91. American Bar Association. 2003. Report of Task Force on Corporate Responsibility. (March 31). Available at: www.abanet.org/buslaw/corporateresponsibility/final_report.pdf.
92. Ibid.
93. Goodman, A., and B. Schwartz. 2004. *Corporate governance: Law and practice.* Matthew Bender & Co.
94. Glass Lewis & Co., LLC. 2006. Available at: www.glasslewis.com.
95. Ibid.
96. Council of Institutional Investors. 2005. About the Council. Available at: www.cii.org/about.
97. Business Roundtable. 2004. Business Roundtable Survey. Available at: www.businessroundtable.com/CEOSurvey/index.aspx.
98. State Board of Administration (SBA) of Florida. 2006. Corporate Governance Annual Report 2006. Available at: www.sbafla.com.

CHAPTER 7

Internal Audit Function

INTRODUCTION

Internal auditing has evolved from the traditional management-driven appraisal activity to an objective, assurance, and consulting activity. Internal auditing is now regarded as a value-added service that assists in improving the organization's governance, operations, risk management, internal controls, and financial reporting. The role of internal auditors has also changed from merely providing input and feedback to management, to directly participating in corporate governance and thus in the decision-making function. Because of recent corporate governance reforms, public companies have established in-house internal audit functions as an integral component of their corporate governance to assist the audit committee and the board of directors to carry out their oversight function. This chapter discusses the role of internal auditors in corporate governance.

INTERNAL AUDITING FUNCTION AND CORPORATE GOVERNANCE

Recent corporate governance reforms require an effective corporate governance structure based on a vigilant board of directors; diligent, competent, and ethical management; a credible independent audit function; and an effective internal audit function. The success depends on the effectiveness of all corporate governance functions. As an integral component of corporate governance, the internal audit function should provide objective and independent assurance and consulting services for all of the company's financial activities, including risk management, internal controls, financial reporting, and other corporate governance functions. The listing standards of national stock exchanges require that listed companies establish an internal audit function.[1] Although privately held companies and not-for-profit organizations are not mandated to have an internal audit function, many companies voluntarily follow the best practices which establish that every organization can benefit from assurance and consulting services provided by their internal auditors.

Internal auditors' services can be viewed as value added in improving the effectiveness of their organization's governance, including effective internal controls.

Internal auditors are now participating in not only the internal corporate governance processes, such as internal controls and enterprise risk management, but also the external corporate governance processes, which include:

- Assisting the board of directors and the audit committee in their oversight function.
- Cooperating with independent auditors in their integrated reports on audits of internal control over financial reporting and financial statements.
- Participating in risk management and control including environmental audits and the preparation of corporate governance and sustainability reports.

The board of directors and the audit committee now expect the internal auditors to play an important role in corporate governance, for example, working to ensure that internal controls over financial reporting are effective and functioning as intended. A survey shows that 79 percent of the respondents report that the internal audit function has assessed their corporate governance structure and has made specific recommendations for its improvements.[2]

To ensure that the internal auditing role is viewed as a value-added function contributing to the improvement of both internal and external aspects of corporate governance, internal auditors should:

- Be independent by directly reporting to the board of directors or to the board's representative, the audit committee.
- Have adequate staff with financial and accounting knowledge and experience.
- Participate in number of corporate governance functions depicted in Exhibit 2.4 and assist all corporate governance participants, including the board of directors, the audit committee, management, external auditors, and legal counsel, in fulfilling their responsibilities.

The Institute of Internal Auditors (IIA), in its 2002 position paper presented to the U.S. Congress, states: "Internal auditors, the board of directors, senior management, and external auditors are the cornerstones of the foundation on which effective corporate governance must be built."[3] The IIA promotes internal auditors as active participants in the corporate governance process yet also independent observers in that process. Internal auditors are adopting emerging corporate governance reforms as the IIA has taken initiatives to revise standards for the practice of internal auditing in the post-SOX era. The external quality assurance review (QAR) is regarded as an important area that internal auditors can contribute significantly to risk assessment, internal control, and governance activities. The chief audit executive (CAE) plays an important role in ensuring that the internal audit function focuses on quality assurance and improvement.

PricewaterhouseCoopers (PwC) suggests six ways to leverage a QAR at a strategic level:

1. Make an up-front commitment to quality.
2. Conduct a sound quality assurance program.

3. Establish forward-thinking protocols.
4. Conduct an external review with integrated benchmarking.
5. Implement corrective actions as necessary.
6. Continuously assess the performance of the internal audit function.[4]

Many organizations that have started to establish or improve their internal audit function realize the benefits of such functions. Five steps are suggested for the establishment or improvement of an effective internal audit function:

1. *Appoint the right person to be the CAE.* The audit committee of the board of directors is "directly responsible" for the appointment, compensation, and, when necessary, dismissal of the company's CAE. The audit committee should also oversee the work of the CAE by approving the internal audit function's budget, audit plan, and scope and by receiving internal audit reports. The CAE's responsibilities are to provide assurance, counsel, and advice to management regarding the company's efficiency, economy, and effectiveness in risk management, financial reporting, internal controls, and governance processes under the oversight function of the audit committee. To fulfill these responsibilities effectively, the CAE should be accepted in the company's "C-Suite" as part of the senior management team. The CAE must participate in relevant management meetings and provide comments, input, and insight on managerial decisions. The CAE is administratively accountable and reports to the company's CEO and also functionally accountable and reports to the audit committee. As the head of the company's internal audit function, the CAE should be competent and knowledgeable in internal auditing standards, tools, methodology, and practices; supervise the internal audit function; communicate effectively with the audit committee, management, and internal audit staff; and demand productive performance and ethical conduct from the internal audit staff.
2. *Establish a written audit charter.* The internal audit charter should specify the purpose, authority, and responsibility of the internal audit function as an integral component of corporate governance in adding value to the company's sustainable performance. The purpose of the function should be clearly described in the charter as providing assurance and consulting services in risk management, financial reporting, internal controls, and governance processes. The authority of the internal audit function is granted by the company's board of directors, particularly the audit committee, to conduct internal audit activities in adding value to the company's performance, have sufficient resources to carry out its responsibilities effectively, and have access to all records, personnel, and property required to conduct internal audits.
3. *Develop an audit strategy.* The internal audit function should have a sound audit strategy that is effective and efficient and adds value to the company's operations in risk management, financial reporting, internal controls, and governance processes. The internal audit strategy should be developed by the CAE in collaboration with management and approved by the audit committee. The strategy should specify audit plans, scope, nature, procedures, and timing of all internal audit activities.

4. *Implement the audit strategy.* An effective implementation of internal audit strategy requires: proper audit plans; sufficient resources including qualified ethical and highly specialized and competent staff; commitment from senior management; and approval of the audit committee. Internal auditors should have adequate training and proficiency in: accounting principles, policies, and practices; internal auditing standards, techniques, tools, and procedures; corporate governance reforms and management principles; and a knowledge base in accounting, economics, taxation, finance, information technology, and quantitative methods.

5. *Establish quality assurance and performance evaluation.* To ensure a high-quality internal audit function that adds value to the company's operations and performance, the internal audit function should be evaluated annually. The performance of internal audit staff should be evaluated by the CAE based on predetermined evaluation benchmarks and process. The performance of the CAE should be evaluated by management (e.g., the chief executive officer [CEO]) and reviewed by the audit committee. The purpose of this evaluation is to improve the quality of the internal audit function and provide a basis for promotion, advancement, and compensation.[5]

Internal Auditors as Assurance Providers

Internal auditors are well trained and positioned to provide numerous assurance services to their organization. The emerging trend toward more emphasis on multiple bottom lines (MBLs) of governance, economic, ethical, social, and environmental performance requires organizations to provide assurance on a variety of their performance measures and achievements. Currently assurance reports on these measures are voluntary, except for audit report on economic measures (four basic financial statements), and should be performed by the organization's internal auditors. The objectivity and credibility of these voluntary assurance services depend on the objectivity, independence, and competence of the individuals providing such services (i.e., internal auditors).

Assurance services provided by internal auditors to their organizations relate to:

- Corporate governance, with a keen focus on risk management and internal control.
- Ethical considerations.
- Social responsibilities.
- Environmental matters.

In addition to these voluntary assurance services, internal auditors can assist external auditors in their integrated audit of internal controls and financial statements. The Public Company Accounting Oversight Board (PCAOB) in its Auditing Standard No. 2 encourages that external auditors use testing results performed by others (internal auditors) in determining nature, extent, and timing of tests of controls in an integrated audit.[6] The extent of reliance on the work of internal auditors in an integrated audit depends on the objectivity, independence, and competence of internal auditors.

Internal auditors may assist management to comply effectively with Sections 302 and 404 requirements of Sarbanes-Oxley (SOX) by reviewing management's certifications on internal controls and financial statements or providing some type of assurance on the completeness and accuracy of those certifications. They should ensure that their services are in compliance with their professional standards and are based on and supported by sufficient and competent audit evidence.

Internal Auditors as Consultants

Internal auditors can provide a variety of consulting services to the company's board of directors, the audit committee, management, and other personnel at all levels to enable them to carry out their assigned responsibilities effectively.

- *Consulting services to the board of directors and audit committee.* One means to achieve the audit committee oversight effectiveness is to ask internal auditors to provide consulting services to the audit committee in overseeing financial reports, internal controls, risk assessment, whistleblower programs, and code of business ethics. Indeed, internal auditors are well trained and knowledgeable to provide such services to the entire board of directors and all board committees, particularly audit committees.
- *Consulting services to management.* Traditionally, the internal auditor role has been defined as providing consulting services to management at all levels to enable it to discharge its responsibilities effectively. In providing consulting services to management, internal auditors assess efficiency, effectiveness, and economy of managerial performance. These services have been in the areas of operational effectiveness and efficiency, internal controls assessment, risk management, financial reporting, safeguarding assets, and compliance with applicable laws, rules, regulations, and standards. To maintain their independence and objectivity, internal auditors should ensure they do not step into the management decision-making function in their consulting activities and should refrain from making decisions on behalf of management.
- *Training services.* Internal auditors should be knowledgeable enough to provide audit training services to all personnel within their organizations. They may provide training on: information technology; internal control procedures and assessment; risk management; financial reporting; compliance with applicable laws, rules, regulations, and standards; and other activities without impairing their objectivity and independence. As the organization's training and educational experts, internal auditors bring more competency and knowledge to the entire organization and assist all personnel to carry out their assigned responsibilities effectively.

TREND AND RELEVANCE OF INTERNAL AUDITORS

Internal auditing has transformed over the past several decades from its beginnings as a financial enforcer and a service function to management to a value-added function as an important component of corporate governance function. This transformation is far from over in light of emerging corporate governance reforms requiring the establishment of internal audit functions for listed companies. The focus of internal auditing has shifted away from compliance and internal controls and moved toward value-added services. The Foreign Corrupt Practices Act (FCPA) of 1977 underscores the important role that internal auditors play in ensuring compliance with internal control provisions.[7] Indeed, the FCPA was labeled the Internal Auditors Full Employment Act of 1977.[8]

The Treadway Commission (COSO) report in 1987 stressed the need for an internal audit function and made several recommendations for enhancing the role of internal auditors: "[I]t is the general belief of our Commission that internal audit function is far too hidden from public view."[9] Treadway recommendations led to significant growth in the internal auditing profession. The IIA, initially in 1947, defined internal auditing as an:[10]

> *independent appraisal activity within an organization for the review of accounting, financial and other operations as a basis for protective and constructive* service to management.

In December 1981, the IIA redefined internal auditing as:

> *An independent appraisal function established within an organization to examine and evaluate its activities as a* service to the organization.[11]

And in 1999, the IIA redefined internal auditing again:

> *Internal auditing is an independent, objective* assurance and consulting activity *designed to* add value *and improve an organization's operations. It helps an organization accomplish its objectives by bringing a systematic, disciplined approach to evaluate and improve the effectiveness of risk management, control, and* governance processes.[12]

Thus, internal auditing had evolved from "serving management" to "a service activity to the company," and now is an "objective assurance and consulting activity." The 2006 PricewaterhouseCoopers (PwC) survey identifies several key trends that continue to influence the internal audit practice. These trends are: (1) significant increase in the use of continuous auditing techniques in response to an ever-increasing dynamic risk environment; (2) firm commitments to equality by utilizing external quality assurance review (QAR); (3) allocating internal audit resources to the organization's activities as SOX compliance demands fewer internal audit resources; (4) shortage of qualified internal auditors; and (5) increasing demand for internal audit services and more focus on the relevance of internal audit reports and conclusions by the company's senior executives and directors.[13]

SOX does not directly address internal auditor responsibilities or internal audit function. Nevertheless, listing standards of national stock exchanges require listing companies to have an internal audit function. Traditionally internal auditors have played an essential role in their organization's internal control structure. The PCAOB has encouraged independent auditors to rely on the work of others, particularly internal auditors, in their auditing and reporting on internal control over financial reporting. The PCAOB in its Auditing Standard No. 2 states that "internal auditors normally are expected to have greater competence and expertise with regard to internal control over financial reporting and objectivity than other personnel."[14] Thus, internal auditors can be of a great assistance to management's compliance with both Sections 302 and 404 of SOX and the external auditor's audit and report on internal controls. However, the PwC study indicates that, in the few years after the passage of SOX, internal auditors were so consumed by SOX compliance that their other priorities suffered and their primary focus on risk-based auditing was diverted.[15]

The 2004 survey of more than 270 internal auditors conducted by PwC reveals that about 60 percent of responding companies devoted half or more of their internal audit resources to SOX compliance.[16] Limited resources were left for internal auditors to address high-risk and nonfinancial areas and add value to their organization's performance. Indeed, PwC's report indicates that "failure to address key strategic, operational, and compliance risk areas in an internal audit program can lead to weak corporate governance, operational inefficiencies, and potentially serious financial losses resulting from weak internal controls."[17] The lack of proper balance between internal auditors' SOX compliance efforts and other activities can be detrimental to the effectiveness of nonfinancial controls and compliance in the company's overall operational effectiveness and efficiency.

The other concerns raised in PwC's report are:

- Internal auditors' objectivity and independence are at risk in situations where they assume an operational role on Section 404 projects.
- A possible reduction in the extent of reliance on the work of the internal auditors by external auditors can occur when internal auditors assume management responsibilities on Section 404 projects.
- There is a potential for conflicts of interest in the roles of internal auditors as specified in their board committee charters approved by the company's board of directors.[18]

Internal auditors in the post-SOX era need to strike an appropriate balance between their priorities and resources to ensure the achievement of their objectives of providing advice and consulting services to their entire organization. The 2005 PwC study on the state of the internal audit profession identified six trends that are impacting the internal auditing profession in the post-SOX period:

1. *SOX requirements continue to affect internal audit priorities significantly.* More than 70 percent of respondents (CAEs) reported that the first year of compliance with Section 404 required more than half of their internal audit resources. To comply with Section 302, management must design and implement effective internal controls and prepare complete and accurate certification for the CEO and CFO to validate. Management is also required to document, test, and assess

the design and operation of internal control over financial reporting. Internal auditors possess knowledge, competence, and objectivity to assist management in complying with Sections 302 and 404 in the four areas of project oversight, consulting and project support, ongoing monitoring and testing, and project audit.

2. *Internal audit strengthens relationships with key stakeholders, particularly the audit committee and management.* More than 88 percent of respondents reported that their internal audit function reports directly to the audit committee or the full board; about 75 percent report administratively to the C-Suite [the CEO, president, or chief financial officer (CFO)].

3. *Risk management and corporate governance take center stage.* Enterprise risk management and the risk-based approach to internal auditing remain vital to the effective functioning of internal auditors. More than 82 percent of responding internal auditors have conducted an enterprise-level assessment, while 79 percent have assessed the corporate governance activities to improve the organization's governance processes.

4. *Rising demands strain internal audit resources and processes.* About a third of surveyed internal auditors have had open internal audit positions for a long time.

5. *Chief audit executives are increasingly asked to provide formal opinions on internal controls.* Of surveyed internal auditors, 38 percent were asked to issue an opinion on the overall condition of internal controls; 33 percent issued an opinion on companies' internal control over financial reporting. Management is primarily responsible for certifying internal controls based on the requirements of SOX. Internal auditors should not be asked to opine on internal controls other than to assess the effectiveness of the overall internal structure.

6. *Continuous auditing and monitoring techniques are gaining momentum.* About 34 percent of survey respondents use continuous auditing techniques.[19]

INSTITUTE OF INTERNAL AUDITORS

The Institute of Internal Auditors is the well-recognized organization representing more than 102,000 members throughout the world. About 46,000 are in 133 chapters established in the United States. The IIA is viewed as the global voice of internal auditors through its issuance of the International Standards for the Professional Practice of Internal Auditing. Since its inception in 1941, the IIA has promoted and played an important role in improving responsible corporate governance, effective internal controls, and reliable financial reporting.

The IIA has adopted a Professional Practices Framework (PPF) that includes new and updated internal auditing standards. The PPF provides a definition of internal auditing, its code of ethics, standards for the professional practice of internal auditing, practice advisories, and development and practice aids.[20] The IIA Code of Ethics consists of two components: principles and rules of conduct. The four principles are integrity, objectivity, confidentiality, and competency; the rules of conduct describe these principles and related ethical conduct.

The Standards for the Professional Practice of Internal Auditing (SPPIA) are composed of three sets of mandatory standards:

1. Attribute standards specifying appropriate features of the individual auditor or audit functions performing internal auditing.
2. Performance standards regarding the performance of internal audit engagements.
3. Implementation standards describing attribute and performance standards and how they can be applied to the specific types of audits.

Internal auditors are required to apply attribute, performance, and implementation standards when performing both assurance and consulting engagements.[21] In an assurance engagement, internal auditors provide an independent assessment of the effectiveness of risk management, internal control, or corporate governance; in a consulting engagement, internal auditors work with audit clients (e.g., department, individual company managers) to specify the nature and scope of their consulting services. In either consulting or assurance services, internal auditors add value to their organization's performance by assisting the entire organization, and its units, departments, and management, to fulfill their responsibilities effectively.

The Institute of Internal Auditors Research Formulation (IIARF) is in the process of establishing the Common Body of Knowledge (CBOK) for internal auditors, which is intended to broaden the understanding of internal auditing practices and the state of the internal auditing profession worldwide. The CBOK will include: (1) the knowledge and skills of internal auditors; (2) the organization and skills of practicing internal auditors; (3) the actual duties performed and responsibilities assumed by internal auditors; (4) the structure of internal audit organizations; (5) the types of industries that practice internal audit; and (6) the regulatory environment of various countries that affect internal auditing.[22]

Internal Auditing Education

The IIA has established the Internal Auditing Education Partnership (IAEP) program to promote internal auditing in colleges and universities in educating the next generation of internal auditors. The IAEP program offers business schools three levels of promoting internal auditing education and practices and their participation with an entry level, partner level, and advanced level known as a Center for Internal Auditing Excellence.[23] The entry level requires a minimum of six hours of internal audit–related subjects covering internal auditing and risk management and control. The partner level requires a minimum of three core course equivalents per year in internal auditing–related subjects. The advanced level requires the establishment of a center for internal auditing excellence with an undergraduate or graduate formal concentration or minor in internal auditing. Exhibit 7.1 presents all three of these internal auditing education levels, refer to the source not to view the full version on the IAA website.

EXHIBIT 7.1   Internal Auditing Education Partnership Continuum
Source: Adapted from the Institute of Internal Auditors. Available at: www.theiia.org/?doc_id=211.

Internal Audit Charter

Internal audit departments should have a charter defining their mission, authority, independence, and responsibilities. Exhibit 7.2 presents a sample internal audit department charter as suggested by the IIA. This sample charter describes the mission and scope of the work of internal auditors and their accountability, independence, authority, and responsibilities. The charter should be signed by the CAE, CEO, and audit committee chair.

AUDIT COMMITTEE RELATIONSHIP WITH INTERNAL AUDITOR

As an integral part of corporate governance, the internal audit function has received well-deserved and long-awaited attention in the post-Enron era. Under the emerging corporate governance reforms, internal auditors are responsible for serving their entire organization and are accountable to the audit committee. Listing standards of national stock exchanges (New York Stock Exchange and Nasdaq) have improved the stature of internal auditors substantially by requiring that listed companies have an internal audit function to assist the company's audit committee and management with continuous assessments of internal controls and enterprise risk management.

EXHIBIT 7.2 Sample Internal Audit Department Charter

Mission and Scope of Work
The mission of the internal audit department is to provide independent, objective assurance and consulting services designed to add value and improve the organization's operations. It helps the organization accomplish its objectives by bringing a systematic, disciplined approach to evaluate and improve the effectiveness of risk management, control, and governance processes.

The scope of work of the internal audit department is to determine whether the organization's network of risk management, control, and governance processes, as designed and represented by management, is adequate and functioning in a manner to ensure:

- Risks are appropriately identified and managed.
- Interaction with the various governance groups occurs as needed.
- Significant financial, managerial, and operating information is accurate, reliable, and timely.
- Employees' actions are in compliance with policies, standards, procedures, and applicable laws and regulations.
- Resources are acquired economically, used efficiently, and protected adequately.
- Programs, plans, and objectives are achieved.
- Quality and continuous improvement are fostered in the organization's control process.
- Significant legislative or regulatory issues impacting the organization are recognized and addressed appropriately.

Opportunities for improving management control, profitability, and the organization's image may be identified during audits. They will be communicated to the appropriate level of management.

Accountability
The chief audit executive, in the discharge of his/her duties, shall be accountable to management and the audit committee to:

- Provide annually an assessment on the adequacy and effectiveness of the organization's processes for controlling its activities and managing its risks in the areas set forth under the mission and scope of work.
- Report significant issues related to the processes for controlling the activities of the organization and its affiliates, including potential improvements to those processes, and provide information concerning such issues through resolution.
- Periodically provide information on the status and results of the annual audit plan and the sufficiency of department resources.
- Coordinate with and provide oversight of other control and monitoring functions (risk management, compliance, security, legal, ethics, environmental, external audit).

(continued overleaf)

EXHIBIT 7.2   *(Continued)*

Independence
To provide for the independence of the internal auditing department, its personnel report to the chief audit executive, who reports functionally to the audit committee and administratively to the chief executive officer in a manner outlined in the section on accountability. It will include as part of its reports to the audit committee a regular report on internal audit personnel.

Responsibility
The chief audit executive and staff of the internal audit department have responsibility to:

- Develop a flexible annual audit plan using an appropriate risk-based methodology, including any risks or control concerns identified by management, and submit that plan to the audit committee for review and approval as well as periodic updates.
- Implement the annual audit plan, as approved, including as appropriate any special tasks or projects requested by management and the audit committee.
- Maintain a professional audit staff with sufficient knowledge, skills, experience, and professional certifications to meet the requirements of this charter.
- Evaluate and assess significant merging/consolidating functions and new or changing services, processes, operations, and control processes coincident with their development, implementation, and/or expansion.
- Issue periodic reports to the audit committee and management summarizing results of audit activities.
- Keep the audit committee informed of emerging trends and successful practices in internal auditing.
- Provide a list of significant measurement goals and results to the audit committee.
- Assist in the investigation of significant suspected fraudulent activities within the organization and notify management and the audit committee of the results.
- Consider the scope of work of the external auditors and regulators, as appropriate, for the purpose of providing optimal audit coverage to the organization at a reasonable overall cost.

Authority
The chief audit executive and staff of the internal audit department are authorized to:

- Have unrestricted access to all functions, records, property, and personnel.
- Have full and free access to the audit committee.
- Allocate resources, set frequencies, select subjects, determine scopes of work, and apply the techniques required to accomplish audit objectives.
- Obtain the necessary assistance of personnel in units of the organization where they perform audits as well as other specialized services from within or outside the organization.

EXHIBIT 7.2 (*Continued*)

The chief audit executive and staff of the internal audit department are not authorized to:

- Perform any operational duties for the organization or its affiliates.
- Initiate or approve accounting transactions external to the internal auditing department.
- Direct the activities of any organization employee not employed by the internal auditing department, except to the extent such employees have been appropriately assigned to auditing teams or to otherwise assist the internal auditors.

Standards of Audit Practice
The internal audit department will meet or exceed the *Standards for the Professional Practice of Internal Auditing* of The Institute of Internal Auditors.

Chief Audit Executive

Chief Executive Officer

Audit Committee Chair

Dated _____

Source: Adapted from the Institute of Internal Auditors. Available at: www.theiia.org/index.cfm?doc_id=73.

These initiatives should encourage companies to invest in and effectively utilize competent and objective internal audit functions.

A close working relationship between the audit committee and internal auditors can improve the effectiveness of corporate governance in three ways.

1. The independence and objectivity of internal auditors can be enhanced when they report their findings directly to the audit committee.
2. The prestige and status of internal auditors can be strengthened when they work with management at all levels for the audit committee. In this regard, the internal auditor's role is considered a value-adding function to improve managerial and employee performance while preserving their independence and objectivity.
3. Internal auditors can be a significant source of assistance to the audit committee to fulfill their oversight responsibilities in functions of such areas as financial reporting, internal controls, external audit, taxes, and working with legal counsel in whistleblowing and ethics matters.

Audit committees should utilize internal auditor services in fulfilling their oversight responsibilities over financial reporting, internal controls, and audit activities. Internal auditors can assist audit committees in establishing and implementing whistleblower programs and a corporate code of business ethics and professional conduct; in assessing the company's enterprise risk management; in developing an agenda for audit committee meetings; and in assisting with the orientation of new audit committee members as well as continuing education and ongoing evaluation of committee members.

In overseeing the company's internal audit function, the audit committee should:

- Consider whether the internal audit function is adding value to the company's long-term objectives.
- Review the goals and mission of the internal audit function.
- Assess the adequacy of resources (budget and personnel) for the internal audit function to achieve its objectives.
- Monitor the performance of the internal audit function.

The audit committee can contribute to the success and effectiveness of internal auditors and the achievement of their value-added activities by ensuring that internal auditors have:

- Sufficient independence from management by reporting and being held accountable to the audit committee.
- Adequate resources, competence, and ongoing training to assess effectiveness of the company's internal controls and enterprise risk management.
- Proper knowledge of the company's corporate governance processes, internal control, financial reporting, and audit activities.
- The mechanisms and confidence to bring forward controversial financial reporting issues without fear of retaliation.
- A process for communicating directly with the company's audit committee on a regular and timely basis.
- Access to the audit committee to discuss concerns related to management activities, financial reporting risk, and potential fraudulent financial reporting without fear of retaliation from management or the board of directors.

INTERNAL AUDITORS' ROLE IN INTERNAL CONTROL

The IIA, in 2004, issued a position paper called "Internal Auditing's Role in Section 302 and 404 of the U.S. Sarbanes-Oxley Act of 2002."[24] Section 302 of SOX requires quarterly certifications from management of both financial statements and financial reporting controls; Section 404 requires management's assessments of the effectiveness of both design and operation of internal control over financial reporting. While management's responsibilities for compliance with both Sections 302 and 404 cannot be delegated or abdicated, internal auditors can assist management considerably in fulfilling its compliance responsibilities. In assisting management to comply with Sections 302 and 404 and other provisions of SOX, internal auditors should maintain their objectivity and independence according to their charter. The CAE should consult with the audit committee in allocating and devoting sufficient internal audit resources and efforts to Sections 302 and 404 without compartmentalizing other internal audit activities.

The IIA's 2004 position paper presents the Section 404 compliance process, several phases of this process, activities within each phase, accountability for each activity, individual(s) responsible to carry out each activity, and recommendations for internal auditor's role for each activity.[25] Exhibit 7.3 provides a summary of phases, activities, accountability, and responsibilities for Section 404 compliance efforts.

The position paper specifies that services performed by the company's internal audit function to assist management in compliance with Sections 302 and 404 of SOX are consistent with internal auditors' professional standards and should not interfere with their professional obligations to maintain their independence and objectivity.[26] The paper suggests four activities of internal auditors to support their company's project to comply with Sections 302 and 404:

1. Project oversight.
2. Consulting and project support.
3. Ongoing monitoring and testing.
4. Project audit.

Exhibit 7.4 summarizes these activities. The extent of the internal auditor's involvement with Sections 302 and 404 depends on the company's internal auditing function and its resources, funding, personnel qualifications, and charter. Any activities performed by internal auditors should be in compliance with the charter, professional standards, and mission of adding value to their organization's operations. The IIA's position paper suggests that internal auditors consider six factors when supporting and consulting with management to comply with Sections 302 and 404:

1. Consulting with management on internal control activities compliance does not impair the internal auditors' independence and objectivity.
2. Making key management decisions in the compliance process impairs the internal auditors' objectivity and independence.
3. Having responsibility for specific operations or participating in making or directing key management decisions impairs internal auditors' objectivity and independence.
4. The design, implementation, and drafting procedures for internal controls to comply with Sections 302 and 404 impair the internal auditor's independence and objectivity.
5. The recommendation of standards for internal controls or review of internal control procedures does not impair the internal auditors' objectivity and independence.

EXHIBIT 7.3   Section 404 Compliance

Phase/Activity	Lead Responsibility	Recommended Internal Auditor Roles
Planning		
Plan	Project sponsor	Provide advice and recommendations. Participate in project team planning.
Scope	Project team	Provide advice and recommendations. Participate in project team planning.
Execution		
Document	Line managers; and/or project team/ and/or specialists	Advise management regarding processes to be used. Perform quality assurance reviews.
Evaluation and Testing	Line managers; project team; specialists	Independently assess management's documentation and testing. Perform effectiveness testing (for highest reliance by external auditors).
Issues	Project team and line managers	Identify control gaps. Facilitate management discussions.
Corrective Action	Line managers	Perform follow-up reviews.
Monitoring Systems	Senior management	Perform follow-up reviews.
Reporting		
Management Reporting	Senior management and line managers	Facilitate determinations (to report). Provide advice.
External Audit Reporting	External auditor	Act as coordinator between management and external auditor.
Monitoring		
Ongoing Monitoring	Senior management	Perform follow-up services.
Periodic Assessment	Project team and/or line managers	Perform periodic audits.

Source: Adapted from IIA, "Internal Auditing's Role in Section 302 and 404 of the U.S. Sarbanes-Oxley Act of 2002" (Altamonte Springs, FL: IIA, May 26, 2004)

EXHIBIT 7.4 Internal Auditors' Activities Pertaining to Sections 302 and 404

Project Oversight	Consulting and Project Support	Ongoing Monitoring And Testing	Project Audit
▪ Participate on project steering committee, providing advice and recommendations to the project team and monitoring progress and direction of the project. ▪ Act as facilitator between external auditor and management	▪ Provide existing internal audit documentation for processes under scope. ▪ Advise on best practices—documentation standards, tools, and test strategies. ▪ Support management and process owner training on project and risk and control awareness. ▪ Perform quality assurance review of process documentation and key controls prior to handoff to the external auditor.	▪ Advise management regarding the design, scope, and frequency of tests to be performed. ▪ Independently is assess management and testing and assessment processes. ▪ Perform tests of management's basis for assertions. ▪ Perform tests of management's basis for assertions. ▪ Perform effectiveness testing (for highest reliance by external auditors). ▪ Aid in identifying control gaps and review management plans for correcting control gaps. ▪ Perform follow-up reviews to ascertain whether control gaps have been adequately addressed. ▪ Act as coordinator between management and the external auditor as to discussions of scope and testing plans. ▪ Participate in disclosure committee to ensure that results of ongoing internal audit activities and other examination activities, such as external regulatory examinations, are brought to the committee for disclosure consideration.	▪ Assist in ensuring that corporate initiatives are well managed and have a positive impact on an organization. This assurance role supports senior management, the audit committee, the board of directors, and other stakeholders. ▪ Use a risk-based approach in planning the many possible activities regarding project audits. Audit best practices suggest internal auditors should be involved throughout a project's life cycle—not just in postimplementation audits.

Source: Adapted from IIA, "Internal Auditing's Role in Section 302 and 404 of the U.S. Sarbanes-Oxley Act of 2002" (Altamonte Springs, FL: IIA, May 26, 2004)

6. Devoting a significant amount of internal auditors' efforts to consulting with management on Sections 302 and 404 compliance can deplete the internal auditors' resources and turn their attention and focus from other value-adding activities to achieve the organization's mission.[27]

EVALUATION OF THE INTERNAL AUDIT FUNCTION

Statement on Auditing Standards (SAS) No. 65, *The Auditor's Consideration of the Internal Audit Function in Audit Financial Statements*, provides guidance for external auditors to consider and evaluate the company's internal audit function and the work of internal auditors in determining the extent, nature, and timing of audit procedures to be performed. SAS No. 65 focuses on the use of internal auditors in the audit of financial statements. However, it provides guidance on evaluating the competence and objectivity of internal auditors. Factors that are articulated in SAS No. 65 and can be used to assess internal auditor's competence are:

- Education and professional certification.
- Professional experience and continuing education.
- Audit plans, policies, programs, and procedures.
- Supervision and review of the auditors' work.
- Practices regarding assignments.
- Quality of work paper documentation.
- Audit reports and recommendations and follow-ups.
- Evaluation of internal auditors' performance.[28]

The effectiveness of the work of internal auditors can be assessed by considering:

- Whether the scope of the work of internal auditors is appropriate to meet the audit objectives.
- Whether the audit programs and procedures are adequate in meeting audit objectives.
- The quality, completeness, and documentation of work papers, including evidence of proper supervision and review.
- Whether audit conclusions are appropriate under the circumstances.
- Whether audit reports are consistent with the audit evidence gathered and work performed.[29]

INTERNAL AUDIT OUTSOURCING

The issue of whether an internal audit function should be established internally or outsourced has not yet been fully properly addressed by regulators and standard-setting bodies. The Conference Board recommends that all public companies should have an internal audit function.[30] The established internal audit function can be either an "in-house" function or an "outsource" function performed by a public accounting firm. To improve internal audit function and internal auditors' independence, internal auditors should have a direct line of communication and reporting responsibility to the audit committee.[31]

The author suggests that all public companies, regardless of their listing status, large private companies, and not-for-profit organizations have an internally established or outsourced internal audit function. The decision whether to establish and maintain an internal audit function or outsource should be made by the company's board of directors in consultation with the audit committee, management, legal counsel, and the independent auditor. A variety of factors, including the company's size in terms of total assets, sales, number of employees, complexity of its operation, financial reporting process, geographic diversity of its operations, enterprise risk management and governance process, and availability of required financial and human capital, should be considered in deciding whether to outsource the internal audit function.

SOX prohibits independent auditors from providing certain internal auditing outsourcing services to public companies contemporaneously with audit services. This does not mean that public accounting firms are not permitted to provide internal audit outsourcing services to public companies; it simply means they cannot perform audit services on financial statements and internal audit outsourcing to the same public client for the same fiscal year. Although independent auditors are not prohibited from performing internal auditing outsourcing services for nonpublic company audit clients, it is still not considered a best practice to do so due to conflict of interest concerns. The SEC, in implementing the provisions of internal audit outsourcing of SOX, issued release Nos. 33-8183 and 34-47265 to clarify the types of internal audit services that are prohibited.[32]

In general, SEC rules prohibit internal audit services that may be subject to audit procedures throughout the audit of a client's financial statements, such as the audit client's internal controls, accounting systems, auditing systems, or financial statements. The SEC rule permits internal audit outsourcing to the client's independent auditor in two areas:

1. Operational internal audits that are not related to the internal accounting controls, financial systems, or financial statements.
2. Nonrecurring assessment of discrete items or other programs unrelated to outsourcing of the internal audit function.

SUMMARY

Internal auditing is regarded as a value-added service that assists in improving the organization's governance, operations, risk management, internal controls, and financial reporting. Thus, internal auditors' competence, objectivity, and independence from management are important determinants of their effectiveness in providing a variety of consulting and assurance services to their organization. The audit committee should be directly responsible for the appointment, compensation, evaluation, promotion, and dismissal of the company's internal audit director, commonly referred to as the chief audit executive. The CAE should have unrestricted access to the audit committee and ultimately be held accountable to the audit committee. The audit committee should participate in the development of the internal audit department's goals and mission, oversee the work of internal auditors and their audit and recommendations, and assess how management is responding to their recommendations.

In summary, internal auditors can play an important role in corporate governance through their active participation in: (1) promoting corporate governance best practices and appropriate ethics and culture within their organizations; (2) communicating important corporate governance issues and practices to their organization's officers and directors; (3) enforcing compliance with applicable laws, rules, regulations, and standards throughout their organization; (4) preventing, detecting, and correcting governance risks, internal control deficiencies, and financial reporting irregularities and fraud; and (5) serving as a vital information source to their organization's board of directors, particularly the audit committee.

NOTES

1. New York Stock Exchange. 2004. Section 303a of Corporate Governance Listing Standards. Available at: www.nyse.com/pdfs/Section303A_final_rules.pdf.
2. PricewaterhouseCoopers. 2006. PwC's state of internal audit profession study: Internal audit post-Sarbanes-Oxley (May 1). Available at: www.pwcglobal.com/extweb/pwcpublications.nsf/docid/acfafd390978cb2785257147005ef9b6.
3. Institute of Internal Auditors. 2002. Recommendations for improving corporate governance: A position paper presented by the IIA to the U.S. Congress (April 8). Available at: www.theiia.org/ecm/guide_pc.fm?doc_id=3602.
4. PricewaterhouseCoopers. 2006. How quality assurance review can strengthen the strategic value of internal auditing. Available at: www.pwc.com/extweb/pwcpublications.nsf/docid/b838f2 da401647 d785257108004a964e.
5. Tarr, R. 2002. Built to last. *Internal Auditor.* (December): 29–33.
6. Public Company Accounting Oversight Board. 2004. Auditing Standard No. 2: *An Audit of Internal Control over Financial Reporting Performed in Conjunction with an Audit of Financial Statements* (Paragraph 17). Available at: www.pcaob.org/standards.
7. Foreign Corrupt Practices Act. 1977. Available at: www.usdoj.gov/criminal/fraud/fcpa.html.
8. Rezaee, Z., and G. H. Lander. 1991. The internal auditor-education and training: The partnership concept. *Managerial Auditing Journal* 6 (2): 4–8.
9. National Commission on Fraudulent Financial Reporting, The Treadway Commission, COSO. 1987. *Report on the National Commission on Fraudulent Financial Reporting.* New York: AICPA.
10. Institute of Internal Auditors. 1947. Definition of internal auditing. Available at: www.theiia.org/index.cfm?doc_id=123.
11. Ibid, 1981.

12. Ibid, 1999.
13. PricewaterhouseCoopers. 2006. PwC's 2006 State of the internal audit profession study: Continuous auditing gains momentum (June 27). Available at: www.pwc.com.
14. Public Company Accounting Oversight Board. 2004. Auditing Standard No. 2.
15. PricewaterhouseCoopers. 2005. How to rebalance internal audit priorities in the Sarbanes-Oxley era. (May 25). Available at: www.pwcglobal.com/ extweb/pwc publications.nsf/docid/07 d11e01f3a2 d1c785256fd30004a331.
16. PricewaterhouseCoopers. 2004. Internal audit alert survey. (November 3). Available at: www.pwc.com/Extweb/manissue.nsf/2e7e9636c6b92859852565 e00073 d2fd/23fdb9805fee7ec085256cd20062978f/$FILE/SurveyResults.pdf.
17. PricewaterhouseCoopers. 2005. How to rebalance internal audit priorities.
18. Ibid.
19. PricewaterhouseCoopers. 2006. PwC's state of the internal control profession study: Internal audit post-Sarbanes-Oxley (May 1).
20. Institute of Internal Auditors. 2005. Professional practices framework. Available at: www.theiia.org/index.cfm?doc_id=1625.
21. Ibid.
22. Institute of Internal Auditors. 2006. The common body of knowledge (CBOK). Available at: www.theIIA.org.
23. Institute of Internal Auditors. 2006. Internal auditing education partnership continuum. Available at: www.theiia.org/academic.
24. Institute of Internal Auditors. 2004. Internal auditing's role in Section 302 and 404 of the U.S. Sarbanes-Oxley Act of 2002. Position Paper. (May 26). Altamonte Springs, FL: IIA.
25. Ibid.
26. Ibid.
27. Ibid.
28. American Institute of Certified Public Accountants. Statement on Auditing Standards (SAS) No. 65. Available at: www.aicpa.org.
29. Ibid.
30. Conference Board. 2003. Commission on Public Trust and Private Enterprise; Part 3: Auditing and accounting. (January). Available at: www.conference board.org/pdf_free/SR-03-04.pdf.
31. Ibid.
32. Securities and Exchange Commission. 2003. Strengthening the Commission's requirements regarding auditor independence. Available at: www.sec.gov/rules/ final/33-8183.htm.

CHAPTER 8

Advisory Function

INTRODUCTION

The advisory function of corporate governance is assumed by professional advisors, including legal counsel, financial analysts, and investment bankers, who normally assist companies in evaluating the legal, financial, and tax consequences of business transactions. Professional advisors participate in corporate governance by providing advisory services to the company's board of directors and management. Management traditionally has engaged professional advisors for the structure, measurement, recognition, and preparation of public filing and disclosures of business transactions. In discharging their fiduciary duty effectively, the boards of directors, particularly outside directors, rely on their advisors (legal counsel, financial advisors, and other consultants). While these advisors are hired by the company and its management, their independence can directly influence director independence and effectiveness. This chapter presents the advisory function of corporate governance normally provided by outside legal counsel, external financial advisors, and investment banks.

Relevance of the Advisory Function

The importance of the role of advisors in corporate governance is well documented in several authoritative sources. The American Law Institute (ALI) states: "The [outside] directors should be entitled to retain legal counsel, accountants, or other experts, at the corporation's expense, to advise them on problems arising in the exercise of their functions."[1] Several provisions of Sarbanes-Oxley Act of 2002 (SOX) deal with the relevance of advisors. For example, Section 301 of SOX states that audit committees must have the authority to engage independent counsel and other advisors to carry out their duties.[2] Section 307 of SOX directs the Securities and Exchange Commission (SEC) to adopt rules "requiring an attorney to report evidence of a material violation of securities laws or breach of fiduciary duty."[3] SOX requires that the audit committee be provided with funding to hire advisors as deemed necessary, including legal counsel and financial advisors.[4] This funding should be provided to the entire board of directors. Starting in 2007, the SEC will require public companies to identify their paid experts in public reports.[5] Thus, these consultants have attempted to force their clients to agree to: (1) limit any legal forces or financial damages they would have to pay in a lawsuit; (2) indemnify them for legal costs and damages; and (3) cap damages at the amount of fees they earn for the provided consulting services.[6]

LEGAL COUNSEL

It should be noted that the role of attorneys as legal counsel addressed in this chapter concerns attorneys "appearing and practicing" before the SEC. In a legal setting, the attorneys' main role is as advocates who represent their client's best interest. Nonetheless, as explained in this section, SEC rules require corporate legal counsel to report violations of securities laws, breaches of fiduciary duty, or similar violations by the company to the chief legal counsel or the chief executive officer (CEO) and eventually to the board of directors. Traditionally, the role of outside legal counsel in the corporate governance process has been to provide independent counsel and advice to company management on a variety of legal matters, including working closely with in-house legal staff to assist with legal compliance matters. Thus, an outside counsel's role in the corporate governance process is that of an outside gatekeeper to promote legal corporate behavior and to protect the interests of the company. Although lawyers (in-house or outside legal counsel) are hired to represent their client's (company) interests, they work with and for client's executives and may be subject to pressure to conform their advice and behavior to the interests of executives. To the extent that corporate executives engage in fraudulent activities, the lawyer's role as gatekeeper can be compromised. In such a case, the company's board of directors should hire outside counsel to investigate allegations of wrongdoing by executives. Typically, however, the general counsel hires outside counsel to help perform legal work related to day-to-day operations to provide additional expertise to supplement its internal legal staff.

A seemingly controversial provision of SOX addresses lawyers' potential conflicts of interest and SEC-issued rules requiring legal counsel practicing before the Commission or representing public companies to report violations of securities laws, reporting up and out of the organization if necessary.[7] A number of legal scholars and organizations, including the American Bar Association (ABA), have written on this matter, expressing concern that this provision erodes the attorney-client privilege and compromises counsel's ability to represent the interests of the client. SOX, by engaging lawyers in policing corporate malfeasance and misconduct and requiring them to report such misconduct, makes the lawyer an important gatekeeper within the corporate governance structure. As an advisor to management, legal counsel plays an important role in identifying financial reporting risks for management and any inaccuracies, misleading information, or noncompliance with applicable laws, rules, and regulations in financial disclosures to investors.

Legal counsel plays an important role in presenting and analyzing relevant information as well as providing valuable advice to the company's board of directors and its committees, officers, and employees in order to discharge their assigned responsibilities effectively. Controversially, Enron's outside legal counsel played a role in advising its board of directors to waive its code of ethics in approving the self-dealing transactions involving the special purpose entities created to hide liabilities and exaggerate earnings.[8] Indeed, the Task Force of the ABA "believes that a prudent corporate governance program should call upon lawyers—notably the corporation's general counsel—to assist in the design and maintenance of the corporation's procedures for promoting legal compliance."[9] Corporate legal counsel, including inside lawyers hired and outside lawyers retained by the company, should coordinate their activities and serve as:

- Counselors to the board, its committees, and directors in effectively carrying out their oversight responsibilities and fiduciary duty.
- Advisors to management in participating in the negotiation, development, process, and documentation of the company's material business transactions.
- Gatekeepers to ensure compliance with all applicable laws, regulations, rules, and standards.
- Enforcement agents to evaluate risks associated with legal issues and to prevent violation of securities, laws, and engagement in corporate malfeasance, misconduct, and fraudulent activities.

Outside counsel should represent the best interests of the company and not necessarily the best interests of any individual executive, particularly when those interests may conflict. However, in reality, their objectivity may be called into question over time if management gives them repeat business. The objectivity and integrity of outside counsel is important to the effectiveness of corporate governance. One example of apparent lack of outside counsel objectivity is the involvement of legal counsel in the board scandal at Hewlett-Packard (H-P).[10] The company's outside legal counsel hired a private investigator in the probe involving the use of a practice called pretexting to obtain the phone records of the company's directors and nine reporters who cover the company.[11] Many consider this practice of seeking phone records as criminal activity. California attorney General Bill Lockyer, on October 4, 2006, filed criminal charges against former H-P chairwoman Patricia Dunn, former chief ethics lawyer Kevin Hunsaker, and three outside investigators who helped the company to discover which of its directors might be leaking information to the press.[12] To promote a culture of compliance within the company, a major role of outside legal counsel is to bring legal compliance issues to the attention of the appropriate authorities in the company, including management, general counsel, the chief compliance officer or its equivalent, the audit committee, or a committee of independent directors.

The Task Force of the ABA suggests that: the company's board of directors should establish a practice of regular and executive session meetings between the general counsel and a committee of independent directors; and the retained outside lawyers should communicate with the employed inside lawyers or general counsel and advise them of material violations or potential violations of applicable laws, regulations, rules, and standards by the company or of material or potential violations of duties to the company.[13] This requires proper communication between general counsel and independent directors as well as between outside counsel and general counsel.

The review of recent reported financial scandals reveals that lawyers played a role by either facilitating management impropriety or not reporting violations of securities laws. Indeed, Powers' report of Enron's internal investigation states there "was an absence of forceful and effective oversight by in-house counsel and objective and critical professional advice by outside counsel."[14] The general understanding is that when management and accountants are attempting to break the law, it is the professional responsibility of legal counsel to detect and prevent the wrongdoing rather than act as facilitators and enablers of wrongdoings. Former SEC chairman William Donaldson raised concerns regarding lawyers not performing their duties as gatekeepers, stating: "This is an area where I have been disappointed by the contribution of some lawyers, who appear in at least some cases to devise their own narrow interpretations of the rules while disclosing as little as possible, rather than to seek helpful disclosure for investors."[15]

Former Enron lawyers elaborate on the lessons that all in-house lawyers could learn from their experiences:[16]

- *Little central control.* The legal department was decentralized in the sense that most of the company's lawyers work for the business unit with little, if any, central control from the company's general counsel.
- *Lawyer's pay.* Attorney fees were effectively determined by business executives who then controlled and provided incentives for lawyers to participate in the gamesmanship as reckless entrepreneurs.
- *Corporate culture.* A company culture of hands-on management and effective governance is more important than legislation (SOX) in promoting an ethical workplace as Enron's lawyers were among the best the profession had to offer.
- *Proper oversight.* There was no oversight by the general counsel. Enron's lawyers were insulated in silos, and more than half worked directly with and were compensated and controlled by business units.
- *Direction from general counsel.* Lack of direction from the top (e.g., general counsel) was a serious flaw in Enron's legal department, and lawyers were presumed to bend to the needs of business executives.

Responsibilities of Legal Counsel

Legal counsel normally provides legal advice to the company's board of directors and management. The role of corporate legal counsel in corporate governance has received significant attention in the post-Enron era. The ever-increasing importance of compliance and legal function of corporate governance in the post-SOX era has also contributed to a continuous increase in in-house attorney pay. In 2006 the base salaries for in-house legal counsel increased by 9.5 percent and bonuses rose by as much as 71 percent.[17] The three primary roles of corporate legal counsel are to:

1. Ensure compliance with all applicable laws, regulations, and rules.
2. Provide legal advice and analysis regarding legal compliance issues in an ethical manner.
3. Communicate material potential or ongoing violations of law and breaches of fiduciary duties to the general counsel and independent directors or a committee of independent directors.

Outside legal counsel objectivity and integrity are important when it comes to corporate governance. Larry W. Sonsini, whose law firm represents about half of the 32 Silicon Valley companies, is under intense scrutiny because of his involvement in both H-P and backdated options scandals.[18] Sonsini's role as corporate legal counsel was influenced by conflicts of interest caused by his multiple roles in corporate affairs as a board member (Brocade's board) and his receipt of stock options from his legal clients. The wave of stock option backdating practices has caused at least 12 in-house lawyers or general counsels at more than 200 implicated companies to leave their jobs, have their contract terminated, or face criminal charges.[19] As rightly stated by Fred Krebs, president of the Association of Corporate Counsel, "If something goes wrong in an organization, the Securities and Exchange Commission looks at the general counsel and says if you didn't stop it, you're at fault."[20]

Legal counsel—either an in-house or outside lawyer—should:

- Serve the interests of the company rather than the personal interests of its directors, officers, employees, shareholders, or other stakeholders.
- Be responsible for implementing an effective legal compliance system under the oversight of the company's board of directors to ensure compliance with all applicable laws, regulations, rules, and standards.
- Advise the board of directors or a board committee on special investigations and report directly to them.
- Have appropriate rules of conduct in conformity with the SEC and the state attorney requirements and effectively enforce these rules.
- Be aware of adherence to their professional codes of ethics and responsibilities in their representation of public companies.

SEC Rules

The SEC issues rules that govern the standards of professional conduct for attorneys appearing and practicing before the Commission on behalf of issuers. These rules require that:

- Attorneys report material violations of federal law and state security law, breaches of fiduciary duty, and other similar violations of state and federal laws.
- Actions be taken by the company when an attorney reports an alleged material violation of state or federal securities laws.
- Reporting up the ladder within the company or, alternatively, to the established qualified legal compliance committee be implemented.[21]

When an attorney, either the company's in-house counsel or outside counsel, becomes aware of such violations by the company or any of its officers, directors, employees, or agents, the attorney must immediately report the matter to the company's chief legal officer, both the chief legal officer (CLO) and chief executive officer (CEO), unless the CEO is involved, or the company's qualified legal compliance committee (if it exists). Upon unsatisfactory responses from either the CEO or chief legal officer, the reporting attorney ultimately may report the violations to the audit committee or another committee consisting solely of independent directors.

The company's CLO must make necessary inquiries to determine if the alleged material violation has occurred or is likely to occur, take appropriate actions upon further evidence about such violations, or otherwise advise the reporting attorney that such violations did not occur. Upon receiving the appropriate response within a reasonable time period, no further action is required by the reporting attorney. If the reporting attorney does not receive a satisfactory response within a reasonable time period, then the attorney must explain the concerns to the CLO and chief financial officer (CFO) (or their equivalents) and then take the matter up the ladder in these four steps:

1. First, to the company's audit committee.
2. If there is no audit committee, then to another committee of the company's board of directors composed of solely independent directors.
3. If there is no such committee, then to the company's board of directors.
4. If the reporting attorney was discharged from employment or a retainer as a result of making such as violation report, the attorney may notify the company's board of directors or its representative on the audit committee.

If the company designates a qualified legal compliance committee (usually composed solely of independent directors), the reporting attorney's only responsibility is to report the alleged material violations to this committee without further follow-up. Alternatively, the reporting attorney can report the violations initially to the company's chief legal counsel, who forwards that report to the pre-established qualified legal compliance committee and notifies the reporting attorney without further obligation to pursue the matter.

A qualified legal compliance committee, under the SEC rule, is a committee that:

- Is comprised of at least one member of the company's audit committee and two or more independent directors.
- Has adopted written procedures for the confidential receipt, retention, and consideration of alleged reported violation(s).
- Has been given proper authority and responsibility to:
  - Inform the CLO and CEO, if necessary, of any report of material violations.
  - Decide whether an investigation is warranted based on the alleged reported material violations, inform the audit committee or the board of directors, initiate an investigation report, and recommend results to the audit committee and/or the board of directors for taking remedial measures in response to the investigated violations.
  - Take, by majority vote, the necessary action to correct the violations, including notifying the SEC if the company fails to implement the recommended remedial measures.[22]

Attorney-Client Privilege

The corporate attorney-client privilege has been under scrutiny in the post-Enron era and, in many cases, has been eroded in corporate criminal investigations. The United States Sentencing Commission modified the Federal Sentencing Guidelines in 2004 for corporations convicted of federal offenses, including the provision that corporations could waive attorney-client privilege to earn credit for cooperation with government.[23] Anecdotal evidence (e.g., Association of Corporate Counsel, the U.S. Chamber of Commerce, and the Business Roundtable) indicates that a majority of the outside counsel has been pressured to waive the privilege in connection with government investigation.[24] The U.S. Chamber of Commerce has raised concerns about two policies of the Justice Department regarding pressuring companies to reveal confidential communications with their lawyers and demanding companies not pay legal fees for their employees who are under investigation.[25] Thus, on April 5, 2006, the Sentencing Commission voted to eliminate language from the Sentencing Guidelines that requires corporations to waive the attorney-client privilege and work production protections to earn sentencing credit for cooperation with a government investigation.[26] However, government attorneys and agents may seek waivers, and the prosecutor may consider the corporation's willingness to waive attorney-client and work product protection and to disclose the complete results of its internal investigation.[27]

The attorney-client privilege relation has long been accepted in the legal system. However, federal authorities deemed waiver of this privilege "cooperation" with government investigations or substantial tax positions.[28] Four recent developments are intended to ensure that attorney-client privilege is preserved.[29] First, in March 2006, the U.S. Sentencing Commission amended its sentencing guidelines to remove waiver of attorney-client privilege as a condition of corporation with regulatory authorities. Second, in June 2006, U.S. District Court Judge Lewis Kaplan ruled that the Department of Justice pressure on companies to withhold paying legal fees for employees under investigation was unconstitutional, a ruling that was viewed by many as a support for preservation of attorney-client privilege. Third, in August 2006, the ABA released its recommendations aimed at: (1) reducing government pressure to use the waiver as part of cooperation in governance investigations; and (2) requesting that the SEC, Public Company Accounting Oversight Board (PCAOB), American Institute of Certified Public Accountants (AICPA), and others adopt standards, policies, procedures, and practices to ensure that attorney-client privilege is preserved in connection with the audit process. Finally, on December 12, 2006, the Department of Justice revised its guidance that establishes approval requirements for federal prosecutors before they can request waivers of attorney-client privileges.

In gathering sufficient competent evidence, auditors may ask their clients to provide them with privileged documents. If clients refuse to provide such documents, the auditors may consider such denial as scope limitation, causing them to either withhold their reports or issue an other-than-unqualified opinion. The release of privileged documents, however, not only makes these documents obtainable by others, but also jeopardizes the attorney-client privilege. The author believes that it is most appropriate for auditors to request whatever information, including privileged documents, they deem appropriate and necessary to reach a conclusion about whether the financial statements are fairly presented. If the clients refuse to provide such information or their attorneys withhold such information from the auditors, these matters should be noted in the audit report to investors. Investors, in turn, should consider such matters when assessing the financial information in the published audited financial statements. Auditors should realize that when misleading audited financial statements are released, it is the auditor, not the clients' legal counsel, who pays the price in reputational damage.

FINANCIAL AND INVESTMENT ADVISORS

Financial and investment advisors, through their discretionary authority to manage investments on behalf of their clients (investors) and participate in proxy voting, play an important role in corporate governance. Investment advisors are required to exercise due diligence, maintain objectivity, and service their clients to the best of their ability. When the advisors have personal or business relationships with the company, its directors, or participants in proxy contents, they may have conflicts of interest. The SEC, in addressing this potential or actual conflict of interest, has adopted a rule that requires investment advisors, in exercising their voting authorities, to act in the best interest of their clients by providing adequate information to them. SEC rules require investment advisors to:

- Establish policies and procedures to guide their proxy voting in the best interest of their clients.
- Disclose adequate information regarding the established policies and procedures and how they have voted their proxies.
- Maintain proper records regarding proxy voting.[30]

The SEC rule requires:

- All investment companies, including mutual funds, to disclose the policies and procedures they use to decide how to vote proxies related to their portfolio.
- Funds to disclose how they voted proxies, either on their Web site or by request, and to file such information with the SEC.
- Funds to let their shareholders know in both their annual and semiannual reports where to go to find the disclosed information.[31]

SECURITIES ANALYSTS

Efficiency, effectiveness, and integrity of capital markets depend on the reliability, quality, and transparency of information received from corporations, securities analysts, and others. Investors need reliable and transparent information to make rational investment decisions and to allocate their capital properly. Securities analysts who cover corporations can play an important role in providing relevant and reliable information to investors. Thus, their objectivity, independence, and integrity are crucial as financial advisors. Unlike other professionals, such as accountants and lawyers who are either hired or retained by companies, securities analysts are hired by brokerage firms to analyze the financial performance of the corporations they follow, assess the quality of the company as an investment, and make recommendations for investment opportunities based on their analysis. In this regard, securities analysts, by influencing investors' investment decisions, can directly or indirectly affect the quality and quantity of financial information that companies disseminate to the public.

Analysts are regulated by the National Association of Securities Dealers (NASD) and its rules designed to prevent bad practices, and they are also subject to the broker/dealer rules issued by the SEC and national stock exchanges. Nonetheless, like accountants and lawyers, securities analysts have been subject to inappropriate pressures and provided with lucrative financial incentives to be biased, rather than objective, toward corporations they follow, particularly when they are associated with firms that also do investment banking and bring in millions of dollars in fees to the investment banking firm each year. Many investors, particularly individual investors, rely on recommendations of analysts without understanding the circumstances under which such recommendations are made. The NASD issued a guide to understanding securities analyst recommendations.[32] The guide addresses two important issues pertaining to analyst recommendations.

1. Analysts' ratings often do not have clear and standardized meanings in the sense that the term "underperformance" means different things to different analysts.
2. Potential conflicts of interest exist and often are not disclosed and therefore are not taken into consideration by investors in assessing the reliability and usefulness of analyst recommendations. For example, investors should consider who the analysts are working for (e.g., large financial firms, institutional money managers) and whether such working relationships can put pressure on the analysts to skew their reports in certain directions.

Role of Securities Analysts

Securities analysts play an important role in recommending stock. During the economic and market boom of the late 1990s, analysts' objective and skeptical mental attitudes became irrelevant. The prudent, objective, skeptical, and diligent analysts who predicted reasonable earnings growth and stock appreciation were ignored—when they could be found. The perception was that the analysts' research was not influenced by investment banking conflicts of interests. However, recent reported financial scandals have raised significant concerns regarding the conflicts faced by research analysts. Popular press and academic research allude to analysts' conflicts of interest in the sense that:

- While the Nasdaq Composite Index was dropping by more than 60 percent, less than 1 percent of analysts' recommendations were to "sell."
- About 99 percent of all research sell-side analysts' recommendations in 2000 were to "hold," "buy," or "strong buy."
- Companies often withheld business from firms whose analysts issued unfavorable reports.[33]

Lawmakers' (Congress) and regulators' concerns have been that investors, particularly small investors, may not know about research analysts' conflicts of interest in situations when: (1) analysts' compensation and other payments may be determined based on the promotion and achievement of investment banking businesses each year; and (2) favorable analysts' research reports could be used to market and sell the investment banking services. Thus, activities in investment banking firms' research departments have come under increasing scrutiny. In May 2002 the SEC approved the proposed NASD Rule 2711 and the amended New York Stock Exchange (NYSE) Rule 472 designed to manage, monitor, and disclose research analysts' conflicts of interest in connection with research reports on equity securities and public appearance.

Section 501 of SOX directs the SEC to issue rules addressing securities analyst conflicts of interest issues. The SEC, on February 20, 2003, adopted a Final rule, Regulation Analyst Certification (Regulation AC).[34] SOX and Regulation AC address concerns regarding the independence of research from investment banking and the analysts' actual or perceived conflicts of interest. Regulation AC requires brokers, dealers, and certain other associated persons to include in their research reports certification by the research analyst that: (1) the views expressed in the research reports accurately reflect the analyst's personal views; and (2) whether the analyst received any compensation in connection with the expressed recommendations or views and, if so, the source, amount, and purpose of such compensation, along with the possible influence of such compensation on the research report.

The distribution by a broker/dealer of any report that does not contain such certifications is a violation of Regulation AC. Furthermore, Regulation AC requires that brokers, dealers, and certain other associated persons obtain from research analysts certifications, so that: (1) the views expressed in all public appearances during the prior calendar quarter accurately reflect the analysts' personal views; and (2) no part of such analysts' compensation is connected to any specific recommendations or views expressed in any public appearances during the prior calendar quarter. Research analysts who are not able to provide these required certifications must present notice of such failure to their examining authorities. Brokers and dealers must disclose such failures in any research reports provided by the analysts for 120 days following such notification and maintain proper related records for a period of at least three years.

Ethical Guidelines for Securities Analysts

Chartered Financial Analysts (CFA) Institute, formerly known as the Association for Investment Management and Research (AIMR), and the National Investor Relations Institute have jointly proposed ethical guidelines governing the relationship between public companies and their securities analysts.[35] The proposed guidelines require analysts to refrain from any conflicts of interest with companies they cover, conduct thorough and diligent research, and be objective and unbiased in their research reports. Corporations must not:

- Discriminate among analysts based on their research and recommendations.
- Withhold relevant information from analysts or deny their access to the company's representatives in order to influence their research.
- Exert pressure on analysts vis-à-vis other business relationships, including investment banking.

The proposed guidelines address the fact that analyst-compensated research is appropriate when: (1) companies engage qualified, competent, and objective analysts; and (2) analysts fully disclose in their research report the nature and extent of the compensation received. The guidelines provided five standards of best practices governing the relationship between corporations and their analysts, which are summarized in the next sections.[36]

Standard I: Information Flow

Analysts, investors, and public companies must not disrupt or threaten to disrupt the free flow of information among corporations, investors, and analysts in any matters that inappropriately influence the behavior of those with whom they are communicating.

Standard II: Analyst Conduct

Analysts must conduct their research and recommendations with utmost objectivity, independence, fairness, and unbiased opinion by:

1. Issuing objective research and recommendations that have a reasonable bias and sufficient evidence supported by thorough, diligent, and appropriate investigation and research.
2. Differentiating between fact and opinion.
3. Ensuring the transparency and completeness of the information presented in their reports.
4. Engaging in no threat to use their research reports or recommendations in order to improve their relationship with the corporations they cover.

Standard III: Corporate Communications and Access

Corporations must not:

1. Discriminate among recipients the information disclosed based on the recipient's prior research, recommendations, earnings estimates, conclusions, and opinions.
2. Deny or threaten to deny information or access to company representatives in order to influence the research recommendations or actions of investment professionals and analysts.
3. Influence the research, recommendations, or actions of analysts or investment professionals by exerting pressure through other business relationships.

Corporations must provide access to the company's management, officers, and other knowledgeable officials to qualified persons or entities, including analysts and investors, and establish and adhere to policies that address how the company defines access, prioritizes requests for access or information, and responds to each request, and under what circumstances and to whom different types or levels of access will be granted.

Standard IV: Issuer-Paid Research Reports

Analysts who can engage in research paid by corporations must:

1. Accept only accept cash compensation for their work.
2. Not accept any compensation contingent on the contract or conclusions of the research or the potential effect on share price.
3. Disclose in the report the nature and the extent of compensation received from drafting the report, and, in addition, the nature and extent of any personal, professional, or financial relationship they, their firm, or its parent subsidiaries, agents, or trading entities may have with the company.
4. Disclose their credentials, including professional designations and experiences, and any matters that could reasonably be perceived to impair their objectivity.
5. Certify that the analysis or recommendations in the report represent the opinion of the author or authors.

The company that hires analysts to produce research and report must:

1. Engage analysts who are qualified and committed to produce objective and thorough research, including disclosure of any matters that could reasonably be expected to impair their objectivity.
2. Pay for the research in cash and only in a manner that does not influence the content and conclusions of the research.
3. Not attempt explicitly or implicitly to influence the research, recommendations, or behavior of analysts to produce research or recommendations favorable to the company.
4. Ensure that all of the disclosures required by the analyst are fully included in the research report that is published or distributed by the company.

Objectivity of Post-SOX Securities Analysts

Analysts' objectivity and performance have improved in the post-SOX era. However, there is still much more room for improvement in some areas to ensure that analysts maintain their objectivity and relevance. Sudden and unexpected departures of executives have been viewed by investors as a warning signal for corporate financial difficulty and a clear warning to sell the stocks. For example, departures of Jeffrey K. Skilling, Enron's former CEO, and of Todd S. Nelson, chairman, president, and CEO of the Apollo Group, caused a substantial decrease in stock prices and significant losses of market capitalization. However, many analysts in high-profile Wall Street firms have advised investors not to worry as these departures do not change the fundamental health and outlook of the company; in many cases analysts advise investors of a buying opportunity as they think the company can be fixed. They often rely solely on the company's earnings releases and personal discussion with its executives rather than investigating the reasons for material and sudden changes or events at the company (e.g., departure of top executives, change audit firm) by examining regulatory filings (e.g., Form 8-K), and their judgment is often biased by their research recommendations.

It appears that even in the post-SOX era, "too many [analysts] still act as mouth-pieces for corporate management. Sell recommendations and straight talk from these people remains all to rare. If analysts don't change their all-rosy-all-the-time outlook, irrelevance will be their reward."[37] Analysts' perceived lack of objectivity can also have a negative impact on brokerage firm research as institutional investors will continue to spend less on analysts' research and "investors will do their own analysis and rely more heavily on work done by independent research shops."[38] Indeed, a study predicts that "Wall Street firms' share of the equity research market would decline to 33 percent by 2009 from 58 percent in 2004," which amounts to a loss of about $1.5 billion.[39]

INVESTMENT BANKS

More than 90 million Americans invest in financial markets, and investment banks usually assist public companies in raising capital funds and arranging their debt financing. Thus, investment banks may play a role in corporate governance by advising companies on their financing and investment decisions and investors on the effective allocation of their investment. Morgan Stanley agreed to pay $186.7 million to settle charges for knowing that Parmalat was failing and yet helping the company to raise billions of dollars in capital worldwide. For example, they arranged a $362 million bond for Parmalat in June 2003, six months prior to its $18 billion fraud, which was discovered in December 2003.

Investment banks have been criticized for their involvement in reported financial scandals. Several investment banks that once were the major players in providing financial advice and financing Enron's operations, including J. P. Morgan, Chase and Co., Toronto-Dominion Bank, Citigroup Inc., Deutsche Bank, AIG, Merrill Lynch and Co., Barclays PLC, and Credit Suisse Group, are now being sued by Enron for helping it hide liabilities and inflate earnings. Enron filed lawsuits against these banks, contending that they could have prevented the company's collapse if they had not "aided and abetted fraud," and is now settling its suits with them. For example, J. P. Morgan and Chase & Co. paid $350 million in cash and dropped $660 million in claims against the company. Toronto-Dominion paid $60 million in cash and dropped $60 million of its claims. These investment banks also settled several billion dollars with Enron shareholders, some paying a total of $8.11 billion in settlements for helping Enron's executives commit fraud. Exhibit 8.1 provides a summary of these settlements.

EXHIBIT 8.1 Enron Settlements by Investment Bankers

Date	Bank	Amount	Description
August 2005	J. P. Morgan	$350 million	Agreed to pay to Enron to settle claims for helping management commit fraud.
August 2005	Toronto-Dominion	$130 million	Agreed to pay Enron $70 million and its shareholders and creditors to settle a lawsuit alleging helping management defraud investors.
July 2005	Canadian Imperial Bank of Commerce	$2.4 billion to investors; $274 million to Enron	Agreed to pay Enron and its shareholders and creditors to settle lawsuits alleging helping management to defraud investors.
June 2005	Citigroup	$2.0 billion	Settlement over the sale of stock and bonds before the Enron's collapse.
June 2005	J. P. Morgan	$2.2 billion	Agreed to pay to settle a class-action lawsuit filed by Enron's investors.
November 2004	Lehman Brothers	$222.5 million	Agreed to pay investors for participating in sale of Enron notes shortly before its bankruptcy proceedings.
July 2004	Bank of America	$69 million	Agreed to pay investors for their losses related to Enron's collapse.
December 2003	Canadian Imperial Bank of Commerce	$80 million	Agreed to pay to SEC civil charges for helping Enron manipulate its financial statements.
July 2003	Citigroup, J. P. Morgan	$305 million	Agreed to pay for financial deals related to loans and trades the banks made with Enron and Dynegy.
February 2003	Merrill Lynch	$80 million	Agreed to pay to settle with regulators to resolve civil charges for allegedly helping Enron fraudulently overstate earnings.
February 2003–August 2005	All of Enron's assisted investment banks	$8.11 billion	Settlements by investment banks as of August 16, 2005.

Source: "Billions in Enron Settlements," *Wall Street Journal*, August 6, 2005. Available at: http://online.wsj.com/article/0,,BS111847500600 5629,00.html.

EXHIBIT 8.2 Revenues, Compensations, and Bonuses of the Five Biggest Securities Firms in the United States in 2006

	Firm				
	(Figures are in billions except for percentages and averages)				
	Goldman	Morgan	Merill	Lehman	Bear
Total Revenue	$35.7	$33.6	$32.50	$17.4	$9.00
Comp/Revenue	47.4%	41.80%	49.50%	50.1%	48.80%
Total Comp	$16.9	$14.0	$16.10	$8.7	$4.40
Bonus Pool	$10.20	$8.4	$9.7	$5.2	$2.60
Employees	25,647	54,349	55,300	24,775	13,000
Average Comp	$658,946	$257,594	$291,139	$351,160	$338,462
Average Bonus	$397,707	$154,556	$174,683	$210,696	$203,077

Source: Harper, C. 2006. "Bonus Pay for Wall Street Big Five Surges to Record $36 Billion," Bloomberg News (November 6)

In the post-SOX era, investment banks and the major brokerage firms have grown rapidly and generated record revenue. Exhibit 8.2 shows the estimated revenue, compensation and benefits (bonus), number of employees, and average bonuses for each of the five biggest U.S. Securities firms in 2006. These firms, Goldman Sachs Group Inc., Bear Stearns Co., Morgan Stanley, Lehman Brothers Holdings Inc., and Merrill Lynch & Co., are expected to reward their 173,000 employees with $36 billion of bonuses in 2006 which is up 30 percent from 2005.[40] These statistics suggest the importance and relevance of investment banks in the economy and its capital markets as well as the important role they play in corporate governance in the post-SOX period.

SUMMARY

Professional advisors, such as legal counsel, financial advisors, and investment banks, assist public companies in the determination and execution of business transactions and in the assessment of their risk, legal, and financial consequences. By virtue of their associations with public companies, professional advisors can influence corporate governance and financial reports. The existence of information asymmetry between management and outside directors demands that the directors rely on advice received from their advisors in overseeing and monitoring management plans, actions, and performance. Legal counsel assists companies to comply with applicable laws, rules, and regulations and often advises them in structuring business transactions to ensure full disclosure and compliance with accounting standards. By providing financial advice to corporations, their directors, officers, and other key personnel, and also by providing coverage and stock recommendations, financial analysts and investment bankers can have significant influence on corporate governance.

NOTES

1. American Law Institute. 1994. Principles of corporate governance: Analysis and recommendations. Section 3.04. Available at: www.ali.org/ali/A459_CorpGov_Brochure.pdf.
2. Sarbanes-Oxley Act of 2002 (SOX). Public Law No. 107-204, Section 301. Available at: www.sarbanes-oxley.com/section.php?level=2&pub_id=SEC-Rules&chap_id=SEC12.
3. Sarbanes-Oxley Act of 2002. Public Law No. 107-204, Section 307. Available at: www.sarbanes-oxley.com/index.php.
4. Sarbanes-Oxley Act of 2002. (July 30). Available at: www.sec.gov/about/laws/soa2002.pdf.
5. Schmidt, R. 2006. Pay consultants seek shield from suits spawned by new U.S. rule (November 15). Bloomberg News. Available at: www.bloomberg.com/apps/news?pid=20601109&sid=aI2Y06xicSqU&refer=exclusive.
6. Ibid.
7. Securities and Exchange Commission. 2003. Standards for attorneys practicing before the SEC. (August 5). Rules 33-8185.34-617276. Available at: www.sec.gov/rules/final/33-8185.htm.
8. Mason, J. 2002. Houston law firm probed for role in fall of Enron. *Houston Chronicle* (March 14).
9. American Bar Association. 2003. Adopted by the House of Delegates report on the Task Force on Corporate Responsibility (August 11–12). Available at: www.abanet.org/buslaw/corporateresponsiblity/home.html.
10. Stecklow, S., C. Forelle, J. R. Wilke, and R. Buckman. 2006. H-P scandal puts chairman, lawyer in awkward light. *Wall Street Journal* (September 8). Available at: http://online.wsj.com.
11. Ibid.
12. Waldman, P., and D. Clark. 2006. California charges Dunn, 4 others in H-P scandal. *Wall Street Journal* (October 5). Available at: online.wsj.com/article/SB115997015390082371.html.
13. American Bar Association. 2003. Adopted by the House of Delegates report on the Task Force on Corporate Responsibility.
14. Powers, W. C. 2002. Report of investigation by the Special Investigative Committee of the Board of Directors of Enron Corp. (February 1). Available at: http://news.findlaw.com/wp/docs.
15. Donaldson, W. H. (2005). Speech by SEC chairman: Remarks before SEC Speaks Conference. (March 4). Available at: www.sec.gov/news/speech/spch030405whd.htm.
16. Hechler, D. 2006. Ex-Enron lawyers take a look back. *National Law Journal* (February 20). Available at: www.law.com/jsp/nlj.
17. Qualters, S. 2006. In-house pay continues to climb. *National Law Journal* (November 8). Available at: www.law.com/jsp/ihc.
18. Burrows, P., and R. D. Hof. 2006. Sonsini under scrutiny. *Business Week* (October 2).

19. Masters, B. 2006. General counsels feel stock options heat. *Financial Times* (November 27). Available at: www.ft.com.
20. Ibid.
21. Securities and Exchange Commission. 2003. Standards for attorneys practicing before the SEC.
22. Ibid.
23. United States Sentencing Commission. 2005. Guidelines manual, Section 3E1.1 (November). Available at: http://ussc.gov/2005/g12005.pdf.
24. Gibson Dunn Update. (April 6, 2006). Available at: www.gibsondunn.com/practices/publications/detail/611/?pub/tem/d=8068.
25. Schmidt, R. 2006. Prosecutors should be curbed, say U.S. business organizations. Bloomberg (May 8). Available at: www.bloomberg.net.
26. Gibson Dunn Update. (April 6, 2006).
27. Ibid.
28. Orenstein, E. 2006. Has "privilege" lost its reward? *Financial Executives International*. Available at: www.fei.org.
29. Ibid.
30. Securities and Exchange Commission. 2003. Disclosure of proxy voting policies and proxy voting records by registered management investment companies (January 31). Available at: www.sec.gov/rules/final/finalarchive/finalarchive2003.shtml.
31. Ibid.
32. National Association of Securities Dealers. 2006. NASD guide to understanding securities analyst recommendations. Available at: www.nasd.com/web/idcplg?IdcService=SSGETPAGE&nodeID=580.
33. Coffee, J. C. 2001. Virtue of the securities analysts. *New York Law Journal* (July 19). Miller, S. S., and B. Q. Boyd. 2001. Analysts under fire. *Insights* (December): 8. Arkin, S. S. 2001. Shoot all the analysts. *Financial Times* (March): 22. Arkin, S. S. 2002. Analysts' conflicts of interest: Where's the crime. *New York Law Journal* (February): 3.
34. Securities and Exchange Commission. 2003. Regulation analyst certification (February 20). Available at: www.sec.gov/rules/final/33-8193.htm.
35. Chartered Financial Analysts Institutes. 2004. Securities analysts and Investor Relations Association jointly forge guidelines for ethical conduct in the analyst-corporate relationship. Available at: www.cfainstitute.org/pressroom/04release/20040311_01.html.
36. Ibid.
37. Ibid.
38. Ibid.
39. Ibid.
40. Harper, C. 2006. Bonus Pay for Wall Street Big Five Surges to Record $36 Billion, Bloomberg News (November 6). Available at: www.bloomberg.com/apps/news?pid=20601087&refer=home&sid=atEk12XYMerk.

CHAPTER 9

External Audit Function

INTRODUCTION

The external audit function should be regarded as an external corporate governance mechanism. It serves to protect investors from receiving incomplete, inaccurate, and misleading financial information. External auditors are responsible for auditing the company's financial statements and for opining on their fair presentation in conformity with generally accepted accounting principles (GAAP). External auditors, practicing before the Securities and Exchange Commission (SEC), have also been required to express an opinion on management's assessment of the effectiveness of the design and operation of internal control over financial reporting (ICFR) as well as an opinion on the effectiveness of internal control itself for large public companies.[1] The external audit function is intended to lend credibility to financial reports and reduce information risk that reports are biased, misleading, inaccurate, and incomplete. It is argued whether external auditors played a role in the reported financial scandals, either through audit failures and negligence, which allowed financial misstatements to go undetected and/or unreported, or through unethical actions that facilitated and/or enabled corporate malfeasance and management impropriety.[2] This chapter addresses the role of the external auditor in corporate governance and financial reporting.

EXTERNAL AUDITING AND CORPORATE GOVERNANCE

As depicted in Exhibit 2.3, the audit function performed by external auditors can play an important role in achieving effective corporate governance and reliable financial reports. The external audit function can be viewed as a value-added function when lending reliability and credibility to published financial reports. The Securities Exchange Act of 1934 set the requirements that companies that offer stock to the public in raising capital must have their financial statements audited by an independent public accountant. Thus, the auditor's role in corporate governance and the financial reporting process is to provide independent assurance to shareholders regarding fair presentation, in all material respects, of the company's financial statements in conformity with GAAP.

Independent auditors have traditionally stood outside of the corporate governance structure as gatekeepers to audit financial statements to ensure their conformity with GAAP. Before the Sarbanes-Oxley Act of 2002 (SOX), the auditing profession was mainly a self-regulated profession except for limited SEC disciplinary jurisdiction. Auditing standards were issued by the American Institute of Certified Public Accountants (AICPA), and auditors themselves conducted the peer review of audit quality. These traditional aspects of the auditing profession left auditors—the corporate gatekeepers—subject to business pressures, the quest for larger fees and profit margins, and the influence of paying clients who wanted certain accounting treatment and tax results. SOX drastically improved these characteristics of the accounting profession in three ways:

1. It created the Public Company Accounting Oversight Board (PCAOB) to regulate the auditing profession.
2. It connected the audit function to the corporate governance structure.
3. It requires that the audit committee be directly responsible for not only hiring, compensating, and firing external auditors but also for overseeing their work, monitoring their independence, and avoiding actual or potential conflict of interest situations.

Recent corporate governance reforms (SOX, SEC rules, PCAOB standards, and listing standards) improve audit quality in several aspects, including:

- Reaffirming the importance of the external audit function in the corporate governance context.
- Mandating that external auditors be independent of their client's management.
- Requiring that external auditors report directly to the company's audit committee.
- Limiting the scope of services (nonaudit, consulting services) that external auditors may provide to their audit clients.
- Requiring an integrated audit approach by expanding auditors' reporting responsibility to express opinions on both internal control and financial statements.

The six largest global accounting networks state three benefits of audits for the global economy and capital markets: (1) audits improve the allocation of capital among global companies regardless of their location by facilitating investors' decisions to channel funds to companies that offer the highest risk-adjusted returns; (2) audits help insulate the global financial system against systemic risk by providing transparency of the financial status of companies in their home economy; and (3) audits facilitate good corporate governance by empowering global investors with the right information.[3] Chief executive officers (CEOs) of the six largest global audit networks believe these benefits can be achieved when: (1) there are global accounting and auditing standards that guide the preparation and audit of financial statements; (2) regulators that oversee audits are formally coordinated and globally established; (3) audit quality is improved; and (4) consistency of audits across different countries within the global audit networks is observed.[4]

EXTERNAL AUDITOR RESPONSIBILITIES

Current auditing standards require that independent auditors provide *reasonable assurance* that the financial statements are free from material misstatements, whether caused by error or fraud, in order to render an unqualified opinion on the financial statements.[5] This is regarded as a high level of assurance but not absolute assurance. However, "reasonable assurance" as a practical matter may mean different things to different groups (auditors, investing public). Investors in the post-Enron era expect independent auditors to discover and report on all material misstatements, including errors, irregularities, and fraud.[6] Independent auditors, nonetheless, in complying with their professional standards, should provide reasonable assurance that financial statements are free from material misstatements.[7] When independent auditors fail to detect significant problems threatening the reliability and integrity of the financial statements, including the failure to detect fraud, the investing public has the right to question the value added, provided by an external audit.

The discussion of the difference between what constitutes a reasonable level of assurance as opposed to a high level reveals an expectation gap that has cast some doubt on the relevance, purpose, and usefulness of external audits. To narrow this perceived gap and to clarify what "reasonable assurance" means, the PCAOB states in Auditing Standard No. 2: "Reasonable assurance includes the understanding that there is a remote likelihood that material misstatements will not be prevented or detected on a timely basis. Although not absolute, reasonable assurance is, nevertheless, a high level of assurance."[8] The International Auditing and Assurance Standards Board (IAASB) also defines "reasonable assurance" to be a high, but not absolute, level of assurance in an assurance audit engagement.[9]

Both reasonable assurance and a high level of assurance are subject to professional interpretation. Independent auditors are required to document their assessment of reasonable assurance through the use of the materiality concept and the audit risk model. Materiality guides independent auditors in the amount of evidence they should gather to form an opinion on the financial statements; the audit risk model justifies the means of gathering sufficient competent evidence through tests of controls and substantive tests. These two concepts will be further discussed in this chapter.

External auditors are not and should not be expected to provide absolute assurance regarding reliability of financial statements primarily because:

- The nature and limitation of evidence-gathering procedures are conducted on selective testing.
- Management assertions and financial representations include accounting estimates that are not certain by nature.
- Judgment in the preparation and audit of financial statements.
- There is the possibility of collusion, false documentation, management override, or engagement in fraud.

The yet-to-be-resolved issue is what type and level of assurance the public desires and whether auditors are willing and able to provide that level. It appears that the public currently desires a high level of assurance, not just reasonable assurance, about fair and true presentation of financial statements. Lee Seidler, former senior managing director at Bear, Stearns & Co. and the Price Waterhouse Professor of Auditing at New York University, states:

> *People tend to think of auditors as detectives. They're not—they're accountants. Even if they look carefully, auditors miss many, maybe even most, fraud. But it would be silly to expect accountants to be society's experts on fine points of law and morality.*[10]

The central issue vital to the audit quality is the nature and extent of auditors' responsibility to detect financial statement fraud. Nevertheless, there is a widening expectation gap between what auditors should be doing and what auditors are willing and capable of accepting to discover fraud according to their auditing standards and the audit fees collected for their service. Users of audited financial statements generally expect external auditors to detect financial statement fraud, employees' illegal acts, and fraud, which affects the quality and integrity of financial reports. External auditors, however, in recognizing the importance of fraudulent financial activities, are more concerned with material misstatements in the audited financial statements.[11] Time will tell whether auditors and the accounting profession will live up to this task. In gaining a better understanding of a financial audit, its nature, and its inherent limitations, the public will be helpful in narrowing the expectation gap. An interesting article regarding limitations of the accounting profession states:

> *Everyone wants to see financial accounting get closer to the truth—and everyone has his own idea of what "the truth" is. Many people would like to require the accountants to be watchdogs of public and business morality. Pressure on the accountants is intense . . . most businessmen [Feel] that the accountants have already gone to ridiculous extremes to assure "realistic" accounting; activist politicians accusing the accountants and businessmen of being in bed together.*[12]

To better understand the intended communications contained in the auditor's report, the American Institute of Certified Public Accountants (AICPA), IAASB, and American Accounting Association (AAA) have initiated a request for proposal (RFP).[13] The RFP is intended to identify and provide information about users' perceptions of the financial statement audit and the communication that is conveyed through an unqualified auditor's report.[14] Examples of relevant questions regarding the value of the financial statement audits are: (1) Who is responsible for the financial statements? (2) What level of assurance does the auditor provide? (3) What information is the subject of the auditor's assurance? (4) Have the auditors looked for fraud? (5) Are internal controls adequate and effective? (6) Do the financial statements present a true and fair view? (7) What type of assurance can auditors provide (e.g., reasonable, high level, absolute)? and (8) How do users perceive the auditor's responsibilities for providing assurance concerning the detection of misstatements due to error or fraud?[15] These questions are addressed in this chapter and in Chapter 14.

AUDITOR COMPETENCIES

Auditor competencies in providing reasonable assurance that financial statements are free from material misstatements, whether caused by errors or fraud, can be classified into four areas: professional competencies, technical competencies, process competencies, and reporting competencies.

1. *Professional competencies.* The first general standard of the so-called ten generally accepted auditing standards (GAAS) requires that auditors have professional training and proficiency to conduct the audit. This means auditors should have education, experience, and certification in performing financial statement audits. To audit public companies, auditors should register with the PCAOB and meet all registration and inspection requirements.
2. *Technical competencies.* Technical competencies refer to auditor knowledge of relevant professional standards, rules, laws and regulations, and the technical understanding and knowledge of their clients' industry and business, corporate governance, financial reporting process, and internal controls in effectively conducting the audit. Public accounting firms are often criticized for assigning inexperienced staff auditors to audit engagements with no proper supervision or technical competencies.
3. *Process competencies.* Process competencies pertain to auditors' ability to choose appropriate evidence-gathering procedures (tests of controls, substantive tests) and to execute auditing procedures effectively. Many auditors use a risk-based approach of focusing their procedures on risk areas that threaten the effectiveness of internal control over financial reporting and the reliability and integrity of financial statements. An integrated audit approach should be used to ensure process competencies in auditing both internal controls and financial statements.
4. *Reporting competencies.* Reporting competencies refer to auditors' ability and willingness to both discover material misstatements and report the discovered misstatements. Auditors have been criticized for failure to detect errors, irregularities, and fraud as well as failure to report discovered misstatements.

TRENDS IN AND THE RELEVANCE OF AUDITING

The problems associated with the growing separation of ownership and control in public companies, as family-run firms slowly began to be replaced by larger public companies with larger numbers of shareholders, created the need for independent auditors to verify management's reporting performance. The passage of the Securities Act of 1933 and the Securities Exchange Act of 1934 established the demand for independent audits of financial reports of public companies filed with the SEC. In effect,

> *[t]he SEC handed the public accounting industry a franchise [the audit] to serve every single public corporation on behalf of the investing public. ...*

By the late 1980s, the major CPA firms ... turned the audit [the franchise] into a commodity.[16]

The performance of the audit as a commodity encouraged public accounting firms to reduce the overall auditor fees by lowering the cost and quality of the audit and instead focus on expanding its nonaudit consulting services, which deteriorated audit quality. In the late 1900s, public accounting firms expanded their services from the "grassroots," prestigious, and conspicuous product of audit services to the performance of a wide range of nonaudit services. Indeed, already by the 1980s and 1990s, the audit was considered a low-margin, loss leader activity that was simply a means of getting new clients to generate revenue by selling them more lucrative consulting services (e.g., tax, internal control and internal audit outsourcing, information technology). This gradual deterioration in audit quality was not evident during the market boom of the 1990s, but became apparent starting with the economic downturn and dot.com bomb of the early 2000s. Unfortunately for investors, the concept of "one-stop shopping" for all audit and nonaudit consulting services became a common practice for many public accounting firms and their clients. This concept and its practice impaired auditor independence as well as public trust and investor confidence due to the concern that auditors serve the self-interests of management, who hire them, rather than the shareholders, who ultimately paid their fees.[17] The words "public accounting firm" were replaced with "professional services firm" by almost all the Big Five (now Big Four) accounting firms to market their nonaudit products and consulting services. Eventually they became sales-driven firms rather than professionals whose job it was to serve and protect the investing public.

The public trust in auditors' judgments and reputation is vital in regarding the audit function as a value-added service that lends credibility to a company's published financial reports. The wave of financial scandals and financial restatements by high-profile public companies and related audit failures eroded investor confidence in financial reports and in the entire external audit function. Barry Melancon, the president of the AICPA, states: "We must restore our most priceless asset—our reputation. We must reach back to our core roots which earned us enormous respect as trusted advisers."[18]

The capital markets and market participants are concerned about the possibility that another big public accounting firm will fail and the ability of the accounting profession to attract, train, and maintain adequate, qualified individuals to perform quality audits. The American Assembly at Columbia University, in May 2005, gathered to discuss the future of the accounting profession. The assembly, consisting of more than 50 leaders from the fields of accounting, academia, law, finance, and the business community, issued its report entitled "The Future of the Accounting Profession: Auditor Concentration." Among other things, it suggests that the collapse of another major public accounting firm may result in the end of the public company audit profession and the beginning of statutory audits of public companies.[19] The assembly concluded that:

- Although concentration limits the choices, the current state of the Big Four accounting firms is sufficient, but a loss of a Big Four firm would create an intolerable situation.
- Global reach, technical expertise, specialization, and the size required to audit large public companies are beyond the reach of even the largest of the midtier accounting firms.
- Regulators (SEC, PCAOB) should create a limited safe harbor to protect auditors against undue litigation for using good faith judgments.

In January 2006, the U.S. Chamber of Commerce released "Auditing: A Profession at Risk," which asserted that the auditing industry faces substantial dangers that threaten its existence. If not properly addressed, these dangers could destabilize the U.S. capital market and thus the nation's economy.[20] The Chamber has committed itself to helping provide stability and worth in the auditing profession. To achieve its objectives, the Chamber proposed a three-part action plan:

1. Help the profession become insurable.
2. Clarify PCAOB standards.
3. Support expansion of and competition among Big Four firms.

Business is booming at the global large public accounting firms; their revenues have grown at a double-digit pace in the post-SOX era. However, auditing firms are still facing several challenges. The first and most continuous challenge remains how to attract the best, brightest, and most talented staff and how to provide them with adequate training to be competent and ethical in meeting the huge demand for audit and nonaudit services. The second challenge facing public accounting firms is the nature and extent of their liability for audit failures. The issue of auditor liability cap is further discussed in this chapter. Finally, the issue of auditor viability is yet to be addressed adequately. The viability issue includes the nature and extent of auditor challenges, likelihood of their failures, ramifications of such failures, consequences of failures, and development of contingency plans in case of failures.

The six largest global public accounting firms—BDO International, Deloitte and Touche, Ernst & Young, Grant Thornton International, KPMG International, and PricewaterhouseCoopers—in November 2006 issued a report entitled "Global Capital Markets and the Global Economy.[21] The report calls for: (1) relaxed liability standards for public accounting firms; (2) efforts to standardize accounting and auditing standards worldwide; (3) creation of a new business reporting model that provides more relevant and reliable financial and nonfinancial information more rapidly; (4) establishment of forensic audits in addition to financial audits to thoroughly investigate the occurrences of financial statement fraud and ways to prevent, deter, detect, and correct such fraud; and (5) the development of an effective recruitment process to attract outstanding individuals and train them in multiple disciplines (e.g., accounting, tax, finance, information technology) to ensure delivery of consistent and high-quality audit services.[22]

Bevis Longstreth, former Reagan SEC Commissioner, calls for the government to audit public companies similar to the way government bank examiners audit banks.[23] Longstreth stated, "There is an inherent tension between doing a good audit job and maximizing your profits. The tension between those two is too great. You can't expect both objectives to be well served by a single institution."[24] The bank regulatory model for the audit of public companies is not a new idea; the initial drafts of the 1933 Securities Act provided for audits of public companies consistent with such a model where auditors are employed by the regulatory agency. Audit failures of recent years, profit-maximizing rather than public interest focus of many public accounting firms, lack of proper competition in the auditing profession, and attempts by public accounting firms to limit their liabilities raise the question as to whether the original drafter of the 1933 Securities Act had the right idea of not franchising audits of public companies to the private sector.

AUDIT QUALITY AND AUDIT FAILURES

There are many cases of auditors' failures to report discovered misstatements in the financial statements. For example, Andersen, then the auditor of Qwest, warned the company and its directors that the SEC would challenge the company's accounting policies and practices concerning revenue recognition and then signed off on its financial statements. The auditor at Adelphia urged management to provide additional disclosures on its related party loans and then rendered a clean, unqualified opinion on its financial statements despite management refusal to provide such disclosures to investors. Xerox's auditor was warned about accounting problems at the company; however, the auditor chose to ignore them and then issued a clean, unqualified opinion on its financial statements. Auditors at HealthSouth were alerted to the potential financial fraud, but they ignored such warnings and issued a clean, unqualified opinion on its financial statements. At Raytheon, auditors issued a clean, unqualified opinion where in fact financial statements were misleading. These cases of egregious behavior by auditors and obvious audit failures contributed to the loss of investor confidence as many investors asked the question of "where were the auditors?"

Audit failure occurs when a company with reported unqualified financial statements discloses low-quality and misleading financial information or has to restate the previously audited statements. Audit failure—the failure of auditors to issue an appropriate audit opinion—can be separated into two categories: an audit process failure and an independent audit failure. This distinction is important because:

- Reported financial scandals and the related audit failures provide evidence of impairments in auditor independence.
- Regulator (e.g., SEC, PCAOB) rules and standards are more concerned with and address the incidence of independent audit failure rather than audit process failure.

- The audit process has often discovered misstatements, but auditors failed to disclose them due to financial and personal ties to their clients.
- Audit process failures are often unintentional, resulting from a lack of exercising due professional care and the imperfection in audit methodology.
- Independent audit failure is caused by auditors intentionally compromising their independence and professional responsibilities.
- Auditors are more likely to benefit directly from compromising their independence in order to secure the quasi rents (e.g., fees collected for nonaudit services in addition to audit fees) in their future audit engagements and for management's side payments associated with current engagements.

VALUE OF REGULATORY AUDIT OPINION

The current regulatory audit opinion conveys whether financial statements and their notes are presented fairly in conformity with GAAP. The value-relevance of the regulatory audit opinion has been questioned by many in terms of its coverage, structure, content, and level of assurance, accountability, and transparency.

- *Coverage.* The current regulatory audit opinion covers four basic financial statements (balance sheet, income statement, statement of cash flow, and statement of owner's equity), the notes to the financial statements, and their consistency with the other information presented in the management discussion and analysis (MD&A) section of the annual report. Recently, registered public accounting firms have been required to opine on both financial statements and internal control over financial reporting only of large public companies (so-called accelerated filers). Public companies provide a variety of financial and nonfinancial information (e.g., market shares, corporate governance, social, ethical, and environmental information, forecasts, projections, and regulatory information) valuable to investors and other users of their annual reports. The regulatory audit opinion provides only reasonable assurance that financial statements are free from material misstatements caused by errors or fraud. Companies often post their financial reports on their Web sites, which normally are hyperlinked to other nonfinancial information. The audit opinion pertains only to financial statements. Independent auditors do not provide any assurance on financial and nonfinancial information other than financial statements. However, as contained in annual reports and this, electronic financial statements are hyperlinked to other information, users of financial reports may get a wrong impression that the regulatory audit opinion pertains to the entire annual report.
- *Structure of audit reports.* The structure of the regulatory audit report consists of the uniform three paragraphs of introductory/opening paragraph, scope paragraph, and opinion paragraph. The introductory paragraph identifies financial statements being audited and differentiates between the responsibilities of management and the auditor regarding the statements. The scope paragraph describes the scope, extent, and nature of the audit, including auditing standards used, audit procedures applied, and audit evidence gathered. The opinion

paragraph expresses the auditor's opinion on the financial statements. Unless it is an unqualified opinion, an explanatory paragraph should precede the opinion paragraph. This structure of the audit report, while providing uniformity, consistency, and comparability, is not tailored to a company's unique specifications and attributes and does not allow auditors to use their judgment regarding quality of financial statements, financial performance, and the associated risk.

- *Content.* The information content of the regulatory audit opinion has been challenged on the grounds that it only opines on fair presentation of financial statements in conformity with GAAP. Statements can be fairly presented in compliance with GAAP and still contain misleading information. The independent auditors should opine on both quality of financial information in terms of its "true presentation" and compliance with GAAP in terms of its "fair presentation." The current audit report approach—"on or off," "comply/do not comply," "black and white," "pass or fail" audit opinion—does not have much value relevance to investors. A better approach could be the degree of a company's compliance with GAAP. Investors may demand that auditors express their opinion on overall financial health and future prospects of the company. Auditors express their judgment on both financial and nonfinancial information in a more customized audit report. The U.K. Companies Act of 2006 requires the company's auditor to report on: (1) its annual accounting in expressing an opinion on a true and fair view of financial accounts, including the balance sheet and the profit and loss, in accordance with the applicable financial reporting framework; (2) the directors' report, opining whether the information given in it is consistent with that of those financial accounts; and (3) the auditable part of the directors' remuneration report, opining whether it has been properly prepared as required by the Act.[25] It is expected that external auditors will be hired to provide different levels of assurance on both financial and nonfinancial information.

- *Level of assurance.* The level of assurance provided in the regulatory audit report is "reasonable assurance." There is a perceived expectation gap between what the users of audit reports consider as "reasonable assurance" and what auditors are willing and able to accept as their responsibility according to their professional standards. Investors often interpret this notion of "reasonable assurance" as "absolute assurance" that audited financial statements are free from any material misstatements and thus that auditors are certifying a "clean bill" of financial health for the company. Auditors, however, can provide only reasonable assurance that financial statements are free from material misstatements, whether caused by errors or fraud. Given that the restatement error rate for audited published financial statements has traditionally been between 5 and 15 percent, the reasonable assurance should be interpreted as high as 95 percent and as low as 85 percent. Recently, the International Auditing Standards and PCAOB Standards assert that a "reasonable assurance" means a "high level of assurance" without quantifying it.

- *Accountability.* The current regulatory audit report is signed by the engagement partners in the name of the public accounting firms. For example, Mr. Jack

Smith, the engagement partner of Ernst & Young, signs the report as Ernst & Young. The name of the engagement partner should be included in the signature in order to make the partner personally accountable for the audit report thus improving the accountability of the report. The new U.K. Companies Act of 2006 requires that the audit report be signed by the senior statutory auditor (the lead auditor) in his or her own name, for and on behalf of the audit firm.[26] The requirement of the printed name and signature of the lead partner along with the name of the company's public accounting firm will bring auditor accountability in line with that of other professionals (e.g., lawyers, physicians, financial executives) and is expected to encourage further personal responsibility for the audit conduct.

- *Transparency.* Recent corporate governance reforms require independent auditors to work with management under the oversight of the audit committee of the company's board of directors for the benefit of shareholders. Thus, shareholders, the primary beneficiaries of a financial audit, are concerned about audit quality and transparency. The U.K. Companies Act of 2006 requires disclosures of the terms on which a company's auditor is appointed and remunerated and the audit services are performed.[27] The Audit Quality Forum identified four measures that may improve audit quality and transparency, and bring real benefits to the shareholder and healthy competition in the accounting profession.[28] These measures address auditor engagement letters, shareholder rights to question auditors, auditor resignation standards, and lead partner's signature on audit reports.

- *Publication of audit engagement letters.* The public disclosure of the content of audit engagement letters should improve transparency of the audit process and enable investors to better understand the scope and terms of the audit, including the presence of auditor limitation of liability provisions. Auditor limited liability agreements (LLA) (so-called liability cap) will be discussed later in this chapter.

- *Shareholders' rights to question auditors.* Shareholders should be given the opportunity to question the auditor in advance of the company's annual meeting by communicating with the auditor via the company regarding the conduct of the audit and the content of the audit report.

- *Publication of auditor resignation statements.* Comprehensive, full, and public disclosure of information in auditors' resignation letters could provide relevant information about the reasons for the resignation and their impacts on the company's corporate governance, financial reporting, and audit process. More than 1,322 public companies have changed their auditors in 2006 and in the post-SOX period, and from 2002 to 2006, about 6,543 public companies changed their public accounting firms, which constitutes about one-half of all the public companies.[29] Auditor changes and their consequences for investors are discussed later in this chapter.

SAFEGUARDING THE AUDITING PROFESSION

Arthur Andersen, one of the Big Five firms (now Big Four), was convicted of obstruction of justice for shredding documents of its Enron audits. This caused the demise of Andersen and reduced the number of big public accounting firms to four; the subsequent Supreme Court overturn conviction ruling did not save Andersen. KPMG, another Big Four accounting firm, agreed, in 2005, to pay $456 million to the government to avoid criminal prosecution for offering illegal tax shelters to its clients. Eight partners of KPMG were also indicted for fraud associated with selling illegal tax shelters. PricewaterhouseCoopers (PwC), the world's largest public accounting firm, is being audited by the Internal Revenue Service for possible violation of its tax reporting. These incidents of audit failures raise concerns about the public accounting firms' ability and willingness to safeguard themselves. The auditing profession has traditionally been regarded as a watchdog of corporate financial reporting and a gatekeeper of the financial reporting process. The rash of financial scandals, the failure of independent auditors as gatekeepers, many incidents of auditor involvement with or ignorance of corporate malfeasance, and enormous lawsuits filed against public accounting firms for the alleged audit failures undermined investor confidence in the auditing profession. Although public accounting firms generally value their reputation and public trust in their profession, unethical actions of a small number of their partners have had adverse impacts on their reputation.

The question that remains unanswered is how the accounting profession should be safeguarded and specifically: "Should all of the safeguards put in place for normal companies not also apply to [independent] auditors?"[30] This and similar questions have been raised despite SOX measures, SEC rules, and PCAOB standards. Several suggestions have been provided to address the unethical, illegal, and damaging actions of a few partners and provide incentives and enforcements to do the right thing of honoring public trust in their profession. One suggestion is to address auditors', particularly partners', judgment bias. Another suggestion is to establish an independent board of directors for public accounting firms similar to the one for public companies in overseeing the firm's audit quality. Indeed, "accounting firms need independent directors, just as their clients do."[31] The Cohen Commission recommended and the author agrees that the Big Four accounting firms be required to have independent boards of directors and prepare annual financial reports similar to those produced by public companies and filed with the SEC.

On May 25, 2006, the PCAOB proposed rules for annual and special reporting of information and events by registered public accounting firms. These proposed rules would: (1) require each registered firm to provide basic information once a year about the firm and the firm's issuer-related practice over the most recent 12-month period; and (2) identify certain events that must be reported by the firm within 14 days if they occur with respect to a registered firm.[32]

A consultation document in July 2006 in the United Kingdom seeks views on the mandatory transparency reporting by some audit firms.[33] The U.K. government is expected to delegate to the Professional Oversight Board of the Financial Reporting Council (FRC) the responsibility for requiring, as a minimum, auditors of U.K. public companies to publish annual transparency reports.[34] These reports are intended to: (1) provide information on certain audit firms regarding their structure, governance, and quality controls; (2) promote audit quality; and (3) furnish transparency disclosures over and above those set forth in the revised eighth Company Law Directive.[35]

Bias in Judgment

To restore public trust and investor confidence in financial reports and auditing, we need to address the requirements of compliance with applicable laws, regulations, standards, and rules (SOX, SEC, FASB) and also recognize the existence of unconscious bias and its devastating effects. For example, David Duncan, the Andersen partner in charge of Enron's audit, was torn by conflicting responsibilities of ensuring Enron's financial statements were not misleading and making the huge monthly payroll of audit and consulting teams. Although Enron was a risky client for Andersen, the threat of losing its $54 million in annual cash flow was considered a high business risk. Duncan compromised his professional responsibilities in favor of keeping Enron as a client and securing jobs for hundreds of Andersen's Houston office professionals. As public accounting firms grow, they accept larger clients, and their business risk and likelihood of judgment bias increases. The self-serving bias can influence one's judgment even in a highly regulated and monitored environment. Bazerman, Loewenstein, and Moore identified three structural aspects of accounting in addition to potential conflicts of interest that provide opportunities for bias to influence judgment.[36] These three structural factors are:

1. *Ambiguity.* Bias enters into judgment and self-serving conclusions are often reached whenever ambiguity exists. Not all of the accounting policies and practices are straightforward. Ambiguity also exists in auditing standards and practices, which may cause self-serving bias and its ill effects.
2. *Attachment.* Auditors and accountants in general are provided with incentives to remain in their clients' good graces. After all, auditors provide audit and nonaudit professional services for fees collected from their clients. Under the current fee system, even with the audit committee being directly responsible for hiring, firing, and compensating external auditors, management cuts the check and works with auditors, on a daily basis, in conducting the audit. This type of relationship with management provides incentives and opportunities for attachment to a particular client and equating auditors' interests with those of management; eventually it could cause self-serving bias. Even if a large accounting firm can observe the loss of major clients as a result of irresolvable disputes and disagreement with a client's management, an individual auditor's (partner) job, career, and compensation may depend on the retention of specific clients. One way to diminish this self-serving bias is to require the lead partner and the review partner to rotate off the audit client engagement every several years. Indeed, SOX and SEC rules require rotation of the lead and review partners every 5 years. The most effective alternative would be the rotation of the audit firm every several years, which has already, in effect, been happening

given the number of audit firm changes recently, as further discussed in this chapter.

3. *Approval.* External auditors ascertain management assertions that may be biased, as management is motivated to make the company look good financially. In effect, auditors endorse or reject management judgments regarding fair presentation of financial statements in conformity with GAAP. Academic research suggests that self-serving biases become more apparent when one endorses biased judgments of others.[37] In other words, auditors are more likely to accept more aggressive accounting policies and practices when managers' biased judgments align with their own biases.

In addressing auditor bias in judgment and their ethical conduct, one should realize that accountants do not work in isolation—teams—and their work, compensation, ethics, and behaviors are influenced by the work ethic and conduct of coworkers; compensation, authority, and pressure of superiors; and actions of even subordinates within the company. Like other human beings, they can be pressured and motivated when the opportunity is given and they are tempted to engage in unethical behavior (e.g., manipulation of financial reports). The creation of the PCAOB, which is discussed in the next section, was intended to positively influence auditors' objectivity, independence, ethical conduct, and professional practice.

PUBLIC COMPANY ACCOUNTING OVERSIGHT BOARD

The auditing profession has traditionally been regarded as a self-regulatory profession in which auditors imposed on themselves a set of ethical, quality control, and auditing standards with a peer review system to adhere to those standards. The financial scandals and related audit failures in the early 2000s and thereafter eroded investor confidence in the accounting profession, calling into question the ability of the auditing profession to self-police; SOX effectively ended the self-regulatory environment of the accounting profession by creating the PCAOB. The PCAOB is a not-for-profit organization that functions under SEC oversight. It consists of five members, two of whom are certified public accountants (CPAs), and is chaired by a member who has not practiced as a CPA for at least five years before appointment. In 2006, Federal Reserve Board Governor Mark W. Olson became the PCAOB's second permanent chairman, succeeding the first chairman, William McDonough, who previously was the president of the New York Federal Reserve Bank.

The PCAOB's mission is to improve the audit quality of public companies. Its primary functions are to:

- Register public accounting firms that audit public companies.
- Inspect the registered public accounting firms on a regular basis.
- Establish auditing, attestation, ethics, quality control, and independence standards.
- Conduct investigations and disciplinary proceedings.

William H. Donaldson, former SEC chairman, stated:

A central purpose of the Act [SOX] was to restore confidence in the accounting profession. *I am very pleased that the centerpiece of the necessary reform
is now on very sound footing and in the midst of important implementation
phases. I am of course speaking of the* Public Company Accounting Oversight Board—*which is awkwardly named and has for a year been resistant
to efforts by the press and others to capture it with a catchy acronym. The
Board is absolutely vital to our markets going forward.*[38]

The PCAOB, since its inception in 2003, has shaped the auditing profession and
helped to move it in the right direction, which would ultimately result in public trust
and investor confidence in profession. PCAOB chairman William J. McDonough
stated:

*PCAOB oversight has already changed the environment of registered public
accounting firms and their partners and staff that participate in audits, and
it has triggered a profound shift in the overall* character of public company
auditing. *Most important, our oversight has changed auditors'* attitudes
toward their accountability . . . *auditors understand that their work is much
more likely to be reviewed within months or even weeks by the PCAOB's
well-experienced, full-time inspectors.*[39]

The PCAOB has provided a unique opportunity to improve audit quality
through its:

- Principles-based audit standards that promote and foster auditors' professional
  judgments.
- Implementation guidance and staff questions and answers to further facilitate
  a smooth implementation of PCAOB Auditing Standards (e.g., May 16, 2005,
  policy statement and November 30, 2005, report on implementation of PCAOB
  Auditing Standards No. 2) and audit practice alerts (e.g., Staff Audit Alert No.
  1, *Matters Related to Timing and Accounting for Option Grants*).
- Inspections program through which the PCAOB influences the application of its
  auditing standards in improving audit quality as inspectors identify deficiencies
  and provide insights on improving standards.
- Enforcement of noncompliance with auditing standards.[40]

The PCAOB has also appointed a standing advisory group (SAG) of 30
members with expertise in accounting, auditing, corporate governance, investments,
and corporate finance to assist the PCAOB in carrying out its standard-setting
responsibilities. The PCAOB is authorized to register both U.S. and non-U.S. public
accounting firms auditing U.S. public companies. As of April 3, 2007, 1,763 public
accounting firms have been registered by the PCAOB. These registered firms audit
over 18,000 public companies; more than 80 percent are audited by the Big
Four public accounting firms (Deloitte & Touche, Ernst & Young, KPMG, and

PricewaterhouseCoopers). These firms pay annual registration fees depending on the size of the firm and number of their clients.

The Public Company Accounting Oversight Board, in 2004, established the office of Internal Oversight and Performance Assurance (IOPA) to ensure the efficiency, effectiveness, and integrity of its programs and operations.[41] IOPA conducts performance reviews and continuous quality assurance of PCAOB functions and programs through its annual and special reviews and inquiries. This internal examination is aimed at ensuring that the PCAOB: (1) constantly identifies and addresses risks to the integrity of its operations; (2) identifies and implements opportunities to improve the effectiveness and efficiency of its programs; (3) reports material and relevant financial and operating information in a fair, complete, and transparent manner to the SEC, Congress, and public; (4) complies with applicable laws, regulations, rules, and policies; (5) appropriately safeguards and uses its resources in an efficient manner; and (6) conducts its programs and operations in a manner consistent with protection and promotion of the public interest in the integrity of audits.[42]

PCAOB Auditing Standards

SOX authorized the PCAOB to adopt or revise the existing auditing standards and/or issue new auditing standards. The PCAOB initially adopted as its interim standards the AICPA's Statements on Auditing Standards (SAS) that existed on April 16, 2003. It has decided to take on the responsibility of issuing auditing, attestation, ethics, and independent standards for registered public accounting firms that audit financial statements of public companies. Meanwhile, it is also reviewing all of the adopted interim standards and deciding whether to modify, repeal, or permanently adopt them as its own standards. As of April 15, 2007, the PCAOB has issued four auditing standards and one ethics rule.

Auditing Standard No. 1 The first PCAOB Auditing Standard (AS No. 1) makes two minor changes in the language of the AICPA standard unqualified audit report. The first change is in the scope paragraph of the report, replacing the phrase "we conducted our audits in accordance with generally accepted auditing standards (GAAS)" with "we conducted our audits in accordance with the standards of the PCAOB (United States)." With respect to the second change, PCAOB AS No. 1 added the state and city in which the public accounting firm prepared the audit report.[43] Exhibit 9.1 presents the standard audit report format adopted by the PCAOB.

The current audit reporting model has been criticized for not reflecting auditor's assurance on the quality of financial statements by focusing on a "pass/fail" approach to audit reporting. The pass/fail approach states that financial statements are presented fairly in conformity with GAAP (pass) or they are not presented fairly (fail). The two advantages of this approach are: (1) the audit report is standard pass/fail language, which provides uniformity and improves comparability; and (2) this approach is commonly accepted by the investing public. The three disadvantages are: (1) the pass/fail approach does not reflect the quality of the financial statements; (2) this approach does not provide relevant and useful information to investors

EXHIBIT 9.1 Report of Independent Registered Public Accounting Firms (Financial Statements)

We have audited the accompanying balance sheets of X company as of December 31, 20X3 and 20X2, and the related statements of operations, stockholders' equity, and cash flows for each of the three years in the period ended December 31, 20X3. These financial statements are the responsibility of the Company's management. Our responsibility is to express an opinion on these financial statements based on our audits.

We conducted our audits in accordance with the standards of the Public Company Accounting Oversight Board (United States). Those standards require that we plan and perform the audit to obtain reasonable assurance about whether the financial statements are free fo material misstatement. An audit includes examining, on a test basis, evidence supporting the amounts and disclosures in the financial statements. An audit also includes assessing the accounting principles used and significant estimates made by management, as well as evaluating the overall financial statement presentation. We believe that our audits provide a reasonable basis for our opinion.

In our opinion, the financial statements referred to above present fairly, in all material respects, the financial position of the Company as of [at] December 31, 20X3 and 20X2, and the results of its operations and its cash flows for each of the three years in the period ended December 31, 20X3, in conformity with U.S. generally accepted accounting principles.

[*Signature*]

[*City and State or Country*]

[*Date*]

Source: Adapted from the Public Company Accounting Oversight Board (PCAOB). Auditing Standard No. 1, *References in the Auditors' Reports to the Standards of the PCAOB*. Available at: www.pcaobus.org.

regarding the quality of the company as investment or credit risk; and (3) this approach focuses on fair presentation rather than true and accurate presentation of financial position and results of operations.

The author suggests the following changes within the framework of the pass/fail model:

- Combine the audit report on the company's financial statements with the report on its internal control over financial reporting in an integrated audit report.
- Expand the description on management's responsibility by stating that financial reports, including the financial statements and internal controls, are prepared and certified by management in terms of their completeness, accuracy, and true presentation.

- State that the audit committee is responsible for overseeing both internal controls and financial reports.
- Present more in-depth details of: audit procedures performed; evidence gathered; conclusions reached (including auditor opinion on the appropriateness of the accounting policies and practices selected by management); reasonableness of the accounting estimates and reserves used by management; the quality, relevancy, reliability, and transparency of financial statements; and whether the financial statements provide sufficient disclosures of the company's material transactions and events.
- Include the name of the lead partner and the review partner in the audit report signature.

Auditing Standard No. 2   In June 2004, the PCAOB issued its AS No. 2, an audit of internal control over financial reporting (ICFR) performed in conjunction with an audit of financial statements.[44] AS No. 2 requires that the independent auditor express an opinion on management's assessment of the effectiveness of ICFR. The independent auditor must also test and express an opinion on the effectiveness of ICFR. In performing tests of controls, the independent auditor must assess the nature and extent of management's documentation of internal controls in providing reasonable support for management's assessment and factors pertaining to the effectiveness of the audit committee in overseeing the company's external financial reporting and its ICFR.

Management and the independent audit reports on the company's ICFR require:

- Management to design and maintain internal controls.
- Management to document the design and operation of ICFR.
- Management to assess (test) the effectiveness of both the design and operation of the company's ICFR.
- Management to prepare its report on a timely basis.
- The audit committee to review management's assessment of the effectiveness of ICFR.
- The independent auditor to perform tests of controls to gather sufficient competent evidence in evaluating both management's assessment of the effectiveness of internal control and internal control itself.
- The independent auditor to issue the report on the company's ICFR on a timely basis.
- The audit committee to review the independent auditor's report on ICFR.
- The independent auditor to communicate significant deficiencies in internal control to the company's audit committee and disclose material weaknesses in internal control in the audit report.
- Management to take remediation actions to correct the identified material weaknesses.
- The independent auditor to issue a report regarding the correction of the identified material weaknesses in internal control.

Identification of Internal Control Deficiencies PCAOB AS No. 2 provides a list of circumstances that may result in a significant deficiency indicating that a material weakness in ICFR exists. These circumstances include:

- Restatement of previously issued financial statements reflecting the correction of a misstatement.
- Identification of a material misstatement in the current period financial statements that were undetected by the company's ICFR.
- Ineffective oversight functions of the company's audit committee regarding its financial reporting and ICFR.
- Ineffective internal control or risk assessment function to monitor the company's risk assessment related to complex business events or transactions.
- Ineffective regulatory compliance function to ensure compliance with applicable laws and regulations, particularly for complex companies in highly regulated industries.
- Identification of any financial statement fraud.
- Uncorrected significant deficiencies that were previously communicated to the company's management and the audit committee by the independent auditor and remain uncorrected after some reasonable period of time.
- An ineffective control environment that creates opportunities for the occurrence of significant deficiencies or material weaknesses in the company's ICFR.

Classification of Internal Control Deficiencies PCAOB AS No. 2 states that when internal control deficiencies are identified, they should be classified into three categories.

1. *Inconsequential deficiencies.* These are internal control deficiencies that either are not material or do not have significant adversarial effects on fair presentation of financial statements in conforming to GAAP.
2. *Significant deficiencies.* Significant deficiencies can be a combination of deficiencies that cause ICFR to be ineffective. These significant control deficiencies adversely affect the company's ability to initiate, measure, authorize, recognize, process, and report financial information in accordance with GAAP.
3. *Material weaknesses.* Material weaknesses are either a significant control deficiency or a combination of significant deficiencies that result in more than a remote likelihood that a material misstatement in financial statements (annual or interim) will not be prevented or detected. That is, it is probable or reasonably possible that a company's ICFR is not effective in preventing and detecting material misstatements in financial reports.

Independent Auditor's Opinion on Internal Controls The independent audit report on ICFR can be a separate report or combined with the audit report on the financial statements. Exhibit 9.2 shows the format and content of an audit report on ICFR. It is expected that eventually the auditing profession will move toward

EXHIBIT 9.2   Report of Independent Registered Public Accounting Firms
(Integrated Audit)

[Introductory paragraph]

We have audited management's assessment, included in the accompanying
[title of management's report], that W Company maintained effective Internal control over financial reporting as of December 31, 20X3, based on
*[Identify control criteria for example, "criteria established in Internal Control—
Integrated Framework issued by the Committee of Sponsoring Organizations of
the Treadway Commission (COSO)."]*. W Company's management is responsible for maintaining effective Internal control over financial reporting and for
its assessment of the effectiveness of internal control over financial reporting.
Our responsibility is to express an opinion on management's assessment and
an opnion on the effectiveness of the company's Internal control over financial
reporting based on our audit.

[Scope paragraph]

We conducted our audit in accordance with the standards of the Public Company
Accounting Oversight Board (United States). Those standards require that we
plan and perform the audit to obtain reasonable assurance about whether
effective internal control over financial reporting was maintained in all material
respects. Our audit included obtaining an understanding of internal control over
financial reporting, evaluating management's assessment, testing and evaluating
the design and operating effectiveness of internal control, and performing such
other procedures as we considered necessary in the circumstance. We believe that
our audits provide a reasonable basis for our opinions.

[Definition paragraph]

A company's internal control over financial reporting is a process designed to
provide reasonable assurance regarding the reliability of financial reporting and
the preparation of financial statements for external purposes in accordance with
generally accepted accounting principles. A company's internal control over
financial reporting includes those policies and procedures that (1) pertain to the
maintenance of records that, in reasonable detail, accurately and fairly reflect the
transactions and dispositions of the assets of the company; (2) provide reasonable
assurance that transactions are recorded as necessary to permit preparation of
financial statements in accordance with generally accepted accounting principles
and that receipts and expenditures of the company are being made only in
accordance with authorizations of management and directors of the company;
and (3) provide reasonable assurance regarding prevention or timely detection of
unauthorized acquisition, use, or disposition of the company's assets that could
have a material effect on the financial statements.

EXHIBIT 9.2 (*Continued*)

[Inherent limitations paragraph]

Because of its inherent limitations, internal control over financial reporting may not prevent or detect misstatements. Also, projections of any evaluation of effectiveness to future periods are subject to the risk that controls may become inadequate because of changes in conditions, or that the degree of compliance with the policies or procedures may deteriorate.

[Opinion paragraph]

In our opinion, management's assessment that W Company maintained effective internal control over financial reporting as of December 31, 20X3, is fairly stated, in all material respects, based on [*Identify control criteria, for example, "criteria established in Internal Control— Integrated Framework issued by the Committee of Sponsoring Organizations of the Treadway Commission (COSO)."*]. Also in our opinion, W Company maintained, in all material respects, effective internal control over financial reporting as of December 31, 20X3, based on [*Identify control criteria, for example "criteria established in Internal Control— Integrated Framework issued by the Committee of Sponsoring Organizations of the Treadway Commission (COSO)."*].

[Explanatory paragraph]

We have also audited, in accordance with the standards of the Public Company Accounting Oversight Board (United States), the [*Identify financial statements*] of W Company and our report dated [*date of report, which should be the same as the date of the report on the effectiveness of internal control over financial reporting*] expressed [*include nature of opinion*].

[*Signature*]

[*City and State or Country*]

[*Date*]

Source: Adapted from the Public Company Accounting Oversight Board. Available at: www.pcaobus.org.

an integrated audit approach that utilizes the combined audits. An integrated audit approach necessitates the use of an integrated audit report. The author suggests that an integrated audit report be issued particularly when the independent auditor issues an unqualified opinion on both financial statements and ICFR. Nevertheless, management's report on internal control should be separate and be placed right after the MD&A section of Form 10-K and immediately before the financial statements section.

There are three possible types of audit opinions on ICFR:

1. *Unqualified opinion.* The unqualified opinion can be rendered when there are no identified material weaknesses in ICFR and no scope limitations. In this case the audit report states: "In our opinion, management's assessment of the effectiveness of the company's internal control over financial reporting is fairly stated."
2. *Adverse opinion.* The adverse opinion should be rendered when there are significant deficiencies in the company's ICFR that result in one or more material weaknesses. In this case the audit report states: "In our opinion, management's assessment of the effectiveness of the company's internal control over financial reporting is not fairly stated."
3. *Qualified/disclaimer opinion.* The disclaimer of opinion should be given when there is a scope limitation and the auditor cannot express an opinion on management's assessment of the effectiveness of the company's ICFR.

PCAOB AS No. 2 mentions some circumstances where management may conclude that the company's ICFR is ineffective. If the auditor concurs with management's assessment, the auditor may issue an unqualified opinion on management's assessment and render an adverse opinion on the effectiveness of ICFR. There may be situations where management reports that the company's internal control is effective but the independent auditor discovers material weaknesses that were not corrected and issues an adverse opinion on the effectiveness of the company's ICFR. This could happen only under rare circumstances where there is a strong disagreement between management and the independent auditor regarding the company's ICFR and the audit committee is unable to resolve this disagreement.

On December 19, 2006, after two years of monitoring the implementation of AS No. 2, holding two roundtable discussions (April 2005, May 2006), and assessing the feasibility, efficiency, effectiveness, and scalability of AS No. 2, the PCAOB proposed for public comment a new auditing standard to supersede AS No. 2.[45] The proposed auditing standard would provide guidance in four areas including:

1. Focus the audit on the matters most important by:
   - Incorporating the top-down approach of beginning with an assessment of company-level controls and financial statement elements and then linking them to significant accounts, relevant assertions, and finally significant processes.
   - Using the risk-based approach by assessing the risk related to significant controls and its impact on the extent, nature, and timing of both tests of controls and substantive tests, and evaluating results of both substantive and control audit procedures in determining the overall risk related to control.
   - Revising definitions related to the evaluation of deficiencies including replacing the term "more than remote likelihood" with the term "reasonably possible" within the definition of material weakness and significant deficiency; focusing the audit only on identifying material weaknesses in internal controls; replacing the term "more than inconsequential" with the term

"significant" in the definition of a significant deficiency; and using the same materiality threshold in both the audit of annual financial statements and ICFR.

2. Eliminate unnecessary procedures by focusing the audit on important matters that assist in identifying material weaknesses including:
   o Requiring auditors to obtain an understanding of management's processes pertaining to internal controls rather than evaluating such processes.
   o Allowing the auditor to exercise judgment in determining the nature and extent of control tests based on knowledge obtained from prior years' audits.
   o Using a risk-based approach of focusing on company-level controls and its control environment.
   o Requiring the auditor to obtain an understanding of the work of others at the client's company and to use the work of others in an integrated audit of both ICFR and financial statements.
   o Requiring a walk-through test for each significant process rather than for each major class of transaction within each significant process with the possibility of using the assistance of others.

3. Scale the audit for smaller companies by tailoring the audit of ICFR to each audit client in terms of their size and complexity by first identifying attributes of smaller companies and then using such attributes in planning and performing the audit.

4. Simplify the audit requirements by:
   o Encouraging the auditor to apply professional judgment in determining the extent and nature of the audit.
   o Making audit guidance more understandable to audit clients and auditors.
   o Providing a better sequential flow of an audit of internal control.[46]

The proposed AS No. 5 would allow auditors to rely on third parties and companies themselves to assess the effectiveness of ICFR rather than the auditor opinion on the management's assessment of ICFR. On April 4, 2007, the SEC approved a framework for changes in the implementation rules of SOX, particularly Section 404, by promoting greater use of a more flexible principles-based approach rather than "iron-clad rules."[47] Specifically, the proposed changes would allow auditors to: (1) scale their audits by taking into consideration the client's particular circumstances; (2) use their professional judgment in the Section 404 process; and (3) have the flexibility to determine when they can rely on work previously done by others. Critics argue that allowing public companies and their auditors more latitude to assess potential financial reporting risk undermines the congressional intent in passing SOX. The SEC and the PCAOB are reconciling their differences between the SEC's "management guidance" and the PCAOB's "auditor guidance" in order to fine-tune AS No. 5.

Auditing Standard No. 3 PCAOB AS No. 3, *Audit Documentation*, was approved by the SEC on August 25, 2004. It establishes general requirements for documentation that the auditor should prepare and retain in an audit of financial statements and requires auditors to prepare and maintain documentation "in sufficient" detail to support the conclusion reached in their reports.[48] Section 1520(a) of SOX requires an auditor who performs financial statement audits in compliance with the SEC requirements to maintain all audit papers for a period of five years pursuant to the audit.[49] The SEC rule extended the retention period to seven years after the auditor concludes the audit.[50] Audit evidence and records to be retained include work papers and other audit documents that contain conclusions, analyses, financial data, and opinions. Section 802 of SOX addresses fines and imprisonment for anyone who knowingly alters, mutilates, conceals, destroys, or falsifies documents or records with the intent to influence or obstruct an investigation conducted by regulators.

PCAOB Auditing Standard No. 4 PCAOB AS No. 4, *Reporting on Whether a Previously Reported Material Weakness Continues to Exist,* establishes guidance for auditors to report on whether a previously reported material weakness in ICFR continues to exist as of a date specified by management.[51] Management may engage the auditor to report on one or more previously reported material weaknesses in internal controls. The auditor's objective, according to AS No. 4, is to provide reasonable assurance as to whether the previously reported material control weakness continues to exist pursuant to management's most recent annual assessment.

AS No. 4 requires auditors to:

- Evaluate whether conditions for engagement performance have been met (e.g., management accepts responsibility for the effectiveness of internal control).
- Plan the engagement (e.g., overall understanding of ICFR).
- Evaluate whether to use the work of others (e.g., management, internal auditors).
- Obtain sufficient competent evidence about the effectiveness of controls.
- Obtain written representations from management and evaluate management's reports.
- Form a conclusion and report.
- Communicate with the audit committee regarding whether a material weakness continues to exist.

PCAOB Rules on Auditor Independence, Ethics, and Taxes On April 19, 2006, the SEC approved the PCAOB's proposed independence and ethics rules.[52] The new rules set guidelines for auditors providing tax services to public company audit clients and prohibit contingent fee arrangements for tax services. The important provisions of the new rules follow.

- A foundation for the independence component of the PCAOB's ethics rules has been introduced by requiring that registered public accounting firms and their associated persons be independent of their audit client throughout the audit and professional engagement period.
- Circumstances in which performance of tax services impairs auditor independence, including services pertaining to marketing, planning, or opining in favor of the tax treatment of transactions that are based on aggressive interpretations of applicable tax laws, are identified.

- Any contingent fee arrangements may impair auditor independence.
- Performance of tax services for certain members of the audit client's management who serve in financial reporting oversight roles (e.g., CEO, CFO) and their immediate family members impairs auditor independence. On October 31, 2006, the PCAOB approved adjusting the implementation schedule for one part of its Rule 3523, entitled *Tax Services for Persons in Financial Reporting Oversight Roles*, by extending its implementation to April 30, 2007.[53] Rule 3523 was originally adopted by the PCAOB on July 26, 2005, and was subsequently approved by the SEC on April 19, 2006.
- SOX requirements that the audit committee preapproves tax services must be complied with.
- The principle that persons associated with registered public accounting firms (e.g., individual accountants) can also be held responsible when their actions contribute to the firms' violations of applicable regulations has been codified.

The new rules have four implications for audit committees.

1. The PCAOB's new rules provide specific guidance for audit committees to preapprove permissible tax services to be performed by the company's independent auditor. The independent auditor must:
   a. Provide a written description to the client's audit committee itemizing the nature and scope of the proposed tax services, including the fee structure for the proposed services.
   b. Discuss the possible implications of the proposed tax services on auditor independence.
   c. Disclose any amendments to tax service engagements and document all communications with the audit committee pertaining to tax services.
2. The audit committee is not required to review or approve the engagement letter for each tax service. However, the audit committee should examine its policies and procedures to ensure their compliance with the new requirements for preapproving tax services.
3. The new rules will not apply to ad hoc preapproval obtained from the audit committee on or before June 19, 2006 (e.g., within 60 days of the SEC's April 19, 2006, order).
4. In cases where tax services are preapproved pursuant to audit committee policies and procedures, the new rules will not apply to any tax service that starts on or before April 19, 2007.

Aggressive tax planning is defined as any planning or opinion that meets all of these four tests:

1. The auditor provides any service related to the plan or opinion.
2. The idea was not initiated by the client.
3. A significant purpose of the idea was to avoid taxes.
4. The plan has a less than 50-50 chance of prevailing if challenged by the Internal Revenue Service.[54]

Critics have expressed three major concerns about the determination of aggressive tax services.

1. The word "any service" could be viewed as the mere preparation of a tax return if embodied in the aggressive tax idea regardless if initiated by the client, the auditor, or even an unrelated third party.
2. The phrase "significant purpose" can be broadly applied to any tax planning with the intention of avoiding taxes. Perhaps the more appropriate wording to use is the term "principal purpose" rather than "significant purpose."
3. Auditors are not prohibited from performing tax services for directors and audit committee members who oversee their audit functions. Permitted tax services include routine tax return preparation and tax compliance, general tax planning and advice, employee personal tax services, and international assignment tax services.

Inspection of Public Accounting Firms

The PCAOB ended several decades of self-regulation and peer reviews for registered public accounting firms. Firms that audit more than 100 public companies are inspected by the PCAOB annually; other firms are inspected triennially. The PCAOB is authorized to refer violations of its professional standards, SEC rules, quality controls, ethics, independence, or other applicable rules, regulations, and standards to the SEC and appropriate state regulatory authorities along with inspection reports and audit firms' letters of response. The inspection reports, including violations, may be made available to the public if concerns and issues included in the reports are not properly addressed by the accounting firm within 12 months after the date of the inspection report.

In 2004, the PCAOB inspected the eight largest U.S. public accounting firms and 91 smaller firms; in 2005, in addition to the eight largest firms, it inspected about 280 smaller firms. The inspection process consists of 20 steps:

1. Select the audit clients based on the PCAOB's assessment of the likelihood of material misstatements or significant audit deficiencies.
2. Review aspects of the selected audits by each firm.
3. Choose the engagements to review according to the PCAOB's criteria.
4. Prevent the accounting firm from limiting or influencing the engagement selection process or any other aspect of inspection review.
5. Review the selected audit clients' financial statements and certain SEC filings.
6. Select certain higher-risk areas for review (e.g., revenue recognition, confirmation).
7. Review the selected areas of revenues, reserves or estimated liability, income taxes, related party transactions, derivatives, supervision of work performed by foreign affiliates, internal control assessment and documentation, and risk assessment.
8. Analyze end-of-the-year closing and adjusting entries, particularly adjustments that were suggested by the auditor and were not booked by the client.

9. Review written communication between the auditor and the client's management.

10. Review written communication between the auditor and the client's audit committee.

11. Conduct an interview with the chairperson of the audit committee of the selected audit client.

12. Discuss unresolved aspects of the inspection process with the personnel from the firm's national offices if the issues cannot be resolved through review of the work papers and discussion with the engagement team.

13. Select additional audits if necessary to follow leads to the root of audit deficiencies (e.g., other audits performed by the same audit partner or engagement team).

14. Review other work performed by internal reviewers who missed the reviewed partner's errors.

15. Identify and resolve audit deficiencies and problems early in their development.

16. Invite the public accounting firm to comment on the discovered potential material accounting errors and significant audit deficiencies.

17. Discuss the discovered problems with audit firm representatives, including members of the engagement team, the firm representative responsible for the inspection process, national office experts, the managing partner, or the firm's CEO.

18. In the discussion, address audit problems, lack of performance of necessary audit procedures, and quality control requirements.

19. Disclose the public portion of the inspection report on the PCAOB Web site.

20. Disclose the nonpublic portion of the inspection report, primarily regarding the firm's quality control system, and other PCAOB communication to the audit firm out of public view unless the firm fails to take proper action to correct the identified audit failures in due time.[55]

In 2005, about 365 audits performed by the largest nine public accounting firms and 623 audits performed by smaller firms were reviewed by PCAOB inspectors. The PCAOB issued its 2005 inspection reports in December 2006; they show several shortcomings in audits conducted by registered public accounting firms. These shortcomings were significant enough that they resulted in making changes in accounting or disclosure practices of audit clients, and in some cases the auditors failed to obtain sufficient competent evidence to support their opinion on audited financial statements.

As of December 15, 2006, the PCAOB had issued more than 320 inspection reports of registered public accounting firms. The reports serve five primary purposes of:

1. Improving audit effectiveness by identifying and requiring resolution of audit failures.

2. Identifying and properly addressing the emerging and common accounting and auditing issues.

3. Improving the audit firm's system of quality control and evidence-gathering procedures.

4. Assisting the PCAOB in establishing appropriate auditing, quality control, and ethics standards.
5. Enhancing public trust and investor confidence in the auditing profession.

PCAOB chairman McDonough summarizes the results of inspection reports:

Two years of inspecting the audits of the largest eight accounting firms has done nothing to shake my view that these firms, operating at their best, are capable of the highest quality auditing. But it has also done nothing to shake my view that the Congress acted wisely in creating independent oversight of the profession to help move [auditing] firms in the direction of consistently operating at their best.[56]

On May 1, 2006, the PCAOB released a statement regarding its approach to inspections of audits of ICFR for the 2006 inspection cycle.[57] The PCAOB combines reviews of audits of ICFR with financial statement audit procedures. Inspections will focus on how efficiently the public accounting firms perform audits pursuant to AS No. 2 by evaluating:

- The degree of integration between the audit of ICFR and financial statement audits.
- The use of a top-down approach to the integrated audit.
- The use of a risk-based approach in properly evaluating and responding to identified risk.
- Reliance on the work of others.[58]

The inspection process is conducted at three levels:

1. Meetings with senior firm leadership to determine the firm's strategies in achieving efficiencies in light of four given guidelines (e.g., integrated audit, risk-based and top-down approaches, and reliance on the work of others).
2. National office inspection procedures to assess how well the firms' guidance and audit tools address the four areas of efficiency.
3. Engagement inspection procedures in which at least one of the four areas of efficiency, including integrated audit, risk-based approach, top-down approach, and utilizing the work of others, will be selected for inspection for each accelerated filer audit that is reviewed.

PCAOB Enforcement Investigations

The PCAOB initiated its enforcement actions against several registered auditors who were alleged to have concealed information requested by the PCAOB through its inspection process. The PCAOB investigation process is very similar to the SEC's enforcement investigations. This process starts with the staff of the Enforcement and Investigation Division issuing document requests that are called accounting board documents (ABDs) and subsequently requests for testimony from partners and managers of the audit firms.[59] The staff then proceeds pursuant to a board "formal order" of investigation. PCAOB enforcement investigations pertain to any financial statement that is included within statements that are filed with the SEC after the audit firm registered with the PCAOB in 2003. PCAOB enforcement investigations are often coordinated with those of the SEC in that:

- The PCAOB staff meets frequently with the SEC staff.
- The PCAOB staff attends SEC testimony of auditors.
- SEC staff sits in on PCAOB testimony without asking questions.

SOX has authorized the PCAOB to inspect registered public accounting firms that audit public companies and discipline them and their associated persons for any violations of securities laws. Thus, registered public accounting firms can be sanctioned by the PCAOB and barred from practicing in public company audit engagements for audit failures. However, only state boards of accountancy can revoke a firm's or an individual's CPA license. PCAOB inspections do not limit a state board's investigation authority. It is also the author's understanding that some registered public accounting firms have decided not to share Part 2 of the PCAOB inspection reports with their client's audit committee that is "directly responsible" for hiring, firing, evaluation, and compensation. This decision sends a troubling signal of substandard and monopolistic behavior by those firms. There have been some concerns that public accounting firms may be disciplined by the PCAOB and the SEC and barred from auditing public companies, but yet keep their licenses granted under state law to provide accounting and auditing services to private companies. The New York State Board of Regents has revised the definition of "unprofessional conduct" for practicing CPAs who are disciplined at the federal level by either the SEC or the PCAOB.[60] The purpose is to hold practicing CPAs accountable for their professional conduct at both the state and federal levels.

AUDIT COMMITTEE OVERSIGHT OF EXTERNAL AUDITORS

The emerging corporate governance reforms have expanded audit committee oversight responsibility over the external audit function. The extended responsibilities of the audit committee make the independent auditor responsible to the committee, not management. These reforms hold the audit committee directly responsible for overseeing the external audit function, and the external auditor is ultimately accountable to the audit committee. The eight extended oversight responsibilities for the audit committee are:

- Appointment, compensation, and retention of the registered public accounting firms.
- Preapproval of audit services and permissible nonaudit services.

- Review of independent auditor plans for the integrated audit of both internal control over financial reporting and annual financial statements.
- Review and discussion of financial statements audited or reviewed by the independent auditor.
- Monitoring of the auditor's independence.
- Auditor rotation requirement.
- Audit firm selection.
- Communication with the independent auditor.

Appointment, Compensation, and Retention of Auditors

Section 301(2) of SOX states that the audit committee is "directly responsible" for hiring, compensating, and firing the company's independent auditor. The committee is also "directly responsible" for overseeing the work of the company's independent auditor in performing all audit and nonaudit services, including audit of financial statements, audit of internal control over financial reporting, review of interim financial statements, and performance of permissible nonaudit services such as tax services. These provisions are intended to reduce potential conflicts of interest between the company's management and its independent auditor.

SOX provides the audit committee with the authority to obtain funding for the compensation of the independent auditor. Management traditionally has negotiated the fees for the performance of audit and nonaudit services in the context of reducing the cost of both services. The audit committee now directly participates in the negotiation process for determining the audit fees and in approving fees for both audit and permissible nonaudit services. It is expected that the committee will place more emphasis on audit quality in light of recent substantial increases in fees due to an extended audit scope, which includes an audit of internal control over financial reporting. Nevertheless, the 2004 KPMG survey indicates that the majority of the participants (about 70 percent) believed that senior executives (CEOs, CFOs) had the most influence over the determination of audit fee and compensation of independent auditors; only about 27 percent thought the audit committee had the most influence.[61]

Exhibit 9.3 shows the percentage of audit fee increases in 2004 for Standard & Poor's (S&P) 500, Russell 300, and other public companies. The average audit

EXHIBIT 9.3   2004 Audit Fees Statistics

Category	Increase	Percentage (%)
S&P 500	$1.2 billion	56
Russell 300 (non S&P 500)	$1.2 billion	85
COS > $100M (Revenues)	$217.2 million	51.7
SB Filers	$20.2 million	21
Russell 300 executive compensation increased 67 percent		

Source: Turner, L. 2005. BLB&G Institutional Investor Forum presented October 20–21, 2005 in New York.

fee increase for S&P 500 and Russell 3000 companies is 56 percent and 85 percent, respectively. Of that figure, much of the increase can be attributed to the first-year compliance with SOX's Section 404 mandatory audit report on ICFR. As the audit of financial reports moves toward an integrated audit of the financial statements and ICFR, we expect that the cost of the audit would substantially increase and the audit committee could be directly responsible for compensating auditors.

Preapproval of Audit Services and Permissible Nonaudit Services

Sections 201 and 202 of SOX require that all audit and permissible nonaudit services performed by the company's independent auditor must be approved by the audit committee. The preapproval process can be done engagement by engagement, or the company can establish preapproval policies and procedures for all audit and permissible nonaudit services. The preapproval of permissible nonaudit services may be delegated to a member of the company's audit committee. However, such a decision by a member of the audit committee must be presented to the committee at its next meeting and should be approved by the company's board of directors.

Review of Independent Auditor Plan for the Integrated Audit

SOX has substantially increased audit committee involvement with the quality and quantity of working relations with independent auditors. A typical once-a-year short meeting between external auditors and the audit committee has been replaced with more frequent and more extensive discussion regarding audit work. Independent auditors obtain more information from the committee regarding the company's financial reporting process, internal controls, and enterprise risk management. Audit committees gather information regarding audit scope, complex accounting policies and practices, alternative accounting treatments, accounting estimates and reserves, and other significant accounting and auditing discussed with management. In conducting the audit, auditors interact with management, which includes gathering evidence, evaluating evidence, and making decisions. Thus auditors should establish a cooperative working relationship with management. Nevertheless, independent auditors should understand that under recent corporate governance reforms and the regulatory environment, they are ultimately accountable and professionally responsible to the audit committee as a representative and guardian of the company's investors and other stakeholders.

The audit committee should review the independent auditor plan for performing audit services, including audit of the company's annual financial statements and audit of internal control over financial reporting. After approving the services, the committee should discuss the audit plan, including audit scope, supervision, staffing, review process, audit sites to be visited, reporting date, areas that require special audit attention (special purpose entities, related party transactions, fraud risk), and any arrangements for audit of the company's subsidiaries, particularly foreign affiliates.

Review and Discussion of Financial Reports

The audit committee should review and discuss annual audited financial statements and interim reviewed financial statements with the company's independent auditor. The purpose of this review and discussion is for the committee to obtain:

- An understanding of the financial reports.
- Assurance from auditors on the financial reports.
- Resolution of any disagreements between management and the auditor regarding the content, format, and presentation of financial reports.
- Recommendations for the company's board of directors for the filing and distribution of financial reports.

The audit committee should meet with the company's CFO, internal auditor, independent auditor, and legal counsel to discuss the integrated audit of annual financial statements, including management's assessment of the effectiveness of ICFR, the auditor's report on management's assessment, and audit of annual financial statements, to evaluate the overall integrity and quality of financial reports before they are filed or distributed.

Issues that should be addressed in the audit committee meeting with the CFO, internal auditor, independent auditor, and legal counsel include but are not limited to:

- The quality and integrity of financial reports in terms of their content, format and disclosure, and presentation in conformity with GAAP.
- All critical accounting policies and practices used by management in measuring and recognizing the company's transactions and events as well as the preparation of financial statements.
- All alternative treatments within GAAP for accounting policies and practices related to material financial items used by management and approved by the independent auditor.
- Disagreements between management and the independent auditor regarding accounting and internal control issues and presentation of financial statements.
- All material communications (oral and written) between management and the independent auditor, including audit adjustments, fraud risk factors, significant deficiencies, and material weaknesses in ICFR.
- All material unusual transactions, significant fluctuations, accounting estimates and reserves, and significant internal control issues.
- Independent auditor disagreements with management about the scope of the integrated audit and material weakness in ICFR and the wording of the audit (reports).
- Any difficulties or lack of cooperation and coordination by management during the audit engagement, including any delays in providing requested information, schedules, records, and documents.
- Substantial changes in the audit fee resulting from departures from the initial integrated audit plan.

■ Any suspected fraud by management or material employee fraud affecting reliability and integrity of financial statements and/or illegal acts by senior management, including violations of applicable laws and regulations.

Monitoring the Auditor's Independence

Auditor independence is the backbone of the auditing profession, affecting the auditor's planning, evidence-gathering procedures, findings, judgment, and credibility, and the public trust in the auditor's opinion. Thus it is essential that the audit committee monitor auditor independence in fact and in appearance while:

■ Planning the audit to ensure that management is not influencing the audit plan and scope of the audit.
■ Gathering evidence to ensure that the auditor has access to all information, records, schedules, and financial statements and the scope of the audit was not limited.
■ Reporting audit findings to ensure that the auditor's judgment and opinion were not influenced by management or by a sense of loyalty to the company.

The SEC requires that the audit committee indicate in its annual report whether the committee has received disclosures about auditor independence and discussed it with the independent auditor.[62] To ensure proper disclosures of auditor independence, the committee should receive an auditor independence confirmation from the company's independent auditor prior to the filing and distribution of audited financial statements. Auditor's independence is discussed further in the next section of this chapter.

Lead Auditor Rotation Requirement

Section 203 of SOX and SEC-related rules require the lead and concurring partners to rotate off the company's audit after five years and stay off for five years (five years on and five years off). Audit partners other than the lead and concurring partners involved in an engagement must rotate off no more than seven years and are subject a two-year time-out. The audit committee should monitor rotation requirements for audit partners prior to an audit engagement. In addition, the committee should ensure that no employee of the company with a financial reporting oversight role, including the CEO, CFO, controller, and CAO, was a member of the current audit engagement team at any time within a one year period (the cooling-off period).

Corporate governance reforms do not require, although they suggest in special circumstances, audit firm rotations. However, the upward trend in audit firm switches in the post-SOX era has received the attention of regulators, the accounting profession, and the investing community. Auditor changes can occur as a result of auditor dismissal by the company's audit committee or the auditor's resignation. In either case, the SEC must be notified of auditor changes by filing Form 8-K. Auditors usually resign when there is an unresolved dispute with a client or when a client's financial health deteriorates, which increases the likelihood of litigation risk. Auditor dismissals often result from disagreements about key issues pertaining to financial reporting, internal controls, and audit fees.

Rotation of Public Accounting Firms

The Conference Board recommends that the company's audit committee consider rotating their public accounting firm when its independence from management is severely in doubt.[63] The Board specifically states that the existence of some or all of these circumstances merits consideration of audit firm rotations:

- One or more former partners or managers of the audit firm hold key financial positions (CFO, controller, chief accountant) in the company.
- The audit firm has been performing audit and assurance services to the company for a substantial period of time (e.g., over 10 years).
- The audit firm has performed significant non-audit services for the company.[64]

In 2005, 1,430 public companies changed their independent public accounting firms, including 77 companies that changed their auditors at least twice.[65] The SEC has yet to adequately address this important issue of audit change disclosure in its rules. In many cases when companies dismiss their auditors, they provide limited or no information related to the reason for the dismissal. Investors are entitled to know the reasons for these changes in auditors. For example, Computer Associates International Inc. (CA) fired Ernst & Young as its independent auditor in 1999 and disclosed in its public filings that there were no disputes, including accounting disagreements or other reportable events, with the dismissed auditors. However, the SEC investigation indicated that CA replaced Ernst & Young with KPMG after Ernst & Young directed CA to make proper disclosure about its executive stock option (ESO) plans. This and many other similar cases underscore the need for more transparent disclosures of reasons for auditor dismissals. The SEC Form 8-K does not require companies to disclose specific reasons for auditor changes in all circumstances, and auditors do not voluntarily provide particular reasons, as they are not required to disclose their agreements and disagreements.

Auditor rotation is mandatory in Italy. The European Commission (EC) is considering requiring mandatory audit rotation of either lead or audit partners every five years or of the audit firm every seven years in member states.[66] Some argue that audit firm rotation helped discover the wrongdoings at Parmalat, the so-called Enron of Europe. Others argue that audit firm rotation practice is useless as fraud had gone on for some time at Parmalat. It can be argued that when an auditor (predecessor auditor) knows that another auditor (successor) will be checking up on the audit work and will be responsible for responding to such inquiries, then it is more likely that the predecessor will pay more attention, be more skeptical, and perform a more thorough audit. Companies normally switch their auditors for a variety of reasons. The SEC, while requiring public companies to disclose to their shareholders in their proxy statement changes in the auditor and the appointment of a new auditor, does not mandate the disclosure of the reason(s) for such changes, nor does it require shareholder ratification of a new auditor.[67] SEC rules require public companies that change their public accounting firms to file a Form 8-K, Item 4.01 to disclose changes within four days, whereas auditors are required to provide standard letters within ten days stating whether they agree with the company's disclosure, without specifying any reasons. The public filings of auditor changes should reveal whether certain items occurred within the previous two years, including: (1) whether the former accountant resigned or was dismissed; (2) whether the auditor's opinion on the company's financial statements was other than unqualified (e.g., adverse, disclaimer, qualified or modified); (3) whether there were any disagreements with the former auditor regarding accounting principles and practices, audit scope, or financial statement disclosures; and (4) whether there was any advice from the auditors regarding the effectiveness of ICFR (e.g., identified material weakness) lack of reliance in management's representations, or new information that materially affected the fairness or reliability of previously issued financial statements (e.g., restatement of financial statements).[68]

SEC regulations require companies to provide their outgoing auditor with a copy of auditor change filings. An outgoing auditor's disagreement with the company's stated reason for the change is rare; there were only 20 cases in 2005 out of a total of 1,430 auditor changes.[69] The disagreements often pertain to undisclosed material weakness, going-concern modifications, disputes over audit fees or services provided, disagreements over accounting principles and practices, and the chain of events leading to dismissals or resignations.

SOX commissioned the Government Accountability Office (GAO, formerly the General Accounting Office) to conduct a study of the potential impact of requiring public companies to rotate their auditors. The GAO's report, issued in 2003, indicates:

- The average length of auditor tenure of Fortune 1000 companies was about 22 years.
- The majority (79 percent) of public companies and their auditors reported that changing audit firms increases the risk of audit failures in the early years of the audit due to the lack of sufficient experience with new clients.
- The majority of public accounting firms and their clients believe that mandatory audit firm rotation would not affect the conduct of the lead partner in dealing with material financial reporting issues.
- The estimated increase in the cost of audit is about 20 percent if mandatory audit firm rotation is imposed.[70]

The GAO report concludes that the SEC and the PCAOB should continue to monitor the effectiveness of existing requirements and compliance with independent standards for enhancing auditor independence and audit quality. The general perception is that audit firm rotation can be very costly, complex, and ineffective without adding much to the objectivity and independence of financial statement audits. However, in the post-SOX period (from 2003 to 2005), about 4,000 public companies changed their audit firm, which is roughly a third of all public companies; in particular, about 11 percent of public companies changed their audit firm

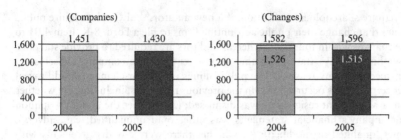

EXHIBIT 9.4 Number of Companies that Changed Auditors, and Number of Auditor Changes
Source: Glass Lewis and Co. 2006. Mum's the word, Yellow Card Trend Alert (July 27). Available at: www.glasslewis.com.

in 2005. This suggests that in reality public companies often change auditors and any mandatory audit firm rotation every several years (e.g., ten years) may not be a bad idea. Exhibit 9.4, presents the number of public companies that changed auditors and the number of auditor changes in 2005 and 2004. The author suggests that the company's audit committee consider all relevant factors, including potential increases in audit cost and the possibility of audit failure in the first few years, as well as the benefit of bringing a fresh perspective in deciding to change auditors.

Audit Firm Selection

The audit committee is now directly responsible for the appointment, compensation, and retention of the company's independent auditor. In selecting the company's public accounting firm, the committee should pay particular attention to auditor independence (e.g., not engaging in prohibited nonaudit services), auditor industry specialization, auditor reputation (e.g., quality control system including independence policies and the latest PCAOB inspections), adequacy and reasonableness of the audit fee, and the requirement for rotation of the lead partner. If the committee at any time becomes aware of a violation of auditor independence, inappropriateness of audit services, significant damages to auditor reputation, or substantial difficulties between management and the independent auditor, they should consider changing the company's independent auditor. The committee should then prepare a short list of potential independent auditors, interview the potential candidates (CFO and the director of the internal audit department may participate in the interview process), and then select at least two independent auditors to submit the formal proposal and advise other auditors that they are no longer being considered.

The two selected public accounting firms should be given the opportunity to: investigate the company; study the integrity of its management; investigate its financial solvency, business risk, financial records, books, and filing requirements; visit the company's important plants and offices, including key personnel; contact the company's current and past business associates; and communicate with the preceding auditor. The two potential independent auditors should show their intent and interest in the audit client by submitting a formal proposal indicating the proposed audit fee or method of determining audit fee and other important issues (auditor independence, rotation requirements). Finally, the audit committee should select one firm and ask it to prepare and sign a written contract (engagement letter). The appointed independent auditor then signs the contract to perform the audit.

Independent Auditor Communication with the Audit Committee

Corporate governance reforms require and/or suggest a variety of formal and informal communications between the audit committee and the independent auditor.

Communications from the audit committee to the independent auditor include, but are not limited to:

- Appointment and retention approval of the independent auditor.
- Formal approval of audit and permissible nonaudit services.
- Formal approval of fees for both audit and nonaudit services with a keen focus on improving the quality of both services.
- Any concerns or risks threatening management reputation and integrity, the reliability of financial reporting, or effectiveness of internal controls known to the audit committee that could possibly affect audit activities and the quality of audit services.
- Allegations of financial statement fraud known to the audit committee that affect the integrity and reliability of financial statements and the effectiveness of a related audit.

Communications from the independent auditor to the audit committee include, but are not limited to:

- The seeking of audit committee preapproval of all audit and nonaudit services in a timely manner.
- The critical accounting policies and practices used by management in the preparation of financial statements.
- All alternative treatments of financial information within GAAP that have already been discussed with management, the ramifications of the use of such alternative accounting treatments, and the treatment preferred by the auditor.
- Any accounting disagreements between the independent auditor and the company's management.
- Any material written communications between the independent auditor and the company's management throughout the course of the audit.
- Significant deficiencies and material weaknesses of ICFR.
- The audit report on annual financial statements.
- The review report on quarterly financial statements.

- The audit report on management's assessment of the effectiveness of ICFR.
- The audit report on the effectiveness of ICFR.
- Financial risks associated with financial reports.

Exhibit 9.5 describes the independent auditor communication with the audit committee under an integrated audit approach. In summary, best practices suggests that the audit committee ask the independent auditor four questions relevant to the integrated audit of internal controls and financial statements:

1. Are there any significant accounting judgments or estimates made by management that the auditor would have made differently had the auditor been responsible for the preparation of the financial statements?
2. Are there any alternative accounting policies and practices that the independent auditor would have preferred to use?
3. Based on the auditor's experience and knowledge of the company, do the financial statements truly and fairly present the company's financial position and results of operations in conformity with GAAP?
4. Has the company implemented internal controls and internal audit procedures that are adequate and effective and are appropriate for the company?

AUDITOR INDEPENDENCE

Auditor independence is the cornerstone of the auditing profession and one of the fundamental aspects that makes audits function value-adding services to society and the investing public. External auditors are independent contractors hired to independently assess and lend credibility to the accuracy of the financial statements. Thus, auditor independence in both fact and appearance is important in assessing the value of audit services provided to clients. Auditor independence is influenced by the entire audit process, from the selection and appointment of auditors, to acceptance of clients, planning the audit engagement and scope of the audit, audit fees, conducting the audit, and reporting audit findings and opinion. Auditor independence is derived from the three basic independence principles as specified in the SEC rules:[71]

1. Auditors cannot be part of management or its team.
2. Auditors cannot audit their own works.
3. Auditors cannot serve in advocacy roles as specified by the SEC and as depicted in Exhibit 9.6.

SOX addresses auditor independence in five of its provisions:[72]

1. Section 206 prohibits auditors from performing an audit for a company whose CEO, CFO, controller, CAO, or person in an equivalent position was employed by the accounting firm during the one-year period preceding the audit (the cooling-off period).

EXHIBIT 9.5 Independent Auditor Communications with the Audit Committee Under an Integrated Audit Approach

To the Chairman of the Audit Committee:
We have audited the internal control over financial reporting and the financial statements of XYZ company as of and for the year ended December 31, 20X5, and have issued our integrated audit report thereon dated March 15, 20X6. Public Company Accounting Oversight Board (PCAOB) standards require that we advise you of the following matters relevant to our integrated audit.

Our Responsibility under the Standards of the PCAOB

Our responsibilities as described in the PCAOB Professional Standards, are to: (1) conduct an audit of internal control over financial reporting; and (2) perform financial audits to obtain reasonable assurance that the financial statements are free of material misstatements whether caused by error or fraud. We conduct our integrated audit in accordance with the Standards of the Public Company Accounting Oversight Board (United States). Our integrated audit does not provide absolute assurance about the effectiveness of internal control nor does it provide absolute assurance about the accuracy of the financial statements. Thus, there is an inherent risk that (1) material weaknesses or significant deficiencies exist in internal control and were undetected; and (2) material misstatements caused by errors, fraud, or illegal acts may exist and were not discovered.

Material Weaknesses

Management is primarily responsible for the effective design and operation of internal control over financial reporting. Our integrated audit detects the following material weaknesses in internal controls that may cause financial statements to be misleading as specified in our audit report.

Significant Deficiencies

The following significant deficiencies have detected that deserve the audit committee's attention.

Significant Accounting Policies

Management is responsible for the selection and application of appropriate accounting policies. A summary of the adopted accounting policies is included in Note [X] to the financial statements, and were consistently applied and appropriate.

Management Judgments and Accounting Estimates

Accounting estimates are an integral component of the financial statements prepared by management and are based on management's judgments. The key accounting estimates affecting the financial statements are [describe]. We evaluated the major factors and assumptions used in developing these statements and accordingly determined that they were reasonable in relation to the basic financial statements taken as a whole.

(*continued overleaf*)

EXHIBIT 9.5 (*Continued*)

Audit Adjustments

Adjustments listed in this report consist of those that have already corrected and booked and those that management decided not to book. These adjustments may not have been detected except through our integrated audit. Adjustments are misstatements detected during the course of the audit that are material and should be corrected and recorded in order for the financial statements to be presented fairly in conformity with GAAP. We did not propose any audit adjustments that could have a significant effect on the reliability of the financial statements.

Other Information in Documents Containing Audited Financial Statements

We are not aware of any inconsistency between other information (e.g., presented in MD&A) and financial information presented in the financial statements nor are we aware of material misstatements of fact that could cause financial statements to be misleading.

Disagreements with Management

All the matters that arose during the course of the audit were resolved to our satisfaction except for [*describe: e.g., classification of internal control deficiencies*].

Consultation with other Accountants

There were no consultations with other accountants relevant to auditing and accounting matters.

Major Issues Discussed with Management Prior to Retention

We did not discuss with management any major issues pertaining to the application of accounting principles and auditing standards that could be perceived as a condition to our retention as the Company's auditors.

Difficulties Encountered in Performing the Audit

We encountered no serious difficulties in dealing with management during the course of our audit.

Lead and Review Partner Rotation

We are in compliance with the requirements of lead and review partner rotation.

Inspection Report

The following portion of our inspection report conducted by the PCAOB is relevant to our integrated audit of the company.

The report is intended solely for the information and use of the audit committee, board of directors, and management of XYZ company and is not intended to be and should not be used by anyone other than these specified parties.

Signature of auditor
Date

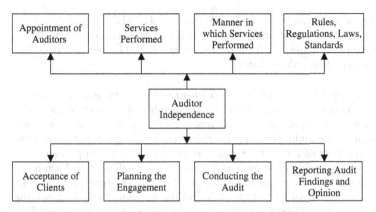

EXHIBIT 9.6 Auditor Independence

2. Section 201 prohibits auditors from providing nine specific nonaudit services (discussed in the next section) to the company contemporaneously with audit services.
3. Section 203 requires the lead audit or coordinating partner and reviewing partner to rotate off the audit every five years.
4. Section 204 requires auditors to report to the audit committee all critical accounting policies and practices used, all alternative treatment of financial information within GAAP, ramifications of the use of such alternative disclosures and treatments, the preferred treatment, and other material written communication between the auditor and management. It also prohibits registered auditors from setting an audit partner's compensation or allocation of partnership based on the revenue generated by providing nonaudit services to clients.
5. Section 103 requires a second-partner review and approval of each public company audit report.

These provisions of SOX were intended to strengthen auditor independence. Thus, public companies should establish proper policies and procedures for the implementation of these provisions, and the company's audit committee should oversee the effectiveness of the established policies and procedures to ensure auditor independence. Listing standards of national stock exchanges require that the listing company's audit committee establish hiring policies for employees or former employees of the company's public accounting firm.[73] The author suggests that the required one year cooling off be extended to a few years, at least two years, for auditors at the managerial or supervisor level.

SEC Rules on Auditor Independence

On January 28, 2003, the SEC issued its final rule amending requirements of auditor independence to enhance independence of auditors who review or audit public companies' financial statements in the post-SOX era.[74] The SEC rule recognizes the important role that the audit committee plays in monitoring auditor independence and in improving the quality of financial reporting. The SEC rule addresses five issues relevant to auditor independence.[75]

1. *Conflicts of interest resulting from employment relationships.* Auditor independence is impaired if the company employs a member of the audit engagement team in a financial reporting oversight role within the year preceding the commencement of the audit procedures for the year that the company hired the auditor. Members of the audit engagement team include a lead partner, concurring review partner, audit staff, and other professionals who perform more than ten hours of service in an audit capacity. The financial reporting oversight role is defined as a role in which an individual has direct responsibility for overseeing those who prepare the company's financial statements (e.g., CEO, CFO, chief accountant, controller).
2. *Scope of services provided by auditors.* The SEC rule permits auditors to provide all permissible nonaudit services to their audit clients as long as they are preapproved by the audit committee. Nine nonaudit services specified in Section 201 of SOX are prohibited:
    a. Bookkeeping or other services pertaining to the accounting records or financial statements of the audit clients.
    b. Financial information systems design and implementation.
    c. Appraisal or valuation services, fairness opinions, or contribution-in-kind reports.
    d. Actuarial services.
    e. Internal audit outsourcing.
    f. Management functions and human resources.
    g. Broker/dealers, investment advisor, or investment banking services.
    h. Legal services and expert services.
    i. Any other nonaudit services that the PCOAB determines.
    The permissible nonaudit services are tax services, internal control reviews, employee benefit plan audits, and acquisition due diligence. The PCAOB Independence Rule prohibits auditors from engaging in aggressive and abusive tax services for their audit clients, which may impair auditor independence.[76]
3. *Partner rotation.* The SEC rule requires the lead audit and concurring review partners to rotate every five years (e.g., five years on, five years off). Audit partners at significant (greater than 20 percent of assets or revenues) subsidiaries and at the parent company who have significant involvement with senior management are required to rotate after seven years and are subject to a two-year time-out period. This rule does not require tax partners to rotate.
4. *Audit committee administration of the engagement.* The audit committee is responsible for approving audit and permissible nonaudit services to be performed by the independent auditor. This preapproval can be obtained directly from the audit committee, or the company can establish preapproval policies and procedures adopted by the committee that are detailed and specified as to the type of service.

5. *Audit partner compensation.* SOX did not directly address audit partner compensation. The SEC rule, however, requires audit partner compensation (e.g., bonuses, commissions) to be linked to the audit quality and not be related to selling nonaudit services.

Public companies were required to disclose fees paid to their independent auditor in three categories of audit fees: financial information systems design, implementation fees, and all other fees since February 2001. This classification of auditor fees often caused confusion as to the extent of nonaudit services provided to clients by the independent auditor. The SEC's final rule, on January 28, 2003, in implementing Section 202 of SOX, expanded auditor fee categories into four classifications of audit fees, audit-related fees, tax fees, and all other fees.[77]

1. *Audit fees.* Audit fees are fees paid for all services performed to comply with generally accepted auditing standards (GAAS) as adopted by the PCAOB and auditing standards of the PCAOB, including the audit of internal control over financial reporting and the audit of financial statements. Audit fees also include services that the independent auditor usually performs in connection with statutory and regulatory filings (e.g., comfort letters, attest services, statutory audits, certain tax services, and consulting services in connection with the financial statement audit).
2. *Audit-related fees.* This category of fees includes assurance and audit-related services that are normally provided by the independent auditor, such as employee benefit plan audits, due diligence and consultations related to acquisitions, and other attest services that are not required by statute or regulation.
3. *Tax fees.* These are fees that are traditionally paid for tax services, such as tax compliance, tax planning, and tax advice performed by independent auditors. Tax fees include fees paid for all tax services that are not classified as the audit or audit-related services.
4. *All other fees.* This category consists of fees paid to the independent auditor for services performed that cannot be classified as audit, audit-related, or tax service categories, including financial information system design and implementation, valuation services, and accounting and auditing consulting services.

The SEC rule requires that:

- Auditor fees and related categories be disclosed for a two-year comparative presentation.
- The independent auditor provide a qualitative description of types of services provided in all categories except for the audit fee category for two comparative years.
- The company's preapproval policies and procedures be disclosed either in a detailed description or through inclusion with the audit committee preapproval policy.
- Public companies disclose the auditor fee classifications in their annual reports and proxy statements.

Auditor independence implies that auditors who do not make managerial decisions should be directly involved in assisting their clients to identify, understand, and apply appropriate accounting policies and practices. As stated by Donald T. Nicolaisen, then the SEC's chief accountant, this mentality and lack of auditor engagement by saying "finish all of your discussion, decide on what the proper accounting is, put it in a memo and then we'll review it" has to change.[78] An emerging issue relevant to auditor independence is the inclusion of auditor limited liability provisions in the audit engagement. This issue is discussed in the next section.

AUDITOR LIMITED LIABILITY PROVISIONS

There has recently been a heated debate concerning the possible establishment of a liability cap for public accounting firms in securities class action lawsuits.[79] The Big Four public accounting firms, auditing more than 90 percent of public companies, want to limit their liability for their audit failures despite the fact that their revenues have substantially increased in the post-SOX period while the number of class-action lawsuits citing them as defendants has significantly decreased, from 31 in 2002 to 26 in 2003, 23 in 2004, 9 in 2005, and just 1 in the first half of 2006.[80] Limitation of liability provisions imposed by audit firms vary, but may include: (1) elimination of or severe restrictions on the right to discovery and document production, which is particularly important in audit-related disputes; (2) denial of access to the public court system and the right to a jury trial by requiring only mandatory, private alternative dispute resolution proceedings; (3) restrictions on the right to assign or transfer a claim against the auditor to a new entity if the company is bought or merged; (4) imposition of a version of the British rule requiring the company to pay all audit firm legal fees and costs under certain circumstances where audit problems arise; and (5) a ban on punitive damages.

These provisions are not in the best interest of either the company or the investing public. Auditor limitation of liability provisions may serve as a disincentive to auditors to perform high-quality audits since the financial consequences to the audit firm for a failed audit are either greatly reduced or eliminated through the use of these provisions. In addition, such provisions are harmful to investors because they generally eliminate any and all access to the public court system, and therefore any notice to shareholders of accounting and audit problems, by requiring the use of mandatory, private arbitration or mediation proceedings where discovery is severely restricted; the proceedings are strictly confidential and no legal precedent is established, making it an inefficient and often costly process with limited value. These provisions are particularly troubling in light of companies such as United Rentals and Semtech Corp., which are currently under investigation by the SEC for significant accounting problems. It is interesting to note that: (1) the public disclosure of these provisions suggests that companies are acknowledging pressure from their external auditors to agree to these types of provisions; otherwise the auditor will refuse to conduct the audit; (2) the provisions may have already existed but were previously undisclosed to investors; and (3) almost all of the 90 companies that have disclosed their auditor limitation of liability agreements are clients of KPMG or Ernst & Young.[81]

Any auditor limitation of liability provision may create incentives and opportunities for auditors to engage in conflict of interest situations that may adversely affect audit reliability, effectiveness, and quality as well as the auditor's judgment, professional skepticism, and accountability. Furthermore, any such provision may impair auditor independence as set forth in independence rules of the SEC, PCAOB, and AICPA. The potential impairment of auditor independence, in fact or even in appearance, will adversely affect investor confidence and public trust in audits and raise safety and soundness concerns regarding auditor objectivity, impartiality, and performance. Federal banking agencies are opposed to any liability caps and bar large banks from agreeing to them because they may lead to less rigorous audits. Investor activists will withhold their vote to approve the auditors who include such agreements in their audit engagement agreements or side letters.[82] The Council of Institutional Investors (CII) in its 2006 spring meeting approved a new corporate governance policy calling on companies to avoid consenting to limitation of auditor liability arrangements.[83] The PCAOB has discussed the issue of auditor liability caps and has yet to issue a statement of position on this topic. The SEC's position is that when a company indemnifies its auditor from liability and related costs from knowing misrepresentations by the company's management, the auditor is not independent.[84]

The Big Four and other public accounting firms, while enjoying a substantial increase in their revenue in the post-SOX period, seek a liability cap or protection from lawsuits that investors filed against them for flawed audits of public companies. A report entitled "Global Capital Markets and the Global Economy" by the six largest global audit networks calls for relaxed liability standards for public accounting firms.[85] Two influential groups (the committee studying the competitiveness of U.S. financial markets and the U.S. Chamber of Commerce) are considering recommending that the government enact new protections for auditors concerning their liability limitations.[86] It is difficult to assess the risk public accounting firms are facing resulting from the threat of lawsuits and other liabilities and whether their revenues are adequate to ensure substantial growth, profitability, and coverage of malpractice suits for several reasons.[87] First, public accounting firms are private partnerships (limited liability partnerships or limited liability corporations) that usually do not disclose their financial condition and results of operations; thus, their financial information is not transparent. Second, public accounting firms typically distribute their profit annually among their partners and ask them to give back money as needed; thus the actual capital of their firm is unknown. Finally, public accounting firms have grown in size and profitability in the post-SOX era as their audit activities and fees substantially increased while changes in their level of profitability and even insurance is not known.[88] Thus, it is difficult to assess whether auditor liability is in proportion to their capital, profitability, or participation in any problem or audit failure.

The U.K. Companies Act states that public companies may: (1) indemnify an auditor of any liability incurred in defending proceedings in which judgment is given in favor of the auditor; and (2) authorize auditor liability limitation agreements to limit the amount of auditor liability provided that such agreements are passed by a resolution in the company's general annual meeting in advance for the amount considered fair and reasonable in all the circumstances.[89] Any indemnification, limitation of liability, and ADR clause in audit engagement letters, while possibly reducing audit costs, may impair auditor independence and reduce audit quality and objectivity. The Committee on Capital Markets Regulation recommends auditor liability be curtailed by either capping auditors' potential courtroom damages or creating protection for some auditing activities.[90] A cap on auditor liability has been a controversial issue backed by the auditing industry and the U.S. Chamber of Commerce suggesting that an outsized court failure could lead to the demise of one or more of the Big Four public accounting firms, which may negatively affect the global capital markets. The committee fails to realize that: (1) no big accounting firms have collapsed because of a significant court award in recent years (Andersen's demise was caused by a criminal conviction); and (2) the pervasiveness of financial restatements in the post-SOX era (e.g. 1,200 in 2005 and about 1,300 in 2006) does not support the committee's assertion that auditors may have incentive to engage in defensive auditing driven by claimed overzealous regulations.

INTEGRATED AUDIT APPROACH

Auditing standards issued by the PCAOB recommend the use of an integrated audit approach consisting of an audit of ICFR and the financial statements. The integrated audit requires independent auditors to express an opinion on: management's assessment of the effectiveness of ICFR; the effectiveness of both design and operation of ICFR; and fair presentation of financial statements in conformity with GAAP. The phrase "integrated audit" appeared for the first time in the title of professional standards when the PCAOB issued its proposed audit standard entitled *An Audit of Internal Control over Financial Reporting that is Integrated with an Audit of Financial Statements*. The new proposed auditing standard when approved would become AS No. 5 and supersede PCAOB AS No. 2. AS No. 5 was developed in response to the perceived ineffectiveness, inefficiency, and lack of scalability of AS No. 2 and in an attempt to encourage auditors to use a principles-based, top-down, risk-based audit, and to apply professional judgment to tailor the integrated audit to the facts and circumstances of each audit engagement. The proposed AS No. 5 is intended to improve the audit by: (1) focusing the audit on the matters most important to internal control; (2) eliminating unnecessary audit procedures; (3) simplifying the auditor requirements; and (4) scaling the integrated audit for smaller companies. The author's review of a sample of 2005 audit engagements letters of Big Four public accounting firms reveals that the engagement letters were prepared based on the performance of integrated audits. An integrated audit requires auditors to change their audit strategy.

Audit Strategy

Independent auditors traditionally have performed a combination of tests of controls and substantive tests to provide reasonable assurance that financial statements are free of material misstatements, whether caused by errors or fraud. This level of assurance requires auditors to reduce the risk of material misstatements to an appropriately low level. The performed level of tests of internal controls, including understanding of the client's internal control structure, is not sufficient to opine on internal controls. Tests of controls must be broadened to include understanding of ICFR and provide reasonable assurance about the effectiveness of both design and operation of internal controls. Auditors have often performed limited tests of controls, used cycle rotation approach to test controls, or conducted dual internal controls or substantive tests. These audit approaches are less relevant to an integrated audit. In an integrated audit there is:

- No *limited tests of controls.* The second standard of fieldwork requires auditors to obtain a sufficient understanding of internal controls to plan the audit and to determine the nature, timing, and extent of audit procedures (mainly substantive tests) to be performed. This requires only an understanding of internal control and does not require the performance of tests of controls. In complying with this standard, independent auditors have performed limited tests of controls only when: (1) adequate controls exist (built in the internal control system); and (2) it is cost justifiable/feasible to perform some limited tests of controls to possibly reduce the extent of substantive tests. This approach of performing limited tests of controls is no longer acceptable under integrated audit of public companies in accordance with the PCAOB No. 2 and the proposed AS No. 5.
- No *use of cycle rotation in tests of controls.* To comply efficiently and effectively with the second standard of fieldwork, in the past auditors have used cycle rotation in tests of controls. This approach involves:
  a. Identifying and classifying the client's transactions into groups of interrelated transactions (cycles), depending on the nature of the client's business and industry (e.g., for manufacturing companies, typical transaction cycles are: (1) revenue and collection cycle; (2) acquisition and payment cycle; (3) conversion cycle; (4) payroll and personnel cycle; and (5) finance and investment cycle).
  b. Obtaining an understanding of internal controls of all relevant transaction cycles.
  c. Performing tests of controls on several of these transaction cycles while conducting a "walk-through" test to ensure the absence of control changes in the remaining cycles previously tested.
  Auditors under integrated audit should express opinions on the effectiveness of both design and operation of ICFR on an annual basis. Thus, the cycle rotation approach to tests of controls is no longer acceptable for auditing public companies in accordance with PCAOB AS No. 2.
- *Dual internal controls and substantive tests.* Independent auditors, in performing dual tests of internal control and substantive audit procedures, have in the past primarily focused on transaction-level prevention, detection, and correction controls as well as transactions and account balances substantive tests. Under the integrated audit approach, auditors should test controls at both the entity level and transaction level. Entity-level controls are relevant to: the effectiveness

of the company's governance; vigilance of its board of directors; integrity and reputation of its management; possibility of management overriding the control system; and its overall corporate culture and code of conduct. The effectiveness of the entity-level controls is important in expressing an opinion on ICFR under an integrated audit approach.

Auditors should focus on prevention, detection, and correction of internal controls at both the entity level and transaction level. They should use evidence gathered by performing tests of controls in determining the nature, timing, and extent of substantive tests of details and analytical procedures for classes of transactions and account balances. Auditors should perform tests of controls as a basis of forming an opinion on the effectiveness of ICFR. They should also perform substantive tests as a basis of expressing an opinion on fair presentation of financial statements regardless of the identified significant deficiencies and material weaknesses in internal controls.

AUDIT OF DEFINED BENEFIT PENSIONS

Recent large corporate bankruptcies and the related transfer of unfunded pension liabilities to the Pension Benefit Guaranty Corporation have caused both the U.S. government and Congress to focus on the minimum funding rules relevant to private sector defined benefit pension plans.[91] In 2005, the government issued a proposal for strengthening the annual funding requirements for pension plans, and Congress subsequently introduced bills for such plans. Employer-defined benefit pension reforms as proposed by the administration and introduced by both the House and the Senate would require plan sponsors to make minimum funding contributions equal to the greater of: (1) the contributions required under the plan's funding standard account estimated based on the plan's actuarial accrued liability; or (2) deficient reduction contributions calculated under the current liability rules.[92] These reforms would replace the current law's "double barrel" system with a single measure of assets and liabilities and required funding method.[93]

Auditors of public companies' employee benefit plans are receiving a consider-able amount of attention in the post-SOX era. Public companies are required to file with the SEC an 11-K report regarding their employee benefit plans.[94] The report requires an audit report on a plan financial statement filed with the SEC. Sections 404 and 906 of SOX may also apply to employee benefit plans (11-K plan reporting).[95] Many public companies have included Section 404 and 906 certifications with Form 11-K filed in light of uncertainties and lack of guidance from the SEC regarding the statutory language. The general understanding is that Section 404 and 906 certifications do not apply to SEC Form 11-K. Nonetheless, the company's audit committee and the independent auditor should pay attention to any developments in 11-K reporting.

Several prominent companies have announced that they will go out of business unless they are allowed to terminate their pension plans. One example is Pittsburgh Brewing, which informed the Federal Pension Benefit Guaranty Corporation that unless its pension plan is terminated, it will not be able to continue in business.[96] The

FASB, as discussed in Chapter 5, is undertaking a two-phase project on overhauling the accounting for pension and postretirement plans and has already issued its accounting standards concerning the first phase. SFAS No. 158, which was issued on September 29, 2006, requires employers to fully: (1) recognize on their balance sheet an asset for a pension plan's underfunded status; (2) measure a plan's assets and obligations as of their fiscal year; and (3) record changes in the funded status of a plan through comprehensive income in the year in which the changes occur. Auditors can be engaged to audit the company's employee benefit plans.

AUDIT OF EXECUTIVE COMPENSATION INCLUDING STOCK OPTIONS

The perceptions that executives are overpaid, their compensation is not linked to their performance, and more serious concerns about the timing of their stock option grants have received considerable attention from lawmakers, regulators, boards, shareholders, and employees. First, lawmakers, including Congressman Barney Frank (D-MA), introduced a legislative proposal that would allow shareholders to vote on executive compensation arrangements. Second, regulators such as the SEC have approved the proposal to improve disclosures and transparency of executive compensation plans. Third, standard setters such as the FASB issued SFAS No. 123(R), requiring companies to begin recognizing stock options as an expense. Finally, federal authorities (e.g. the SEC and Justice Department) have probed more than 250 companies for their alleged illegal backdating practices of stock option grants to unjustifiably benefit their executives and key employees. The reforms on executive compensation are likely to continue for the foreseeable future. It is expected that the compensation committee will pay more attention to executive compensation.

The potential cost to shareholders can be significant as companies with backdating practices are restating their financial statements. For example, Broadcom Corp. reported the change to its earnings for its backdating practices is about $1.5 billion. As probed companies delay to file their financial reports they come under more scrutiny by regulators and increase market reactions to such probes. The stock option backdating scandal is becoming more widespread as more companies are probed for their grant backdating practices. Traditionally, auditors have not paid sufficient attention to client backdating practices for several reasons. First, accounting standards prior to the issuance of SFAS No. 123(R) did not require companies to recognize their compensation cost as an expense, and often when financial items are not reported in financial statements, they do not receive adequate audit consideration. Second, although auditors are responsible for reviewing footnotes to the financial statements to ensure they are consistent with financial items, footnotes are usually not subject to the same scrutiny as financial statement amounts. Third, financial ties and dependence on nonaudit consulting fees had prevented auditors from being adequately skeptical concerning the involvement of their clients' directors and executives with option backdating practices. Fourth, auditors had not been required to report on internal control over financial reporting, which could have uncovered weaknesses in companies' internal controls concerning backdating policies and practices. Finally, companies were not required to file changes in option grants for weeks and months in the pre-SOX period, which presented opportunities to manipulate backdating practices.

Lawmakers, regulators, and investor activists, among others, are raising concern requiring independent auditors' involvement in grant backdating practices and want to know what roles corporate directors, including the compensation committee, play outside. The AFL-CIO, one of the largest investors in public companies, has raised severe concerns about the role that public accounting firms play in the reported backdating probes. They sent a letter to all Big Four public accounting firms asking them to describe what role they may or may not have had in executive stock options (ESO) backdating scandals.[97] Attorneys, compensation consultants, and independent committees might have played a role in the reported ESO grant backdating practices and subsequent probes. More than 250 public companies are under scrutiny by the Department of Justice, the SEC, and the IRS for possible tax-law violations, and by their own internal investigations for their ESO grant backdating practices.

On July 28, 2006, the PCAOB announced an initiative to publish "Audit Practice Alerts" to address the emerging auditing issues.[98] The first audit practice alert was issued to address auditing matters related to timing and accounting for ESO grants. The alert is prepared by the PCAOB Office of Research and Analysis and addresses auditors regarding reports and disclosures about public companies' practices related to the granting of ESOs including possible backdating of such grants. The reported backdating practices, whether legal or not, may have implications for audits of both financial statements and ICFR particularly when companies announced restatements of their financial statements as a result of these practices.

The recorded value of ESO is a function of market value of underlying stock on the grant date and the specified exercise price. ESOs are regarded as those money options or discounted options when the exercise price is less than the market price of related stock on the date of grant. When the grant date is manipulated or managed to the date when the underlying stock is low, improper value may be assigned to ESOs. The value of ESOs may be managed by several options grant schemes including the backdating of grant date practices, spring-loading or bullet dodging. There is a wide range of backdating practices including: (1) selecting exercise prices based on market prices on dates earlier than the grant date; (2) allowing the option holder to obtain an exercise price equal to the lower of the market price of the stock at the grant date or during the period subsequent to the grant date; (3) preparing or subsequently modifying option documentation in order to manage a lower exercise price than the market price at the actual grant date; and (4) inappropriately selecting a grant date when all of the prerequisites to a grant had not yet occurred.

Auditors should review with the compensation committee the company's:

1. *Current compensation policies and practices.* The SEC rules require public companies to file the new compensation discussion and analysis (CD&A). The CD&A requires companies to disclose their compensation policies and practices and the role that executive officers play in the compensation process. The

SEC approved comprehensive changes in the disclosure requirements for: (1) the compensation of directors and officers; (2) related-person transactions; (3) director independence; (4) ownership of securities by officers and directors; and (5) other corporate governance matters.[99] To comply with these requirements, public companies should provide greater disclosure in their proxy statements, annual reports, and registration statements regarding total compensation of their directors, principal executive officer, the principal financial officer, and the three highest-paid officers. Other requirements pertain to disclosure of the grant-date fair value of the stock options, changes in pension values and non-qualified deferred compensation earnings, and the company's CD&A section. Auditors should work with compensation committees in assessing whether the company's compensation policies and practices are in compliance with the new rules.

2. *Disclosure of perquisites.* Auditors should review the required disclosure of dollar thresholds for perquisites to ensure that they are completely and appropriately disclosed. The SEC reduced the threshold on the disclosure of perquisites by requiring the disclosure of executive perks of more than $10,000.

3. *Related-person transactions.* The SEC released its final rules, in August 2006, to reform disclosure requirements regarding related person transactions. These changes will include: (1) increasing the dollar threshold for the related-person transactions from the current benchmark of $60,000 to $120,000; (2) requiring disclosure of policies and procedures for review, approval, and ratification of related-person transactions; (3) eliminating the distinction between indebtedness and other types of related-person transactions and arrangements as well as requirements for disclosure of specific types of director relationships.[100]

4. *Employees covered under Section 162(m)-compliant plans.* Section 162(m) of the Internal Revenue Code limits the deductibility of compensation paid to "covered employees" unless the compensation is "performance based." The auditor should ensure that covered employees are in compliance with SEC and tax rules.

SUMMARY

External auditors play an important role in corporate governance by lending credibility to published financial reports. The emerging integrated audit of both internal control over financial reporting and financial statements is expected to: improve audit quality, efficiency, and effectiveness; enhance reliability of financial reports; strengthen the effectiveness of design and operations of ICFR; restore investor confidence in public financial information; and contribute to the efficiency and integrity of the financial markets. Progress has been made in the accounting profession to regain investors' confidence since the accounting scandals that began to emerge in 2000 and still continue. Nevertheless, much more improvement is needed in the areas of auditor independence, responsibility for detecting financial statement fraud, relationship with the audit committee, continuous auditing, and auditing of fair value and auditor liability.

NOTES

1. The terms "external auditors," "independent auditors," "registered auditors," and "outside auditors" are used interchangeably in the business literature. These terms are also used interchangeably throughout the book to describe any auditor who is considered as an independent accountant for the company within the meaning of the Securities Acts administered by the SEC. The term "registered auditors" refers to independent auditors registered with the Public Company Accounting Oversight Board.

2. Powers, Jr. W. C. 2002. Report of investigation of the Special Investigation Committee of the board of directors of Enron Corp. (February). Available at: www.CAA.com/2002/Law/02/02/enronreport/powers.report.pdf.

3. International Audit Networks. 2006. Global Networks and the Global Economy: A Vision from the CEO of the International Audit Networks (November). Available at: www.globalpublicpolicysymposium.com.

4. Ibid.

5. American Institute of Certified Public Accountants. 2002. Statement on Auditing Standards No. 99: Consideration of Fraud in a Financial Statement Audit. Available at: www.aicpa.org/download/auditstd/summarysas99.doc.

6. Rezaee, Z. 2004. Restoring public trust in the accounting profession by developing anti-fraud education, programs, and auditing. *Managerial Auditing Journal* 19 (1).

7. Harrington, C. 2003. The new accounting environment: Companies face a paradigm shift in how they conduct business. *Journal of Accountancy* 196.

8. Public Company Accounting Oversight Board. 2004. Auditing Standard No. 2: *An Audit of Internal Control over Financial Reporting Performed in Conjunction with an Audit of Financial Statements* (Paragraph 17). Available at: www.pcaob.org/standards.

9. International Auditing and Assurance Standards Board. 2005. *2005 handbook of international auditing, assurance & ethics pronouncements* (December). Available at: http://www.ifac.org/Store/Category.tmpl?Category=Auditing%2C%20Assurance%20%26%20Related%20Services.

10. Seidler, L. J. Why everybody's jumping on the accountants these days. *Forbes* 2006. Available at: www.forbes.com/free_forbes/1977/0315/037.html.

11. Rezaee, Z. 2002. Forensic accounting practices, education and certifications. *Journal of Forensic Accounting* 3 (2) (July–December): 207–224.

12. Seidler, L. J. Why everybody's jumping on the accountants these days. *Forbes* 2006. Available at: www.forbes.com/free_forbes/1977/0315/037.html.

13. American Institute of Certified Public Accountants (AICPA). 2006. AICPA, IAASB, and AAA Request for Proposals and Research on Unqualified Auditor's Report Communications. Available at: http://www.aicpa.org.

14. Ibid.

15. Ibid.

16. Imhoff, E. A. Jr. 2003. Accounting quality, auditing, and corporate governance. *Accounting Horizons* (supplement): 117–128.

17. *Economist*. 1990. Blowing the whistle on accountancy. (December 22): 17.

18. Melancon, B. C. 2002. A new accounting culture: Speech made by president and CEO of the American Institute of Certified Public Accountants to the Yale Club. New York. (September 4). Available at: www.aicpa.org/pubs/jofa/oct2002/melance.htm.

19. American Assembly, Columbia University. 2005. The future of the accounting profession: Auditor concentration. Available at: www.americanassembly.org/programs.dir/report_file.dir/AUDIT_report_report_file_Auditor%20Concentration%208th%20pass%2010.20.05.pdf.

20. U.S. Chamber of Commerce. 2006. Auditing: A profession at risk. Available at: www.uschamber.com/NR/rdonlyres/ewj43d74z5pemtshnkdi3fvko6azefuio2npyjeicyanm3hj4spkg7ivliac62faaieqewp4vdktk4ozqfv4ucilwpe/0601auditing.pdf.

21. The big six largest global audit networks. 2006. Global Capital Markets and the Global Economy: A vision from the CEOs of the international audit networks (November). Available at: www.pwc.com.

22. Ibid.

23. Corporate Crime Reporter. 2007. Former Reagan SEC Commissioner Calls for Public Auditor 21 *Corporate Crime Reporter* 8 (February 12). Washington, DC.

24. Ibid.

25. Office of Public Sector Information. The Companies Act 2006. Available at: http://search.opsi.gov.uk/search?q=companies+act+2006+pdf&output=xml_no_dtd&client=opsisearch&proxystylesheet=opsisearch&site=default_collection.

26. Ibid.

27. Ibid.

28. Audit Quality Forum. 2005. Audit quality: Shareholder involvement audit resignation statements. Institute of Chartered Accountants in England and Wales. Audit and Assurance Faculty. (March). Available at: www.icaew.co.uk/auditquality.

29. Glass Lewis and Co. 2007. Speak No Evil. Yellow Card Trend Alert. (May 21). Available at: www.glasslewis.com.

30. Norris, F. 2005. Applying safeguards to auditors. *International Herald Tribune* (September 2). Available at: www.iht.com/protected/articles/2005/09/01/business/norris02.php.

31. Ibid.

32. Public Company Accounting Oversight Board (PCAOB). 2006. Rulemaking Docket 019: Periodic Reporting by Registered Public Accounting Firms (May 23). Available at: http://www.pcaobus.org/Rules/Docket_019/index.aspx.

33. Financial Reporting Council 2006. Transparency Reporting by Auditors of Public Interest Entities (July). Available at: http://www.frc.org.uk.

34. Ibid.

35. Ibid.

36. Bazerman, M. H., G. Loewenstein, and D. A. Moore. 2002. Why good accountants do bad audits. *Harvard Business Review* (November): 97–102.

37. Ibid.

38. Donaldson, W. H. 2003. Remarks to the National Press Club. (July 30). Available at: www.sec.gov/news/speech/spch073003whd.htm.

39. McDonough, W. J. 2005. Speech text: Chairman McDonough speaks to Financial Executives International. Current Financial Reporting Issues Conference. New York. (November 18). Available at: www.pcaob.org/news_and_events/events/2005/speech/11-18_mcdonough.aspx.

40. Gradison, B. 2006. Testimony of the acting chairman of Public Company Accounting Oversight Board before the U.S. House of Representatives Committee on Financial Services Subcommittee on Capital Markets, Insurance, and Government Sponsored Enterprises (March 29). Available at: financialservices.house.gov/media/pdf/032906bg.pdf.

41. Public Company Accounting Oversight Board (PCAOB). 2004. Internal Oversight. Available at: www.pcabus.org/About_the_PCAOB/Internal_Oversight/index.

42. Ibid.

43. Public Company Accounting Oversight Board. 2004. Auditing Standard No. 1: *References in Auditors' Reports to the Standards of the Public Company Accounting Oversight Board*. (May 14). Available at: www.pcaob.org/Standards/Standards_and_Related_Rules/Auditing_Standard_No.1.aspx.

44. Public Company Accounting Oversight Board. 2004. Auditing Standard No. 2: *An Audit of Internal Control over Financial Reporting Performed in Conjunction with an Audit of Financial Statements* (Paragraph 17). Available at: www.pcaob.org/standards.

45. Public Company Accounting Oversight Board (PCAOB). 2006. Proposed Auditing Standard. An Audit of Internal Control over Financial Reporting that is Integrated with an Audit of Financial Statements (December 19). Available at: www.pcaob.org/standards/proposed_standards_and_related_rules.aspx.

46. Ibid.

47. U.S. Securities and Exchange Commission. 2007. SEC Commissioners Endorse Improved Sarbanes-Oxley Implementation to Ease Smaller Company Burdens, Focusing Effort on 'What Truly Matters.' (April 4). Available at: www.sec.gov/news/press/2007/2007-62.htm.

48. Public Company Accounting Oversight Board. 2005. Auditing Standard No. 3: *Audit Documentation*. Available at: www.pcaob.org/Standards/Standards_and_Related_Rules/Auditing_Standard_No.3.aspx.

49. Securities and Exchange Commission. 2003. Final rules: Retention of records relevant to audits and review. Release Nos. 33-8180, 34-4741. (January 24). Available at: www.sec.gov/rules/final/33-8180.htm.

50. Ibid.

51. Public Company Accounting Oversight Board. 2006. Overview of Auditing Standard No. 4: Reporting on Whether a Previously Reported Material Weakness Continues to Exist. (April 27). Available at: www.pcaobus.org.

52. Public Company Accounting Oversight Board. 2006. SEC approves PCAOB rules on auditor ethics, independence and tax services. (April 21). Available at: www.pcaob-us.org/news_and_events/news/2006/04_21.aspx.

53. Public Company Accounting Oversight Board (PCAOB). 2006. Implementation Schedule for Certain Ethics and Independence Rules Concerning Independence, Tax Services, and Contingent Fees (October 31). Available at: www.pcaob.org.
54. Public Company Accounting Oversight Board. 2006. SEC approves PCAOB rules on auditor ethics, independence and tax services. (April 21). Available at: www.pcaob-us.org/news_and_events/news/2006/04_21.aspx.
55. McDonough. 2005. Speech text: Chairman McDonough Speaks to Financial Executives International. Public Company Accounting and Oversight Board (November 18). Available at: http://www.pcaobus.org/News_and_Events/Events/2005/Speech/11-18_McDonough.aspx.
56. Ibid.
57. Public Company Accounting Oversight Board. 2006. Statement regarding the Public Company Accounting Oversight Board's approach to inspections of internal control audit in the 2006 inspection cycle. Release No. 104-2006-105. (May 1). Available at: www.pcaobus.org.
58. Ibid.
59. Gibson Dunn Update. 2005. PCAOB initiates enforcement investigations. (June). Available at: www.gibsondunn.com/practices/publications/detail/id/766/?publtemld=7794.
60. Accounting Web. 2006. NY Crackdown on Bad Accountants Addresses Long-Term Concern. Accounting Web (July 17). Available at: http://www.accountingweb.com/cgi-bin/item.cgi?Id=102351.
61. KPMG. 2004. Oversight of audits: Audit Committee Roundtable Highlights. Audit Committee Institute. (Spring). Available at: www.kpmg.com/aci.
62. Securities and Exchange Commission. 2003. Commission adopts rules strengthening auditor independence. (January 22). Available at: www.sec.gov/news/press/2003-9.htm.
63. Conference Board. 2003. Commission on Public Trust and Private Enterprise; Part 3: Auditing and Accounting. (January). Available at www.conference-board.org/pdf_free/SR-03-04.pdf.
64. Ibid.
65. Glass Lewis and Co. 2006. Mum's the Word, Yellow Card Trend Alert (July 27). Available at: http://www.glasslewis.com.
66. Willsher, R. 2004. Riding the audit merry-go-round. *Accountancy Age* (May 26). Available at: www.accountancyage.com/accountancyage/analysis/2040820/riding-audit-merry-round.
67. Securities and Exchange Commission. 2003. Commission adopts rules strengthening auditor independence (January 22). Available at: http://www.sec.gov/news/press/2003-9.htm.
68. Glass Lewis and Co. 2006. Mum's the Word, Yellow Card Trend Alert (July 27). Available at: http://www.glasslewis.com.
69. Ibid.
70. United States General Accounting Office. 2002. Financial restatements. GAO-03-138. Available at: www.gao.gov/new.items/d03138.pdf.

71. Securities and Exchange Commission. 2003. Commission adopts rules strengthening auditor independence (January 22). Available at: http://www.sec.gov/news/press/2003-9.htm.
72. Sarbanes-Oxley Act of 2002. (July 30). Available at: www.sec.gov/about/laws/soa2002.pdf.
73. New York Stock Exchange. 2004. Final NYSE corporate governance rules. Available at: www.nyse.com/pdfs/finalcorpgovrules.
74. Securities and Exchange Commission. 2003. Strengthening the Commission's requirements regarding auditor independence: Release No. 33-8183. Available at: sec.gov/rules/final/33-8183.htm.
75. Ibid.
76. Public Company Accounting Oversight Board. 2006. SEC approves PCAOB rules on auditor ethics, independence and tax services (April 21). Available at: www.pcaobus.org/news_and_events/news/2006/04-21.aspx.
77. Securities and Exchange Commission (SEC). 2003. Strengthening the Commission's requirements regarding auditor independence. Available at: http://www.sec.gov/rules/final/33-8183.htm.
78. American Institute of Public Accountants (AICPA). 2006. A Future that Matters: An Exit Interview with the Chief Accountant of the SEC (February). Available at: http://www.aicpa.org/pubs/jofa/feb2006/pickard.htm.
79. Reilly, D. 2006. Booming audit firms seek shield from suits. *Wall Street Journal* (November 1): page C1. Available at: online.wsj.com/article/SB116235111161209823.html.
80. Audit Analytics. 2006. Big 4 Securities Class Action Litigation—Citing Auditor as Defendant (November 9). Available at: www.auditanalytics.com.
81. Rapaport, M. 2006. (Much) More about Auditor Liability Caps. Dow Jones Newswires (June 26). Available at: http://www.dowjones.com.
82. Schmidt, R. 2005. Ernst, KPMG liability caps draw fire from regulators, investors. Bloomberg. (December 12). New York. Available at: http://www.bloomberg.com/apps/news?pid=10000103&sid=aVGCZaozSkAI.
83. Council of Institutional Investors. 2006. 2006 spring meeting. Council meetings. Available at: www.cii.org/meetings/index.html.
84. Securities and Exchange Commission. 2004. Office of the Chief Accountant: Application of the Commission's rules on auditor independence—Frequently asked questions. (December 13). Available at: www.sec.gov.
85. The Big Six Largest Global Audit Networks. 2006. Global capital markets and the global economy: A vision from the CEOs of the International Audit Networks (November). Available at: http://www.globalpublicpolicysymposium.com/.
86. Reilly, D. 2006. Booming audit firms seek shield from suit. *Wall Street Journal* (November 1): page C1. Available at: www.online.wsj.com/article/SB111161209823.html?.
87. Ibid.
88. Ibid.
89. Office of Public Sector Information. The Companies Act 2006. Available at: http://search.opsi.gov.uk/search?q=companies+act+2006+pdf&output=xml

_no_dtd&client=opsisearch&proxystylesheet=opsisearch&site=default_ collection.

90. The Committee on Capital Markets Regulation. 2006. Interim report of the Committee on Capital Markets Regulation. (November 30). Available at: www.capmktsreg.org/research.html.

91. PricewaterhouseCoopers. 2005. Comparison of defined benefit pension reform proposals. *PwC's HRS Insight* (October 6). Available at: www.cfodirect.com/CFOPrivate.nsf.

92. Ibid.

93. Ibid.

94. Securities and Exchange Commission. 2002. Annual report pursuant to Section 13 or 15(d) of the Securities Exchange Act of 1934 (September 25). Available at: www.sec.gov/divisions/corpfin/forms/11-k.htm.

95. Gibson, Dunn & Crutcher, LLP. 2003. Application of Sections 404 and 906 of the Sarbanes-Oxley Act to employee benefit plans. (October 16). Available at: www.gibsondunn.com/practices/publications/detail/id/766/?pubItemId=7136.

96. Boselovic, L. 2005. Pittsburgh Brewing says it's in deep trouble. *Pittsburgh Post Gazette* (June 29).

97. Union to accounting firms: Backdating? 2006. *Smart Pros* (September 13). Available at: http://www.accounting.smartpros.com/x54687.xml.

98. Public Company Accounting Oversight Board (PCAOB). 2006. Staff Audit Practice Alert No 1: Matters Related to Timing and Accounting for Option Grants (July 28). Available at: http://www.pcaob.us.org.

99. Securities and Exchange Commission (SEC). 2006. Executive Compensation and Related Disclosure (August 29), Release 33-8732A. Available at: http://www.sec.gov/rules/final/2006/33-8732a.pdf.

100. Ibid.

CHAPTER 10

Monitoring Function

INTRODUCTION

The monitoring function of corporate governance is the direct responsibility of shareholders and other stakeholders (e.g., employees, customers, creditors, suppliers). The monitoring function of corporate governance can be achieved through direct participation of investors in the business and financial affairs of corporations or through intermediaries, such as security analysts, institutional investors, and investment bankers. A 2006 PricewaterhouseCoopers (PwC) survey reveals that more than half of the 1,300 surveyed directors (51 percent) report institutional investors influence their board the most; 26 percent say analysts and 15 percent report that Institutional Shareholder Services (ISS) rating agencies influence the board the most; still others mention that the plaintiffs' bar and activist hedge fund also play a role (4 percent and 3 percent, respectively).[1] This chapter discusses the monitoring role of these individuals in corporate governance.

SHAREHOLDERS

The wave of financial scandals at the turn of the twenty-first century proved that a lack of monitoring by shareholders could be very costly and devastating to them. As depicted in Exhibit 2.3 and further explained in this chapter, active participation and monitoring by shareholders in the company they own is an important component of effective corporate governance. Shareholders can effectively fulfill their monitoring function by:

- Attending annual and special shareholder meetings.
- Participating in director elections.
- Submitting proposals to be included as shareholder resolutions at the annual meeting.
- Continuously communicating with the company's directors and officers by staying abreast of corporate development and events.

Shareholders have a legal right to monitor boards of directors, and they often act as a check on the boards. State and federal laws are aimed at protecting shareholder rights by allowing shareholders to: (1) inspect and copy the company's stock ledger, its list of shareholders, and certain books and records; (2) approve certain business transactions (e.g., merger and acquisition); (3) receive proxy materials; and (4) obtain significant disclosures for related-party transactions.

Shareholders have the right to:

- Vote for the election of directors.
- Receive accurate and reliable annual audited financial statements and quarterly reviewed financial statements.
- Demand access to corporate documents, including minutes of board meetings.
- Submit shareholder resolutions that are placed in the annual proxy statement.
- Vote on important business transactions, such as mergers and acquisitions.
- Bring shareholder derivative lawsuits.

These and other issues relevant to the shareholder monitoring function are discussed in this chapter.

Shareholder Monitoring

The Working Group on Corporate Governance, in 1991, suggested five corporate governance principles for shareholders, which are still relevant to the effectiveness of monitoring function of investors:

- Institutional shareholders of public companies should see themselves as owners, not just investors.
- Shareholders should not be involved in the conduct of the company's day-to-day operations.
- Shareholders should evaluate the performance of the directors regularly.
- In evaluating the performance of directors, shareholders should be informed.
- Shareholders should recognize and respect that the only goal common to all shareholders is the ongoing prosperity of the company.[2]

The level of trust and confidence that investors have in reported financial information may relate directly to the reliability, quality, and transparency of the information; that confidence is adversely affected by differing motivations and information asymmetries. Several corporate governance mechanisms are suggested to align the interests of management with those of shareholders, allow investors to assess and monitor the behavior of management, and reinforce shareholders' trust in management. For example, shareholders' approval of executive compensation packages and ability to influence executive tenure are effective mechanisms to ensure alignment of management interests with those of investors. The extent of managerial incentives and monitoring mechanisms depends on the trustworthiness of management and amount of trust investors have in management. In one scenario, no executives are trustworthy and they attempt to make themselves better off at the expense of investors. This scenario suggests that investors should place very little trust, if any, in executives and must rely on corporate governance mechanisms to align interests. Another scenario is that executives are indeed trustworthy and always work in investors' best interests. Here little, monitoring is needed. The real business world functions as a continuum demanding trust but still requiring monitoring.

The effectiveness of the monitoring and control functions by investors is determined based on the interrelated factors of:

- Property rights established by law or contractual agreements that define the relations between a company's investors and its management, as well as the existence of such relations between different types of investors.
- Financial systems facilitating the supply of finance among households, financial intermediaries, and corporations.
- Networks of intercorporate competition and cooperation establishing relations between corporations in the marketplace.

Property Rights Investors' influence, monitoring, and control are significantly affected by the property rights set forth by state corporate law, company articles of incorporation and bylaws, and any contractual agreements. Property rights establish the legal relations between a company's investors and its management, as well as the relations among different types of investors (e.g., equity owners, debt holders). Effective property rights create a well-balanced and proper division of power between investors and management in the sense that investors are provided with adequate control, while management autonomy is preserved for acting within its own discretion. Property rights, particularly corporate law, specifically define how shareholder rights translate into voting rights in corporations, including the voting rights of shareholders, rules on proxy votes, voting thresholds for particular decisions, and investor meeting quorums. Corporate and securities laws, including state and federal statutes, also establish the fiduciary duty, structure, role, and composition of the company's board of directors.

Financial System The financial system provides a means of financing and corporate ownership that fundamentally constitutes the supply side of capital markets. The supply side of financial markets is significantly influenced by regulatory measures, pension regimes, and labor rules.[3] Financial systems provide two alternative modes of financial mediation between households (investors) and corporations.[4] The first mode is bank-based finance, where banks take deposits from households and channel this savings into loans made to companies. The second mode is market-based finance in which households, directly or indirectly through retirement plans, invest in equity or debt securities issued by corporations. Household savings levels, time horizons (short term, long term), and types of financing (regular, retirement) affect the incentives and investment policies of financial institutions, including pension funds and mutual funds. In return, these institutions can impact corporate governance by providing different types of financing requiring different reforms of financial and corporate governance systems.

Intercorporate Networks   Investor influence in corporate governance is affected by the patterns of intercorporate networks.[5] Intercorporate networks determine the relation between the company and other corporations or organizations, the structure of power and opportunity, and access to critical resources, information, and strategic decisions. These intercorporate relations, by creating a coalition of power and opportunities, can influence corporate governance and the ways these networks are managed. The nature and extent of corporate control within networks is affected by state regulation, market competition, and antitrust laws. For example, market competition regulations discourage capital ties between competing corporations, which may force them to merge. These mergers might reduce the concentration of ownership within large corporations and strategic interests within corporate governance.

Shareholder Power

Corporate law provides shareholders with voting rights to monitor their companies in several ways. Shareholders have the right to vote to:

- Elect directors.
- Amend the company's bylaws.
- Approve charter amendments and mergers.

Power to Elect Directors   The most important monitoring mechanism of shareholders is their voting right to elect directors. This voting right can be constrained by constitutional arrangements that limit shareholders' ability to exercise their power. One obvious example of such constraints is the provision of staggered boards or classified boards. In staggered boards, directors are typically grouped into classes, normally three, with only one class of directors coming up for reelection each year. Therefore, shareholders are not able to replace a majority of the directors in any given year regardless of how dissatisfied they may be with them. Staggered boards are a powerful defense against control challenges and removal of directors in proxy contents. Board declassification, or destaggering the board, recently has been one of the most common types of shareholder resolutions.

The plurality voting provision is another example of constraints imposed on shareholders to limit their voting power to remove directors. In accordance with the existing plurality voting system, shareholders receive ballots enabling them to vote "for" a director or to "withhold" their votes without being given the opportunity to vote against a director. Thus, directors can be elected and reelected with even a single vote cast in their favor. The plurality voting system should be replaced by a majority voting system that requires individual directors who do not receive at least 50 percent voting support from shareholder to resign from the board.

Power to Amend Bylaws   Shareholders have the power to vote to amend their company's bylaws in addition to the power to vote to elect or remove directors. Shareholders' power to amend the company's bylaws can be constrained by provisions included in the corporate charter or bylaws. An example of such constraints is the provision of supermajority requirements (e.g., two-thirds of outstanding shares), which can make it difficult for shareholders to pass a bylaw amendment that management opposes.

Power to Approve Charter Amendments and Mergers   Shareholders also have the power to vote to approve charter amendments and mergers. However, this power can be constrained by the provision of supermajority requirements for passing charter amendments or approving a merger if opposed by management, primarily because nonmanagement shareholders are less likely to vote and management can influence some votes. When such constraints exist, management can influence charter amendments or mergers significantly.

Strengthening Shareholder Rights

Shareholders have been inattentive and traditionally have not participated in corporate governance effectively by letting their preferences and voices be heard by the company's board. The lack of transparency, accountability, and proper communication between shareholders and the board of directors is perhaps the most detrimental factor to the effectiveness of corporate governance. Inattentive shareholders resulted in a system where the chief executive officer (CEO) would have undue influence on the election of directors and their compensation, and also have a significant role on the board in the dual roles of both chair and CEO. When the CEO is given the opportunity to shape the structure of the board of directors because of a lack of shareholder engagement, the likelihood of directors challenging the CEO's preferences or effectively overseeing the managerial function can be reduced substantially. This perceived compromise or gamesmanship creates a boardroom culture that can adversely impact the effectiveness of corporate governance at a company. Thus, the strengthening of shareholders' rights by providing timely access to information, enhancing shareholders' voting power, and promoting shareholder democracy can have a positive effect on corporate governance.

Access to Information   Shareholders, by engaging in the monitoring function, play an important role in corporate governance through holding the company's board of directors accountable for business strategies, performance, and investment decisions. In the era of information technology and the Internet, shareholders should be provided with timely electronic access to all relevant information in advance of shareholders' annual meetings. The U.K.-proposed Company Law Reform provides several measures to improve shareholder communication and engagement, including:

- Requiring shareholder approval for the directors' remuneration report.
- Holding the company's annual general meeting (AGM) within six months of the end of the financial year.
- Making the company's annual results, full accounts, and reports electronically available to all members and the public.
- Disclosing any resolutions to the AGM and results of polls at general meetings on the company's Web sites.

- Enabling shareholders to require an independent scrutiny of any polled vote.
- Promoting the use of electronic communications with shareholders as the default position.
- Enhancing the ability of indirect investors who do not hold legal titles to their shares to exercise rights through proxy, governance rights, and the right to information power.[6]

To ensure effective monitoring of corporate business and affairs, shareholders should be able to communicate regularly with the corporate directors. In May 2005 the Business Roundtable released its shareholder-director communications guidelines.[7] The report indicates that 90 percent of its member companies have established policies and procedures for shareholder communications with directors, and 85 percent of nominating committees showed willingness to consider shareholder recommendations for board nominees. Exhibit 10.1 presents the Business Roundtable recommendations and comments regarding shareholder-director communications.

The Business Roundtable recommends five principles for fair and respectful treatment of shareowners and their views.

1. Public companies should have effective procedures for shareholders to communicate with the board and for directors to respond to shareholders' concerns. Traditionally, shareholders have raised their concerns with management, particularly the CEO. Often their concerns were ignored or not addressed appropriately. Corporate governance reforms in the post–Sarbanes-Oxley (SOX) era enable shareholders to communicate their concerns with independent directors.
2. All communications with shareholders should be consistent, fair, transparent, clear, and candid. Leading research and proxy advisory firms, corporate governance rating organizations, and investor activists, including the Council of Institutional Investors (CII), the Conference Board, the Corporate Library, the ISS, Glass, Lewis & Co. (Glass Lewis), and the State Board of Administration (SBA) of Florida have established proxy voting guidelines and corporate governance principles that address a wide range of governance and financial issues, from board structures, director independence, executive compensation, and auditor independence, to financial reporting quality, reliability, and transparency.
3. The established shareholder communication procedures should be readily available to shareholders. The Securities and Exchange Commission (SEC) has released proposed rules that would allow public companies to submit proxy materials electronically to their shareholders.[8] The SEC's attempts to reduce printing costs of proxy materials by using Internet availability should be balanced against its overall mission of protecting investors by ensuring that they receive proxy materials easily. Forrester Research, Inc. conducted a survey of shareholders that indicates that if the SEC-proposed rules are adopted immediately without modification, shareholder participation in the proxy voting process would decline substantially. Specifically, the survey reveals:

EXHIBIT 10.1 Recommendations and Guidelines for Shareholder–Director Communications

Guidelines for Shareholder–Director Communications	Additional Comments
1. Every publicly owned corporation should have effective procedures for shareholders to communicate with the board and for directors to respond to shareholders' concerns.	▪ Procedures for shareholder communications should be established and overseen by the board or independent committee. ▪ Directors should meet with shareholders to address concerns; note, however, that the directors' views are not always the same as the board's. ▪ The board shall designate a member of management to collect, organize, and review shareholder communications and likewise report the findings to the board or independent committee. ▪ The corporation should be aware of the SEC's Regulation Fair Disclosure and other legal restrictions before disseminating potential nonpublic information. ▪ Continuous improvement of the communications process is beneficial to remain effective.
2. A corporation's relationship with its shareholders should be characterized by candor. All communications with shareholder should be consistent, clear, and candid.	▪ Directors and management should never mislead or misinform shareholders. ▪ The goal of communications is to educate the shareholders of the corporation's business and the decision-making process of the board.
3. A corporation's procedures for shareholder–director communications, and its corporate governance practices generally, should be readily available to shareholders.	▪ Corporate governance information, such as corporate governance principles and the code of ethics, should be clearly disclosed. ▪ Disclosure regarding procedures for communication among shareholders and directors should be transparent, accessible, and understandable.
4. The board should be notified of all proposals submitted by shareholders, and the board or its corporate governance committee should oversee the corporation's response to shareholders' proposals.	▪ Management should report to the board or corporate governance committee on proposals submitted by shareholders for inclusion in the corporations proxy statements. ▪ Management should also report to the board or corporate governance committee on proposals it may be able to resolve outside the formal proxy process.

(continued overleaf)

EXHIBIT 10.1 (*Continued*)

Guidelines for Shareholder–Director Communications	Additional Comments
	▪ Communication with the proponents of shareholder proposals should be encouraged.
	▪ Shareholder proposals should be given serious consideration, and responses should be communicated to the proponents and all shareholders.
5. Directors should attend the corporation's annual meeting of shareholders and should respond, or ensure that management responds, to appropriate shareholder questions concerning the corporation.	▪ Corporate policy should be established stating that all directors are to attend the annual meeting of shareholders.
	▪ The corporation should have a process for responding to shareholder questions submitted before, during, and after the meeting.

Source: Adapted from Business Roundtable, "Guidelines for Shareholder–Director Communications," May 2005. Available at: www.businessroundtable.org/pdf/20050527001 ShareholderCommunicationsGuidelines-FINAL-5.26.05.pdf.

    a. The majority of surveyed shareholders reported they will not take the extra steps required to obtain proxy information.

    b. About 38 percent of participating active shareholders would be less likely to vote under the SEC-proposed rule.

    c. The majority of shareholders (67 percent) prefer the existing SEC voting process.

    d. Over 46 percent believe the SEC-proposed rules would make it harder to participate in the voting process.

    e. Less than half of the online shareholders have broadband, enabling them to engage in online financial activities.

    f. More than half of shareholders in the category of 50 years or older are less likely to be online.

    g. The majority of shareholders who are less likely to have the technological expertise to be online prefer not to read online or believe that paper mail is more secure and reliable.[9]

4. The company's board should be notified of all shareholder proposals, and the board or its corporate governance committee should oversee the company's response to the proposals. According to Peter Clapman, the retired chief investment counsel of TIAA-CREF, independent directors prefer to learn about serious issues directly from institutional investors because "sometimes the information they get about differences of opinion has been filtered by management.... Directors need to understand fully and fairly when there is a dispute between institutional shareholders and management."[10]

5. Directors should attend the annual meeting of shareowners and respond, or ensure that management responds, to all relevant questions. Annual shareholder meetings provide opportunities for shareholders to ask the company's board of directors and management questions regarding the company's performance and future prospects relevant to their voting and investment decisions. The meetings also enable the company's directors and officers to present their views and provide relevant and convincing responses to shareholder questions.

The CII and the National Association of Corporate Directors (NACD) issued a joint task report in 2004 that presents five determinants of the effective board-shareholder communication.[11] These determinants require:

1. A continuous communication program, including regular, comprehensive, and publicly available disclosures pertaining to the company's important topics, such as performance and governance issues.
2. Detailed contact information for the company's secretary and/or other management representative and for at least one independent director. The most appropriate contact for board-shareholder communications is the independent board chair, the lead independent director, or the independent chair of the nominating/governance committee.
3. Differentiation of issues that are appropriate for the company's board to address from those that are appropriate for management. For example, board-shareholder communications should include governance issues and major business strategic decisions, such as mergers, acquisitions, and divestitures; more routine matters should be communicated by management.
4. The development and disclosure of the company's communication policies, including in-person meetings, telephone calls, e-mail, and other written communication.
5. Effective adherence to the established communication policies and continuous monitoring of these policies. The company's board should ensure that board-shareholder communication policies are appropriate, effectively implemented, and reviewed and updated on a regular basis.

PricewaterhouseCoopers (PwC) provides a general reference guide to assist management and the board of directors in preparing for the annual meeting. The guide presents a list of 300 questions that shareholders may ask regarding the company's stock prices, corporate governance, executive compensation plans, business strategy and operations, information technology, financial reports, and corporate social responsibility.[12] Examples of some prominent questions are:

- *How has the company's stock performed compared with the market overall and with their competitors?*

- *What is the company's dividend policy and how does it compare with other companies in the industry?*
- *How many shares are outstanding and what percentage is owned by the company's directors and officers?*
- *What is the company doing to improve shareholder democracy and relations?*
- *Is the company in compliance with all applicable laws, regulations, rules, and standards, including SOX, SEC rules, and listing standards?*
- *How does management assess the adequacy and effectiveness of the company's internal control over financial reporting, and what are the significant deficiencies and material weaknesses in internal controls?*
- *How is the quality of the integrated audit of financial statements and internal control over financial reporting performed by the company's independent auditors?*
- *Are there any limited liability arrangements in the integrated audit engagement letter?*
- *Does the company have an internal audit department, and what is its function and reporting responsibility?*
- *Does the company have a code of conduct and ethics establishing an appropriate "tone at the top" promoting ethical behavior?*
- *Is the company's executive compensation approved by the board of directors and voted on by shareholders?*
- *Do the company's financial statements reflect true and fair presentation of the financial position and results of operations?*
- *What is the company's overall mission and strategy?*
- *What are management's short-term goals, and are they compatible with the long-term goal of achieving sustainable shareholder value creation and enhancement?*
- *Does the company consider itself an industry leader in the use of information technology?*
- *How does the company measure its multiple bottom lines (MBL) in areas of economic, governance, social, ethical, and environmental performance?*[13]

Enhancing Shareholders' Voting Power   The existing SEC rules allow companies to reject any shareholder proposals pertaining to director election. The U.S. Second Circuit Court of Appeals, on September 5, 2006, issued a ruling that enables shareholders in its jurisdiction (New York, Connecticut, Vermont) to nominate corporate directors.[14] The court ruled that the SEC was wrong to block an attempt by the American Federation of State, County and Municipal Employees (AFSCME) to include a shareholder proposal on the company proxy. The SEC staff sided with AIG attempts to exclude shareholder proposals concerning director elections from its proxy materials. The court rejected the SEC approach. The SEC, on October 12, 2006, decided to delay a key decision on whether to permit shareholders more access to company proxies. This has been interpreted to mean that the election of the board of directors is a challenging issue concerning shareholder democracy;

"a key battleground in corporate governance—has become entangled in US mid-term election politics."[15] This delay, however, allows the decision by the court to stand, which investor activists consider positive.

Public companies usually send proxy ballots to shareholders, including the names of directors up for election. A director candidate can get nominated by a board committee and placed on the ballot. Shareholders, of course, can nominate their own candidate through separate ballots, which is often a complicated and costly process. The court ruled that under the existing SEC rules, shareholders should have access to the proxy for purposes of nominating their choice of candidate for director. In October 2003 the SEC issued a proposal to give shareholder access to the proxy; no action has been taken by the SEC to finalize the proposal. Pursuant to the court decision, the SEC announced that it will recommend an amendment to Rule 14a-8 under the Securities Exchange Act of 1934 pertaining to director nominations by shareholders. The decision by the Second Court of Appeals is important because: (1) it states that shareholders should be able to access the proxy for the purpose of nominating their choice of candidate for director, which disagrees with the SEC staff's long-standing interpretation of the proxy rules; (2) a large number of public companies are subject to the jurisdiction of the Second Circuit Court of Appeals; and (3) the SEC is expected to revise its proxy rules to ensure consistent rational application of its rules to shareholder proposals.

The exercising of shareholders' rights should be enhanced by allowing them to:

- Nominate directors to be included on the company's proxy.
- Ask questions and raise concerns.
- Table resolutions.
- Vote in absentia.
- Participate in general meetings via electronic means.

The CII recommends six shareholder voting rights:

1. *Access to the proxy.* Companies should provide access to management proxy material for long-term investors (those owning shares for at least three years or a group of long-term investors owning, in aggregate, at least 5 percent of a company's voting shares) to nominate less than a majority of directors.
2. *One share, one vote.* Companies should allow one vote for each share of their common stock with no classes of common stock having disparate voting rights. The company's board should not issue unauthorized common stock with unequal voting rights without shareholder approval.
3. *Confidential voting.* Companies shall have confidential policies and practices for proxy vote casting, counting, and verifying.
4. *Voting requirements.* Supermajority votes should not be required in any circumstance. A majority vote should be adequate for amending the company's bylaws or taking other actions requiring a shareholder vote. A majority vote of common shares outstanding should be required to approve:
   a. Major corporate decisions concerning a sale or pledge of the company's assets whose value exceeds 10 percent of the total consolidated assets.

  b. The acquisition of 5 percent or more of the company's common shares at above-market prices except for tender offer to all shareholders.
  c. Poison pills.
  d. Abridging or limiting the rights of common shareholders to take a variety of actions (e.g., election or removal of directors, nominations of directors, call for special meetings).
  e. Decisions for the issuance of debt to the extent that it would excessively leverage the company.
5. *Broker votes.* Broker nonvotes and abstentions should be counted only for purposes of a quorum.
6. *Bundled voting.* Companies should permit shareholders to vote on unrelated issues separately. No bundled voting should be permitted for actions concerning amendment of the company's charter, bylaws, or antitakeover provisions.[16]

Shareholder Democracy   The relationship between the company's board of directors and its shareholders has received a considerable amount of attention in the post-Enron era. Traditionally, the accountability and transparency between the board and shareholders has not been effective in the sense that the board was not informed of what shareholders were expecting of it and shareholders were not aware of the board's activities and its effectiveness. Shareholders have voting rights to elect directors as their agents; however, individual directors have no direct responsibility or accountability to shareholders. Shareholder democracy of empowering shareholders to nominate, elect, or remove directors has been debated extensively in the literature. Under the current plurality voting system of uncontested director elections, even a single vote for a nominee will elect that director to a board, regardless of the number of votes withheld.

The majority voting system, which would require a director who received a majority of "against" votes to resign, has received a great deal of attention. Despite some legal concerns (e.g., plurality voting is allowed under state law), institutional investors and investor activists strongly support a majority vote default rule. A modified version of majority voting, better known as majority voting lite or Pfizer majority voting, has been suggested, but is not as widely supported by investors. Under one version of a majority voting lite rule, directors who receive a majority of "no" or withhold votes would be required to submit their resignation to the board. The company's board of directors (as opposed to shareholders) would then decide whether to accept the resignation, and, if so, would appoint its own candidate (rather than accept shareholder-nominated director candidates). The Committee on Capital Market Regulation endorses majority rather than plurality voting.[17] The committee wrote the first bipartisan report that supports majority rule, bringing U.S. shareholder election in line with that of other developed countries. The committee also discusses whether broker votes should be counted in the company's director election as is currently being practiced. The New York Stock Exchange has already proposed to change the current practice by disallowing the counting of votes cast by brokers, which are almost always in favor of management resolutions.[18]

A *New York Times* article states that "investors may think they live in the United States of America but when it comes to electing corporate directors, shareholders' intended watchdogs in the boardrooms, they are definitely back in the U.S.S.R."[19] Investors can only vote for a director or withhold votes. For anyone who opposes a candidate, the election is an exercise in futility.[20] It is expected that investors who own the company, and ultimately have residual claims over its assets, should be empowered to elect directors who are supposed to be the guardians of their investment. A proposal that would have given investors such power to influence the nomination and election process was put forward by the SEC but has not been finalized in a rule. A recent incident of what is seemingly a case of abuse of the plurality voting method is the board vote at Career Education Corp., which shareholder activists view as a "corporate governance double whammy."[21] Democratic voting is not practiced when directors are elected even with the opposition of an overwhelming majority of votes and when brokers can vote for management in place of silent shareholders.[22] Under the plurality voting model, the withheld votes (symbolic votes against directors on the proxy cards) at Career Education were more than 62 percent of outstanding shares for the three management-backed nominees.[23] This suggests that three directors were given a complete vote of no confidence by the majority of shareholders, yet they were elected under the plurality-voting model, a common voting practice in corporate America.

Investment funds have raised their concerns regarding the lack of democracy in the boardroom. One example is a letter submitted by an investment fund requesting an SEC review of no-action determination regarding a shareholder proposal to Computer Associates, Inc. (CA) in which shareholders were being denied the opportunity to vote on whether the two directors remaining on its board from the period when CA got into trouble should continue to serve.[24] CA was required to restate its financial statements in 2006; has been under an SEC investigation, which has resulted in several convictions and penalties; and has lost senior executives, including the chief operating officer, chief financial officer [CFO], and chief of global sales, in recent months; its stock price is about 35 percent below what it was in 1996. There are signs of ineffective corporate governance, particularly an irresponsible board of directors, which shareholders are not allowed to change. The SEC has ruled that CA can exclude the proposal for its proxy that disallows shareholders to exercise their right to vote for or against the two directors. Institutional investors and investor activists requested the SEC to review its position on the CA proposal by stating:

> The issue is whether the Commission will interpose itself between a company and its shareholders when shareholders believe that certain directors should be removed from office and when state law empowers such removal.[25]

Several of the world's largest investment mangers (e.g., the Association of British Insurers, F&C Asset Management, Dutch Pension Fund Manager, the Third Swedish Pension Fund, the Australian Reward Investment Alliance, and Scottish-based Standard Life Investments) that collectively manage about $34 trillion in assets have called on the SEC to give shareholders power to change the composition of U.S. companies' boards.[26] Investors in other countries (e.g., the United Kingdom, Australia, and the Netherlands) are given more opportunities to remove underperforming or unfit directors than their counterparts in the United States. The shareholders' basic ownership rights of having unrestricted access to company proxies for board elections are not aligned with those of other developed countries, which undermines the effectiveness of corporate governance in the United States and shareholder democracy.

Shareholders' ready access to companies' proxies, in order to put forward director nominees, and other resolutions have received considerable interest from shareholder activists and have been the focus of a couple of court cases. Regarding shareholder democracy and its role in the free enterprise system, Arthur Levitt, the former SEC chairman, states:

> *Shareholder capitalism enables our markets to thrive, our companies to grow, and our economy to remain strong. And central to this system is the principle that shareholders can have a voice in the running of companies that they own, that their votes will count. How the SEC handles this [proxy access] can have a profound effect on the future of shareholder democracy, corporate governance and the future of markets.*[27]

Levitt suggests that the SEC strengthen shareholder democracy by: (1) passing its 2003 proxy access proposal; (2) including safeguards, such as minimum required shares to be eligible to put forward director nominees; (3) increasing the number of exempt solicitations from 10 persons to 20 in order for investors, particularly institutional investors, to easily communicate with each other; (4) allowing the electronic transmission of proxy materials; and (5) endorsing the principle of majority of directors.[28]

In the post-SOX era, investors are becoming more active in their monitoring function by submitting proposals to refine their companies' corporate governance. Shareholder resolutions from 2007 contain several important proposals including: (1) an advisory vote on executive compensation packages—Aflac is the first major U.S. company that would give its shareholders a nonbinding advisory vote on its corporate pay practices in 2009; (2) say-on-pay resolutions that pressure companies to link their compensation policies and practices to executive performance; (3) proposals to allow shareholders to run opposing board candidates; and (4) majority voting for the nomination and election of directors.[29] The number of shareholder proposals increased marginally in 2006 to 634 proposals from 625 in 2005 with: (1) more than 120 receiving majority levels of support; (2) the elimination of supermajority voting requirements; (3) the declassification of the board (destaggering director terms); (4) the independence of the board chairman; (5) the award of performance-based stock options; and (6) the issue of sustainability reports.

In summary, the seven most prevailing concerns of shareholders and their expectations and issues that they want directors to understand in 2007 and onward are:

1. *Shareholders seek a meaningful say in who sits on the board.* Board democracy and accountability driven by majority voting and shareholder access to proxy materials for nominating directors can significantly improve the effectiveness of shareholder monitoring function.

2. *Shareholders lack trust in a board that lacks independent leadership.* The effectiveness of the oversight function of the company's board of directors can be significantly influenced by the board's independence. An independent board should have a board leader who is either a nonexecutive chair or a lead director with a defined set of responsibilities designed to promote the board independence.

3. *Shareholders expect disclosure to reveal the company's true condition.* Shareholders expect more transparent financial and nonfinancial information reflecting their company's true condition, and fair presentation of its key financial indicators above and beyond generally accepted accounting principles (GAAP) and the line item disclosure rules.

4. *Shareholders are skeptical of complex compensation schemes.* Shareholders are concerned about outsize and complex executive pay influenced by backdating and spring-loading practices. Shareholders expect more fair, transparent, performance-based, and reasonable executive compensation which meet their advisory vote and approval.

5. *Shareholders want exit scenarios to be reasonable.* Shareholders expect reasonable severance packages for departing CEOs due to their inappropriate behavior or lack of adequate and effective performance.

6. *Shareholders expect the board to take responsibility—and change the board—when necessary.* Shareholders demand their company's board to accept responsibilities for their actions (bad or good), be held accountable for their consequences, and change its behavior and/or composition accordingly to remediate the problems.

7. *Shareholders should be able to effect change.* When shareholders lose confidence and trust in the ability of their company's board of directors and its top management team to effectively discharge their fiduciary duty, they should not face insurmountable barriers to effecting change.[30]

INSTITUTIONAL INVESTORS

The direct ownership of stocks by American households has decreased substantially in the past several decades, from 91 percent in 1950 to just 32 percent in 2004, whereas stock ownership for financial institutions has increased substantially, from 9 percent in 1950 to more than 68 percent in 2004 for all stocks.[31] These changes in the ownership structure from individual investors to institutional investors have several profound effects on corporate governance. The formation of institutional shareholders, including mutual funds and public and private pension funds, has changed the traditional agency concept of the separation of ownership control from decision control. Under the emerging agency-dominated investment society, the majority of individual investors indirectly participate in the capital markets by investing in public and private pension plans and mutual funds. Consequently, financial institutions acquire stocks of public companies.

Institutional investors should also share some of the blame for reported financial scandals due to their lack of monitoring of their companies' governance. The publicized financial scandals of the early 2000s originated from the use of overly aggressive accounting and earnings management practices during the late 1990s. Financial irregularities and earnings management practices of many companies in the late 1990s definitely sent strong signals of forthcoming financial scandals. Nonetheless, investors either did not want to ask tough questions about their companies' governance or did not care as long as the stock prices were going up. Earnings management practices of even prominent companies, such as Tyco, General Electric, and Cisco, were reported in the press, but investors, particularly institutional shareholders, did not raise much concern about the irregularities of these companies, which were making profits for them. The economic downturn; the stock market plunge of 2000 and 2001; the failures of Enron, WorldCom, Adelphia, and Global Crossing, among others; and the ineffectiveness of their corporate governance made investors angry, especially when the root of these problems were caused by large-scale fraud and audit failures. The two biggest corporate bankruptcies in U.S. history, Enron and WorldCom, and the failures of other high-profile companies were caused primarily by fraud, which cost investors and pensioners over $500 billion and made investors take notice and demand corporate accountability. Investors' outcry against corporate greed, malfeasance, and fraud encouraged lawmakers and regulators to respond.

Institutional investors—insurance companies, public and private pension funds, investment trusts, mutual funds, and investment management groups—often hold substantial outstanding shares of public companies. The company's board of directors should obtain an understanding of each of their key institutional investors. Institutional investments in the United States have grown significantly in the past five decades, from about 6.1 percent of aggregate ownership of equities in 1950 to over 50 percent by 2002; that rate will continue to grow as more employees participate in pension funds.[32] Indeed, there are currently more than 2,600 public pension funds that hold more than 20 percent of publicly traded U.S. equity. Corporate ownership in the United States is highly dispersed and diffused, meaning that a large number of small shareholders own a significant portion of corporate ownership (equities); more than 50 percent of U.S. households own shares of corporations. The incentive and opportunity for individual investors to monitor the company's governance, in a highly diffused ownership structure, is very remote. Individual investors cannot afford the high costs of monitoring, particularly where inattentive shareholders will also enjoy the benefits of monitoring at no cost. Thus, only large shareowners and, particularly, institutional shareholders have the incentives and resources to monitor companies' governance and benefit from the actions of monitoring institutional investors without incurring the costs.[33]

Academic research suggests that the involvement of large shareholders, including institutional investors (e.g., the California Public Employees' Retirement System [CalPERS], in the monitoring function of corporate governance has the potential to limit agency problems associated with the separation of ownership and control in public companies. Institutional investors can play an important role of reducing information asymmetry between management and shareholders by obtaining private information from management and conveying that to shareholders and, thus, to the capital markets.[34] The integrity and credibility of such information determines its relevance and usefulness to investors.[35] A joint report by the CFA Institute and the Business Roundtable Institute for Corporate Ethics suggests that companies get their investors more engaged by: (1) encouraging widespread corporate participation in continuous dialogues with asset managers and other financial market participants to better understand how their companies are valued in the marketplace; (2) educating institutional investors and their advisors on the issue of their short-term and long-term fiduciary duties to their constituents; and (3) supporting education initiatives for individual investors to promote focus on sustainable shareholder value creation and enhancement.[36]

Institutional Investor Monitoring

Institutional investors normally monitor their holdings by using a screening system based on financial performance (e.g., benchmarks), identifying problem areas and concerns, and determining causes and effects of the problems. Although institutional investors do not micromanage the companies in which they invest, they may monitor their holdings by ensuring that the company is well managed and has a clear and attainable strategy. Institutional investors do not regularly intervene in a company except in rare circumstances. Intervention may occur in situations where there are significant concerns about financial performance, corporate governance, strategy, operational performance, mergers and acquisitions strategy, lack of proper oversight function by independent directors, reported material weaknesses in internal controls, inadequate succession planning, inappropriate compensation schemes, or lack of commitment to social, environmental, and ethical issues.[37]

Institutional investors may intervene by:

- Meeting with management.
- Expressing concerns through the company's advisors.
- Meeting with directors, particularly independent directors, lead directors, or the independent chair of the board.
- Collaborating with other institutional investors.
- Making a public statement in advance of the annual shareholder meeting.
- Submitting resolutions at the annual shareholders meeting.
- Calling for a special meeting to change the company's board.[38]

Institutional investors may serve as lead plaintiff in a class action securities lawsuit under the Private Securities Litigation Reform Act of 1995. As part of negotiated settlements, they have tried to positively influence corporate governance. For example, the California State Teacher's Retirement System (CalSTRS) brought a class action suit against Homestore, an Internet real estate company, and then settled the suit by:

- Obtaining $64 million in cash and stock for shareholders.
- Demanding that the company agree to appoint a shareholder-nominated director to the board.

- Asking the company to ban the use of stock options in compensating directors, and getting the company to agree to eliminate the staggered terms for its directors and to increase the number of independent directors and board committees.[39]

Institutional shareholders play an important role in corporate governance by:

- Exercising their right to elect directors.
- Raising their concerns about the company's governance with either company management or the board of directors.
- Assisting in reducing information asymmetry by providing a mechanism to convey the relevant information they obtained from management to investors.
- Improving the efficiency of the capital markets by transmitting relevant information they obtain from management to the financial markets and reducing agency problems by possessing resources, incentives, opportunities, and expertise to monitor managerial and oversight functions more effectively.

The ever-increasing presence of institutional investors in the capital markets empowers them to influence corporate governance. For example, institutional investors claimed that they have played an important role in increasing board independence and, through close monitoring of management, encouraged them to focus more on the company's sustainable performance rather than short-term profit maximization. Institutional investors are not only seeking a more active role in the nomination process, but also are trying to influence the process. For example, in March 2004, after months of negotiations, Marsh and McLennan Co. agreed to nominate a director, who was recruited by institutional investors, to be put to a shareholder vote.[40]

Opponents to institutional investor activism argue that the primary role of institutional shareholders is to manage pension funds on behalf of their beneficiaries, and they claim that investors' monitoring activities detract them from their main responsibilities. Institutional investors believe that the monitoring function is an integral part of fulfilling their fiduciary duty to act in the best interests of its plan participants. To perform the monitoring function effectively, institutional investors should maintain the investment for a sufficiently long period of time and hold a sufficient number of shares over the long term to reduce the free-rider problem of incurring the monitoring costs while all investors enjoy the benefits of such monitoring.[41] Most, if not all, large public pension funds are heavily indexed and therefore are the ultimate long-term investment. Furthermore, academic research suggests that there is evidence of positive short-term market reactions to the announcement of certain types of activism whereas there is little evidence of long-term capital market reactions; and there are some changes in the real activities of companies subsequent to shareholder pressure.[42]

In the post-SOX era, there has been strong shareholder support for major corporate governance reforms, and many of the shareholder proposals led by investor activists and institutional investors have received more than 50 percent support.[43] During the 2005 proxy season majority voting proposals received the highest level of support with an average 44 percent on 57 different company ballots. Board declassification was next in amount of shareholder support. Shareholder proposals regarding expensing stock options, independent board chairmen, and executive compensation also received considerable support. The State Board of Administration (SBA) of Florida, as a member of the ICGN and the Conference Board Governance Center, voted on about 3500 corporate proxies in 2006. The SBA has developed a comprehensive set of proxy voting guidelines that cover a wide range of corporate governance issues including independent boards, performance-based executive compensation, succession planning, shareholder monitoring, auditor independence, shareholder democracy, and meaningful participation.[44] During the 2006 proxy season, the number of shareholder proposals increased marginally to 634 proposals from 625 in 2005 with: (1) more than 120 receiving majority levels of support; (2) the elimination of supermajority voting requirements; (3) the declassification of the board (destaggering director terms); (4) the independence of the board chairman; (5) the award of performance-based stock options; and (6) the issue of sustainability reports.

Governance of Institutional Investors

America's 100 largest money managers now hold about 58 percent of stocks of public companies in the country.[45] It is expected that these giant financial institutions will be actively involved in monitoring public companies' governance, business, and affairs. These financial institutions, on one hand, are agents of individual shareholders with the fiduciary duty of managing these funds for the best interests of their principals (individual investors). On the other hand, they own and manage public companies' stocks; principals of these institutions are responsible for monitoring public companies' (agents) governance, business, and affairs. This dual responsibility of institutional investors as agents of individual investors and principals of public companies may create conflicts of interest for them. This real or potential conflict of interest has, in many cases, caused institutional investors to refrain from active monitoring of corporate affairs and governance.

Lack of effective monitoring by institutional investors can be attributed to and explained by three reasons:

1. Institutional investors, with a few exceptions (e.g., state and local public pension funds, unions, TIAA-CREF), have their own interests to serve aside from the interests of their investor-principals. For example, corporate pension plans are often controlled by the company's executives whose compensation is linked to the reported earnings. Compensation of mutual fund managers is often based on the return on funds' assets. Money managers who manage corporate 401(k) assets have a fiduciary duty to vote those proxies in the best interests of the plan participants (individual employees who contribute to a 401(k)), but may feel pressure to vote with management on proxies in order to ensure a continued business relationship with the company and its top executives.
2. Financial institutions have a tendency and motivation to focus on short-term speculation of stock price changes rather than long-term investing based on sustainable intrinsic corporate value.

3. Managers of mutual funds and pension plans are less likely to support a proxy proposal that is opposed by the management of a corporate client.[46]

MUTUAL FUNDS

Mutual funds are means by which ordinary investors can become shareholders by investing in the capital markets and are an investment vehicle they can use to try to achieve their financial goals, including saving for comfortable retirement and adequate investment for their children's education. As a conduit for investment by individual investors, mutual funds play an important role in the nation's continuing economic growth and vibrancy of its capital markets. Thus, it is vital that they be managed in the interests of their individual investors. More than 95 million Americans invest in and entrust their savings to mutual funds, an industry with over $7 trillion assets. However, critics have argued mutual fund companies are failing to fulfill their responsibility of representing shareholders' best interests despite their more than 25 percent control of U.S. stocks.[47] Anecdotal evidence indicates that large mutual funds companies overwhelmingly vote in support of management (80–92 percent) and marginally vote in favor of resolutions sponsored by shareholders (30–53 percent).[48] Many managers of mutual funds earn big fees while choosing their stocks to invest in based on the market index.[49]

Fidelity, the nation's largest mutual fund, which oversees more than $1 trillion in investor assets, can play an important role in corporate governance through casting hundreds of thousands of votes on its client's behalf at public companies' annual shareholder meetings.[50] Fidelity has distinguished itself from other large mutual funds (e.g., T. Rowe Price, Vanguard) by: (1) siding with corporate management and directors in 92.5 percent of its votes; (2) supporting 99 percent of directors whom management nominated; (3) voting against proposals concerning separation of the positions of chair of the board and the chief executive officer at many companies; (4) voting for all directors and against shareholders across almost all of its actively managed portfolios; and (5) infrequently voting in favor of key shareholder proposals and against management recommendations (e.g., 33 percent compared with 51 percent for Vanguard, 67 percent for T. Row Price, and 70 percent for American Funds). Investor activists view these voting records of Fidelity as evidence by that Fidelity: (1) "rarely exercise[s] its unprecedented muscle to push for improved corporate governance"; (2) "has frequently declined to join its rivals and other investors in confronting dubious company management"; and (3) "has lagged the benchmark Standard & Poor's 500-stock index in eight of the past 12 years."[51]

The rash of mutual fund scandals in 2003 indicates significant ineffectiveness in fund governance structures that caused the erosion of investor confidence in the mutual fund industry. The gradual transformation of stock ownership from individual investors to institutional investors run by professional money managers and corporations has contributed to two distinct levels of agency problems. The first level is associated with potential conflicts of interest between individual investors and their trustees and fiduciaries, namely professional money managers and corporations (mutual funds, public and private pension plans). The second level is related to the potential conflicts of interest between the professional money managers and corporations (financial intermediation) and their corporate clients. These levels of agency problems will continue to exist as long as individual ownership is diminishing and the agency (intermediate) society is monitoring public companies' governance, affairs, and business. These actual and potential conflicts of interest encouraged Congress to address the governance deficiencies of mutual funds.

Congress passed the Investment Company Act in 1940 to set requirements for prohibiting investment companies (mutual funds) from engaging in certain transactions that may create conflicts of interest.[52] The Act also requires that a fund's board of directors provide oversight over management to align management interests with those of shareholders while granting broad authority to the SEC to provide exemptions to this act (conditionally or unconditionally) when the exemptions are in the public interest and provide protections for investors.[53] The SEC has brought enforcement actions against troubled mutual funds and obtained over $2.2 billion in disgorgements and civil penalties, which has been used to compensate injured investors.[54] To improve the independence and director oversight of mutual funds, the SEC requires mutual funds to have independent chairs. This condition was adopted to strengthen independent oversight of potential conflicts of interest.[55]

The SEC's staff further investigated the association between an independent chair of mutual funds, fund performance, and fees; results were inconclusive, although other studies have shown the association. Nevertheless, the staff found that an independent chair can improve fund compliance with applicable rules and regulations. Commissioners Cynthia A. Glassman and Paul S. Atkins dissented on the grounds that the SEC report did not adequately justify the requirement that the chair of the board of directors of a mutual fund be an independent director or whether mutual funds chaired by independent directors: (1) perform better; (2) have lower expenses, or (3) have better compliance records than those chaired by interested (inside) directors.[56]

In July 2004 the SEC, in a three-to-two vote, adopted mutual fund governance reforms that require mutual funds to have an independent chair (nonexecutive) and require that 75 percent of board members be independent. The independent directors must have the authority to hire staff to support their oversight function, engage in an annual self-assessment, and hold separate executive sessions with fund management present. The SEC initially approved this rule in 2004; the U.S. Chamber of Commerce brought a lawsuit against the rule; and the U.S. Court of Appeals nullified the rule in the last week of June 2005, on the grounds that the SEC failed to consider the cost to mutual fund companies in promulgating the rule. On June 29, 2005, one day before William Donaldson stepped down as chairman, the SEC reapproved that rule.[57]

The Mutual Fund Director's Forum (MFDF), in August of 2005, conducted a survey that found that the implementation cost of the SEC rules for affected mutual funds is likely to be less than $50,000 and that such a cost could be marginal for those large family complex funds (e.g., Fidelity, Vanguard).[58] The survey also reveals that the majority (90 percent) of the 45 surveyed fund companies were already in compliance with the SEC rules regarding 75 percent supermajority independent requirements, and about 80 percent had independent board chairs.[59]

A joint report by the CFA Institute and the Business Roundtable Institute for Corporate Ethics makes several recommendations to reduce potential bias and conflicts of asset managers including: (1) align asset manager compensation with sustainable performance and long-term client interest; (2) improve disclosure of asset managers incentive metrics, fee structures, and personal ownership of funds they manage; and (3) encourage asset managers to consider sustainable pay-for-performance criteria for corporate executive compensation in their decision in which companies to invest.[60] The report also recommends that corporate leaders (CFOs, CEOs): (1) communicate long-term strategic goals and related sustainable performance benchmarks to investors, including asset managers, rather than just providing quarterly earnings guidance; (2) promote analysts and asset managers in using a long-term focus in their analyses and capital investment decisions; and (3) promote an institutional investor focus on sustainable value for themselves and in the assessment of their asset managers.[61]

For the third time during the past several years, the SEC has considered whether to require the mutual funds to have an independent chair and be composed of 75 percent independent directors. On two occasions (Rule Release 26520, July 27, 2004, and Rule Release No. 26985, June 30, 2005), the SEC approved these requirements; both have been rejected by the D.C. Circuit for inadequacies in the rulemaking process.[62] The court remanded these governance enhancement rules to the SEC for further consideration. As of September 1, 2006, federal law permits funds to be composed of a simple majority of independent directors and have an interested chair.

Several mutual funds have responded to the SEC's request for additional comments regarding the investment company governance proposals. The AARP Funds support the SEC's proposal to require 75 percent independent directors on the fund's board and an independent director to serve as chair.[63] The AARP Funds believe that compliance costs of these governance enhancement rules would be small compared with the total operating expenses of the fund and the benefits afforded to shareholders.[64] The Mutual Funds Directors Forum supports these governance enhancements rules and believes that: (1) the implementation of these rules would improve investor confidence in mutual funds and, thus, the integrity and efficiency of the capital markets; and (2) costs of implementing these rules are negligible in relation to fund assets and operating expenses, such as fund advisory fees.[65] In support of the new requirements for the independence of the chairman of mutual funds and at least 75 percent of the board to be independent directors, John C. Bogle, a 55-year veteran of the mutual fund industry, founder of Vanguard, and former CEO of the Wellington Management Company, states:

> *I have many concerns about the prevailing levels of conducts and values in today's mutual fund industry. But my overriding concern is that funds are operated largely in the concern of their management companies, rather than in the interest of their shareholders. To begin to address this imbalance, I am strongly in favor of requiring the chairman of the fund board of*

directors to be independent of the management company I continue to believe that 100 percent of the board should be independent.[66]

Mutual funds, by virtue of casting their annual proxy votes on behalf of their customers, play an important role in protecting investors' interest by putting their clients' interests ahead of their own in supporting shareholder-friendly company practices. For example, Putnam Funds, in 2006, opposed directors in 16 percent of elections and voted against 34 percent of the proposals by 1,150 companies to adopt or amend restricted stock plans or stock options for company directors or executives.[67] Putnam's trustees, by using a benchmark of "if a proposed stock option or restricted stock plan would add more than 1.67 percent to a company's existing shareholder base [to] vote against it," show their commitment to shareholders to do the right thing. The Four Horsemen of mutual fund governance as promoted by the State Board of Administration (SBA) of Florida are: (1) no more than one management company on the fund's board; (2) independent chairman of the board; (3) dedicated fund staff; and (4) federal statute of fiduciary duty.[68]

Chief Compliance Officer

The SEC, in December 2003, adopted initiatives that require mutual funds and their advisors to have comprehensive compliance policies and procedures and to appoint a chief compliance officer (CCO) to assist the board in improving the governance structure. The CCO is accountable to the fund's board and can be terminated only by the board's decision. Mutual funds and their advisors should establish the required compliance policies and procedures, including the position of the CCO, and can substantially benefit from doing so. A fund's CCO plays an important role by monitoring and ensuring that the fund and its advisors effectively comply with applicable laws, rules, and regulations, including the securities laws, and providing appropriate information regarding such compliance to the fund's board.

Code of Ethics

To reinforce ethical behavior and integrity in the investment management industry, the SEC, in July 2004, issued rules that require registered investment advisors, including advisors to mutual funds, to adopt a code of ethics that sets forth the standards of ethical conduct for each employee. Mutual funds and their advisors should comply with the requirements of their code of ethics.

Soft-Dollar Trading

It is reported that mutual fund companies have hidden use of customers' money to pay brokers for buying and selling stocks in funds and have used what amount to kickbacks from these commissions to buy everything from analyst reports, to data feeds, to office furniture.[69] This soft-dollar trading can cause more than

"$33.6 billion lost by fund shareholders each year and in most cases it's not disclosed and it's coming right out of the pocket of the investor."[70] Furthermore, this soft-dollar system promotes many other problems, including:

- Generating excessive trading, which causes higher transaction costs and capital gain trades and inversely affects fund performance.
- Causing inefficient trading because funds routinely trade with less efficient brokerages at higher rates to generate soft-dollar goodies.
- Misallocating resources for using commissions to compensate brokerage firms for selling their funds to retail investors.
- Inadequate disclosing by funds for commission spending particularly to buy research.
- Victimizing unsophisticated investors due to their inability to press investments managers and brokers to limit soft-dollar use.

Overall, the lack of proper disclosure of soft-dollar trading and inability of the small investors to demand more information or to monitor their investment managers and brokerages for excessive soft-dollar use underscore the important role that independent directors of mutual funds can play in protecting shareholders. But the problem is that many directors of mutual funds are not independent from fund management companies, and even directors who are independent may not fully understand the issues of soft-dollar inefficiencies. It is suggested the most effective way to protect investors from soft-dollar abuses would be to "require fund managers to pay for everything except trade executions out of the corporate kitty" through legislation.[71]

HEDGE FUNDS

Hedge funds and other private equity investors play an important role in financing and corporate governance issues by promoting investor protection as their primary goal. Investors, in general, and hedge and mutual funds, in particular, can influence corporate governance by demanding that boards of directors act independently from management, holding boards accountable for their decisions, and holding the compensation committee accountable for approving excessive executive pay. Hedge funds are usually private investment partnerships, and traditionally they have been exempt from most federal regulations, primarily because traditionally they have served sophisticated investors and institutional investors.

Recently hedge funds have been closely watched and scrutinized by lawmakers, regulators, and the investing public due to the fact that: (1) they increasingly manage money for small investors through pension funds; (2) several fund companies have recently collapsed resulting from fraud allegations, including Stamford, Atlanta-based International Management Associates, and Connecticut-based Bayou Management; (3) the civil cases brought against hedge funds by the SEC substantially increased to 29 in 2005 compared with only 10 in 2002; and (4) the corporate fraud task force is currently investigating the fraud in the $1.2 trillion lightly regulated hedge fund industry.[72] Pequot Capital Management, one of the nation's most prominent hedge funds, is under SEC investigation for possible insider trading.[73] The investigation has not resulted in any charges against the hedge fund, and Pequot has denied any wrongdoing.[74] It is expected that corporate governance of hedge funds will be further addressed by regulators.

EMPLOYEE MONITORING

The agency theory aspect of corporate governance focuses primarily on the relation between investors and management with shareholders, considered the only bearers of residual risk. In modern corporations, particularly in the era of technological advances, labor resources are becoming an important part of corporate governance as capital resources. The balance of power and association among property rights (investor protection), managerial control (management prerogative), and employee participation rights (labor management and employee protection) can play an important role in the effectiveness of corporate governance. Employees' participation in corporate governance can influence managerial control and authority and can influence their participation in decision making and cooperation in the implementation of decisions. After all, it was an employee whistleblower at Enron and at other companies who uncovered the widespread fraud present at the highest levels of the company.

The shape and extent of employees' participation in corporate governance is a function of their level of investment in the company's stock through retirement plans and whether their skills are firm-specific. In a situation in which employees invest in skills specific to their company and their retirement funds and pensions are tied in the company's stock, their incentives to exercise a voice and participate in corporate governance are greater. Alternatively, when employees' skills are portable across companies and their investments in the company are insignificant, they may prefer strategies of exit over voice in response to dissatisfaction and grievances. Thus, employees' interests in corporate governance are shaped by their economic, investment, and employment ties to the company, as well as their participation in managerial decisions.

Employees' participation rights can be defined by employment contracts, employer action, labor law, ownership, and/or collective bargaining. Employees' participation may be established by the employment contract in terms of involvement in decision making, or it may be determined through decisions made by the employer. Participation rights may also be established by the labor law or statutory law, or by direct ownership as shareholders or through employee share ownership plans (ESOPs). Finally, collective bargaining can be an important vehicle for establishing contractual participation rights. In addition, employee stock options and other performance-related incentives may shape employee participation. The financial scandals and bankruptcies of Enron and WorldCom, which caused significant loss of jobs and employee pension funds, underscore the importance of employee participation in corporate governance.

There are several advantages of employee participation in corporate governance:

- Employees, through their ownership of the company's shares, have more incentives to align their interests with those of shareholders, but may feel pressure to support management in order to stay employed.
- It is a learning process for employees to advance their position, show their commitment, and improve the company's operation efficiency and effectiveness.
- It can be regarded as an internal mechanism to monitor managerial performance and prevent management opportunistic conduct. The only concern is whether employee governance and monitoring conflict with shareholder governance and monitoring. Academic research suggests that these two forms of governance are indeed complementary and mutually beneficial in the sense that cooperative monitoring provides more incentives for management to align its interests with those of employees and shareholders.[75]

SUMMARY

In the post-SOX era, institutional investors have continued their monitoring of public companies and attempted to influence governance of the public companies in which they are invested. Institutional investors have put forth many proposals intended to improve corporate governance effectiveness. Shareholders should monitor the board of directors' effectiveness and performance because the company's board represents its shareholders and should be held accountable to them. Most public companies use plurality voting, which is permitted by state law. In this type of voting, management can nominate a director and, if the election is uncontested, the nominated director can be elected with just a single vote. The author suggests that companies adopt a true majority voting default rule for the election of directors, allow shareholder access to their proxy materials to make this process more democratic and meaningful, and permit a shareholder advisory vote on executive compensation.

NOTES

1. PricewaterhouseCoopers (PwC). 2006. What directors think. (November). Available at: www.pwc.com.
2. The Working Group on Corporate Governance. 1991. A new compact for owners and directors. *Harvard Business Review* (July–August): 141–143.
3. Jackson, G., and S. Vitols. 2001. Between financial commitment, market liquidity and corporate governance: Occupational pensions in Britain, Germany, Japan and the USA. In *Comparing Welfare Capitalism: Social Policy and Political Economy in Europe, Japan and the USA*, ed. B. Ebbinghaus and P. Manow. London: Routledge.
4. Zysman, J. 1983. *Governments, markets and growth: Finance and the politics of industrial change*. Ithaca, NY: Cornell University Press.

5. Stokman, F. N., and F. W. Wasseur. 1985. National networks in 1976: A structural comparison. In *Networks of corporate power*, ed. F. N. Stokman, R. Ziegler, and J. Scott. Cambridge: Polity Press. Windolf, P., and J. Beyer. 1996. Co-operative capitalism: Corporate networks in Germany and Britain. *British Journal of Sociology* 47 (2): 205–231.

6. U.K. Proposed Company Law Reform. 2005. Available at: www.publications. parliament.uk/pa/Id200506/Idbills/034/2006030pdf.

7. Business Roundtable. 2005. Guidelines for shareholder-director communications (May). Available at: www.businessroundtable.org/pdf/20050527001 ShareholderCommunicationsGuidelines-FINAL-5.26.05.pdf.

8. Securities and Exchange Commission. 2005. SEC votes to propose rule to provide investor with Internet availability of proxy materials. (November 29). Available at: www.sec.gov/news/press/2005-166.htm.

9. Forrester Research, Inc. 2006. ADP phone survey: Shareholder communications. (January 23). Available at: http://ics.adp.com/release11/public_site/comment/ images/Forrester_Research-Results_of_TelephoneSurvey.pdf.

10. Clapman, P. 2005. Commentary: The 2005 survey of the Spencer Stuart Board Index (SSBI). (December 5). Available at: www.spencerstuart.com.

11. Council of Institutional Investors/NACD. 2004. Task Force Report: Improving board-shareowner communications. (February 26). Available at: www. nacdonline.org/images/white.CIITaskForce-2004-2-26-04.pdf.

12. PricewaterhouseCoopers. 2006. Questions that may be asked at the 2006 shareholders meetings (January). Available at: www.pwc.com.

13. Ibid.

14. Pender, K. 2006. Board drama in East (September 10). Available at: www.sfgate. com/cgi-bin/article.cgi?file=Chronicle/archive/2006/09/10/BUGJ9L1IPA1.DTL.

15. Grant, J. 2006. SEC postpones decision on company proxies. *Financial Times* (October 12). Available at: www.ft.com.

16. Council of Institutional Investors. 2004. Corporate governance policies. (October 13). Available at: www.cii.org.

17. Committee on Capital Markets Regulation. 2006. Interim report of the Committee on Capital Market Regulation. (November 30). Available at: www.capmktsreg.org/research.html.

18. Ibid.

19. Morgenson, G. 2005. Who's afraid of shareholder democracy? *New York Times* (October 2). Available at: www.nytimes.com.

20. Ibid.

21. Plitch, P. 2005. Career Ed vote lays bare contentious governance practices. (May 24). *Wall Street Journal Online*. Available at: http://online.wsj.com/article/ BTCO20050524005927.00html.

22. Ibid.

23. Ibid.

24. Amalgamated Bank Long View Collective Investment Fund. 2006. Request for commission review of no-action determination regarding shareholder proposal to CA, Inc. (June 23). Available at: www.hitchlaw.com.

25. Morgenson, G. 2006. Soviet-style proxies. Made in the U.S.A. *New York Times* (June 25). Available at: www.nytimes.com.

26. Burgess, K., and J. Grant. 2006. Investors "lack basic rights" on US boards. *Financial Times* (October 24). Available at: www.ft.com.

27. Levitt, A. 2006. Commentary: Stock populi. *Wall Street Journal* (October 27). Available at: www.online.wsj.com/article/SD116194105035055582.html.

28. Ibid.

29. Tse, T. M. 2007. Score one for dissident: Aflac to be 1st U.S. firm to allow advisory votes on pay. *Washington Post* (February 15). Available at: washingtonpost.com.

30. Millstein, I. M., H. J. Gregory, and R. C. Grapsas. 2007. Seven things shareholders want directors to understand in 2007 (January 10). Available at: www.weil.com.

31. Bogle, J. C. 2005. Individual stockholder, R.I.P. *Wall Street Journal Commentary*. (October 3). Available at: www.wsj.com.

32. Board of Governors of the Federal Reserve System. 2003. Flow of funds accounts of the United States: Annual flows and outstandings. Washington, DC. Available at: www.federalreserve.gov/releases/z1.

33. Gillan, S., and L. T. Starks. 2003. Corporate governance, corporate ownership, and the role of institutional investors: A global perspective. *Journal of Applied Finance* 13(2) (Fall): 4–30.

34. Ibid.

35. Ibid.

36. CFA Institute Center and Business Roundtable Institute for Corporate Ethics. 2006. Breaking the short-term cycle. (July 24). Available at: www.cfapubs.org/toc/ccb/2006/1.

37. London Stock Exchange. 2004. A practical guide to corporate governance. Available at: www.rsmi.co.uk.

38. Commission of the European Communities. 2003. Modernising company law and enhancing corporate governance in the European Union. Available at: http://eur-lex.europa.eu/LexUriServ/site/en/com/2003/com2003_0284en01.pdf.

39. Goodman, A., and B. Schwartz. 2004. Corporate governance: Law and practice. New York: Matthew Bender & Co. *Financial Times*. 2003. CalSTRs' ethical victory. (August 25). Available at: www.ft.com.

40. Solomon, D., and J. S. Lubin. 2004. Democracy looks for an opening in the boardroom. *Wall Street Journal*. (March 22).

41. Gillan, S., and L. T. Starks. 2003. Corporate governance, corporate ownership, and the role of institutional investors. *Journal of Applied Finance* 13 (2) (Fall/Winter): 4–22.

42. Ibid.

43. State Board of Administration of Florida. 2005. Corporate governance 2005 annual report. Available at: www.sbafla.com.

44. State Board of Administration (SBA) of Florida. 2006. Corporate Governance Annual Report 2006. Available at: 222.sbafla.com.

45. Gillan and Straks. 2003. Supra.

46. Ibid.

47. Lauricella, T., and K. Whitehouse. 2006. No secrets: How funds vote your shares. *Wall Street Journal* (October 3). Available at: www.online.wsj.com/article/SB115921504081573380.html.

48. Ibid.

49. Lauricella, T. 2006. Professors shine a light into "closet indexes." Measurement may help investors see how much of their holdings are actively managed. *Wall Street Journal* (July 18). Available at: www.online.wsj.com/article/SB1158676981639076.htm.

50. Morgenson, G. 2006. Fidelity, staunch defender of the status quo. *New York Times* (October 6). Available at: www.nytimes.com.

51. Farzad, R. 2006. Fidelity's dividend loyalties. *BusinessWeek* (October 16).

52. U.S. Congress. The Investment Company Act. 1940. Available at: www.sec.gov/about/laws/ica40.pdf.

53. Ibid.

54. Securities and Exchange Commission (SEC). 2005. Exemptive rule amendments of 2004: The independent chair condition. A report in accordance with the Consolidated Appropriateness Act, 2005. (April). Available at: www.sec.gov.

55. Ibid.

56. Commissioners Glassman and Atkins. 2005. Letter from Commissioners Glassman and Atkins re: Staff report on the Exemptive Rule Amendments of 2004: The Independent Chair Condition (April 29). Available at: www.sec.gov/news/speech/spch05205cagpsa.htm.

57. Securities and Exchange Commission. 2005. Commission response to remand by Court of Appeals. Final rule: Investment Company Governance: IC-26520. (June 30). Available at: www.sec.gov/final/finalarchive/finalarchive2005.shtml.

58. Mutual Fund Directors Forum. 2005. Report of the Mutual Fund Directors Forum on the cost implications of an independent chair and a 75 percent independent board. Available at: www.mfdf.com/UserFiles/File/ReportofSurvey.pdf.

59. Ibid.

60. CFA Institute Center and Business Roundtable Institute for Corporate Ethics. 2006. Breaking the short-term cycle.

61. Ibid.

62. U.S. Securities and Exchange Commission (SEC). 2004. Investment Company Governance. Release No. 1 C-26520 (July 27, 2004) and Release No. 1 C-26985 (June 30, 2005). Available at: www.sec.gov/rules/final/findarchive/finalarchive2005.html.

63. AARP Funds. 2006. Response to requested additional comments in Investments Company Governance Proposal (August 18). Available at: www.aarpfunds.com.

64. Ibid.

65. Mostoff, A. S. 2006. Comments to the SEC on its mutual funds governance enhancement rules. Mutual Fund Directors Forum (August 21). Available at: www.mfdf.com.

66. Bogle, J. C. 2006. Request for additional comment: Investments company governance. File Number 57-03-04 Bogle. (August 21). Financial Markets Research Center, Malvern, PA.

67. Morgenson, G. 2006. Related apologies in proxy land. *New York Times* (August 20). Available at: www.nytimes.com.
68. State Board of Administration (SBA) of Florida. 2006. Corporate Governance Annual Report 2006. Available at: www.sbafla.com.
69. Shack, J. 2005. Sins of commissions. *Institutional Investor* (December 14). Available at: www.iimagazine.com/Article.aspx?ArticleID=1025848.
70. Ibid.
71. Ibid.
72. Schmidt, R. 2006. Hedge fund fraud is an emerging threat, McNulty says (July 7). Available at: www.bloomberg.net.
73. Bogdanich, W., and G. Morgenson. 2006. SEC is reported to be examining a big hedge fund. *New York Times* (June 23). Available at: www.nytimes.com.
74. Ibid.
75. Boatright, J. R. (2004). Employee governance and the ownership of the firm. *Business Ethics Quarterly* 14 (1): 1–21.

Contemporary Issues in Corporate Governance

Corporate Governance in Private and Not-for-Profit Organizations

INTRODUCTION

The emerging corporate governance reforms discussed in the previous chapters normally are aimed at improving corporate governance of for-profit organizations, particularly public companies. Not-for-profit organizations (NPOs or nonprofits) usually are established to achieve philanthropic purposes rather than maximizing the wealth of their stakeholders. However, private companies and nonprofits, such as government entities, healthcare organizations, colleges and universities, and charitable organizations, have been under scrutiny for their governance. For example, the scandal in the Roslyn (New York) schools shows that an outside accountant hired to perform the bookkeeping in a school district assisted in covering up the alleged theft by school administrators of $11.2 million in public money.[1] In the context of corporate governance and accountability, private companies and NPOs have the same stewardship responsibilities as business corporations. This chapter discusses corporate governance in private companies and state and local government entities, healthcare, colleges and universities, and other nonprofits.

CORPORATE GOVERNANCE OF PRIVATE COMPANIES

Recent corporate governance reforms, including the Sarbanes-Oxley Act (SOX), Securities and Exchange Commission (SEC) rules, listing standards, and best practices, are applicable to public companies. They are intended to improve corporate governance, financial reporting, and accountability of public companies. Congress's intent in passing SOX was to significantly improve the corporate governance practices, financial reporting, and audit activities of public companies. However, many of its provisions are relevant and feasible for private companies and nonprofits. It was expected that these provisions would eventually be adopted by all organizations (private, public, and not-for-profit) as part of "best practices." The trend toward the adoption of the best practices of corporate governance by all businesses will continue as they have the flexibility to choose the most relevant and cost-effective aspects of corporate governance reforms.[2] Many of these reforms, particularly some provisions of SOX, can be very beneficial to private companies that have no intention of ever going public. Furthermore, SOX has become so pervasive that many stakeholders of private companies, including customers, suppliers, investment banks, and auditors, demand that they voluntarily conform to some of the key provisions of SOX.

There are several reasons why private companies may choose to adopt some of the emerging corporate governance reforms including SOX. Among the reasons are: (1) owners of closely held companies may in the long term desire to go public or sell the company (Goss International Corp.); (2) private companies and their directors may believe that compliance with corporate governance reforms can promote sustainable benefits by making their business more effective and efficient; (3) owners at private companies may believe that effective internal controls can improve efficiency (Goss International Corp); (4) suppliers, customers, and even the government may require compliance with a set of corporate governance reforms (Wells Fargo & Co); and (5) lenders may require private companies to comply with emerging corporate governance reforms (Financial Engines Inc).[3]

Some of the less cumbersome provisions of SOX relevant to nonpublic companies are:

- Improving their corporate governance of creating an appropriate balance of power-sharing between owners, management, and the board of directors.
- Improving the quality of their financial reports.
- Strengthening their code of ethics and business conduct.
- Prohibiting loans to their officers.
- Enhancing their communications with their shareholders and other constituencies through holding conference calls or meeting with them and/or distributing periodic quarterly and annual financial statements.
- Increasing the effectiveness of the board oversight function through establishing independent audit and governance committees to oversee financial reporting, internal controls, audit activities and governance matters.
- Improving their internal control over financial reporting by implementing some of the key provisions of SOX, including internal control reports by management and audit reports by the independent auditor.

An interview of chief executive officers (CEOs) of 340 of the fastest-growing U.S. privately held companies conducted by the PricewaterhouseCoopers (PwC) Trendsetter Barometer reveals that:

- These CEOs are more in favor of fewer government regulations.
- They have, in general, a positive view of SOX and its impact on public companies' corporate governance, accountability, and transparency.
- More than 25 percent of them have implemented best practices from the SOX compliance experience of public companies.
- About 75 percent are opposed to mandating SOX's provisions across the board on companies that are not publicly traded.[4]

A 2006 survey conducted by Foley & Lardner, a law firm that practices in corporate governance, indicates that:

- 86 percent of respondents (directors and officers) believed that SOX would continue to have a significant impact on private companies.
- 70 percent of the surveyed private organizations have self-imposed corporate governance reforms, including many provisions of SOX.
- Corporate governance participants who promote and influence the decision to adopt corporate governance reforms are the organizations themselves, their board members, and their auditors.
- Private companies have the flexibility of adopting most cost-effective provisions of SOX and other corporate governance reforms and tailoring them to their organization's governance structure.
- The most common aspects of corporate governance reforms adopted as "best practices" by private companies are audited financial statements, establishing independent directors, requiring the audit committee oversight of auditors, and the development of a corporate ethical code.
- It is expected that the trend toward the adoption of some aspects of the emerging corporate governance reforms as "best practices" by private companies will continue to increase.
- The average annual implementation cost of best practices of corporate governance for private companies is estimated as $105,000, which is about 26 percent higher than their estimated cost prior to SOX.[5]

Private companies, like public companies, are subject to the requirements of state law and these five corporate governance best practices:

1. Establishing an appropriate "tone at the top" promoting ethical, legal and professional conduct throughout the company.
2. Developing and maintaining adequate and effective internal controls in general and internal controls over financial reporting to ensure operational effectiveness and efficiency, reliability of financial reports, and compliance with applicable laws, rules and standards.
3. Establishing antifraud programs to prevent, detect, and deter misappropriation of assets and misstatements of financial reports.
4. Using the best practices and provisions of SOX to improve governance, transparency, and accountability.
5. Establishing whistleblower programs.

Effect of SOX on Private Companies

Private companies are not currently required to comply with corporate governance, financial reporting, internal control, audit activities, and other provisions of SOX. Nevertheless, a survey conducted by PwC reveals that CEOs from 17 percent of the surveyed fast-growing private companies reported that SOX has already had an effect on their business, and another 13 percent anticipate such effects in the near future.[6]

Private companies are experiencing the impacts of SOX in these areas of their business practices, listed based on their importance:

- Improving control documentation and testing.
- Refining corporate governance policies and procedures.
- Strengthening the code of business conduct/ethics.
- Adopting public company best practices.
- Establishing and updating whistleblower programs and policies.
- Creating an independent and effective audit committee.
- Establishing an independent and vigilant board of directors.[7]

Surveyed companies that did not believe that the benefits of compliance with SOX outweigh costs still will adopt some provisions of SOX in order to:

- Achieve a best business practice.
- Address future or potential problems.
- Respond to recommendations of outside constituents (leaders, advisors, vendors, and shareholders).
- Consider future sale of the business to another company.
- Resolve current business problems.
- Consider going public (initial public offering [IPO]).[8]

Financial reports of private companies are important and relevant to financial decisions made by these companies' owners and management. The Financial Auditing Standards Board (FASB) has taken the initiative to improve the quality of the financial reporting of private companies.[9] The FASB and the American Institute of Certified Public Accountants (AICPA) have traditionally studied whether financial accounting and reporting standards should be different for private companies. The general consensus has been that accounting policies and practices of measuring, recognizing and reporting business transactions and economic events should be the same and companies of all sizes and types (small versus large, private versus public) benefit from uniform accounting and reporting standards. The AICPA has issued an invitation to comment on its proposal entitled *"Enhancing the Financial Accounting and Reporting Standard-Setting Process for Private Companies."*[10] The FASB is considering this proposal in assessing the differences in accounting standards for private companies within the framework of generally accepted accounting principles (GAAP). The FASB and the AICPA are committed to finding ways to improve the quality, value, transparency, and cost effectiveness of financial reporting for private companies. To achieve this goal, they are jointly proposing: (1) improving the FASB's current processes of assessing whether differences are needed in the current and future accounting standards for private companies; and (2) sponsoring a committee designed to increase input and insights from private company constituents in the standard-setting process.[11]

The FASB/AICPA's invitation to comment on financial reporting for private companies has generated discussions as to: (1) whether it is appropriate to diverge from generally accepted accounting principles (GAAP) merely because an entity is nonpublic; (2) whether and how differing for private companies would increase the complexity of the financial reporting standards setting process; and (3) whether the establishment of separate accounting standards for private companies would cause dilution in the FASB's resources and efforts to focus on principles-based accounting standards for all entities, private, public, small, or large.

Corporate Governance and the Initial Public Offering

The IPO is viewed as the beginning of the formation of corporate governance in a newly established public company while the initial owners attempt to maximize their wealth generated from the sale of the company's ownership (blockholders). Traditionally, the composition of the board of directors of newly established public companies has been dominated by outside directors in an attempt to move the board away from both inside and instrumental directors (e.g., lawyers, investment banks, consultants).[12] The structure of corporate governance of these companies in terms of the percentage of ownership of blockholders and outside directors on the board can change once the company is past the IPO stage.

The process of going public begins with the preparation to file a registration statement with the SEC. This statement contains the owner's letter of intent for the offering, the estimated range of the offer price, the number of shares being offered, the ownership concentration, the governance structure, a description of the financial condition, and the use of proceeds. The information contained in the statement along with the underwriters' identities is reported in the preliminary initial public offering prospectus. The issuing company then chooses the lead and comanaging underwriters to assist the company to register with the SEC and provide credible certification of their financial condition.

During the preregistration period right before the issuing company registers with the SEC, regulations prohibit the company from conducting promotions that may boost its stock price. The underwriter reviews the prospectus to ensure that no information is omitted or incorrectly reported. The underwriter should exercise due diligence review and analysis to reduce any risk of potential legal liabilities. This preliminary prospectus is prepared and submitted to the SEC for review. The lead underwriter then begins to establish a syndicate of underwriters that are willing to participate in underwriting the IPO. During this quiet period, the issuing company and underwriters are not permitted to make any solicitations to potential outside investors. After the submission of the prospectus to the SEC and before the SEC decision to accept or reject the IPO prospectus (the waiting period), the underwriter and the issuing company communicate with institutional investors and solicit indications of interest. This process of book building should help the issuing company to estimate the demand for its newly issued stock. During this period, no written communication with potential investors is permitted, with the exception of the preliminary prospectus, and no binding sales of shares or commitments to buy shares are allowed.

Shortly before the SEC declares the right to issue shares, and when there is an indication that the SEC will approve the IPO prospectus, the issuing company and the underwriter sign the underwriting agreement that finalizes the offer and the number of shares to be offered. This agreement binds the underwriter to buy the amount issued at the established price. On the effective day (the day the SEC declares the right to issue the shares), the underwriter sells the shares to investors. Upon completion of the IPO, insiders including management, the founders of the company, and the directors who own shares of the company are bound by Rule 144, which requires the company to report insider ownership changes that exceed one percent of the total outstanding shares.[13]

Insiders usually have a binding contract with the underwriter (known as a lockup agreement) not to sell their shares before the lockup period expires, which is typically 180 days after the IPO. After the lockup period expires, Rule 144 allows insiders to sell up to 1 percent of the total outstanding shares per quarter without reporting to the SEC or participating in the primary seasoned equity offerings (SEOs) to raise more funds. Compliance with applicable IPO rules and regulations requires the formation and effective functioning of corporate governance mechanisms. The SEC in its securities offering reform has decided to end the so-called quiet period during which company executives and other personnel were prohibited from making public statements prior to an IPO of stock.[14] This securities offering reform is intended to increase the amount of information (public presentations, written materials in addition to the prospectus) about shares that are being offered to the public in order to promote the sale of stocks and bonds to investors and improve the efficiency of the capital markets without mandating delays in the offering process. SOX is being criticized for not addressing issues related to IPOs that contributed to the Refco debacle.

Recent corporate governance reforms (SOX, SEC rules, listing standards, and best practices) relevant to public companies have made going public a challenging endeavor for private companies. Private companies going public and raising capital through IPOs must now comply with corporate governance reforms imposed on public companies. The author suggests that these companies begin complying with some of these reforms well in advance of their IPO process to get themselves ready for when the market conditions are right. Examples of reforms that can be planned in advance of the IPO process are:

- Formation of a board composed of a majority of independent directors.
- Formation of board committees (audit, compensation, nomination/governance) that contain all independent directors.
- Designation of one of the members of the audit committee as the audit committee financial expert.
- Establishment of financial relationships with directors and officers that comply with SOX (e.g., no personal loans to directors and executive officers).
- Establishment of new arrangements with independent auditors to conduct and integrate the audit of both internal control over financial reporting and audit of financial statements as well as prohibition of the performance of nonaudit services.

- Preparation for executive certifications of internal control under Sections 302 and 404 of SOX and financial statements as well as annual filing (Form 10-K) and quarterly filing (Form 10-Q) deadlines for accelerated filings.
- More than 50 global exchanges list domestic and foreign IPOs. However, typically only about 10 percent of the IPOs are listed abroad.

NOT-FOR-PROFIT ORGANIZATIONS

Purpose of Not-for-Profit Organizations

The primary purpose of nonprofits is to serve the public rather than to maximize shareholder wealth through earning profits. NPOs are created to serve the public, often individuals other than organizations, and are usually tax-exempt when complying with Internal Revenue Service (IRS) rules. NPOs have a fundamental difference from business corporations with respect to their relationship with their stakeholders. NPOs may receive grants, which are funds from their constituencies, to provide services to the community. Governance of NPOs is crucial in managing and monitoring their activities and balancing their budgets. NPOs receive their budgets through grants or contributions from their stakeholders or fees or membership dues charged for their services or memberships. Thus, NPO activities for generating funds are similar to the activities of profit-oriented business firms for generating revenue. Section 501(c) of the Internal Revenue Service code defines tax-exempt organizations as those that are operated for philanthropic purposes. The organization must serve the public good and not benefit a private shareholder or individual. The organization cannot be a lobbying organization, attempt to influence legislation by propaganda or otherwise, or be an organization participating in a political campaign.[15]

NPOs are required to pay taxes on their unrelated business income (UBI) when the revenue is generated from nonphilanthropic services. Tax exemption is usually given to NPOs that meet and continue to meet IRS requirements. NPOs that wish to obtain federal tax-exempt status file the request with the IRS and upon approval receive the exemption. Tax-exempt organizations can be subject to tax on revenue generated from engagement in a trade or business unrelated to their exempt purposes, and must file an annual return with the IRS to maintain their tax-exempt status. Donations to tax-exempt organizations that have received approval by the IRS as 501(c) entities are tax-deductible by donors.

Recently the Panel on the Non-Profit Sector was organized to demonstrate the role of charitable organizations in American life and to strengthen NPO accountability, transparency, and governance.[16] The panel developed eight principles regarding the role of charitable organizations, the responsibilities of the charitable community, and the need for balanced government oversight, and it made a set of recommendations to improve transparency, governance, and accountability of charitable organizations based on its established principles.[17] The panel's suggested principles are:

1. A vibrant charitable community is vital for a strong America.
2. The charitable sector's effectiveness depends on its independence.

3. The charitable sector's success depends on its integrity and credibility.
4. Comprehensive and accurate information about the charitable sector must be available to the public.
5. A viable system of self-regulation and education is needed for the charitable sector.
6. The government should ensure effective enforcement of the law for charitable organizations.
7. Government regulation should deter abuse in the charitable sector without discouraging legitimate charitable activities.
8. Compliance with applicable laws and high standards of ethical conduct should be required and commensurate with the size, scale, and resources of the organization.[18]

The panel's recommendations call for improvement within the nonprofit sector, more effective oversight, and changes in the law. The panel's recommendations are:

■ Effective oversight of the charitable sector requires vigorous enforcement of federal and state law.
■ The annual information returns filed to the Internal Revenue Service (IRS) by charitable organizations (Forms 990, 990-EZ, and 990-PF) should be improved by providing more accurate, complete, and timely information for federal and state regulators, managers of charitable organizations, and the public.
■ Congress should require charitable organizations with annual revenues of between $250,000 and $1 million to have their financial statements annually reviewed and those with more than $1 million audited annually by independent auditors.
■ Charitable organizations should provide more detailed information about their operations and performance of their programs to the public through their annual reports, Web site, or other means.
■ Charitable organizations should be discouraged from providing compensation to their board members. When such compensation is provided, it should be fully disclosed, including the amount, reason, and method of determining reasonableness of the compensation.
■ A charitable organization should have a minimum of three members on the governing board to be qualified for recognition as a 501(c)(3) tax-exempt organization, and at least one-third of the members of the governing board should be independent to be qualified as a public charity rather than a private foundation.
■ Charitable organizations should adopt and enforce a conflict of interest policy, and the IRS should require them to disclose on their Form 990 series whether they have such policies.[19]

Governance of Not-for-Profit Organizations

In the business environment, the board of directors represents the owners (shareholders) of the company. NPOs typically are owned by their members (e.g., trade associations, professional societies), their communities (e.g., social services, education, hospitals), or their constituencies (e.g., state, local governments). Thus, the board of directors or its equivalent, the board of trustees, represents the members, communities, or constituencies in a NPO. Regardless of the type of NPO and the nature of their ownership, the board has total authority over the organization, is directly responsible for its activities and ultimately accountable to its ownership, and delegates its authority to others to carry out the organization's activities. In the business sector, the chief executive officer (CEO) manages the company; in NPOs, the CEO may be called executive director, president, general manager, superintendent, or director-general. The board grants its authority to the CEO.

To regain public confidence, particularly that of donors, NPOs should improve their governance by demonstrating integrity, honesty, ethics, and transparency in their performance. William H. Donaldson, then the chairman of the SEC, in his remarks before the Annual Conference of Independent Sector, stated that the public lack of confidence in NPOs is very serious.[20] Donaldson suggests some type of self-regulation for NPOs with the goal being:

> *not simply to avoid unwanted legislation, but rather to advance a regime of self-regulation that produces better results than any congressional proposal or regulatory overseer can achieve. The ultimate goal of a self-regulatory approach should be for leaders throughout the non-profit sector to mobilize in support of improved governance standards, greater accountability, and a higher ethical code.*[21]

Four major documents make up the governance documents of NPOs: two organization documents (mission statement and code of conduct) and two legal documents (charter and bylaws).

1. *Mission statement.* A mission statement defining an organization's vision, mission, and goals is regarded as the most important document. It sets an appropriate tone for directors, management, and volunteers to direct their activities toward achieving the organization's objectives. A mission statement is not a legal document per se but an important document describing an organization's goals and reasons for existence.
2. *Code of conduct.* The organization's code of conduct is currently required by law for NPOs; SOX requires public companies to establish a code of conduct for their financial executives. Codes of conduct set an appropriate "tone at the top" and related guidance for directors, management, employees, and volunteers to follow in carrying out their responsibilities in dealing with sensitive information and avoiding conflicts of interest.
3. *Charter.* An organization's charter, which is also referred to as articles of organization or certification of incorporation, is a legal document that should be filed with the secretary of state of its state. This charter serves as the constitution of the NPO and a prerequisite for official status as a not-for-profit organization. For not-for-profit groups established as trusts, the official governance document

is often called a declaration of trust or the trust instrument; it also requires periodic filings or reporting obligations.
4. *Bylaws*. Bylaws spell out the basic operating procedures and the way an organization is structured and governed. Bylaws establish rules and procedures for selection of directors, appointment of officers, meetings, voting, and indemnification.[22]

Corporate Governance Reforms Relevant to NPOs

Regulators in several states, including New York, California, and Virginia, are considering applying provisions of SOX to NPOs. Many NPOs are adopting some of the provisions of SOX in order to improve their corporate governance, financial reporting, internal control, and audit activities even though it is not required. Examples of NPOs that are implementing some of the provisions of SOX are New York's Juilliard School, which is adopting transparency and board involvement, and the International Swimming Hall of Fame in Florida, which is recruiting board members who can understand and review audits.[23] Eight provisions of SOX that would be more appropriate and applicable to NPOs are:

1. *More vigilant and independent directors.* More vigilant and independent directors on the board of trustees of NPOs can improve the effectiveness of their corporate governance.
2. *Audit committees.* The audit committees of public companies in the post-SOX era are important components of corporate governance in overseeing financial reporting, internal control, risk management, and audit activities. It is expected that NPOs will establish or revise their audit committee charter by adopting requirements of SOX regarding the independence and financial expertise of audit committees.
3. *Improvements in the financial reporting process.* NPOs can benefit significantly from the provisions of SOX that require more transparent and timely financial reports in the areas of contingent liabilities and prevention of fraudulent financial activities.
4. *Risk management and internal controls.* Risk management assessment and internal controls are vital to the sustainable success of NPOs. Provisions of SOX, SEC rules, and Public Company Accounting Oversight Board (PCAOB) standards pertaining to internal control over financial reporting are applicable and beneficial to both private companies and NPOs.
5. *Audit quality.* Recent corporate governance reforms, including SOX, SEC rules, and PCAOB standards, are intended to improve audit quality and strengthen audit independence of public companies. The requirements for an integrated audit approach of audits of both internal controls and financial statements are well suited for NPOs. More independent and better-quality audits are also essential to the integrity, relevance, and transparency of financial reports of private companies and NPOs.
6. *Codes of conduct.* Public companies are required to establish codes of conduct and business ethics for their employees in general and financial officers in

particular. Section 406 of SOX and the SEC-related rule require that public companies subject to the Exchange Act reporting requirements, except for registered investment companies, disclose whether they have adopted written codes of ethics for their principal executive, financial, or accounting officers, controllers, or persons performing under their supervisions.[24] There is no doubt that every organization, private, public, or nonprofit, would benefit from the culture of promoting ethical conduct.

7. *Whistleblower programs.* Public companies are now required to establish proper whistleblower programs to facilitate employees voicing their concerns and reporting corporate wrongdoing to authorities without the risk of retaliation or losing their job. SOX created the opportunity for confidential and anonymous submissions of complaints by requiring the company's audit committee to establish procedures for the receipt, retention, and treatment of such complaints.[25] NPOs can benefit significantly from similarly appropriate whistleblower programs.

8. *Document destruction.* Sections 802 and 1102 of SOX make it illegal to knowingly alter, destroy, conceal, mutilate, cover up, or falsify any record, document, or other object to impair the document's or object's integrity or availability for use in official proceedings. PCAOB auditing standards also require retention of audit evidence for at least seven years. These requirements to preserve integrity and availability of relevant documents, including audit evidence, are also applicable to NPOs.

A 2004 survey conducted by Foley & Lardner indicates that more than 40 percent of the surveyed NPOs reported that they have voluntarily adopted these provisions of SOX:

- Executive certifications of financial statements, particularly CEO/CFO financial statement attestation.
- Whistleblower initiatives.
- Board approval of nonaudit services provided by external auditors.
- Adoption of corporate governance policy guidelines.[26]

A study shows that NPOs are practicing good governance and focusing on their accountability in the post-SOX era.[27] The next list presents several of the NPOs' good governance practices.

- The vast majority of the 247 boards of surveyed NPOs are highly or significantly involved in the major strategic oversight functions.
- The majority of NPOs' boards (93 percent) set organizational missions and objectives.
- 83 percent of surveyed boards are involved in the approval of significant monetary functions, including organizational budgets and finances.
- 83 percent review accounting and auditing standards and practices.
- 88 percent engage in establishing executive compensation.
- 73 percent are involved in setting ethical standards.

- The majority (97 percent) of the surveyed organizations have undergone an independent audit within the past two years and distributed their financial reports to the boards.

Governance Mechanisms

The corporate governance mechanisms of NPOs are different from those of corporations discussed in the previous chapters. Unlike business firms, NPOs do not have the external corporate governance mechanisms of the capital markets, the market for corporate takeovers, or product market competitions. Thus, NPOs must rely primarily on internal governance mechanisms to assess performance, monitor and reward good performance, and monitor and discipline poor performance. The primary governance mechanisms of NPOs are their governing and advisory boards. The governing board is directly responsible and ultimately accountable for the organization's affairs. In a large NPO with sufficient competent staff, the governing board provides more of an oversight function rather than the managerial function of directly making decisions. However, in a small NPO, the governing board may perform both managerial and oversight functions.

The advisory board of a NPO typically provides advice and gives counsel rather than engaging in governing the organization. The advisory board often is composed of volunteers rather than elected or appointed members. For example, in a state-supported university, the governing board is usually appointed by the state at the university level; the voluntary advisory board for all colleges and departments within the university (law, business, medical, engineering, and education schools) is composed of members of the community and student body. Unlike their counterparts in business firms, who are largely motivated by substantial compensation, volunteers serve on the board by committing their time, efforts, and even money because of their dedication, beliefs, and interests for good cause. Furthermore, the board of NPO organizations does not often have resources to hire advisors and relies on the commitment, dedication, and competence of its members for giving counsel.

NPO directors or trustees must avoid conflicts of interest by not engaging in material transactions with the NPO, serving as an attorney, or providing other services for substantial fees. Like business firms, NPOs should have an adequate and effective internal control system to ensure the organization:

- Performs efficiently and effectively within given resources and budgets.
- Achieves its program results.
- Presents financial reports that are reliable and transparent.
- Complies with applicable laws and regulations, particularly the IRS tax-exempt statutes.

The NPO's internal control structure should also prevent and detect errors, irregularities, and fraud, particularly employee embezzlements. Fraudsters perpetrate fraud and steal money even from NPOs. It is not uncommon that the funds donated or the grants and contributions to a NPO are appropriated and restricted for activities for achieving the intended philanthropic purposes. Thus, the NPO's internal control system should ensure that appropriated funds are spent on designated programs to achieve the intended purposes. The directors or trustees of the NPO typically are volunteers or are appointed by the sponsoring organization to oversee the NPO's activities and affairs.

The chair of the board is also selected by the sponsoring organization or by directors for a limited number of terms. Often the board chair is rotated among the members of the board or trustees. NPOs, like business firms, organize their work through the establishment of committees. The types, structure, and number of committee members depend on the size of the organization and the size of its board of trustees. The most common structured committees of NPOs are:

- Governance or nominating.
- Development or fundraising.
- Finance, budget, or audit.
- Operations.
- Programs.
- Personnel.
- Executive.

Not-for-profit organizations are normally managed and function through the committee assignments. The committees often have proper staff, make decisions, take actions, and report their activities to the board or trustees.

Duties of the Board of Directors/Trustees

Boards of directors or trustees are regarded as governing bodies primarily responsible for affairs. Members of boards of directors/trustees, depending on the organization's size and activities, may provide oversight functions, or with smaller organizations engage in both oversight and managerial functions. This section examines duties and responsibilities of boards of directors, their composition, member qualification, committees, and effective meetings. Much of these discussions are from the publication of Society of Corporate Secretaries and Governance Professionals.[28] Directors and trustees of NPOs have three major fiduciary duties:

1. *Duty of obedience*, which requires directors and trustees to carry out their assigned responsibilities in accordance with the organization's rules, standards, and procedures as specified in its articles of incorporation, bylaws, and mission statements.
2. *Duty of care*, which requires directors and trustees to exercise due care, diligence, and skill that an ordinary, prudent person would exercise under similar circumstances.
3. *Duty of loyalty*, which requires directors and trustees to carry out their activities in pursuing the best interests of the organization by avoiding self-dealing and self-serving activities.

Board Committees

The work of the board of directors or trustees is best performed and more effective in the form of committees. The chair of each committee should present the committee's findings and recommendations to the entire board for approval and action. These board committees are relevant to NPOs:

- *Audit committee*, consisting only of independent directors or trustees, responsible for overseeing financial reporting, internal control, audit activities, and compliance with applicable laws, rules, and regulations.
- *Executive committee*, composed of officers and committee chairs who can act on behalf of the entire board between the board meetings if circumstances require.
- *Development/fundraising committee*, which organizes and oversees fundraising events and capital campaigns.
- *Finance committee*, which oversees financing and investment activities including budget and tax activities.
- *Nominating committee*, which identifies the board members' needs and makes recommendations to the board about vacant board positions.
- *Program committee*, which is responsible for the organization's programs and activities, the accomplishment of the programs, and its future initiatives.
- *Personnel committee*, which develops compensation and benefit plans for the organization's paid staff.

Responsibilities of the Board of Directors/Trustees

The 15 primary responsibilities of the board of directors/trustees of NPOs are to:

1. Establish the organization's mission and goals.
2. Develop strategies to achieve these goals.
3. Appoint officers and executives to run the organization.
4. Determine compensation of executives, oversee their work, and evaluate their performance.
5. Review the organization's programs and services.
6. Oversee financial reporting, internal controls, and audit activities.
7. Oversee compliance with applicable laws, rules, and regulations, particularly tax rules.
8. Promote ethical behavior and accountability throughout the organization.
9. Ensure adequacy and effective use of resources.
10. Evaluate the board's performance.
11. Approve directors'/trustees' compensation, if any.
12. Assess the board's vacancies and recruit new board members.
13. Ensure executives and staff provide the board with relevant and timely information to carry out its fiduciary duties effectively.
14. Set an appropriate "tone at the top" promoting ethical conduct throughout the organization.

15. Ensure that all board members participate in orientation and continuing education programs.

Attributes of Board Members

The effectiveness of the organization's board depends on the attributes, personal integrity, competence, dedication, insight, and professional qualifications of its members. The six important qualities of an effective board member are:

1. *Vision.* The ability to see the big picture and establish the organization's mission.
2. *Leadership.* The ability and courage to set direction to achieve the organization's mission and related goals.
3. *Stewardship.* The sense of accountability and integrity to pursue the organization's goals and serve the interests of the organization, its intended beneficiaries, constituents, and the public.
4. *Skill.* Knowledge and ability to provide effective oversight of the organization's operations, programs, activities, and performance.
5. *Diligence.* The ability to exercise due care, dedication and commitment to carry out oversight responsibilities in achieving the organization's goals.
6. *Collegiality.* The ability to work as a member of a team and respect colleagues and their views.

Audit Committees of Not-for-Profit Organizations

The American Institute of Certified Public Accountants (AICPA) has developed a tool kit to improve audit committee effectiveness of NPOs.[29] This tool kit provides audit committee charter metrics to assist NPOs to tailor their audit committee charter to their own specifications and size by using best practices.

Some of the most important attributes of audit committees for NPO organizations provided in the tool kit are:

- All members of the committee should be independent.
- The chair of the committee should be a member of the board of directors in good standing.
- The committee should have access to financial expertise.
- The committee's charter should be reviewed annually.
- The committee should meet as needed to address matters on its agenda, but not less frequently than twice a year.
- The committee should conduct executive sessions with external auditors, internal auditors, and chief financial officers.
- The committee should be authorized to hire independent auditors, counsel, or other consultants as deemed necessary.
- The committee should review and approve the appointment, replacement, reassignment, or dismissal of the chief audit executive (CAE) or the director of the organization's internal audit function.

- The committee should appoint the independent auditors, approve their audit fees, and preapprove nonaudit services to be provided by independent auditors.
- The committee should review management policies and procedures.
- The committee should review with management and independent auditors the audit findings and auditors' judgments about the quality, not just the acceptability, of accounting policies and practices.
- The committee should review the organization's code of conduct and ethics.
- The committee should review the organization's whistleblower programs, policies, and procedures.
- The committee should review the organization's compliance with applicable laws, rules, regulations, and standards.
- The committee should annually evaluate its own performance as well as the performance of independent auditors and internal auditors.[30]

The AICPA has also developed a tool kit for audit committees of government organizations to help them improve their effectiveness.[31] This tool kit is designed to provide guidance and best practices for audit committee oversight functions. The AICPA's audit committee charter metric for government organizations specifies these attributes:

- Committee members should be appointed by the governing body.
- At least one member of the committee should have financial experience.
- The audit committee charter should be reviewed annually to ensure its adequacy, effectiveness, and compliance with all applicable rules, laws, and regulations, including government auditing standards (yellow book).
- The committee should meet at least four times per year or more as deemed necessary.
- The committee should have executive sessions with the CEO, CFO, independent auditor, internal auditor, legal counsel, and other key personnel involved in the financial reporting process.
- The committee should have the authority to hire professional consultants as necessary.
- The committee should review and approve the appointment, replacement, reassignment, or dismissal of the CAE.
- The committee should oversee the appointment of the independent auditors to be engaged for external reporting of government organizations.
- When the use of a particular independent auditor is not specified by law or regulation, the committee should establish related audit fees and a regular schedule for periodically rebidding the audit contract with public accounting firms.
- The committee should review with management the policies and procedures relevant to the use of expense accounts, public monies, and public property by management, key personnel, and public officials.
- The committee should review with management the organization's risks and steps taken to minimize risks.

- The committee should review periodically the audit plan, scope, and findings of both internal and external auditors.
- The committee should ask management (CEO, CFO) about the financial health of the government organization, including the financial status in relation to its adopted budget.
- The committee should review with management and the independent auditor the effects of regulatory and accounting initiatives on the organization's financial reporting process.
- The committee should periodically review the government organization's code of conduct to ensure its adequacy and effectiveness.
- The committee should review the organization's whistleblower programs, policies, and procedures for the receipt, retention, and treatment of complaints received by the organization.
- The committee should perform an annual evaluation of independent and internal auditors as well as its own oversight effectiveness.
- The committee should review and approve of the audit committee's agenda.[32]

Internal Control in Not-for-Profit Organizations

Internal control over financial reporting, operations, and compliance with applicable laws and regulations, particularly tax-exempt status, are important internal governance mechanisms of nonprofit organizations. Internal controls over fundraising and operations are important to ensure donations, grants, and other financial supports are properly accounted for and assets are safeguarded against misappropriation. Internal controls over financial reporting of NPOs are designed to prevent, detect, and correct misstatements to improve reliability, integrity, and quality of financial reports. Internal controls pertaining to compliance with applicable laws and regulations are essential in a NPO to ensure continuation of tax-exempt status of the entity, as many NPOs benefit from the tax-exempt status.

COLLEGE AND UNIVERSITY GOVERNANCE

College campus governance is evolving as many universities are moving away from state-supported or sponsored colleges to self-supported units, and their top administrators enjoy high compensation. Indeed, recent disclosures of compensation (pay and perquisites) of campus leaders resulted in resignations and indictments of universities such as American University and Texas Southern University.[33] It appears that business scandals and outsourcing over outsized executive pay have reached into academia as Congress is considering strengthening a federal prohibition on excessive compensation for leaders of universities and other charitable organizations.[34] University boards of trustees are getting more involved in their governance, as evidenced by the board of Vanderbilt University scrutinizing the budget and other financial items of the university and taking an active role in university affairs, including strategic planning, capital expenditures, and management compensation.[35]

Colleges and universities are also under scrutiny for more effective governance. Recent ethical violations and cheating in highly ranked business schools (e.g., Duke, Texas A&M) that train future business leaders underscore the importance of university governance in adopting and enforcing zero tolerance ethics and honor codes. A report issued by a federal commission urges significant improvement in the governance of U.S. higher education by calling for: (1) public universities to measure student learning with standardized tests; (2) federal monitoring of colleges' quality; (3) sweeping changes to the financial aid system; (4) public universities to find new ways of controlling costs; and (5) college tuition not to grow faster than median family income.[36] The Career Education Corporation, a for-profit education company that operates on about 86 campuses offering career-oriented programs in cooking, healthcare, photography, and other fields, is currently under investigation by the Justice Department. It has been put on probation by the Southern Association of Colleges and Schools, is being sued by former employees, students, and shareholders, and is being investigated by the SEC. To improve corporate governance at the Career Education Corporation, five proposals were put forth by shareholders, with some of them already approved by about two-thirds of shareholders. These proposals are: (1) declassifying its board in requiring the company's directors to stand for election every year; (2) eliminating the company's poison pill; (3) allowing shareholders to call a special meeting with a two-thirds vote; (4) adopting a majority voting provision requiring that directors receive more than 50 percent of the votes cast to be reelected; and (5) adding one more independent director to the company's board.[37]

SUMMARY

The corporate governance structure of private companies and NPOs plays an important role in the organization's governance, financial reporting, and audit functions. NPOs are expected to improve their stewardship and accountability, which can be achieved through effective corporate governance. Important attributes of effective corporate governance of private companies and NPOs are independence of members of the board of trustees, written charters, and regular meetings of the board with management, officials, internal auditors, and external auditors. In the absence of the regulatory requirements for NPOs to reform their governance practices, they should voluntarily adopt strong governance and accountability principles, guidance, and practices to:

- Improve the performance of their board by requiring board members to be independent and establish an audit committee.
- Enhance the reliability and transparency of their financial information and public disclosures.
- Manage their organization effectively and efficiently.
- Protect the interests of their constituencies and public trust.
- Design and implement adequate and effective internal controls to ensure operational efficiency, reliable financial reporting, and compliance with applicable laws, rules, regulations, and standards.

NOTES

1. News Staff. 2005. Accountant pleads guilty in Roslyn Schools Scandal. (November 11). Available at: www.nysscpa.org/home/2005/1105/2week/article 40.htm.
2. Broude, P. D. 2006. The impact of Sarbanes-Oxley on private and non-profit companies. (March 9). Available at: www.foley.com/files/tbl_s31Publications/FileUpload137/3261/ndi%202006%20private%20study.pdf.
3. Badal, J., and P. Dvorak. 2006. Sarbanes-Oxley gains adherents. *Wall Street Journal* (August 14). Available at: www.online.wsj.com/article/SB1155-51450520734692.html.
4. PricewaterhouseCoopers. 2006. PwC's trendsetter barometer: Some companies finding government regulations helpful. (January 11). Available at: www.barometersurveys.com.
5. Broude. 2006. The impact of Sarbanes-Oxley on private and non-profit companies.
6. PricewaterhouseCoopers. 2005. Trendsetter barometer survey. Available at: www.pwc.com/extweb/ncpressrelease.nsf/docid/2718F909C8D0198985256FF6005758EF.
7. Ibid.
8. Ibid.
9. Financial Accounting Standards Board. 2006. Private Company Financial Reporting. (June 26). Available at: www.fasb.org/project/private_company_finanical_reporting.shtml.
10. Ibid.
11. Ibid.
12. Baker, M., and P. Gompers. 2003. The determinants of board structure at the initial public offering. *Journal of Law and Economics* 46: 569–598. Available at: http://web.lexis-nexis.com/universe/document?_m=8a7208820d2cbcad05 19751aa4601057&_docnum=1&wchp=dGLbVtb-zSkVA&_md5=64626dca 298a35ef7732363a9cc27a5f.
13. Securities and Exchange Commission. 2003. SEC Rule 144. Available at: www.sec.gov/investor/pubs/rule144.htm.
14. Securities and Exchange Commission. 2005. Securities offering reform. (July). Release Nos. 33-8591; 34-52056; IC-26993; FR-75. Available at: www.sec.gov/rules/final/finalarchive/finalarchive2005.shtml.
15. Internal Revenue Service. Section 501(c). Available at: www.irs.gov/publications/p557/ch03.html.
16. Panel on the Non-Profit Sector. 2005. A final report to Congress and the non-profit sector on strengthening governance, transparency, and accountability. (June). Available at: www.nonprofitpanel.org/final/Panel_Final_Report.pdf.
17. Ibid.
18. Ibid.
19. Ibid.

20. Donaldson, W. H. 2004. Speech by SEC chairman: Remarks before the annual conference of *Independent Sector*. (November 8). Available at: www.sec.gov/news/speech/spch110804whd.htm.

21. Ibid.

22. Society of Corporate Secretaries and Governance Professionals. 2005. Governance for nonprofits: From little leagues to universities. Available at: www.governanceprofessionals.org.

23. Hymnowitz, C. 2005. In Sarbanes-Oxley era, running a nonprofit is only getting harder. *The Wall Street Journal*. (June 21). Available at: www.careerjournal.com/columnists/inthelead/20050622-inthelead.html.

24. Sarbanes-Oxley Act. 2002. Section 406: Code of ethics for senior financial officers. Available at: www.sec.gov/about/laws/soa2002.pdf.

25. Ibid.

26. Foley & Lardner. 2004. The cost of being public in the era of Sarbanes-Oxley: The impact of Sarbanes-Oxley on private companies. Available at: www.fei.org/download/foley_6_16_2005.pdf.

27. Salamon, L., and S. Geller. 2005. Communique No. 4: Nonprofit governance and accountability. Johns Hopkins University. Available at: www.jhu.edu/listeningpost/news/pdf/comm04.pdf.

28. Society of Corporate Secretaries and Governance Professionals. 2005. Governance for nonprofits.

29. American Institute of Certified Public Accountants. 2005. Audit committee toolkit for not-for-profit organizations. AICPA Audit Committee Effectiveness Center. Available at: www.aicpa.org/Audcommctr/toolkitsnpo/homepage.htm.

30. Ibid.

31. Ibid.

32. Ibid.

33. Lubin, J. S., and D. Golden. 2006. Vanderbilt reins in lavish spending by Star Chancellor. *Wall Street Journal*. (September 26). Available at: www.online.wsj.com.

34. Ibid.

35. Ibid.

36. Dillon, S. 2006. Panel endorses Standards for Colleges. (August 11). Available at: www.signonsandiego.com/uniontrib/200608/news_lnllcolleges.html.

37. Morgenson, G. 2006. Can a for-profit college learn a lesson? *New York Times*. (May 7). Available at: www.nytimes.com.

CHAPTER 12

Corporate Governance and Business Ethics

INTRODUCTION

An academic survey of 50,000 students at 69 business schools reveals that 26 percent of business majors admitted to cheating on exams; another 54 percent admitted to cheating on written assignments.[1] The survey, conducted during the past 15 years, shows that cheating has increased over time, perhaps due to technology that makes cheating easier, increased pressure to perform, and student rationale for using recently reported corporate and accounting scandals to justify their behavior (e.g., cheating at Duke, Texas A&M).[2] These students will be future business leaders whose ethical conduct could continue to be adversely affected by the pervasiveness of financial and political scandals. This chapter on business ethics starts with the general definition of "ethics" and its field of study, including metaethics, normative ethics, and applied ethics, and proceeds with business ethics. Ethics is broadly described in the literature as moral principles about right and wrong, honorable behavior reflecting values, or standards of conduct. Honesty, openness, responsiveness, accountability, due diligence, and fairness are the core ethical principles.

DEFINITION OF ETHICS

Ethics is defined in *Webster's Dictionary* as "a set of moral principles: a theory or system of moral values."[3] In the literature, ethics is defined as value systems by which individuals assess their and others' behavior according to a set of previously established standards derived from a variety of religious, cultural, societal, or philosophical sources.[4] Ethics is also described as "a process by which individuals, social groups, and societies evaluate their actions from a perspective of moral principles and value."[5] Metaethics focuses on ethical theories, their evolution, and the social, religious, spiritual, and cultural influences shaping those theories. Normative ethics emphasizes the practical aspects of ethics by providing principles of appropriate behavior and guidance for what is right or wrong, good or bad in behavior (e.g., principles of justice, honesty, social benefits, and lawfulness). Applied ethics deals with the application of moral principles and reasoning as well as codes of conduct for a particular profession or segment of society (e.g., business ethics, environmental ethics, and medical ethics).

Business ethics, the focus of this chapter, is a subset of applied ethics that deals with the ethical issues, conflicts of interest, and morality of business decisions. The definition of business ethics adopted in this chapter is based on the one described by Velasquez:

> Business ethics is a specialized study of moral right and wrong. It concentrates on moral standards as they apply to business policies, institutions, and behavior....It includes not only the analysis of moral norms and moral values, but also attempts to apply the conclusion of this analysis to that assortment of institutions, technologies, transactions, activities, and pursuits that we call business.[6]

CORPORATE CODE OF ETHICS

An enforceable code of ethics that sets the appropriate "tone at the top" of promoting ethical and professional conduct and establishing the moral structure for the entire organization is the backbone of effective corporate governance. Integrity and ethical conduct are key components of an organization's control environment as set forth in both reports of the Committee of Sponsoring Organizations of the Treadway Commission (COSO), "Internal Control, Integrated Framework" and "Enterprise Risk Management."[7]

Ethical crises have occurred throughout the history of humankind and will continue to occur particularly when there is a conflict of interest. Many tragedies and scandals can be traced back to the ethical behavior of individuals involved and their activities. For example, reported financial scandals might have been prevented had executives, directors, and auditors behaved more ethically. Academic research, which focuses on corporate misconduct or misrepresentation of financial position, indicates that three factors normally increase a company's probability of engaging in such misconduct. Companies are more likely to misrepresent their financial position when:

1. Their performance is below their industry's average performance.
2. Their performance is significantly above their own past performance.
3. Their chief executive officer (CEO) receives a high proportion of total compensation as stock options.[8]

Codes of business ethics and conduct are intended to govern behavior, but they cannot substitute for moral principles, culture, and character. There has been a discussion of whether ethics and ethical behavior can be taught. Some believe that moral principles and ethics are part of family values that cannot be taught. There is a general consensus, however, among academicians and practitioners that corporate governance and business ethics should be a key part of business education. Nonetheless, the means of and strategy for providing such education is not clear. There are some who believe that ethical thinking, behavior, and accountability should be experienced throughout the educational process by either integrating them into business courses and programs or teaching them as a stand-alone subject. The author believes that business ethics can be promoted and should be taught to improve accountability, integrity, judgment, and other valuable qualities that should be part of the business decision-making process. Setting the appropriate "tone at the top" promoting ethical culture and policies can influence individual behavior. Teaching business ethics should provide incentives and opportunities for individuals, particularly professionals, to enhance their personal integrity and professional accountability.

A 2006 Dark Reading "Security Scruples" survey reveals that entities operate differently in private than they say they do in public.[9] A survey of 648 information technology (IT) and security professionals was conducted to determine their beliefs and behaviors in both real and hypothetical security situations. The survey results indicate that: (1) a large majority agreed on how to do the "right thing"; (2) more than 27 percent have accessed unauthorized data; (3) only 53 percent of respondents said they would report a colleague who was abusing security privileges; and (4) while many entities maintain codes of ethics and related policies to protect their ethical and legal positions, their actual enforcement of these policies vary with the situation.[10] These results suggest that the situational ethics and "organizational ethical culture" where "the ends justify the means" prevail more in the workplace than the codes of ethics focusing on "good versus bad" or "acceptable behavior versus unacceptable conduct."

The phrase "organizational ethical culture" consists of three root words:

1. *Organization*, which is defined as a group of individuals or entities bound to achieve a shared goal.
2. *Ethics*, which is honorable behavior that conforms to the norm of the group.
3. *Culture*, which is a pattern of shared beliefs adopted by the group in dealing with its internal and external affairs.

Thus, organizational ethical culture is described as beliefs, ethical behavior, and practices shared by members of a group in pursuing their goals and fulfilling their responsibilities. Ethical behavior and value creation may produce the same consequences in many decisions in the real world. Management has a fiduciary responsibility to create long-term shareholder value and to act within the boundaries of commonly accepted ethical standards.

Securities and Exchange Commission Rules on Corporate Code of Ethics

Section 406 of the Sarbanes-Oxley Act (SOX) requires public companies to disclose whether they have adopted codes of ethics for their senior financial officers and have disclosed in their public filings if their code of ethics changes or if any waivers from the code are granted.[11] The Securities and Exchange Commission (SEC) established its rules in implementing Section 406 and extended codes of ethics requirements to both the company's principal financial officers (Section 406) and principal executive officers (Section 407). SEC rules also expanded the definition of "code of ethics" as the company's written standard designed to deter wrongdoing and to promote:

- Honest behavior and ethical conduct, including the ethical handling of actual or apparent conflicts of interest between personal and professional relationships.
- Avoidance of conflicts of interest, including disclosure of any material transaction or relationship that could be reasonably expected to give rise to such a conflict to the appropriate person or persons identified in the company's adopted code.
- Full, fair, accurate, timely, and understandable disclosure in public reports and documents, either filed with the SEC or made available to the public.
- Compliance with applicable governmental laws, rules, and regulations.
- The prompt internal reporting of violations of the code to an appropriate person or persons identified in the company's code of ethics.
- Accountability for adherence to the company's adopted code of ethics.[12]

The SEC rules in implementing Section 406 of SOX require public companies to disclose whether they have adopted a code of ethics for their principal officers, including principal executive officers, principal financial officers, principal accounting officers, controller, or other personnel performing similar functions, in the annual report filed with the SEC. If the company has not adopted such a code of ethics, it must disclose the reason for not doing so.

Public companies must make their code of ethics publicly available in any of these ways:

- Filing their code of ethics as an exhibit to their SEC annual reports.
- Posting their code of ethics on their Web site and specifying the Web site address and its purpose in the annual reports filed with the SEC.
- Disclosing in their annual reports that a copy of their code of ethics is available without charge upon request.

The SEC rules on corporate codes of ethics neither specify the content and format of such code nor prescribe the procedure for ensuring monitoring, compliance, enforcing, or sanctioning of any violations. The SEC adopted code of ethics recommends:

- Public companies should adopt codes of ethics that are more comprehensive and broader than ones that mainly just meet the new disclosure requirements.
- The established code of ethics should describe the company's policies and procedures for internal reporting of code violations.
- Individuals with adequate authority and status (e.g., the chair of the audit committee and ethics officer) within the company should be designated to receive, investigate, and take actions on the reported code violations.

- Guidelines should be provided for avoiding material transactions or relationships associated with potential conflicts of interest.
- Consequences of noncompliance or violation of the company's established code of ethics should be disclosed.
- Policies and procedures should be established to ensure that individuals receiving code violations are recused when they are involved in any matters related to an alleged violation.

SEC rules require public companies to report to the SEC significant amendments to their code of ethics or any waiver affecting specified officers, pursuant to the filing of their first annual report on their code of ethics. The required amendment and waiver disclosures should be disclosed within 5 business days and can be provided in a Form 8-K filed with the SEC or disclosed on the company's investor relations Web site. The Web site disclosure, designed for the reporting of the company's code of ethics and subsequent amendments and waivers, must be maintained online for at least 12 months or otherwise be retained for at least 5 years. Public companies that do not have a code of ethics must establish one that meets the requirements of the SEC final rule. Public companies with an existing code of ethics must ensure that their code satisfies SEC requirements or otherwise revise it, or be prepared to disclose reasons why they have not adopted a qualifying code of ethics.

Listing Standards

The listing standards of the New York Stock Exchange (NYSE) further expand on the SEC rules by requiring listed companies to adopt and disclose a code of business conduct and ethics for directors, officers, and employees and promptly disclose any waivers of the adopted code for directors and executive officers.[13] The NYSE listing standards, while suggesting that each listed company determine its own business conduct and ethics policies, provide an extensive list of important matters that should be addressed by the company's code, including conflicts of interest, corporate opportunities, confidentiality, protection of proper use of the company's assets, fair dealing, reporting of any illegal or unethical conduct, and compliance with applicable laws, rules, and regulations.[14] National Association of Securities Dealers (NASD) ethics rules for Nasdaq-listed companies are similar to those of the NYSE and further require the company's adopted code to provide for an enforcement mechanism and any waivers of the code for directors or executive officers to be approved by the board and disclosed no later than the next periodic report.

The process of making ethical decisions starts with the commitment to do the right thing by:

- Recognizing the relevant issue, event, or decision.
- Evaluating all alternative courses of action and their impacts on one's well-being as well as the well-being of others possibly affected by the decisions.
- Deciding on the best course of action available.
- Consulting appropriate ethical guidance.

- Continuously assessing the consequences of the decision and adopting appropriate changes.
- Implementing the decision.

ETHICS IN THE WORKPLACE

Ethics in the workplace is receiving a considerable amount of attention as the emerging corporate governance reforms require setting an appropriate "tone at the top" that promotes ethical conduct. A review of the reported financial scandals proves that most ethical dilemmas have financial consequences and dimensions. In the post-SOX era, there are increased interactions among the board of directors, audit committees, internal auditors, external auditors, executives, and employees, in general, regarding ethical conduct in the workplace.

A survey conducted by the Conference Board in February 2004 examines the role of the board of directors of a large sample of global companies in promoting ethical conduct.[15] The survey reveals that the oversight activities and involvement of the board, particularly of the audit committee, in establishing, maintaining, and monitoring ethics programs are growing. About 66 percent of all surveyed companies in the United States report that their companies' codes of ethics were established by a board resolution. The increasing trend toward more involvement of the board in the company's ethics program is influenced by the devastating consequences of reported financial scandals rooted in the unethical conduct by directors, officers, and auditors of high-profile companies and the development of corporate governance reforms that promote ethical conduct throughout the organization.

The survey also reports that:

- More than half of the surveyed board members indicate that they review their company's ethics programs regularly with the range of 54 percent in Japan to 78 percent in the United States.
- About 50 percent said they review their company's ethics training programs with the range of 42 percent of companies in western Europe to 61 percent in the United States.
- Audit committees in the United States were more involved in overseeing their companies' ethics program than in other countries (77 percent in the United States compared to 63 percent in Japan and 40 percent in India).
- Independent directors made up the ethics oversight committees in 85 percent of U.S. companies, 82 percent of Japanese companies, and 37 percent of western European companies.[16]

Overall, the survey results indicate that all 165 of the surveyed global companies have taken measures to ensure compliance with adequate and effective corporate ethics programs. Companies in the United States are leading the effort.

BUSINESS ETHICS

Business ethics is described as the moral principles and standards that guide business conduct and ensure ethical behavior. Four different levels of business ethics have been identified based on what type of business, and their actions are evaluated. These levels are:

1. *The business systems level,* which defines ethical behavior and assessment of business and their effects on society.
2. *The industry level,* which suggests that different industries have their own sets of ethical standards (e.g., chemical industry versus pharmaceutical industry).
3. *The company level,* under which different companies have their own sets of ethical behaviors.
4. *The individual manager level,* in which each manager and other corporate governance participants are responsible for their own behavior.[17]

Although there is not a single commonly accepted definition of business ethics, there are numerous examples of possible violations of ethics in business ranging from backdating practices of executive stock options grants to spying on outside directors. Ethical violations include the behavior of the convicted executives of the high-profile companies of Enron, WorldCom, Adelphia, and Tyco. The trend in business shows declining business ethics in recent years. The actual decline or the perception of decline in business ethics is not good for business and modern society. This trend of declining business ethics should be reversed through: (1) more education about business ethics; (2) establishment of business codes of ethical conduct; (3) enforcement of ethical conduct; and (4) changing business culture and promoting ethical behavior as described in the following section.

Business ethics deals with ethics and integrity in the business environment with an important underlying postulate that the majority of business leaders, managers, and other personnel are honest and ethical in conducting their business and that the minority who engage in unethical conduct will not prevail in the long term. Thus, the corporate culture and compliance rules should provide incentives and opportunities for the majority of ethical individuals to maintain their honesty and integrity and provide measures for the minority of unethical individuals to be monitored, punished, and corrected for their unethical conduct. Companies should promote a spirit of integrity that goes beyond compliance with the established code of business ethics or compliance to the letter of the law by creating a business culture of doing what is right.

An important aspect of the emerging trend toward increased corporate accountability and governance is reflected in the role and relevance of business ethics and codes of professional conduct. The diversity of people, existence of various value systems, and sensitivity of moral issues make it difficult to achieve a consensus and central theme for ethics. Thus, the "situation ethics theory" is used in this chapter to build a consensus as to the appropriate ethical practices, professional responsibilities, and honorable behavior through the promotion of, establishment of, and compliance with business and professional codes of conduct.[18] Situation ethics "is a moral pattern allowing circumstances to overrule principle and allegiance. Principle here is interpreted as definable moral, criminal, or civil law. Allegiance refers to group loyalty."[19] This definition suggests that individuals should do what is right rather than comply with specific principles when facing ethical challenges.

The creation of a culture which ensures that employees comply with the company's code of conduct and carry out its ethics policies and procedures is the key to an ethical work environment. Attributes of an ethical corporate culture or an integrity-based culture are:

- Sense of employee responsibility.
- Freedom to raise concerns without fear of retaliation.
- Managers modeling ethical behavior and emphasizing the importance of integrity.
- Leadership understanding of the pressure points that drive unethical behavior.
- Processes to find and fix these areas of pressure.[20]

Companies need to have ethics and business programs to address:

- Their diversity of personnel and human resources.
- The expectations of the public and their stakeholders.
- Their legal, professional, and regulatory environment.
- Compliance with applicable laws, regulations, rules, standards, and guidelines, including SOX, federal sentencing guidelines, SEC rules, and listing standards of national stock exchanges.
- Integration of ethics and business conduct programs into their corporate governance.

Triangle of Business Ethics

Exhibit 12.1 shows the triangle of business ethics, which consists of ethics sensitivity, ethics incentives, and ethical behavior.

Ethics Sensitivity

An organization consists of diverse individuals with a variety of value systems and ethical theories. An individual (e.g., an accountant) in an organization works in collaboration and coordination with others in fulfilling his or her responsibilities. Gamesmanship, loyalty, peer pressure, and other factors influence one's ethical decisions and actions. Ethics sensitivity is defined as moral principles, workplace factors, gamesmanship, loyalty, peer pressure, and job security that influence one's ethical decisions and are derived from the organization's ethical culture.

Ethics Incentives

People typically are motivated and responsive to incentives; they may face conflicts of interest where there are conflicting incentives. For example, to increase shareholder

Ethics
Sensitivity

Business
Ethics

Ethical
Behavior

Ethics
Incentives

EXHIBIT 12.1 Triangle of Business
Ethics

wealth, the agency theory suggests that managerial compensation plans be linked to the company's performance or stock returns.[21] Ethics incentives encompass rewards, punishments, and requirements for behaving either ethically or unethically. Examples of such incentives are an organization's appropriate "tone at the top" promoting ethical conduct, various professional codes of conduct (e.g., the American Institute of Certified Public Accountants [AICPA] Code of Conduct), and ethics rules (SEC's ethics rule for principal financial officers). Incentives for ethical behavior come from several sources:

- Individual-based incentives.
- Organization-based incentives.
- Market-based incentives.
- Profession-based incentives.
- Regulatory-based incentives.

Individual-Based Incentives Individual-based incentives for ethical behavior pertain to one's ethical values and moral principles to do the right thing. The fundamental individual-based incentives are the needs and desires of individuals to maximize their own good and minimize their own discomfort. Thus, the purpose of having ethical principles is not to force individuals to care about ethics but to provide incentives for those who already care to behave ethically.[22]

Organization-Based Incentives Organization-based incentives come from the organization's appropriate tone set at the top in promoting ethical behavior by establishing, maintaining, and enforcing such behavior throughout the organization. Organization-based incentives go beyond promoting corporate values of integrity, fairness, and honesty. They include a set of principles that require ethical behavior. Organization-based incentives are practical measures for motivating and mandating individuals to comply with the company's applicable rules, regulations, laws, and ethical standards and to act within ethical and legal constraints.[23]

Profession-Based Incentives   Profession-based incentives for ethical behavior are defined by a professional affiliation of individuals. For example, practicing accountants should observe the codes of professional ethics of the AICPA and the Public Company Accounting Oversight Board (PCAOB). Professional codes of conduct serve as references and benchmarks for individuals, establish rules of conduct relevant to the profession, and provide a means of facilitating enforcement of rules and standards of conduct. In June 2005 the International Ethics Standards Board for Accountants (IESBA), part of the International Federation of Accountants (IFAC), issued its revised code of ethics for use by professional accountants worldwide. The key principles of the IESBA's code are (1) integrity; (2) objectivity; (3) professional competence and due care; (4) confidentiality; and (5) professional behavior.[24]

Market-Based Incentives   Market-based incentives for ethical behavior are provided by markets by imposing substantial costs on organizations and individuals who engage in unethical behavior. For example, a consequence of reducing costs by lowering the quality of products and services can have the adverse effect of substantialy reducing revenues.

Regulatory-Based Incentives   Regulatory-based incentives for ethical behavior are induced through rules and regulations by imposing sanctions, fines, and penalties on organizations and individuals who engage in unethical and unacceptable behavior. In making decisions, organizations and individuals assess expected future loss in terms of potential penalties and the probability of being caught and the gains from opportunistic behavior.

     Ethical and professional conduct in business addressed in this chapter is based on the premise that:

- Individuals respond to a variety of incentives provided to them in logical, systematic, and creative ways.
- Individual-Based incentives relate to personal integrity and are the primary driver of ethical behavior.
- Organization-based incentives should be established through corporate culture.
- Profession-based incentives define individuals' professional behavior and responsibility.
- Market-based incentives relate to the reputation of and impose potentially significant costs on organizations and individuals who engage in unethical behavior.
- Regulatory-based incentives impose severe penalties on organizations and individuals who engage in unlawful and unethical behavior.

     These incentives, alone or in the aggregate, should be identified, addressed, and utilized to promote and enforce ethical behavior.

Ethical Behavior

Corporate governance should create an ethical business environment in which the company's officers, directors, and all employees are encouraged and empowered to do "the right thing." Henry Paulson, the secretary of the Treasury, believes that "we must rise above a rules-based mindset that asks 'is this legal?' and adopt a more principles-based approach that asks 'is this right?' "[25] Ethical behavior is the five-step process of:

1. Recognizing ethical issues.
2. Considering all alternative courses of action.
3. Referring to ethical incentives to guide the best actions.
4. Evaluating the consequences of ethical decisions.
5. Proceeding with confidence and adaptation.

The company's directors and executives should demonstrate, through their actions as well as their policies, a firm commitment to ethical behavior throughout the company and a culture of trust within it. Although a right "tone at the top" is very important in promoting an ethical culture, actions often speak louder than words. Directors and executives, through their actions, can set examples for ethical behavior. The quotes that follow were made by high-profile executives who were subsequently indicted and convicted of corporate malfeasance.[26] These CEOs promoted ethical and social values in words yet violated them in their actions.

> *Boards should be absolutely certain that the company is run properly from a fiduciary standpoint in every degree. I am a great believer in the audit committee having full access to the auditors in every way, shape and form.*
> *—Al Dunlap (Sunbeam)*

> *You'll see people who in the early days...took their life savings and trusted this company with their money. And I have an awesome responsibility to those people to make sure that they've done right. —Bernard Ebbers (WorldCom)*

> *We are offended by the perception that we would waste the resources of a company that is a major part of our life and livelihood, and that we would be happy with directors who would permit that waste....So as a CEO, I want a strong, competent board. —Dennis Kosloski (Tyco)*

> *It's more than just dollars. You've got to give back to the community that supported you. —John Rigas (Adelphia)*

> *People have an obligation to dissent in this company. —Jeffrey Skilling (Enron)*

REPORTING BUSINESS ETHICS AND CONDUCT

As corporate scandals come to light, even three years after the passage of SOX (e.g., AIG, Freddie Mac, Fannie Mae, Refco, backdating of stock options), the issue of business ethics becomes more prominent. Section 406 of SOX requires public companies to disclose in their annual financial statements the establishment (or lack) of corporate code of conduct. Nevertheless, public companies may choose to report their business ethics and conduct as a separate report to their shareholders or as part of their regular filings with the SEC.

The defense industry has been under scrutiny to improve its business ethics and conduct. Certain defense contractors have adopted six principles of business ethics and conduct set forth in the Defense Industry Initiatives (DII) on Business Ethics and Conduct, better known as Initiatives. DII was established in 1986 to adopt and implement a set of business ethics and conduct principles. These six principles require that defense contractors:

1. Comply with a written code of business conduct.
2. Provide sufficient training to all personnel within their organization regarding personal responsibility under the code.
3. Encourage internal reporting of violations of the code with the promise of no retaliation for such reporting.
4. Self-govern their activities by implementing controls to monitor compliance with all applicable laws and regulations (e.g., federal procurement laws).
5. Share their best practices in implementing the DII principles through participation in an annual Best Practices Forum.
6. Be accountable to the public.[27]

The first of these principles, the requirement for a written code of business conduct, calls for defense contractors' public accountability for their commitment to the Initiatives through the completion of an annual Public Accountability Questionnaire.

The defense contractors participating in the Initiatives (signatory companies) are required to complete the questionnaire by answering a series of questions regarding their policies, procedures, and programs designed to comply with the Initiatives during their reporting period. As part of their public accountability process, these signatories are required to conduct internal audits, assess their compliance, and provide officer certifications regarding the completeness, accuracy, and timeliness of their responses to the questionnaire. Alternatively, signatories may engage an independent public accountant (practitioner) to examine or review their responses to the questionnaire and express a conclusion regarding the appropriateness of those responses in a public report. The performance of such engagements by a practitioner raises several questions about whether this engagement is considered an attest engagement under Section 101 of the AICPA's Attest Engagements, including what criteria the practitioner should use for such an engagement, what procedures should be applied to the questionnaire responses, and what report format should be used for an attest engagement.

The AICPA, in offering guidance to practitioners for performing such services to signatories, provides interpretations of Section 101 Attest Engagements and has answered those questions. The AICPA states that:

EXHIBIT 12.2 Illustrative Defense Contractor Assertions and Examination Reports

Defense Industry Questionnaire on Business Ethics and Conduct

Unqualified Opinion Unrestricted with Criteria Attached to the Presentation

Defense Contractor Assertion

Statement of Responses to the Defense Industry Questionnaire on *Business Ethics and Conduct for the period from* _____ *to* _____.

The affirmative responses in the accompanying *Questionnaire on Business Ethics and Conduct with Responses by the XYZ Company for the period from* _____ *to* _____ are based on policies and programs in operation for that period and are appropriately presented in conformity with the criteria set forth in the *Defense Industry Initiatives on Business Ethics and Conduct*, including the Questionnaire.

Attachments:

Defense Industry Initiatives on Business Ethics and Conduct

Instructions and Questionnaire on Business Ethics and Conduct with Responses by the XYZ Company for the period from _____ to _____.

Examination Report

Independent Accountant's Report

To the Board of Directors of the XYZ Company

We have examined the XYZ Company's *Statement of Responses to the Defense Industry Questionnaire on Business Ethics and Conduct for the period from* _____ *to* _____, and the Questionnaire and responses attached thereto. XYZ Company's management is responsible for its responses to the Questionnaire. Our responsibility is to express an opinion based on our examination.

Our examination was conducted in accordance with attestation standards established by the American Institute of Certified Public Accountants and, accordingly, included examining, on a test basis, evidence as to whether XYZ Company had policies and programs in operation during that period that support the affirmative responses to the *Questionnaire* and performing such other procedures as we considered necessary in the circumstances. We believe that our examination

(continued overleaf)

EXHIBIT 12.2 *(Continued)*

provides a reasonable basis for our opinion. Our examination procedures were not designed, however, to evaluate whether the aforementioned policies and programs operated effectively to ensure compliance with the Company's *Code of Business Ethics and Conduct* on the part of individual employees or to evaluate the extent to which the Company or its employees have complied with federal procurement laws, and we do not express an opinion or any other form of assurance thereon.

In our opinion, the affirmative responses in the Questionnaire accompanying the *Statement of Responses to the Defense Industry Questionnaire on Business Ethics and Conduct for the period from* _____ *to* _____ referred to above are appropriately presented in conformity with the criteria set forth in the *Defense Industry Initiatives on Business Ethics and Conduct*, including the Questionnaire.

Source: Adapted from AICPA's Professional Standards, AT §9101.21

EXHIBIT 12.3 Illustrative Defense Contractor Assertion and Review Reports Restricted Because Criteria Are Available Only to Specified Parties

Defense Industry Questionnaire on Business Ethics and Conduct

Defense Contractor Assertion

Statement of Responses to the Defense Industry Questionnaire on *Business Ethics and Conduct for the period from* _____ *to* _____ .

The affirmative responses in the accompanying *Questionnaire on Business Ethics and Conduct with Responses by the XYZ Company for the period from* _____ *to* _____ are based on policies and programs in operation during that period and are appropriately presented in conformity with the criteria set forth in the *Defense Industry Initiatives on Business Ethics and Conduct*, including the Questionnaire.

Attachments: None

Review Report

Independent Accountant's Report

To the Board of Directors of the XYZ Company

(continued overleaf)

EXHIBIT 12.3 *(Continued)*

We have reviewed the XYZ Company's *Statement of Responses to the Defense Industry Questionnaire on Business Ethics and Conduct for the period from* _____ *to* _____. XYZ Company's management is responsible for the Statement of Responses to the Defense Industry Questionnaire on Business Ethics.

Our review was conducted in accordance with attestation standards established by the American Institute of Certified Public Accountants. A review is substantially less in scope than an examination, the objective of which is the expression of an opinion on the affirmative responses in the Questionnaire. Accordingly, we do not express such an opinion. Additionally, our review was not designed to evaluate whether the aforementioned policies and programs operated effectively to ensure compliance with the Company's *Code of Business Ethics and Conduct* on the part of individual employees or to evaluate the extent to which the Company or its employees have complied with federal procurement laws and we do not express an opinion or any other form of assurance thereon.

Based on our review, nothing came to our attention that caused us to believe that the affirmative responses in the Questionnaire referred to above are not appropriately presented in conformity with the criteria set forth in the *Defense Industry Initiatives on Business Ethics and Conduct*, including the Questionnaire.

This report is intended solely for the information and use of the XYZ Company and [*identify other specified parties— e.g.*, the Defense Industry Initiative] and is not intended to be and should not be used by anyone other than these specified parties.

Source: Adapted from AICPA's Professional Standards, AT §9101.25

- Section 101 is applicable when a practitioner is engaged by a signatory (defense contractor) to review or examine its certification of annual public accountability questionnaire.
- The criteria for assessing the defense contractor's responses to the questionnaire and its related instructions should be used by the practitioner in the review or examination engagement.
- The objective of procedures performed is to gather sufficient and competent evidential matter that the defense contractor has designed and implemented policies and programs to respond adequately to all questions in the questionnaire. The objective is not to provide assurance on the effectiveness of the designed policies and procedures in compliance with the signatory's code of business ethics and conduct.[28]

The standards of reporting in Exhibits 12.2 and 12.3 provide guidance on report content and wording appropriate in various circumstances.

SUMMARY

A well-established and effectively enforced code of conduct provides ethical standards and guidelines on: resolution of conflicts of interest; compliance with applicable laws, rules, and regulations; confidentiality of proprietary information; and fair dealing with investors, customers, suppliers, employees, and other interested parties. The emerging corporate governance reforms require public companies to establish a code of conduct for their executives and other key personnel and to publicly disclose their business code of conduct, which sets an appropriate tone at the top promoting ethical behavior and compliance with applicable laws, rules, regulations, and standards.

NOTES

1. Beucke, D. 2006. Biz majors get an F for honesty. *Business Week* (February 6).
2. Ibid.
3. *Merriam-Webster Dictionary*. 2006. Available at: www.m-w.com/dictionary/ethics.
4. Hurley, M. 1992. Ethical Problems of the Association Executive in Study Guide for Institutes of Organizational Management, Chamber of Commerce of the United States, Washington, DC, p. 2.
5. Cordiero, W. P. 2003. The only solution to the decline in business ethics: Ethical managers. *Teaching Business Ethics* (August): 7, 3; ABI/INFORMGLOBAL.
6. Velasquez, M. 2002. Business ethics: Concepts and cases, 5th ed. Englewood Cliffs, NJ: Prentice-Hall.
7. Committee of Sponsoring Organizations. 1998, 2004. Internal control: Framework. Enterprise risk management: Integrated framework. Available at: www.coso.org/publications.htm.
8. Harris, J., and P. Bromiley. 2005. Financial misrepresentation, executive compensation, and firm performance: An empirical study. Working paper, University of Minnesota.
9. Dark Reading. 2006. Security's Rotten Apples (October 4). Available at: www.darkreading.com/document.asp?doc_id=105282print=trace.
10. Ibid.
11. Sarbanes-Oxley Act. 2002. Section 406: Code of ethics for senior financial officers. Available at: www.law.uc.edu/CCL/SOact/soact.pdf.
12. Securities and Exchange Commission. 2003. Rules implementing Sections 406 and 407 of the Sarbanes-Oxley Act of 2002. Available at: www.sec.gov/rules/final/33-8177a.htm.
13. New York Stock Exchange. 2003. Final NYSE corporate governance rules. Available at: www.nyse.com/pdfs/finalcorpgovrules.pdf.
14. Ibid.
15. The Conference Board. 2004. Ethics programs—The role of the board: A global study. (February). Available at: www.conference-board.org/publications/describe.cfm?id=762.
16. Ibid.

17. Steiner, G., and J. Steiner. 2006. *Business, government and society,* 7th ed. New York: McGraw-Hill, pp. 206–208.
18. McCarthy, I. N. 1997. Professional ethics code conflict situations: Ethical and value orientation of collegiate accounting students. *Journal of Business Ethics* 16 (September): 1467–1474.
19. Milton, D. G. 1971. Entrepreneurial style and the situation ethic. *Business* 11 (2): 18.
20. Gebler, D. 2005. Why is it so hard to create an ethical culture? (May/June). Available at: http://accounting.smartpros.com/x48460.xml.
21. Jensen, M. L., and K. J. Murphy. 1990. CEO incentives—It's not how much you pay, but how. *Harvard Business Review* (May–June): 138–149.
22. Cohen, J. 2001. Appreciating, understanding and applying universal moral principles. *Journal of Consumer Marketing* 18 (7): 578–594.
23. Jenkins, R. 2001. Corporate codes of conduct: Self-regulation in a global economy. Technology, Business and Society Programme Paper No. 2. Available at: www.unrisd.org/unrisd/website/document.nsf/0/e3b3e78bab9a886f80256b5 e00344278/$FILE/jenkins.pdf.
24. International Federation of Accountants. 2005. Code of ethics. Available at: www.ifac.org/ethics.
25. Paulson, H. M. 2006. Remarks by Treasury Secretary on the competitiveness of U.S. capital markets Economics Club of New York, New York. (November 20). Available at: www.treas.gov/press/releases/hp174.htm.
26. Grace, H. S. 2005. Effective governance in an ethicless organization. *The CPA Journal.* Available at: www.nysscpa.org/cpajournal/2005/505/perspectives/p6.htm.
27. Defense Industry Initiatives on Business Ethics and Conduct. Defense industry initiative principles. Available at: www.dii.org/statement.htm.
28. American Institute of Certified Public Accountants. 2001. Attest engagements: Engagements interpretations of Section 101, AT Section 9101. Available at: www.aicpa.org/members/div/auditstd/Cod_Pro_std_sec_Num.htm.

CHAPTER 13

Globalization, Technology, and Corporate Governance

INTRODUCTION

C orporate governance should be responsive to the emerging challenges and opportunities of the twenty-first century. These challenges are globalization, technology, and regulations. Regulations and their relevance to corporate governance were discussed in Chapter 6. This chapter discusses the impact of globalization and technology on corporate governance. Technology plays an important role in corporate governance, particularly in improving and automating the compliance process in the postcorporate governance reforms era. A survey conducted by CFO Research Service in collaboration with Virsa Systems and PricewaterhouseCoopers indicates that:

- More than 75 percent of the surveyed executives assigned either "top priority" or "moderate priority" to the automation of their compliance and control environment in the post–Sarbanes-Oxley (SOX) era.
- Over 56 percent plan to scrutinize their underlying business process.
- About 43 percent will turn their attention to improving and automating manual controls, such as reconciliation and security.[1]

Corporate governance structures can be differentiated across countries in terms of degree of ownership and control. For example, the corporate governance structure in the United States, the United Kingdom, and Canada is characterized by widespread ownership, which may create conflicts of interest between decision control (management) and ownership control (widespread shareholders). In Germany and Japan, the ownership is concentrated in the hands of a few blockholders (e.g., banks, organizations); the potential conflict of interest is between controlling shareholders and minority shareholders. The corporate governance structure in different countries is influenced by cultural, political, and historical factors as well as the legal and regulatory environment, as discussed in the next section.

CORPORATE GOVERNANCE: A GLOBAL PERSPECTIVE

Globalization in this chapter is defined as the extent of "inter-linkages among countries in the trade of goods and services, or capital flows, and to a much lesser extent, movement of people."[2] One important aspect of the extent of globalization is the volume of total cross-border capital flows into and out of a country. Exhibit 13.1 shows cross-border capital flows for a sample of industrialized countries from 1999 to 2003. Despite the increasing cross-border capital flows, no single set of globally accepted corporate governance standards currently exists. However, a common set of global corporate governance best practices is beginning to emerge. The minor corporate governance variations reflect the nature of cultural, social, legal, regulatory, business, and economic systems of different countries. The corporate governance structure in the United States focuses on managerial functions to maximize shareholders' wealth; the German structure emphasizes interests of a wide range of stakeholders, including shareholders, creditors, employees, and communities.

Four factors differentiate corporate governance structures across different countries:

1. Legal infrastructure.
2. Regulatory environment.
3. Information infrastructure.
4. Market infrastructure.[3]

A country's legal infrastructure can influence the corporate governance structure significantly, including its principles, internal and external mechanisms, and functions. The infrastructure defines the legal right of corporations and the fiduciary

EXHIBIT 13.1 Globalization Measured in Terms of Capital Flows (1999 to 2003)

	Capital Inflows		Capital Outflows	
	Billion $	% of GDP	Billion $	% of GDP
United States	4,167	38	1,922	17
Euro Area	3,569	44	3,609	44
United Kingdom	2,387	133	2,247	125
Switzerland	343	111	510	165
Canada	223	26	297	34
Australia	212	42	124	24
Sweden	190	63	223	74
Denmark	143	68	167	79
Norway	121	55	196	89
Japan	106	3	664	15

Source: Philip R. Lane and Gian Maria Milesi-Ferretti, "Financial Globalization and Exchange Rates," IMF Working Paper WP/05/3, January 2005.

duties of their directors and officers to the shareholders. In the United States, state and federal statutes constitute legal infrastructure for corporate governance. The rule of law and order is vital to the effectiveness of corporate governance. Various types of country laws shape the structure of corporate governance, including corporate law, tort law, and bankruptcy law.[4] Corporate law plays a vital role by determining how companies are established, defining the rights of shareholders, and establishing fiduciary duties of directors and officers.

Securities law, determined by federal statutes, is also important in protecting investor interests and rights by setting minimum requirements for companies offering securities to the public regarding accurate, relevant, and useful financial information. Although bankruptcy law may not play an important role in corporate governance and the way companies are governed, it defines the rights of creditors, investors, and other stakeholders as well as settlement procedures regarding liquidation or restructuring of an insolvent company. Corporate governance is vital in protecting the interests of equity holders and debt holders in crisis situations, such as hostile takeovers and bankruptcy. Vigorous enforcement of corporate laws significantly impacts the overall effectiveness of corporate governance.

Market infrastructure consists of rules, regulations, and best practices that determine how capital markets function, directly impacting corporate governance. Specifically, listing standards of organized global stock exchanges govern the independence of company directors, board committee responsibilities, shareholder voting process, and financial reporting requirements.

Globalization and information technology enable the development of global business and financial markets that create profound challenges for businesses and regulators seeking to protect investors worldwide. The speed with which financial transactions can be conducted around the world has encouraged regulators to establish a global financial infrastructure and global corporate governance standards. The International Monetary Fund (IMF), the World Bank, the Basel Committee for Banking Supervision, the Organization for Economic Cooperation and Development (OECD), the International Organization of Securities Commissions (IOSCO), and U.S. regulators (SOX and the Securities and Exchange Commission [SEC] rules) have taken initiatives to provide guidance and sources of supervisory standards for national and international business and financial markets. Thus, countries and their companies that conduct business in global markets have to comply with global standards and regulations provided by those organizations. However, global best practices in corporate governance are still emerging.

Corporate governance structure is shaped by the availability, efficiency, and effectiveness of both internal and external corporate governance mechanisms. These mechanisms and their collective functions differ by country, industry, and company environments. Specifically, each country has its own corporate governance structure tailored to and suitable for its legal, political, cultural, business, and regulatory environment. There are four main and distinct global corporate governance structures: the United States, the United Kingdom, Germany, and Japan. Other structures seem to be derivatives of these four structures. For example, the Canadian corporate governance structure is similar to the United Kingdom's structure, whereas Dutch and Swiss structures are closely modeled after the German structure.

Determination of differences in corporate governance in the United States and other countries centers around four areas:[5]

1. *Corporate ownership and control.* Corporate ownership in countries other than the United States is much more highly concentrated through large banking institutions of family ownership. The concentration of corporate ownership and control and government ownership of a large portion of corporate shares can influence corporate governance in those countries significantly.

2. *Capital raising.* Public companies in the United States raise capital, both equity and debt securities, directly from the public through the financial markets. In other countries (e.g., Europe, Asia), banks are the primary source of capital for companies. Lending arrangements with banks and ownership of large blocks of shares by banks empower banks to monitor and control the companies' affairs and influence their corporate governance.

3. *Culture.* Under the U.S. market-based corporate governance structure, shareholder value creation and enhancement is the primary objective of public companies. In many other countries, corporations are responsible for protecting the interests of a variety of stakeholders, including shareholders, employees, customers, suppliers, government, and the public. Thus, the corporate governance structure in other countries is driven by the need to balance the interests of all stakeholders. The corporate decision-making process is also affected by the closed and family culture in those countries compared with the open and social culture in the United States.

4. *Legal system.* The country's legal system is the key driver of corporate governance in determining corporate responsibility, authority, structure, and fiduciary duties of its directors and officers. Extant literature in accounting and finance examines the relationship between the legal protection of investors and the development of financial markets and corporate governance, and concludes that the legal system is an important integral component of corporate governance. Thus, better legal systems contribute to market liquidity.[6] Corporate governance listing standards do not normally exist outside the United States.

The three primary differences between the corporate governance measures in the United States and other countries follow.

1. *Audit committees.* Audit committees in the United States must be composed of at least three independent directors, with at least one being designated as the audit committee financial expert. Audit committees in other countries are recommended to be established through nonbinding corporate governance codes. For example, the U.K. combined code recommends listed companies to form a committee of at least three directors with the majority being independent, nonexecutive directors. In U.K. companies, directors have the authority and are responsible for managing and running the company. Indeed, directors act as trustees for shareholders, and their duties are established in common law and under statute. German public companies are recommended to have an audit committee consisting of supervisory board members. Japanese corporate

governance principles recommend that public companies establish an audit committee composed of majority nonexecutive directors.

2. *Shareholder approval.* Listing standards in the United States require shareholder approval for certain issuances of securities that are typically addressed in state corporate law. In other countries, shareholder approval requirements usually are imposed by the corporate law. For example, in the United Kingdom, public companies are required to grant preemptive rights to their shareholders upon any issuance of equity for cash. The U.K. Companies Act requires that auditors be appointed by and report to shareholders on the truth and fairness of the company's financial statements that are prepared by the board of directors.

3. *Voting rights.* Unlike listing standards in the United States, other countries usually permit the issuance of nonvoting preferred shares or restricted ordinary shares without limitations.

Global Reach of Sarbanes-Oxley

Foreign companies with 300 or more U.S. shareholders must comply with provisions of SOX. There are over 470 non-U.S. companies listed on New York Stock Exchange (NYSE) with an aggregate market capitalization of $3.8 trillion, which accounts for more than 30 percent of the total market capitalization of NYSE listed companies.[7] Traditionally, multinational corporations have benefited from listing on U.S. stock exchanges primarily because of ready access to a large group of active investors and potential acquisitions. Nevertheless, the high compliance costs of SOX could reduce some of these benefits. These additional compliance costs, estimated in the range of $5 million to $10 million per company per year, may encourage non-U.S. companies to delist in U.S. exchanges.

On December 13, 2006, the SEC voted to repropose amendments to the current rules that permit a foreign private issuer to exit the Securities Exchange Act of 1934 registration and reporting regime if the class of the issuer's securities has less than 300 U.S. security holders.[8] The reproposed Exchange Act Rule would allow the termination of registration of foreign private issuers that meet a quantitative benchmark designed to measure relative U.S. market interest for that class of securities regardless of head count of the issuer's U.S. security holders.[9] The reproposed benchmark would require the comparison of the average daily trading volume of an issuer's securities in the United States with that in its primary trading market (no greater than 5 percent during a recent 12-month period).[10] Under the reproposed rules, an issuer of equity securities may choose to terminate its Exchange Act registration and related reporting requirements, if the average daily trading volume of the subject class of securities in the United States has been 5 percent or less of the average daily trading volume of that class of securities in its own primary trading market during a recent 12-month period. These rules, while making the exit from the U.S. stock exchanges easier by foreign issuers, are intended to protect U.S. investors by: (1) allowing deregistration only by foreign registrants in whose securities U.S. market interest is relatively low; (2) requiring that the delisted issuer whose trading exceeds the five percent benchmark at the time of delisting to wait at least a year before it terminates its Exchange Act reporting obligations; and (3) discouraging foreign private issuers to delist their securities from U.S. exchanges at the time when the U.S. market for their securities is still relatively active.[11]

The deregulation of foreign securities started with the SEC's rule No. 144A, in 1990, which allowed the sale of securities by foreign issuers to institutional investors and rich individuals in the United States without complying with securities disclosure rules.[12] The reproposed rules would significantly reduce the scope of regulations in global financial markets, which may result in less protections for all investors in the United States. The new rules are being criticized for allowing foreign private issuers to "keep the money that was raised from the securities, but they will no longer have to comply with the rules. Thousands of companies will be eligible to deregister from the United States."[13]

Provisions of SOX and SEC-related implementation rules have reached beyond the boundaries of the United States, as many of the provisions and related rules are equally applicable to foreign private issue and domestic issuers. Thus, foreign private issuers are subject to all previously discussed corporate governance measures except for these four:[14]

1. *Section 16(a) of the Securities Act of 1934.* Foreign private issuers are not subject to Section 16(a) of the Securities Act of 1934 and are not affected by the accelerated filing deadlines for insiders. Therefore, the disclosures that U.S. public companies provide to the SEC on Form 8-K are normally disclosed by foreign private issuers on an annual basis.

2. *Audit committee charter.* Listing standards of national stock exchanges (NYSE, Nasdaq) are more lenient toward foreign private issuers in the sense that these companies are not required to maintain an audit committee charter, which is mandatory for U.S. listed companies.

3. *Code of ethics.* Foreign private issuers are not required to provide the "immediate disclosure" on Form 8-K of any changes to their code of ethics or waiver from the code for their senior financial officers and principal executive officers. These changes and waivers should be disclosed in the company's annual report to the SEC.

4. *Internal control certifications and attestation.* Although executive certifications of internal control and financial statements are equally applied to both domestic and foreign issuers, foreign private issuers are not required to file interim certifications. However, the SEC, in August 2005, released rules requiring foreign private issuers traded on Nasdaq to provide "semi-annual balance sheets and income statements."[15] Specifically, foreign private issuers listed on Nasdaq:

   a. Must submit the interim reports (semiannually) within six months of the end of the company's second fiscal year.

   b. Must translate the interim financial statements into English and submit on Form 6-K.

   c. Are not required to have their interim financial information be reviewed by external auditors or reconciled to U.S. generally accepted accounting principles (GAAP).[16]

Global Collaborations and Challenges

Technological advances and globalization have developed to the point that, as elaborated by Thomas L. Friedman, the world has become flat in the sense that countries can see where they are compared to other countries.[17] In a flat world, cross-border investments are common as investors consider the global financial markets in making investment decisions. Effective corporate governance can improve the efficiency and integration of global financial markets and provide better information on which investors can base their decisions. A survey indicates that:

- Over 58 percent of CEOs felt that globalization would have a somewhat or very positive impact on their organizations.
- There are several barriers to globalization, including overregulation, trade barriers/protectionism, political instability, and social issues.
- CEOs are investing the most resources in China, followed by India, Brazil, and Russia, commonly known as BRICs (Brazil, Russia, India, and China).
- Globalization strategies have shifted from purely cost cutting to moving into the emerging-market countries (BRICs) to find new customers and to serve existing ones.
- Globalization is not without challenges or complexity.
- More than 75 percent of responding CEOs reported that the level of complexity in their organization in 2006 is higher than it was three years ago.
- Expansion into new territories, launching new products, and mergers and acquisitions are the most complex issues.[18]

Regulators worldwide have collaborated to improve the effectiveness of global corporate governance. Examples of such collaborations are the SEC's continuous efforts and financial dialogue with its counterparts in Europe and Asia, as elaborated by the SEC commissioner Cynthia A. Glassman.[19] The SEC has been very active in developing financial dialogue with its counterparts in the European Union (EU). The United States and the EU should establish better cooperative efforts in promoting the development of a principles-based regulatory framework that is sensitive and responsive to different cultures, histories, political and legal regimes, economic systems, and regulatory philosophies. Economic developments in Asia, particularly China and India, will soon have unprecedented effects on the global economy, financial markets, and cross-border investments. The SEC and the Japanese Financial Service Agency have had continuous bilateral dialogue to enhance the quality of regulatory discussions and participate in a working group to discuss financial sector developments in both countries.[20] SEC chairman Christopher Cox, along with Treasury secretary John Snow and Federal Reserve chairman Alan Greenspan, have participated in a U.S.-China Joint Economic Committee to discuss with their counterparts a range of policy issues and regulatory matters relevant to financial markets in both countries and possible collaboration initiatives.[21]

On March 16, 2004, the European Commission (EC) proposed the 8th Company Law Directive on statutory audit and annual accounts and consolidated accounts. It was approved by the European Parliament on September 28, 2005, and by the council on October 11.[22] Objectives of the Directive on Statutory Audit are to:

- Restore credibility of financial reporting of all member states.
- Enhance the EU's protection against financial scandals of high-profile companies, such as Parmalat and Ahold.
- Bring EU financial reporting into the twenty-first century through more effective and ethical audit processes.
- Require the application of international auditing standards.
- Restore credibility in the auditing profession that was undermined by recent financial scandals.
- Reinforce and harmonize the statutory audit function throughout the EU.
- Establish principles for public supervision of the statutory audits in all member states.
- Establish requirements for external quality assurance and duties of statutory auditors.
- Improve auditor independence by requiring listed companies to establish an audit committee.
- Facilitate cooperation between regulators in the EU and regulators in other countries (Public Company Accounting Oversight Board [PCAOB]-U.S.).
- Create an audit regulatory committee to implement its measures.[23]

There has been a growing international interest in corporate social responsibility, including environmental, social, and governance (ESG) issues.[24] The ESG issues can influence the performance of investment portfolios and thus should be considered in assessing investment decisions and ownership practices. To address this important global issue, in 2005, the United Nations Secretary-General invited a group of representatives from 20 investment organizations in 12 countries to establish a set of global best practice principles for responsible investment.[25] The process of developing principles for responsible investment (PRI) was coordinated and overseen by the UN Financial Initiative and the UN Global Compact. The PRI are voluntary and aspirational rather than prescriptive, providing a framework for incorporating ESG issues into investment decision making and ownership practices.[26] Compliance with the PRI is expected to lead not only to a more sustainable financial return but also to a close alignment of investors' interests with those of global society at large. The PRI provides a common framework for the integration of ESG issues and consists of:

- Integration of ESG issues into investment analysis and decision-making processes.
- Incorporation of ESG issues into investment ownership policies and practices.
- Promotion of appropriate disclosure on ESG issues by the entities in which institutional investors invest.
- Promotion of acceptance and implementation of the principles within the investment industry.
- Collaboration among institutional investors to enhance the effectiveness of implementing the principles.
- Reporting on initiatives, activities, and progress toward implementing these principles.[27]

Corporate Governance in Multinational Corporations

Multinational corporations (MNCs) play an important role in the world economy and in trade. As the number of MNCs increases and they continue to be more relevant and important, their corporate governance becomes essential in aligning the interests of their headquarters (parents) with those of subsidiaries, which usually have divergent political, economical, cultural, and environmental interests. International Accounting Standard (IAS) No. 27 entitled *Consolidated and Separate Financial Statements* states that a parent-subsidiary relationship arises when one enterprise (the parent) is able to control another enterprise (the subsidiary); "control" is defined as the power to govern the operating and financial policies of the subsidiary by owning the majority of the voting shares of the subsidiary, being able to govern the operating and financial policies of the subsidiary, or being able to influence the subsidiary's decisions substantially.[28]

In purely domestic corporations, corporate governance mechanisms are designed to align the interests of management and shareholders and arise from the separation of ownership and control. In an MNC, corporate governance mechanisms are designed not only to align the interests of subsidiaries with those of the parent company, but also to align the interests of management of the parent company with those of both its majority and minority shareholders. Thus, the potential conflicts of interest between the subsidiaries and the parent company as well as between the parent company and its shareholders create agency costs. In an MNC, a parent company can be both an agent (management) and a principal (owner): an agent in relation to its own shareholders and a principal in relation to its subsidiaries, with shareholders of the parent company being the ultimate residual risk-bearing owners (principals). Thus, in order to align their interests with those of shareholders, the agents should be monitored, controlled, and bonded through a set of contracts that are costly to write and enforce.

In the absence of interest alignment, the management of subsidiaries may make decisions to maximize their own interests, which may be detrimental to the long-term performance of the parent company. Likewise, the management of the parent company may make decisions that may result in reducing shareholder value. Thus, the nexus of contracts (monitoring, bonding, and controlling) to reduce agency costs constitutes the corporate governance structure between the parent company and its subsidiaries and between shareholders of the parent company and its management. Both internal and external corporate governance mechanisms of companies have evolved over time to monitor, bond, and control management. These mechanisms are the capital markets, the managerial labor markets, regulations, investors (particularly institutional investors), and the board of directors, which may act independently, substitutionally, or complementarily to align the interests of stockholders and management. The parent-subsidiary corporate governance structure is designed to align the interests of subsidiaries with those of the multinational corporation's headquarters.

The parent-subsidiary corporate governance structure is shaped by both the host and the home country's legal, political, cultural, and regulatory systems; the business practices and historical patterns of countries; the global capital, labor, and managerial markets; global institutional investors; and the boards of directors. Other factors that may influence the parent-subsidiary corporate governance structure are the international strategy of MNCs and the subsidiary's industry, size, and relative importance to the entire system of MNCs. Particularly when the subsidiary is wholly owned by the parent company and is managed automatically (independently) by a management that has little, if any, ownership interest in the multinational or the subsidiary, the effectiveness of parent-subsidiary corporate governance becomes more crucial in monitoring and controlling the managerial actions of the subsidiary.

INFORMATION TECHNOLOGY

Information technology (IT) can play an important role in improving the efficiency and effectiveness of corporate governance. IT is an effective means of delivering timely and accurate information for planning, monitoring, and reporting purposes. The IT manager is an important senior executive working with other senior executives (CEO, chief financial officer [CFO], controllers) as part of the managerial function of corporate governance. The chief information officer (CIO) or IT manager is responsible for effective management and operation of the IT function to support other corporate governance functions. The effective functioning of all corporate governance functions depends on the quality of support received from the IT function. The IT function enables other corporate governance functions to operate in real-time online processes facilitating simultaneous decision making, continuous monitoring, instantaneous assessment electronic reporting, and continuous auditing. A 2006 survey of the CEOs of 312 of the fastest-growing companies indicates that: (1) their company's total operating budget devoted to IT development averaged 8.14 percent in 2005, which is up 24 percent compared with 6.56 percent reported in 2002; and (2) several areas of IT development including security applications, wireless networks, faster data transactions, Internet technology, and data convergence continue to have significant impacts on their business.[29]

Compliance with Sections 404 (real-time disclosures) and 802 (criminal penalties for altering documents) of SOX necessitates the use of IT solutions for timely access to secure and complete business documents. IT governance is defined as a set of policies, procedures, and practices used by the company to manage risk and create value through information management by establishing IT strategy and assessing and improving its performance.[30] The primary goals of IT strategy are to create value by aligning IT capabilities with business objectives and to sustain value by effectively managing portfolio of IT investments.[31] IT and its integration across all corporate governance functions ensure more timely financial information, more effective regulatory compliance (SOX), more efficient use of IT systems, and more efficient and effective use of software applications. Many companies are still using IT infrastructures based on stand-alone systems to achieve their goals. The emerging issue in IT infrastructures is integrating IT services and business processes based on Web services. Web services are developed based on a Web-enabled descriptive taxonomy of eXtensible markup language (XML).

The company's executives, particularly the CFO, can ensure the achievement of IT objectives by:

- Aligning IT performance goals with strategic business performance.
- Aligning communication and transaction processing capabilities with operational business objectives.
- Integrating IT strategy and performance throughout the company by linking performance of IT employees to the overall business objectives.
- Establishing policies and procedures to measure, monitor, and realize the value delivered by IT.
- Establishing the position of CIO to manage IT activities.
- Aligning IT to support interaction with external business parties.
- Assessing feedback from users of IT against agreed service levels.
- Designing a flexible IT infrastructure to accommodate future operational growth, changes, and opportunities.
- Monitoring IT innovations to identify solutions for operational and competitive advantage.
- Ensuring that the company's board of directors is aware of IT's contribution to the overall performance and compliance with applicable laws and regulations.
- Managing risks across the IT department.
- Ensuring system reliability and infrastructure integrity, confidentiality, and privacy.
- Continuously monitoring IT performance.
- Properly allocating IT costs to all user departments within the company.
- Providing sufficient capital resources to support essential IT infrastructure.[32]

The important role that IT can play in improving the effectiveness of corporate governance, particularly regarding financial reporting and disclosure, is not yet well recognized in the business literature and the financial reporting process. Information technology, specifically the use of the Internet and e-commerce, has had a significant impact on the way companies operate and, accordingly, on their governance. The SEC has recently accepted, on a voluntary basis, public companies filing their financial reports on eXtensible Business Reporting Language (XBRL) format along with statuary filings under the Electronic Data Gathering, Analysis, and Retrieval (EDGAR) system.[33] Technology solutions and software packages are being developed to document compliance with provisions of SOX, particularly Section 404 on internal control over financial reporting. The SEC has announced a series of roundtables to be held throughout 2006 to address the implementation of new Internet tools to assist investors, analysts, and other users of financial reports to receive more timely information. The roundtables will discuss the experiences of the first year of a pilot program of using interactive data for public company filings with the SEC. The SEC is also seeking written feedback from registrants, investors, auditors, and others on their experience with XBRL and interactive data.

CYBERCOMPANY MODEL

The future extensive use of IT in the areas of shareholder communication, electronic commerce, electronic financial reporting, and electronic continuous auditing eventually would cause companies to move toward the "cybercompany" model. The emerging cybercompany model would require changes in many components of the corporate governance structure presented in Chapter 2. Corporate governance goals of shareholder value creation and enhancement as well as other stakeholder value protections remain the same. Corporate governance principles of fairness, honesty, transparency, responsiveness, accountability, and resilience would also be applicable to the cybercompany model. However, corporate governance structure, including internal and external mechanisms, would change to some extent. Corporate governance objectives, principles, and functions would be the same, but the manner in which these functions operate (oversight, managerial, internal audit, compliance, external audit, advisory, and monitoring) will differ. Thus, the full and effective use of IT may shape and improve corporate governance functions.

The cybercompany model is characterized by:

- Electronic communication with shareholders.
- Electronic commerce.
- Electronic financial reporting.
- Electronic continuous auditing.

Electronic Communication with Shareholders

Shareholders can cast votes electronically using the same technologies utilized in local and national elections. Thus, it is expected that, in the future, the majority, if not all, of the company communications, including annual meetings and voting, will be conducted in electronic form. In 2005 the United Kingdom proposed Corporate Law Reform recommendations, subject to shareholder approval, for companies to use electronic means, such as Web sites and e-mails, to communicate with their shareholders.[34] The SEC, in November 2005, released its proposed rule to provide investors with proxy materials on the Internet.[35] This proposed rule would allow public companies and their shareholders to use the Internet to satisfy requirements regarding the delivery of proxy materials. If approved, investors would no longer receive their pre–annual meeting proxy materials through the regular mail in paper form. Instead, they would receive an e-mail that their materials would be made available online through a Web site.

The use of electronic communication, in lieu of traditional communications on paper, can be beneficial to both companies and their shareholders. Companies can save substantial costs of paper-based production and dissemination of annual proxy and financial statements and improve the timeliness and transparency of communications with shareholders by using electronic means. Shareholders can also benefit by using electronic means in communicating with their companies and in participating in meetings that might otherwise be inaccessible or difficult to attend because of the constraints of time or location. Nevertheless, the existing corporate laws require the use of paper-based shareholder communications; these laws prevent both companies and their shareholders from reaping the benefits of electronic means of communicating.

Modern video conferencing, or "Web cam" technology, enables companies to conduct meetings, including board and even shareholder meetings, electronically without requiring everyone to be physically present. In the future, shareholders' annual meetings can be arranged in a specified physical location, date, and time, but the means of participation may be either physical or electronic. If shareholders have access to the required technology and the discussion can be managed effectively, a more advanced electronic shareholder annual meeting would be through a "virtual" meeting, in which there is no chosen physical location for the meeting, but discussions are organized through the use of an electronic bulletin board.

Electronic Commerce

During the past several decades the global economy has changed from an industrial economy to an information economy. Recently, with the Internet, it has transformed into a digital economy. The digital economy is significantly changing the way businesses, governments, and individuals interact and exchange goods and services. IT, in general, and the Internet, in particular, enable the establishment of cybercompanies, such as Google, Yahoo, eBay, CNET, E-cost, and Amazon.com. Almost all traditional retailers have established online trades. Electronic commerce (e-commerce) has become an integral component of business strategies and has altered the way organizations conduct their daily operations. The business framework has transformed from "brick-and-mortar" to "brick-and-click" infrastructure. E-commerce can be broadly defined as conducting business affairs, transactions, and communications over the Internet or through private online networks.

In today's digital and information knowledge economy, companies rely on IT to conduct their business and to communicate with customers, suppliers, branches, and employees. IT is becoming an integral part of the company's strategic planning process. Thus, the board of directors should ensure ten things:

1. Management periodically assesses the technology needs of the company and has a strategic IT plan that monitors and updates IT facilities.
2. Management periodically assesses the required technology expertise and conducts employee training and education in technology.
3. Management has invested in and utilized IT adequately.
4. Management continuously communicates IT policies to personnel.
5. Management periodically conducts risk assessments of the company's use of IT.
6. Management has established privacy policies.
7. The company is in compliance with laws and regulations relevant to IT.
8. Management effectively protects the company's e-commerce activities from internal and external attacks by unauthorized persons.
9. Management has addressed legal implications of the use of IT including software, hardware, service agreements, and related copyright laws.
10. Management has established and effectively communicated policies and procedures pertaining to licenses, copyrights, and agreements to all personnel.

E-commerce strategies are classified into:

- Business to business (B2B), the online exchanges of products, services, and business transactions between businesses and suppliers.

- Business to consumer (B2C), conducting business online with consumers.
- Consumer to consumer (C2C), where consumers trade among themselves.
- Business to government (B2G), or exchanging transactions between business and governmental entities.
- Government to government (G2G), consisting of online programs and activities between governmental agencies.
- Government to consumers (G2C), where online transactions are exchanged between governmental entities and consumers.[36]

E-commerce transactions have grown from about $100 billion in 1999 to more than $8 trillion in 2004 worldwide and are expected to increase at about 20 percent compound annual growth over the next five years.[37] This exponential growth in e-commerce activities significantly affects the way companies are operated, managed, and monitored. E-commerce has had profound implications for corporate governance and has raised several policy, legal, and business issues that need to be addressed.

Electronic Financial Reporting

The effectiveness of corporate governance and the efficiency and integrity of the capital markets are greatly influenced by the amount, timeliness, accuracy, and completeness of public financial information provided by public companies. Accurate and reliable public financial information enables investors to monitor public companies' governance effectively and assess their operating, financing, and investment performance. High-quality financial information can be produced only under effective accounting and internal control systems guided by sound accounting policies and practices and audited by competent and independent auditors. In other words, the quality of public financial information is influenced by the competence and integrity of providers of information; soundness of accounting principles, policies, and practices; effectiveness of the related internal controls; credibility of the audit process; and timeliness of information. Users of financial statements, including analysts and investors, can search the full text of every SEC document filed by public companies within the last two years. The SEC tool that enables real-time, full-text research of filings on the SEC's EDGAR database can be found at: www.sec.gov/edgar/resarchedgar/webusers.htm.

Information Infrastructure The information infrastructure determines the way financial information is generated, processed, analyzed, audited, and used in making business and investment decisions. The information infrastructure of corporate governance is affected by the company's:

- Directors in overseeing the financial reporting process, internal controls, and audit activities.
- Top management team in designing sound accounting and internal control systems and in certifying its financial statements and internal control over financial reporting.

- Independent auditors by providing opinions on both financial statements and internal controls.
- Legal counsel in assisting management with financial disclosures.
- Financial analysts in accurately and objectively forecasting their earnings quantity and quality.
- Standard-setting bodies in promulgating accounting and auditing standards to be used in financial reporting and audit activities.

Internal Controls   Several sections of SOX require the use of IT solutions to comply with these provisions. The use of IT solutions can be more effective in compliance with Sections 302, 404, 409, and 802. Effective and timely compliance with provisions of SOX requires public companies to utilize their IT resources or obtain IT solutions required to access and process the data. About half of the surveyed senior executives indicated that their company made only satisfactory use of technology in the first year (2004) of compliance with Section 404 of SOX.[38] However, about 75 percent of U.S. multinationals plan to make significant technology changes in the second year and beyond of compliance with provisions of SOX, particularly as related to their control environment and the compliance process.[39]

Information Security   Information security and privacy of technology companies have received significant attention. Technology company executives worldwide are facing intense competition and changes in their corporate governance. The global convergence to digital services and worldwide economic expansions in China, Europe, and India encourage technology companies to be flexible in strategies, business models, corporate governance, and culture. A survey conducted by PricewaterhouseCoopers of 126 technology executives in 34 countries reveals that technology companies should:

- Manage their business risks properly by remaining flexible in their governance, strategies, business models, and cultures.
- Develop partnerships and alliances with other technology companies to profit from changes in technologies.
- Pay close attention to customers' needs and changes in products and markets.
- Become more adaptable and better able to assess and manage risks and opportunities.[40]

eXtensible Business Reporting Language (XBRL)

The emerging regulatory and corporate governance reforms demand more reliable, timely, and transparent financial information. Currently many companies post their financial statements on their Web sites. The Web-based financial reports are basically electronic reproductions of the printed annual reports with no value added except that they are readily available. The use of the Internet in the electronic financial reporting process should make financial information easily accessible and readable by a wide variety of applications. The electronically published business and financial information is often integrated through hyperlinks, which makes separation of financial information from other information quite difficult. The eXtensible Business Reporting Language (XBRL) enables business reporting information to be transferred automatically between different computer platforms and applications. XBRL allows the selection, analysis, storage, and exchange of tagged data that can be displayed automatically in various platforms and *tailored* to specifies presentation format.

The standardized XBRL format allows all market and corporate governance participants, including companies, investors, auditors, analysts, and government agencies, to share financial information electronically to the extent that investors have access to the same information as analysts. XBRL provides a computer-readable identifying tag for each individual item in financial reports rather than treating those items as a block of computer text or printed documents. The XBRL tags are prepared according to the applicable taxonomies: GAAP for financial reporting, tax rules for tax purposes, or specific regulatory definitions for regulatory filings. The tagging process can handle financial information in different accounting standards and languages to serve a wide range of users.

XBRL is an XML-based platform for analysis, exchange, and reporting of financial information with the purpose of integrating business reports and technology solutions. XBRL International currently freely licenses the XBRL standard and framework.[41] Under XBRL format, descriptions in the form of tags or labels are attached to the business data in terms of an agreed-on vocabulary known as taxonomy. Development of the appropriate taxonomy is the key to the application of XBRL in financial reporting simply because XBRL is not dependent on any particular hardware platform, software system, programming language, or application standards (accounting, tax, or regulatory).

Companies should integrate their financial and operational activities and data by using Web services. The use of Web-based programs such as XML and XBRL enable companies to do six things:

1. Eliminate manual processes and their related costs.
2. Integrate their automated operational and financial activities.
3. Improve their control environment.
4. Enhance efficiency, effectiveness, accuracy, and timeliness of financial reports.
5. Enable convergences in global financial reporting by identifying, automating, and tagging financial information in any language and financial standards used by the company and linking to other sources of authoritative guidance, such as International Financial Reporting Standards (IFRS).
6. Shorten turnaround between events and decisions and provide more time for analysis and decision making by automating inefficient manual information gathering and analysis.

Costs and Benefits of XBRL   There are potential costs of providing supplementary XBRL-related documents, as in Exhibit 100, to the SEC's EDGAR system. Costs are also associated with the initial adoption of the XBRL-tagged data system, including the costs of testing and evaluating the XBRL format. Nevertheless, the use of an

XBRL-tagged data system holds significant potential for the future of electronic financial reporting. Perceived benefits include:

- XBRL can be used on any computer hardware equipment or operating system to store data that can be shared easily without having to rekey data, which reduces errors and results in productivity improvements for all users.
- XBRL data do not change from the time and place of origination to their eventual designation and use, which results in more transparency in financial reporting.
- The XBRL format can provide time and cost savings for users of financial statements by enabling them to analyze key financial ratios, compare companies to peers or indices, and perform other financial analyses without having to rekey or reformat financial information.
- The use of XBRL might result in improvements in internal control over financial reporting by enabling the use of continuous monitoring and automatically checking electronic information and its related internal controls.
- The improvements in internal controls might lead to less cost of compliance with Section 404.
- The consistency and comparability provided by the use of XBRL might result in more efficient and effective filings and analysis of financial information by the SEC.
- XBRL improves the transparency of financial information by allowing organizations to respond much more quickly to changes in business conditions, regulatory requirements, and economic developments.[42]

XBRL Operation XBRL contains several components and documents that enable XBRL operation, as depicted in Exhibit 13.2. XBRL components and documentations are the XBRL specifications, taxonomies, instance documents, reports, and assurance.[43]

XBRL Specification In April 2005 the XBRL Specification Group released the current XBRL specification, Version 2.1, which provides a technical explanation of XBRL and its operation, including the framework, taxonomies, and instance documents. The XBRL specification is available for download from the XBRL Web site (www.xbrl.org).

XBRL Taxonomies Taxonomies are XBRL's dictionary, which describes the key data elements (numbers and text) included in XBRL instance documents designed for particular financial reporting purposes and in compliance with requirements of regulatory, financial reporting provisions, or tax authorities. Various taxonomies have been released based on U.S. GAAP and IFRS.

XBRL Instance Documents XBRL instance documents are a collection of data elements and explanatory tags in a machine-readable format designed based on the rules and concepts of particular taxonomies to ensure the data are moved reliably and consistently between systems.

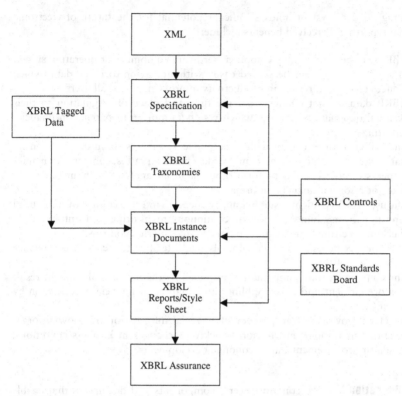

EXHIBIT 13.2 XBRL Operation
Source: Extracted from the Canadian Institute of Chartered Accountants, Information Technology Advisory Committee, "Audit and Control Implications of XBRL," December 2005. Available at: www.cica.ca/itac.

XBRL Style Sheets XBRL style sheets are used to convert instance documents that are in machine-readable format to human-readable reports. Style sheets can present XBRL data in the format of financial statements in HTML, PDF, word processing, or other specified presentation formats.

XBRL Controls Three control issues of XBRL need to be addressed:

1. Organizations using the XBRL format should ensure that they utilize an appropriate taxonomy suitable for their financial reporting, regulatory, and tax purposes.
2. Organizations should establish policies, procedures, and controls to ensure that the tagging of data is accurate and complete, and meets the requirements of the selected taxonomies.

3. Control policies and procedures should be designed for the approval of the selected taxonomy, tagged data, and reporting of XBRL data applicable to financial reporting and other regulatory and tax purposes.

XBRL Assurance   Online and real-time financial reports prepared based on the XBRL format require continuous assurance to ensure their integrity and accuracy. Computer-assisted audit and assurance techniques should be developed to monitor XBRL tagged data continuously to ensure their integrity, completeness, accuracy, consistency, and comparability. Auditors may be engaged in providing assurance on financial statements generated with XBRL. The objective of such an assurance engagement is similar to the engagement for other financial statements: to provide reasonable assurance that financial statements are fairly presented in accordance with the selected taxonomy (e.g., GAAP, IFRS, tax rules, regulations). Auditors should apply an integrated audit approach in expressing an opinion on the effectiveness of internal controls of both design and operation of instance documents to ensure the integrity of the XBRL tags and the fair presentation of financial statements generated with XBRL. XBRL assurance will be further discussed in the next section under continuous auditing.

XBRL Standards Board   To improve the quality of its technical materials and its standard-setting process, XBRL International is establishing the XBRL Standards Board (XSB).[44] The XSB's primary responsibilities will be to:

- Increase the quality, consistency, and stability of technical materials of XBRL International.
- Enhance the level of openness and formality of the standard-setting process of XBRL.
- Improve the effectiveness of the standard-setting process, which should accelerate adoption of XBRL standards.

XBRL Application   The SEC, in September 2004, proposed a voluntary plan to all public companies to submit their financial statements to the commission using XBRL beginning with the 2004 calendar year-end report filings.[45] The SEC's intent in adopting voluntary XBRL filings was to enhance users' ability to search the filings database, extract and analyze financial information and perform financial comparisons within industries, and facilitate the SEC's review of filings.[46]

The SEC issued a release, in February 2005, adopting amendments to establish a voluntary program relating to XBRL.[47] The SEC permits voluntary XBRL financial reporting filings with the SEC as a way of supplementing required filings on the EDGAR system. The supplemental data would be submitted as Exhibit 100 to the filings under EDGAR. The SEC rule indicates that:

- No preapproval is required to submit the XBRL data.
- One submission will not require or commit a registrant to future XBRL supplemental submissions.

- The use of XBRL for the notes to the financial statements is optional.
- The XBRL data on Exhibit 100 should provide the same information that the registrant includes in its filing under the Exchange Act of 1934 or the Investment Company Act of 1940.
- Cautionary language must be exercised to advise investors that the XBRL protocol is still in the testing stages and that they should not rely on the XBRL data to make investment decisions.
- The XBRL-related documents must be labeled as "unaudited for annual filings" and "unreviewed for quarterly financial statements."
- Submitted XBRL-related documents that provide information related to a different filing must reference the official filing from which the XBRL data were derived.[48]

The SEC, in February 2005, announced an XBRL Voluntary Filing Program (VFP) promoting registrants to tag their financial information using XBRL. Microsoft was the first company to provide its full set of financial statements including footnotes tagged in XBRL. Microsoft's first quarter of using the VFP program in Form 10-Q required 175 hours of effort, including 75 hours for XBRL taxonomy extension and customization, 60 hours to create and validate the XBRL document, and 40 hours for quality assurance review; the second time the quarterly Form 10-Q was submitted, the effort was reduced by two-thirds, to 60 hours.[49] Microsoft was also the first company to submit its annual reports in Form 10-K (for the year ending June 30, 2005) in XBRL format in September 2005.[50] In the second year (2006), 17 companies participated in the XBRL pilot program, including Adobe Systems, Bowne & Co, Business Objects, RR Donnelley & Sons, EDGAR Online, EMC, InfoSYS, Microsoft, United Technologies, MCO, Bristol Meyers, Squibb, Dow Chemical Co., and Xerox Corp.

The first mandatory e-filing using XBRL format is now being implemented under the system of the Call Report Modernization Project for about 8,400 financial institutions.[51] The call report uses the Central Data Repository (CDR), a secure shared database of the quarterly schedules of the nation's commercial banks. The project is designed to simplify and increase the transparency of the call report process to supervise and evaluate financial conditions and results of operations of financial institutions. Call report filings are used to compile and verify financial reports of financial institutions used by the Federal Deposit Insurance Corporation (FDIC), the Federal Reserve Bank (FRB), the office of the comptroller of the currency (OCC), and the public. The Federal Financial Institutions Examiners Council (FFIEC) estimates that about 192,500 hours are spent compiling and filing call reports composed of 2,000 fields of data, including 400 pages of instructions and 1,500 formulas to support the data. The e-filing system using XBRL reporting is required for the fourth quarter of 2005 for financial institutions. The system is expected to substantially reduce the cost of filing call reports and significantly improve their accuracy and transparency.[52]

Regarding the use of technology in financial reporting, Christopher Cox, the chairman of the SEC, states:

*We are really on the threshold of a "revolution in corporate reporting"...
to bring our system of corporate disclosure and financial reporting into
the 21st century.... . Interactive data will also make disclosures more
useful to investors, and to every market participant. Interactive data [by
using XBRL] could make it possible for issuers to reduce the cost of
substantiating the numbers that appear in their financial statements.*[53]

On January 11, 2006, Cox announced that the SEC staff would offer expedited
reviews of registration statements and annual reports filed with the commission
to companies that voluntarily participate in a test group designed for the SEC's
interactive data initiative.[54] The SEC's interactive data program is an extension of
its voluntary program for receiving financial information using the XBRL format.
Companies that use the commercial, industrial, banking, investment management,
and insurance industry classification in XBRL are encouraged to participate in
the voluntary test group program. On September 25, 2006, the AICPA announced
that XBRL-US will become an independent, not-for-profit organization. XBRL was
initially formed as a volunteer committee of the AICPA and now, as the Chartered
U.S. jurisdiction of XBRL International., Inc., XBRL-U.S. will continue to pursue
two goals: (1) supporting the implementation of XBRL for financial reporting in
the United States through the development of taxonomies for use by the public
and private sectors; and (2) promoting adoption of XBRL through conferences,
pilot interviews, educational materials and events.[55] SEC chairman Cox, at the 14th
International XBRL Conference, reaffirmed the SEC's strong support of the goal
of XBRL-US to document every necessary taxonomy to produce XBRL-financial
statements for every industry by no later than midyear 2007.[56] The SEC has also
launched a demonstration release of its new software tool for reviewing and analyzing
the interactive data filings thus far submitted by a number of U.S. public companies.

Technology Solutions   In the post-SOX era, companies, their accountants, and
their auditors are searching for any technology solutions or tools that can assist
them in complying with provisions of SOX. Several XBRL solutions have been
suggested and/or developed to improve and simplify the use of XBRL in business
and financial reporting:

- A PDF document containing embedded XBRL for the U.S. GAAP or any
  other XBRL taxonomy is paving the way toward successful implementation of
  electronic financial reporting. Embedding XBRL with PDF enables organizations
  to create a single document, which makes compliance and regulatory filing
  possible through system-to-system filings simultaneously.
- The Microsoft Office tool for XBRL is now available to be used with Microsoft
  Office Professional Edition 2003, particularly Microsoft Office Word 2003
  and Microsoft Office Excel 2003, to create and analyze documents in XBRL
  format.[57]
- Financial Reporting and Auditing Agent with New Knowledge (FRAANK)
  has been developed to provide integrated and automated access to financial
  information available on the Internet.[58] FRAANK enables organizations to:

○ Extract accounting numbers from natural-text financial statements available from the SEC EDGAR system.
○ Develop an understanding of financial information and accounting numbers by matching the line-item labels to synonyms of tags in an XBRL taxonomy.
○ Convert the consolidated financial statements, including the balance sheet, income statement, and statement of cash flows, into XBRL-tagged format.
○ Integrate the accounting numbers with other financial information publicly available on the Internet, including stock quotes and analysts earnings forecasts.[59]

Continuous Auditing

Technological advances enable corporations to conduct a material portion of their transactions online and prepare their financial statements electronically and, eventually, on a real-time basis using the XBRL format. In a real-time accounting system using XBRL taxonomies, the traditional source documents, such as purchase orders, sales inventories, and checks, are replaced with electronic messages, and much of the financial information and related audit evidence is available only in electronic form for a certain period of time.[60] The use of electronic, real-time, XBRL-format financial reporting processes by clients necessitates that auditors utilize a continuous auditing approach. Continuous auditing is defined as "a comprehensive electronic audit process that enables auditors to provide some degree of assurance on continuous information simultaneously with, or shortly after, the disclosure of the information."[61] This definition is comprehensive and covers all professional services provided by auditors to their clients, including review, attestation, and audit services. Continuous auditing enables auditors to use the integrated audit approach of both an audit of internal control over financial reporting and an audit of financial statements. Continuous auditing can offer four benefits:

1. Reduce the cost of an audit engagement by enabling auditors to test a larger sample of a client's transactions.
2. Reduce the amount of audit resources needed to manually perform tests of controls and substantive tests.
3. Increase the quality of financial statement audits by allowing auditors to use the integrated audit approach of understanding the client corporate-level controls.
4. Specify transaction selection criteria to choose transactions or transaction cycles and perform integrated audits.[62]

The 2006 survey of PricewaterhouseCoopers reveals that: (1) half of the surveyed U.S. companies are using continuing auditing techniques in 2006, which is up 35 percent from that of 2005; (2) of those companies that do not yet have continuous auditing techniques in place, more than 31 percent have implemented plans to do so.[63] This significant increase in the use of continuous auditing techniques will eventually change the way both internal and external auditors have traditionally conducted the audit. On May 25, 2005, the PCAOB released staff questions and answers regarding XBRL attest engagements based on data furnished to the SEC under the XBRL Voluntary Financial Reporting Program on the EDGAR system.[64] The PCAOB's guidance addresses the audit report on whether XBRL data accurately reflects the corresponding financial information. Currently the voluntary XBRL program does not require companies to obtain auditor assurance on XBRL data. However, the PCAOB's staff questions and answers provide guidance on the application of PCAOB's attestation standards to auditors engaged in performing attestations to XBRL data for companies seeking to obtain assurances. On August 15, 2006, the International Accounting Education Standards Board (IAESB) of the International Federation of Accountants (IFAC) proposed new guidance to assist professional accountants worldwide to meet ongoing and ever-changing technology challenges.[65] The proposed guidance outlines the knowledge and skills necessary to prepare accountants to perform competently in one or more information technology roles, including: (1) assurance provider or information systems auditor; (2) manager of information systems; and (3) designer of business systems.[66]

The American Institute of Certified Public Accountants (AICPA), in its AT 101, *Interpretation Attest Engagements of Financial Information*, included in XBRL instance documents, addresses practitioners' considerations when they are engaged to examine and report on XBRL data.[67] The AICPA has taken initiatives on both XBRL and the Enhanced Business Reporting (EBR) project. To provide better coordination between the two projects, the AICPA has combined them under one assurance services executive committee. Practitioners (certified public accountants) may be engaged to examine and report on whether the XBRL instance document accurately reflects the financial information provided through the XBRL tag process, which also may include reference to other financial items in a PDF format.

SUMMARY

Globalization and technological advances have made the world "flat" by enabling corporations, organizations, and individuals worldwide to conduct their business electronically using the Internet. The ever-increasing use of e-commerce encourages companies to utilize electronic financial reporting, such as XBRL format, to produce and disseminate financial reports and independent auditors to employ continuous auditing methodologies to conduct audits. Thus, IT is expected to influence all seven functions of corporate governance discussed in Chapter 2 and, particularly, Chapters 3 to 10.

NOTES

1. PricewaterhouseCoopers. 2005. Compliance and technology: A special report on process improvement and automation in the age of Sarbanes-Oxley. (August 11). Available at: www.pwc.com/extweb/pwcpublications.nsf/docid/9B5A0370 D3722DE98525704B003B9357.

2. Increasing globalization of capital markets. Serving global capital markets and the global economy: A View from the CEOs of the International Audit Networks (November 2006).
3. These four factors are used in Standard & Poor's Corporate Governance Scores in ranking corporate governance both at a country and at a company level. Available at: www.standardandpoors.com/NASAPP/cs/contentserve?pay.
4. LaPorta, R., F. Lopez-de-Silanes, A. Shleifer, and R. Vishny. 1997. Legal determinants of external finance. *Journal of Finance* (52): 1131–1150.
5. American Bar Association. 2002. Special study on market structure listing standards and corporate governance. A special study group of the Committee on Federal Regulation of Securities. American Bar Association, Section of Business Law (August). *57 Business Law.* 1487.
6. LaPorta, et al. 1997. Legal determinants of external finance.
7. PricewaterhouseCoopers. 2005. *World Watch: Governance and Corporate Reporting.* Iss. 1. Available at: www.pwc.com/extweb/pwcpublications.nsf/docid/f031ba1c684f50b980256fb10036400d/$file/World_Watch_Issue1_2005.pdf.
8. U.S. Securities and Exchange Commission (SEC). 2006. SEC votes to repropose rules allowing foreign private issuer deregistration under the Exchange Act (December 13). Available at: www.sec.gov/news/press/2006/2006-207.htm.
9. Ibid.
10. Ibid.
11. Staffin, E. Speech by SEC Staff: Opening Remarks at the SEC Open Meeting (December 13). Available at: www.sec.gov/news/speech/2006/spch121306es.htm.
12. Norris, F. 2006. S.E.C. to firms: Keep money. Forget rules. *New York Times* (December 15). Available at: www.nytimes.com.
13. Ibid.
14. Deloitte & Touche. 2003. Audit committee resource guide. (February). Available at: www.us.deloitte.com.
15. SEC Release No. 34-53020. 2005. Termination of a Foreign Private Issuer's Registration of a Class of Securities Under Section 12(g) and Duty to File Reports Under Section 15(d) of the Securities Exchange Act of 1934. (December 5). Available at: www.sec.gov/rules/proposed/proposedarchive/proposed2005.shtml.
16. Ibid.
17. Friedman, T. L. 2005. *The world is flat: A brief history of the twenty-first century.* New York: Farrar Straus & Giroux.
18. PricewaterhouseCoopers. 2006. 9th annual global CEO survey: Globalization and complexity. Available at: www.pwc.com.
19. Glassman, C. A. 2005. The SEC in a global market place: Current issues. Remarks before the Center for the Study of International Business Review. Breakfast Roundtable Services. (October 7). New York. Available at: www.sec.gov/news/speech/spch100705cag.htm.
20. Ibid.
21. Ibid.

22. European Commission. 2005. The Council Agreement on the 8th company law directive on statutory audit (October 11). IP/05/1249. Available at: europa.ue.int/comm/internal_market/auditing/index.

23. Ibid.

24. United Nations Environment Programme Finance Initiative and the UN Global Compact. 2006. Principles for responsible investment. (April 27). Available at: www.unepfi.org/principles or www.unglobalcompact.org/principles.

25. Ibid.

26. Ibid.

27. Ibid.

28. International Accounting Standard Board. International Accounting Standards (IAS) No. 27: *Consolidated and Separate Financial Statements*. Available at: www.iasb.org/standards/summaries.asp.

29. PricewaterhouseCoopers. 2006. Trendsetter Barometer (October 11). Available at: www.cfodirect.pwc.com/CFODirectweb/controller.jpf?contentcode= FASE-6UE.htm.

30. Canadian Institute of Chartered Accountants. 2005. Aligning investment information technology with business strategy: What CFOs need to consider. Information Technology Advisory Committee (June). Available at: www.cicar.ca.ifac.

31. Ibid.

32. Ibid.

33. Securities and Exchange Commission. 2005. XBRL voluntary financial reporting program on the EDGAR system. (February 3). Available at: www.sec.gov/rules/final/33-8529.htm.

34. U.K. Department of Trade and Industry. 2005. The proposed Corporate Reform Bill. (March). Available at: www.dti.gov.uk.

35. Securities and Exchange Commission. 2005. SEC votes to propose rule to provide the investor with Internet availability of proxy materials. (November 29). Available at: www.sec.gov/news/press/2005_166.htm.

36. Rezaee, Z. 2002. *Financial statement fraud: Prevention and detection*. Hoboken, NJ: John Wiley & Sons. Chapter 13.

37. Ibid.

38. PricewaterhouseCoopers. 2005. U.S. multinationals look to technology for improvements in future Sarbanes 404 efforts. PwC's Management Barometer. (October 6). Available at: www.cfodirect.com/cfopublic.nsf.

39. Ibid.

40. PricewaterhouseCoopers. 2005. Technology executive connections: Embracing change in the technology industries. (October 6). Available at: www.cfadirect.com/CFOPrivate.nsf.

41. XBRL International. Available at: www.xbrl.org.

42. Organizations interested in the emerging developments of XBRL taxonomies, tools, and solutions should visit the XBRL Web site at: www.xbrl.org.

43. Canadian Institute of Chartered Accountants. 2005. Information technology advisory committee: Audit & control implications of XBRL. (December). Available at: www.cica.ca.itac.

44. eXtensible Business Reporting Language. 2006. XBRL International forms standards board to strengthen its technical output. (April 4). Available at: www.xbrl.org/Announcements/XSB-PR-final-4April2006.htm.

45. Securities and Exchange Commission. 2004. Comments on proposed rule: XBRL voluntary financial reporting program on the Edgar system. Available at: www.sec.gov/rules/proposed/s73504.shtml.

46. Ibid.

47. Securities and Exchange Commission. 2005. XBRL—Voluntary financial reporting program on the EDGAR system. Available at: www.sec.gov/answers/xbrl.htm.

48. Ibid.

49. Sinnett, W. M. 2006. XBRL: A "revolution" in corporate reporting? (March 2). Available at: www.cfodirect.com/CFOPrivate.nsf/vContentPrint/EFA90A67.htm.

50. Ibid.

51. Accounting Web. 2005. A closer look at the first mandatory e-filing system using XBRL. (September 1). Available at: www.accountingweb.com/cgi-bin/item.cgi?id=101260.

52. Ibid.

53. Cox, C. 2005. Speech at the 12th XBRL International Conference. Tokyo. November 7. Available at: www.sec.gov/news/speech/spch110705cc.htm.

54. Securities and Exchange Commission. 2006. SEC offers incentive for companies to file financial reports with interactive data. (January 11). Available at: www.sec.gov/news/press/2006-7.htm.

55. eXtensible Business Reporting Language (XBRL). 2006. XBRL-US to become independent organization (September 25). Available at: www.xbrl.org/us.

56. Cox, C. 2006. Speech by SEC chairman: The promise of interactive data (December 5). Available at: www.sec.gov/news/speech/2006/spch120506cc.htm.

57. Microsoft Office Online. (2005). Improving financial analysis and reporting using XBRL and the Microsoft Office System. Available at: www.microsoft.com/office/solutions/xbrl/defalt.mspx.

58. Bovee, M., A. Kogan, K. Nelson, R. P. Srivastava, and M. A. Versarhelyi. 2005. Financial Reporting and Auditing Agent with Net Knowledge (FRAANK) and Extensible Business Reporting Language (XBRL). *Journal of Information Systems* 19(1) (Spring): 1–18.

59. Ibid.

60. Rezaee, Z. A. Sharbatoghlic, R. Elam, and P. L. McMickle. 2002. Continuous auditing: Building automated auditing capability. *Auditing: A Journal of Practice and Theory* 21(1) (March): 147, 163.

61. Ibid.

62. Ibid.

63. PricewaterhouseCoopers (PwC). 2006. PwC's 2006 State of the Internal Audit Profession Study: Continuous Auditing Gains Momentum (June 27). Available at: www.pwc.com.

64. Public Company Accounting Oversight Board. 2005. Attest engagements regarding XBRL financial information furnished under the XBRL Voluntary Financial

Reporting Program on the Edgar system. (May 25). Available at: www.pcaobus.org/Standards/Staff_Questions_and_Answers/index.asp.

65. International Accounting Education Standards Board. 2006. Proposed guidance and information technology for professional accountants. (August). Available at: www.ifac.org/EDs.

66. Ibid.

67. American Institute of Certified Public Accountants. 2003. AT 101 interpretation attest engagements on financial information included in XBRL instance documents. (September). Available at: www.pwccomperio.com/contents/english/external/us/ps/at9101.htm.

CHAPTER 14

Corporate Governance Emerging Issues

INTRODUCTION

The Committee for Economic Development (CED), which is regarded as a public-policy organization and consists of current and retired business leaders, identifies four challenges facing corporate America in the post–Sarbanes-Oxley (SOX) era: (1) presentation of key financial and nonfinancial Performance indicators of public companies; (2) assurance on independent and fair audit process; (3) executive compensation; and (4) nomination and election of corporate boards. This chapter presents these and other corporate governance emerging issues, including challenges, opportunities, and improvements, along with the author's suggestions. The issues presented in this chapter are classified into sections pertaining to:

- Investor confidence and global markets.
- Multiple bottom-line performance and reporting in areas of corporate governance and social, ethical, and environmental activities.
- The corporate governance structure, including director independence diversity,and accountabilty, shareholder challenges, and executive compensation.
- Internal controls and risk management, including Section 404 compliance.
- Financial reporting, including complexity, transparency, and convergence in financial reporting standards and stock option expensing, pension liability recognition, electronic financial reporting, and financial reporting disclosure.
- Audit function, including integrated audit procedures and reports, liability caps, and fraud auditing.

INVESTOR CONFIDENCE AND GLOBAL FINANCIAL MARKETS

Investor confidence in global financial markets is the key driver of economic growth, global competition, and financial stability in the sense that when confidence increases, consumers buy more goods, and investors are willing to invest at prevailing prices. This is a complex issue with no worldwide, well-established indicator. Generally speaking, investors are considered confident when stock prices are on an upward trend and the news about future stock performance is optimistic. The fear of terrorist attacks, the economic downturn in many countries, instability in the governments of some countries, and the bad news of pervasive global financial scandals, have eroded investor confidence in global financial markets.

Technological advances and global competition have enabled companies and their investors to "largely meet in the jurisdiction of their choosing... [they] have choices about where to invest, where to raise capital, and where secondary trading is to occur."[1] Thus, companies can choose the regulatory regime they desire to operate under, and investors have a choice of safeguards and protections provided under different regulatory reforms. Effective regulatory reform creates an environment under which companies can operate in achieving sustainable performance, being held accountable for their activities, and providing protections for their investors. Regulatory reforms, in terms of their effectiveness and context, can be classified into three concepts of: (1) a race to the bottom; (2) a race to optimality; and (3) a race to the top.[2] The race-to-the-bottom concept suggests that global securities regulators, in an effort to attract issuers, deregulate to the point that issuers are provided with maximum flexibility for their operations at the expense of not securing adequate protections for investors. The race-to-the-top concept suggests that global securities regulators provide maximum protection for investors through rigid regulations and highly scrutinized enforcements at the expense of putting globally competing companies at a disadvantage with noncost-justified regulations. The race-to-optimality concept is a hybrid of the first two concepts, in which both issuers (companies) and investors prefer a regulatory regime and jurisdiction that provides cost-justified investor protection. In real-world global competition, a combination of these three concepts may work best, as many provisions of SOX have been globally adopted.

Global Financial Markets

More than three-quarters of the 184 members of the International Monetary Fund (IMF) have experienced financial crisis, including the 1997–98 Asian crisis.[3] These crises have continued into the twenty-first century. The IMF and World Bank have assessed the strength of financial regulations in member countries and have set forth standards and prerequisite conditions for access to IMF funds. Globalization and information technology (IT) create profound challenges for businesses and regulators to protect investors worldwide. The speed with which financial transactions can be conducted and money can be moved around the world encourages regulators to establish global financial infrastructure and corporate governance.

A report published by PricewaterhouseCoopers (PwC), entitled *The World in 2050*, projects the relative size of the 17 largest economies in the world in terms of their purchasing power parity (PPP) and market exchange rate (MER) in the period from 2005 to 2050.[4] The 17 largest economies in the world are composed of the so-called G7 countries of the United States, Japan, the United Kingdom,

Germany, France, Italy, and Canada, plus Spain, Australia, and South Korea, and the seven emerging market economies of the E7, including China, India, Brazil, Russia, Turkey, Mexico, and Indonesia. The report concludes that:

- There is no single right way to measure the relative size of the E7 as compared to the established G7 (Organization for Economic Co-operation and Development [OECD] economies).
- As of 2005, the E7 are about 20 percent of the size of the G7 at MER and about 75 percent of the size in PPP terms.
- By the year 2050, the E7 will be about 25 percent larger than the current G7.
- Within the E7, both China and Russia are expected to experience substantial declines in their working-age population between 2005 and 2050; India, Indonesia, Brazil, Mexico, and Turkey are expected to experience a significant increase in their working-age population over this period.
- India is expected to be the fastest-growing large economy in the world over the period to 2050, with a projected gross domestic product (GDP) of about 60 percent of that of the United States in terms of MER and close to 100 percent of that of the United States in terms of PPP.
- China is projected to be about 95 percent of the size of the United States at MER by 2050 and about 40 percent larger in terms of PPP.[5]

A 2006 PwC survey reveals that the majority of the 1300 surveyed directors (52 percent) say that China is the most discussed emerging market by boards, followed by India (38 percent) and Brazil (11 percent).[6] Standard & Poor's conducted ratings of European companies in the past two decades and documented three key findings: (1) corporate Europe still remains predominantly investment grade with the "A" rating category in 2006 compared with "AA" rating 15 years ago; (2) the proportion of companies rated with speculative grade in Europe is about 19 percent compared with the comparable ratio of 49 percent in the United States; (3) continuing changes in corporate risk orientation have caused the declining prominence of "AAA" for companies both in the United States and Europe.[7]

After many decades of European and American domination of global markets, trades and investments are now flowing between the Middle East and Asia. With oil prices riding high, Middle Eastern countries and their investors and companies have funds to invest and Asian countries have the capabilities to attract such investments. It is inevitable that governments in both Asia and the Middle East will create a more hospitable business and investment climate, allowing investments to reach their global potential. Islamic financial resources are estimated to be more than $200 billion. The total savings of 60 percent of the world's 1.2 billion Muslims are expected to be managed in compliance with Shariah law, which practically prohibits interest-bearing notes or interest being earned in bank accounts.[8] The Accounting and Auditing Organization for Islamic Financial Institutions (AAOIFI) has started to establish international Islamic accounting and auditing for Islamic financial services and businesses since the International Organization of Securities Commissions (IOSCO) acknowledged that international accounting standards and generally accepted accounting principles (GAAP) do not adequately address and capture Islamic transactions.[9] These emerging changes have significant implications for countries' political, economic, and business infrastructures worldwide. Sir Howard Davies, a director of the London School of Economics and former chairman of the U.K. Financial Services Authority, provides this advice to all emerging countries participating in global business and financial markets:[10]

1. *Make a strategic decision on whether to participate in global competitive markets with their overwhelming rules, regulations, and measures.*
2. *Establish independent institutions for developing proper regulations which are minimally influenced by the political process.*
3. *Separate central banking from banking and financial supervision.*
4. *Decide on a regulatory structure that best serves the country's business and financial products as either a single regulator for all financial services or separate regulators for banking, insurance, and securities.*
5. *Acquire and train skilled and independent regulatory staff and, when warranted, seek technical assistance from more developed countries.*
6. *Establish a strategy to improve and update corporate governance and disclosure policies.*

The IMF, the World Bank, the Basel Committee for Banking Supervision, the OECD, IOSCO, and U.S. regulations (SOX and SEC rules) have taken initiatives to improve global corporate governance and provide guidance and sources of supervisory standards for national and international business and financial markets. Thus, countries and their companies that conduct business in global markets have to comply with global standards of regulations and guidance provided by those organizations. Several initiatives have been taken in an attempt to roll back some provisions of SOX despite the continuing corporate scandals. An article published on November 1, 2006, points out the possibility of London taking over New York's current standing as the global financial capital and states the perceived overregulation (SOX) is a contributing factor to that change.[11] Traditionally, New York has provided the broadest, most efficient, and most liquid capital markets worldwide and the most prosperous business environment for all businesses, particularly financial firms. The article argues four factors that shape the global financial markets: globalization, overregulation, frivolous litigation, and incompatible accounting standards. The first factor, globalization of the capital markets, will continue to play a major role as advances in technology and communication enable the establishment of financial markets anywhere in the world and more free flow of capital worldwide. The other three factors deserve more attention from U.S. lawmakers, regulators, and standards setters. First, it appears that the seeming overregulation in the United States is putting U.S. markets at a global competitive disadvantage as: (1) there are more than ten federal, state, and industry regulatory bodies in the United States compared to only one such body in the United Kingdom; (2) the British regulatory body appears to be more collaborative and solutions oriented than its counterparts in the United States; and (3) it has been estimated that the gross financial regulatory reforms driven by SOX need to be revisited to promote the best practices of reducing frivolous lawsuits without eliminating meritorious ones. Finally, convergence to international accounting standards needs to be expedited.

Globalization along with higher compliance costs of corporate governance reforms in the United States have made the London and Hong Kong exchanges more favorable for investors in general and initial public offerings (IPOs) in particular. Capital is attracted to the most efficient, safe, prosperous, and cost-effective global exchanges, and it remains there as long as it is fairly treated. Several factors have contributed to the shift to global exchanges rather than U.S. exchanges including: (1) global markets are more aggressive in pursuing start-up companies and facilitating their IPOs; (2) global markets are more responsive to the needs of smaller companies by getting global investors interested in their listed companies and by providing proper analyst coverage for them; (3) the cost of compliance with listing requirements in the global markets is relatively lower than that of the U.S. capital market; in particular, underwriting fees from investment banks in the United States are about 7 percent compared to less than 4 percent in the United Kingdom; and (4) the global perception is that the United States is politically and culturally adverse to the international market system.[12]

Globalization of capital markets is evidenced by mergers of global stock exchanges, including the recent merger of the NYSE and Euronext and the potential merger of Nasdaq and the London Stock Exchange, which create challenges and opportunities for the U.S. capital markets, policymakers, and regulators that should be properly addressed. For example, in the absence of an agreement amongst the global regulatory bodies (SEC, EC), non-U.S. exchanges may be able to convince companies worldwide to list on their markets to avoid the compliance costs of SOX. NYSE's chief executive officer (CEO), John Thain, said:

> *A partnership with Euronext fulfills our shared vision of building a truly global marketplace with great breadth of product and geographic reach that will benefit all investors, issuers, and our shareholders and stakeholders.*[13]

The merged NYSE Euronext created the first trans-Atlantic exchange and the world's largest and most liquid global securities with about $28.5 trillion total market capitalization. The author suggests that U.S. regulators and their counterparts in Europe and on other continents work together to assess the possibility and feasibility of convergence in global capital markets to improve their efficiency, effectiveness, safety, and integrity and to prevent a global crisis that would eventually affect the economies and financial markets of countries worldwide.

A report coauthored by Michael R. Bloomberg, the mayor of New York, and Senator Charles E. Schumer (D-NY) makes these recommendations to ensure the future competitiveness of U.S. and New York financial services:

- *Provide clear guidance for implementing the Sarbanes-Oxley Act.* The SEC and the Public Company Accounting Oversight Board (PCAOB), in implementing provisions of SOX, must ensure that their implementation rules and related auditing standards are cost-justifiable, efficient, and scalable.
- *Implement securities litigation reform.* Legislative reform and the SEC's rules should address the long-term structural problems that underpin the trend

toward increasing litigation in the securities industry to reduce overall legal burden on listed companies.

- *Develop a shared vision for financial services and a set of supporting regulatory principles.* These principles should be aimed toward maintaining U.S. global competitiveness, promoting innovation to meet customer needs, improving the management of systemic risks, fostering the ethical conduct of business, enhancing the financing of a growing economy, and contributing to the creation of new jobs.
- *Ease restrictions facing skilled non-U.S. professional workers.* Skilled professional workers worldwide should be welcomed and encouraged to join the U.S. workforce.
- *Recognize International Financial Reporting Standards (IFRS) without reconciliation and promote the convergence of accounting and auditing standards.* The U.S. FASB and PCAOB should work with their international counterparts toward ultimate convergence in accounting and auditing standards.
- *Protect U.S. global competitiveness in implementing the Basel II Capital Accord.* U.S. banking institutions should implement the Basel II Capital Accord in requiring U.S. banks capital at the same level as their non-U.S. peers by protecting the structural integrity of the U.S. financial system while preserving the global competitiveness of U.S. banks.
- *Form an independent, bipartisan National commission on financial market competitiveness to resolve long-term structural issues.* The commission should study and assess long-term structural issues that affect the sustainability, health, competitiveness, and leadership of U.S. financial markets and their contribution to the national economy.
- *Modernize financial services charters.* U.S. policymakers and regulators should assess and, where appropriate, modernize U.S. financial services charters, holding company models, and operating structure to ensure they are competitive by international standards.[14]

The U.S. financial markets have traditionally been the world's largest, deepest, vibrant, and most liquid. To maintain this global leadership and competitiveness, U.S. policymakers, regulators, standard setters, and private and public businesses should address emerging global governance and structural issues presented throughout this book and consider best practices of other nations.

Corporate Governance in the Post-SOX Era

A 2005 survey of boards of Standard & Poor's (S&P) 500 companies reveals that much progress has been made in corporate governance in the post-SOX era, but there is still room for improvement.[15] Progress has been made in these areas of corporate governance:

- Many boards have moved beyond mere compliance with applicable regulations and now engage more proactively in independent stewardship and accountability.

- The overall makeup of boards is more independent. More than 40 percent of boards have only one nonindependent director (the CEO), and the median number of inside directors is two compared with four nearly 20 years ago.
- All mandatory board committees (audit, compensation, nomination/governance) are composed of independent directors.
- The supermajority (94 percent) of boards have designated an independent lead or presiding director in order to improve the independence of board leadership.
- The lead or presiding director has made independent directors more accountable for and invested in oversight functions.
- CEO succession has been addressed more proactively by the board of directors.
- Institutional investors are more engaged in effective monitoring of corporations by approaching the board directly to voice their governance concerns.
- Some boards implemented best practices of corporate governance above and beyond mere compliance with rules and regulations (e.g., change to majority voting systems).[16]

The substantial decrease in investor lawsuits has been interpreted as a sign of improvements in corporate governance and accountability for corporate America in 2005, and a sign that the emerging reforms (SOX, SEC rules, listing standards, and best practices) are working and making positive impacts on American businesses. Such a decline can also be attributed to a less volatile stock market in 2005, passage of time since reported high-profile scandals, economic recovery since the economic downturn of the early 2000s, and significant decline (141 percent) in cases brought before the Ninth U.S. Circuit Court of Appeals, which covers California, home to many technology companies.

Regulatory reforms, including SOX in the United States, are aimed at protecting investors who have provided both U.S. and non-U.S. businesses with the lowest cost of equity capital in the world.[17] This is made possible in the United States for three reasons:

1. Individual investors in the United States have provided companies with low-cost and long-term funding at a level unparalleled in any other country.
2. The high level of investor protection provided through regulations in the United States has promoted the cross-listing premium offered in the U.S. capital markets.
3. The benefits of the low cost of equity capital in the United States exceed compliance costs associated with investor protection laws.[18]

Corporate governance practices that need much more improvement are:

- *Shareholder democracy.* Shareholders' ready access to companies' proxies in order to put forward director nominees and other resolutions has received considerable interest from shareholder activists and has been the focus of a couple of court cases. The Second Circuit U.S. Court of Appeals ruled that the SEC was wrong to block an attempt by the American Federation of State, County and Municipal Employees (AFSCME) to include a shareholder proposal on the company proxy. The SEC staff sided with AIG attempts to exclude shareholder proposals concerning director elections from its proxy materials. Shareholder democracy is discussed further in the next section.

- *The separation of the chair of the board and the CEO roles.* Only about 30 percent of S&P 500 companies split the CEO/chairman position, and, of them, only 9 percent have a truly independent chair. (In the other cases, the new chair is the former CEO or is connected to management.)
- *Narrower definition of "financial expert."* Although the number of audit committee members designated as financial experts has increased substantially (the majority of boards now identify more than one financial expert on the audit committee), the quality of their financial expertise is undermined due to the acceptance of a broad definition of a financial expert.
- *Board diversity in terms of expertise, race, and gender.* About 12 percent of boards still have no female directors, and women continue to make up only 15 percent of all independent directors. In addition, the recruitment of active CEOs or chief operating officers (COOs) as directors is becoming more difficult.
- *A trend toward boards with fewer directors.* The average board size in 2005 was 10.7 directors compared with 12 directors in 1998.
- *The requirement that all mandated board committees (audit, compensation, and nomination) be composed of at least three independent directors and 75 percent of all directors be independent.* This trend suggests that an ideal board size is 12 directors, particularly for large companies.
- *Ambiguous definition of director liability.* The personal liability of directors needs to be addressed in light of developments in cases that involved directors of Enron, WorldCom, and Disney.
- *Executive compensation reforms.* The year 2006 is regarded as the period of executive compensation scrutiny and reforms. The SEC rules require more relevant and transparent disclosure of executive pay, including the total compensation figure, incentive stock- and options-based rewards, pensions and other postemployment benefits (OPEB) plans, and perquisites, for the company's CEO, CFO, and the three other highest-paid executive officers as well as directors. These rules also require a new compensation discussion and analysis (CD&A) to replace the current compensation committee report and performance graph. Public companies should require a shareholder advisory vote on their executive compensation.

The Committee for Economic Development (CED), in March 2006, published its recommendations for improving corporate governance in the post-SOX era.[19] Its recommendations are:

- *Ensure that audit committees are autonomous and vigorous.* The company's board of directors, particularly the audit committee, should be competent and independent, have access to all pertinent data, and oversee financial reporting and both internal and external audit activities.
- *Inform users of financial statements, particularly investors, that financial information is inherently judgmental.* Public companies should inform and educate the investing public, stock analysts, regulators, and other users of financial

reports that financial statements are based on judgments. To improve these judgments, companies should:

- ○ Provide ranges of values rather than precise numbers.
- ○ Use fewer rules and more principles.
- ○ Present both financial and nonfinancial information on key indicators.

■ *Give Sarbanes-Oxley a chance to work.* Many provisions of SOX have proven to be relevant and effective in improving corporate accountability and enhancing the professional responsibility of individuals involved in the financial reporting process (e.g., board of directors, audit committees, management, external auditors, internal auditors, legal counsel, and financial advisors). Although small companies should not be exempted from SOX's provisions, the SEC and the PCAOB should consider compliance costs associated with issuing rules to implement provisions of SOX, particularly for smaller companies.

■ *Tame excessive executive compensation.* The widening disparity of income between top corporate executives and average employees (400 to 1) has raised serious concerns that executive compensation often reflects neither market conditions nor individual performance.

■ *Use independent nominating committees to select and evaluate directors.* An independent nominating committee should be directly responsible for recommending and nominating new board candidates, recommending committee assignments, and evaluating the performance of directors.[20]

Global Corporate Governance

Several differences exist between the U.S. and European models of corporate governance. The most significant differences are:

1. *Definition of corporate governance.* Corporate governance in the United States primarily focuses on aligning the interests of management with those of the shareholders. In contrast, European corporate governance emphasizes the protection of all stakeholders' interests, including shareholders, and particularly alignment of interests of controlling shareholders with those of minority or individual shareholders.

2. *Dispersed vs. concentrated ownership.* The capital ownership structure in the U.S. is more dispersed as about 100 million Americans own shares of public companies through direct or managed ownership. Conversely, capital ownership in Europe is more concentrated with majority ownership and controlling shareholders. Thus, corporate governance mechanisms in Europe are designed to protect the rights of minority individual shareholders and protect divergent controlling shareholders.

3. *Fiduciary duties.* The so-called Anglo-Saxon legal regime in both the U.S. and U.K. establishes an enforceable set of fiduciary duties for directors to act as agents in the best interest of both controlling and minority shareholders. In civil law countries (most of Europe) the fiduciary principle is not well developed and thus the rules-based approach often allows controlling shareholders to extract private benefits at the expense of individual or minority shareholders.

4. *Regulator-led vs. shareholder-led approach.* The U.S. disclosure system is viewed as a regulator-led approach in the sense that state statutes enact laws pertaining to corporate governance matters and federal statutes establish rules regarding disclosures and other matters relevant to public companies. Conversely, the U.K. promotes shareholder monitoring, giving the appearance that shareholders have more rights in the U.K. than in the U.S. regarding director nomination and election as well as major business transactions.

5. *Plurality vs. majority voting.* The board election process in the U.S. is governed by plurality voting by shareholders coupled with limited ability to even nominate director candidates. Conversely, in the U.K. and other European countries, directors are elected by simple majority voting, which empowers shareholders to remove incompetent and unethical directors at annual or extraordinary meetings. Shareholders in the U.S. are lagging behind their counterparts in Europe to have access to proxy materials for the nomination of director candidates to vote against underperforming directors and to have advisory votes in approving executive compensation.

6. *Different types of fraud.* Different capital ownership systems, namely dispersed vs. concentrated, may be susceptible to different types of fraud. The U.S. dispersed ownership structure is more prone to short-term earnings management and quarterly reporting fraud perpetrated to overstate earnings to influence stock prices and increase the value of executive stock options. Conversely, in Europe, shareholders are concerned about the extraction of private benefits from the company and its controlling shareholders to the detriment of minority shareholders.[21]

Several initiatives have been taken during the past decade to improve corporate governance worldwide. Many of these initiatives addressing improvements in corporate governance are primarily national. No globally accepted set of corporate governance principles or global regulatory framework governs corporations, global financial institutions, or capital markets worldwide. Regulators in the United States, the SEC, IOSCO, and the World Federation of Exchanges (WFE) have yet to agree on a global regulatory framework or a global corporate governance structure. The OECD's international standards of corporate governance have not achieved global acceptance to be included in the global regulatory framework.

The International Corporate Governance Network (ICGN) was founded in 1995 by institutional investors, companies, financial intermediaries, academics, and other parties interested in the establishment of global corporate governance practices.[22] The ICGN adopted corporate governance principles developed by the OECD as minimum acceptable standards for companies and investors worldwide and highly recommends that companies use the adopted principles as best practices. In July 2005 the ICGN revised its Global Corporate Governance Principles, as summarized in Exhibit 14.1. The ICGN's principles are comprehensive enough to be applicable to corporations throughout the world. However, companies worldwide should establish their own corporate governance code comparable to ICGN principles and tailored to their political, cultural, economic, legal, and regulatory environment. The author suggests that global corporate governance principles address governance, social, environmental, and ethics performance of companies, in addition to their economic performance, also known as multiple bottom lines (MBL).

MULTIPLE BOTTOM LINES PERFORMANCE AND REPORTING

Responsible investment (RI), commonly referred to as socially responsible investment (SRI), focuses on multiple bottom lines (MBL) performance of companies in the areas of economic, ethical, environmental, corporate governance, and social activities. The Global Reporting Initiative (GRI) is planning to release its third version (G3) of nonfinancial reporting guidelines, which provides a framework to report on economic, environmental, and social performance.[23] Currently, about 750 companies worldwide are using the GRI guidelines, and it is expected that about 5,000 companies will begin using them.

Investors who pay attention to company MBL believe that these factors affect their investments and decisions, and, thus, they should be properly managed. A survey conducted by Mercer Investment Consulting indicates:

- Moderate growth in SRI strategies in the next two years with participation by responding investors is expected to increase from 22 percent to 28 percent.
- The majority of investors who pursue an SRI approach believe that it will reduce risk and improve returns.
- The majority of participating investors feels that environmental, social, ethical, and corporate governance factors are very important in their investment decisions.[24]

An interesting article in the *Wall Street Journal*, written by former Vice President Al Gore and David Blood, underscores the importance of the sustainability reporting of corporate MBL performance. The article states:

Capitalism and sustainability are deeply and increasingly interrelated. After all, our economic activity is based on the use of natural and human resources. Not until we more broadly "price" in the external costs of investment decisions across all sectors will we have a sustainable economy and society. . . . The interests of shareholders, over time, will be best served by companies that maximize their financial performance by strategically managing their economic, social, environmental and ethical performance.[25]

There has been a growing international interest in MBL performance reporting, including environmental, social, and governance (ESG) issues.[26] The ESG issues can influence the performance of investment portfolios and, thus, should be considered in assessing investment decisions and ownership practices. To address this important global issue, in 2005 the United Nations Secretary-General invited a group of representatives from 20 investment organizations in 12 countries to establish a

EXHIBIT 14.1 International Corporate Governance Network Statement on Global Corporate Governance Principles

Corporate Objective—Shareholder Returns
Optimizing Return to Shareholders
A corporation's overall objective should be to maximize shareholder returns over
  time.
Long-Term Prosperity of the Business
This can be achieved through structuring and implementing a strategy to improve
  the corporate equity.

Disclosure and Transparency
Objective
Relevant and material information should be disclosed on a timely basis to provide
  shareholders with enough facts to make informed decisions.
Disclosure of Ownership and Voting Rights
Outside information disclosures, such as a description of the relationship of the
  company to other companies in the corporate group, data on major shareholders
  and others that control or may control the company, and information on
  differential voting rights and related party transactions, are recommended.

Audit
Accounting Principles
ICGN supports the development of a complete and high-quality set of international
  accounting and financial reporting standards.
Audit Independence
Annual audits should be completed on the behalf of shareholders by independent,
  external auditors chosen by the audit committee and approved by shareholders.
Annual Audit
The audit should provide an external and objective opinion stating whether the
  financial statements are a fair representation of the company.
Scope of Audit
The law determines the scope of an audit, dependent on the shareholders right to
  expand that scope.
Approval of Financial Statements and Internal Controls
The board of directors and the appropriate officers of the corporation should attest,
  on at least an annual basis, to the accuracy of the company's financial statements
  or financial accounts and the adequacy of its internal controls.

Shareholders' Ownership, Responsibilities and Voting Rights and Remedies
Shareholder Ownership Rights
Shareholders should not be restricted in their exercising ownership rights.
Protections
Boards should not discriminate among any shareholders.

Unequal Voting

"One-share, one-vote" should be the typical voting power, and any divergence should be disclosed to the shareholders.

Access to the Vote

Voting channels should be developed to provide opportunities and access to shareholder in voting situations.

Shareholder Participation in Governance

Shareholders should have the opportunity to participate in key corporate governance decisions.

Shareholders' Right to Call a Meeting of Shareholders

"Every corporation should provide holders of a specified portion of the outstanding shares of a corporation, not greater than ten percent (10%), with the right to call a meeting of shareholders for the purpose of transacting the legitimate business of the corporation."

Shareholder Resolutions

Laws should be established to provide fair opportunities for shareholders to place resolutions before the shareholder body.

Shareholder Questions

Shareholders should be granted access to the board, management, and the external auditor at meetings of shareholders with opportunities to ask questions.

Major Decisions

Shareholder approval is required in order to implement major changes to the core business of a corporation or any other items that may affect shareholder rights and privileges.

Duty to Vote

Systems should be designed to facilitate institutional investors in their voting responsibilities.

Institutional Shareholder Responsibilities

"Institutional investors should discharge their responsibilities as shareholders as set out in the ICGN Statement on Institutional Shareholder Responsibilities."

Consultation Amongst Institutional Shareholders

Laws should be enacted to allow institutional investors ways to consult with management on issues.

Vote Execution

Intermediaries shall cast votes in accordance to the owners' instructions.

Record of Ownership of a Corporation's Shares

Corporations shall maintain records on the owners of its shares.

Disclosing Voting Results

Voting results shall be released in a timely manner with equal counting procedures given to present and absentee votes.

Shareholder Rights of Action

Shareholders should be granted accessible opportunities to discuss potential disputes with the corporation.

(*continued overleaf*)

EXHIBIT 14.1 (*Continued*)

Corporate Boards
Duties of the Board
Duties of the board include, but are not limited to: reviewing, approving, and guiding corporate strategy; monitoring the effectiveness of corporate governance practices; hiring, firing, and compensating key executives; and ensuring the integrity of the corporation overall.
Director Competencies
The board should consist of members with a variety of skills and qualifications.
Directors Are Fiduciaries
Members of the board of directors and supervisory boards must act in the best interest of the shareholders or the corporation.
Independent-Minded Directors
Judgments by directors are most effective when made free of any external influences that are not in the best interest of the corporation.
Factors Affecting Independence
Independence can be affected by consulting engagements and relationships with significant shareholders.
Disclosing the Meaning of Independence
"Every corporation should disclose its definition of independence and should disclose its determination as to whether each member of its board of directors whether such member is independent."
Independent Board Members
Boards should be staffed with a "strong presence" of independent directors.
Nonexecutive Nonindependent Board Members
Boards may include a minority of nonexecutive, nonindependent directors who can effectively assist in the operations of a corporation.
Election of Directors
Directors should be rotated individually on a minimum three-year basis.
Board Chairs
The chair of the board should be independent and not a former or current CEO.
Board Committees
Duties of board committees should be well defined and disclosed.
Independent Committees
"All corporations should establish the key committees of the board which include the audit, compensation and nomination/governance committees."
Related Party Transactions
Corporations should have established processes to review and monitor related party transactions.
Director Conflicts of Interest
Corporations should have procedures for identifying and managing any conflicts of interest that directors may have.
Board Evaluation
Regular evaluations of the board and individual directors performance should take place and be disclosed.

Nonexecutive Director Meetings
Nonexecutive directors should hold meetings without the presence of executives of the corporation.
Share Ownership
Ownership of shares by senior managers and directors should be disclosed in order to maintain the parallelism of shareholders and senior managers and directors.

Corporate Remuneration Policies
Aligning Remuneration with the Interests of Shareholders
"Corporations should follow the best practices for remuneration set out in the most current policy of the ICGN."

Corporate Citizenship, Stakeholder Relations and the Ethical Conduct of Business
Board Responsibilities and Duties in Relation to Stakeholders
"The board is accountable to shareholders and responsible for managing successful and productive relationships with the corporation's stakeholders."
Compliance with Laws
Corporations are to follow all laws governing their locality.
Disclosure of Policies
Policies involving stakeholders should be disclosed.
Employee Participation
Aligning employee interests with those of shareholders and stakeholders can be achieved through the development of performance-enhancing programs.
Corporate Social Responsibility
Corporations should be governed economically, socially, and environmentally through an effective code of ethics.
Integrity
"The board is *responsible* for determining, implementing and maintaining a culture of integrity."

Corporate Governance Implementation
Compliance with and Disclosure of Governance Codes and Systems
Corporations should comply with a corporate governance code comparable to the ICGN Principles.
Resolution of Governance Issues
"Corporate governance issues between shareholders, the board and management should be addressed through dialogue and, where appropriate, with government and regulatory representatives as well as other concerned bodies, so as to resolve disputes, if possible, through negotiation, mediation or arbitration."

Source: Adapted from the revised *International Corporate Governance Network Statement on Global Corporate Principles*, released July 8, 2005. Available at: www.icgn.org/organisation/documents/cgp/revised_principles_jul2005.pdf.

set of global best practice principles for responsible investment.[27] The process of developing principles for responsible investment (PRI) was coordinated and overseen by the UN Financial Initiative and the UN Global Compact. The PRI are voluntary and aspirational rather than prescriptive; compliance with the PRI is expected to lead not only to a more sustainable financial return but also to a close alignment of the interests of investors with those of the global society at large.[28] The PRI provide a common framework for the integration of ESG issues and consist of:

- Integration of ESG issues into the investment analysis and decision-making process.
- Incorporation of ESG issues into investment ownership policies and practices.
- Promotion of appropriate disclosure on ESG issues by the entities in which institutional investors invest.
- Promotion of acceptance and implementation of the principles within the investment industry.
- Collaboration among institutional investors to enhance the effectiveness of implementing the principles.
- Reporting on initiatives, activities, and progress toward implementing these principles.[29]

Previous chapters focused on public companies' financial reports and ways to improve the financial reporting process in measuring and reporting a company's economic performance. The sections that follow discuss the performance and reporting of public companies in the areas of corporate governance, social responsibility, environmental matters, and ethical issues.

Corporate Governance Performance and Reporting

The agency theory suggests that effective corporate governance can reduce agency costs, which in turn leads to improved firm performance. Academic studies find a positive relation between the company's corporate governance and its performance.[30] More specifically, companies with high (low) governance rankings significantly outperformed (underperformed) the S&P index. The stocks of the five top-rated corporate governance companies rose 23.1 percent, the top 15 companies showed on average an increase of 3.4 percent, and the lowest-ranked governance companies experienced a 4.1 percent decline compared to the average decline of 2.3 percent for all S&P companies over the three-year period, which ended on March 20, 2003.[31] These results suggest that companies with top corporate governance performance and ratings can, over time, generate superior financial performance (return on assets), effect more favorable investments, and lower their financing costs (cost of capital). Conversely, companies with poor corporate governance can incur increased investment risks and, thus, a higher cost of capital.

Disclosures of corporate governance measures and their effectiveness can attract fund managers and individual investors to buy shares, which in turn may increase stock prices and lower cost of equity capital, and thus improve corporate governance. Theoretically, if effective corporate governance can encourage participants to improve their performance, and their roles can be counted as value-added functions, then one would expect an improvement in corporate performance. However, overregulated corporate governance that would cause executives to become unjustifiably risk averse or discourage talented and knowledgeable executives from taking managerial positions in public companies can be detrimental to the long-term success of a company by damaging innovation, entrepreneurial spirit, and corporate competitiveness.

Corporate governance reporting is the new phenomenon that has emerged since the passage of SOX. Methodologies and standards are yet to be established. A framework of reporting and assurance is suggested by the GRI guidelines, which promote accountability reports.[32] In 2002 more than 600 companies worldwide issued sustainability reports in compliance with GRI's reporting guidelines, focusing primarily on the company's environmental performance. Examples of companies that issued sustainability reports are Conoco, Dow Chemical, Ford Motor Co., Johnson & Johnson, British Airway, Canon, Nissan, and Shell Petroleum. The author recommends that companies worldwide issue reports to disclose transparent and relevant information about their corporate governance principles, structure, mechanism, and functions, as discussed in Chapters 2 to 10.

Corporate Social Responsibility

A global survey of 4,238 corporate executives in 116 countries reveals that executives worldwide overwhelmingly support corporate social responsibility that goes beyond creating shareholder value.[33] However, the majority of global executives reported that sociopolitical issues, including environmental matters, present real risks and their companies should address these risks through effective involvement of the CEO.[34] The survey suggests that companies often take the wrong approach in addressing their social responsibility and managing the related risk; about half of the respondents reported that their companies lobby regulators and governments and use public relations and the media to manage social and political challenges.[35] The majority of executives felt that the most effective strategy to manage social issues was to establish policies on ethics, engage shareholders, and increase transparency about the risks of products and processes.[36]

A survey of investors in SRI mutual funds finds that 54 percent reported in 2005 that they are interested in investing in these companies, compared with 40 percent and 44 percent in 1999 and 2002, respectively.[37] More than 55 percent of Americans believe that SRI plays an important role in motivating corporations to act more socially responsible by contributing to product safety, corporate honesty, and environmental safety, and generating fairer wages for employees. In the same survey, 52 percent believe that SRI mutual funds are at least somewhat successful in promoting socially responsible activities; more than 70 percent of Americans either invest in more socially responsible companies or purchase their products and services; and the majority of the respondents (55 percent) stated that they believe socially responsible companies carry less risk and deliver better returns. Thus, public companies should engage in and report on their social activities in order to fulfill and disclose their commitments to a wide range of stakeholders (e.g., customers, suppliers, employees, regulators, and shareholders).

Environmental Performance and Reporting

Environmental matters, particularly climate change, currently are receiving a considerable amount of attention from the socially responsible and investment community. Goldman Sachs, a leading global financial institution, regards a healthy environment as a necessary factor for the well-being of society, the success of businesses, and a sustainable and strong economy, and as such plays a constructive role to address the challenges facing the environment.[38] Goldman Sachs' environmental policy framework is designed to address environmental matters and promote policy measures with a keen focus on providing real solutions to problems to ensure the achievement of sustainable shareholder value creation.

Goldman Sachs' environmental initiatives are:

- Working with government and private sectors in establishing policies that guide environmental public policy development based on market-based mechanisms, mandatory actions, and global solutions to mitigate environmental problems.
- Reporting its own environmental performance to ensure that its facilities and business practices adopt leading-edge environmental safeguards (e.g., greenhouse gas emissions).
- Acting as a market maker by seeking investment opportunities and investing in the environmental markets (e.g., $1 billion investment in energy projects).
- Increasing its commitment to systematically incorporate governance, social, and environmental criteria into the fundamental analysis of companies.
- Establishing and funding a Center for Environmental Markets to conduct independent research with partners in academia and other research organizations to develop appropriate environmental public policies.
- Taking into consideration environmental issues, policies, and practices in business selection decisions.
- Applying its environmental policy to the Goldman Sachs Group, Inc. and its majority-owned subsidiaries.[39]

Thus, a socially responsible strategy and focus on environmental issues are expected to receive more attention from institutional investors. Risks and opportunities of focusing on environmental issues should be considered by boards of directors of public companies as the investing community values company environmental initiatives and responses in developing new "green" products. The 2005 Investor Summit on Climate Risk was hosted by the United Nations with more than 300 participants, including representatives of pension programs, both domestic and foreign.[40] Traditionally, pension programs have supported initiatives to ensure that companies owned in their portfolios provide adequate disclosures on their environmental liabilities. Several companies, including General Electric and DuPont, have announced that they seek to increase their profit by focusing on the environment and offering environmentally friendlier products and services. Some insurance companies, such as Swiss Re, are providing coverage for environmental liabilities and have established procedures to assess and consider environmental risk.[41] Thus, public companies should evaluate their environmental risk and performance and report to their constituencies regarding their environmental activities. The International Organization for Standardization's (ISO) 14,000 standards provide guidance for organizations worldwide to manage their environmental issues and report on their environmental performance.[42]

Ethics Performance and Reporting

The emerging corporate governance reforms require public companies to adopt a code of conduct for key financial officers. Public companies have adopted codes of conduct, offered employee training programs in ethics, and often appointed chief ethics officers to oversee the establishment and maintenance of codes of ethics and ethics programs. The established codes of conduct and ethics programs address:

- Avoidance and resolution of conflicts of interest between the company and employees.
- Compliance with all applicable laws, rules, regulations, standards, and policies.
- Emphasis on customer relations to enhance the company's reputation.
- Proper use of the company's confidential information.
- Encouragement of whistleblowers to reveal dishonesty or wrongdoing.

The author believes that, although the primary focus and goal of corporate governance in the foreseeable future will continue to be on economic issues to create sustainable long-term shareholder value, the issues of social, ethical, and environmental performance of companies will gain momentum, thus making it appropriate for public companies to start paying more attention to such matters.

SHAREHOLDER CHALLENGING ISSUES

Corporate governance reforms in the United States generally are intended to protect shareholders even though they benefit other stakeholders, including creditors, customers, employees, suppliers, government, and society, by providing some means of protecting their interests. This section presents several emerging shareholder issues pertaining to the nomination process, voting system, proxy statements, and regulations, along with the author's suggestions for possible improvements in these areas.

Nomination Process

Existing SEC rules do not grant shareholders the right to place the names of director-nominees, or even resolutions regarding the election process, on the corporate ballot, although management uses the company's assets (shareholder residual claims) to distribute those ballots to campaign for its candidates. Of course, shareholders can access management's proxy card by filing a shareholder resolution; however, it is difficult to place a proxy card on the corporate proxy.

One important unresolved issue concerning shareholder democracy is whether investors should be provided with the same access to the proxy as a company gives to its management team. The recent court cases involving AIG by the U.S. Court of Appeals for the Second Circuit issued a ruling that permits shareholders in its jurisdiction to nominate directors, unlike the SEC rules, which permit companies to reject any shareholder proposal pertaining to director election. Investor activists and organizations (e.g., the Council of Institutional Investors [CII]) have urged the SEC to sustain the recent decisions in the AIG case by permitting investors access to the proxy, provided a bylaw amendment is adopted. The Business Roundtable, an association of CEOs, on the other hand, has urged the SEC not to adopt a shareholder access rule.[43]

Regarding shareholder democracy and its role in the free enterprise system, Arthur Levitt, the former SEC chairman, states:

> [S]hareholder capitalism enables our markets to thrive, our companies to grow and our economy to remain strong. And central to this system is the principle that shareholders can have a voice in the running of companies that they own, that their votes will count. . . . How the SEC handles this [proxy access] can have a profound effect on the future of shareholder democracy, corporate governance, and the future of our markets.[44]

He further suggests that the SEC strengthen shareholder democracy by: (1) passing its 2003 proxy access proposal; (2) including safeguards such as minimum required shares to be eligible to put forward director nominees; (3) increasing the number of exempt solicitations from 10 persons to 20 in order for investors, particularly institutional investors, to communicate easily with each other; (4) allowing the electronic transmission of proxy materials; and (5) endorsing the principle of majority of directors.[45]

Current proxy rules do not enable shareholder control and effective monitoring of the companies they own and have caused a lack of proper communication between shareholders and the board of directors, which could result in more frequent litigation. Investors in other countries (e.g., the United Kingdom, Australia, and the Netherlands) are given more opportunities to remove underperforming or unfit directors than their counterparts in the United States. On December 6, 2006, the SEC for the second time postponed its scheduled vote on whether to allow shareholders to nominate corporate directors at annual meetings. Thus, the court's decision will stand in giving shareholders power to nominate directors until the SEC makes its decision in this regard. In the United Kingdom and Europe shareholders are granted the same right to use the proxy as management, whereas their counterparts in the United States are not provided with that right, exposing them to significant additional risk. The author strongly suggests that the SEC, in conjunction with its recently adopted rules of allowing online proxy statements, take proper action to finalize the proposed shareholder nomination rule.

Voting System

The majority of U.S. public companies currently apply plurality voting, which permits uncontested management nominees to be elected to their boards without even a single vote, definitely with less than majority vote.

Under the commonly practiced plurality voting:

- Nominated candidates can vote for themselves.
- A single affirmative vote, even by the candidate, is sufficient for a director to be elected, regardless of how many (majority) shareholders oppose the candidate.
- The nominating committee provides shareholders with the option of voting for nominees or choosing not to vote at all.
- The majority of shareholders, up to 99 percent, can vote against a nominee and he or she can still be elected.

Directors should be elected annually by a majority of the votes cast when, under state law, the company's charter and bylaws permit majority voting. Alternatively, when state law requires plurality voting for directors' elections, the company's board can adopt policies requiring that directors tender their resignation if the number of votes withheld from the director exceeds the number of votes for the director. If such a director decides not to tender a resignation, he or she should not be renominated after the expiration of the current term. The company's board should consider shareholder proposals that receive a majority of votes cast for and against.

The trend towards the adoption of a majority voting system is evidenced by the fact that: (1) more than 70 public companies have already adopted a majority voting standard for their directors' elections; (2) about 150 companies have adopted a director recognition policy concerning directors who receive more "against" votes that "for" votes; (3) the 2006 Delaware corporate law amendment prohibits any shareholders' approved bylaw that prescribes a required vote for director elections (majority vote) for being replaced or altered by company's board; and (4) the American Bar Association passed amendments allowing the company's board of director's elections. The Committee on Capital Markets Regulation endorses majority rather than plurality voting.[46] The committee wrote the first bipartisan report that supports majority rule to bring U.S. shareholder election in line with that of other developed countries. The author strongly supports this trend toward the adoption of a majority voting standard for director election that allows investors to vote "no" to underperforming incumbent directors. The majority vote lite or even the plurality voting system could be used only in rare cases when multiple nominees are nominated for the same directorship.

Proxy Statements

On November 29, 2005, the SEC voted to propose a rule to provide investors with Internet availability of proxy materials.[47] The SEC's proposal would permit public companies and other persons to use the Internet to satisfy requirements relevant to the delivery of proxy materials. Under the existing SEC rules (Rule 14a-3), the proxy statement and annual report must be delivered in paper unless contested by shareholders to be delivered electronically (e.g., through e-mail). The proposed rules would provide two significant benefits: substantially reducing the cost of complying with the proxy rules, and enabling persons other than the company with more cost-effective means to undertake their own proxy solicitations.[48]

The proposed rule is expected to reduce the $1 billion annual costs of printing and mailing proxy statements to shareholders, who often do not exercise their right to vote.[49] The proposal would:

- Allow the solicitation of proxy votes by simply mailing a postcard-type notice informing shareholders of the Internet location of the company's proxy statement.
- Include on the postcard the information on shareholder meetings required by the state statute.
- Include the notion of proxy ballots and voting instructions on the postcard.
- Permit shareholders to request a paper copy of the proxy statement if they desire.
- Make it less expensive and easier for institutional investors that are dissatisfied with incumbent directors to wage proxy contents for board representation.
- Apply equally to public companies and others, such as dissident shareholders, in a proxy contest.
- Provide options to companies to either mail proxy material to shareholders or post them on their Web site.

The goal of the SEC in proposing the use of e-proxy is to simplify the process, reduce company costs of printing and making proxy materials, and make the process less tedious and more flexible for investors. Nonetheless, four issues pertaining to e-proxy deserve further consideration:

1. E-proxies may impact investor preference and behavior, resulting in lower response rates by individual investors. The majority of individual/retail investors do not want e-proxy because of:
   a. Security concerns related to financial information over the Internet.
   b. The difficulty of reading materials on a computer screen.
   c. Not having Internet access at all times.
2. E-proxy delivery may not be successful in the long term if the majority of individual investors decide to opt back in to receive printed proxy materials.
3. E-proxies may not result in lower costs for investor-to-investor communications and may shift the cost of printing proxy materials from companies to investors.
4. E-proxies may further complicate compliance with NYSE Rule 452, the so-called Broker Vote or ten Day Rule. The only shortcoming of simple postcards is that any promanagement summary postcard has the potential of driving down turnout or encouraging automatic "yes" voting in contentious annual general meetings.[50]

On December 13, 2006, the SEC voted to adopt amendments to its proxy rules that would allow public companies to furnish proxy materials to their shareholders through a "notice and access" model using the Internet.[51] Companies choosing to follow this model: (1) must post their proxy materials on an Internet Web site and send a Notice of Internet Availability of Proxy Materials to their shareholders at least 40 days before the meeting date; and (2) may send a paper proxy card accompanied by another copy of the notice ten days after the initial notice was sent.[52] This alternative "notice and access" model is intended to substantially decrease the costs associated with paper proxy materials. SEC rules allow online proxy statements, which bring U.S. proxy rules in line with rules in other countries (e.g., the United Kingdom), enable dissidents seeking board seats to level the playing field with incumbent directors who usually use corporate funds to support their candidacies, and make it easier and less costly for institutional investors by offering them the option of proposing their own slate of directors. A report by the Shareholder Voting Working Group (SVWG) indicates that the use of electronic voting has almost doubled in the United Kingdom, from 22 percent in 2004 to 42 percent in 2005, which contributed to more investors participating in corporate meetings.[53] The author suggests that e-proxy rules should be flexible by allowing investors to "opt-in" by selecting electronic delivery rather than requiring electronic proxy voting and material distribution.

Shareholder Resolutions

Shareholder resolutions are less likely to induce changes in the nominating and election process, as SEC rules allow companies to omit resolutions that would permit shareholders to list candidates for directors. The SEC rules should empower shareholders to replace underperforming directors and provide them with incentives to spend more time and effort in monitoring corporate activities and performance. More effective shareholder democracy is likely to increase market mechanisms for corporate control, reduce management entrenchment devices, and elect independent directors who focus on long-term sustainable shareholder value creation and enhancement.

During the 2006 proxy season, shareholders started acting like owners by demanding greater involvement in the election process.[54] Proposals that would require corporate directors to obtain more than half of the shareholders' votes to secure a board seat were put forth in 140 companies in 2006. The NYSE has appointed a special committee, which has recommended abolishing its traditional rule of allowing brokerage firms holding stock for their clients to vote those shares in director elections without receiving voting instructions from the clients. The author hopes that these developments and the fact that shareholders have started to act like owners will bring more transparency and accountability to corporate boardrooms.

In summary, as of January 2007, the SEC has yet to address three important issues relevant to shareholder democracy: majority vote for the election of directors, shareholder access to the proxy materials for the nomination of directors, and shareholder advisory vote on executive compensation. Indeed, in a response letter concerning the shareholder proposal to amend Hewlett-Packard's (HP) bylaws to require HP to include the name and other information of any person nominated by shareholders, the SEC's staff refused to express any view on whether HP may exclude the proposal.[55] Europe's most powerful pension fund managers, who collectively manage assets of $765 billion from which more than $100 billion is invested in the United States, have warned U.S. regulators that shareholders' rights should be strengthened to maintain confidence in U.S. capital markets.[56]

CHALLENGES FACING DIRECTORS

Corporate governance reforms have addressed many important issues pertaining to directors, including director independence, nomination, compensation, composition, and evaluation. Nonetheless, several prevailing challenges facing directors have remained unresolved. These challenges are:

- Director accountability and liability.
- The separation of chair and CEO roles.
- Executive compensation.
- Board diversity.

This section presents these director challenges and the author's suggestions regarding them.

Director Accountability and Liability

Until recently, it was very rare, and almost unheard of, for outside directors of public companies to pay money from their own pockets to settle shareholder lawsuits relevant to their liability. In January 2005 former outside directors of Enron and WorldCom agreed to pay a total of $31 million ($18 million WorldCom and $13 million Enron) out of their own pockets, in addition to a total of $191 million paid by their directors' and officers' (D&O) insurance ($155 million Enron, $36 million WorldCom) to settle securities class action lawsuits.[57] These settlements are viewed by many as the start of a new litigation strategy, even though the settlement amounts are far less than the losses to investors resulting from corporate failures. Indeed, some institutional investors are taking lead plaintiff roles and attempting not only to hold directors and officers personally liable in incidents of fraud, but also to effect corporate governance changes.[58]

In the Walt Disney case, although the court did not find directors liable, it reinforced their responsibility for considering all material available information in making business decisions, as many aspects of directors' conduct fell short of corporate governance best practices. Disney's board was criticized for an inappropriate boardroom culture that allowed directors to be passive and the CEO to influence the board for personal benefit, the CEO's excessive influence on independent directors' actions and decisions, and the imperial CEO who acted unilaterally in making important decisions. While the court's opinion indicates the governance failures at Disney, it stopped short of finding directors liable.[59] The court's opinion here was perceived by many as "signals to investors that they should not look to the courts for protection from governance failures."[60] Thus, investors should rely on other external corporate governance mechanisms (e.g., capital markets) to discipline management failures. This court opinion of not holding directors liable for governance failure definitely underscores the need for reforms, such as majority shareholder voting, to enable shareholders to hold directors accountable.

Separation of the Chair of the Board and CEO Roles

One of the most controversial and unresolved issues in corporate governance worldwide, particularly in the United States, has been CEO duality. The issue is whether the chair of the board should be distinct from the company's CEO. Opponents of CEO duality argue that:

- The separation of the roles of CEO and chairman avoids concentration of power and authority in one individual.
- CEO duality prevents the separation of leadership of the board from management of the business.
- The ever-increasing responsibilities and accountability of the chair of the board and the CEO make it difficult for one person to perform both roles effectively.
- The oversight function assumed by the chair of the board of directors is totally distinct from the managerial function exercised by the company's CEO.

Proponents of CEO duality argue that:

- The CEO, by serving as a bridge between executives and the board, can coordinate the oversight function with the managerial function effectively.
- The combined role of CEO and chair of the board can ensure the long-term well-being of the company.
- The combined leadership of the board and management of the business better aligns management interests with those of shareholders.

The author suggests that the positions of board chair and CEO be separated, particularly when the CEO can influence the nomination of the independent directors and has the ability and tendency to dominate the board leadership and process. In cases where there is CEO duality, the author suggests that the lead director be in charge of managing and running the board. The establishment of the lead presiding director position has made independent directors more effective and accountable in their oversight role of corporate governance, according to the 2005 survey of the Spencer Stuart Board Index (SSBI).[61] Nonetheless, oversight responsibilities of lead/presiding directors can vary significantly from board to board or from time to time. PwC suggests that lead/presiding directors be empowered to add substantial value in three roles:

1. Setting a more effective and robust agenda for the board and assessing the quality of briefing materials received from management.
2. Orchestrating a richer and more thoughtful discourse with management.
3. Providing ballast in turbulent times when the company is in a crisis or during a CEO transition.[62]

Executive Compensation

Anecdotal evidence is mixed regarding the relation between CEO pay and the nation's economic performance. A survey of directors documented that 65 percent believed that executive pay has contributed to positive U.S. economic performance in the sense that good executives help to create jobs and sell products that contribute to the economic performance and prosperity of the nation.[63] However, a survey of institutional investors found that only 22 percent reported that the executive pay system has helped the nation's economic growth, whereas 90 percent felt top executives were significantly overpaid.[64] The contrasting views of investors and directors on the reasonableness and relevance of executive pay suggest: (1) despite recent corporate governance reforms, management decides who gets on the board and, thus, directors have incentives to support pay arrangements that favor senior executives; (2) directors are more aligned with CEOs than with shareholders; and (3) outsized executive pay will continue to grow until shareholders are empowered to easily replace directors.[65]

The laws on executive compensation are likely to continue for the foreseeable future. It is expected that the compensation committee will pay more attention to executive compensation and stock option grant accounting practices. Effective compliance with various provisions of SOX and SEC-related rules should assist companies to provide more timely, accurate, and reliable information about their executive compensation and stock option grants. Management certification of financial statements and internal controls, the auditor's report on internal control over financial reporting, and disclosure requirements on Form 4 should prevent further occurrences of stock option grant backdating practices in the post-SOX period. Current regulations and rules require proper disclosures of executive compensation without dictating any guidance in determining such compensation. However, two recent court decisions are warning directors that they may violate their fiduciary duty of care for making defensible pay decisions.

The majority of 2006 surveyed directors (88 percent) felt that full disclosure of executive compensation is a positive step in bringing more transparency to executive pay, whereas about 30 percent were concerned about meeting the new SEC rules. In addition, more than 66 percent believed boards of directors in the United States are having trouble controlling the outside CEO compensation, whereas 34 percent felt shareholders, particularly institutional investors, will be the primary driver of curtailing outrageous CEO pay; only 1 percent believed Congress would have to get involved.[66] The general consensus is that directors and shareholders should determine the nature and extent of executive compensation. However, compensation policies and practices that result in outsized and unjustifiable transfers of wealth from shareholders to the company's directors and others will come under scrutiny as those compensations must be fully disclosed, transparent, and limited to performance.

The CED believes that "the solution to excessive executive compensation must be regarded as a matter of process and disclosure."[67] The CED makes these recommendations pertaining to executive compensation:

- Compensation committees should adopt attainable, measurable, and specific performance metrics for their businesses and use those metrics as benchmarks in assessing management.
- The compensation process must be run by compensation committees composed of independent directors who are advised by independent consultants.
- Management should possess a substantial equity interest in the company.
- Executive compensation should be transparent and fully disclosed to shareholders.
- Compensation plans should promote sustainable value creation rather than exploit favorable accounting or tax treatment.
- Severance compensation plans should be thoroughly reviewed by the compensation committee, approved by the board of directors, and disclosed to shareholders.
- Companies should reserve the right to recapture the portion of executive compensation affected by restatements of financial statements.

The author suggests these seven practices in executive compensation.

1. *No tenure for senior executives.* Senior executives, including the CEO and CFO, should not have multiyear contracts *or* any contract in excess of two years must be approved by the company's shareholders.
2. *Annual performance reviews.* Senior executives' performance should be reviewed annually, and continuation of their employment and reappointment should be approved either annually or every few years.
3. *Link compensation to performance.* Senior executive compensation should be linked to performance.
4. *Fully disclose compensation packages.* The senior executive compensation package including salary, short-term bonuses, long-term incentives (stock options, restricted stocks), pension and postemployment benefits, and perquisites should be fully disclosed to shareholders.
5. *Limit influence of outside consultants.* The influence of outside consultants on compensation committee decisions should be limited, and the entire board of directors should consider the committee's recommendation in approving senior executive compensation.
6. *Reasonable CEO pay.* Chief executives' pay should be reasonable relative to their peers and should be limited to a predetermined and preferably relatively small multiple (5 to 10 times) of the compensation of the company's top 20 most senior managers.
7. *Shareholder advisory vote.* Public companies should obtain a shareholder advisory vote an executive compensation and establish "say on pay" policies.

Board Diversity

During the past several years, several institutional investor groups, including the CII, California Public Employees' Retirement System (CalPERS), and TIAA-CREF, have advocated more diversity in the boardroom in terms of gender and ethnic background. Some have argued that director independence requirements and other corporate governance reforms in the post-SOX period should have positive impacts on director diversity by race and gender. Overall, director diversity has been enhanced slightly in the post-SOX period; however, as discussed in Chapter 3, the proportion of seats held by members of racial minorities and women continues to remain low in comparison with their representation in the nation's management positions and entire workforce.

It is expected that the trend toward increasing the demand for board diversity by gender and race will continue as companies add new independent directors to their boards and as the demand for individuals with a financial background to serve on boards increases. From the total of 49,783 U.S. directors in 2006, only 4,043 directors are women, representing an average of 0.7 women directors per company.[68] Larger company boards have a significantly higher representation of women (about 1.5 percent on average) compared with smaller companies (about 0.5 percent on average).[69] The author suggests that public companies specifically make reference to board diversity by race and gender in their proxy statements.

SOX CHALLENGES

Public companies are facing several challenges in complying with SOX provisions, particularly Section 404. The first challenge is transitioning from "compliance project mentality" to "sustainable compliance processes." Companies should integrate the SOX compliance process into their corporate governance structure, risk and compliance processes, internal controls, financial reports, and audit activities. The second challenge is who will lead the SOX compliance process. The author suggests that SOX and other corporate governance processes be viewed as everyone's responsibility, from the oversight function to managerial, advisory, audit, and monitoring functions. However, the leadership of future SOX matters and compliance with other emerging corporate governance reforms should be assigned to the chief compliance officer (CCO) or the equivalent. Assigning such leadership to financial officers (CFO, controller, and chief accountants) can cause a focus only on financial compliance (e.g., executive certifications of internal controls and financial reports) and less emphasis on compliance regarding corporate governance, risk management, corporate culture, and applicable laws and regulations. Placing leadership in the internal audit function can exhaust internal audit resources to perform quality control activities, may impair internal auditor independence, and may deemphasize the importance of financial reporting compliance. The third challenge is the compliance cost of Section 404. It has been asserted that compliance is too costly for public companies, particularly smaller ones. Some argue that the emerging corporate governance reforms, including SOX, SEC-related implementation rules, and listing standards, have caused smaller companies to incur compliance costs that are disproportionate to the induced incremental benefits and divert the attention of company management away from strategic decisions and operational activities.

The author suggests the following in addressing these challenges:

- Management should use the integrated compliance approach according to Sections 302, 404, and 906 of SOX in providing certifications of both ICFR and financial statements. On July 18, 2006, the SEC released a proposed rule, a concept release, intended to provide a better understanding of the need and concerns of public companies regarding management's assessment of ICFR.[70] The SEC approved a framework, in April 2007, for changes to implementation rules of SOX that would ease the form, extent, and nature of documentation to support its ICFR assessment.

- Management should report on ICFR annually, and also annually assess both the design and operating effectiveness of internal controls over all relevant financial statement assertions, using the suggested Committee of Sponsoring Organizations of the Treadway Commission (COSO) internal control framework for smaller companies. COSO, in June 2006, issued a report entitled "Internal Control over Financial Reporting—Guidance for Smaller Public Companies."[71] This report neither replaces nor modifies the previously issued framework, but provides management guidance in establishing and monitoring effective ICFR as well as the assessment of the internal control effectiveness.

- Independent auditors should audit and report on the effectiveness of both the design and the operation of ICFR by performing walk-through tests of controls and the assessment of the control environment, while relying on the work of others (e.g., internal auditors) in determining the extent, timing, and nature of other tests of controls. The audit focus should be on the effectiveness of ICFR rather than management's assessment of the effectiveness of ICFR.

- Smaller companies should not be exempted from compliance with Section 404, even though their compliance costs may be disproportionably high. The Committee on Capital Markets Regulation recommends to Congress that small companies under $75 million in market capitalization be exempted from the need for an external audit of their internal controls under Section 404, but should not be totally exempted from compliance with Section 404.[72] Exemptions of certain companies (smaller companies) or the position of voluntarily compliance with Section 404 of SOX can result in four negative consequences: (1) noncompliant companies will continue to produce financial reports that are inferior to those of compliant companies; (2) investors, in the long term, will adjust the cost of capital to reflect the discrepancy in the quality of financial information of compliant versus noncompliant firms; (3) audit costs, insurance costs, and litigation costs will increase for noncompliant companies to compensate for the increased level of risk; and (4) as investors in noncompliant companies start to lose money, litigation will increase for these companies and their boards, management, and auditors.

- There should be only one set of financial reporting standards, namely GAAP, which provides guidelines for measuring, recognizing, and reporting business transactions and economic events, and it should apply equally to small and large companies.

■ Listing standards of national stock exchanges (e.g., NYSE, American Stock Exchange [AMEX], Nasdaq) regarding director independence, formulation of board committees (audit, compensating, nominating), and designated audit committee financial experts should be applied uniformly and consistently to both small and large companies.

■ The SEC should not differentiate in its application of financial reporting and disclosure requirements between small and large companies.

■ Standard setters (e.g., PCAOB, FASB) should issue accounting and auditing standards that are applicable to companies of all sizes with proper consideration being given to smaller companies.

■ Congress should not consider compromising, revising, or relaxing provisions of SOX while regulators should fine-tune their implementation rules.

FINANCIAL REPORTING CHALLENGES

In the post-SOX era, several unresolved financial reporting issues exist. This section addresses some of these issues.

Financial Restatements

Financial restatements have remained a major contributing factor to eroding investor confidence and public trust in public financial information, even in the post-SOX era. The 2006 Government Accountability Office (GAO) report reveals that: (1) the total number of public companies disclosing financial restatements from 2002 through September 2005 rose from 3.7 percent to 6.8 percent; (2) the number of reported financial restatements increased about 67 percent from 2002 to September 2005; (3) greater scrutiny and focus on the quality of financial reporting by company management, audit committees, external auditors, and regulators was the primary contributing factor in identifying financial restatements; (4) cost- or expense-related reasons accounted for about 35 percent of the reported restatements; (5) the majority of restatements (58 percent) were prompted by an internal party, such as management and internal auditors; (6) noncompliance and/or ineffective compliance with existing SEC regulations (e.g., items on Form 8-K) were the primary causes of lack of proper disclosures of financial restatements; (7) the capital markets reacted negatively to the reported financial restatements, as evidenced by substantial reduction in market capitalization ($63 billion) of companies that announced restatements between July 2002 and September 2005; and (9) reported financial restatements could have negative impact on investor confidence.[73]

The upward trend of financial restatements in the post-SOX period indicates, on average, an annual increase of about 38 percent, with 24.3 percent, 31.8 percent, 17.8 percent, and 78.4 percent increases in 2002, 2003, 2004, and 2005, respectively. More than 10 percent of listed U.S. companies restated their financial statements in 2006, up 13 percent compared to 2005. Overall, in the post-SOX period, about

2,931 companies filed at least one restatement. On the surface, these financial restatements can be interpreted as financial problems with companies and reveal the fact that management and auditors were not able to detect the problems. Causes and effects of these restatements should be evaluated to determine their impacts on investor confidence and stock prices. Many of these restatements were driven from remediation actions taken to correct significant deficiencies and material weakness in internal control over financial reporting. The number of these types of restatements is expected to decline as companies continue to improve their internal control over financial reporting in 2006 and onward. These restatements may cause short-term negative market reactions, but, in the long term, they should have a positive impact on stock prices as investors may take the view that changes made in improving the reliability of financial statements and internal controls are working in providing them with a true picture of company finances.

Glass Lewis applies the term "stealth restatements" to companies that did not amend previous financial statements to reflect a restatement, failed to report the restatement in a standard SEC filing Form 8-K, and did not inform investors of a looming restatement in their late filing of annual or quarterly financial statements with the SEC.[74] These stealth restatements constitute about 14 percent of the total number of restatements in 2005, compared with 2 percent in 2004. They are worrisome to investors and signal red flags to regulators. Smaller companies with market capitalization of less than $75 million accounted for about two-thirds of so-called stealth restatements, suggesting that these companies should be held more accountable for compliance with the provisions of SOX, particularly requirements for executive certifications and auditor reports on their internal control over financial reporting. Although the majority of more than 2,500 financial restatements in the post-SOX period were not caused by violations of securities laws or intentional manipulation of earnings, the SEC has yet to implement Section 304 of SOX, which requires executives to give back their bonuses when financial statements are subsequently restated. Investor confidence in financial reports is adversely affected as restatements continue to grow at an increasing rate. For this reason, the SEC and the PCAOB should increase their efforts to reverse this trend.

Enhanced Business Reporting

The value relevance and information content of historical financial statements are being questioned as many investors and other users of financial reports do not use these statements in making financial decisions. Dennis Nally, chairman of PwC, has stated that the current system of financial reporting has several shortcomings that are confusing for both institutional and retail investors and, thus, will limit its usefulness and relevance in the future.[75] Nally suggested the need for creation of a "National Commission on Corporate Reporting" to improve the usefulness of corporate and financial reporting.[76] Enhanced business reporting (EBR), focusing on both financial and nonfinancial information about current and future performance, is suggested as an alternative to improve the quality, transparency, and integrity of financial reporting.[77] The Enhanced Business Reporting Consortium was established through the cooperative efforts of several professional organizations, including the American Institute of Certified Public Accountants (AICPA), Business Roundtable, Confederation of British Industry, International Chamber of Commerce, Nasdaq, National Association of Corporate Directors, National Investor Relations Institute, Open Compliance and Ethics Group, and XBRL International.

The Enhanced Business Reporting Consortium (EBRC) is in the process of trying to develop a voluntary, global disclosure framework for EBR that will provide a structure for the presentation of nonfinancial components of business reports. This framework will integrate financial and nonfinancial components of business reporting, including key performance indicators, on an industry-by-industry basis to better reflect the company's opportunities and risks, complexities of modern business, and the quality of both earnings and cash flows.[78] The improved transparency provided by the EBR framework will ensure the effectiveness of the company's corporate governance process. Investors and other users of financial reports are demanding more forward-looking and nonfinancial information on all relevant key performance indicators (KPIs) regarding economic, governance, social, ethics, and environmental issues, in addition to historical financial information.

Stock Options Accounting

Stock options have been used as a part of compensation plans to provide long-term incentive measures for directors, officers, and key personnel. Accounting for the recognition and pricing of stock options has been controversial and, recently, has come under increased scrutiny by lawmakers (Congress), regulators (SEC), and standard setters (FASB, PCAOB). The FASB, in its Statement of Financial Accounting Standards SFAS) No. 123(R), requires recognition of employee stock options as an expense. When the FASB was deliberating on accounting for stock options, many public companies opposed an accounting standard that would require expensing their stock options. Opponents argued that such a requirement would: (1) substantially reduce their reported earnings; (2) compromise their ability to attract talented key personnel; and (3) put them in the global competitive disadvantage.[79] Some of the companies that opposed the issuance of SFAS No. 123(R) are among those that are being probed by the SEC and the Justice Department for their alleged illegal backdating practices of their stock option grants (KLA-Tencor Corp, Macrovision Corp, United Health Group, Inc., and Altera Corp).

The backdating probe of stock option grants is still in its early stage, as more companies are being scrutinized and questioned about their backdating polices and practices. Prior to the passage of SOX, options grants did not need to be disclosed for weeks, or even months, which could allow executives to retroactively choose favorable grant dates. In the post-SOX period, companies are required to disclose their executive options within two business days of granting. Backdating option grants may have the effect of benefiting executives by securing low stock price by essentially using "stockholder money to buy high and sell even lower than their filings had previously disclosed."[80] Whether the company intentionally manages the timing of grants retroactively by setting the exercise price of stock options to correspond with the lower market price of the stock or unintentionally records stock option grant dates incorrectly, the end result is an understatement of stock option expenses in their financial statements.

The list of companies with option grant backdating probes is growing daily. As of April 2007, more than 250 U.S. public companies have been implicated for backdating practices. Ineffective corporate governance and internal controls can create incentives and opportunities for option backdating that violate GAAP, SEC filing requirements, and IRS tax rules. Similarly, option backdating practices and subsequent probes can cause disruption in implicated companies' operations resulting from costly internal or external investigations by federal authorities, ineffectiveness in corporate governance resulting from departures of directors and officers, and financial reporting problems caused by late filings, internal control deficiencies, and restatements. Thus, option backdating practices and probes are detrimental to implicated companies' operations, governance, internal controls, and financial reports.

The author believes that stock option backdating schemes violate:

- Proxy disclosure rules if they were not disclosed to shareholders.
- The fiduciary duty under state law if executives backdated their stock options without approval of the company's board of directors.
- Fair trading rules because shareholders are not provided the same opportunity to retroactively buy stocks at past market lows.
- Fair representation of financial statements because an incorrect value is assigned to stock options and their related compensation expense, which may cause restatements of financial statements.
- Section 409A of the Internal Revenue Code, which determines the tax treatment of deferred compensation, including stock options, by requiring that these options have a fixed exercise date or otherwise are subject to a 20 percent penalty tax.
- IRS Code Section 162(m), which sets a limit of $1 million for tax-deductible executive compensation, except for payments that qualify as performance-based compensation or commissions.

Backdating practices raise concerns about the effectiveness of the compensation committee's oversight function in overseeing the fairness, accuracy, and transparency of options; the integrity of management to engage in a gamesmanship scheme to unfairly benefit from the company's compensation practices; and the efficacy of audits conducted by independent auditors in determining whether the right value is being recorded for options. All corporate governance functions presented in this book should attempt to ensure that proper values are assigned to option awards. The best practices of stock options recommend public companies: (1) adopt "blackout" periods to preclude stock options when executives have material, nonpublic information in hand; (2) adopt fixed grant date schedules that provide for option grants on a periodic basis (e.g., monthly, quarterly, annually); (3) adopt grant policies for the establishment of option exercise prices on the predetermined grant dates; (4) refrain from making grants on these fixed dates for scheduled grants when executives have market-moving news; and (5) provide full transparency about option grants by disclosing the rationale for making grants on a certain date and the proper explanation for scheduled grants.[81]

The author suggests that:

- Public companies adopt more transparent executive stock option policies and practices that disclose not only the expiration date of options, but also the grant date and board-preapproved policies for granting stock options.
- The SEC address executive stock option grant procedures and controls and bring enforcement actions against companies that improperly backdated their executive stock options. The pervasiveness of backdating practices encouraged the SEC to provide some backdating guidance as elaborated on in a letter sent by Carol A. Stancey, Chief Accountant, Division of Corporate Finance, to CFOs of public companies.[82] The letter addresses guidance regarding restatement of errors in accounting for grants of stock options to the company's executives and officers and indicates that while backdating practices are inappropriate, companies must restate their financial statements to correct their backdating problems, and following the guidance would not ensure there would be no further review by the SEC.
- The PCAOB bring the issue of stock option backdating to the auditor's attention when it conducts an integrated audit of financial statements and the internal controls. The PCAOB, in July 2006, issued its first Audit Practice Alert, which advises auditors that backdating practices may have implications for the integrated audit of both financial statements and internal control over financial reporting.[83]

Antifraud Program and Plan

Corporate malfeasance, executive misconduct, and fraudulent financial activities have contributed to the reported financial scandals of the past few years. Lawmakers (Congress), regulators (SEC), and standard setters (PCAOB, FASB) have responded to the pervasiveness of fraudulent financial activities that have eroded investor confidence and public trust in corporate America and its financial reports. The 2005 Global Economic Crime study conducted by PwC indicates that the threat of fraud in the post-SOX era is more prominent than ever with companies having no adequate antifraud program to assess the scale of the problem.[84] The four primary findings of the survey are:

1. More than 45 percent of the surveyed companies experienced fraud in the past two years after the passage of SOX in 2002.
2. The number of companies that reported cases of corruption and bribery in the past two years (2004, 2005) increased over 71 percent; money laundering increased by 133 percent.
3. The number of companies reporting financial misrepresentation increased by about 140 percent in the post-SOX period.

4. Fraud cost companies, on average, over $1.7 million, whereas 40 percent suffered significant loss of reputation, damaged business relations, and decreased staff motivation.[85]

In discussing the limitations of SOX, SEC rules, and PCAOB audit standards in addressing antifraud programs and controls beyond financial statement fraud, PwC suggests a five-step antifraud program applicable to all sorts of fraud.

Step 1. Establish a baseline for a project team to assess existing antifraud programs and controls, develop a remediation plan, and communicate with the audit committee and independent auditors.

Step 2. Conduct a fraud risk assessment independently or integrated with the overall risk assessment process to identify the company's risks and strengthen its effectiveness in preventing and detecting fraud.

Step 3. Assess and test the design and operating effectiveness of internal controls to prevent and detect fraud.

Step 4. Assign the internal audit function to address the residual risks that are not mitigated adequately by antifraud programs and controls.

Step 5. Standardize the processes for fraud incident investigation and remediation and enable prompt responses to allegations or suspicions of fraud.[86]

These suggested steps cover antifraud programs and controls relevant to both financial statement fraud and occupational fraud.

The author suggests that companies use these five steps and integrate them into their corporate governance structure to emphasize that fraud prevention and detection are everyone's responsibility, from directors to all personnel. The PCAOB should also establish further guidance and auditing standards on auditor responsibility for detecting financial statement fraud. The author suggests that the SEC:

- Improve its resources to review public company periodic filings annually for large accelerated filers.
- Develop a selective review approach using factors signaling greater risk of disclosure problems, such as reported material weaknesses in internal controls, noncompliance with applicable laws and regulations, and reported material financial restatements.
- Consider company-level factors, such as the corporate governance structure, high-level volatility in stock price, disparities in price to earnings ratios, earnings growth, and quality in selecting the review process.

Global Financial Reporting Standards

There have been extensive and inconclusive debates over the past several years on whether International Financial Reporting Standards are making steady progress to become globally generally accepted standards for financial reporting. The U.S. FASB and regulators (SEC) should work closely with their international counterparts, the

IASB and the European Association for Listed Companies (EALIC), to achieve convergence in financial reporting standards and practices. The FASB and IASB have made significant progress by agreeing to conduct their major accounting standard projects jointly and convincing the SEC to allow foreign companies to use IFRS to raise capital in the United States. Thousands of listed companies throughout the world, particularly in the European Union, presented their first annual financial statements in 2005 on a mandatory IFRS basis. In 2007 more than 100 countries will require their public companies to prepare their financial statements under IFRS. Convergence between U.S. GAAP and IFRS has been gaining momentum. IFRS are being regarded as a principles-based approach to financial reporting that is flexible and sensible in dealing with different countries' political, legal, and cultural environments.

In March 2006, as part of their road map to convergence, the FASB and the IASB released a joint memorandum of understanding (MOU) that lists 11 separate areas where convergence progress is to be achieved by 2008.[87] The road map referred to in the MOU is an agreement between the U.S. SEC and the European Union Internal Market Commission (EUIMC) that the SEC would accept IFRS developed by the IASB as comparable to U.S. GAAP by 2009. IFRS became mandatory for European companies as of January 2005. The IASB announced, in July 2006, that it will not require public companies to adopt any new IFRS that are under deliberation before January 1, 2009. Both leaders of the IASB and FASB have predicted that by 2011, significant progress towards convergence in the global financial reporting process will be made.[88] These initiatives have created a landscape for the move toward ultimate convergence. It is also expected that the global standard setters will present a major overhaul of accounting standards that redefine the format of the balance sheet and income statement to provide more transparent financial information on KPIs.

Pension and OPEB Plans Accounting

Pension and other postretirement employee benefits plans are now under extensive scrutiny. Many companies are failing to contribute sufficient funds to worker retirement plans, pension benefits are becoming too expensive, and many companies have switched from traditional pensions to so-called defined contribution plans, such as 401(k)s. The application of existing accounting standards for pensions and OPEB has created misleading and meaningless financial statements that often overstate reported total assets. For example, in 2004, the S&P 500 companies reported $99 billion in net pension assets on their balance sheets while their pension plans were underfunded by $165 billion, indicating a total overstatement of $264 billion.[89] A report issued by the GAO revealed that more than half of the 29,000 private pension plans were underfunded. This fact suggests that companies' obligations to their retirees exceed the assets for their defined benefit plans and that the underfunded pension plans and OPEBs have been kept off the balance sheet.[90]

At the turn of the century, public pension plans held an average of 100 percent of the fund required to meet obligations to workers. However, many public pension plans lost money when the stock market dropped, and, by 2004, the average funding level of these plans had decreased to 87.8 percent; some plans fell to as low as about 50 percent funded.[91] Several prominent companies have announced that they will go out of business unless they are allowed to terminate their pension plans. One example is Pittsburgh Brewing, which informed the Pension Benefit Guaranty Corporation (PBGC) that unless its pension plan is terminated, it will not be able to continue in business.[92] On January 23, 2006, Sprint Nextel reported its decision to freeze pension plans for almost half its 80,000 employees by not offering a fixed retirement benefit to new workers in order to be able to compete with other wireless carriers.[93]

The FASB, in September 2006, issued its Statement of Financial Accounting Standards (SFAS) No. 158, "*Employer's Accounting for Defined Benefit Pension and other Postretirement Plans*," which requires companies to recognize on their balance sheet the funded status of their pension and OPEB Plans as of December 31, 2006, for calendar-year companies. SFAS No. 158 will also require fiscal year-end measurements of plan assets and benefit obligations, which will be effective for fiscal years ending on or after December 15, 2008. SFAS No. 158 completes the first phase of FASB's project on pension and OPEB plans. The next phase will provide accounting standards concerning measuring plan assets and obligations and the determination of net periodic benefit cost.[94]

The FASB is planning to move forward with Phase II of its project, which could result in a comprehensive overhaul of accounting standards for pension and OPEB plans. SFAS No. 158 is intended to improve the accuracy, completeness, and transparency of financial statements to all users of financial reports, including shareholders, creditors, employees, donors, and retirees, by getting the balance sheet to better reflect the economics of the entity's pension and OPEB plans. Eventually it will improve the transparency of the postemployment benefits and compliance with funding requirements of pension and OPEB plans. To mitigate the substantial decline in equity resulting from the implementation of the proposed standards, companies may take four initiatives:

1. Companies may choose to fund their OPEB and pension plans through either debt financing (borrowing) or using their excess cash. The Credit Suisse report indicates that 235 of the S&P 500 companies could fully fund their OPEB and pension plans with the cash that is on their balance sheet; 128 companies, constituting about 70 percent of underfunded plans, would have to borrow money to fully fund their pension and OPEB plans.[95]
2. Companies may attempt to reduce their OPEB and pension-funded status by shrinking their plan obligations by passing on some costs to their plan participants.
3. Companies may attempt to limit the growth in the plan's obligations by closing the OPEB and pension plans to new employees or by freezing the plans.
4. Companies may try to totally shut down or terminate their pension and OPEB plans.[96]

The author recommends that the FASB expedite its second phase project on pension and OPEB accounting by addressing the perceived "glaring measurement problems," providing guidelines for the measurement of future retirement-benefit obligations to employees, and addressing assumptions that companies are making in estimating future interest rates and salary inflation. The primary concern regarding pension accounting is the determination of a company's pension capability by projecting future salary increases and other costs through the projected benefit obligation (PBO) method. The PBO is determined by calculating the present value of the future benefit payments, including expected salary. It is not clear why future pay increases should be regarded as a current liability on the balance sheet. Perhaps the accumulated benefit obligations (ABO) method that does not require estimate of future obligations is a better method to use in calculating pension liabilities.

Use of Derivatives Speculation

Derivatives have been used to offset risk from fluctuations in interest rates and currency. A study shows that many high-profile companies (e.g., Procter & Gamble, Gibson Greetings) are using derivatives for speculative purposes by actively taking positions in interest rate and currency derivatives on the basis of likely market movements.[97] These companies consider speculation a profitable activity, and their CFO (not CEO) compensation-related incentives are associated with the likelihood that the company engages in derivative speculations.[98] Investors are not able to differentiate derivatives used for risk management purposes from those used for speculation purposes. Companies with a governance structure that enables greater managerial power and fewer shareholder rights and those with stronger derivative internal controls are more likely to use derivatives for profit-making motives than for speculative purposes.[99]

The current GAAP do not provide adequate guidance for companies to properly disclose their speculative activities, and, thus, reported financial statements do not adequately reflect them. The Government Accounting Standards Board (GASB) issued its Preliminary View (PV) on April 28, 2006.[100] The PV proposes that the fair value of derivatives and any changes in their fair value be reported in the financial statements. However, if a derivative is effectively hedging (reducing) the risk, then the annual changes in its fair value would be deferred and reported on the balance sheet.

Enterprise Risk Management

Enterprise risk management (ERM) has recently received considerable attention from public companies, the business community, and the accounting profession. Financial scandals of the early 2000s and recent world events, including the September 11, 2001, terrorist attacks, have generated more interest in the issue of overall ERM. Natural disasters, such as hurricanes, earthquakes, and floods, require companies to design adequate and effective disaster recovery plans and assess their risk of occurrence and their consequence on operations. Companies should conduct risk assessment periodically to identify potential risks and design appropriate controls to mitigate their adversarial impacts. The board of directors, particularly the audit committee, should oversee the company's ERM, and both internal and external auditors should be involved in assessing risks of natural disasters and the protection of important electronic and other information by implementing guidelines provided in the COSO framework on ERM.[101]

XBRL-Generated Financial Reports

eXtensible business reporting language (XBRL) is an application of extensible markup language (XML) in business and financial reporting. XBRL is now commonly accepted as the electronic method of business and financial reporting worldwide. XBRL tools, techniques, and taxonomies have been developed by the XBRL International Steering Committee available at the XBRL Web site (www.xbrl.org). XBRL enables computer systems to assemble data electronically in instance documents, retrieve data directly from XBRL instance documents, and convert data to human-readable financial reports. A move toward the global acceptance of XBRL for electronic business and financial reporting requires auditors to provide assurance by conducting an integrated audit on XBRL-generated financial statements. This type of audit should be conducted in accordance with PCAOB Auditing Standard No. 2, the PCAOB's Interim Attestation Standard (AT 101), and the PCAOB's Staff Questions and Answers document on XBRL released May 25, 2005.

The objective of an integrated audit on XBRL-generated financial statements is the same as other financial statement audits: to express an opinion on the effectiveness of both the design and the operation of internal controls over XBRL-generated financial reports, particularly the posting of XBRL instance documents on the Internet, and the fair presentation of XBRL-generated financial statements in conformity with the selected XBRL taxonomy (e.g., U.S. GAAP, IFRS). The primary difference between the audit objective of the conventional reports and XBRL reports is that the conventional financial statements and their internal control reports are presented at a particular point in time (e.g., the end of the fiscal year), whereas XBRL-generated financial statements and their related internal controls are made on a real-time basis. This presents challenges to auditors in providing continuous assurance on XBRL-generated real-time financial statements and internal control reports.

An important issue for regulators (SEC), standard setters (FASB, PCAOB), public companies, and the accounting profession is to decide whether to require public reporting on XBRL-generated financial statements and internal control reports at a point in time (periodic filing report dates, quarterly 10-Q, or annual 10-K form), or on a real-time basis. The author recommends that regulators and standard setters require public disclosures of both only at periodic report filing dates. Companies, however, should use XBRL-generated financial statements and related internal controls on a real-time basis for internal purposes.

An integrated audit of periodic XBRL-generated financial statements and internal controls requires auditing of:

- Internal controls over XBRL taxonomy, the tagging of data, preparation of the instance documents, the integrity of the tagged data, and the consistent application of both taxonomy and the tagged data.
- The effectiveness of both the design and operation of XBRL internal controls, including authorization procedures and selection of the appropriate taxonomy and tagged data in producing financial statements.

- The XBRL instance documents to ensure the integrity and reliability of XBRL-generated financial statements and comparability of data contained in the instance documents and the audited financial statements.
- XBRL-generated financial statements in conformity with the selected XBRL taxonomy.

The end result is an integrated audit report, expressing an audit opinion on management's assessment of the effectiveness of internal controls over XBRL financial reporting and fair and true presentation of XBRL-generated financial statements in conformity with the selected taxonomy (GAAP). Auditors should use continuous auditing when their clients report XBRL-generated financial statements on a real-time basis.

EMERGING AUDITING ISSUES

The emerging auditing issues in the post-SOX period are:

- Auditor independence.
- Auditor changes.
- Engagement letters.
- Audit failure.
- Integrated audit approach.
- Concentration of and competition in public accounting firms.
- Continuous auditing.
- Confirmations.
- Diversity in accounting.
- Auditor liability.
- Auditor communication with those charged with governance.

Auditor Independence

SOX and SEC rules have addressed auditor independence in several ways, as discussed in Chapter 9. The SEC has approved the PCAOB proposal addressing auditor independence in performing tax services. The PCAOB rules on ethics and independence prohibit independent auditors from offering two types of tax services for their audit clients: tax shelters and tax services to individuals within the client's organization who are in a financial oversight role. The AICPA, in October 2005, issued Ethics Interpretation 101-15, *Financial Relationships*. This interpretation provides the definition of "direct" and "indirect" financial interests by auditors in their client's business and types that are considered direct or indirect. Auditor independence is a cornerstone of the auditing profession. As such, it should be monitored continuously by regulators and standard setters, as changes in legal, regulatory, business, and global environment create new challenges for auditors.

Auditor Changes

Emerging corporate governance reforms, including SOX, SEC-related rules, and listing standards, require lead audit partner rotation every five years. Nevertheless, it appears that audit committees are seriously considering circumstances that warrant audit firm rotations, even though the existing corporate governance reforms do not require such. This issue is extensively, and yet inconclusively, debated in the literature. The general perception is that audit firm rotation can be very costly, complex, and ineffective without adding much to the objectivity and independence of financial statement audits. However, a recent report shows that in the post-SOX period (from 2003 to 2005) about 4,000 public companies changed their audit firms, which is roughly a third of all public companies, and, in particular, about 11 percent (1,430) changed their audit firm in 2005.[102] This suggests that, in reality, public companies frequently change their auditors and any mandatory rotation every several years (e.g., 10 years) may not be a bad idea.

Changes in auditors may be classified into legitimate changes and manipulative changes. Examples of legitimate changes are appointing a auditor who would charge less, company growth beyond the capabilities of the audit firm, changes in senior executives, or acquisition by another company. Examples of manipulative changes are disputes between management and auditors over accounting policies and practices. A study by Glass Lewis and Company shows that: (1) the turnover is highest at smaller public companies; (2) about 60 percent of the auditor changes are characterized by the companies as firings and the remaining 40 percent as resignations; (3) in more than 72 percent of these cases, the companies chose not to give any reason when they notified the SEC about the auditor departure; and (4) larger companies audited by the Big Four are less likely to give reasons, with 82 percent is being silent about their auditor changes.[103] The existing SEC rules require disclosure of a reason for changes in an auditor if it pertains to certain issues. The audit committee is now directly responsible for hiring, compensating, and firing external auditors. This responsibility should also extend to providing shareholders with transparent information regarding changes in auditors and justifiable explanations for such changes. The independent auditor should also be annually ratified by shareholders.

Engagement Letters

There is no requirement that the engagement letter (a written contract between the company and its independent auditor) must be signed by a member of the audit committee. Management has the authority to sign the letter. The author recommends that the engagement letter be reviewed, approved, and/or signed by the chair of the company's audit committee or a designated member of that committee. This practice ensures that a common understanding exists among the audit committee, management, and the independent auditor that the auditor works with management for the audit committee; it also assures that the audit committee regularly evaluates the performance of the independent auditor.

Audit Failure

A review reported on high-profile financial scandals (e.g., Enron, Global Crossing, WorldCom, Adelphia, Qwest, Parmalat, and Royal Ahold) suggests that they were the result of failures in business, financial reports, and audit functions. These scandals demonstrate that, as a company approaches business failure, the incentive to "cook the books" increases. If opportunities exist, management may engage in financial statement fraud and, through gamesmanship schemes, pressure auditors not to report discovered fraud, which, in turn, increases the likelihood of both reporting and audit failures. The PCAOB, as the watchdog of the auditing profession, should issue appropriate auditing standards, ethics rules, and quality control standards to assist auditors in improving the quality of financial audits, reducing audit failure, and, thus, protecting investors from receiving misleading audited statements. The issuance of robust auditing standards on financial fraud can be very effective in reducing audit failures.

Integrated Audit Approach

An integrated audit covers the audit of both internal control over financial reporting and the audit of financial statements. The PCAOB, in March 2004, adopted its Auditing Standard (AS) No. 2 regarding an integrated audit as directed by Sections 103 and 404(b) of SOX. The SEC approved AS No. 2 in June 2004. Large public companies, known as accelerated filers, have been required to comply with: (1) Section 404(a) of SOX, which requires companies to annually provide their management's assessments of the effectiveness of internal control over financial reporting; and (2) AS No. 2 of the PCAOB, which requires an integrated audit for fiscal years ending after November 14, 2004. The SEC is planning to require compliance with both Section 404(a) and AS No. 2 for smaller companies, known as nonaccelerated filers, for their fiscal year ending on or after December 15, 2008. Large public companies hired registered public accounting firms in 2004 to conduct an integrated audit, which substantially increased the cost of audit. These companies have been through two years of integrated audit and have substantially improved their efficiency and reduced the Section 404 compliance costs by about 40 percent.[104] The costs decreased in the second year because both auditors and companies gained experience with integrated audit. Also, a significant portion of the first-year implementation cost resulted from start-up costs. Public companies and their auditors were also challenged by inadequate staffing, insufficient training, and lack of proper experience in conducting an integrated audit, as stated in the PCAOB report.[105]

The PCAOB provides auditors with a set of recommendations to improve their audit strategies, policies, procedures, and training in applying an integrated audit. As public companies and their auditors enter the third year of integrated audit, the approach has received considerable attention from public companies, the investing public, regulators, standard setters, and the accounting profession. The PCAOB released its four-point plan to improve the effectiveness, efficiency, and scalability of an integrated audit, particularly auditors' implementation of internal control reporting requirements of Section 404 of SOX.[106] This four-point plan and the proposed PCAOB Auditing Standard No. 5, as discussed in Chapter 9, will refine the integrated audit approach.

Concentration of and Competition in Public Accounting Firms

Public accounting firms play an important role in promoting efficiency of capital markets as they lend credibility to the financial statements of over 7,800 public companies trading on U.S. stock exchanges in 2006. More than 51 percent of these companies are audited by the Big Four public accounting firms (Ernst & Young, PricewaterhouseCoopers, KPMG, and Deloitte & Touche) and about 49 percent by other public accounting firms (e.g., Grant Thornton, BDO). In the post-SOX period, the Big Four audit firms had a net loss of almost 800 audit clients to non–Big Four audit firms.[107] However, in terms of market capitalization, the share of Big Four audits is 97.7 percent of total market capitalization. Thus, healthy competition in public accounting firms is important to the sustainability of audit services provided by those firms.

Section 701 of SOX directs the Government Accountability Office to study the factors contributing to consolidation in public accounting firms in the 1980s and 1990s in the United States.[108] The GAO report concludes that while there is no evidence of adverse impact of consolidation of accounting firms, further concentration in auditing firms would not be good for healthy competition within the profession. The SEC's chairman, Christopher Cox, raised his concerns by stating that "intense concentration isn't desirable" and adding that regulators need to consider whether their rules are inhibiting competition in the field.[109]

The CEOs of the six largest international audit networks suggest these ways of reducing concentration and improving competition in the auditing profession:

- *Focus enforcement.* Enforcement authorities should focus on penalties for individual audit failures and related auditor negligence and wrongdoing rather than penalizing the entire firm, as the loss of another major auditing firm could be detrimental to the financial health of the capital markets.
- *Liability reform.* Meaningful liability reform should promote competition and reduce concentration in the audit industry.
- *Scope of service reform.* Meaningful reform in relaxing the current scope of service restrictions should go beyond those measures needed to preserve auditor independence and objectivity.[110]

These suggested measures fail to realize that lack of proper enforcement through ineffective self-review, performance of conflicting consulting services, and relaxed regulations on auditor liability were the main cause of audit failures and the current concentration in the auditing profession from the Big Eight a couple decades ago to the Big Four now.

The author recommends that regulators (SEC) and standard setters (PCAOB) encourage public companies to use public accounting firms other than the Big Four (e.g., the Second Big Six) for their audit and permissible nonaudit services. Doing so would improve competition in the auditing industry, which would result in high audit quality and lower audit cost, both of which eventually contribute to the achievement of shareholder value enhancement and protection. William Parrett, chief executive of Deloitte & Touche, predicts that "both from a business standpoint and a regulatory standpoint, larger firms will evolve into a global partnership over the next decade."[111] The existing structure of public accounting firms consists of networks of member partnerships established in the countries in which they operate.[112] The major force behind the push for a single global partnership structure comes from regulators, but liability policies in certain countries must change significantly before the global partnership structure can be adopted.[113]

Continuous Auditing

The use of the Internet has had a significant impact on companies' operations and financial reporting. The financial reporting process is moving toward electronic reporting as more companies use the XBRL format. Regarding the importance of XBRL for future financial reporting, SEC Chairman Cox states, "I certainly agree with you [AICPA] that XBRL will do for business reporting what bar coding did for product distribution. But I believe its possibilities extend much further than that."[114]

The use of the XBRL format allows investors to have online, real-time access to their company's financial reports, as discussed in Chapter 13. The e-filing system using XBRL reporting is now required for financial institutions. It is the author's hope that public companies expeditiously move toward using electronic filing and financial reporting utilizing the XBRL format, which would result in reducing the cost of financial reporting, improving the accuracy and transparency of financial reports, and also necessitating the utilization of electronic, continuous auditing. The 2006 PwC survey reveals that: (1) half of the surveyed U.S. companies used continuous auditing techniques in 2006, which is up 30 percent compared to 2005; and (2) of those companies that do not yet have continuous auditing techniques in place, more than 31 percent have implemented plans to do so.[115] This significant increase in the use of continuous auditing techniques eventually will change the way both internal and external auditors have traditionally conducted the audit.

Confirmations

Confirmations provide audit evidence about several management assertions, including valuation and allocation, existence, completeness, and rights, or even the absence of certain conditions (e.g., side agreements). Confirmation of accounts receivable is required under the existing auditing standards. Auditors should maintain control over confirmations to ensure the integrity and reliability of the process and reduce the possibility of receiving false or colluded information. Where electronic media is used during the confirmation process, auditors should verify the source and content. To do so and to ensure the integrity of the confirmation process, auditors can utilize service providers with a secure clearinghouse for confirmations. The use of a secure clearinghouse or a secure electronic confirmation solution (e.g., Capital

Confirmation Inc.) can assist auditors in obtaining secure electronic confirmations where all the parties involved are preauthenticated. In this way, auditors can be assured that an appropriate person responded to the confirmation request.

The current manual confirmation process fails to authenticate who completed the confirmation request and led to the audit failures of ZZZZ Best, Parmalat, and CF Foods. According to current auditing standards and practices, the audit client provides the identity and addresses of banks, customers, and others, and auditors monitor the initial mailing of the confirmation process without controlling that confirmation letters are received and completed by an objective, competent, third-party respondent. This process is expensive, time consuming, and ineffective, and lacks authentication. Using available technology to automate the confirmation process can substantially improve the efficiency and effectiveness of confirmation as persuasive audit evidence. To ensure the integrity of the automated process, the privacy and security of the confirmation communication should be secured and authentication of parties involved should be established.[116] Doing this requires an appropriate infrastructure to facilitate cooperation among the auditor, audit client, and third-party respondent within a secure network similar to the one developed by Capital Confirmation Inc. [117]

Diversity in Accounting

A study by the AICPA, in 2005, indicates that women account for 19 percent of all public accounting firm partners, compared with 12 percent a decade ago.[118] To help women cope with children, aging partners, or other issues, about 38 percent of public accounting firms offer a variety of alternative career paths that do not lead to partnership, including choosing to stay as a senior manager or moving into a recruiting area.[119] Other findings of the study are:

- There is still a gender gap in the desire for partnership in the sense that, among senior managers, only 41 percent of women, compared with 65 percent of men, expressed the desire to become a partner.
- The two most commonly cited reasons for leaving public accounting are working conditions (e.g., schedules, hours, assignments) and work/life issues.
- Women are gravitating to smaller accounting firms where the opportunity for advancement is greater and in which women represent 47 percent of the workforce as opposed to 40 percent at larger firms.
- Female professionals are less likely to be aware of networking opportunities, practice development training, and leadership development programs.
- Male professionals are becoming as interested in and as affected by work/life policies as female professionals in public accounting firms.
- Public accounting firms that focus on the personal needs of their professional staff are experiencing productivity gains as more motivated and self-fulfilled employees reciprocate by nurturing the firm's valued client base.[120]

The author recommends that public accounting firms continue to improve gender diversity within their companies.

Auditor Liability

A lawsuit filed with the trustee of the bankrupt company Impath against its independent auditor, KPMG, indicates:

- Impath employees involved with the fraud were former KPMG auditors who had worked on the audit.
- KPMG had designed an accounts receivable system that was involved with the problems.
- Public accounting firms are attempting to prevent this type of lawsuit by imposing a limited liability agreement, a so-called liability cap, on their client's company, which would also continue to a bankrupt trustee.[121]

This case clearly suggests that the currently practiced limited liability provisions, as discussed in Chapter 9, can prevent plaintiffs from taking auditors to court for audit failures and recovering damages from auditors. Auditors have claimed that the auditor liability provisions contained in their audit engagements have been a common practice for controlling audit costs without adversely affecting the opportunities for shareholder class actions. The Investment Company Institute and the Federal Financial Institutions Examination Council (FFIEC) have viewed this practice as unsafe and unsound. The SEC's position is that auditor limited liability provisions, including indemnification, impair auditor independence. However, the SEC has stopped short of requiring disclosures of any agreements that limit auditor liability. The PCAOB has yet to take any position on auditors' clauses in client engagement letters (e.g., limitation of liability, agreements to waive jury trial, and the use of alternative dispute resolution [ADR]). The author recommends that: (1) public companies disclose any auditors' limited liability clauses to their audit committees and in their proxy statements to shareholders and that regulators (SEC) and standard setters (PCAOB) should properly address the impacts of these clauses on auditor independence and objectivity; and (2) public accounting firms publicly disclose their financial statements providing public information on their profits and distribution of their annual profits to their partners.

Auditor Communication with Those Charged with Governance

Traditionally, independent auditors have communicated certain material and relevant accounting, financial reporting, and audit information to the audit committee. In the post-SOX era auditors are more closely working with the audit committee as the committee is directly responsible for the appointment, retention, compensation, and oversight of independent auditors. However, the independent auditor working relationship with other commonly formed board committees (nomination, compensation), particularly the compensation committee, has yet to be addressed. The adoption of SFAS No. 123(R) requires companies to expense their stock options rather than disclose them in notes to the financial statements. The recognition of costs of options as expenses necessitates that auditors pay considerably more attention to stock option grants and the timing of such grants than pre-SFAS No. 123(R). The pervasiveness of option backdating practices requires auditors to communicate with their client company's compensation committee for the proper valuation and disclosure of employee stock options.

As an important gatekeeper, auditors should communicate with other gatekeepers, including the board of directors and corporate legal counsel. The PCAOB has yet to issue an auditing standard concerning the communication between the audit committee and the independent auditor. The Auditing Standards Board (ASB) of the American Institute of Certified Public Accountants issued Statement of Auditing Standards (SAS) No. 114 entitled *The Auditor's Communication with Those Charged with Governance,* which superseded SAS No. 61, *Communication with Audit Committees.*[122] SAS No. 114 requires auditors to conduct more robust two-way communication with those charged with governance concerning certain significant matters pertaining to the audit of financial statements of all nonissuers. SAS No. 114 also provides guidance on: (1) which matters should be communicated; (2) who they should be communicated to; and (3) the form and timing of the communication. The author suggests that the PCAOB, in a comprehensive auditing standard, address auditors' communication with all corporate governance participants including the board of directors, management, internal auditors, and legal counsel as discussed throughout this book, particularly Chapters 3 to 10.

INVESTOR PROTECTION: CONFIDENCE IN AND COMPETITIVENESS OF THE U.S. CAPITAL MARKETS

The U.S. capital markets have been through much turmoil since their inception in the 1790s, and each time the markets lost public trust and investor confidence and thus suffered significant declines in value.[123] The history of U.S. capital markets indicates that, during the good times, investors invest in new technologies with the expectation to gain from rising stock prices. Examples are the periods leading up to the 1929 market crash and the 2000 dot-com bubble burst, when the markets were built on a foundation of false numbers that did not create wealth and market corrections caused losses of billions of dollars in market capitalization. These losses could have been avoided by greater transparency and independence, fair and true financial information, more oversight and regulation, and avoidance of conflicts of interest.

The series of problems that contributed to the financial scandals which encouraged Congress to pass SOX include: (1) severe conflicts of interest that affected independence and objectivity of auditors and financial analysts; (2) a weak self-regulatory peer review system of the auditing industry with an unspoken code of "don't tell on me, and I won't tell on you"; (3) lack of proper accountability for financial statements by management; (4) compromised financial reporting standards that failed to reflect economic reality; (5) ineffective corporate governance of major accounting firms; (6) the availability of votes of some members of Congress to serve the views of well-funded special interests; (7) lack of accountability and responsibility on the part of well-paid corporate executives; (8) lack of proper congressional funding for the SEC to effectively review and enforce compliance with its rules; (9) insufficient penalties for white-collar crime and violations of securities laws; (10) ineffective oversight function of the audit committee in appointing, retaining, and compensating external auditors; (11) simple greed and arrogance; (12) market pressure on short-term earnings and management attempts to exceed or at least beat analysts' forecast estimates; (13) imbalance of power-sharing among management, directors, and shareholders; and (14) lack of vigilant and effective corporate governance.

SOX has contributed to the restoration of confidence of about 90 million Americans in the capital markets. Nonetheless, eight emerging challenges in the post-SOX period have demonstrated the need for the continuation of SOX: (1) the number of restatements reported by public companies soared to 1,295 in 2005 and is estimated to exceed 1,300 in 2006, many of which resulted from auditors' testing of internal controls; (2) about 15 percent of public companies with over \$75 million in market capitalization that implemented Section 404 for the first time in 2005 disclosed material weaknesses in their internal controls; (3) the self-reporting of internal controls under Section 302 as being certified by many CEOs and CFOs is not accurate, as only one out of eight companies that disclosed material weaknesses reported control deficiencies in the quarter preceding the disclosed weaknesses; (4) the disclosure of accounting firms' involvement in activities such as promoting illegal tax shelters, destroying audit documents, and withholding important information from courts of law; (5) failure of financial statements to reflect the economic reality and the extensive obligations for the promised pension plans; (6) the pervasiveness of questionable backdating practices of stock option grants at more than 200 companies, which is regarded by many as the second wave of financial scandals in the twenty-first century; (7) continuous excessive executive pay at many public companies that is not linked to the company's performance; and (8) lack of proper shareholder democracy, as evidenced by shareholders' inability to have access to their company's proxy materials and the continuation of plurality voting for director elections.

Investor protection is the bedrock of the capital markets. Recent corporate governance reforms including SOX, SEC rules, listing standards, court decisions, and best practices have restored investor confidence in public financial information and capital markets. Continuous reforms in 16 areas are needed to ensure investor protection and vibrancy and global competitiveness of U.S. capital markets: (1) dissemination of relevant financial information to the capital markets, which focuses on the long-term performance of creating sustainable shareholder value rather than short-term earnings guidance; (2) a requirement for public companies to disclose information pertaining to key performance indicators, which is useful to investors in assessing long-term financial prospects and health of a company; (3) more participation and inclusion of investors in the standard-setting process through membership in both the Financial Accounting Standard Board and the International Accounting Standard Board; (4) the issuance of new and improved objective-based accounting standards in a timely manner, which reflect the economic reality of a company's transactions and report both the historical costs and fair values of assets and liabilities, including pensions and leases, key assumptions affecting financial statements, and performance of ongoing operations that are within the control of management; (5) development of independent governance for the major international audit networks that is modeled after requirements currently in place for boards of public companies, including independence, authority over partners, compensation, and responsibility; (6) proper public disclosure of annual financial reports and filing of financial statements by major public accounting firms with the PCAOB consistent with the filing requirements of public companies; (7) more timely and transparent inspection reports on public accounting firms by the PCAOB, and better cooperation between the SEC and the PCAOB regarding inspections of and enforcement actions against public accounting firms; (8) improvements in the information provided by external auditors to the investing public, which reflects a more true and fair presentation and quality of financial statements than the current "pass or fail" audit reports; (9) narrowing the perceived expectation gap by requiring that auditors search for and find fraud, unless the amounts involved are immaterial or the auditor was misled through false documents and representations provided by management; (10) a requirement for mandatory rotation of audit firms every 10 years, during which the auditor could not be fired unless the company first received the permission of the PCAOB for changing auditors—this would alleviate the need for partner rotation every 5 years and reduce the excessive number of auditor changes (about 4,800 between 2003 and June 2006); (11) a catastrophic cap on auditors' liability linked to a standard, such as 15 times the charged audit fees, only if auditors agreed to the demands of investors for more improved governance, transparent and public disclosure of their financial reports, improved audit reports, a new financial statement fraud standard, and mandatory rotation of audit firms; (12) an increase in the financial expertise on audit committees from the currently less than 10 percent of audit committee members being former CFOs, controllers, or CPAs; (13) a move toward electronic financial reporting, with the use of the XBRL platform or a similar application to improve easy accessibility, comparability, timeliness, and consistency of electronic financial information; (14) preparation of financial statements and disclosures in plain English; (15) enhancement of shareholder rights through majority voting rather than plurality voting, and easy access to the company's proxy materials for director election; (16) requirement of shareholder advisory vote on executive compensation; and (17) promotion of professional schools of accountancy that train accountants with a knowledge-based education comparable with that of other professions, such as medicine and law, which have changed their education curriculum from undergraduate programs to advanced degrees with specializations.

More than 50 stock exchanges worldwide assist companies in conducting their initial public offerings. Stock exchanges in India, Italy, and South Korea have recently attracted many domestic IPOs, and many state-owned enterprises in China and France have done their fund-raising domestically and have listed their IPOs on their home exchanges. Companies traditionally have listed on their domestic stock exchanges, and only about 10 percent have chosen to list abroad.[124] Indeed, in the first half of 2006, only 8 of the 110 IPOs in the United States listed abroad, of which the 6 listed on London's Alternative Investment Market (AIM) raised $323 million in total.[125] Thus, this perception that the high compliance cost of SOX has forced U.S. companies to list their IPOs overseas is not warranted, and the fact that smaller foreign companies choose to go public in their domestic exchanges provides no justifiable evidence about the global competitiveness of U.S. capital markets.

Recent corporate governance reforms including SOX, SEC rules, state corporate laws, listing standards, and best practices are intended to protect the 90 million Americans who have placed their hard-earned money in capital markets to achieve a comfortable retirement or save toward the education of their children. These protections were designed to prevent another catastrophic scandal that could wipe out the entire lifetime efforts and future dreams of American investors. A report of security class action filings in 2006 in the United States indicates that the number of securities fraud class actions fell from 178 in 2005 to 110 in 2006, which is the lowest level since the adoption of the Public Securities Litigation Reforms Act (PSCRA) of 1995.[126] It is also interesting that, in 2006, only one case was filed against public accounting firms and only five against underwriters. SOX has been a contributing factor along with improvement in listing standards, a stable stock market, and more effective enforcement actions in reducing the number of lawsuits. Any attempts to roll back these reforms or relax related regulations could have detrimental effects on the long-term sustainability and global competitiveness of U.S. capital markets. Rather, these corporate governance reforms should address the three important shareholder issues of majority vote, access to proxy materials, and shareholder advisory vote on executive pay in order to maintain global competitiveness and leadership of U.S. capital markets.

SUMMARY

Recent reforms have made significant improvements in corporate governance policies, structure, and practices of public companies. Nevertheless, much more improvement needs to be made in several emerging corporate governance issues. The most prevailing challenges are related to director liability, the majority voting system, CEO turnover and succession, separation of the positions of chair of the board and CEO, board independence and the role of lead directors, and directors' and executives' compensation and stock ownership. The three emerging financial reporting issues are: (1) whether the current financial reporting model is relevant to investors and analysts in assessing public companies' financial performance and risk; (2) whether the convergence of U.S. GAAP with IFRS standards is helpful in enhancing the usefulness of financial reports; and (3) whether financial audits add value by lending credibility to financial reports.

NOTES

1. Ethiopis, T. 2006. Statement by SEC Staff: A race to the top. International Regulatory Reforms Post Sarbanes-Oxley (September 15). Available at: www.sec.gov/news/speech/2006/spch091106et.htm.
2. Ibid.

3. PricewaterhouseCoopers. 2005. Investment management perspectives (July). Available at: www.pwc.com.

4. PricewaterhouseCoopers. 2006. The world in 2005: How big will the major emerging market economies get and how can the OECD compete? (March). Available at: www.pwcglobal.com/extweb/ncpressrelease.nsf/docid/91A9EA 1716F47125852571290000886AB/$FILE/Size_of_emerging_economies-March_2006.pdf.

5. Ibid.

6. PricewaterhouseCoopers. 2006. What directors think. (November). Available at: www.pwc.com.

7. Standard & Poor's. 2006. European ratings distribution: Two decades of visible change. *Global Fixed Income Research* (November). Available at: www.standardandpoors.com.

8. PricewaterhouseCoopers. 2005. Investment management perspectives (July). Available at: www.pwc.com.

9. Ibid.

10. Ibid.

11. Schumer, C., and M. R. Bloomberg. 2006. To save New York, learn from London. *The Wall Street Journal* (November 1). Available at: http://online.wsj.com/article/SB116234404428809623.html.

12. Risen, C. 2006. Is London the world's new financial capital? The New York. *New Republic* (November 17). Available at: www.tnr.com.

13. CNN Money. 2006. NYSE, Euronext in trans-Atlantic exchange deal. (June 2). Available at: http://money.cnn.com/2006/06/01/markets/nyseeuronext.reut/?cnn=yes.

14. Bloomberg, M. R., and C. E. Schumer. 2007. Sustaining New York's and the U.S.'s Global Financial Services Leadership. Available at: http://schumer.senate.gov/SchumerWebsite/pressroom/special_reports/2007/NY_REPORT%20_FINAL.pdf.

15. Spencer Stuart Board Index. 2005. What really changed in the three years since the Sarbanes-Oxley Act (SOX): Survey of S&P 500 companies. (December). Available at: www.spencerstuart.com.

16. Ibid.

17. Niemeier, C. D. 2006. *American competitiveness in international capital markets*: Background Paper for the Atlantic's Ideas Tour Commemorating the Magazine's 150th Anniversary. Washington, DC. U.S. Public Company Accounting Oversight Board.

18. Ibid.

19. Committee for Economic Development. 2006. Private enterprise, public trust: The state of corporate America after Sarbanes-Oxley. (March 21). Available at: www.ced.org/docs/summary/summary_2006corpgov.pdf.

20. Ibid.

21. Campos, R.C. 2007. Speech by SEC Commissioner: Remarks before the CNMV Corporate Governance and Securities Markets Confidence. U.S. Securities and Exchange Commission (February 8). Available at: www.sec.gov/news/speech/2007.spch02807rec.htm.

22. International Corporate Governance Network. 2005. Global corporate governance principles. (July). Available at: www.icgn.org/organization/documents/cgp/revisedprinciplesJul2005.pdf.

23. Global Reporting Initiative (GRI). 2006. G3 Guidelines. Available at: www.grig3.org/guidelines.html.

24. Mercer Investment Consulting. 2006. Perspective on responsible investment. (January). Available at: www.mercerIC.com.

25. Gore, A., and D. Blood. 2006. For people and planet: When will companies start accounting for environmental costs? (March 28). *Wall Street Journal*. Available at: www.opinionjournal.com/editorial/feature.html?id=110008151.

26. United Nations Environment Programme Finance Initiative and the UN Global Compact. 2006. Principles for responsible investment. (April 27). Available at: www.unepfi.org/principles or www.unglobalcompact.org/principles.

27. Ibid.

28. Ibid.

29. Ibid.

30. Mikkelson, W., M. Partch, and K. Shah. 1997. Ownership and operating performance of companies that go public. *Journal of Financial Economics* 44: 218–307.

31. Ibid.

32. Global Reporting Institute. 2002. The sustainability reporting guidelines. Available at: www.globalreporting.org.

33. *McKinsey Quarterly*. 2006. The McKinsey Global Survey of business executives: Business and society (April 2). Available at: www.mckinseyquarterly.com/article_abstract_visitor.aspx?ar=1741&L2=39&L3=29.

34. Ibid.

35. Ibid.

36. Ibid.

37. Schneyer, F. 2005. Investors linking SRI funds to keep firms in line. (January 23). Available at: www.plansponsor.com.

38. Goldman Sachs. 2005. Goldman Sachs environmental policy framework. Available at: www.gs.com/our_firm/our_culture/social_responsibility/environmental_policy_framework/index.html.

39. Ibid.

40. United Nations Foundation. 2005. Institutional investor summit on climate risk. (May 10). Available at: www.unfoundation.org/features/2005_inst_investor_summit_climate_risk.asp.

41. Ibid.

42. International Organization for Standardization. 2002. Environmental management: The ISO 14000 family of international standards. Available at: www.iso.ch/iso/en/prods-services/otherpubs/iso14000/index.html.

43. The Business Roundtable. 2006. SEC Response to AFSCME vs AIG Decision (September 29). Available at: www.businessroundtable.org.

44. Levitt, A. 2006. Commentary: Stock populi. *Wall Street Journal* (October 27). Available at: www.online.wsj.com/article/SD116194105035055582.html.
45. Ibid.
46. Committee on Capital Markets Regulation. 2006. Interim Report of the Committee on Capital Markets Regulation. (November 30). Available at: www.capmktsreg.org/research.html.
47. Securities and Exchange Commission. 2005. SEC votes to propose rule to provide investor with Internet availability of proxy materials. (November 29). Available at: www.sec.gov/news/press/2005-166.htm.
48. Ibid.
49. Ibid.
50. Automatic Date Processing Inc. Brokerage Services Group. 2005. Letter sent by ADP to the chairman of the SEC regarding the e-proxy proposal. (November 22).
51. U.S. Securities and Exchange Commission (SEC). 2006. SEC votes to adopt e-proxy rule amendments and propose mandatory model (December 13). Available at: www.sec.gov/news/press/2006/2006-209.htm.
52. Ibid.
53. Automatic Data Processing Inc. 2005. Supra.
54. Morgenson, G. 2006. Finally, shareholders start acting like owners. *New York Times* (June 11). Available at: www.nytimes.com.
55. U.S. Securities and Exchange Commission. 2007. Staff Response to Hewlett-Packard Company Incoming Letter dated November 3, 2006. (January). Available at: www.sec.gov.
56. Johnson, S. 2007. Pension funds urge greater shareholders' rights. *Financial Times* (January 22). Available at: www.ft.com.
57. Klausner, M., N. Munger, C. Munger, B. S. Black, and B. R. Cheffins. 2005. Outside directors' liability: Have WorldCom and Enron changed the rules? *Stanford Lawyer* 71 (Winter). Available at: www.law.stanford.edu/publications/lawyer/issues/71/sl71_klausner.pdf.
58. Bradford,M. 2005. D&O suits increasingly seek to tap personal funds. *Business Insurance* 39 (7) (February 14): 23–24.
59. Ibid.
60. Bebchuk, L. 2005. The Disney verdict shuts out investors. *Financial Times*. (August 12). Available at: www.ft.com.
61. Spencer Stuart Board Index. 2005. What's really changed in the three years since the Sarbanes-Oxley Act.
62. PricewaterhouseCoopers. 2006. Spencer Stuart 2005 Board Index. (January 12). Available at: www.cfodirect.com/CFOPrivate.nsf.
63. Hymowitz, C. 2006. Sky-high payouts to top executives prove hard to curb. *Wall Street Journal* (June 26). Available at: http://online.wsj.com/artile/SB115127720534290299.html.
64. Ibid.

65. Ibid.

66. Corporate Board Member/PricewaterhouseCoopers 2006 Survey. What directors think.

67. Committee for Economic Development. 2006. Private enterprise, public trust: The state of corporate America after Sarbanes-Oxley. (March 21). Available at: www.ced.org/docs/summary/summary_2006corpgov.pdf.

68. Corporate Board Member/PricewaterhouseCoopers 2006 Survey. What directors think.

69. Ibid.

70. U.S. Securities and Exchange Commission (SEC). 2006. Concept Release Concerning Management's Reports on Internal Control over Financial Reporting (July 18). Available at: www.sec.gov.

71. Committee of Sponsoring Organizations of the Treadway Commission (COSO) 2006. Internal control over financial reporting—Guidance for smaller public companies. Available at: www.aicpa.org/copyright.htm.

72. Committee on Capital Markets Regulation. 2006. Interim Report of the Committee on Capital Markets Regulation.

73. Government Accountability Office. 2006. Report to the Ranking Minority Member, Committee on Banking, Housing, and urban Affairs, U.S. Senate. Financial Restatements: Update of Public Company Trends, Market Impacts, and Regulatory Enforcement Activities (July). Available at: www.gao.gov/new.items/d06678.pdf

74. Glass Lewis & Co. 2006. Getting it wrong the first time. Restatement Trend Alert (March 2). Available at:www.glasslewis.com.

75. Hanford, D. J. 2006. PricewaterhouseCoopers chair reporting needs improvement. Dow Jones News Service (June 6). Available at: http://cfodirecto.pwc.com/CFODirectWeb/cfocontent/contentCo.

76. Ibid.

77. Anderson, A., P. Herring, and A. Pawlicki. 2005. EBR: The next step. *Journal of Accountancy* (June): 71–74.

78. Ibid.

79. Reilly, O. 2006. FASB appears in a new light on stock options. *The Wall Street Journal* (August 14). Available at: http://online.wsj.com/article/SB115552025107534780.html.

80. Morgenson, G. 2006. Options fiesta and investors paid the bill. *The New York Times* (July 30). Available at: http://www.nytimes.com.

81. State Board of Administration (SBA) of Florida. 2006. Corporate Governance Annual Report 2006. Available at: www.sbafla.com.

82. U.S. Securities and Exchange Commission. 2007. A letter sent by Chief Accountant, Division of Corporation Finance, in response to inquiries related to filing restated financial statements for errors in accounting for stock option grants (January). Available at: www.sec.gov/divisions/corpfin/guidance/oilgasltr012007.htm.

83. Public Company Accounting Oversight Board. 2006. Staff Audit Practice Alert No. 1: Matters Related to Timing and Accounting for Option Grants (July 28). Available at: www.pcaob.org.

84. PricewaterhouseCoopers. 2005. Global Economic Crime Survey 2005 (December 1). Available at: www.pwc.com/pwc_2005_global_crimesurvey.pdf.
85. Ibid.
86. PricewaterhouseCoopers. 2005. Predicting the unpredictable: Protecting utilities against fraud, reputation and misconduct risk. (November 3). Available at: www.cfodirect.com/cfopublic.nsf.
87. International Accounting Standards Board and U.S. Financial Accounting Standards Board. 2006. A roadmap for convergence between IFRS and U.S. GAAP 2006–2008. Memorandum of understanding between the FASB and IASB. (February 26). Available at: www.fasb.org.
88. Accounting Web. 2006. IASB chairman calls for accounting standards convergence by 2011. (June 20). Available at: www.accountingweb.com.
89. Zion, D., and B. Carcache. 2005. Let the games begin: FASB to tackle pension and OPEB. (November 11). *CSFB's Research and Analysis.*
90. United States Government Accountability Office: Report to Congressional Committees. 2005. Private pensions: Recent experiences of large defined benefit plans illustrate weaknesses in funding rules. Available at: www.gao.gov/new.items/d05294.pdf.
91. Geller, A. 2005. Walkout points to more tension on public pensions. (December 29). Associated Press.
92. Boselovic, L. 2005. Pittsburgh Brewing says it's in deep trouble. *Pittsburgh Post Gazette* (June 29).
93. Eckert, B. 2006. Sprint Nextel freezes pensions for half its workforce. *Washington Business Journal* (January 23). Available at: www.bizjournals.com/washington/stories/2006/01/23daily6.html.
94. Financial Accounting Standards Board. 2006. Statement of Financial Accounting Standards (SFAS) No. 158, *Employer's Accounting for Defined Benefit Pension and other Postretirement Plans* (September 29). Available at: www.fasb.org.
95. Financial Accounting Standards Board. 2006. Exposure draft to improve accounting for postretirement benefit plans, including pensions. (March 31). Available at: www.fasb.org.
96. Ibid.
97. Geczy, C., B. A. Minton, and C. M. Schrand. 2005. Taking a view: Corporate speculation, governance, and compensation. (November). Available at: ssrn.com/abstract=633081.
98. Ibid.
99. Ibid.
100. Governmental Accounting Standards Board. 2006. Preliminary views: Accounting and financial reporting for derivatives. (April 28). No. 26-4P.
101. Committee of Sponsoring Organizations. 2004 enterprise risk management. (September). Available at: www.erm.coso.org.
102. Norris, F. 2006. Deep secret: Why auditors are replaced. *New York Times* (July 28). Available at: http://www.nytimes.com.
103. Glass Lewis and Co. 2006. Mum's the word, Yellow Card Trend Alert (July 27). Available at: http://www.glasslewis.com.

104. CRA International. 2006. Sarbanes-Oxley Section 404 costs and implementation issues: Spring 2006 survey update. Available at: www.crai.com.

105. Public Company Accounting Oversight Board. 2005. Report on the initial implementation of Auditing Standards No. 2. An Audit of Internal Control over Financial Reporting Performed in Conjunction with an Audit of Financial Statements. PCAOB Release No. 2005-023 (November 30). Available at: www.pcaobus.org.

106. Public Company Accounting Oversight Board. 2006. Board announces four-point plan to improve implementation of internal control reporting requirements. (May 17). Available at: www.pcaob.org/New_and_Events/News/2006/05_17.aspx.

107. KPMG. 2006. Audit market share analysis (November). Available at: www.kpmg.com.

108. United States Government Accountability Office. 2003. Accounting firm consolidation: Selected large public company views on audit fees, quality, independence and choice. GAO-03-1158. Available at: www.gao.gov/new.items/d031158.pdf.

109. Burns, J. 2005. SEC's COX wants simpler rules, more competition for accounting. *Wall Street Journal Online*. (December 6). Available at: www.online.wsj.com/article_print/SB113381176660114298.html.

110. International Audit Networks. 2006. Global networks and the global economy: A Vision from the CEO of the International Audit Networks (November). Available at: www.globalpublicpolicysymposium.com.

111. Parker, A. 2005. Accounting head unveils "remarkable" strategy: Deloitte's global chief is aware that the firm's main objective could make it a hostage to fortune. *Financial Times*. (December 13).

112. Accounting Web. 2005. Deloitte head predicts single global partnership structure for Big 4. (December 16). Available at: www.accountingweb.com/cgi-bin/item.cgi?id=101585&d=815&h=817&f=816&dateformat=%25B%20%25e,%20%25Y.

113. Ibid.

114. Cox, C. 2005. Speech by SEC chairman: Remarks before the 2005 AICPA national conference on current SEC and PCAOB developments. (December 5). Available at: www.sec.gov/news/speech/spch120505cc.htm.

115. PricewaterhouseCoopers (PwC). 2006. PwC's 2006 State of the Internal Audit Profession Study: Continuous auditing gains momentum (June 27). Available at: www.pwc.com.

116. Adlhizer, G. R., and J. D. Cashell. 2006. Automating the confirmation process: How to enhance audit effectiveness and efficiency. (April). Available at: www.cpaj.com.

117. Ibid.

118. American Institute of Certified Public Accountants. 2006. A decade of changes in the accounting profession: Workforce trends and human capital practices. (February). Available at: www.aicpa.org/members/div/career/wofi/research.htm.

119. Ibid.

120. Ibid.
121. Impath v. KPMG. 2005. United States District Court District of New Jersey Case. 2-05-CV-03756-DMC-MF, filed 07/27/05.
122. American Institute of Certified Public Accountants. 2006. Statement of Auditing Standards (SAS) No. 114. *The Auditor's Communication with Those Charged with Governance.* Auditing Standards Board (ASB). Available at: www.aicpa.org.
123. Much of the discussion in this section is from Turner, L. E. 2006. Learning from accounting history: Will we get it right this time? *Issues in Accounting Education* 21 (4) (November): 383–407.
124. Ernst & Young. 2007. Global capital market trends (January). Available at: www.ey.com.
125. Ibid.
126. Cornerstone Research. 2006. Securities Class Action Case Filings 2006: A year in review (December). Available at: www.cornerstone.com and www.securities. standford.edu.